T0181998

Lecture Notes in Computer Science 14023

Founding Editors

Gerhard Goos
Juris Hartmanis

The series Lecture Notes in Computer Science (LNCS), including its subseries Lecture Notes in Artificial Intelligence (LNAI) and Lecture Notes in Bioinformatics (LNBI), has established itself as a medium for the publication of new developments in computer science and information technology research, teaching, and education.

LNCS enjoys close cooperation with the computer science R & D community, the series counts many renowned academics among its volume editors and paper authors, and collaborates with prestigious societies. Its mission is to serve this international community by providing an invaluable service, mainly focused on the publication of conference and workshop proceedings and postproceedings. LNCS commenced publication in 1973.

Pei-Luen Patrick Rau

Editor

Cross-Cultural Design

15th International Conference, CCD 2023
Held as Part of the 25th International Conference, HCII 2023
Copenhagen, Denmark, July 23–28, 2023
Proceedings, Part II

 Springer

Editor
Pei-Luen Patrick Rau
Department of Industrial Engineering
Tsinghua University
Beijing, China

ISSN 0302-9743   ISSN 1611-3349 (electronic)
Lecture Notes in Computer Science
ISBN 978-3-031-35938-5   ISBN 978-3-031-35939-2 (eBook)
https://doi.org/10.1007/978-3-031-35939-2

This Springer imprint is published by the registered company Springer Nature Switzerland AG
The registered company address is: Gewerbestrasse 11, 6330 Cham, Switzerland

Foreword

Human-computer interaction (HCI) is acquiring an ever-increasing scientific and industrial importance, as well as having more impact on people's everyday lives, as an ever-growing number of human activities are progressively moving from the physical to the digital world. This process, which has been ongoing for some time now, was further accelerated during the acute period of the COVID-19 pandemic. The HCI International (HCII) conference series, held annually, aims to respond to the compelling need to advance the exchange of knowledge and research and development efforts on the human aspects of design and use of computing systems.

The 25th International Conference on Human-Computer Interaction, HCI International 2023 (HCII 2023), was held in the emerging post-pandemic era as a 'hybrid' event at the AC Bella Sky Hotel and Bella Center, Copenhagen, Denmark, during July 23–28, 2023. It incorporated the 21 thematic areas and affiliated conferences listed below.

A total of 7472 individuals from academia, research institutes, industry, and government agencies from 85 countries submitted contributions, and 1578 papers and 396 posters were included in the volumes of the proceedings that were published just before the start of the conference, these are listed below. The contributions thoroughly cover the entire field of human-computer interaction, addressing major advances in knowledge and effective use of computers in a variety of application areas. These papers provide academics, researchers, engineers, scientists, practitioners and students with state-of-the-art information on the most recent advances in HCI.

The HCI International (HCII) conference also offers the option of presenting 'Late Breaking Work', and this applies both for papers and posters, with corresponding volumes of proceedings that will be published after the conference. Full papers will be included in the 'HCII 2023 - Late Breaking Work - Papers' volumes of the proceedings to be published in the Springer LNCS series, while 'Poster Extended Abstracts' will be included as short research papers in the 'HCII 2023 - Late Breaking Work - Posters' volumes to be published in the Springer CCIS series.

I would like to thank the Program Board Chairs and the members of the Program Boards of all thematic areas and affiliated conferences for their contribution towards the high scientific quality and overall success of the HCI International 2023 conference. Their manifold support in terms of paper reviewing (single-blind review process, with a minimum of two reviews per submission), session organization and their willingness to act as goodwill ambassadors for the conference is most highly appreciated.

This conference would not have been possible without the continuous and unwavering support and advice of Gavriel Salvendy, founder, General Chair Emeritus, and Scientific Advisor. For his outstanding efforts, I would like to express my sincere appreciation to Abbas Moallem, Communications Chair and Editor of HCI International News.

July 2023   Constantine Stephanidis

HCI International 2023 Thematic Areas and Affiliated Conferences

Thematic Areas

- HCI: Human-Computer Interaction
- HIMI: Human Interface and the Management of Information

Affiliated Conferences

- EPCE: 20th International Conference on Engineering Psychology and Cognitive Ergonomics
- AC: 17th International Conference on Augmented Cognition
- UAHCI: 17th International Conference on Universal Access in Human-Computer Interaction
- CCD: 15th International Conference on Cross-Cultural Design
- SCSM: 15th International Conference on Social Computing and Social Media
- VAMR: 15th International Conference on Virtual, Augmented and Mixed Reality
- DHM: 14th International Conference on Digital Human Modeling and Applications in Health, Safety, Ergonomics and Risk Management
- DUXU: 12th International Conference on Design, User Experience and Usability
- C&C: 11th International Conference on Culture and Computing
- DAPI: 11th International Conference on Distributed, Ambient and Pervasive Interactions
- HCIBGO: 10th International Conference on HCI in Business, Government and Organizations
- LCT: 10th International Conference on Learning and Collaboration Technologies
- ITAP: 9th International Conference on Human Aspects of IT for the Aged Population
- AIS: 5th International Conference on Adaptive Instructional Systems
- HCI-CPT: 5th International Conference on HCI for Cybersecurity, Privacy and Trust
- HCI-Games: 5th International Conference on HCI in Games
- MobiTAS: 5th International Conference on HCI in Mobility, Transport and Automotive Systems
- AI-HCI: 4th International Conference on Artificial Intelligence in HCI
- MOBILE: 4th International Conference on Design, Operation and Evaluation of Mobile Communications

List of Conference Proceedings Volumes Appearing Before the Conference

1. LNCS 14011, Human-Computer Interaction: Part I, edited by Masaaki Kurosu and Ayako Hashizume
2. LNCS 14012, Human-Computer Interaction: Part II, edited by Masaaki Kurosu and Ayako Hashizume
3. LNCS 14013, Human-Computer Interaction: Part III, edited by Masaaki Kurosu and Ayako Hashizume
4. LNCS 14014, Human-Computer Interaction: Part IV, edited by Masaaki Kurosu and Ayako Hashizume
5. LNCS 14015, Human Interface and the Management of Information: Part I, edited by Hirohiko Mori and Yumi Asahi
6. LNCS 14016, Human Interface and the Management of Information: Part II, edited by Hirohiko Mori and Yumi Asahi
7. LNAI 14017, Engineering Psychology and Cognitive Ergonomics: Part I, edited by Don Harris and Wen-Chin Li
8. LNAI 14018, Engineering Psychology and Cognitive Ergonomics: Part II, edited by Don Harris and Wen-Chin Li
9. LNAI 14019, Augmented Cognition, edited by Dylan D. Schmorrow and Cali M. Fidopiastis
10. LNCS 14020, Universal Access in Human-Computer Interaction: Part I, edited by Margherita Antona and Constantine Stephanidis
11. LNCS 14021, Universal Access in Human-Computer Interaction: Part II, edited by Margherita Antona and Constantine Stephanidis
12. LNCS 14022, Cross-Cultural Design: Part I, edited by Pei-Luen Patrick Rau
13. LNCS 14023, Cross-Cultural Design: Part II, edited by Pei-Luen Patrick Rau
14. LNCS 14024, Cross-Cultural Design: Part III, edited by Pei-Luen Patrick Rau
15. LNCS 14025, Social Computing and Social Media: Part I, edited by Adela Coman and Simona Vasilache
16. LNCS 14026, Social Computing and Social Media: Part II, edited by Adela Coman and Simona Vasilache
17. LNCS 14027, Virtual, Augmented and Mixed Reality, edited by Jessie Y. C. Chen and Gino Fragomeni
18. LNCS 14028, Digital Human Modeling and Applications in Health, Safety, Ergonomics and Risk Management: Part I, edited by Vincent G. Duffy
19. LNCS 14029, Digital Human Modeling and Applications in Health, Safety, Ergonomics and Risk Management: Part II, edited by Vincent G. Duffy
20. LNCS 14030, Design, User Experience, and Usability: Part I, edited by Aaron Marcus, Elizabeth Rosenzweig and Marcelo Soares
21. LNCS 14031, Design, User Experience, and Usability: Part II, edited by Aaron Marcus, Elizabeth Rosenzweig and Marcelo Soares

47. CCIS 1836, HCI International 2023 Posters - Part V, edited by Constantine Stephanidis, Margherita Antona, Stavroula Ntoa and Gavriel Salvendy

https://2023.hci.international/proceedings

Preface

The increasing internationalization and globalization of communication, business and industry is leading to a wide cultural diversification of individuals and groups of users who access information, services and products. If interactive systems are to be usable, useful and appealing to such a wide range of users, culture becomes an important HCI issue. Therefore, HCI practitioners and designers face the challenges of designing across different cultures, and need to elaborate and adopt design approaches which take into account cultural models, factors, expectations and preferences, and allow development of cross-cultural user experiences that accommodate global users.

The 15th Cross-Cultural Design (CCD) Conference, an affiliated conference of the HCI International Conference, encouraged the submission of papers from academics, researchers, industry and professionals, on a broad range of theoretical and applied issues related to Cross-Cultural Design and its applications.

A considerable number of papers were accepted to this year's CCD Conference addressing diverse topics, which spanned a wide variety of domains. A notable theme addressed by several contributions was that of service and product design for the promotion of cultural heritage and local culture. Furthermore, a considerable number of papers explore the differences in cultural perceptions of technology across various contexts. Design for social change and development constitutes one of the topics that emerged this year, examining the impact of technology on society, for vulnerable groups, for shaping values, and in promoting social movements and folk beliefs. Another growing topic is that of sustainable design, which delves into methodologies, cultural branding, and design for sustainability in various areas such as travel, transportation and mobility, climate change and urban public spaces. Emerging technologies, future-focused design and design of automated and intelligent systems are also prominent themes, exploring culturally informed innovative design methodologies, User Experience aspects and user acceptance angles, as well as evaluation studies and their findings. Furthermore, papers emphasized the design of technological innovations in domains of social impact such as arts and creative industries, cultural heritage, immersive and inclusive learning environments, and health and wellness.

Three volumes of the HCII 2023 proceedings are dedicated to this year's edition of the CCD Conference:

- Part I addresses topics related to service and product design for cultural innovation, design for social change and development, sustainable design methods and practices, and cross-cultural perspectives on design and consumer behavior.
- Part II addresses topics related to User Experience design in emerging technologies, future-focused design, and culturally informed design of automated and intelligent systems.
- Part III addresses topics related to cross-cultural design in arts and creative industries, in cultural heritage, and in immersive and inclusive learning environments, as well as cross-cultural health and wellness design.

Papers in these volumes were included for publication after a minimum of two single-blind reviews from the members of the CCD Program Board or, in some cases, from members of the Program Boards of other affiliated conferences. I would like to thank all of them for their invaluable contribution, support and efforts.

July 2023   Pei-Luen Patrick Rau

15th International Conference on Cross-Cultural Design (CCD 2023)

Program Board Chair: **Pei-Luen Patrick Rau,** *Tsinghua University, P.R. China*

Program Board:

- Na Chen, *Beijing University of Chemical Technology, P.R. China*
- Zhe Chen, *Beihang University, P.R. China*
- Kuohsiang Chen, *Fuzhou University of International Studies and Trade, P.R. China*
- Wen-Ko Chiou, *Chang Gung University, Taiwan*
- Paul L. Fu, *Wish Inc., USA*
- Zhiyong Fu, *Tsinghua University, P.R. China*
- Hanjing Huang, *Fuzhou University, P.R. China*
- Yu-Chi Lee, *Ming Chi University of Technology, Taiwan*
- Xin Lei, *Zhejiang University of Technology, P.R. China*
- Sheau-Farn Max Liang, *National Taipei University of Technology, Taiwan*
- Pin-Chao Liao, *Tsinghua University, P.R. China*
- Rungtai Lin, *National Taiwan University of Arts, Taiwan*
- Po-Hsien Lin, *National Taiwan University of Arts, Taiwan*
- Na Liu, *Beijing University of Posts and Telecommunications, P.R. China*
- Ta-Ping (Robert) Lu, *Sichuan University – Pittsburgh Institute, P.R. China*
- Liang Ma, *Tsinghua University, P.R. China*
- Xingda Qu, *Shenzhen University, P.R. China*
- Huatong Sun, *University of Washington Tacoma, USA*
- Hao Tan, *Hunan University, P.R. China*
- Pei-Lee Teh, *Monash University Malaysia, Malaysia*
- Lin Wang, *Incheon National University, South Korea*
- Hsiu-Ping Yueh, *National Taiwan University, Taiwan*
- Runting Zhong, *Jiangnan University, P.R. China*
- Xingchen Zhou, *Beijing Normal University, P.R. China*

The full list with the Program Board Chairs and the members of the Program Boards of all thematic areas and affiliated conferences of HCII2023 is available online at:

http://www.hci.international/board-members-2023.php

HCI International 2024 Conference

The 26th International Conference on Human-Computer Interaction, HCI International 2024, will be held jointly with the affiliated conferences at the Washington Hilton Hotel, Washington, DC, USA, June 29 – July 4, 2024. It will cover a broad spectrum of themes related to Human-Computer Interaction, including theoretical issues, methods, tools, processes, and case studies in HCI design, as well as novel interaction techniques, interfaces, and applications. The proceedings will be published by Springer. More information will be made available on the conference website: http://2024.hci.international/.

General Chair
Prof. Constantine Stephanidis
University of Crete and ICS-FORTH
Heraklion, Crete, Greece
Email: general_chair@hcii2024.org

https://2024.hci.international/

Contents – Part II

Future-Focused Design

Culturally-Informed Design of Automated and Intelligent Systems

User Experience Design in Emerging Technologies

An Exploration of How Aesthetic Pleasure is Related in Lighting Design

Jen-Feng Chen[✉], Po-Hsien Lin, and Rungtai Lin

Graduate School of Creative Industry Design, National Taiwan University of Arts,
New Taipei City, Taiwan
jenfeng0328@gmail.com, t0131@ntua.edu.tw, rtlin@mail.ntua.edu.tw

Abstract. In the past, the emphasis of many products was on functionality, as people were primarily concerned with whether items could meet their daily needs, thus emphasizing rationality and functionalism has always influenced modern industrial design. With the development of society, people's increasing emphasis on product aesthetics and emotions, by increasing the pleasure generated by the appearance of the product, the product can more easily attract consumers, and therefore the pleasure of the product has become an important design consideration. This study explores the relationship between three product appearance factors: form, color, and function, and pleasure and preference through literature review and questionnaire survey. Data was obtained from 72 untested participants, and the results indicate that product color is an important attribute that affects pleasure, and product preference is significantly correlated with pleasure.

Keywords: product aesthetics · pleasure · preference · product appearance factors

1 Introduction

Traditionally, human factors have tended to focus on making products "usable" by emphasizing utilitarian and functional benefits. However, as people's emphasis on aesthetics and emotions increases, they not only want products to be functional but also want to experience pleasure in the process of use. Product design has shifted from the past emphasis on Design for Function that focused on functionality, to Design for Feeling that emphasizes human inner experiences. The core value of design has moved from rational values that emphasize function and physiological needs, towards emotional values that emphasize aesthetics and psychological needs [30]. Product development must also abandon the pursuit of function and cost, and emphasize a human-centered design approach. Pleasure is a psychological experience that refers to feelings of happiness or satisfaction. The Oxford English Dictionary defines "pleasure" as a condition or feeling caused by experiencing or anticipating something that is good or desirable. Therefore, the pleasure issues in product use not only involve usability, but also include product functionality, usability, aesthetics, performance, and reliability [24]. Product pleasure is

P.-L. P. Rau (Ed.): HCII 2023, LNCS 14023, pp. 3–15, 2023.
https://doi.org/10.1007/978-3-031-35939-2_1

a hot topic in the field of product design, and people are increasingly interested in understanding and researching various aspects of products that bring emotional experiences to people [4, 12, 20], because it not only affects the user's acceptance of the product, but also can increase the frequency of product use [34]. Product appearance design is one of the important factors that influence users' sense of pleasure. An aesthetically pleasing appearance can attract users' attention and increase the product's appeal [17]. At the same time, the product appearance can also influence users' perceptions of the product, making it perceived as high-quality, efficient, and usable [1]. Product appearance features such as shape and color can affect consumer product choices, and a deeper understanding of users' perception of appearance can better optimize product appearance to meet market demands [8]. Understanding the appearance attributes perceived by consumers in product design can help designers convey certain pre-specified meanings in the product [3], and incorporating "pleasure" into the design of the product can make it more attractive [2].

In recent years, the advantages of price and production volume brought about by the maturation of LED technology have led to an increase in its popularity, making it the mainstream light source of the 21st century. The development of LED lighting fixtures has progressed from pursuing high brightness and efficiency, and intelligent system control with technological breakthroughs at its core, to being people-oriented, emphasizing the users' sensory pleasure, comfort, and happiness [21]. With the trend in product design gradually moving towards selling designs that appeal to emotions and are close to the heart of people [31], LED light sources have features such as rich colors, small size, low heat, and energy efficiency, leading to many creative and emotionally pleasing design ideas. For example, Philips Lighting's Living Colors demonstrates the rich color characteristics of LED light sources by quickly changing the atmosphere of the space by switching to different light source colors to meet people's different situational needs.

Taiwanese lighting brand QisDesign combines design, creativity, technology, and aesthetics to give LED lighting a new look and meet users' functional and aesthetic needs. Its products have won numerous awards and are marketed worldwide, establishing a unique brand image in the high-priced lighting market. As LED lighting technology becomes more mature, the threshold for entering the lighting market is lowered, and designers must move away from a function-oriented technical mindset and focus on people's emotional needs. Therefore, this study conducted a questionnaire survey using QisDesign lighting to explore the impact of different attributes of product appearance on user pleasure and preference, making lighting more human-centered and creating emotional value.

2 Literature Review

2.1 Aesthetic Pleasure and Product Appearance

The term "aesthetics" comes from the Greek word "aesthesis," which refers to sensory perception and understanding or sensual knowledge. The concept of beauty was first proposed over 2,000 years ago by the Pythagorean school in ancient Greece, who believed that beauty was harmony and proportion [36]. Plato elevated the discussion of beauty to the level of philosophical inquiry. Aesthetics became a standard discipline within philosophy, dealing with concepts such as beauty, ugliness, sublimity, comedy, and so on, and is applicable to art… And the study of beautiful things that are related to the senses and emotions" [15]. In Chapter Seven of "Poetics," Aristotle proposed that "beauty consists in size and order." In rhetoric, it is said that "beauty is a kind of goodness, and beautiful things cause pleasure because they are also good". In the Middle Ages, Saint Augustine and Thomas Aquinas believed that beautiful objects should have proper proportions and pleasing colors [38]. When aesthetics is mentioned in design practice, it usually refers to the beautiful appearance. Eighteenth-century empiricist philosophers such as David Hume and Edmund Burke emphasized the connection between aesthetic experience and sensory pleasure [6, 13]. Baumgarten redefined aesthetics as the satisfaction of the senses or sensory pleasure, delving deeper into the nature and meaning of beauty. After that, aesthetics is generally regarded as an abstract, subjective feeling, and it also became an independent discipline for the first time [11].

With the changing times, the consumption pattern has gradually shifted from a rational consumption model to emotional one [10]. Consumers no longer blindly pursue products with high efficiency or low prices, but are willing to spend more money on products that can satisfy their psychological and emotional needs [22]. A good appearance design can attract consumers to use the product, communicate with them, and increase the value of the product by improving the quality of the related usage experience. Therefore, the appearance or design of the product is undoubtedly the decisive factor for its market success [5]. To create a truly enjoyable product, it is important to consider whether the product's functionality and aesthetics are in line with the values, desires, and lifestyles of its target audience. With the changing consumer concept and functional homogenization, the impact of product appearance design on purchase decisions is increasing. Evaluating the aesthetic pleasure of product appearance is an important research direction, including how to investigate users' more subjective perceptions and preferences, predict consumers' preferences for product appearance, and provide product appearance design recommendations for manufacturers [29, 35]. The visual attributes of product appearance are usually di-vided into three categories: psychophysical attributes, organizational attributes, and meaningful attributes. Psychophysical attributes are the formal characteristics of the object, such as its shape, size, and color. The aesthetic effects of these attributes are highly correlated and quantifiable [22, 26]. Therefore, how product appearance de-sign can make users feel pleasure, and the form, color, and functional use can be-come the main research evaluation attributes.

2.2 Elements of Lighting Design that Bring Pleasure

A good lighting design not only enhances visual performance and physiological com-fort but also affects sleep quality, alertness, happiness, and health [19]. In 2016, the Lighting Europe published the "Strategic Roadmap 2025," which sets three stages of development for the lighting market. The first stage focuses on the efficient and widespread application of LED light sources in daily life. The second stage aims to achieve energy efficiency and environmental friendliness through intelligent lighting control systems for sustainable development. The third stage emphasizes "Human-centered" lighting design, focusing on people's feelings and emphasizing the improvement of happiness and health through the improvement of light quality. There-fore, many studies focus on improving light source comfort and work efficiency, as well as the two main design directions of how to improve people's pleasure and happiness through the improvement of light quality. Therefore, many research focus on improving lighting comfort and work efficiency, as well as improving people's pleasure and well-being through the improvement of light quality. Regarding the improvement of work efficiency and comfort, many studies on office lighting environments have shown that improving office lighting has a positive impact on employees. Good lighting can enhance the comfort, health, and productivity of modern office environments [16, 32]. The international lighting company PHILIPS Lighting mentions on its official website that improving lighting conditions can increase comfort and have a positive impact on employee performance, including a 25% improvement in psychological and memory function, a 12% increase in telephone processing efficiency, and a 23% increase in productivity.

In terms of pleasure and well-being, Kruithof proposed the combination principle of illuminance and color temperature based on psychophysical data drawn from a curve, which can create the most comfortable and pleasant atmosphere when high illuminance is combined with high color temperature, and low illuminance is combined with low color temperature [18]. Many studies have shown that lighting can create an appropriate spatial atmosphere and bring a pleasant feeling to people by changing the lighting effects in different environments. For example, in commercial shopping spaces, different color temperatures and color rendering indices can change the emotional response of consumers' shopping behavior and bring them pleasure [14, 23]. Good lighting in the office environment can make users feel happier, more satisfied with the work environment, and more engaged in work [33].

From the above lighting development trends, it can be seen that lighting design has shifted from focusing primarily on users' basic needs, including physical function, brightness, and cost, to today's requirement for a good lighting product to not only have good functionality and aesthetics, but also to understand users' emotional needs and incorporate elements that bring pleasure into the product. Jordan once introduced the term "pleasure" into the context of product design, and defined pleasure products as those that give people a sense of pleasure from three types of benefit experiences when interacting with the product: emotional, hedonic, and practical. The so-called emotional benefits explore how the product moves a person's emotions, hedonic benefits explore how the product inspires a person's positive and pleasant feelings, and practical benefits explore how people use the product to complete tasks and accumulate results [25]. Many studies have shown that users are more likely to choose a product that they find visually pleasing, and that viewing a product's appearance can generate pleasure [28, 37]. This study only focuses on the relationship between the appearance of the product and the feelings of pleasure and preference.

2.3 From Rational Needs to Emotional Needs

As the times change, the trend of consumption has shifted from rational consumption to emotional consumption, which is in line with Maslow's hierarchy of needs theory. The theory states that there are hierarchical levels of needs, and the satisfaction of needs will start from the lowest level of Physiological needs, then Safety needs, Social needs,

Esteem needs, and finally self-actualization needs. When one level of needs is satisfied, individuals will pursue the next higher level of needs [7]. This indicates that if users are satisfied with practicality, safety, and comfort, the focus of needs may shift towards decorative, emotional, and symbolic design attributes. Looking at the three development stages of the lighting market, lighting design has also evolved from meeting the basic lighting functional needs at the bottom of the pyramid, to high-quality lighting and ultimately to human-oriented emotional needs. How to make users feel comfortable and happy is the focus of today's lighting design. As there have been many studies on improving the quality of light, the relationship between the appearance and user's pleasure of the lighting fixture is worth exploring.

Norman pointed out that the emotional aspect of design may be more critical to the success of a product than its practical elements. Demirbilek and Sener (2003) also believed that designers should understand the emotional, user, and product design aspects, which all affect purchasing and usage choices [9]. In terms of emotional design, Norman proposed three levels in his book "Emotional Design": (1) visceral level, which is the user's first impression of the product, including its appearance, texture, and feel. The visceral level is more primitive than conscious thinking, and we make rapid responses and decisions on good or bad, beautiful or ugly, safe or dangerous, based on our direct reaction to the product's visual and first impression. (2) behavioral level, which relates to the product's use and experience, and whether it has effective functions, is easy to recognize, understand, and operate, which deter-mines the feelings during use. (3) reflective level, which emphasizes the message, culture, and meaning of the product or its utility.

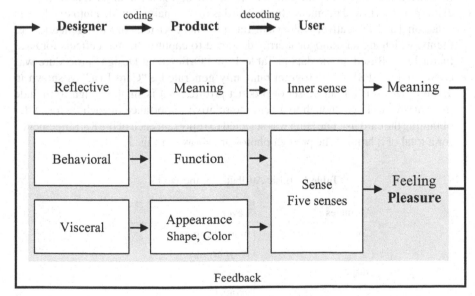

Fig. 1. Communication in Different Design Levels Between Designers and Users

This article focuses on the relationship between product appearance and aesthetic pleasure, which belongs to the instinctive level proposed by Norman. Based on Norman's Design Model, Users' Mental Model, and System Image, it is known that designers do not have direct interaction with users, but communicate with them through the product. However, there may be cognitive differences between the designer's interpretation and the user's understanding due to the effects of encoding and decoding. Therefore, further research is needed to explore how the visual first impression of a product can generate pleasure for users. Combining Norman's System Image with the three design levels, as shown in Fig. 1, can help understand the communication between designers and users at different design levels and serve as the main frame-work for this study.

3   Research Methodology

This study intends to construct an accessible criticism model that is easy to understand for the relationship between product appearance and pleasure. A five-point scale questionnaire is used to examine the pleasure and preference of QisDESIGN brand lighting products' appearance shape, color, and functionality given to the sub-jects, and to further understand the impact of appearance attributes on user pleasure and the correlation between pleasure and preference.

(1) Sampling explanation of lighting products: Based on the subjects' feedback on the works and through literature review and expert discussions, three basic attributes are considered important components of product appearance. First is color, divided into two levels: monochrome and multicolor. Second is form, divided into two levels: organic form and geometric form. Third is functionality, divided into two levels: functional and decorative, as shown in Table 1. There is a total of 8 different arrangements, which are an orthogonal array designed to capture the main effects for each factor level. Based on the data in Table 1, an "Orthogonal Design" procedure was conducted in SPSS. The program randomly generated a "Card List," as shown in Table 2, which is a reduced set of product profiles that is small enough to include in a survey but large enough to assess the relative importance of each factor. After obtaining the card list, one lamp was selected to represent each of the 8 arrangements, for a total of 8 lamps. The product photos are shown in Fig. 2.

Table 1. Basic Attributes of the Works

Attributes	Level
Color	monochrome
	polychrome
Shape	organic
	geometry
Function	functional
	decorative

Table 2. Card List Generated for Conjoint Analysis

Card List			
Card ID	Color	Shape	Function
P1	monochrome	organic	functional
P2	monochrome	organic	decorative
P3	monochrome	geometry	functional
P4	monochrome	geometry	decorative
P5	polychrome	organic	functional
P6	polychrome	organic	decorative
P7	polychrome	geometry	functional
P8	polychrome	geometry	decorative

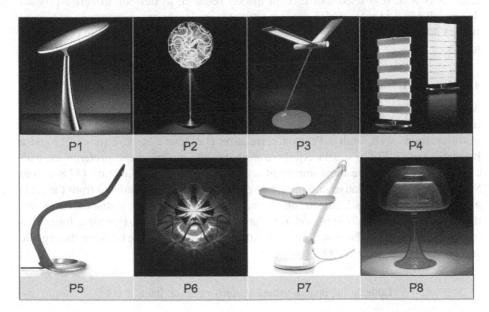

Fig. 2. Eight Chosen products in accordance with the Card List Generated by SPSS

(2) Questionnaire design: Eight lamps were evaluated using a 5-point Likert scale to assess the pleasure and preference for each lamp, and then ranked accordingly.

(3) Testing procedure: Prior to the questionnaire testing, the 8 lamps were displayed in a separate space. Participants scanned a QR code with their mobile phones upon entering the room to access the Google form for the questionnaire. During the testing process, participants were allowed to touch the lamps, turn them on and off, and adjust the lighting angle to fully experience the lamp products. A total of 72 valid questionnaires were collected in this survey (Fig. 3).

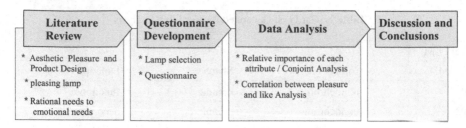

Fig. 3. Research procedure and experimental analysis flowchart

4   Results and Discussions

In the process of selecting research subjects, the product chosen was QisDesign, a Taiwanese brand of LED lighting fixtures. To further investigate participants' responses to stimuli, this study employed a statistical technique called "Conjoint Analysis". Conjoint analysis is a survey-based tool used in market research to develop effective product designs. It can determine which product attributes are important or unimportant to consumers and which levels of product attributes are most or least desirable in consumers' minds.

4.1   Conjoint Analysis for Relative Importance of Each Attribute of the Products

According to the statistical results of Table 3 and Fig. 4, we have summarized the importance of product attributes. The results show that the correlational model of this study performs well, with a Pearson correlation coefficient of .852 (p < .01) and a Kendall's tau of .772 (p < .01). All three attributes affect consumers' preferences, with color (42.3%) being the most important attribute, followed by Function (34.8%) and Shape (29.9%). The relative importance of each attribute was calculated from the tools given in Table 3 and Fig. 5. Regarding the overall utility of color, the statistical data show that monochrome (r = .788) is more popular than polychrome. For Function, functional (r = .330) is more popular than decorative, and there is no difference between the organic and geometry shapes (r = .000).

Table 3. Importance value and utility of the attribute levels

Factor	Level	Utility	Importance Value %
Color	monochrome	.788	42.347
	polychrome	−.788	
Shape	organic	.000	22.882
	geometry	.000	
Function	functional	.330	34.771
	decorative	−.330	
Pearson's R: .852**		Kendall's tau: .772**	

** p < .01.

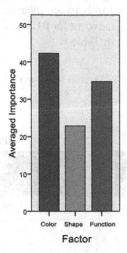

Fig. 4. Average Importance of Product Attributes

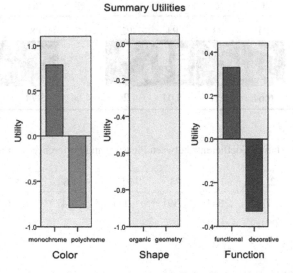

Fig. 5. Preference Levels Associated with Color, Proportion, and Shape

4.2 Correlation Between Pleasure and Happiness

The pleasure and preference scores of each light were statistically evaluated and ranked based on their scores, as shown in Tables 4 and 5. P4 had the highest pleasure score with an average of 4.38, followed by P1 with an average of 4.25 and P7 with an average of 3.79. P1 had the highest preference score with an average of 6.64, followed by P3 with an average of 5.18 and P4 with an average of 5.04. Pearson correlation analysis was conducted to examine the relationship between pleasure and preference, and the Pearson correlation coefficient was .731* (p < .01), indicating a significant positive correlation between overall pleasure and preference for the products. Furthermore, individual analysis was conducted to examine the relationship between pleasure and preference for each light, and the results showed that all lights, except for P1, had a significant correlation between pleasure and preference, as shown in Table 6.

Table 4. Overall pleasure ranking

Rank	1	2	3	4	5	6	7	8
No.	P4	P1	P7	P3	P8	P6	P5	P2
Product								
Mean Scores	4.38	4.25	3.79	3.83	3.68	3.29	3.07	3.04

Table 5. Overall preference ranking

Rank	1	2	3	4	5	6	7	8
No.	P1	P3	P4	P2	P7	P8	P6	P5
Product								
Mean Scores	6.64	5.18	5.04	4.29	4.04	3.74	3.61	3.46

Table 6. Correlation Coefficients between Pleasure and Preference for Each Products

Product	P1	P2	P3	P4	P5	P6	P7	P8
r	.063	.347**	.384**	.391**	.431***	.447***	.367**	.466***

** $p < .01$. *** $p < .001$.

5   Conclusions

This study investigates the relationship between the visual attributes of lighting products and the feelings of pleasure and preference through literature review, expert discussion, and questionnaire analysis. The study aims to provide important reference for product designers and to create emotional value for lighting products. Based on the research and analysis, the following recommendations are proposed:

(1) The core value of design has shifted from focusing on functionality to emphasizing user emotions, and aesthetics can satisfy human sensory pleasure. The attractiveness of a product can be enhanced by making it visually pleasing, which is a key element

in providing users with pleasure. Since ancient Greek times, many scholars and artists have proposed theories of the formal principles of beauty. These theories are related to product design, including form, color, and usage function, and they can be regarded as the visual attributes of a product that provide pleasure.

(2) The research results indicate that color is the most important attribute that affects users' preference for lighting products, followed by function, and shape is the third. Subjects preferred monochromatic object over polychrome object, with silver and white being the most popular monochromatic colors and polychrome Color is based on bright warm colors. Functional attributes can be classified into functional and decorative, where functional refers to reading lighting and decorative refers to ambient lighting. Subjects preferred reading lighting to ambient lighting, indicating that different lighting source characteristics may affect user preferences and require further investigation. The styling attributes can be divided into organic and geometric styling, but subjects did not have a preference for either category.

(3) The research results indicate that there is a correlation between the pleasure and preference of subjects for the appearance of lighting products. The ranking of pleasure and preference showed that P1 and P4 were both in the top three, indicating that the visual attributes of these two lighting products are worth further exploration. In addition, by examining the attributes of the top three lighting products for both pleasure and preference, it was found that all were reading lights, and their even and soft lighting characteristics may be the reason why subjects found them enjoyable and pleasing. This phenomenon is consistent with the literature review that light sources can bring pleasure to users, and further research can be conducted on the relationship between lighting source characteristics and pleasure.

References

1. Sonderegger, A., Sauer, J.: The influence of design aesthetics in usability testing: effects on user performance and perceived usability. Appl. Ergon. **41**(3), 403–410 (2010). ISSN 0003-6870
2. Bi, W., Lyu, Y., Cao, J., Lin, R.: From usability to pleasure: a case study of difference in users' preference. Engineering **13**, 448–462 (2021)
3. Blijlevens, J., Creusen, M., Schoormans, J.: How consumers perceive product appearance: the identification of three product appearance attributes. Int. J. Des. **3**(3), 27–35 (2009)
4. Blijlevens, J., et al.: The aesthetic pleasure in design scale: the development of a scale to measure aesthetic pleasure for designed artifacts. Psychol. Aesthet. Creat. Arts **11**, 86–98 (2017)
5. Bloch, P.H.: Seeking the ideal form: product design and consumer response. J. Mark. **59**(3), 16–29 (1995)
6. Burke, E.: A Philosophical Enquiry Into the Origin of Our Ideas of the Sublime and Beautiful. Oxford University Press, Oxford. (Original work published in 1757) (2015)
7. Chien, C.-W., Lin, C.-L., Lin, R.-T.: The study of period style in products. J. Natl. Taiwan Coll. Arts **99**, P1–27 (2016)
8. Creusen, M.E.H., Schoormans, J.P.L.: The different roles of product appearance in consumer choice. J. Prod. Innov. Manag. **22**, 63–81 (2005)
9. Demirbilek, O., Sener, B.: Product design, semantics and emotional response. Ergonomics **46**(13–14), 1346–1360 (2003)

10. Gobe, M.: Emotional Branding: The New Paradigm for Connecting Brands to People. Allworth Press, New York (2001)
11. Goldman, A.: The aesthetic. In: Gaut, B., McIver Lopes, D. (eds.) The Routledge Companion to Aesthetics, pp. 181–192. Routledge, London (2001)
12. Hekkert, P.: Design aesthetics: principles of pleasure in design. Psychol. Sci. **48**, 157–172 (2006)
13. Hume, D.: A Treatise of Human Nature. Penguin Books, London (1985)
14. Quartier, K., Vanrie, J., Van Cleempoel, K.: As real as it gets: What role does lighting have on consumer's perception of atmosphere, emotions and behaviour. J. Environ. Psychol. **39**, 32–39 (2014). ISSN 0272-4944
15. Lin, P.H., Yeh, M.L., Lin, H.Y.: Design for aesthetic pleasure. In: Rau, P.L. (eds.) HCII 2019. LNCS, vol. 11576. Springer, Cham (2019). https://doi.org/10.1007/978-3-030-22577-3_37
16. Manav, B.: An experimental study on the appraisal of the visual environment at offices in relation to colour temperature and illuminance. Build. Environ. **42**(2), 979–983 (2007)
17. Berkowitz, M.: Product shape as a design innovation strategy. J. Prod. Innov. Manag. **4**(4), 274–283 (1987). ISSN 0737-6782
18. Hsieh, M., Li, G.: Effects of illumination types and color temperatures on office worker's moods and task performance from the viewpoint of eco-efficiency –a case of subjects at the age of 20–28. J. Archit. **102**, P1–18 (2017)
19. Aarts, M.P.J., Aries, M.B.C., Straathof, J., van Hoof, J.: Dynamic lighting systems in psychogeriatric care facilities in The Netherlands: a quantitative and qualitative analysis of stakeholders' responses and applied technology. Indoor Built Environ. **24**, 617–630 (2015)
20. Norman, D.: Emotional Design: Why We Love (or Hate) Everyday Things, pp. 17–24. Basic Books, New York (2005)
21. Ogando-Martínez, A., López-Gómez, J., Febrero-Garrido, L.: Maintenance factor identification in outdoor lighting installations using simulation and optimization techniques. Energies **11**(8), 2169 (2018)
22. Danziger, P.: Why People Buy Things They Don't Need: Understanding and Predicting Consumer Behavior, Kaplan Trade (2005)
23. Park, N., Farr, C.A.: The effects of lighting on consumers' emotions and behavioral intentions in a retail environment: a cross-cultural comparison. J. Inter. Des. **33**(1), 17–32 (2007)
24. Jordan, P.W.: Human factors for pleasure in product use. Appl. Ergon. **29**(1), 25–33 (1998). ISSN 0003-6870, 46(13–14), 1346–1360
25. Jordan, P.W.: Designing Pleasurable Products, Taylor & Francis, UK (2000)
26. Hecht, P., Ryder, H.: 10 - Product Aesthetics. Product Experience, Elsevier, pp. 259–285 (2008). ISBN 9780080450896
27. Lu, P., Hsiao, S.-W.: A product design method for form and color matching based on aesthetic theory. Adv. Eng. Inform. **53**, 101702 (2022). ISSN 1474-0346
28. Karkun, P., Chowdhury, A., Dhar, D.: Effect of baby-like product personality on visually perceived pleasure: a study on coffeemakers. Ergon. Caring People, 273–279 (2017)
29. Dou, R., Li, W., Nan, G., Wang, X., Zhou, Y.: How can manufacturers make decisions on product appearance design? A research on optimal design based on customers' emotional satisfaction. J. Manag. Sci. Eng. **6**(2), pp. 177–196 (2021). ISSN 2096-2320
30. Lin, R.-T.: The integration of human needs and technology- the cultural Innovation. Sci. Dev. **396**, 68–75 (2005)
31. Lin, R., Su, C.-H., Chang, S.-H.: from cultural creativity to qualia. In: Conference of Taiwan Institute of Kansei, Tunghai University, Taiwan (2010)
32. van Bommel, W., van den Beld, G.: Lighting for work: a review of visual and biological effects. Light. Res. Technol. **36**(4), 255–266 (2004)
33. Veitch, J.A., Stokkermans, M.G.M., Newsham, G.R.: Linking lighting appraisals to work behaviors. Environ. Behav. **45**(2), 198–214 (2013)

34. Westbrook, R.A.: Product/consumption-based affective responses and postpurchase processes. J. Mark. Res. **24**(3), 258–270 (1987)
35. Green, W.S., Jordan, P.W.: Pleasure With Products. CRC Press. Chapter 5, p. 7 (2002)
36. Tatarkiewicz, W.: The great theory of beauty and its decline. J. Aesthet. Art Crit. **31**(2), 165–180 (1972)
37. Wu, TY., Chang, Wc., Hsu, YH.: Designing a Lighting with Pleasure. Human Centered Design, pp 139–146 (2009)
38. Zhang, X.: Western Aesthetics in the 20th Century. Wuhan University Press (2009)

Effect of Editing Photos by Application on Chinese Facial Impression Perception

Wen Qi Fang[1] (ID) and Yu-Chi Lee[2](✉) (ID)

[1] School of Design, South China University of Technology, Guangzhou 510006, China
[2] College of Management and Design, Ming Chi University of Technology, New Taipei City 243303, Taiwan
yclee@mail.mcut.edu.tw

Abstract. Using editing applications to edit face and post it on social media platforms has become the norm. The aim of this study was to assess the effect of Chinese young men and women using popular editing applications to edit their faces on underlying facial impressions. Four targets (half males) edited their own facial photos, original photos and edited photos were collected as experimental stimulus materials. Attractiveness, trustworthiness, and dominance of two types of photos were rated by 30 Chinese young females. The results showed that no significant difference was found in the two photo types of male targets. Female edited photos were significantly more attractive and dominant than the original photos. However, the female editing did not improve the trustworthiness of the face impression. The result revealed that the effect of retouching on facial impressions is different for male and female perceiver. Additionally, editing faces does not necessarily lead to a better impression, especially for male perceivers. The findings of this research can be taken into account in the future use and design of editing applications.

Keywords: Retouching · Impression · Gender gap

1 Introduction

In recent years, by using advanced photo editing applications (e.g., Facetune), people can easily manipulate their facial features, such as smoothing, filtering, and reshaping [1]. Approximately 62.2% of young women reported that they "sometimes" and "very often" engage in selfie editing [2]. Editing brings variations in photos of the same face. The variations of facial features can modulate facial impression formation, and the influence extends to many aspects of life, such as whom to date, whom to hire, and whom to make friends with [3]. On social media, posting edited photos of oneself is becoming very popular [4]. It is a behavior of self-presentation, that is, to convey some information about oneself to others [5]. Individuals have more control over their self-presentational behavior in the social network than in face-to-face communication [6]. By strategically managing their self-presentations, people can present the aspect of their personalities and the best image they want to present [6]. Nowadays, it is very common in daily life.

© The Author(s), under exclusive license to Springer Nature Switzerland AG 2023
P.-L. P. Rau (Ed.): HCII 2023, LNCS 14023, pp. 16–24, 2023.
https://doi.org/10.1007/978-3-031-35939-2_2

For those who edit their facial photos, the edited photos are certainly considered better than the original ones. However, in various comments online, some negative attitudes toward editing photos by others have also emerged. Some studies have answered the issue of whether photo editing makes a better impression. For example, Nakano & Uesugi [4] found a positive effect on attractiveness perception after moderate modification of Asian female faces. Meanwhile, they found that extreme editing can reduce attractiveness and naturalness. Judgment criteria for facial impressions may vary across cultures. In terms of the impact of editing photos in real life, Cristel et al. [7] reported that three races subjects had no significant first impression (social skills, academic performance, dating success, occupational success, attractiveness, financial success, relationship success, and athletic success) differences between selfies and selfies with added filter. Hence, self-face editing in daily life cannot certainly enhance one's impression.

With the discovery of three underlying dimensions of facial evaluation (attractiveness, trustworthiness, dominance) [8, 9], these facial dimensions have become important variables in assessing facial impressions. Although many studies concerning the impact of photo editing, the effect of facial editing on these three facial impressions according to Asian preferences is unclear. In addition, females are the main users of various photo editing applications, and relatively few males use editing software. Therefore, most studies on photo editing focus on women, and gender difference in facial impressions obtained from the male and female editor was rarely noticed.

Hence, this study aims to complement upon previous research, ratings the basic facial impression of two types of photos in the context of Asian aesthetics. The two types of photos used in the study were original facial photos and edited facial photos edited by male and female targets. This study can contribute to a better comprehension of the photo impression edited by the male and female in the Asian cultural context.

2 Method

2.1 Participants

A total of 30 Chinese young women aged 17 to 24 years (M = 20.03, SD = 1.81) were recruited in the photo rating experiment. Females were recruited because they were found to have higher levels of perceptual accuracy in previous first impression studies [10]. Recruited participants use social media on a daily basis. The frequency of their facial editing is evenly distributed between no editing at all and almost daily editing. All participants had normal or corrected-to-normal vision, and they had no visual deficiency (e.g., color blindness). Participants signed informed consent at the start of the experiment, and each of them have no prior knowledge of the scientific purpose of the study.

2.2 Experimental Materials

Four targets (two males and two females) were recruited for the preparation of the experimental material, and their ages ranged from 21 to 25 years (M = 23, SD = 1.58). The average body mass index (BMI) of all targets were within the normal range (18.5 < BMI < 24.9). No abrupt features in the appearance of the four targets. They often edit and post their facial photos to social media platforms (e.g., Qzone and Facebook).

Material preparation start with a shot of the targets' faces. Targets were asked not to wear any accessories or glasses, and no beards or visible makeup on their face. To avoid the impact of clothing, targets wore the same style of clothing. Subsequently, targets were sitting in front of a white background, smiling naturally, a professional photographer took photos of the four targets' front faces in turn. After the original photos of the four targets were collected, the researchers standardized the four photos: the photos were scaled to regulate the proportion of the face in the photo and cropped to a uniform ratio as well as to ensure the high definition of the photo.

After the photos were taken, four targets came to a quiet laboratory for photo editing separately. Each target was required to install the editing applications they were interested in or frequently used, on an iPad (11 inches, 2388 × 1668 pixels). Then, they were asked to edit their own facial photo aiming to upload on social media platforms, without a time limit. Three editing applications were used by the four targets: Meitu, Facetune, and VSCO. After completing the photo editing, a total of eight different photographs (4 targets × 2 types) were collected, examples of the two types of photos are shown in Fig. 1 and Fig. 2 for male and female, respectively.

Fig. 1. Original and edited photo of a male target.

2.3 Photo Rating Experiment

The photo rating experiment was performed in the laboratory. The light conditions in the laboratory are constant. No indication of any impact on the consequence would be provided to participants before the experiment. Each participant was requested to sit in front of a table, iPad was placed on the table as a display to show photo materials. Participants were able to move the iPad freely to view the images. A questionnaire about the basic facial impression dimensions was sent to the participants' phones for them to rate the photos appearing on the iPad.

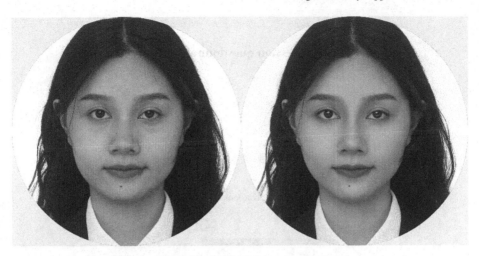

Fig. 2. Original and edited photo of a female target.

Prior to the experiment, participants were informed of the experiment procedure, and an additional photograph was used to improve the familiarity of procedure. In the experiment, participants rated two photo types (original, retouched) from each of the targets twice, a total of 16 photos (4 target * 2 types * 2 repetitions) appeared on the iPad in random order. Participants rated each photo continuously with no time limit. After seeing a photo displayed on the iPad, the participant rated the attractiveness, trustworthiness, and dominance of the photo through a questionnaire on their phone correspondingly. Each facial impression rating from 0 to 100 by dragging a slider that displayed the scores accordingly. Slider scales can have a more precise reading of a participants' views than using Likert scales [11]. Figure 3 illustrates the state of the participant while performing the assessment and shows the facial impression questionnaire used in the study. The participant is shown a blank page lasting 5 s before the next photo is displayed to avoid the continuous appearance of photos leading to a comparison between two photos. After completing scoring the eight photographs (having completed half of the experiment), participants rested for at least five minutes. No acquaintance between targets and participants to avoid interference of familiarity on impression rating.

2.4 Data Analysis

To understand the changes in impressions caused by male targets and female targets editing respectively, the scores were divided into two groups by target gender. Then, the differences in the facial impression scores between the two photograph types were tested using independent samples t-tests separately. An alpha level of 0.05 was applied for significance testing. All the data were analyzed by using SPSS 26.0 software.

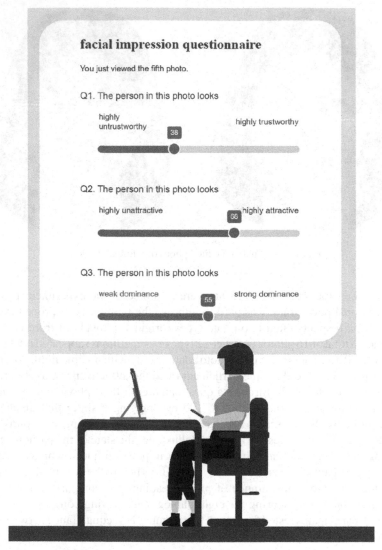

Fig. 3. The scenario of photo rating experiment.

3   Results and Discussion

Table 1 shows the results of independent samples t-tests on two types of photos with different gender targets, the average scores and standard deviations are also shown in the table. According to the photo impressions result, no significant differences in three facial impressions were found between the two photographs of male targets (all $p > 0.05$). The average attractiveness and dominance impression scores of male target's edited photos (attractiveness: 36.17 ± 18.32, dominance: 45.32 ± 18.52) have improved compared to the original photos (attractiveness: 34.17 ± 17.49, dominance: 41.52 ± 19.24). For trustworthiness, the average score of male edited photos is lower than original one (original: 42.67 ± 20.62, edited: 37.42 ± 19.22). However, the differences mentioned above are too small to reach the significance. This might cause by the sample size issue. For female targets, the attractiveness (p < 0.01) and dominance (p < 0.05) scores of the edited photos (attractiveness: 55.25 ± 19.24, dominance: 53.58 ± 17.99) are significantly higher than the original photos (attractiveness: 44.90 ± 17.78, dominance: 47.02 ± 16.95). There is no significant difference in trustworthiness (original: 51.75 ± 19.25, edited: 52.95 ± 17.34; p = 0.720). Figure 4 shows the average scores of the three impression ratings for all targets. All photos of the four targets did not show extreme impression scores. Most of the edited photos of the four targets all showed different degrees of average improvement compared to the original photos. However, editing leads to a decrease in the mean attractiveness and trustworthiness of the second male target, as well as a decrease in the mean trustworthiness of the first male and second female targets. It seems that editing a photo has the potential to cause a specific impression of someone to fall.

Table 1. Mean, standard deviations and significance of impressions scores for male and female targets.

Male targets					
	Original		Edited		
	Mean	SD	Mean	SD	Significance
Attractiveness	34.17	17.49	36.17	18.32	p = 0.542
Trustworthiness	42.67	20.62	37.42	19.22	p = 0.152
Dominance	41.52	19.24	45.32	18.52	p = 0.273
Female targets					
Attractiveness	44.90	17.78	55.25	19.24	p = 0.003**
Trustworthiness	51.75	19.25	52.95	17.34	p = 0.720
Dominance	47.02	16.95	53.58	17.99	p = 0.042*

*p < 0.05; **p < 0.01.

In terms of results, facial editing improved facial attractiveness and dominance of female targets, the trustworthiness of female targets remains unchanged, and the facial impression of male targets to others also remained the same. Therefore, photo editing may enhance the first impression of the face (attractiveness and dominance), but there are differences between male and female editors. The results are inconsistent with the study of Cristel et al. [7], they pointed out that there was no first impression difference between unfiltered photos and filtered photos, although the targets liked the filtered photos best. The difference in results may be attributed to that the current study's focus on the difference between male and female targets and splitting the data off. In addition,

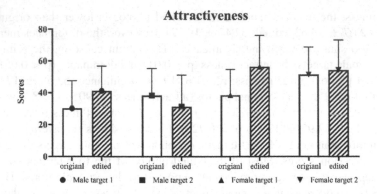

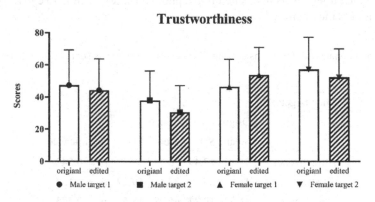

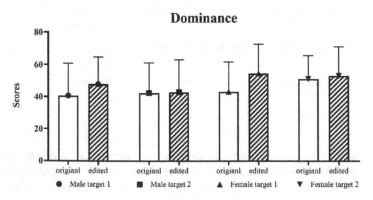

Fig. 4. Average scores of attractiveness, trustworthiness and dominance of the four targets.

there were no restrictions on how the target edited the photos in the current study, whereas the study by Cristel et al. [7] required subjects to use two preset filter types. A natural and realistic context is important when shooting and editing. In future studies of edited photo impressions, attention needs to be paid to the influence of gender and self-other perspective. Besides, this study used a subjective assessment method, which has limitations in terms of the number of targets and participants in the sample. Future studies could concern for the impact of retouching between different ethnic groups and recruit a larger number of more representative samples for studying.

In this study, the edited photos of the male targets not only did not show a significant increase in impressions but even a decrease in the mean score of trustworthiness. Considering that the current main users of popular editing applications are women, these results may be caused by the default photo processing of editing applications. For example, when dragging the dots in apps to increase the beauty level, it is usually accompanied by a pointed chin and fairer skin, it makes the edited face more feminine. Thus, the photos edited by popular applications of the day can have a more negative impression on males, editing apps focused on enhancing male image need to be developed. It is important to note that the subjects who participated in the scoring in this study were all female. If there has scores from the male perspective, it may differ from the present results.

Additionally, women's edited photos make them look more attractive and dominant. Editing applications can enhance facial symmetry and feminine features, while easily bringing the face closer to the average human face. These facial changes are the key to biologically enhancing the attractiveness of the female face [12]. There is another possible reason why women look better in edited photos. Women are better at creating their own visual self-worth than men in terms of aesthetic, emotional, self-reflective and aesthetic-symbolical aspects of photography [13]. Besides, a previous study focusing on the role of makeup has found that more attractive women tend to be perceived as more likely to adopt dominance tactics and give a stronger sense of dominance [14]. The role of editing and makeup may be similar in this regard, facial editing would also lead to dominance enhancement.

Furthermore, trustworthiness remains unaffected regardless of the target's gender. In some studies, editing has been considered as having a potentially negative impact on trustworthiness. Similarly, makeup has been found to make salespeople less trustworthy [15]. One of the important reasons for this untrustworthiness is the unnatural feeling, some editing such as smoothed skin texture and enlarged eyes can bring unnatural feeling [4, 7]. The current study revealed that photo editing did not inevitably result in photo enhancement. As photo retouching tools and photo editing applications become accessible and integrated with other social media platforms, providing more guidelines for users and warning of the appropriate consequences becomes increasingly important to prevent future negative effects caused by facial editing [16].

4 Conclusion

This study assesses the impact of facial self-edit and target's gender on basic facial impression among Chinese people. Two types of photos from four targets were rating in experiment, to get the average score of attractiveness, trustworthiness and dominance for each photo. The edited photos of female targets were more attractive and dominance than their original photos, no change in trustworthiness was found. For male targets, there were no impressions difference between the edited photo and the original photo. Females editing their photos can get an impression boost, while males can't. As more and more males start using editing applications, they need to beware of such impression problems. The findings of this study provided information about the current editing situation. The use of more delicate subjective measures paired with objective measures and an expanded sample size could be considered in future studies.

References

1. Vendemia, M.A.: The effects of engaging in digital photo modifications and receiving favorable comments on womens selfies shared on social media. Body Image **37**, 74–83 (2021)
2. Cohen, R., Newton-John, T., Slater, A.: 'Selfie'-objectification: the role of selfies in self-objectification and disordered eating in young women. Comput. Hum. Behav. **79**, 68–74 (2018)
3. White, D., Sutherland, C.A.M., Burton, A.L.: Choosing face: the curse of self in profile image selection. Cognit. Res. **2**, 23 (2017)
4. Nakano, T., Uesugi, Y.: Risk factors leading to preference for extreme facial retouching. Cyberpsychol. Behav. Soc. Netw. **23**, 52–59 (2020)
5. Baumeister, R.F.: A self-presentational view of social phenomena. Psychol. Bull. **91**, 3–26 (1982)
6. Krämer, N.C., Winter, S.: Impression management 2.0: the relationship of self-esteem, extraversion, self-efficacy, and self-presentation within social networking sites. J. Media Psychol. Theor. Methods Appl. **20**, 106–116 (2008)
7. Cristel, R.T., Dayan, S.H., Akinosun, M., Russell, P.T.: Evaluation of selfies and filtered selfies and effects on first impressions. Aesthet. Surg. J. **41**, 122–130 (2021)
8. Oosterhof, N.N., Todorov, A.: The functional basis of face evaluation. Proc. Natl. Acad. Sci. U.S.A. **105**, 11087–11092 (2008)
9. Sutherland, C.A.M., Oldmeadow, J.A., Santos, I.M., Towler, J., Michael, B.D., Young, A.W.: Social inferences from faces: ambient images generate a three-dimensional model. Cognition **127**, 105–118 (2013)
10. Chan, M., Rogers, K.H., Parisotto, K.L., Biesanz, J.C.: Forming first impressions: the role of gender and normative accuracy in personality perception. J. Res. Pers. **45**, 117–120 (2011)
11. Chyung, S.Y., Swanson, I., Roberts, K., Hankinson, A.: Evidence-based survey design: the use of continuous rating scales in surveys. Perform. Improv. **57**, 38–48 (2018)
12. Rhodes, G.: the evolutionary psychology of facial beauty. Annu. Rev. Psychol. **57**, 199–226 (2006)
13. Siibak, A.: Constructing the self through the photo selection - visual impression management on social networking websites. Cyberpsychology **3**, 1 (2009)
14. Schneider, Z., Moroń, M.: Facial makeup and perceived likelihood of influence tactics use among women: a role of attractiveness attributed to faces with and without makeup. Curr Psychol. **41**, 1–12 (2022)
15. Mittal, S., Silvera, D.H.: Makeup or mask: makeup's effect on salesperson trustworthiness. J. Consum. Mark. **37**, 271–277 (2020)
16. Beos, N., Kemps, E., Prichard, I.: Photo manipulation as a predictor of facial dissatisfaction and cosmetic procedure attitudes. Body Image **39**, 194–201 (2021)

Design Optimization of Adjustable Filter Rod Based on User Experience

Ning Hou[1], Yanggang Ou[1], Qiang Liu[1], Jing Che[1], Lei Wu[2], and Huai Cao[2](✉)

[1] China Tobacco Hubei Industrial Co., Ltd., Wuhan 430051, People's Republic of China
[2] School of Mechanical Science and Engineering, Huazhong University of Science and
Technology, Wuhan 430074, People's Republic of China
caohuai@hust.edu.cn

Abstract. With the transformation and upgrading of the market consumption structure, the market demand for new filter rods with innovative experience is rising. Based on user experience and computational fluid dynamics theory, the rule and mechanism of filter rod suction resistance are systematically studied, and the change rule of filter rod suction resistance is visual quantified through big data. Aiming at the appearance and functional structure design of arbitrary rotating filter rod, an innovative industrial design solution is proposed to change the flow direction and output of filter rod flue gas, so as to improve the user experience of filter rod suction. The experimental results show that: 1) the accuracy of suction resistance adjustment of filter rod is improved; 2) When the filter rod angle is rotated to 280°, the flue gas flow is the shortest, the suction resistance is the smallest, and effectively enhanced the user experience; 3) When the molding speed is 150 m/min, the qualification rate reaches 99.98%, which can meet the requirements of stable production of filter rods. The research results provide theoretical and practical reference for industrial design optimization and user experience evaluation in the related research fields.

Keywords: User experience · Computational fluid dynamics · Adjustable filter rod · Industrial design · Structural design

1 Introduction

Donald Norman put forward the concept of "user experience" (UX) in the mid-1990s [1, 2]. Many scholars interpret user experience from different perspectives. Most definitions have both similarities and differences. For example, most definitions emphasize interaction, while ISO9241-210 focuses on use, which is also the most recognized definition by scholars, that is, people's perception and response to using or participating in products, services or systems [3]. User experience originates from human-computer interaction of computer science and spreads rapidly. Its content continues to expand, becoming a typical cross integration of highly interdisciplinary, and has been deeply applied in many fields, including usability design, ergonomics, information aesthetics, and specific applications of information technology and product design [4].

P.-L. P. Rau (Ed.): HCII 2023, LNCS 14023, pp. 25–35, 2023.
https://doi.org/10.1007/978-3-031-35939-2_3

Furthermore, Liu Yi [5] believes that user experience design can be analyzed and understood from the three levels of available, ease of use and integration. Chen Wei [6] also put forward a similar point of view. Only when the product achieves functionality is the basis, and only when it meets self needs is the highest level. Inspired by Maslow's view on the hierarchy of human needs, he summarized six elements of user experience design: "product functional demand → product sensory demand → product interaction demand → product emotional demand → product social demand → product self demand". Coincidentally, Jordan [7] believes that the user experience dimension model should be a pyramid layered form, with functionality, usability and pleasure from bottom to top. User experience design generally has two forms. One is to improve existing products through user experience testing and evaluation to improve user satisfaction. The other is to let users participate in the design of new products. Through user research and proposing design prototypes, users can experience and constantly improve until they meet user experience needs [8]. This paper is aimed at the second kind of design research on new product development.

2 Literature Review

It is difficult for traditional design categories to transform user needs into possible service features by observing the scenario of the entire service system [9]. Therefore, HP, IBM, YAHOO, Microsoft, Lenovo and other major enterprises have established user experience research institutions in their early years [10]. In recent years, Internet enterprises with fierce competition have found that the success of their products depends largely on how many users will choose to use them and continue to use them. Therefore, they have also set up user experience design departments, such as Huawei UCD, Taobao UED, Tencent CDC, Baidu XDC, Netease UEDC, etc., to facilitate rapid product updates and iterations based on user needs.

In the academic field, Hu Fei [11] collected and screened 70 user experience design methods. Xin Xiangyang [12] has put forward the academic idea of taking experience as the design object at the International Experience Design Conference (IXDC) and the Australian User Experience Conference (UX Australia) since 2014. In TEDx activities in 2015, it was clearly pointed out that there is an essential difference between user experience (UX) and experience design (EX). He believed that user experience (UX) is not a feeling, but a process from beginning to end, and experience is the design criterion. What users do, think and feel when operating or using a product/service. The user experience is flat, neutral, intuitive and easy to understand, focusing on the product itself; Focus on means of life, designers are creators. Experience design (EX), on the other hand, not only focuses on the process, but also contains expectations and continues to have influence. Experience as a design object. The experience of personal growth through a series of meaningful events under the guidance of specific goals. Multiple dimensions, dynamic, bring a higher level of surprise. Focus on the meaning of life. The designer is upgraded to an enabler. He proposed the Experience EEI (Expectation Event Impact) model to support his view.

3 User Experience of Adjustable Filter Rod

The use of filter rods is growing and showing a trend of diversification. On the one hand, the filter rod with single function cannot meet the market demand. On the other hand, in order to alleviate consumers' sense of contradiction between health and smoking, the tobacco industry has increased supervision and promoted research on harm reduction and coke reduction in many aspects [13]. As an important part of cigarettes, cigarette filter rods are round rods made of filter materials through processing and rolling, which can reduce the content of tar and nicotine in cigarettes and reduce the harm of tobacco to human body.

In recent years, with the transformation and upgrading of cigarette consumption structure, the market demand for new filter rods with innovative technologies is also rising. The new filter rod has been widely used in the production because it can improve the cigarette smoking quality, and the technical requirements and process requirements for the filter rod manufacturers have become higher. After the filter rod is cut, it is connected to the cigarette suction end, namely the filter tip, which can effectively filter and intercept harmful substances in the smoke [14]. For consumers, avoid the discomfort caused by cigarette dust sticking on their lips, reduce the spicy taste and tar content of cigarettes, eliminate impurities and improve the experience. For tobacco manufacturing enterprises, filter rods can effectively reduce the consumption of tobacco leaves, indirectly improve the anti-counterfeiting characteristics, and also improve functionality, such as increasing smoke regulation.

With the improvement of consumption level, consumers' attention has shifted from the traditional consumption concept of "value for money" to the new modern consumption concept of "people-oriented". Improving the user experience has become a problem that needs to be considered. We should not only consider the functions that can be achieved by the filter rod, but also start to consider green, convenient use, and whether it can bring a unique experience. However, the rapid development of new technologies has not fully digested the complex functions. On the one hand, some technologies cannot be mass produced, and on the other hand, how to improve the functional experience by improving the usability of filter rod products. How to save time and effort when using the filter rod, so as to improve the technical experience. The appearance of the design is dazzling and gives users aesthetic experience.

In order to improve the user experience and satisfaction of the filter rod, it is necessary to have higher requirements on the structural design optimization and materials of the filter rod firmware. Li Jie [15] designed a comprehensive evaluation method for cigarette quality by using the efficacy coefficient method and the objective weight assignment method. The results showed that the weight coefficient ranked first among the six physical indicators, including circumference, hardness, length, weight, and total ventilation rate. Peng Bin [16] studied the influence of filter rod suction resistance on the release of tar, CO and nicotine in mainstream cigarette smoke, and found that filter rod suction resistance was negatively correlated with the release of tar and CO in mainstream cigarette smoke. Pan Lining [17] analyzed the influence of filter rod suction resistance on the release of acidic flavor components in mainstream cigarette smoke by GC/MS. The results showed that with the increase of suction resistance, the release of six acidic flavor components in mainstream cigarette smoke gradually decreased. Wang Yiheng [18] pointed out that cigarette smoking resistance is a key factor affecting the sensory quality of cigarettes and one of the key indicators in cigarette design. Suction resistance is one of the key factors that affect the internal quality of cigarettes, and also an important factor that directly affects the user's smoking experience. Xing Jianji [19] in order to control the stability of cigarette suction resistance, studied the correlation analysis between filter rod pressure drop and cigarette suction resistance (Y), and found that the correlation coefficient r $=$ 0.8307, resulting in a one-dimensional linear regression equation: $Y = 0.446x - 108.38$.

In summary, there is little research on adjustable filter rods among cigarette filter rods, and the research perspective on filter rods is basically focused on the discussion of such quality indicators as suction resistance, length, hardness, circumference, weight and ventilation of cigarette filter rods. There is little research on integrating user experience design into filter rod products. In view of this, this paper takes the arbitrary rotating filter rod as an example to carry out targeted optimization design research. By improving the knob to adjust the smoke size, it is convenient for users to adjust according to their own needs, so as to effectively improve the user experience.

4   Optimization Design Method of Adjustable Filter Rod Based on User Experience

4.1   Experimental Materials

Polybutylene succinate (PBS) biodegradable plastic materials are used. Customized filter rod and firmware for cigarettes are processed by Shenzhen Dijia Machinery Co., Ltd. and raw materials are provided by Hubei Zhongyan Cigarette Factory.

4.2   Experimental Equipment

Micro injection molding machine; Inspection equipment for nozzle bar integrated test bench; Creo 8.0 model drawing software, PTC; Aperture simulation software, PTC; Three coordinate measuring instruments; CNC machining center, as shown in Fig. 1 and Fig. 2.

Fig. 1. Three coordinate measuring instruments in the experiment

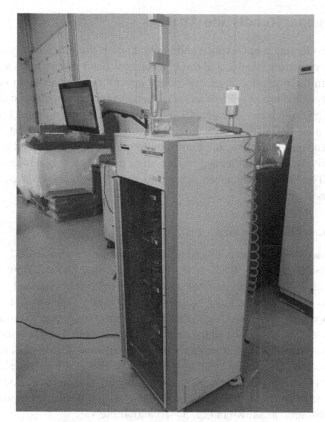

Fig. 2. Comprehensive test bench for filter rod

4.3 Participants

A total of 35 relevant technicians were randomly recruited into this experiment, including 20 male and 15 female, average age 31.5 years. All participants had normal or corrected-to-normal color vision. All participants were in normal mental and physical state.

4.4 Experimental Process

Take the arbitrary rotating filter rod fastener as an example, carry out targeted optimization design, select (molding/die-casting) injection molding method to design the plastic molding mold, adopt computational fluid dynamics and visualization methods, record and test the pressure drop and suction resistance of filter rod adjusted at different angles, and obtain the influence mechanism and law of user experience. The product design process based on user experience in this paper: user demand analysis - preliminary structure design - optimization design and simulation experiment-3D printing sample - mold opening test-final mass production. The experiment use descriptive statistics method, such as frequency statistics.

5 Experimental Results and Analysis

This research collecting users' explicit and implicit needs through telephone calls, interviews and other user interviews, and through internal team discussion and analysis of users' needs. In the process of user experience optimization experiment of adjustable filter rod, the dynamic law of air flow and suction resistance distribution in cigarette was explored through fluid dynamics calculation and analysis. Computational Fluid Dynamics (CFD) is calculated with Creo 8.0. By using the scientific visualization software, the pressure drop and outlet pressure corresponding to different included angles can be recorded intuitively after the filter rod rotates, so as to analyze the suction resistance of the filter rod. The blue, yellow green and red in the visual analysis diagram represent the distribution of air flow.

5.1 Preliminary Scheme Design

After preliminary structural analysis and research, scheme 1 and scheme 2 are obtained. Scheme 1: two flue gas inlet holes at the bottom and two flue gas flow holes in the middle partition. The upper and lower two injection parts can be adjusted intermittently every 60°. This 2-hole scheme has 3 gears 0–60–120° and 3 gears rotating in the same direction, respectively corresponding to different flue gas flow distances, so as to achieve the purpose of suction resistance adjustment. Scheme 2: three flue gas inlet holes at the bottom and three flue gas flow holes in the middle partition. The upper and lower two injection parts can be adjusted intermittently every 60°. This 3-hole scheme has two gears 0–60°, and the two gears rotate in the same direction and change circularly, respectively corresponding to different flue gas flow distances, so as to achieve the purpose of suction resistance adjustment, as shown in Fig. 3, 4, 5 and Table 1.

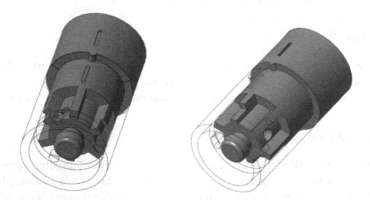

Fig. 3. Structure design of adjustable filter rod: from left to right scheme 1 and 2

5.2 Optimize Scheme Design

With several hydrodynamic calculations and analyses, the optimized design scheme is obtained. The outer cylinder of the paper wrapping is 6.95 mm in average, and 14 mm

Table 1. Comparison of pressure drop and suction resistance of Scheme 1 and Scheme 2

Structure	Angle	Pressure drop	Suction resistance
2 holes + 3rd gear	0°	817.8 pa	83.4 mmWG
	60°	2240 pa	228.4 mmWG
3 holes + 2nd gear	0°	355 pa	36 mmWG
	60°	1030 pa	105 mmWG

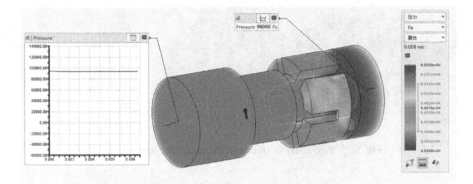

Fig. 4. Visual analysis of fluid dynamics of Scheme 1

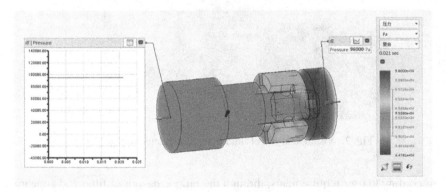

Fig. 5. Visual analysis of fluid dynamics of Scheme 2

in total after being buckled. When the scribed line is aligned, it is the maximum position of suction resistance, and is set as the starting point of 0°. Set it to the right rotation direction to adjust the suction resistance, which can be continuously adjusted within the rotation angle of 0–280°. 280° to 360° is the transition zone, where the absorption resistance changes discontinuously. The clearance of this section after being buckled is 0.1 mm, and it can return to the starting point of 0° only after forced rotation. The smoke inlet and outlet of the firmware shall be marked on the smoke inlet and outlet drawing.

The smoke receiving direction of the inlet and outlet shall not be changed. 35 relevant technicians were randomly selected for the experiment and used frequency statistics. The composite shall be conducted according to the direction of the inlet and outlet, and the import and outlet directions shall also be recognized when the cigarette sticks are rolled, as shown in Fig. 6, 7, 8 and Table 2.

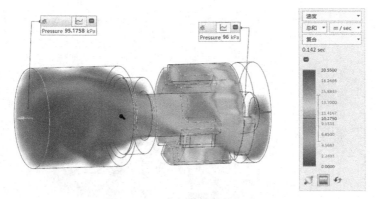

Fig. 6. Visual analysis of fluid dynamics calculation in 0°

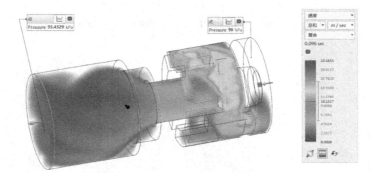

Fig. 7. Visual analysis of fluid dynamics calculation in 140°

According to user requirements, through the unique design of filter rod appearance and functional structure, this research proposes innovative solutions for industrial design to change the flow direction and output of filter rod flue gas. Three types of adjustable modes have been developed: circular half cut type, separated type and arbitrary rotation type. Circumferentially semi cut type requires uniform circular cutting at the fixed position of the filter rod body; For the separation type, it is proposed to cut a section of filter rod virtually, which can be removed or installed to change the filter rod structure during use; The arbitrary rotation type can realize the arbitrary rotation of the filter rod, thus improving the user experience of the final filter rod product, as shown in Fig. 9.

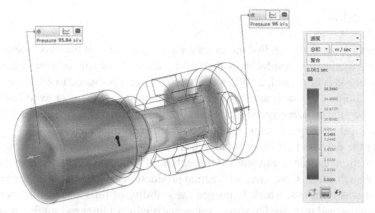

Fig. 8. Visual analysis of fluid dynamics calculation in 280°

Table 2. Relationship between suction resistance and user experience

Angle	Pressure drop	Suction resistance	User experience state
0°	824.2 Pa	84.1 mmWG	Poor (91.4%), The suction resistance is the largest
70°	697.6 Pa	71.18 mmWG	Average (88.5%), The suction resistance gradually decreases
140°	567.1 Pa	57.86 mmWG	Good (82.8%), The suction resistance gradually decreases
210°	494.2 Pa	50.4 mmWG	Good (85.7%), The suction resistance gradually decreases
280°	160 Pa	16.33 mmWG	Excellent (94.3%), Minimum suction resistance

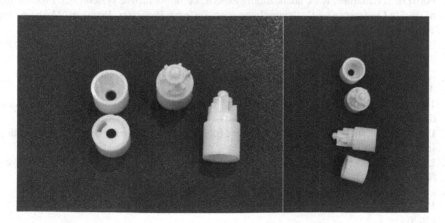

Fig. 9. 3D printing of adjustable filter rod

6 Conclusion

This paper systematically studied the structural characteristics of filter rod suction resistance. The experimental results show that: 1) the accuracy of suction resistance adjustment of filter rod is improved; 2) When the filter rod angle is rotated to 280°, the flue gas flow is the shortest, the suction resistance is the smallest, and the user experience is the best; 3) When the molding speed is 150 m/min, the qualification rate reaches 99.98%, which can meet the requirements of stable production of filter rods.

Taking the design of arbitrary rotating filter rod as an example, the variation law of filter rod suction resistance was studied through fluid dynamics calculation analysis and scientific visualization. Combined with actual production and personnel operation, mass production was achieved, which improved the stability of filter rod suction resistance from the source, and improved the user experience quality of filter rod suction resistance. The research results of this paper explore the user experience field of adjustable filter rod, and provide theoretical reference for experience optimization in this field.

Acknowledgments. The research supported by the Hubei Zhongyan Science and Technology Project Fund (2021JSGY3CL2B040).

References

1. Norman, D.: The Design of Everyday Things. Zhongxin Press (2003)
2. Norman, D., Miller, J., Henderson, A.: What you see, some of what's in the future, and how we go about doing it: HI at apple computer. In: Proceedings of the ACM Conference on Human Factors in Computing Systems (1995)
3. ISO/TC 159/SC 4 Ergonomics of Human-System Interaction: ISO 9241-210, Ergonomics of Human-System Interaction: Part 210: Human-Centred Design for Interactive Systems (2010)
4. Forlizzi, J, Battarbee, K.: Understanding experience in interactive systems. In: Proceedings of the 5th Conference on Designing Interactive Systems: Processes, Practices, Methods, and Techniques. ACM (2004)
5. Liu, Y.: On the status of the user experience design in china market. Packag. Eng. **32**(04), 70–73 (2011)
6. Chen, W.: User experience design elements and application in product design. Packag. Eng. **32**(10), 26–29+39 (2011)
7. Jordan, P.W., Persson, S.: Exploring users' product constructs: how people think about different types of product. CoDesign **3**(S1), 97–106 (2007)
8. Lei, Y., Hu, J.: The discussion about the user experience design from the perspective of product innovation. Art Des. **2**(11), 107–109 (2011)
9. Luo, S.J., Zhu, S.S.: User Experience and Product Innovation Design. China Machine Press (2010)
10. Luo, Y.: Lenovo: design is king. Glob. Entrep., 2–14 (2006)
11. Hu, F., et al.: User experience design: from concept to method. Packag. Eng. **41**(16), 51–63 (2020)
12. Xin, X.Y.: From user experience to experience design. Packag. Eng. **40**(08), 60–67 (2019)
13. Yue, X.F., et al.: Study on the technology of reducing harm and coke of cigarette. Ke Ji Feng (06), 15 (2018)

14. Wu, J.Z., et al.: Filtration structure progress of cigarette filter. Light Ind. Mach. **35**(05), 86–90 (2017)
15. Li, J., et al.: The evaluation method and application of cigarette quality based on some physical indexes. Manag. Sci. Eng. **4**(02), 30–40 (2015)
16. Peng, B., et al.: Effects of material's parameters on deliveries of tar, nicotine, and CO in mainstream smoke of virginia type cigarettes. Tob. Sci. Technol. **2**(2), 63–67 (2012)
17. Pan, L.N., et al.: Effects of cigarette material parameters on deliveries of acidic aroma components in mainstream cigarette smoke. Tob. Sci. Technol. **49**(3), 55–61 (2014)
18. Wang, Y.H., et al.: Research summary of the influential factors on cigarette draw resistance. Anhui Agric. Sci. Bull. **23**(8), 139–141 (2017)
19. Xing, J.J., et al.: Effect of filter rod pressure drop on cigarette suction resistance. China Sci. Technol. Overv. **05** (2013)

Lighting Cognition Predict Model From Physiological Signals - A Pilot Study

Chi-Lun Hung and Chin-Mei Chou(⊠)

Department of Industrial Engineering and Management, Yuan Ze University, No. 135,
Yuan-Tung Rd, Chung-Li, Taoyuan 32003, Taiwan, R.O.C.
kinmei@saturn.yzu.edu.tw

Abstract. This research aimed to design a personal lighting cognition predict model based on machine learning techniques. As a pilot study, we will investigate the relationship between lighting conditions and physiological signals. The experiment involved four different illuminance levels: 30 lx, 100 lx, 200 lx, and 500 lx, under the slack correlated color temperature (CCT) of 3000 K. Fifty-five participants, ranging in age from young adults (20–40 years) to older adults (over 60 years), were recruited. For each illuminance state, 5 min of physiological data and lighting cognition questionnaire were collected. Our results showed that two feature extraction methods, one from the time domain and one from the frequency domain, led to different outcomes. Furthermore, specific features of physiological signals that can reflect subjective cognition under different lighting conditions.

Keywords: Lighting Cognition · Physiological Signal · Emotion Recognition

1 Introduction

Ambient lighting has the potency of changing people's mood in accordance with its atmosphere, which is defined as the personal perception of external elements and internal sensations of the surroundings (Vogels 2008). Light exposure can activate the physiological changes in human body within 1 to 5 min (Prayag et al. 2019), and the same effect is obtained on subjective cognition (Fotios 2017). Therefore, lighting can be used as an atmosphere-induced stimulant to alleviate negative emotions and improve positive perceptions and comfort (Yu et al. 2018; De Ruyter and Van Dantzig 2019).

Physiological signal analysis is a reliable method to identify the emotional state by recording the reaction of the autonomic nervous system (ANS). In 1997, Picard and Healey proposed a concept of "affective wearables", which were portable sensors to capture signals able to assess emotion patterns such as galvanic skin conductivity (GSR), electromyogram (EMG), blood volume pressure (BVP), and heart rate (HR). Recently, automatic emotion recognition has been an interesting topic, and several studies demonstrated the feasibility of physiological signals in predicting cognitive status (Domínguez-Jiménez et al. 2020). For instance, GSR and photoplethys2020mography (PPG) are used to build the emotion recognition classifier (Udovičić et al. 2017; Lee and Yoo 2020). As the review has shown, most predictive models classify arousal and valence

© The Author(s), under exclusive license to Springer Nature Switzerland AG 2023
P.-L. P. Rau (Ed.): HCII 2023, LNCS 14023, pp. 36–46, 2023.
https://doi.org/10.1007/978-3-031-35939-2_4

states based on a two-dimensional model of emotions proposed by Russell (1980) that are easy to quantify multiple emotions.

The purpose of this study is to design a personal lighting cognition predict model based on machine learning techniques. We collected physiological signals under different light to reflect subjective cognition of emotion induced and assess by the emotion-dimensional model. The features are extracted time domain and frequency domain from physiological signals and then attempts to recognize the arousal or valence state of lighting induced. In this pilot study, we record GSR, Skin Temperature (SKT), and PPG in 56 participants to examine the relationship between physiological features and emotional state. Finally, the features with a significant distribution in the emotional dimension were used as input to the cognitive prediction model.

2 Methodology

2.1 Data Collection

A total of 56 participants were exposed to four different lighting conditions designed to induce emotion. The group consisted of 27 males and 29 females, ranging in age from 20 to 30 and 40 to 60, respectively. The illuminance levels were set at 30 lx, 100 lx, 200 lx, and 500 lx, with the color temperature fixed at 3000K. Each participant underwent a four-phase experiment, lasting a total of 60 min, with the sequence of light settings being randomly assigned. Physiological data was collected using three signals: GSR, SKT, and PPG frequency at 40 Hz, collected by Biofeedback 2000 x-pert. The experiment began with a 5-min rest period to adapt and measure the baseline physiological data. Participants then completed a questionnaire as a baseline. Next, they were asked to relax under the lighting for 5 min while their physiological signals were recorded. Afterward, they completed the questionnaire again as an after-assessment. To avoid carry-over effects, participants rested for 5 min under the same baseline lighting condition before the next induction. This process was repeated until all lighting conditions were completed (see Fig. 1).

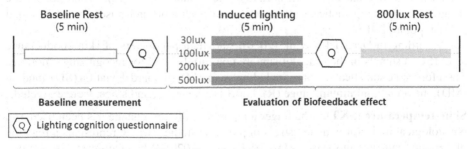

Fig. 1. Experimental procedure.

The lighting cognition questionnaire in this study was developed based on the following research. Flynn et al. (1979) organized a series of adjective scales to investigate user impressions of lighting scenarios. Adjective vocabularies such as visual perception, lighting valence, and subjective feeling were rated to describe the user's affect towards the current environment. Therefore, 26 cognition adjectives were used to create the questionnaire in this research. The questions related to environmental cognition, subjective valence, and emotional state of lighting. A 7-point Likert scale was used for investigation.

2.2 Experiment Questionnaire Validation

To validate the assessment of lighting cognition, the questionnaire responses underwent a reliability analysis. Factor analysis was conducted on the 26 cognition adjectives associated with different lighting conditions to group related questions and identify the primary cognitive aspects. The Kaiser-Meyer-Olkin (KMO) measure of sampling adequacy was used to determine the necessary sample size for reliable factor extraction. Principal Component Analysis (PCA) was used to extract the primary scope of the questionnaire, with loadings below 0.5 considered to have an insignificant impact on a factor.

2.3 Feature Extraction

Prior to feature extraction, all physiological signals underwent pre-processing to eliminate noise and were normalized against each subject's last 1-min baseline values. This was done to minimize variance between individual subjects' responses (Plarre et al. 2011; Lee and Yoo 2020). A total of 35 features were extracted from each participant. Two methods were used to analyze the characteristics of physiological signals for feature computation. First, the percentage change was computed for the raw signals of GSR, SKT, and PPG after the lighting induction. Next, the signal was split into moving windows of one-minute length (n = 5), and time-domain features were extracted.

Galvanic Skin Conductivity (GSR). The skin conductance level (SCL) measures the slow-varying electrical field of the skin that responds to a tonic stimulus of GSR (Tronstad et al. 2022). Unlike Skin Conductance Responses (SCR), which reflect the occurrence of a stimulus, Skin Conductance Level (SCL) changes over time and is used to measure nonspecific or internal feelings (Posada-Quintero and Chon 2020). When people are stimulated, the sympathetic nerve affects sweat secretion and raises the SCL signal (Christopoulos 2019).

According to Dzedzickis et al. (2020), statistical parameters of skin conductance level (SCL) signals in the time domain are commonly used for recognizing emotions. Therefore, nine statistical features, including mean (M), standard deviation (SD), median (MD), maximum, minimum, range (R), kurtosis, skewness, and slope, were extracted.

Skin Temperature (SKT). The finger temperature (Temp) change has been used as a physiological indicator to assess stress in previous studies, which represents a reaction of the autonomic nervous system (Dzedzickis et al. 2020). When feeling stressed, blood vessels constrict, blood supply decreases, and extremity temperature drops (Wallin 1981; Riva et al. 2003). The same parameters as those from SCL were computed for analysis.

Photoplethysmography (PPG). Changes in heart rate (HR) are related to the parasympathetic nervous system and can be used to assess the ANS. Activation of the sympathetic nervous system can result in an increased HR (Lang et al. 1993). Traditionally, heart rate variability (HRV) was measured by electrocardiography (ECG) using the R-R interval in the time domain. However, PPG has been shown to calculate frequency domain parameters of HRV using the P-P interval (Selvaraj et al. 2008; Pinheiro et al. 2016). Both time and frequency domain data can provide information on ANS through HRV (Ziemssen and Siepmann 2019).

Castaldo et al. (2019) evaluated the performance of short HRV recordings (~5 min) and ultra-short HRV recordings (less than 5 min) for the analysis of HRV. The results showed that R-R interval, HR, and HF features exhibited correlation within both 5-min and sub-1-min recordings. Hence, the HRV features in this study would be extracted from 5-min data.

2.4 Feature Analysis

In order to create a more precise lighting cognition model, we conducted feature extraction for all physiological features using the Pearson correlation test. This allowed us to evaluate the connection between physiological features and the scope of lighting cognition.

3 Result and Discussion

3.1 Lighting Cognition

In the factor analysis, a KMO result of 0.903 indicates a reliable sample size. Four factors were found to explain 69.75% of the variables. Factor 1, which includes eight personal preference adjectives, explains 35.09% of the variance in the dataset and constitutes the first factor. Factor 2, which includes eight negative adjectives, explains 16.75% of the variance. The negatively formulated items in this questionnaire constitute the second factor. Factor 3 covers seven adjectives related to visual fatigue and explains 11.65% of the variance. Factor 4 consists of four positive adjectives and explains 5.57% of the variance. Table 1 shows the results of factor loadings and Cronbach's alpha for each scope. The Lighting Cognition Questionnaire was assessed for reliability and validity using Cronbach's α. The α values for the four domains were all above 0.7, indicating high internal consistency and reliability.

The Friedman test results showed significant differences in cognition between different lighting illuminance levels for the following categories: factor 1 of Preference scope ($\chi2(3) = 29.518$, $p = 0.001$), factor 2 of Negative Emotion scope ($\chi2(3) = 12.404$, $p = 0.06$), factor 3 of Visual Fatigue scope ($\chi2(3) = 32.967$, $p = 0.001$), and factor 4 of Positive Emotion scope ($\chi2(3) = 13.286$, $p = 0.04$). As shown in Fig. 2-a, post-hoc analyses for all scenarios indicate that participants had a lower preference for 30 and 100 lx compared to 200 lx ($p = 0.001$) and 500 lx ($p = 0.001$). The factor analysis showed an inverse relationship between factors 2 and 4. Negative Emotion at 30 lx differed significantly from that at 200 lx ($p = 0.006$) and 500 lx ($p = 0.03$). Similarly, Positive Emotion at 30 lx was significantly lower than that at 100 lx ($p = 0.048$), 200 lx ($p = 0.005$), and 500 lx ($p = 0.002$), which is consistent with the result from factor 2 (see Fig. 2-b, 2-d).

Table 1. Result of Factor analysis and Cronbach's alpha

Adjective verb	Scope				Cronbach α
	1	2	3	4	
Feel Like	0.873				0.932
Feel Satisfying	0.857				0.936
Feel Interest	0.846				0.935
Feel Impressive	0.817				0.934
Feel Nature	0.808				0.936
Feel Familiar	0.732				0.947
Feel Uniform	0.732				0.939
Feel Relaxed	0.678				0.948
Factor 1 Cronbach α					0.946
Feel Dislike		0.884			0.887
Feel Fear		0.865			0.891
Feel Anger		0.859			0.893
Feel Tense		0.840			0.891
Feel Discord		0.724			0.903
Feel Depress		0.716			0.896
Feel Unpleasant		0.644			0.909
Feel Frustrating		0.528			0.909
Factor 2 Cronbach α					**0.909**
Feel Dry Eyes			0.836		0.862
Feel Fatigue			0.834		0.854
Feel Hazy			0.731		0.860
Feel Unfocused			0.686		0.857
Feel Vague			0.659		0.883
Feel Sleepy			0.600		0.867
Feel Dizzy			0.599		0.883
Factor 3 Cronbach α					**0.884**
Feel Soft				0.815	0.806
Feel Warm				0.787	0.819
Feel Simple				0.731	0.874
Feel Chilled				0.665	0.817
Factor 4 Cronbach α					**0.867**

(*continued*)

Table 1. (*continued*)

Adjective verb	Scope				Cronbach α
	1	2	3	4	
explained variation	35.09%	16.75%	11.65%	5.57%	
cumulative variation	35.09%	51.84%	63.49%	69.06%	

Both factors indicated that a 30 lx illuminance resulted in the least positive mental state valence. Visual Fatigue was significantly different between 100 lx ($p = 0.033$), 200 lx ($p = 0.001$), and 500 lx ($p = 0.001$), respectively (see Fig. 2-c). The fatigue of the eyes increased as the illuminance decreased.

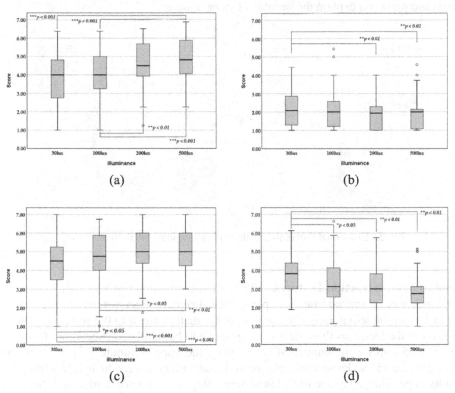

(a)   (b)

(c)   (d)

Fig. 2. Lighting cognition in four illuminance levels: (a) Factor 1 of Preference scope; (b) Factor 2 of Negative Emotion scope; (c) Factor 3 of Visual Fatigue scope (d) Factor 4 of Positive Emotion scope (* $p < 0.05$, ** $p < 0.01$, *** $p < 0.001$).

3.2 Physiological Feature Selection

Validation of Physiological Signals. The lighting cognition questionnaire identified four factors: "preference", "negative emotion", "visual fatigue" and "positive emotion". According to the Pearson test, the percentage change in SCL had a low correlation with "preference" (r = 0.180) and "visual fatigue" (r = −0.175) based on subjective measurements. Both factors were related to arousal. No correlation was found between the change in Temp and any of the four factors (r < 0.1). However, a significant correlation was found between the change in pulse and "preference" (r = 0.168). Figure 3 shows the relationship between the three physiological signals, presenting two dimensions of arousal and valence states. A clear correlation was found between SCL and Temp (r = 0.396), and between Pulse and Temp (r = 0.277). There was a weaker correlation between SCL and Pulse (r = 0.176). These results suggest that the features of SCL can explain the variable of arousal level in the emotional dimension, while the features of Temp and pulse can explain the variable of valence state.

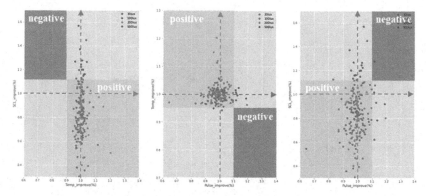

Fig. 3. Emotional Dimensions - three physiological signals scatter plot.

Validation of Extraction Features. The Pearson correlation test was applied to time domain features extracted from three physiological signals, as shown in Figs. 4, 5, 6 and 7. For further modeling, only correlations greater than or equal to 0.2 were considered relevant to the factor, as those below 0.1 appeared to be unrelated. Regarding factor 1, no related features were found in SCL, except for the slope in minute 3. In addition, ten features of Temp and Pulse showed less correlation with factor 1, which differs from the results in percentage change of SCL and Temp. Regarding Factor 2, nine SCL features exhibited a clear correlation, and twelve features in Pulse had a correlation greater than 0.1. However, only two Temp features were related to the factor of negative emotions. For Factor 3, six SCL features and four Pulse features had a correlation greater than 0.2. Additionally, there were two Temp features related to this factor. The correlated features of SCL and Temp, which were the same as those for SD, slope, and range in factor 2. Factor 4 has shown no correlation with Pulse features. Regarding SCL and Temp, there were 13 and 10 features, respectively, that had a correlation over 0.1. Overall, we found

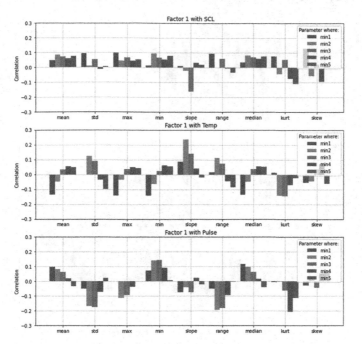

Fig. 4. Correlation coefficient between Factor1 and features

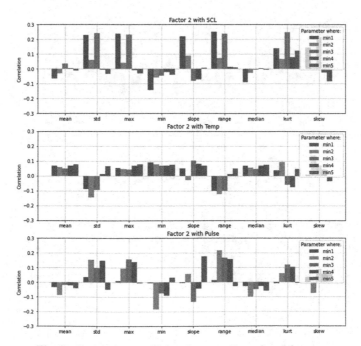

Fig. 5. Correlation coefficient between Factor2 and features

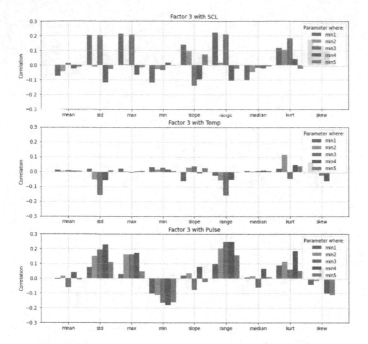

Fig. 6. Correlation coefficient between Factor3 and features

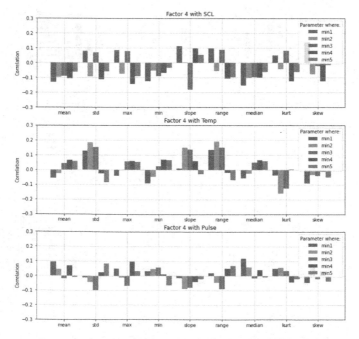

Fig. 7. Correlation coefficient between Factor4 and features

that the extraction of the SD, slope, max, and range features from three signals was related to cognitive responses to lighting.

As shown in Fig. 8, the frequent domain features of LF, HF, and TP were correlated with factor 1 and factor 2. For factor 4, there was a correlation with LF%, HF%, and LF/HF ratio.

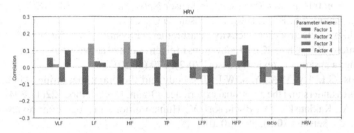

Fig. 8. Correlation coefficient between four Factor and HRV features

4 Conclusion

Comprehensive results have shown that physiological signals can reflect subjective cognition in different lighting conditions. This study utilized two feature extraction methods. However, we found that the time domain features split per minute may be too long due to the faster changing of emotional cognition. Therefore, it is suggested to divide the signals into shorter lengths to obtain valuable features.

References

Vogels, I.M.L.C.: Atmosphere metrics: a tool to quantify perceived atmosphere. Probing Experience: from Assessment of User Emotions and Behaviour to Development of Products, pp. 25–41 (2008)

Prayag, A.S., Jost, S., Avouac, P., Dumortier, D., Gronfier, C.: Dynamics of non-visual responses in humans: as fast as lightning? Front. Neurosci. **13**, 126 (2019)

Fotios, S.: A revised Kruithof graph based on empirical data. Leukos **13**(1), 3–17 (2017)

Yu, B., Hu, J., Funk, M., Feijs, L.: DeLight: biofeedback through ambient light for stress intervention and relaxation assistance. Pers. Ubiquit. Comput. **22**(4), 787–805 (2018)

De Ruyter, B., Van Dantzig, S.: Ambient lighting atmospheres for influencing emotional expressiveness and cognitive performance. In: European Conference on Ambient Intelligence, pp. 1–13 (2019)

Picard, R.W., Healey, J.: Affective wearables. Pers. Technol. **1**(4), 231–240 (1997)

Domínguez-Jiménez, J.A., Campo-Landines, K.C., Martínez-Santos, J.C., Delahoz, E.J., Contreras-Ortiz, S.H.: A machine learning model for emotion recognition from physiological signals. Biomed. Signal Process. Control **55**, 101646 (2020)

Udovičić, G., Đerek, J., Russo, M., Sikora, M.: Wearable emotion recognition system based on GSR and PPG signals. In: Proceedings of the 2nd International Workshop on Multimedia for Personal Health and Health Care, pp. 53–59 (2017)

Lee, J., Yoo, S.K.: Recognition of negative emotion using long short-term memory with bio-signal feature compression. Sensors **20**(2), 573 (2020)

Russell, J.A.: A circumplex model of affect. J. Pers. Soc. Psychol. **39**(6), 1161 (1980)

Flynn, J.E., Hendrick, C., Spencer, T., Martyniuk, O.: A guide to methodology procedures for measuring subjective impressions in lighting. J. Illum. Eng. Soc. **8**(2), 95–110 (1979)

Plarre, K., et al.: Continuous inference of psychological stress from sensory measurements collected in the natural environment. In: Proceedings of the 10th ACM/IEEE International Conference on Information Processing in Sensor Networks, pp. 97–108. IEEE, April 2011

Tronstad, C., Amini, M., Bach, D.R., Martinsen, Ø.G.: Current trends and opportunities in the methodology of electrodermal activity measurement. Physiol. Meas. **43**(2), 02TR01 (2022)

Posada-Quintero, H.F., Chon, K.H.: Innovations in electrodermal activity data collection and signal processing: a systematic review. Sensors **20**(2), 479 (2020)

Christopoulos, G.I., Uy, M.A., Yap, W.J.: The body and the brain: measuring skin conductance responses to understand the emotional experience. Organ. Res. Methods **22**(1), 394–420 (2019)

Dzedzickis, A., Kaklauskas, A., Bucinskas, V.: Human emotion recognition: review of sensors and methods. Sensors **20**(3), 592 (2020)

Wallin, B.G.: Sympathetic nerve activity underlying electrodermal and cardiovascular reactions in man. Psychophysiology **18**(4), 470–476 (1981)

Riva, G., Davide, F., IJsselsteijn, W.A.: Measuring presence: subjective, behavioral and physiological methods. In: Being There Concepts, Effects and Measurement of User Presence in Synthetic Environments, vol. 5, pp. 110–118 (2003)

Lang, P.J., Greenwald, M.K., Bradley, M.M., Hamm, A.O.: Looking at pictures: affective, facial, visceral, and behavioral reactions. Psychophysiology **30**(3), 261–273 (1993)

Selvaraj, N., Jaryal, A., Santhosh, J., Deepak, K.K., Anand, S.: Assessment of heart rate variability derived from finger-tip photoplethysmography as compared to electrocardiography. J. Med. Eng. Technol. **32**(6), 479–484 (2008)

Pinheiro, N., et al.: Can PPG be used for HRV analysis?. In: 2016 38th Annual International Conference of the IEEE Engineering in Medicine and Biology Society (EMBC), pp. 2945–2949 (2016)

Ziemssen, T., Siepmann, T.: The investigation of the cardiovascular and sudomotor autonomic nervous system—a review. Front. Neurol. **10**, 53 (2019)

Castaldo, R., Montesinos, L., Melillo, P., James, C., Pecchia, L.: Ultra-short term HRV features as surrogates of short term HRV: a case study on mental stress detection in real life. BMC Med. Inform. Decis. Mak. **19**(1), 1–13 (2019)

Research on User Satisfaction of Gamification Elements in Short Video Applications: A Comprehensive Method Based on Kano Model

Huiqing Li, Junran Zhang, Qianqian Tang, and Weixing Tan[✉]

Hunan University, Changsha 410082, China
2500923755@qq.com

Abstract. There are few studies on how to attract and satisfy users, despite the fact that short video attracts users worldwide. Gamification is a popular form of auxiliary design that makes a product more appealing and functional. Existing research on gamification focuses primarily on fundamental research and education. This study divides gamification into three dimensions and classifies gamification elements in short videos to examine the relationship between gamification and user satisfaction. Simultaneously, the questionnaire based on the KANO model (n = 221) quantitatively categorizes gamification elements into different quality categories and provides a user satisfaction score to quantify the relationship between gamification elements and user satisfaction, demonstrating that gamification applications with different dimensions have different effects on user satisfaction.

Keywords: application of gamification elements · Short video · User satisfaction

1 Introduction

Today, as a result of the Internet's diversification, short videos are constantly evolving and innovating to enrich people's daily lives. Due to the abundance of short video applications, numerous short video applications are continually seeking a viable method to enhance the short video user experience and increase user retention. In the communication process, the integration and infiltration with various platforms and media has become a trend in the development of short video applications. However, "gamification" includes the game's inherent user stickiness. The concept of incorporating game elements into non-game scenes has significant research and reference value for the form and content creation of short videos. Under the development of short video applications, the question of whether gamification can increase the user retention of short videos has become a topic of research. This paper classifies and discusses gamification elements in short videos based on the theoretical model of gamification. Using the KANO model, it is determined whether gamification elements have an effect on user satisfaction. According to the KANO model, all gamification elements in short videos are categorized into four distinct demand levels, and the category for research is determined. This study provides a reference for users to experience and utilize functions with different gamification elements in short video applications, demonstrates that gamification applications of different dimensions have different effects on user satisfaction, offers suggestions for the future development of short video applications, and generates new ideas.

2 Related Research on Gamification Elements

2.1 The Discussion of Gamification Elements

With the advancement of Internet technology, "Gamification" has once again captured the attention of the public. The term "gamification" was first proposed at the GDC conference in January 2011, where the concept of "gamification" was first introduced. Even a decade ago, gamification as a design and guidance method continued to play an active role in various fields and industries, providing new ideas and methods for numerous Internet-based products.

In academic circles, there is still no unified definition of gamification. Hamari J. and Koivisto J. [1] studied the relationship between utilitarianism, hedonism, social motivation, continuous use intention, and users' attitude towards gamification design by collecting user data from gamification services. They concluded that gamification is the apex of a hedonic self-goal system, and that gamification refers to technologies that attempt to increase people's intrinsic motivation for various activities. According to Deterding, Dixon, and others [2], gamification refers to "using game design elements in non-game context," which is a widely accepted definition. Using PBL theory, Michael Sailer analyzes the influence of game elements such as badges, leaderboards, and performance charts on users' psychological needs [3]. He believes that the primary goal of gamification, or the application of game design elements to non-game purposes in the real world, is to cultivate human motivation and performance for particular activities. In conclusion, although the academic community has not described gamification in a unified and authoritative term, "gamification" is generally applied to the functions of products in a gamification mechanism in order to motivate, provide feedback, and guide users to alter their behaviors and form habits. Compared to traditional games, gamification is a mechanism that can be implemented in a variety of settings. It applies game elements to product design and user behavior. In the highly developed Internet of today, gamification provides product development ideas.

2.2 Characteristics and Categories of Gamification Elements

Gamification includes gamification elements. Famous gamification professor Kevin Weibach defines gamification as "the technology of using game elements and gamification design in non-game situations." [4] Gamification elements must be extracted from games using design thinking [5] and implemented in non-game contexts. The application of gamification mechanisms or gamification elements to design objectives can increase user satisfaction [6].

Characteristics of Gamification Elements. Today, gamification elements tend to be more diverse, and they play a crucial role in gamification design. Wang Qi believes [7] that a gamification element is a specific component that can be used in games, and the key to achieving the design objective of a gamification system is the correct selection and application of this element.

The essence of gamification derives from the game itself, and the game's components are essential to the game's design. JesseSchell argues in "The Art of Panoramic Exploration Game Design" [8] that a game consists of four fundamental elements: game mechanism, story setting, aesthetic expression, and implementation technology. Each of the four components of the game is equal and essential. The interconnectedness and complementarity of the game's four elements runs throughout the entirety of the player's experience. The game mechanism describes the player's objective so that the player can obtain a better game experience by completing the game's characters. The story setting creates the world view of the game by establishing the game's storyline, and constantly strengthens the player's immersion in order to launch a series of game events. Aesthetic expression begins with the visual, auditory, and other perceptual systems of the human body. Good audio-visual artistic language effects can create a more immersive game environment, thereby fostering a stronger connection between players and the game. The realization technology serves as the game's material foundation. Whether the interactive mode of the game or the design of the game's content, it requires specialized technical support to achieve the desired results.

Regarding the investigation of gamification elements, Zhang Zhendong [5] discovered the game's description in the literature. A large number of documents were created in relation to the structural elements of the game, the emotions and interactions of the players, the game world, and its relationship to the outside world. On the basis of these findings, six game characteristics were summarized: voluntariness and freedom, enjoyment and other emotions, game goals, game rules, interaction, and relative independence. And combine it with gamification elements to illustrate the connection between games and gamification elements.

In general, gamification elements resemble game elements, which are based on the perspective of players or users and increase user retention. The author believes that by elaborating game elements, gamification elements can be extracted and gamification design can be explored more thoroughly. In her book "Game Changes the World," Jane McGonigal [9] proposes four game characteristics, namely game objective, game rules, feedback, and voluntariness, which have an effect on the characteristics of gamification elements.

(1) In different game designs, the game's objective influences the final direction of the player's efforts. In gamification design, the goal is also established to direct the player's actions, so the goal setting must be clear.
(2) Rules are, generally speaking, the ways to play a game. Players must understand the game's rules and consistently complete tasks in order to achieve their objectives.
(3) Feedback, users must receive timely product feedback and relevant information throughout the experience.
(4) Voluntary, voluntary signifies that users have the freedom to make their own decisions and actively participate in the entire game process.

King [10] classifies game elements into five categories for the description of gamification characteristics by analyzing the characteristics of psychological structure factors.

Social characteristics, characteristics of manipulation and control, narrative and identity, characteristics of reward and punishment, and performance characteristics. According to Guo Qianqian's [11] theory of social interdependence, the gamification characteristics are divided into four categories: individualism, teamwork, competition, and cooperation-competition.

In conclusion, the game's features prioritize the design of the game's actual content. Comparing the characteristics of the game elements with those of the gamification features reveals a degree of similarity. However, due to the different settings used in gamification design, the characteristics brought by each type of gamification are distinct, and the characteristics of gamification require further academic investigation.

Categories of Gamification Elements. The gamification element is a game element refined and summarized from various game products, and its applicability to non-game settings is investigated. It is summarized on the basis of a large number of user experiences, which can stimulate user participation and generate enjoyment in specific scenes, and is a significant example of gamification learning from games. Some scholars believe that gamification elements can be divided into the following categories: challenges, scores, badges and paper stickers, leaderboards, user experience journeys, and restrictions. PBL theory, including points, leaderboards, and badges, is a common component of gamification.

The DMC theory is a well-recognized explanation according to the literature. According to Werbach et al.'s DMC theory [12], game elements are divided into dynamics, mechanics, and components, with the dynamics layer including constraints, emotions, and narratives, among other things. The game mechanism layer contains elements such as competition, difficulty, opportunity, etc. The game component layer includes elements such as integral, feedback, and reward.

Koivisto and others [13] examined and analyzed a large number of empirical research documents pertaining to gamification and concluded that gamification elements in literature research can be roughly divided into five categories: Achievement, Social, Immersion, Non-digital elements, and Miscellaneous elements.

Social networking features, cooperation and teamwork, among other things, are examples of social gamification aspects in these five areas. The immersive gamification elements include Avatar and Dialogues, etc. Non-digital elements mainly refer to game elements from reality, which are different from virtual game elements; Mixed elements mainly include Virtual pets, Virtual currency and Trading. In general, there is no single classification for gamification components. The categories of gamification aspects vary depending on the settings, technologies, and dimensions, but the fundamental idea is to use the virtual game features as a point of reference in various real-world settings and create various gamification designs for various users.

Gamification is mainly inspired by games, and usually uses game mechanism. [14, 15] and other writers separate three categories of game design and gamification mechanisms that are directly connected to game motivation: (1) immersion (2) achievement and (3) social dimension. The immersion-related features use role-playing, storytelling, or avatars as the game mechanism to immerse users in self-directed activities. On the other hand, the immersion-related features use role-playing, storytelling, or avatars as the game mechanism to immerse users in self-directed activities. Finally, The social function is meant to get users to interact with each other, and the game mechanism is cooperation and working together. The game mechanism is cooperation and working together.2.3 Gamification element design and application.

Gamification has its own distinct qualities in various industries, which generates innovative design concepts for various Internet products. The author classifies and arranges the relevant product cases of gamification design on the market based on a case study and a survey of the relevant literature. Education and learning, efficiency behavior, and sports and fitness are the primary categories analyzed.

Education and Learning Classes. Whether in education or study, more researchers and scholars have found that gamification can arouse greater enthusiasm and interest in users' learning. In this age of fragmentation, it has become hard for many people to read a book and learn a language.

In terms of education, China MOOC has also continuously integrated gamification elements in the process of optimization. Large-scale open online course (hereinafter referred to as MOOC). Since 2012, the online course platform has developed rapidly. MOOC of China University collects excellent courses from top universities in China and gives lectures online. According to the analysis and research conducted by Qu Qianmei [16], there are clear benefits in terms of student behavior, learning outcomes, and course evaluation because MOOCs use game mechanics to present content based on hypothetical scenarios. There are three primary facets that reveal how well a MOOC supports game talk: the job, the role, and the cooperation. MOOC rewards the course by awarding the certificate of qualification, and drives the homework of the course by the task elements. Only by completing the task in a difficult way can learners obtain the certificate. At the same time, in terms of roles, learners need to evaluate each other with other learners after completing the weekly tasks. Learners and revisers symbolize the roles of students and teachers. Through the transformation of the two roles, they not only meet the teaching needs, but also add a brand-new identity and perspective to learners' experience. Additionally, through review and feedback, the interactive cooperation in the comment section reduces the distance between students, teachers, and other learners. Additionally, gamification aspects are used here, and each course's progress is indicated by a visible progress bar.

In terms of learning, a huge number of learning applications also constantly enrich the user's learning experience in the form of gamification. For example, English learning apps such as Hundred Words Chop, Scallop Words, Ink Words, and English Fun Dubbing in language learning can better guide users to complete English learning by integrating different gamification elements. In the "Hundred Words Chop", Ning Lianju [17] and others divided the "Hundred Words Chop" into three levels: task, interaction and socialization. In the process of users memorizing words, the "chop" behavior formed by the sliding of fingers interacts with the interface, which is very similar to the game mechanism in the game "Fruit Ninja" in which players get points through the game behavior of "cutting" fruits. By repeatedly "cutting off" words, users can finish the daily number of words to recite and improve their word memory. At the same time, the interesting graphics, text, and voice encourage users to keep working on their daily learning goals. Simultaneously, the Hundred Words Chop also carries out a challenge, in which users constantly get points for ranking through the competition of memorizing words, and display their rankings through the leaderboards, so as to improve their own grades, which not only enhances users' sense of accomplishment, but also achieves the purpose of learning. Other language learning apps are also gamified in the same way. In addition to language learning applications, ideological and political applications also adopt gamification design. Using a PBL approach, the Learning Power app, for instance, assigns daily assignments and leaderboards so that users can continuously learn party and government ideas by completing one job after another, compete with other team members, and create various index categories for ranking. The ranking of users is determined by the amount of points earned in several categories.

Efficiency Behavior. Gamification has played an important part in the growth of effective behavior habits in the cultivation of behavior. In the market, applications such as Forest focusing on forests and tomato to do improve users' time efficiency in a gamification way. Forest, as a time-efficient app, is a way to improve users' time efficiency by keeping users away from mobile phones. The interface and operation of the product as a whole are straightforward. The objective of directing users to "plant trees" to get time is to decrease the amount of time people spend on their mobile devices. When the interface is opened, you need to set the length of time you need to focus on. After the setting is completed, the mobile phone will enter the frequency locking state, making it impossible for users to enter the mobile phone desktop normally and use other applications. If the user is absent from his or her mobile phone for an extended period of time, the application's tree will grow from a bud to a towering tree. In contrast, the sapling will indicate that the planting failed and become a dead tree, indicating that the user's behavior of avoiding the mobile phone was unsuccessful. Qi Linhui [18] believes that Forest restricts the user's behavior of using mobile phones in four ways: locking screen, planting trees, timer and satisfaction. Among them, the concept of planting trees uses gamification elements to enhance the user experience. In the overall process, screen locking interrupts the interaction between people and smart phones so that users stop receiving feedback from mobile phones and the flow of heart is interrupted, so as to improve users' concentration, while "planting trees" is a metaphor combining saplings with time in the form of gamification elements, with the length of time reflected by the characteristics of saplings. At the same time, with the extension of time, users can obtain corresponding gold coins in the time of improving concentration, so as to exchange and unlock different types of tree species. In addition, to further its goal of enhancing productivity, Forest can also rate users via leaderboards and direct their actions using the gamification components of behaviors, points, and leaderboards.

Fitness Exercise. Keep is a typical sports app. In order to promote users to exercise better, Keep applies gamification elements to the extreme. To encourage users to incorporate sports and fitness into their daily lives, Keep is governed by PBL game theory, and its content includes scores, badges, and leaderboards. Similarly, Ning Lianju [17] and others defined "keep" into three levels: task, interaction, and socializing, laying the groundwork for the gamification-facilitated modification of users' attitudes about sports and the occurrence of fitness behavior as a habit. After obtaining users' needs and information, Keep provides users with more diversified fitness services, establishes corresponding personal sports files for users with personalized sports data, records and analyzes users' sports time, sports length and sports trajectory, and quantifies them according to tasks such as punching in. When users reach a challenge or task every time, they will get corresponding medals and wear them. The achievements can be praised and recognized by other users through sharing, and at the same time, the data after exercise can be displayed in the form of dynamic visualization, forming a sports growth system like a nurturing game, all of which record the results of users' output and physical consumption in fitness, which is easy for users to see their growth and affirm themselves. At the same time, with the continuous improvement of sports level, users and Keepers encourage, share and communicate with each other to enhance their fitness experience. The leaderboard also shows the sports data of each user, and users are easily recognized by others, which not only makes users have a flow of heart during sports and become more involved in sports, but also better cultivates users' awareness of sports and fitness, and attracts attention to their own health. Keep's gamification feature will surely motivate more users to do more sports and participate on a regular basis, allowing more users to acquire sports behavior patterns.

2.3   Gamification Elements in Short Video Applications

Definition and Classification of Short Videos. In the environment of the rapid development of modern network economy, short video applications have sprung up. Compared with online video types such as iQiyi and Youku, short video applications have the characteristics of more individuality, fragmentation, creativity and communication, and they occupy a place in the busy life of modern people [19]. Short video is used in most applications. Short video can be divided into two categories. Except for short video-based applications such as Douyin and Kuaishou, short video-based applications are embedded in major social platforms such as WeChat and Weibo. This paper analyzes the types of short video-based applications and the types of applications embedded with short video.

Short Video and Gamification. Gamification design has outstanding performance in the design of many Internet products and enhancing the user experience. It improves the product interface design and enhances the human-computer interaction function of the system, which makes the product more sticky [20]. Short video application, a popular Internet product, has made an amazing and effective attempt at gamification. According to the observation and use of short video software, the current short video involves not only video brushing, but also live broadcast, independent creation and public interaction.

Gamification Dimension and Short Video Gamification Element Classification. At present, there is no common understanding of the meaning and classification of gamification elements. This hinders the guidance on the analysis and development of gamification concepts, and often leads to invalid gamification design [21]. Sofia Marlena Schöbel (2020) summed up three dimensions of construction elements, motivation and inspirational elements, and improved the classification of construction elements. The classification of gamification elements adopted in this paper refers to this classification method, and Annex 1 classifies and summarizes the gamification elements in short films.

3 Design Method and Data Analysis

3.1 Satisfaction and Satisfaction Measurement

Satisfaction is the overall subjective post-consumption evaluation based on consumer experience [22] (Oliver, 1980). User satisfaction is the degree of customer satisfaction, and it is the degree of feeling state produced by comparing the perceived effect after consumption with the previous expectations of users after consuming a certain product or service [23].

User satisfaction can be regarded as the overall evaluation of the specific products used by users over a period of time. As the essence of product value, satisfaction is influenced by subjective factors such as users' sensory perception and psychological feedback [14]. In order to maintain a high competitive advantage in the ever-changing Internet market, the primary task of short video platforms and companies is to meet the needs of users (CR) and obtain users' satisfaction [24]. Therefore, in order to improve the applicability and operability of gamification in short video applications, it is of certain theoretical significance and practical value to study and test user satisfaction.

Research on satisfaction abroad began in the 1930s. Sweden first established a customer satisfaction index model in 1989, and then more than 30 countries, including the United States, Canada, and Germany, successively established national or regional customer satisfaction index models [25]. The Kano model is an important theoretical model developed by Japanese quality management master Noriaki Kano in the 1980s [26], and it is one of the most widely used satisfaction measurement tools [14]. This model provides the framework for product requirements [14], and it is a useful tool to classify and prioritize customer satisfaction models according to how customer requirements affect customer satisfaction [27].

3.2 KANO Model

The traditional KANO model divides users' needs into five dimensions, namely, essential attributes, expected attributes, attractive attributes, irrelevant attributes, and reverse attributes [28]; it then forms a KANO classification evaluation table [26] according to the influence of whether the needs are met or not on user satisfaction, so as to express the nonlinear relationship between different needs and user satisfaction. Traditional KANO user needs evaluation is subjective and can only provide designers with limited decision support [27, 29–33]. In order to solve the problems of the KANO model, qualitative analysis, and subjective classification, scholars have established different quantitative KANO models [6], such as the KANO index proposed by Qianli Xu (2009) according to the Kano principle, and put forward the A-KANO model [27], such as Yang (2005), which divides the first four categories of Kano into eight categories. Moreover, because the traditional Kano model only considers clear (as opposed to fuzzy) descriptions, it does not consider the inaccuracy and uncertainty of customer requirements due to their language origin [31, 35, 36] or the discontinuity problem caused by qualitative defects. [31] Wang and Ji (2010) put forward the Continuous Fuzzy Kano model, and so on. This questionnaire will adopt the traditional KANO model analysis method, introduce the better-worse coefficient proposed by Berger and others, and further judge the

KANO category of gamification elements in short videos by calculating the satisfaction coefficient.

3.3   KANO Questionnaire Design and Definition of Characteristic Attributes

This paper divides gamification into three dimensions: construction elements, motivation, and inspirational elements. The questionnaire is designed with gamification elements in mind. The questionnaire survey is used to determine whether users are satisfied with this function or whether they are satisfied without it. The questionnaire data is calculated and analyzed, the attributes are classified, and conclusions are drawn.

KANO Questionnaire Design. This part only answers the users who indicated that they have short video application software or have watched short videos in the basic information survey. First of all, we need to design a questionnaire according to the specific mode of KANO theory and ask the 13 functional attributes sorted out in the previous article in a positive and negative way so that the respondents can express their attitude towards whether the product has this function or not. Attitudes are set by Richter's five-level scale, which is divided into five measures, corresponding to five attitudes: very satisfied, satisfied, ordinary, dissatisfied, and very dissatisfied. All kinds of attitude expressions will be explained before answering questions (Table 1).

very satisfied—let you feel satisfied, happy, and surprised.
Satisfied—indicates that you think this is a necessary function or service.
Just so-so-you don't care, but it's fine.
not satisfied—you don't like it, but you can accept it.
very dissatisfied—makes you feel dissatisfied and unhappy about it.

Table 1. KANO Model Questionnaire

1. Sound Feedback *					
Background music during short video playback					
	Very dissatisfied				Very satisfied
How would you feel if you **had** this function?	○ 1	○ 2	○ 3	○ 4	○ 5
How would you feel **without** this function?	○ 1	○ 2	○ 3	○ 4	○ 5

Definition of Feature Attributes. For each index, the KANO model is divided into two directions: positive questions and negative questions to collect data. And after getting the data, the index is mapped to six attributes. A KANO model evaluation results classification comparison table is to show such a comparison table (Table 2).

In this paper, a KANO questionnaire is designed according to the gamification elements in short videos, and user satisfaction is investigated. Then, according to the KANO model comparison table, its attributes are divided into five categories.

Expected attribute: If this function is provided, the user's satisfaction will improve; if it is not provided, the user's satisfaction will decrease. The charm attribute is a function

Table 2. KANO model comparison table

Uncontained / Contain	5 Very Satisfied	4 Basically Satisfied	3 Indifferent	2 Barely Accepted	1Dissatisfied
5 Very Satisfied	Suspicious Result 5-5	Attractive Attribute 4-4	Attractive Attribute 5-3	Attractive Attribute 5-2	Attractive Attribute 5-1
4 Basically Satisfied	Reverse Result 4-5	No Difference 4-4	No Difference 4-3	No Difference 4-2	Mandatory Attribute 4-1
3 Indifferent	Reverse Result 3-5	No Difference 3-4	No Difference 3-3	No Difference 3-2	Mandatory Attribute 3-1
2 Barely accepted	Reverse Result 2-5	No Difference 2-4	No Difference 2-3	No Difference 2-2	Mandatory Attribute 2-1
1 Dissatisfied	Reverse Result 1-5	Reverse Result 1-4	Reverse Result 1-3	Reverse Result 1-2	Suspicious Result 1-1

that surprises users. If this function is not provided, it will not reduce users' satisfaction. Essential attribute: this is the basic requirement of the product. If this requirement is not met, user satisfaction will be greatly reduced. However, no matter how the necessary demand is improved, users will have an upper limit on satisfaction. Reverse result: it does not belong to the user's demand category, and when it does not have this attribute, the user's goodwill is high; when it is available, user satisfaction will decline. No difference results: whether this function is available or not, the user's satisfaction will not change, and it will always remain at the same level. Users will be satisfied with this factor regardless of whether it is available or not. Suspicious results generally do not appear. When suspicious results appear, it is generally because the survey users do not understand the content of the question or the survey collection is wrong. Therefore, this factor needs to be eliminated in the calculation process.

4 Results

4.1 KANO Model Analysis

The questionnaire screened out users who had experience with or a habit of using short videos, set 13 questions in total, and finally recovered 221 copies and got 2873 data points. Table 3 is the questionnaire data output table, that is, the attribute proportion, classification result, better coefficient, and worse coefficient corresponding to each gamification element are obtained.

Table 3. KANO model comparison table

The questionnaire survey results are compared and analyzed with the KANO model comparison table. Through statistical induction and sorting, according to the principle of "maximum" in the traditional KANO model, the KANO category to which each gamification element belongs is obtained.

Table 4. KANO model comparison table

Gamification Element	Desired Attributed	Attractive Attributed	Suspicious Results	Essential Attribute	No Difference Results	Reverse Results	Classification Results
Sound Feedback	9.05%	10.40%	5.43%	11.31%	58.37%	5.43%	No Different Results
Information Feedback	6.33%	9.05%	3.82%	5.88%	69.23%	5.43%	No Different Result
Social Contact	17.19%	8.60%	4.27%	8.14%	54.25%	7.58%	No Different Results
Ranking List	6.33%	5.88%	3.62%	2.71%	71.5%	9.95%	No Different Results
Rank	3.17%	3.62%	3.17%	1.36%	76.02%	12.67%	No Different Result
Progress Bar	32.13%	12.67%	4.07%	3.62%	40.72%	6.79%	No Different Result
Reward	6.79%	9.05%	3.17%	2.28%	66.62%	12.22%	No Different Results
Cooperate	9.05%	11.76%	2.26%	1.36%	69.68%	2.26%	No Different Results
Challenge	5.88%	4.52%	3.62%	2.26%	77.57%	8.14%	No Different Results
Achivement	8.14%	8.60%	3.17%	2.26%	68.76%	9.05%	No Different Results
Ownership	39.82%	10.86%	3.62%	4.98%	36.2%	4.98%	No Different Results
Self-Expression	19.91%	14.03%	4.52%	1.81%	55.06%	4.07%	Desired Attributed
Altruism	12.22%	15.84%	3.17%	1.81%	61.54%	5.43%	No Different Results

As shown in Table 4, the traditional KANNO two-dimensional attribute classification is carried out according to the principle of "maximum value," and one expected attribute is obtained: ownership. We got 12 indifferent results: voice feedback, information feedback, socialization, ranking, grade, progress bar, reward, cooperation, challenge, achievement, self-expression, and altruism.

4.2 Better-Worse Coefficient Analysis

The traditional Kano model classification method uses a simple "maximum" method to determine attributes, which has its own inherent defects. On the one hand, when there are many large values, it is impossible to make a horizontal comparison, and it is easy to ignore other dimensions, which is not conducive to accurately judging the quality attributes of the demand project. On the other hand, it belongs to qualitative analysis in essence, and it is difficult to effectively compare the demand items in the same attribute [37]. Therefore, the better-worse coefficient proposed by Berger and others is introduced into the analysis of this survey result for further quantitative analysis. Through the calculation of the formula, the worse coefficient and better coefficient of each gamification element are obtained to help define their KANO attributes and prioritize them.

The Better-Worse coefficient more clearly shows the influence on user satisfaction when a certain demand is met or not [38].

The Better coefficient indicates the satisfaction degree of users when meeting a certain demand [39], and its value is usually positive. The greater the positive value or the closer it is to 1, the stronger the effect of improving user satisfaction will be and the faster satisfaction will rise.

The specific calculation method is as follows:

Better = (attractive attribute + expected attribute) / (attractive attribute + expected attribute + required attribute + indifferent result).

The Worse coefficient indicates the user's dissatisfaction when a certain demand is not met [39]. The numerical value is usually negative. The greater the negative value is or the closer it is to -1, it means that it has the greatest impact on user dissatisfaction, and the stronger the impact of satisfaction reduction, the faster the decline.

The specific calculation method is as follows:

$Worse = (required\ attribute + expected\ attribute) / (attractive\ attribute + expected$
$attribute + required\ attribute + indifference\ result) \times (-1).$

In addition, when the two gamification elements belong to the same attribute, the greater the Better coefficient or the smaller the Worse coefficient, the higher the priority. In short video applications, the Better coefficient and Worse coefficients corresponding to each gamification element are shown in Table 5.

Table 5. KANO model comparison table

Gamification elements	Better coefficient	Worse coefficient	Classification results
Sound feedback	21.83%	-22.84%	No difference
Information feedback	17.00%	-13.50%	No difference
Social Contact	29.08%	-28.57%	Essential Attributes
Ranking List	14.14%	-10.47%	No difference
Rank	8.06 %	-5.38%	No difference
Progress bar	58.25%	-40.10%	Desired Attributed
Reward	18.72%	-10.70%	No difference
Cooperate	22.66%	-11.33%	No difference
Challenge	11.79%	-9.23%	No difference
Achievement	19.17%	-11.92%	No difference
Ownership	55.17%	-48.77%	Desired Properties
Self-Expression	37.13%	-23.76%	Charismatic attributes
Altruism	30.69%	-15.35%	Charismatic attributes

According to the values of Better and Worse coefficients, the quartile bitmap of Better-Worse coefficients can be drawn (as shown in Table 6). The Better-Worse coefficient chart shows the coordinates of each function, with the absolute value of Worse as the abscissa and the better value as the ordinate, which can visually show the attributes of all function items.

Among them, the first quadrant is the expected attribute, and the Better value and Worse absolute value are both high, that is, providing this service or having this functional attribute will improve the satisfaction of the target users, otherwise it will reduce the satisfaction. The gamification elements in the first quadrant are: ownership and progress bar.

The second quadrant is the charm attribute, with high Better value and low Worse absolute value. Although not providing this function will not significantly reduce the satisfaction of the target users, providing this function or having this attribute will significantly improve the satisfaction. The gamification elements in the second quadrant are: self-expression and altruism.

The third quadrant is the result of no difference, and the absolute values of Better and Worse are both low, so users don't care whether they have this function attribute or not. The gamification elements in the third quadrant are: cooperation, sound feedback, rewards, achievements, information feedback, leaderboards, challenges and grades.

The fourth quadrant is an essential attribute, with a low Better value but a high Worse absolute value, that is, although providing this service or having this function will not significantly improve the satisfaction of the target users, not providing it or not having it will greatly arouse their dissatisfaction. The gamification elements in the third quadrant are: socialization.

Table 6. KANO model comparison table

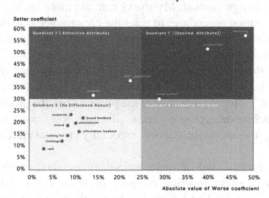

In general, the priority of requirement attribute satisfaction is: required attribute > expected attribute > attractive attribute > indifferent result > reverse result. Therefore, based on the priority level of demand satisfaction, according to the characteristics of each demand level, combined with the absolute value of Better-Worse coefficient and the position of each demand item in the quadrant diagram, we can determine the importance order of 13 gamification elements in short video applications, and finally analyze them as follows: social > ownership > progress bar > self-expression > altruism > sound feedback > indifferent results > achievement > information feedback > reward > leaderboard.

4.3 Short Video Game Satisfaction Analysis

According to the above analysis of KANO model data and Better-Worse coefficient, it can be seen that 13 gamification elements contained in short video applications are in demand among the four demand levels as a whole.

Among the essential attributes, sociality is the only essential attribute, and as the highest priority attribute, social elements play an important role. Socialization not only provides a channel for the rapid spread of short videos, but also contributes a lot of original content and stronger user stickiness to social media. For example, in private messages in the background, users can share a lot of videos and compose ideas, or interact effectively with more users in the comment area of works, which brings huge traffic and attention to short video applications, so social attributes need to be focused on in short videos.

In the expected value attribute, through Kano model analysis, ownership and progress bar are two gamification elements with higher weight. It shows that short video users have greater attention and demand for the content involved in personal accounts in short video APP. For example, for short video applications, my collection works, my works, my praise works and other parts are the key to affect user satisfaction. Whether it is in the gamification application of vision, interaction and content, or in the user experience of performance, behavior and reflection, the higher the completeness and practicability of the design, the higher the satisfaction of users. Among them, the works collected by users must be the works with the highest demand for users, which need better integration and classification of design content; My works can add more interesting elements and more convenient operation procedures to meet the creative needs of users; My favorite and favorite works need to know more accurately the video style and content that users like, and better promote tailor-made personalized content for them. To sum up, for the user account itself, the product needs more in-depth research and design, constantly meet the user's expectations for the account itself, and improve the user's stickiness through gamification. As for the elements of the progress bar, the progress bar is a visual reminder and feedback for time, progress and notification. Reasonable gamification of the progress bar can improve users' satisfaction, especially in visual effects and information visualization.

Charismatic attributes include altruism and self-expression, which respectively represent the personal shooting function category of short video and the function of rewarding public welfare for live broadcast. Although these two functional elements are extremely common in short video, they are mixed in the development of short video market, and the quality of creation is uneven. Under the condition of meeting the necessary needs, short video platform should provide users with more exciting and interesting self-shooting effect elements and improve the rich and better public welfare rewarding function, which is undoubtedly the most ideal to improve user satisfaction.

Undifferentiated results include levels, challenges, leaderboards, rewards, achievements, voice feedback, and information feedback elements of the product that have nothing to do with user satisfaction. According to the survey, the above 8 points account for an equal proportion of users, so these 8 functional elements can be selected in the design.

To sum up, regarding the distribution of different elements in the 13-Year Plan in four levels of demand, the gamification elements of short video should mainly meet the ownership and progress bar in the essential demand and the social attributes in the expected demand. At the same time, combined with the altruism and personal expression in the corresponding charm demand, the short video application should be planned and designed according to the priority level of the four needs, and the user experience should be optimized, so as to improve the user satisfaction and increase the user stickiness of short video products.

5 Discuss

In this study, we focus on the gamification elements in short videos and their relationship with user satisfaction. In the process of collecting and analyzing the questionnaire, we use three gamification dimensions and their corresponding gamification elements to construct a multi-level vocabulary list for subsequent comment text analysis.

However, the traditional Kano model applied in this study also has some limitations. First of all, the traditional Kano model has time difference, the gamification attribute is not static, and the user's cognition of gamification elements will change with time; Secondly, in terms of users, users' backgrounds are different. First, users' cognition of questionnaire topics and options is biased due to different cultural backgrounds. Second, users' own differences, users' use and experience of various short video applications are different. Thirdly, the questionnaire is analyzed from both sides and the answer options are repeated, which will make users feel bored to some extent.

Generally speaking, although KANO model is recognized as the best method to study the relationship between demand and satisfaction [33], because the user's psychology is complex, the answers given by the user must be completely consistent with the user's psychology, which is uncertain, so the traditional Kano satisfaction evaluation is too subjective [32, 33] and the decision-making criteria are more empirical [40]. To make up for this deficiency, we often need to carry out additional quantitative tests, so if conditions permit, we will use fuzzy Kano to better consider the user's motivation, and then accurately obtain the user's needs and implement effective service strategies.

6 Conclusion and Prospect

According to the previous research on gamification elements and the current data, this paper uses Kano model to evaluate the relationship between gamification and user satisfaction in short videos through questionnaires. An overall assessment is given based on the Kano model's quality classification and the quantitative user satisfaction calculation data. This article's main contributions are as follows:

(1) *Exploring the gamification elements in short videos.*
(2) *Based on the questionnaire and Kano model, the relationship between gamification elements and user satisfaction in short videos is established.*

Gamification is a very valuable element to enrich product design [14], but some gamification elements can't be well adapted to the use of products. For short video applications, many and miscellaneous gamification may have a negative impact on it and reduce user satisfaction. Therefore, when using gamification in short video applications, we should carefully consider it, get user feedback in time, and improve and upgrade the gamification elements in it to make users have a better sense of experience.

Appendix 1 Classification of Gamification Elements in Short Videos

Short video application	Gamification dimension	Gamification element	Other terms	Component	Detailed content
Douyin;Xiaohongshu;Kuaishou;Pinduoduo (Duoduo Video)	Building Elements (They are core elements of the gamification concept and are used by system developers and designers as building blocks for implementing information systems)	points	Eperience Points, Loyalty Points, Reputation Points, Scores, Credits, Currencies	Studio; Video page; Homepage	Reward gift points; live broadcast points (game live room win or lose quiz); number of likes; number of comments; number of favorites; number of reposts; number of fans; number of plays; visitors
Douyin; Xiaohongshu		badges	Trophies, Medals, Stamps, Icons	Studio	Rank 1 Badge; Gift Value Badge; Little Sweet Potato (Xiaohongshu user) level
Douyin; Kuaishou; Weishi		Feedback	Audible Feedback	video page	Douyin BGM; Big data information collection and feedback (personalized recommendation)
Xiaohongshu; Douyin		Time pressure	Deadline, Time Banking, Time Limit, Time Constraints	video page	Time-limited activities; Chinese New Year watching Tik Tok swiping red envelopes
Douyin; Weibo; Duoduo Video		leaderboard	Ranking, High-Score Tables, Score Boards, Badge Board, Line Chart	Studio; search page;	Likes and gift rankings; hot search list; hot sale list

(continued)

(continued)

Short video application	Gamification dimension	Gamification element	Other terms	Component	Detailed content
Douyin; Xiaohongshu; Duoduo Video; bilibili		Progress bar	Progress, Performance Graph, Performance Stars, Progress Notification	Studio; video page; Short Video Homepage	PK bar; video duration progress bar; double speed; watching video withdrawal progress
Douyin; Kuaishou;		Level	User level, progression	Studio	fandom level; creator level; creators
Xiaohongshu; Douyin; Kuaishou; Weishi; Duoduo Video		task	missions, quests, assignments, goals	Reporting information; event lottery; task activities; check-in	There are rewards for completing certain reporting tasks; task center; creator tasks; event check-in tasks; invitation tasks; red envelopes
Douyin; Xiaohongshu		virtual goods	Virtual gifts	Studio	virtual gift
Douyin; Weibo; Weishi		avatar	Roles; Virtual Character; Character; User Profile	Homepage Video; Homepage Information; Studio; Comment Area	Video page avatar;homepage avatar;live room avatar;comment area avatar

(continued)

(continued)

Short video application	Gamification dimension	Gamification element	Other terms	Component	Detailed content
		narratives	Meaningful stories	video page	Video interactive narrative communication;
Douyin;Weibo; Xiaohongshu		reminder	History;progression,time line		Year-end summary
Douyin; Kuaishou; Xiaohongshu; bilibili; Pinduoduo(Duoduo Video); Weishi		social contact		Studio;News page;chat page; comment area; sharing page;Douyin Zizai dynamics	Interactive chat with the anchor in the live broadcast room; @ ; new friends; notifications; cartoon stickers on the chat page; exchange views with bloggers/other netizens in the comment area; page sharing; pop-up questions and interactions; user avatars; user dynamic sharing; video/voice chat
Kuaishou; Duoduo Video		Collection system	Badge System, Point System, List of Medals, Point Grading System		watch video credits

(continued)

(continued)

Short video application	Gamification dimension	Gamification element	Other terms	Component	Detailed content
Douyin;Kuaishou;Pinduoduo(Duoduo Video);	Dynamics (Impact of build elements on subjective user experience over time) Describe how users using gamification concepts experience building elements. This experience depends on how the system developer or designer designs the structural elements according to their different characteristics	Reward	Encourage; motivate; prize; something that rewards someone for doing something	Studio;Duoduo Video	Watch the live broadcast of the game to get live broadcast points; lottery/lucky bag/red envelope; watch the video to get cash
Douyin; Xiaohongshu		Cooperation	Collaboration, Team, Team Building, (Social Networking Features)	Studio photo page	fan group cooperative shooting
Douyin; Kuaishou		Competition		Studio	Anchor gift PK

(continued)

(continued)

Short video application	Gamification dimension	Gamification element	Other terms	Component	Detailed content
Douyin; WeChat video number; Weishi		Challenge		Studio	Apply for connection and mic; activity challenge; theme challenge; can receive welfare rewards; encourage users to create original shares
Douyin; Kuaishou;	Motivational elements (Describe the user's motivation and/or their emotional response and user reaction to the build)	Social facilitation		message page; account page	Join the Douyin community maintainer; report user information. Remind the user to reduce the volume; watch for a long time, remind the user to take a break
Douyin; Kuaishou; Xiaohongshu		Ownership		personal account	My favorite works; my works; my favorite works
Xiaohongshu; Douyin;		Achievement			Backpack; Creator Hub
		self-expression		photo page	special effects and props
Douyin		altruism		Studio	Reward (for public welfare)

Appendix 2 Questionnaire

Hello! We are graduate students from the School of Design and Art of Hunan University. We are conducting a questionnaire survey on user satisfaction of gamification elements in short video applications. The questionnaire consists of 13 questions and takes about 3 min. Your data will be kept strictly confidential for internal research only.

Explanation:
Short video: refers to video content played on various new media platforms, suitable for watching in mobile state and short-term leisure state, and pushed by high frequency, ranging from a few seconds to a few minutes. Common short video applications are Douyin, Kuaishou, Volcano short video, Tencent Weishi and so on.

If you have used short video applications or browsed short video related content on the Internet, please continue reading.

Gamification is defined as "the use of game design elements in non-gamified scenarios". It is designed to improve user satisfaction, and common gamification elements include challenges, quests, achievements, rewards, leaderboards, and so on.

1.Sound feedback *

Music plays in the background while the short video is playing.

	Very dissatisfied				Very satisfied
When offering this feature, you feel	○1	○2	○3	○4	○5
When lacking this feature, you feel	○1	○2	○3	○4	○5

2.Information feedback *

Personalized recommendation, short video app through big data analysis for you to recommend your favorite content.

	Very dissatisfied				Very satisfied
When offering this feature, you feel	○1	○2	○3	○4	○5
When lacking this feature, you feel	○1	○2	○3	○4	○5

3.Socialize *

Short video comment section, chat page.

	Very dissatisfied				Very satisfied
When offering this feature, you feel	○1	○2	○3	○4	○5
When lacking this feature, you feel	○1	○2	○3	○4	○5

4.List *

Such as short video search hot list, broadcast hot list, popularity list.

	Very dissatisfied				Very satisfied
When offering this feature, you feel	○1	○2	○3	○4	○5
When lacking this feature, you feel	○1	○2	○3	○4	○5

5.Grade *

For example, fan group level, creator level, creator cultivation, intimacy and honor level in short videos.

	Very dissatisfied				Very satisfied
When offering this feature, you feel	○1	○2	○3	○4	○5
When lacking this feature, you feel	○1	○2	○3	○4	○5

6.Progress bar *

PK bar, video duration progress bar, double speed, watch video withdrawal progress, complete task progress bar.

	Very dissatisfied				Very satisfied
When offering this feature, you feel	○1	○2	○3	○4	○5
When lacking this feature, you feel	○1	○2	○3	○4	○5

7.Reward *

Benefits for actions or achievements, such as leveling up, redeemable points at the store, inviting new people to get cash packets, etc.

	Very dissatisfied				Very satisfied
When offering this feature, you feel	○1	○2	○3	○4	○5
When lacking this feature, you feel	○1	○2	○3	○4	○5

8.Cooperation *

Work together to achieve common goals, such as short video co-shooting, co-creation, joint release.

	Very dissatisfied				Very satisfied
When offering this feature, you feel	○1	○2	○3	○4	○5
When lacking this feature, you feel	○1	○2	○3	○4	○5

9.Challenge *

Set a goal and engage in activities to accomplish it. Such as Dou Yin gesture dance, role imitation and other challenges.

	Very dissatisfied				Very satisfied
When offering this feature, you feel	○1	○2	○3	○4	○5
When lacking this feature, you feel	○1	○2	○3	○4	○5

10.Achievement *

For example, in my Backpack and Creator Center, the user creation level will unlock the corresponding achievement as the task is completed.

	Very dissatisfied				Very satisfied
When offering this feature, you feel	○1	○2	○3	○4	○5
When lacking this feature, you feel	○1	○2	○3	○4	○5

11.Ownership *

Such as my collection of works, my works, my likes.

	Very dissatisfied				Very satisfied
When offering this feature, you feel	○1	○2	○3	○4	○5
When lacking this feature, you feel	○1	○2	○3	○4	○5

12.Self-expression *

In the creation process of short video shooting, I added special effects and props to make my creation more interesting.

	Very dissatisfied				Very satisfied
When offering this feature, you feel	○1	○2	○3	○4	○5
When lacking this feature, you feel	○1	○2	○3	○4	○5

13.Altruism *

In short videos, donations or rewards are used for public welfare activities.

	Very dissatisfied				Very satisfied
When offering this feature, you feel	○1	○2	○3	○4	○5
When lacking this feature, you feel	○1	○2	○3	○4	○5

References

1. Hamari, J., Koivisto, J.: Why do people use gamification services? Int. J. Inform. Manage. **35**(4), 419–431 (2015). https://doi.org/10.1016/j.ijinfomgt.2015.04.006
2. Deterding, S., Dixon, D., Khaled, R., et al.: From game design elements to gamefulness: defining "gamification". In: Proceedings of the 15th International Academic MindTrek Conference: Envisioning Future Media Environments, pp. 9–15 (2011)

3. Sailer, M., Hense, J.U., Mayr, S.K., et al.: How gamification motivates: An experimental study of the effects of specific game design elements on psychological need satisfaction. Comput. Hum. Behav. **69**, 371–380 (2017)

4. (美)瑞宁,克洛林,范库伯,刘松涛译 About Face3交互设计精简.电子工业出版社 (2008)

5. 张振东.游戏化视角下的互联网产品设计策略研究.江南大学 (2015)

6. Recabarren, M., Corvalán, B., Villegas, M.: Exploring the differences between gamer and non-gamer students in the effects of gamification on their motivation and learning. Interact. Learn. Environ. 1–14 (2021)

7. 王琦.游戏化元素对移动阅读APP用户持续使用意愿的影响研究.江苏科技大学 (2021). https://doi.org/10.27171/d.cnki.ghdcc.2021.000023

8. (美) JESSESCHELL著.全景探秘游戏设计艺术.北京: 电子工业出版社 (2010)

9. (美) 简·麦戈尼格尔 (JaneMcGonigal) 著; 闾佳译.游戏改变世界.杭州: 浙江人民出版社 (2012)

10. King D, Delfabbro, P., Griffiths, M.: Video game structural characteristics: A newpsychological taxonomy. Int. J. Mental Health Add. **8**(1), 90–106 (2010)

11. 郭倩倩.游戏化元素及用户类型对用户移动优惠券分享意愿影响的交互设计研究.东北大学 (2019). https://doi.org/10.27007/d.cnki.gdbeu.2019.002422

12. Werbach, K., Hunter, D.: For the Win: How Game Thinking Can Revolutionize Your Business. Wharton Digital Press (2012)

13. Koivisto, J., Hamari, J.: The rise of motivational information systems: a review of gamification research. Int. J. Inform. Manage. **45**, 191–210 (2019). https://doi.org/10.1016/j.ijinfomgt.2018.10.013

14. Yin, S., Cai, X., Wang, Z., et al.: Impact of gamification elements on user satisfaction in health and fitness applications: a comprehensive approach based on the Kano model. Comput. Hum. Behav. **128**, 107106 (2022)

15. Shen, Y., Kokkranikal, J., Christensen, C.P., et al.: Perceived importance of and satisfaction with marina attributes in sailing tourism experiences: A kano model approach. J. Outdoor Recreat. Tour. **35**, 100402 (2021)

16. 曲茜美,曾嘉灵,尚俊杰.情境故事视角下的MOOC游戏化设计模型研究.中国远程教育 **40**(12), 24–33+92–93 (2019).https://doi.org/10.13541/j.cnki.chinade.2019.12.004

17. 宁连举,肖玉贤,崔然.基于说服原则的互联网产品的游戏化设计——以百词斩、Keep、蚂蚁森林为例.北京邮电大学学报(社会科学版) **23**(03), 67–76 (2021).https://doi.org/10.19722/j.cnki.1008-7729.2020.0382

18. 齐琳珲.注意力分散时代的媒介"中断"与"反中断"——"专注森林"的个案考察.山东社会科学 2022(02), 141–147 (2022). https://doi.org/10.14112/j.cnki.37-1053/c.2022.02.014

19. 郑亚.基于用户体验的短视频APP设计分析.大众文艺,2021(06):59–60+71.21.OLIVER,Richard L.A cognitive model of the antecedents and consequences of satisfaction decisions. J. Market. Res. **17**.4, 460–469 (1980)

20. 李月琳,何鹏飞.游戏化信息检索系统用户研究:游戏元素偏好、态度及使用意愿.中国图书馆学报 **45**(03), 62–78 (2019). https://doi.org/10.13530/j.cnki.jlis.190023

21. Schöbel, S.M., Janson, A., Söllner, M.: Capturing the complexity of gamification elements: a holistic approach for analysing existing and deriving novel gamification designs. Europ. J. Inform. Syst. **29**(6), 641–668 (2020)

22. OLIVER, Richard L.: A cognitive model of the antecedents and consequences of satisfaction decisions. J. Market. Res. **17**.4, 460–469 (1980)

23. 洪晓青.我国高等教育领域客户满意度模型比较研究.广播电视大学学报(哲学社会科学版) 2012(02), 8–14 (2012). https://doi.org/10.16161/j.issn.1008-0597.2012.02.021

24. Clegg, B., Wang, T., Ji, P.: Understanding customer needs through quantitative analysis of X Kano's model. Int. J. Qual. Reliab. Manage. **27**(2), 173–184 (2010)

25. 支国平 APS中国区顾客满意度调查研究(硕士学位论文,中国地质大学(北京)) (2021)

26. Kano, N.: Attractive quality and must-be quality. Hinshitsu (Quality. J. Japan. Soc. Qual. Control) **14**, 39–48 (1984)
27. Xu, Q., Jiao, R.J., Xi, Y., Helander, M., Khalid, H.M., Opperud, A.: An analytical Kano model for customer need analysis. Design Stud. **30**(1), 87–110 (2009). https://doi.org/10.1016/j.des tud.2008.07.001
28. Bhardwaj, J., Yadav, A., Chauhan, M.S., et al.: Kano model analysis for enhancing customer satisfaction of an automotive product for Indian market. Mater. Today: Proc. **46**, 10996–11001 (2021)
29. Berger, C., Blauth, R., Boger, D.: Kano's methods for understanding customer-defined quality (1993)
30. Chen, M.C., Hsu, C.L., Lee, L.H.: Investigating pharmaceutical logistics service quality with refined Kano's model. J. Retail. Consum. Serv. **57**, 102231 (2020)
31. Wu, M., Wang, L.: A continuous fuzzy Kano's model for customer requirements analysis in product development. Proc. Inst. Mech. Eng. Part B: J. Eng. Manuf. **226**(3), 535–546 (2012)
32. 孟文,韩玉启,何林.基于模糊Kano模型的顾客服务需求分类方法.技术经济 **33**(06), 54–58 (2014)
33. 赵宇晴,阮平南,刘晓燕,单晓红.基于在线评论的用户满意度评价研究.管理评论 **32**(03), 179–189 (2020). https://doi.org/10.14120/j.cnki.cn11-5057/f.2020.03.018
34. Yang, C.C.: The refined Kano's model and its application.Total Qual. Manage. Bus. Excell. **16**(10), 1127–1137 (2005)
35. Lee, Y.-C., Huang, S.-Y.: A new fuzzy concept approach for Kano's model. Expert Syst. Appl. **36**(3), 4479–4484 (2009). https://doi.org/10.1016/j.eswa.2008.05.034
36. Lee, Y.C., Sheu, L.C., Tsou, Y.G.: Quality function deployment implementation based on Fuzzy Kano model: an application in PLM system. Comput. Indust. Eng. **55**(1), 48–63 (2008)
37. 张静维.老年群体的政务APP服务需求研究.江西财经大学 (2022). https://doi.org/10.27175/d.cnki.gjxcu.2022.000162
38. 虞慧岚, 侯利敏, 宋明亮.基于KANO模型的母婴室服务需求分析.设计 **33**(07), 141–143 (2020)
39. 梁清清.基于KANO模型的运动健身APP用户需求分析及功能设计.设计 **34**(07), 150–153 (2021)
40. 李鹏.KANO模型在汽车产品开发中的应用与改进.汽车工业研究 2014(07), 37–42 (2014)

Visual Attention Analytics for Individual Perception Differences and Task Load-Induced Inattentional Blindness

Zhimin Li, Zexu Li, and Fan Li

The Hong Kong Polytechnic University, Hong Kong 999077, China
fan-5.li@polyu.edu.hk

Abstract. Inattentional blindness (IB) is a detection failure of unexpected stimuli due to the concentration on main tasks. Scholars have applied load theory to provide a potential theoretical explanation for IB from the perspective of cognitive resources and task load, while the underlying visual mechanism is still unknown. In addition, apart from task load, individual perception differences may greatly affect IB frequency. Hence, the study aims to reveal the underlying visual mechanism of individual perception differences and task load-induced IB. Specifically, eye movement patterns across IBs and non-IBs, the respective impacts of individual perception differences and task load on eye movements, and their interaction effects are studied. 40 participants conducted a series of hybrid perceptual load experiments, including perceptual level tests and an IB-induced video viewing task. Our results show that IBs and non-IBs have significant differences in six eye movement metrics, such as saccades magnitude, blink frequency, and pupil diameter. Moreover, perception differences and task load have significant effects on three and four eye movement metrics respectively. Besides, first view time demonstrates the interaction effects between individual perception levels and task load. This research not only provides new evidence for the impacts of individual perception differences and task load on IB, but also elaborates on the changing rules of eye-tracking metrics. The visual attention analyses in this study provide a theoretical basis for the objective identification of IB, promoting the process of human-computer interaction.

Keywords: Inattentional Blindness · Individual Perception Differences · Eye Tracking · Task Load · Load Theory

1 Introduction

Inattentional blindness (IB) occurs when observers focus on resource-consuming tasks and fail to detect unexpected stimuli [1]. It is a common phenomenon in life, and its harm cannot be underestimated. For example, drivers may overlook the incoming vehicles from side roads, resulting in a collision; doctors may fail to recognize clinical warnings, thus threatening patient safety. To reduce the risks of IB-induced serious life and death consequences, IB has long been studied in many fields, such as driving, medical surgery,

P.-L. P. Rau (Ed.): HCII 2023, LNCS 14023, pp. 71–83, 2023.
https://doi.org/10.1007/978-3-031-35939-2_6

aviation, and construction industries [2–5]. These studies demonstrated how IB occurs and poses serious safety risks in different fields. In addition, these studies revealed many influencing factors of IB, such as task load, age, working memory capacity, and work experience [1, 6, 7]. Among them, individual perceptual capacity and task load are found to be the two main influencing factors.

Nevertheless, limited existing studies tried to deeply explain the underlying mechanism of individual perceptual capacity and task load on IB. It is assumed that these impact factors may induce IB by affecting the visual attention allocation of observers. For example, the existing studies have found the ratio of IBs and non-IBs is highly related to fixation times, and fixation duration of areas of interest (AOIs) [8]. Hence, this paper aims to reveal the mechanisms behind individual perceptual capacity and task load-induced IB via eye-tracking technology. Besides these fixation times, other in-depth eye movement parameters that can reflect human spatio-temporal sampling ability can be studied, such as the first view time to stimuli, saccade magnitude, pupil diameter, and blink frequency [9]. The following research questions will be addressed:

(1) What are the different features of visual attention distributions between IBs and non-IBs?
(2) How do individual perceptual capacity and task load affect observers' visual attention respectively, and then trigger IB?
(3) What are the interaction effects between perceptual capacity and task load reflected by eye movements?

This research not only reveals the effects of IB on the visual awareness of observers but also elaborates on the significant features of in-depth eye-tracking metrics. Moreover, we demonstrate the influence mechanism of impacting factors on IB through the underlying visual attention patterns. Further, the interaction mechanism between co-existing impact factors is revealed, i.e., individual perception differences and task load. In addition, the visual functioning analyses in this study provide a data basis for the objective identification of IB, which means a human-centered system could be better designed.

2   Literature Review

Without digging into the potential mechanism of the IB phenomenon, it would be challenging to reduce the risks of IB. Based on load theory, human attention resources are limited, while all the human information processing, including perception, decision-making, and action would consume attention resources [10]. When the task at hand is within the perceptual capacity, unexpected stimuli are easy to be noticed, otherwise, they would be ignored. For example, some participants in a study clicked through a warning in the information security system during a task, and later reported that they had not seen any security warnings [11]. White and O'Hare found that novice pilots failed to find many objects in the visual scene when distracted by cell phone calls [4].

There is a certain history of studying IB with eye movements, containing psychology, medical surgery, magic, and driving [1, 6, 8, 12]. Recording with eye-tracking data is a better method to identify IB than self-reporting or a post-experiment questionnaire [13].

Previous studies suggested that eye-tracking data can evaluate human visual attention [9]. Therefore, we hypothesize that the features of eye movement metrics between IBs and non-IBs are significantly different (H1). However, evaluation metrics of eye movements in previous research are too simple to fully understand IB, mainly including the ratio of IBs and non-IBs, AOI fixation times, and duration [8]. It is expected that the features of sufficient and in-depth visual and cognitive metrics could reveal the human ability to understand warning signals at different spatio-temporal sampling capabilities, such as the first view time to stimuli, saccade magnitude, blink frequency, and pupil diameter [9].

Besides, a few scholars have investigated some impact factors affecting the frequency of IB, including load, perception differences, age, working memory capacity, and work experience [1, 6, 7, 14]. Particularly, Torralbo et al. pointed out that the responses to unexpected stimuli decreased linearly with increasing task load [7]. Eayrs and Lavie applied the load theory to indicate that individual perception differences could lead to a different awareness of IB [14]. Nevertheless, they lacked further elaboration on the mechanism behind these effects, such as whether the influence factors induce IB by affecting eye movements. Since both perception differences and task load were shown to have effects on IB, and IB and eye movements are hypothesized to be strongly correlated in H1, we assume that perception differences and task load have a strong correlation with eye movements respectively (H2, H3).

In addition, most of the above studies focused on the effects of influencing factors on IB, but we know little about how these factors interact with each other. Studying the interaction between co-existing impact factors on the appearance of IB via eye-tracking technology can help alleviate IB at an integrated level. Hence, it is assumed that individual perception differences and task load would have significant interactive effects on eye movement metrics (H4).

Therefore, to enrich the research gap, this paper aims to demonstrate the differences in visual attention distributions between IBs and non-IBs, exploring the interaction mechanism between co-existing impact factors via multi-dimensional eye-tracking analysis. The eye movement metrics include fixation duration, fixation times, first view time, saccade magnitude, pupil diameter, and blink frequency. We also compare the visual attention distributions and the susceptibilities to IB at varying levels of perception and task load that may occur simultaneously and interact with each other in a working environment.

3   Methodology

3.1 Participants

Sixty subjects volunteered to complete the experiments. None of them watched the video of the Invisible Gorilla before, and all of them have normal or corrected-to-normal vision and hearing. Fifty-three subjects obtained valid perceptual capacity test results. After excluding subjects with poor eye tracker calibration or under external disturbance during the experiment, forty subjects (22 male, 18 female) obtained valid eye movement data. The ages of the 40 subjects ranged from 18–30 (M = 22.3, SD = 2.42). Informed consent was obtained from all participants prior to scanning. The study protocol was approved in accordance with the institutional ethics guidelines.

3.2 Apparatus

This research applied Gazepoint 3 (GP3) eye tracker to collect eye movement data, as shown in Fig. 1. GP3 is a desktop-based eye-tracking device, which can collect various types of eye movement metrics with a sampling frequency of 60 Hz. It needs to be connected to a laptop and aim at the eyes of the subjects at an upward angle, which is ideally 30 cm below the eyes and 65 cm away.

Based on the software of GP3, an AOI analysis on the stimuli in the video viewing task was performed to explore the eye movement metrics. Six kinds of eye movement metrics were explored in this study, including fixation duration and times, first view time, blink frequency, pupil diameter, and saccade magnitude, as shown in Table 1.

Fig. 1. Gazepoint 3 eye tracker and software.

Table 1. Explanations on eye movement metrics.

Eye movement metrics	Description
Fixation duration	Total time of fixations on AOI
Fixation times	Total times of fixations on AOI
First view time	Time stamp of fixations firstly enter AOI
Saccade magnitude (SACCADE_MAG)	Saccade magnitude calculated as the distance between the current fixation and last fixation (% of the screen)
Right pupil diameter (RPMM)	The right pupil diameter in millimeters
Left pupil diameter (LPMM)	The left pupil diameter in millimeters
Blink Frequency (BLKMIN)	The number of blinks in the previous 60 s period of time

3.3 Experimental Design

We conduct a series of hybrid perceptual load experiments to answer the research questions. The experimental task requires participants to first complete a test of individual perceptual capacity. After collecting the perception levels, we randomly divided the subjects into two groups with a consistent distribution of perception levels.

Then, subjects are required to watch the most representative IB video called "Invisible Gorilla" with their eye movements being recorded [15], as shown in Fig. 2. The occurrence of IB can be detected by whether the gorilla can be seen. In addition, among the two groups, one has the task of counting balls in the video, and the other has no task. The specific procedures are as follows.

Participants read and signed an informed consent document and completed a background questionnaire to collect the basic information, including age, sex, visual and auditory situation, and viewing experience of invisible orangutans.

Individual Perceptual Capacity Test. Individual perceptual capacity can be identified via observers' subitizing capacities, i.e. the capacity to report a limited number of items in parallel in an enumeration task [16, 17]. Subjects who report a larger number of items in a limited time have a stronger perceptual level. Therefore, we applied the individual perceptual capacity test to evaluate subjects' perception levels, as shown in Fig. 3. In addition, subjects are required to complete 20 times of tests, and the correct rate in 20 tests is considered as the assessment standard of the perceptual level, ranging from 0 to 1.

The Experimental Task. The "Invisible Gorilla" video was designed and completed by Simons and Chabris in 1999 [15]. In the video, subjects can see that two groups of athletes are constantly moving and passing a basketball to each other. The two groups of athletes are wearing black and white T-shirts to be easily distinguished. In the group with a task, subjects were required to count how many times the athletes wearing white T-shirts pass the ball while watching the video. Besides, in the video, a man dressed as a gorilla was the unexpected stimulus who walked among the players playing ball, slaps himself on the chest, and then slips away. In contrast, in the group without a task, subjects were required to watch the video without counting the number of passes.

IB Questionnaire. After watching the experimental video, the subjects answered the number of times the players passed the ball, and they also were asked if anything special has been observed during the viewing task. If the subjects answered that they saw a gorilla, there is no IB phenomenon, otherwise, it will be confirmed as IB [15]. IB can be divided into two situations, including no fixation on stimuli or no awareness of stimuli with fixations.

3.4 Data analysis

Based on the four hypotheses in the literature review, the hypothetical structure shown in Fig. 4 can be derived. Hypothesis 1 assumes a strong relationship between eye movement metrics and IB occurrence. Hypotheses 2 and 3 assume the significant influence of individual perception differences and task load on eye movement metrics, respectively.

Fig. 2. The "Invisible Gorilla" video screenshot [15].

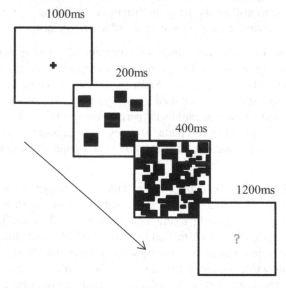

Fig. 3. Individual perception capacity test [16]. A cross appears for 1s, and then it is replaced by a picture containing a variable number (1–9) of squares with random sizes and positions. After 100 ms, the stimulus was replaced by a black-and-white noise mask, lasting for 400 ms. Subsequently, a question mark "?" replaced the noise mask. All participants were asked to respond as soon as possible after the question mark appeared, indicating how many squares they thought there were by writing down the corresponding number.

Hypothesis 4 assumes that the impact of perception differences on eye movements is significantly affected by task load, i.e., perception difference and task load have significant interactive effects on eye movement metrics. The whole structure reveals the incidence relation between perceptual levels, task load, eye movement metrics, and IB.

To verify these hypotheses, analysis of variances (ANOVA) would be applied to reveal the incidence relation of perception differences and task load on IB. Specifically, one-way ANOVA would be applied to analyze eye movement metrics of IBs and non-IBs to verify H1. A two-way, repeated measures ANOVA on the effect of perceptual capacity and task load would be applied to verify H2–H4.

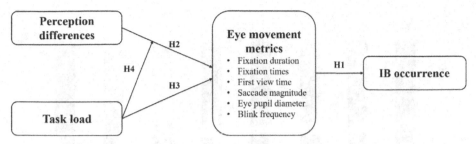

Fig. 4. The hypothetical structure between IB, eye movement metrics, perception differences, and task load.

4   Results

Results showed that the occurrence of IB was different under varying perception levels and task load, as shown in Fig. 5. First, Fig. 5 shows that task load can induce IB. Specifically, in the task group, 9 subjects did not see the gorilla while 11 subjects saw the gorilla, a proportion consistent with previous studies [15]. Based on the above definition of IB, 9 subjects who did not see the gorilla belonged to IBs and the other subjects belonged to non-IBs. Among the 9 IB subjects, 4 subjects had fixations on AOI while the other 5 subjects did not have fixations. By comparison, all 20 subjects in the no-task group saw the gorilla with fixations.

Second, individual perception differences can affect IB frequency, too. The individual perceptual capacity test showed that 40 subjects' perception levels were distributed between 0.5 and 1, which could be divided into four groups: low, comparatively low, comparatively high, and high perceptual capacities (PC). Figure 5 shows that in the task group, all subjects with low PC belonged to IBs while all subjects with high PC belonged to non-IBs. In the two groups of comparatively high and comparatively low PC, nearly half of the subjects had IB.

Moreover, the effects of perception differences on IB can be affected by task load. Compared to the task group, there is no IB occurrence in the no-task group, which objectively shows that the impact of perception differences on IB is affected by task load.

Our experiments confirmed that task load and poor individual perceptual capacity may induce IB. In the following subsections, the hypotheses are tested to answer research questions and explore the underlying visual mechanism of IB.

4.1   *H1*: The Eye Movement Metrics of IBs and Non-IBs are Different

Comparison analyses of eye movement metrics were conducted between IBs and non-IBs, as shown in Table 2. Eye movement data from 9 IB subjects and 9 non-IB subjects were compared. The 9 non-IB subjects were randomly selected from 31 non-IB subjects. A one-way ANOVA has been given respectively on the effect of the between-group difference on six eye movement metrics including fixation duration, fixation times, first view time, saccade magnitude, right and left eye pupil diameter, and blink frequency.

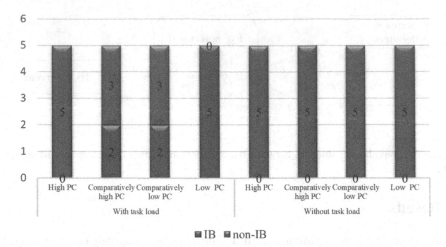

Fig. 5. Effects of perception differences and task load on IB occurrence.

Results indicate that between-group variance exhibited a significant effect on six eye movement metrics including fixation times [$F = 12.20, P < 0.01$], first view time [$F = 42.32, P < 0.01$], fixation duration [$F = 5.57, P < 0.05$], saccade magnitude [$F = 7.07, P < 0.05$], pupil diameter of right eye [$F = 5.39, P < 0.05$] and left eye [$F = 7.23, P < 0.05$] and blink times [$F = 4.57, P < 0.05$].

In other words, compared with non-IBs, IBs have shorter fixation duration, fewer fixation times, shorter first view time, smaller saccade magnitude, larger pupil diameter, and higher blink frequency. Hence, the results showed significant differences in six eye movement metrics between IBs and non-IBs, which verified H1.

Table 2. One-way ANOVA results on eye movement metrics between IBs and non-IBs, $\alpha = 0.05$.

Eye movement metrics	F	P
Fixation duration	12.19852	0.00301**
Fixation times	42.32	7.25E-06***
First view time	5.570159	0.031302*
Saccade magnitude	7.072803	0.017135*
Right pupil diameter	5.389261	0.033786*
Left pupil diameter	7.232966	0.016117*
Blink Frequency	4.572996	0.048252*

Note: * p-value less than .05
** p-value less than .01
*** p-value less than .001

4.2 *H2*: Perception Differences Have a Significant Impact on Eye Movement Metrics

To discuss the influence of the effect of perception differences and task load on eye movement metrics, a two-way, repeated measures ANOVA has been given respectively on six eye movement metrics as illustrated in the 4.1 section (see Table 4 in Appendix).

Table 3 represents the ANOVA results for four eye movement metrics with significant p-value, including fixation duration, fixation times, first view time, and pupil diameter. It shows that perception differences exhibited significant effects on the fixation duration $[F = 11.46, P < 0.01]$, fixation times $[F = 8.08, P < 0.01]$, and first view time $[F = 3.90, P < 0.05]$. In other words, subjects with lower perceptual capacity would have shorter fixation duration, fewer fixation times, and longer first view time. Further, the effect of perceptual capacity on fixation duration would be more notable than fixation times and first view time.

Therefore, a conclusion could be drawn that perception differences have significant effects on three eye movement metrics, including fixation duration, fixation times, and first view time, which verified H2. Besides, according to the verification of H1 and H2, it can be concluded that perception differences can induce IB by mediating eye movements. Specifically, subjects with poor perceptual capacity are more prone to induce IB, and the underlying eye movement changes are shorter fixation duration and fewer fixation times.

Table 3. Two-way ANOVA results of the effect of Perception differences and Task load on eye movement metrics, $\alpha = 0.05$.

Eye movement metrics	Perception differences	Task load	Interaction
Fixation duration	$F = 11.46$ $P = 2.9\text{E-}05***$	$F = 5.38$ $P = 0.027*$	$F = 0.47$ $P = 0.70$
Fixation times	$F = 8.08$ $P = 0.00038***$	$F = 14.95$ $P = 0.00051***$	$F = 0.67$ $P = 0.59$
First view time	$F = 3.90$ $P = 0.018*$	$F = 5.51$ $P = 0.025*$	$F = 3.13$ $P = 0.039*$
Right pupil diameter	$F = 0.77$ $P = 0.53$	$F = 8.31$ $P = 0.0070**$	$F = 0.09$ $P = 0.97$
Left pupil diameter	$F = 1.00$ $P = 0.41$	$F = 4.36$ $P = 0.045*$	$F = 0.23$ $P = 0.87$

Note: * p-value less than .05
** p-value less than .01
*** p-value less than .001

4.3 *H3*: Task Load has a Significant Impact on Eye Movement Metrics

Eye movement data from 40 subjects in the groups with and without task were compared. As shown in Table 3, task load exhibited a significant effect on the fixation duration [$F = 5.38, P < 0.05$], fixation times [$F = 14.95, P < 0.001$], first view time [$F = 5.51, P < 0.05$] and pupil diameter of right eye [$F = 8.31, P < 0.01$] and left eye [$F = 4.36, P < 0.05$]. In other words, subjects with task load have shorter fixation duration, fewer fixation times, shorter first view time, and larger pupil diameters of right eye and left eye. Further, the effect of task load on fixation times would be more notable than fixation duration, first view time, and pupil diameters of right eye and left eye.

Therefore, a conclusion could be drawn that task load has significant effects on four eye movement metrics, including fixation duration, fixation times, first view time, and pupil diameter, which verified H3. Besides, according to the verification of H1 and H3, it can be concluded that task load can induce IB by mediating eye movements. Specifically, subjects with task load are more prone to induce IB, and the underlying eye movement changes are shorter fixation duration, fewer fixation times, shorter first view time, and larger pupil diameters.

4.4 *H4*: Perception Differences and Task Load Have Significant Interactive Effects on Eye Movement Metrics

According to Fig. 5, the effects of perception differences on IB can be affected by task load. In the task group, about half of the subjects had IB, and the subjects with lower perception ability were prone to IB. By comparison, there was no IB occurrence in the no-task group.

A two-way, repeated measures ANOVA was conducted on the interaction effect of perception differences and task load from the perspective of six eye-movement metrics, as shown in Table 3. Results show that the two impact factors have an interactive relationship on the first view time [$F = 3.13, P < 0.05$].

In other words, perception differences and task load have significant interactive effects on the eye movement metric of first view time to the stimulus. Compared with the no-task group, the first view time to stimuli with task load is generally shorter for different perceptual capacities, which verified H4.

5 Conclusions

Understanding the mechanisms behind IB and its impact factors can provide foundations to design interventions and then effectively avoid the occurrence of IB-induced serious safety accidents. This study aims to reveal eye movement features across IBs and non-IBs, the respective impacts of individual perception differences and task load on eye movements, and the interaction effects between these two factors.

Through the multi-dimensional eye-tracking analysis, the results reveal that there are significantly different features of eye movement metrics between IBs and non-IBs. Compared with non-IBs, IBs have shorter fixation duration, fewer fixation times, shorter first view time, smaller saccade magnitude, larger pupil diameter, and higher blink frequency.

Moreover, this research not only verifies the effects of perception differences and task load on IB, respectively, but also reveals that these two impacting factors can induce IB by mediating eye movements. Task load and poor individual perceptual capacity may induce IB. Specifically, subjects with lower perceptual capacity would have shorter fixation duration and fewer fixation times. Also, subjects with task load have shorter fixation duration, fewer fixation times, shorter first view time, and larger pupil diameter. The above effects are consistent with the corresponding eye movement patterns when IB appears, which effectively explains how the influencing factors trigger IB.

In addition, the interaction mechanism between the two co-existing impact factors, i.e., individual perception differences and task load, is revealed in this research. The two impact factors have significant interactive effects on the first view time. In other words, compared with the no-task group, the first view time to the unexpected stimulus in the task group is generally shorter for different perceptual capacities.

This research not only provides new evidence for the role of individual perception differences and task load on IB, but also elaborates on the changing patterns of in-depth eye-tracking metrics. Moreover, this paper demonstrates a scientific basis for the influence and interaction mechanisms of impacting factors on IB by analyzing the underlying visual attention patterns. In addition, the visual functioning analyses in this study provide a data basis for the objective identification of IB, which means a human-centered system could be better designed.

This study is limited by the number of participants. Future studies can expand the subject size to obtain richer eye movement patterns. Besides, in the future, we can further explore other co-existing impact factors in IB-induced fields, such as working memory capacity.

Appendix

Table 4. Overall eye movement metrics and performance of 40 subjects.

No. of users	Task	IB	Perceptual levels	Fixation duration	Fixation times	First view	BLKMIN	LPMM	RPMM	SACCADE MAG
User01	Yes	No	D	0.049	1	31.116	18	5.42	5.85	300.6081
User04	Yes	Yes	A	0.345	2	27.978	9	4.36	4.95	496.7303
User07	Yes	Yes	C	0	0	29.276	11	3.951631	4.144244	335.3916
User09	Yes	No	B	0.345	2	29.112	7	3.83	3.88	161.2319
User12	No	Yes	D	0.197	1	29.966	29	3.96198	3.79997	327.4281
User15	Yes	Yes	A	0.345	2	30.59	14	4.30995	4.43839	298.9361
User17	Yes	Yes	B	0.329	1	31.116	13	3.96342	4.30688	414.4907
User18	Yes	Yes	C	0.214	1	29.736	28	5.33199	5.30795	78.55948
User19	Yes	Yes	B	0.345	2	30.475	8	6.08326	5.59429	740.0174
User20	Yes	Yes	B	0.279	3	29.325	6	4.48	4.53	402.3166
User21	Yes	No	D	0	0	30.492	9	4.66	4.85	346.2608
User22	Yes	Yes	A	1.479	2	26.883	5	4.93382	4.82345	36.33122

(*continued*)

Table 4. (*continued*)

No. of users	Task	IB	Perceptual levels	Fixation duration	Fixation times	First view	BLKMIN	LPMM	RPMM	SACCADE MAG
User23	Yes	No	B	0.296	1	29.457	7	5.83	5.84	481.496
User24	Yes	Yes	C	0.049	1	31.05	20	5.87525	5.73623	158.6623
User25	Yes	Yes	A	0.559	2	33.877	10	3.64457	3.62375	395.2969
User26	Yes	No	D	0	0	33.877	16	4.89	5.08	218.4246
User28	Yes	Yes	A	1.774	3	28.717	21	5.83058	6.06359	32.63993
User29	Yes	No	D	0	0	29.177	15.8	5.25	5.34	296.1736
User30	Yes	No	C	0	0	29.473	13	5.53	5.36	246.3377
User33	Yes	No	D	0	0	29.933	17	5.97	5.66	343.5421
User35	No	Yes	A	0.723	3	29.457	8	3.89	4.05	274.435
User36	No	Yes	B	0.542	2	29.851	7	5.68342	5.36812	113.1984
User37	No	Yes	B	0.625	2	28.191	7	4.22823	4.13751	308.206
User38	No	Yes	B	0.493	2	30.574	16	4.22151	4.16716	375.3857
User40	No	Yes	C	0.411	1	28.291	12	4.14305	4.1398	315.9718
User41	No	Yes	D	0.131	1	28.636	10	5.68516	5.73886	212.0396
User42	No	Yes	B	0.444	4	29.111	5	4.09	4.44	403.5926
User43	Yes	No	C	0.049	1	33.877	3	4.59	4.58	118.0615
User44	No	Yes	A	0.937	4	30.853	12	3.25	3.48	313.0218
User45	No	Yes	B	0.591	3	30.952	18	5.04933	3.49124	210.5933
User46	No	Yes	C	0.395	2	28.816	8	4.76	4.95	565.5875
User47	No	Yes	A	1.808	4	29.604	8	4.29	4.16	418.3489
User50	No	Yes	C	0.394	1	33.877	3	4.21143	3.96615	297.5906
User52	No	Yes	D	0.164	2	28.241	7	4.91801	4.44682	49.62793
User53	No	Yes	C	0.382	3	28.947	4	3.77821	3.75478	61.87143
User56	No	Yes	D	0.082	1	29.489	6	3.66136	3.44367	15.40579
User57	No	Yes	A	1.528	2	30.688	11	5.05264	5.31206	20.88403
User58	No	Yes	A	0.246	1	29.424	25	4.2149	3.90007	113.45
User59	No	Yes	D	0.263	2	28.175	1	5.02	5.22	320.8485
User60	No	Yes	C	1.134	4	29.489	9	4.81	4.78	464.7693

References

1. Richards, A., Hannon, E.M., Vitkovitch, M.: Distracted by distractors: eye movements in a dynamic inattentional blindness task. Conscious Cogn **21**(1), 170–176 (2012)
2. Park, S., Park, C. Y., Lee, C., Han, S. H., Yun, S., Lee, D.-E.: Exploring inattentional blindness in failure of safety risk perception: Focusing on safety knowledge in construction industry. Safety Sci. **145** (2022)
3. Drew, T., Vo, M.L., Wolfe, J.M.: The invisible gorilla strikes again: sustained inattentional blindness in expert observers. Psychol. Sci. **24**(9), 1848–1853 (2013)
4. White, A., O'hare, D.: In plane sight: Inattentional blindness affects visual detection of external targets in simulated flight. Appl. Ergon. **98**, 103578 (2022)
5. Hyman, I.E., Jr.: Unaware observers: the impact of inattentional blindness on walkers, drivers, and eyewitnesses. J. Appl. Res. Mem. Cogn. **5**(3), 264–269 (2016)

6. Memmert, D.: The effects of eye movements, age, and expertise on inattentional blindness. Conscious Cogn **15**(3), 620–627 (2006)
7. Torralbo, A., Kelley, T.A., Rees, G., Lavie, N.: Attention induced neural response trade-off in retinotopic cortex under load. Sci. Rep. **6**, 33041 (2016)
8. Hergovich, A., Oberfichtner, B.: Magic and misdirection: the influence of social cues on the allocation of visual attention while watching a cups-and-balls routine. Front Psychol. **7**, 761 (2016)
9. Mahanama, B., Jayawardana, Y., Rengarajan, S., Jayawardena, G., Chukoskie, L., Snider, J., et al.: Eye movement and pupil measures: a review. Front. Comput. Sci. **3** (2022)
10. Cartwright-Finch, U., Lavie, N.: The role of perceptual load in inattentional blindness. Cognition **102**(3), 321–340 (2007)
11. Xu, J., Park, S.H., Zhang, X., Hu, J.: The improvement of road driving safety guided by visual inattentional blindness. IEEE Trans. Intell. Transp. Syst. **23**(6), 4972–4981 (2022)
12. Simons, D.J., Jensen, M.S.: The effects of individual differences and task difficulty on inattentional blindness. Psychon. Bull. Rev. **16**(2), 398–403 (2009)
13. Vance, A., Anderson, B.B., Kirwan, C.B., Eargle, D.: Using measures of risk perception to predict information security behavior: insights from electroencephalography (EEG). J. Assoc. Inf. Syst. **15**(10), 679–722 (2014)
14. Eayrs, J.O., Lavie, N.: Perceptual load and enumeration: Distractor interference depends on subitizing capacity. J. Exp. Psychol. Hum. Percept. Perform. **47**(9), 1149–1165 (2021)
15. Simons, D.J., Chabris, C.F.: Gorillas in our midst: sustained inattentional blindness for dynamic events. Perception **28**(9), 1059–1074 (1999)
16. Eayrs, J., Lavie, N.: Establishing individual differences in perceptual capacity. J. Exp. Psychol. Hum. Percept. Perform. **44**(8), 1240–1257 (2018)
17. Eayrs, J.O., Lavie, N.: Individual differences in parietal and frontal cortex structure predict dissociable capacities for perception and cognitive control. Neuroimage **202**, 116148 (2019)

Analysis of the Influence of Visual Design Elements of Regional Traditional Culture in Human-Computer Interaction

Mingzhi Li[✉] and Young-Hwa Choe

Honam University, Gwangju 62399, Korea
bestcinema@daum.net, 20228291@my.honam.ac.kr

Abstract. The design of strong regional cultural art expression color occupies a major position in visual design, in which the unique elements derived from the national culture influenced by the regional environment is one of the important factors to highlight the visual design and products. The traditional Chinese art colors have a strong artistic expression, especially in the traditional decorative and expressive, art colors can more prominently show their charm, and fully realize the intersection of art forms and aesthetics, which coincides with the work of modern graphic design, and virtual interactive design is the degree of feedback from the environment after the human manipulation of objects within the virtual environment. Traditional art colors and modern graphic design have the same expressive and artistic flavor in the process of conveying visual effects, and the use and setting of hues are fully reflecting the free and spontaneous form of expression. Artworks can change with human sight and movement, constantly and randomly generating brand-new images, so that the audience can fully feel the changing situation of the works as if the real world in general. Modern visual designers also pay attention to the grasp of the senses in their practice, according to the brightness and splendor of the colors, their preferences, and feelings, so that decorations and colored objects in the color of the embellishment of life, fully realize the perfect integration of color and graphic design Through this way, the audience can feel their own physical and mental state, and more interactive, is the result of the audience's reaction, more unique, in line with contemporary people. It is unique and meets the aesthetic needs of contemporary people.

Keyword: Elements of Chinese Regional · Culture · Contemporary Visual Design · Graphical text · Human Machine Interaction

1 Introduction

China has been a multi-ethnic country living together since ancient times, and this culture is formed by the process of intermingling, migration, settlement, interdependence, and development and evolution of multi-ethnic cultures. During the long-term historical process of ethnic exchange, traditional culture has formed its local characteristics. This process is consistent with the process and laws of the formation and development of

P.-L. P. Rau (Ed.): HCII 2023, LNCS 14023, pp. 84–97, 2023.
https://doi.org/10.1007/978-3-031-35939-2_7

the Chinese nation and is part of the birth and reproduction process of the multi-ethnic Chinese nation. As a part of cultural heritage, its research direction focuses on the organic integration of cultural elements produced by traditional national culture and basic design, and explores the value of the elements produced by its inherited culture in visual design, so that its art products contain the spirit of culture, and make them both modern and international visual aesthetic concepts. The conception and composition of visual design, as well as the meaning of the images that are intended to be expressed, are influenced by the environment in which the creators grew up and the cultural environment they received, which is one of the important reasons why designers from different countries have different styles when creating their works. This is one of the reasons why designers from different countries have different styles when creating their works. The cultural elements and characteristics of the region are one of the main materials in the use of visual design. Elements. Patterns. Color is an important factor in beautifying and highlighting the image, and each element. Patterns. The use of symbols and colors is closely related to the conception and composition of the whole picture design.

In the modern design of Bauhaus, the three basic compositions are plane composition, color composition, and three-dimensional composition. In the basic composition, the visual information of traditional culture is extracted, and the visual elements are reconstructed to form an independent design style, i.e. the design elements of Tout. Visual design covers many design sub-sections, among which graphic design, logo, typography, painting, etc., and regional traditional culture is its exploration of its traditional patterns and visual symbols in the new use of modern visual design, through its visual symbols and ideological expression, the unique regional ethnic culture design elements extracted, build new design ideas and design forms, dig its unique cultural characteristics We can inject soul into a design. It enriches the visual modeling symbols and has a new way of extracting visual information, which makes the use of visual communication design more meaningful and forms a unique way of information expression in human-computer interaction.

The traditional Chinese culture contains many special graphic elements, among which are the characteristic and special patterns and the spiritual aspect of the people's culture and their traditional history and culture as well as the art and philosophy brought by the regional culture. The function of visual design is to convey information to the greatest extent possible, and visual design can use all available visual information to be transformed into symbols with sufficient pheromones, and it has the role of pointing, which can better bring better information in the human-computer interaction experience. Through directional factors, we can bring better information transmission in the human-computer interaction experience, so that people can interact more efficiently in the process of visual experience and feeling information.

Visual design, in a broad sense, includes everything that human beings receive visually. In exploring the use of traditional cultural elements in visual communication design, in its reconstruction and development, a new concept of art is reconstructed, so that its design language is no longer simply to emphasize a purely visual information factor to guide aesthetic behavior but to let the cultural spirit and subjective thought contained therein to dominate prior thinking.

Human beings in the exploration of the world's cognitive form of the pioneering cognition for the visual information of the preceding ideological cognition of its form, color, and symbols. And ideology is refracted in the aggregated life of social forms, thus forming a unique regional cultural system. With the inheritance of the long history and the mingling of their respective national cultures, their unique artistic characteristics have also come to the fore, also for the innovative way of visual design with new information guide, and heavy and give visual design a new art form.

The design of strong regional cultural art expression color occupies a major position in visual design, in which the unique elements derived from the national culture influenced by the regional environment is one of the important factors to highlight the visual design and products. The traditional Chinese art colors have a strong artistic expression, especially in the traditional decorative and expressive, art colors can more prominently show their charm, and fully realize the intersection of art forms and aesthetics, which coincides with the work of modern graphic design, and virtual interactive design is the degree of feedback from the environment after the human manipulation of objects within the virtual environment. Traditional art colors and modern graphic design have the same expressive and artistic flavor in the process of conveying visual effects, and the use and setting of hues are fully reflecting the free and spontaneous form of expression. Artworks can change with human sight and movement, constantly and randomly generating brand-new images, so that the audience can fully feel the changing situation of the works as if the real world in general. Modern visual designers also pay attention to the grasp of the senses in their practice, according to the brightness and splendor of the colors, their preferences, and feelings, so that decorations and colored objects in the color of the embellishment of life, fully realize the perfect integration of color and graphic design Through this way, the audience can feel their own physical and mental state, and more interactive, is the result of the audience's reaction, more unique, in line with contemporary people. It is unique and meets the aesthetic needs of contemporary people.

2   Research Status and Development Trend

Visual design in a broad sense is to includes all things received by human vision, in exploring the use of traditional cultural elements in visual design, in its reconstruction and development, to rebuild a new concept of art, so that its design language is no longer simply to emphasize a is to guide the aesthetic behavior with a simple visual information factor, but to let the cultural spirit and subjective ideas contained therein to dominate prior thinking, which is in the information This is crucial in the interaction between information. The precognitive cognition of humans in exploring the world is for the ideological cognition of the form, color, and symbol of visual information, which is refracted in the aggregated life of social forms, thus forming a unique regional cultural system. With the inheritance of history and the intermingling of respective national cultures, its unique artistic characteristics have come to the fore and also brought a new information guide for the innovative way of visual design and heavily endowed visual design with a new artistic form. Visual communication visuals include visual information factors, images, colors, and totems a series of visual symbols that can show the essence of things, to communicate information factors, ideas, and cultural expression. It contains the richness of regional culture, history, and cultural uniqueness, and its fundamental purpose in how to use and extract this to information derivatives, to cause modern people for the design of beauty and historical and cultural resonance, and its derived consumer products can meet both consumer and cultural psychological needs. The civilization and culture of a region is a long-term accumulation process. The "spirit" formed by the fusion of various ethnic cultures and habits is one of the fundamental reasons for the formation and development of the region. From the perspective of cultural geography, the influence of the region on culture and art is deep-rooted. The unique and deep "cultural" spirit of a region over a long period directly contributes to the relatively stable and orderly unique stylistic characteristics of the region and also creates classic and rich artistic achievements. The cultural and geographical factors formed by the times and the environment The view of cultural geography is that a specific regional ecology produces a specific literary and artistic form. The survival and dissemination activities of human beings are influenced by a certain geographical environment. The Philosophy of Art proposed the three elements of art and culture "era, race, and environment". In terms of cultural geography, the regional culture and natural environment have a profound influence on the artistic thinking and visual expression of the region.

Culture is the sum of the material and its derived spirit born of human activity of a social nature in general, and has three broad dimensions, divided into thought, order, and matter. Thought culture refers to its spiritual dimension derived from the creation of material culture by human beings, in which the material creates the spirit, and then the spirit leads the material to a new value given, although it does not have the characteristics of physical form, the basic properties of a material are too single, the visual symbols extracted are too stereotyped and single, the artistic values given are too monotonous, thought culture as implicit culture can give the manifest culture multiple informative and usable values.

At present, visual art has widely penetrated people's daily life, so the personalized requirements for its design are also increased. To further reflect the personalization of design works, it is also necessary to make use of production and design purposes, which is very helpful to achieve a good combination of design art and people's daily life, to realize human-computer interaction in actual social activities. Therefore, in the process of teaching visual arts, students also need to be guided to connect with people's actual lifestyles in the process of designing their works. Under the combination of cultural heritage, lifestyle, and space-time environment, the meaning of the work is reflected, to reflect their design style and personality, create personalized elements with good application functions, and reflect their value in the process of human-computer interaction. Although in the field of the art design, the most important thing is the personalization of the design, we should not pursue personalization too much, thus neglecting the functionality of the work, visual art must be closely related to the development of business, the lack of functionality of the commodity, it also loses the essence of the commodity requirements. To achieve the harmonious development of functional and personalized works, only in this way can the innovative design concept be truly reflected.

3 Design Principles and Methods of Visual Elements of Regional Traditional Culture in Interactive Media

What is "visual design"? What are its basic characteristics? Through the study of "visual design", we can know that its basic core content is a visually creative design, through the visual expression of different, in the process of design to add some attractive elements, the performance of a visual impact can stimulate the interest of the audience, to attract the attention of the hands, so that the information can be transmitted to the audience. This is the basic principle of visual design, such as product logos, advertising leaflets, advertisements everywhere, etc. The purpose of the process of visual design is to express the information through various things that can be observed by the line of sight so that after the design of the performance method can increase the intensity of the performance effect of infection, can create a visual communication atmosphere conducive to the audience to accept the information, which is a very critical point is the visualization of the specific information of creativity and expression. The visual design also has certain limitations, because of the restrictive way of communication, whether it is an advertisement or a logo, the message it conveys is relatively vague, and what it shows is usually a conceptual thing that cannot accurately and clearly shows the specific content of the message, so on many occasions, in various activities, it plays the role of guiding the audience to learn more information, is a kind of visual communication design that boosts products, services or values, rather than the terminal design of products or services, so it is better to guide people to accept its pheromone and guiding element in the process of interaction so that people can have a better experience while using products and services. Therefore, we can make visual design a design with a "selling" function, which is also the icing on the cake for the process of human-computer interaction. The information carrier used in visual design is usually a variety of graphics and image symbols, which can express some information simply and clearly and can serve the purpose of conveying information and increasing the visual impact. Intuitive image and symbolic expression can make the process of transmitting information more attractive to people's attention and has a good visual impact. Then, the criteria to judge whether the visual design is qualified need to be based on its characteristics to develop, on the one hand, to see whether it can match the release of information media, on the other hand, is the content of the design and to show whether the things have a strong impact, can play a good publicity effect, however, the ultimate measure of its value is whether the process of publicity on the audience to produce, however, the final measure of its value is whether it has a leading role in the process of publicity to the audience, but this is difficult to quantify the indicators, only according to the results of the later to judge the success of the message or not.

3.1 Case Study Analysis

In this study, a qualitative analysis was conducted using the case study method and the literature review method. Here we have selected a representative individual case for analysis, which is an installation titled "Ten Thousand Hairs of Power - Intelligent Dynamic Display of Calligraphy and Painting" by the famous Chinese calligrapher and seal carver "Han Tianheng" at the National Museum of China on October 31, 2019.

The installation titled "Ten Thousand Hairs of Power - Intelligent Dynamic Display of Calligraphy and Painting" at the Han Tianheng Art Exhibition at the National Museum of China on October 31, 2019, was developed by the Han Tianheng Art Museum in cooperation with the Shanghai Institute of Arts and Crafts, reflecting the organic fusion of traditional Chinese culture and contemporary intelligent technology. The installation was developed by the Han Tianheng Art Museum in cooperation with the Shanghai Institute of Arts and Crafts.

The device, through human-machine interaction, can sense the distance between the viewer and the screen in real time and adjust the speed of the video playback in real-time based on this. The closer the viewer is to the screen, the slower the brush strokes move, and the more clearly the viewer can study the delicate brushwork; and when the viewer gradually moves away from the screen and back to the original position, the brush strokes will gradually speed up again to normal speed. In this way, the initiative of viewing and studying is left to the viewer, who is free to choose which part he or she wants to focus on carefully. In this process, not only can the general audience experience the cultural and artistic creation value of calligraphy and painting, but also calligraphy and painting enthusiasts and professional practitioners can get the opportunity to exchange their skills "through space".

The whole installation contains 12 works, except for the prologue "Ink and Wash", "Orchid", "Ink and Bamboo", "Strange Stones of Qing Huang", "Fragrance of the King", and "The Art of Painting". The four ink paintings, "Fragrance of the King", form a special graphic effect on the projection glass, which is different from the effect of traditional physical rice paper.

In addition to traditional calligraphy, painting, and seal engraving work, the most attractive part of the exhibition is a set of installations called "Ten Thousand Hairs of Power - Intelligent Dynamic Display of Calligraphy and Painting". Through a large screen, the installation continuously and dynamically displayed the creation process of calligraphy and painting works, and the creation speed could be intelligently adjusted according to the audience's interaction, which attracted a large number of visitors to stop and watch. In the process of user experience in human-computer interaction, the closer the visual transmission to the audience and the screen, the slower the movement of the brush strokes, the more the audience can study the delicate brushwork; and when the audience gradually moves away from the screen back to the original position, the movement of the brush strokes will gradually speed up to the normal speed. In this way, both painting and calligraphy enthusiasts and professional practitioners will have the opportunity to communicate and exchange their skills "through space".

According to the results generated by the case analysis observation, this is the debut of a traditional culture exhibition combined with human-computer interaction intelligent technology, to integrate technology into the culture, let the culture come alive, and bring the audience a refreshing feeling, in the process of human-computer interaction, "Wan Hao Qi Li" painting and calligraphy intelligent dynamic display can be through a video display, multimedia interaction In the process of human-computer interaction, the "Wan Hao Qi Li" intelligent dynamic display of calligraphy and painting can, through video display and multimedia interaction, let the audience understand the cultural connotation and traditional aesthetic concept behind the painting and calligraphy works while watching them. In this way, viewers can not only appreciate the expression of beauty by watching the painting and calligraphy works but also deepen their understanding of traditional culture through human-computer interaction. In addition, human-computer interaction allows viewers to better experience the charm of traditional calligraphy and painting works. Through human-computer interaction, viewers can choose to watch different works of calligraphy and painting according to their interests and preferences, and deepen their understanding of the works through video display and multimedia interaction. In this way, viewers can further enhance their understanding and appreciation of traditional culture while enjoying viewing works of calligraphy and painting.

Chinese painting, on the other hand, is a unique art form that can be used to represent many different concepts and themes in visual communication. For example, Chinese painting can be used to represent natural scenery, animals, people, architecture, etc. It can also be used to represent the mood, atmosphere, and state of mind.

Calligraphy, on the other hand, is the art of writing Chinese characters with brush and ink. In visual communication, calligraphy can be used to represent the uniqueness and charm of Chinese culture, as well as to convey different emotions and atmospheres. And different genres of calligraphy are chosen to convey different messages depending on the need. In addition, calligraphy can be used in combination with other art forms (e.g., drawing, photography, etc.) to further enrich the visual effect, and in this case, using human-computer interaction for recombination can bring about new concepts and contexts that greatly affect the development of traditional art forms. Digital technology has diversified the language of art, and the output of information can be accomplished more easily with a constant stream of new technologies for painting The design of the composition, and the formation of the style. The traditional painting technique is no longer the only tool for artistic achievement, but the variation of digital art opens another door to art.

Moreover, traditional culture is an important heritage of a country or nation, which carries a long history and rich cultural connotations. Combining traditional culture with human-computer interaction can allow more people to know and understand traditional culture through modern technical means. For example, intelligent dynamic displays can allow viewers to learn about the cultural connotations and traditional aesthetic concepts behind the paintings and calligraphy while viewing them.

At the same time, human-computer interaction can also bring new ideas and ways for the inheritance and promotion of traditional culture. Through modern technological means, the charm of traditional culture can be better presented to attract the attention and participation of the younger generation. For example, we can observe some applications of human-computer interaction, such as using chatbots to help people learn a certain traditional culture, or using games to let people understand the traditional culture. By observing these examples, we can see that human-computer interaction can help people understand the traditional culture in new ways and carry forward the essence of traditional culture.

In addition, we can observe how human-computer interaction can help traditional culture gain wider distribution in modern society. For example, through the use of web and mobile technologies, human-computer interaction can make the knowledge and skills of traditional culture accessible to more people across geographical and time constraints.

The traditional culture exhibit combined with human-computer interactive intelligence is a human-computer interactive technology that provides visitors with an interactive experience related to traditional culture. This approach allows visitors to understand the traditional culture more intuitively and also increases their interest in the exhibit.

As an example, in a traditional culture exhibit, voice recognition technology and virtual reality technology can be used so that visitors can interact with the exhibit using their voices and get information about traditional culture. Touch screen technology can also be used so that visitors can tap on the screen to learn about different aspects of traditional culture. Overall, traditional culture combined with human-computer interaction is a good way to make the traditional culture better protected and inherited, and also to let more people know and understand traditional culture through modern technological means.

4   Innovation of Visual Elements in Human-Computer Interaction

In the innovation process of human-computer interaction, regional cultural characteristics, extracting traditional cultural elements, and combining them with modern graphic design have become a new way of synthesizing visual information. Studying the visual characteristics and visual orientation brought by its traditional culture, and other kinds of orientation factors, finding the similarities between it and interface design, and integrating them, can experience a different blend of unique regional characteristics and modern cultural elements in the process of human-computer interaction.

And in the current highly developed environment of information technology, although the composition of these cultures is not reflected by modern colors, the interface elements need to have good visibility and readability. In the interface color scheme, in addition to the use of regional cultural color elements, the use of traditional colors in the change to achieve unity will give to bring people's hearts unlimited shock. Reflect the strong cultural characteristics and play the purpose of visual communication. To bring the audience the culture of color composition application, only then can it become a work that the public is happy to perceive and easy to understand. Apply traditional art colors to reflect the composition of colors, and use gorgeous colors to make the work bring a strong visual impact to the audience. It produces a strong contrast with other graphic designs, covering multiple influences in religion, literature, ethnicity, region, and history. The traditional philosophical thought, cultural spirit, and ideology are self-contained and reflect the different styles of the times. And people experience unique pleasure in human-computer interaction. Whether the interaction design works are more infectious and attractive, whether they better reflect the interactivity of the interface, and whether they have better affinity and make people pleasing to the eye, determines the success of interaction design.

In practice, designers gradually create patterns that are recognized by most people (patterns include both graphic structure and structural form). In the regional culture, there are also a series of totems and patterns that are different from the traditional ones, and they form a new image with new visual senses and messages after asking. If we want to make design works with rich traditional cultural heritage and distinctive characteristics of the times at the same time, we need to seek the fitting point between the traditional patterns of folk art and modern graphic design and integrate the two. To reshape a new graphic style that organically combines modern creative ideas with the spirit of traditional culture. To understand the cultural connotation of the graphic style, we can use it flexibly and avoid rigid application. Although multimedia interface interaction design integrates design art, aesthetics, sociology, communication science, ergonomics, and other disciplines based on one, it has its structural system. And innovation is the requirement of design essence and the requirement of the times. In the human-computer interaction as "design for communication" visual communication design, how to properly and fully convey the information is the central problem that every designer always has to face. However, in today's society, it is not enough to set the keywords of conveying information correctly and adequately. It is necessary to start from the innovation of each cultural influence, design concept, visual language, and technical expression to convey the message correctly and adequately. In the design of visual media, the use of visual symbols to express and convey information, how do we use some effective information? The word "innovation" is not new to us. Innovation is the innovation of design concepts and thinking based on the unique culture of the region. In short, it is the innovation of past design experience and knowledge. Depending on the nature and degree of innovation, it can be understood as inherited innovation and radical innovation, and the latter has even become a kind of negation and rebellion to a certain extent, especially for a fixed framework of thinking formed by the self-subconscious for a long time.

In terms of visual elements in human-computer interaction, they have a dialectical unity and an inseparable overall relationship. Design concept innovation is the premise and foundation of visual language innovation and technical expression innovation; while visual language innovation is the manifestation of design concept innovation and technical expression innovation; technical expression innovation provides strong technical support and realization for the latter.

5   Results and Discussion

Visual search refers to searching for a target within the range of vision. When a corresponding target is found, information interference from other factors is excluded and target information is determined. When multiple target information detection is performed, recognition is based on the differences in the feature factors, environmental factors, and detail factors of the object to achieve the result of identifying the target. When we are in information recognition, usually we will carry out the visual comparison in the brain, the information in the memory and visual information into a superposition, this superposition state will give a new independent meaning to the product in reality. The visual elements in the human-computer interaction interface will bring a visual perception awareness process to the user. When the user perceives the characteristics of the interface information, the brain will passively omit and strengthen a series of characteristic information when under the influence of the regional environment and culture our thinking form is in a shallow solidified field, which comes from the influence of cultural subtlety. When we visually perceive the interface elements, through the visual elements of strong regional culture to form a superposition of consciousness, is it possible to perceive and obtain the target information quickly, to deepen the user's visual perception and influence?

In terms of design perspective, quick recognition should be the main presentation of the design, the limited space of the human-computer interaction interface should allow users to identify information more effectively, but the visual pheromones in it are also complex, sensory, pheromones, shape, space, etc. will affect the experience with. The difference between the two lies in the complexity and simplicity of the guiding elements, and the difference between complex recognition and simple recognition in the use scenario, which mainly depends on the way the content of the interface is presented. Visual elements with strong regional culture in the interface system, under the integration of thinking state and form, the integration of visual perception and thought cognition can be more effective to assist the process of user experience and cognition, and the guidance of user cognition is more effective, especially the guidance involving pheromone cognition, such as simple interface elements with the basic shape and interface elements with multiple information, while the interface with high information recognition is better to guide the user. The design of special visual elements and interface integration will significantly affect the user's experience, usefulness, and perception in human-computer interaction. The integration with culture will bring a three-dimensional thinking environment to the user, in the case of the integration of memory, cognition, and environment, the way of thinking shows a superposition state, and the design of the integration will bring a better interaction experience.

For example, in some cultures, people may prefer to use language to communicate, while in other cultures, people may prefer to use gestures or eye contact. And regional cultural interface design may influence people's expectations and preferences for HCI interfaces; for example, people in some cultures may prefer simple and intuitive interfaces, while in other cultures they may prefer colorful interfaces. Also in terms of interactive content and purpose, regional cultures may influence people's expectations of HCI content and purpose. For example, in some cultures, people may want to be educated and entertained by HCI, while in other cultures, people may prefer to solve practical problems through HCI. And regional cultures may influence expectations and preferences for HCI rules and etiquette; for example, in some cultures, people may want to be polite and respectful when interacting with HCI, while in other cultures, people may prefer to be direct.

Cultural differences in HCI can manifest themselves in many ways. For example, people in different cultures may have different expectations and habits and may use HCI differently. Therefore, when designing HCI systems, designers should consider the habits and expectations of use in different cultures to better adapt to different cultural environments. For example, in some cultures, people may prefer to talk directly to the robot, while in other cultures, people may prefer to interact with the robot by touching the screen or through gestures.

In addition, cultural differences may influence how robots are perceived and accepted. In some cultures, people may be more receptive to robots and use them as useful tools, while in other cultures, people may have more reservations about robots. Therefore, it is important to design human-robot interaction systems with cultural differences in mind so that they provide a good experience in different cultural environments.

In the current diversified design environment, when designing HCI systems, it is important to take into account the usage habits and expectations in multiple cultures and try to provide multiple interaction methods to provide a good user experience in different cultural environments. Local design, on the other hand, should pay attention to local design when designing for the internationalization of human-computer interaction. This means that designers should understand the characteristics of local cultures and take into account local cultural differences in the design process. Also when designing HCI systems, internationalization testing should be conducted to ensure that the system works well in different cultural contexts. During the testing process, feedback from users from different cultural backgrounds should be collected and improvements should be made based on the feedback. When designing an HCI system, a global team should be assembled that includes members from different cultural backgrounds. This can help designers better understand the habits and expectations of users from different cultures and take these differences into account in the design process.

The gradual shift of visual culture communication from direct visual transmission to digital technology support marks the transformation and formation of a cultural form from paper-based reading to visually influenced reading, promoting the expansion of new modern and even post-modern communication concepts, and bringing about paradigm shift in human thinking. These profound changes to information dissemination and visual senses are completely new, and what they bring is a comprehensive innovation in art forms and concepts, etc. In the current era of multiculturalism, it is a requirement and necessity of the times to accept multiple cultures and to bring art creation and teaching into a new state.

The qualitative discussion in this paper addresses the integration of visual element design in HCI. Through qualitative feedback, different factors affect the recognition of the interface and there is variability in the applicability of different presentation methods in the interaction process, so the interaction process under each factor remains to be explored in future research.

References

1. Lu, L.F., Huang, L.: Exploration and application of graphic design language based on artificial intelligence visual communication. Wireless Commun. Mobile Compu. **2022**, 1–10 (2022). https://doi.org/10.1155/2022/9907303
2. Chen, Y.: Artistic design of real-time image interaction interface for advertising screens based on augmented reality and visual communication. J. Sens. **2021** (2021). https://doi.org/10.1155/2021/1597236
3. Zhang, F.: Research on the internet plus visual communication design – the application of visual design in internet. J. Phys. Conf. Ser. **1915**(4), 042039 (2021). https://doi.org/10.1088/1742-6596/1915/4/042039
4. Gao, G.J., Li, W.Y.: A system architecture for 5G virtual reality-based visual design creation. Int. J. Commun. Syst. **35**(5) (2021). https://doi.org/10.1002/DAC.4750
5. Song, G.: The application of motion graphics in visual communication design. J. Phys. Conf. Ser. **1744**(4) (2021). https://doi.org/10.1088/1742-6596/1744/4/042165
6. Zhao, D., Pan, B.: Psychological cognition and thinking needs in visual communication design. In: e3S Conference Network, vol. 236 (2021). https://doi.org/10.1051/E3SCONF/202123605070
7. Jiang, B., He, Q.: A study on multimedia technology and technological innovation in visual communication. J. Phys. Conf. Ser. **1693**(1) (2020). https://doi.org/10.1088/1742-6596/1693/1/012132
8. Kress, G., van Leeuwen, T.: Reading Images: The Grammar of Visual Design. Routledge, Third edition. | London; New York: Routledge, 2021. (2020). https://doi.org/10.4324/9781003099857
9. Lin, L., Takazawa: Exploring modern visual design thinking in traditional chinese culture with the example of demon image design in Shanhaijing. In: Proceedings of the Fourth International Conference on Culture, Education and Economic Development in Modern Societies (ICCESE 2020) (Advances in Social Sciences, Education and Humanities Research, vol. 416), pp. 269–272. Ed. Atlantis Press (2020)
10. Sun, Y.: Research on the application method of interaction design in human-computer interface design. Front. Art Res. **4.0**(11.0) (2022). https://doi.org/10.25236/FAR.2022.041113
11. Wang, L.J.: The three-dimensionality of visual communication design in the new media era. ArtPin **08**, 243–244 (2019)
12. Wang, X.: A study of information communication in interaction design. Pack. Eng. **31**(12), 12–14 (2010). https://doi.org/10.19554/j.cnki.1001-3563.2010.12.005
13. Wang, K., Kuang, C.: Visual communication design model for new media and public health environment and new communication mode. J. Environ. Public Health 2022 (2022). https://doi.org/10.1155/2022/1177677
14. Zheng, Y.: Study on the application of Chinese traditional visual elements in visual communication design. Math. Probl. Eng. 2022 (2022). https://doi.org/10.1155/2022/1020033

15. Dandan, Z., Bo, P.: Psychological cognition and thinking needs in visual communication design. E3S Web of Conferences, vol. 236 (2021). https://doi.org/10.1051/E3SCONF/202 123605070
16. Chang, L.: The development trend of visual communication design. Front. Art Res. 2.0(9.0) (2020). https://doi.org/10.25236/FAR.2020.020915
17. The opportunities and limitations of human-computer interaction in virtual and augmented reality. Int. J. Recent Technol. Eng. **8.6** (2020). https://doi.org/10.35940/ijrte.f9494.038620
18. Musunuru, G.V.: The opportunities and limitations of human computer interaction in virtual and augmented reality. Int. J. Recent Technol. Eng. **8**(6), 4667–4673 (2020). https://doi.org/10.35940/ijrte.F9494.038620
19. Liming, T.: Research on artistic expression under human-computer interaction scenes. In: Proceedings of 2019 International Conference on Art Design, Music and Culture (ADMC 2019). Ed., p. 15-1. Francis Academic Press, UK (2019)
20. Tian, F.: Human-computer interactions for virtual reality. Virtual Real. Intell. Hardware **1**(3) (2019). https://doi.org/10.1016/S2096-5796(19)30028-2
21. Zhou, J.: Analysis of the application of national cultural symbols in visual communication design. Front. Educ. Res. **3**(1) (2020). https://doi.org/10.25236/FER.2020.030125.
22. Wang, Y.: Research on innovative application of new media in visual communication design. J. Phys. Conf. Ser. **1550**(3) (2020). https://doi.org/10.1088/1742-6596/1550/3/032146
23. Valantinaitė, I., Sederevičiūtė-Pačiauskienė, Ž, Žilinskaitė-Vytė, V.: Culturally conditioned visual communication in creative expression. Creat. Stud. **13**(1), 216–245 (2020). https://doi.org/10.3846/cs.2020.12004
24. Zhu, X., Wu, Q.: Research on the application of chinese traditional cultural symbols in modern visual communication design. Art Educ. Res. **19**, 71–74 (2022)
25. Jing, H., Jin, C., Lijun, Z.: The value and application of fusion of ethnic traditional patterns and visual communication design art. Art View. **29**, 50–52 (2022)
26. Wang, C.: The application of Chinese traditional colors in modern visual communication design. J. Anyang Eng. College **21**(05), 30–32 (2022). https://doi.org/10.19329/j.cnki.1673-2928.2022.05.009
27. Sun, Y.: Study on the application of Chinese traditional elements in visual communication design. J. Changjiang Eng. Vocat. Technol. College **39**(03), 70–74 (2022). https://doi.org/10.14079/j.cnki.cn42-1745/tv.2022.03.017
28. Wang, B.: Research on the integration of visual communication design and traditional cultural elements. Da Guan. **09**, 15–17 (2022)
29. Wang, Y.H.: The application of traditional cultural elements in visual communication design in the new business era. Commerce Exhib. Econ. **16**, 76–78 (2022). https://doi.org/10.19995/j.cnki.CN10-1617/F7.2022.16.076
30. Liu, Y.: A study on the influence of regional culture on visual communication design. Popular Color **08**, 84–86 (2022)
31. Jiu, P.: The application of pen and ink art elements in visual communication design. Art View **23**, 43–45 (2022)
32. Lei, Y.: Innovation and development of visual communication design in the new media era. Art View **23**, 55–57 (2022)
33. Zheng, G.: The application of Chinese traditional elements in the teaching of visual communication design. Art Educ. Res. **12**, 118–119 (2022)
34. Liu, J.: Study on the innovation and development trend of visual communication design in the era of digital media. Art Literat. **06**, 137–139 (2022). https://doi.org/10.16585/j.cnki.mswx.2022.06.040
35. Lan, Z.: The integration of visual communication design and traditional elements. Art View **17**, 69–71 (2022)

36. Li, C.: Analysis of the application of visual communication in interactive online advertising design. Art Market. **06**, 118–120 (2022)
37. Xu, T.: Exploring the innovation mode of visual communication design in the new era. Art Lit. **04**, 142–144 (2022). https://doi.org/10.16585/j.cnki.mswx.2022.04.054
38. Qin, M.: Exploring the integration path of folk art and visual communication design. Art View **09**, 81–83 (2022)

How to Select the Force Setting of the Exoskeleton? The Effect of Working Height, Hand Posture on Assisting Force

Kang-Hung Liu[1]([✉]), Sheng-Chun Yi[2], and Yu-Cheng Lin[1,2]

[1] Department of Mechanical and Computer-Aided Engineering, Overseas Chinese University, Taichung, Taiwan
khliu@ocu.edu.tw
[2] Department of Computer-Aided Industrial Design, Overseas Chinese University, Taichung, Taiwan

Abstract. The technology of passive upper-limb exoskeletons has been developed and improved to reduce the possibility of work-related injury or musculoskeletal discord. At present, each type of exoskeleton wearing guideline has different basis. There is no adjustment guideline for different working heights. This research aimed to explore the effect of working heights, working postures, and the setting of exoskeleton, on the assisting force. A passive upper limb exoskeleton, Comau MATE, was applied as the experimental equipment to explore the effect of above three factors. The results showed that the assisting forces of exoskeleton were significantly affected by working height, spring tension setting, and width between hands. The exoskeleton could provide better assisting force when users' working area are between shoulder to head, and the effect may decrease when user put their hand overhead. When users' two hands were shoulder width apart, the exoskeleton could provide better support. Those finding could provide a guide for the passive upper-limb exoskeleton users to adjust their setting of exoskeleton.

Keywords: Exoskeleton · Working Posture · Assisting Force

1 Introduction

The technology of exoskeletons has been continuously developed and improved to reduce the possibility of work-related injury or musculoskeletal discord [1]. Exoskeletons can be defined as wearable mechanical devices that work collaboratively with the use [2]. Several different exoskeleton products come out and validated by researchers (as shown in Table 1). However, at present, each type of exoskeleton wearing guideline has different basis. There is no adjustment guideline for different working heights. For example, the work area of workers is over shoulder or overhead may cause different risk and need specific assisting forces. There are also different body dimensions such as heights and weights, especially for users from different races. Because the adjustment of exoskeleton assisting force is usually time-consuming or need extra hand tool, people will not adjust it very often. Then, how to adjust the auxiliary force of the exoskeleton depends on situation and body dimensions become ambiguous.

© The Author(s), under exclusive license to Springer Nature Switzerland AG 2023
P.-L. P. Rau (Ed.): HCII 2023, LNCS 14023, pp. 98–107, 2023.
https://doi.org/10.1007/978-3-031-35939-2_8

Table 1. Passive upper-limb exoskeleton designed by different countries.

Product	Company/ Country	Weight	Illustration	Ref.
Paexo	Ottobock/ Germany	1.8 kg		[3]
Vest Exoskeleton (VEX)	Hyundai/ Korea	2.5 kg		[4]
Airframe	Levitate Technologies, Inc./ USA	2.7 kg		[5]
Mascular Aiding Tech Exoskeleton (MATE)	Comau/ Italy	3 kg		[6]
ShoulderX™	SuitX/ USA	6 kg		[7]
Ekso Vest	Ekso Bionics/ USA	4.3kg		[8]
EXHAUSS Stronger	EXHAUSS/ France	9kg		[9]

This research aimed to explore the effect of working heights, working postures, and the setting of exoskeleton, on the assisting force. The results of this research could provide a guide for the passive upper-limb exoskeleton users to adjust their setting of exoskeleton.

2 Methodology

2.1 Experimental Participants

Fifteen volunteer participants were recruited to participate in this study. The range of their age was from 18 to 22. All participants were college students and self-reported normal physical capacity and absence of any physical and/or mental illness.

2.2 Experimental Device

This research applied the exoskeleton named MATE, developed by an Italy company, Comau, a leading automation solutions provider. MATE is a cutting-edge wearable device designed to assist workers with manual tasks in industrial settings. It is a passive upper-limb exoskeleton, complies with the physiological movements of the shoulders, and has adjustable assistance level (see Fig. 1). It is an upper-body exoskeleton that uses spring-based structure to support workers of excessive effort during daily tasks performance. The weight of MATE is approximate 3 kg. The usability of the Comau MATE exoskeleton has been evaluated [10, 11].

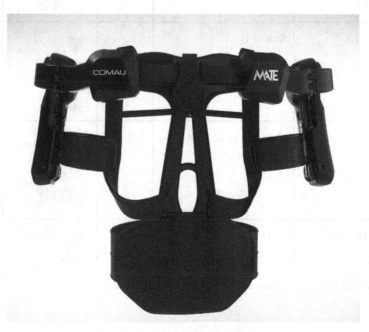

Fig. 1. Comau MATE Exoskeleton.

2.3 Experimental Design

The three main independent variables and one dependent variable were as follow:

Independent Variable I: Spring Tension Setting. The spring tension of the exoskeleton was adjustable. Three levels of the spring tension, maximum, medium, and minimum were included in the experiment. The maximum level of the spring tension can provide stronger torque to raise wearer's arms. On the other hand, the minimum level of the spring tension can only provide limited torque to support wearer's arms.

Independent Variable II: Working Height. There were five levels of working height in this research. Because the passive upper-limb exoskeletons were usually designed to support user work over-shoulder, the working height in this research was from shoulder height (150 cm) to overhead (190). Each level is separated by ten centimeters.

Independent Variable III: Distance Between Hands. The factor of distance between hands had two levels. The first level asked experimental participants place their close to simulate the posture of fine work such as locking screw on the ceiling. The second level asked experimental participants place their hands shoulder width apart to simulate the posture likes lifting a box.

Dependent Variable: Assisting Force. The dependent variable in this research was assisting force. The experimental participants were asked to wear the exoskeleton and grasp a hanging rod with crane scale. The assisting force was the difference between the values measured by the crane scale while the participant wears and does not wear exoskeleton (see Fig. 2).

This research applied a full factorial design with three factors ($5 \times 2 \times 2$) to explore the effect of working heights, working postures, and the setting of exoskeleton on the assisting force.

2.4 Experimental Process

After confirming that the subject was aware of and willing to participate, their height and weight were orally asked and recorded. Then, the experimental process, precautions, and the wearing method of the passive upper limb exoskeleton MATE were explained to the subject. The subject was asked to wear the passive upper limb exoskeleton, with the assistance of two experimenters during the wearing process. The experimenters helped adjust the assistance force of the exoskeleton and ensured that the exoskeleton was attached to the subject's body properly, ensuring that the position of the exoskeleton, tightness, and the assistance force adjustment knobs were all correct. Before the formal experiment began, one of the experimenters demonstrated how to conduct the experiment. After the demonstration was completed, the subject was asked to repeat the trial once, and the experimenters checked that the movements were safe before proceeding with the formal experiment.

Fig. 2. The experimental setting with wearing exoskeleton and the crane scale.

3   Results

3.1   Descriptive Statistics and the Normal Probability Tests

An analysis of variance (ANOVA) was conducted to analyze the experimental data on assisting force. Before analysis, the descriptive statistics of the original values measured by crane scale were shown in Table 2 and the assisting force were shown in Table 3. To use an ANOVA, the data should satisfy the basic assumptions of normality. A normal probability test was applied to determine whether the data fit a normal distribution ($p > 0.05$). The Kolmogorov-Smirnov test was applied to test the normality. The results of the normal probability tests indicated that the data of all five working heights were fitting normal distributions ($p < 0.05$). (see Table 4).

Table 2. Descriptive statistics (mean and standard deviation) of the original values measured by crane scale with exoskeleton support.

Spring tension setting	Working height	Distance between hands	
		Close	Shoulder width
Minimum	150	2.07 (0.84)	1.67 (0.82)
	160	2.72 (1.09)	2.30 (0.96)
	170	3.60 (1.30)	3.11 (1.19)
	180	4.49 (1.40)	3.99 (1.17)
	190	5.91 (2.01)	5.22 (1.68)
Medium	150	1.81 (0.85)	1.44 (0.66)
	160	2.42 (0.98)	1.99 (0.86)
	170	3.28 (1.10)	2.84 (0.97)
	180	4.23 (1.35)	3.56 (1.11)
	190	5.75 (2.06)	4.87 (1.76)
Maximum	150	1.60 (0.71)	1.21 (0.63)
	160	2.24 (0.89)	1.72 (0.77)
	170	2.97 (1.08)	2.47 (0.90)
	180	3.78 (1.15)	3.11 (0.83)
	190	5.43 (2.16)	4.54 (1.80)

Table 3. Descriptive statistics (mean and standard deviation) of assisting force.

Spring tension setting	Working height	Distance between hands	
		Close	Shoulder width
Minimum	150	1.42 (0.61)	1.51 (0.51)
	160	1.36 (0.69)	1.54 (0.69)
	170	1.11 (0.71)	1.35 (0.76)
	180	0.91 (0.65)	1.06 (0.62)
	190	0.36 (0.58)	0.59 (0.80)
Medium	150	1.68 (0.74)	1.75 (0.53)
	160	1.66 (0.58)	1.85 (0.69)
	170	1.43 (0.81)	1.63 (0.80)
	180	1.16 (0.64)	1.48 (0.62)
	190	0.52 (0.77)	0.95 (1.11)

(*continued*)

Table 3. (*continued*)

Spring tension setting	Working height	Distance between hands	
		Close	Shoulder width
Maximum	150	1.89 (0.71)	1.98 (0.60)
	160	1.84 (0.61)	2.12 (0.76)
	170	1.74 (0.76)	2.00 (0.89)
	180	1.61 (0.71)	1.94 (0.84)
	190	0.84 (0.97)	1.27 (1.22)

Table 4. The results of Kolmogorov-Smirnov test

Working height	Test statistic	DF	Sig
150	0.052	90	0.200
160	0.089	90	0.075
170	0.089	90	0.078
180	0.091	90	0.065
190	0.056	90	0.200

3.2 The Results of Experiment

As shown in Table 5 the assisting forces were significantly affected by working height ($F = 26.142$, $p < 0.001$), spring tension setting ($F = 24.693$, $p < 0.001$), and width between hands ($F = 11.000$, $p = 0.001$). There was no significantly interaction among three factors. When participants' two hands were close, the assisting forces of the exoskeleton increase with strong spring tension and lower working height. There was an especially lower assisting force when the working height was far overhead (see Fig. 3). When participants' two hands were shoulder width apart, there were similar effects via spring tension. However, there was a slight difference with working height. The highest assisting force was found when the working height was 160. Both the working height get higher and lower, the assisting force decreases (see Fig. 4).

Table 5. ANOVA summary table

Source	SS	DF	MS	F	p-value
Working height (A)	57.199	4	14.300	26.142	<0.001*
Spring tension setting (B)	27.014	2	13.507	24.693	<0.001*
Distance between hands (C)	6.017	1	6.017	11.000	0.001*
A × B	1.045	8	0.131	0.239	0.983*
A × C	0.899	4	0.225	0.411	0.801*
B × C	0.184	2	0.092	0.168	0.846*
A × B × C	0.227	8	0.028	0.052	1.000*
Error	229.194	419	0.547		

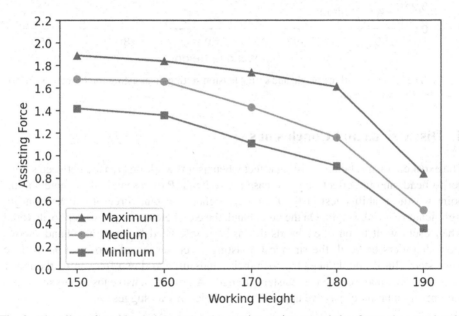

Fig. 3. The effect of working height and spring tension setting on assisting force when two hands were close.

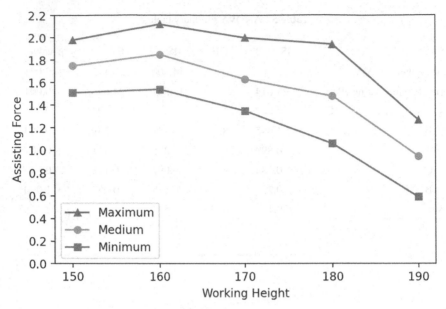

Fig. 4. The effect of working height and spring tension setting on assisting force when two hands were shoulder width apart.

4   Discussions and Conclusions

The exoskeleton has better assisting effect when users' working area are between shoulder to head, and the effect may decrease above head. Past research also found similar point via the usability test [10]. Obviously, higher assistant force of exoskeleton got significant reduced weight. On the other hand, the exoskeleton may cause opposite force when users want to put their hands down. If people need to keep their hands above their shoulders or head, the strongest assisting force setting of exoskeletons will be suggested. But if people need to move their hands up and down frequently, the lower assisting force may reduce the resistant strength. A comprehensive task analysis before the implementation of passive upper-limb exoskeleton was suggested.

5   Limitation and Future Research

The sample of this study was limited and recruited only young adults from university, which could limit generalizability. To develop a comprehensive guide that can work in practice, extended data collection with diversity is necessary in the future.

Acknowledgement. This research was funded by the National Science and Technology Council of Taiwan with project number of 109-2221-E-240-001-MY3 and 111-2813-C-240-005-E.

References

1. Bosch, T., et al.: The effects of a passive exoskeleton on muscle activity, discomfort and endurance time in forward bending work. Appl. Ergon. **54**, 212–217 (2016)
2. Gopura, R., et al.: Developments in hardware systems of active upper-limb exoskeleton robots: a review. Robot. Auton. Syst. **75**, 203–220 (2016)
3. Maurice, P., et al.: Evaluation of PAEXO, a novel passive exoskeleton for overhead work. Comput. Methods Biomech. Biomed. Engin. **22**(sup1), S448–S450 (2019)
4. Hyun, D.J., et al.: A light-weight passive upper arm assistive exoskeleton based on multi-linkage spring-energy dissipation mechanism for overhead tasks. Robot. Auton. Syst. **122**, 103309 (2019)
5. Liu, S., et al.: Solving the surgeon ergonomic crisis with surgical exosuit. Surg. Endosc. **32**(1), 236–244 (2017). https://doi.org/10.1007/s00464-017-5667-x
6. Perez Luque, E.: Evaluation of the Use of Exoskeletons in the Range of Motion of Workers (2019)
7. Alabdulkarim, S., Nussbaum, M.A.: Influences of different exoskeleton designs and tool mass on physical demands and performance in a simulated overhead drilling task. Appl. Ergon. **74**, 55–66 (2019)
8. Kim, S., et al.: Assessing the influence of a passive, upper extremity exoskeletal vest for tasks requiring arm elevation: Part I–"Expected" effects on discomfort, shoulder muscle activity, and work task performance. Appl. Ergon. **70**, 315–322 (2018)
9. Theurel, J., et al.: Physiological consequences of using an upper limb exoskeleton during manual handling tasks. Appl. Ergon. **67**, 211–217 (2018)
10. Luque, E.P., et al.: Evaluation of the Use of Exoskeletons in the Range of Motion of Workers. PhD thesis, University of Skovde, Skovde (2019)
11. Grazi, L., et al.: Design and experimental evaluation of a semi-passive upper-limb exoskeleton for workers with motorized tuning of assistance. IEEE Trans. Neural Syst. Rehabil. Eng. **28**(10), 2276–2285 (2020)

SeeCC: An Online Cross-Cultural Communication Aid to Improve Communication and Cooperation Performance

Nan Qie, Xinyue Kang, and Pei-Luen Patrick Rau[✉]

Department of Industrial Engineering, Tsinghua University, Beijing, China
rpl@mail.tsinghua.edu.cn

Abstract. In this research, we designed an online cross-cultural communication aid SeeCC, which can provide individual-level cultural portrait and real-time communication tips. We conducted an experiment to test the effectiveness of SeeCC in promoting cross-cultural skills and performance. Sixty participants from multiple cultural backgrounds were recruited to complete online collaboration tasks. The results showed that (1) SeeCC significantly improved users' skills in online cross-cultural communication, and (2) the expert-evaluated outcome quality was better with SeeCC than without it, confirming the effectiveness of SeeCC in improving cross-cultural communication and collaboration performance. The results indicated great potential for SeeCC to be used in cross-cultural training and global collaboration support.

Keywords: Cross-cultural communication · Computer-mediated communication · Computer-mediated cooperation · System design and evaluation

1 Introduction

With the development and popularization of the Internet and communication technologies, an increasing amount of cross-cultural communication happens online. It is becoming increasingly common for globally distributed people to collaborate, make decisions, and implement actions in "virtual" collaborative teams (Davison & Ward 1999; Jarvenpaa & Shaw 1998).

In online cross-cultural communication (OCCC), being informed about each other's individual-level information is more difficult in comparison to face-to-face communication, which can make OCCC more challenging. The people who may participate in OCCC are cross-cultural themselves. They may have experienced multi-cultural influences, speak two or more languages, have interacted with people from multiple cultural backgrounds, and have experience of studying, working and living abroad (Agar 1991). Therefore, it is not accurate to define their cultural beliefs and behavior patterns by their nationality alone. As Scollon, Scollon, and Jones (2012) point out, "cultures do not talk

P.-L. P. Rau (Ed.): HCII 2023, LNCS 14023, pp. 108–125, 2023.
https://doi.org/10.1007/978-3-031-35939-2_9

to each other; individuals do". Patel and Salih (2018) also advocated that in this international age, we require the capability to handle culturally different individuals rather than nations.

Beyond the challenges, the rapid development of the Internet and communication technologies has provided new opportunities for cross-cultural communication. Technologies, such as machine learning, provide more opportunities for the media to learn individual-level patterns; and such as natural language processing, can support real-time understanding of the communication process. Compared to an offline setting, an online environment makes it easier to collect and manage users' cultural orientation information and provide support in real time without disturbing the communication process. A system that provides individual-level cultural orientation information and real-time communication tips is practical and can be useful in OCCC.

This study aimed to design and develop an individual-level cross-cultural communication aid that can help promote communication skills and improve OCCC performance. We chose to apply it to a text-based online communication scenario. First, although communication technologies such as voice and video chat are now gaining popularity, research indicated that in both interpersonal context and organizational context, people sometimes prefer text-based communication media to richer communication media, considering formality (Trevino et al. 1990), social influence, individual experience (Carlson & Zmud 1999), and the embedded tools (Aritz et al. 2018). Second, current technology for text processing is more mature than for audio and video processing, so text-based scenario is a good place to start the study of a communication aid. Furthermore, we focused on communication between two persons because it is the minimum number of persons required for communication, and one-to-one interaction is the basic cell of team collaboration.

1.1 Training Tools to Develop Cross-Cultural Skills

Cross-cultural training tools have been developed and applied to help individuals achieve good cross-cultural performance. In addition to traditional forms of lectures, some experiential programs were created to provide more vivid scenarios. Bafa Bafa (Shirts 1977) is an intercultural simulation game. Participants in Bafa Bafa are randomly arranged in two cultural groups. After familiarizing themselves with their culture, individuals from the two cultural groups interact with each other and follow the instructions to perform some intercultural tasks. This process simulates cultural shock and adaption. ExcelL (Mak et al. 1999) provides another form of experiential training. Instead of encouraging people to step out and train themselves by dealing with challenges, ExcelL allows trainees to acquire behavioral knowledge in a realistic and safe environment. The focus of ExcelL is on behavioral training through observational learning and guided practice. Participants learn to adapt to a new cultural environment with the help of a "cultural map", which describes the appropriate behavior for specific scenarios and related cultural knowledge on why things should be done a certain way.

In addition to face-to-face training, researchers in the field of education have developed interactive multimodal learning tools by applying new technology (Moreno & Mayer 2007). Games, simulations, and social robots have been introduced for learning languages and preparing users for different cultures. Maseltov is a mobile game that promotes integration and prevents social exclusion by encouraging migrants to interact with the local population (Schuller et al. 2013). There are also examples of non-digital game products such as How Would You Say It, which uses game-like tools like cards to encourage users to reflect on dilemmas and events in situations and environments where different cultures collide in order to enhance culture awareness and cross-cultural communication skills (Nyman Gomez & Berg Marklund 2018). Johnson and Zaker (2012) integrated Alelo's social simulation approach into instructional practice to teach the Chinese language. Learners "visit" Chinese locations to meet Chinese "locals", and complete communicative tasks in the virtual world. This provides an immersive environment, which maximizes the learners' engagement and learning motivations. Andrés' (2015) article explored the possibility of making robots capable of inter-cultural emotional communication and introduced two approaches: data-driven approach and model-driven approach. With these approaches, a robot can adjust its emotional communication according to users' cultures and can provide users with a safe scenario to practice intercultural emotional communication.

The current tools, used in either face-to-face or non-face-to-face conditions, have some similarities. First, the current tools are used to develop users' cross-cultural knowledge and skills in advance, rather than to support real-time cross-cultural interaction. Second, the current tools aim to train users to deal with one or several national cultures, rather than train users to deal with one after another individuals with multiple cultural orientations. Third, the current tools are set for an offline cross-cultural interaction environment. An online environment requires specific verbal and non-verbal skills; however, there lack tools that are specially designed for OCCC. To design OCCC facilitating tools, it is necessary to know how culture can influence OCCC behavior.

1.2 How Culture Manifests Itself in OCCC

Researchers have used various cultural frameworks to explain cross-cultural differences in communication and collaboration. The most commonly accepted and adopted theory is Hofstede's cultural framework (Hofstede et al. 2010). Although it is established based on the national culture approach, the dimensions in the Hofstede's framework have proved to be effective in describing individuals (Yoo et al. 2011). Hofstede's framework depicts cultural differences in six dimensions, including collectivism-individualism, power distance, uncertainty avoidance, masculinity-femininity, long-term orientation, and indulgence-restriction. People from collective cultures emphasize "we" more than "I," while people from individualistic cultures emphasize "I" more than "we." People who have a collective orientation prefer to use first-person plural pronouns (Na & Choi 2009). People from high power-distance cultures accept and agree with the unequal distribution of power. In highly collective and power-distance cultures, individuals who enter an organization later show special respect to those who entered earlier (Qie et al. 2019). The rest of the dimensions affect how people make decisions. People from high uncertainty-avoidance cultures find it challenging to tolerate unpredictable situations. People from high masculinity cultures emphasize success or money versus love or care. People from long-term orientation cultures attach high importance to future gains over current gains. People from a high restriction culture show a negative attitude of satisfying natural human desires.

Besides Hofstede's framework, Hall's (1989) theory on the communication style is mostly cited in communication behavior studies. Hall divided cultures into those with a high-context style and low-context style. In high-context cultures, people communicate implicitly and the information conveyed is hidden in the context, while in low-context cultures, people communicate mainly by explicit verbal expression. Kayan, Fussell, and Setlock (2006) found that people from high-context cultures rate emoticons as significantly more critical than people from low-context cultures during online communication. Lim and Urakami's (2018) research further indicated that for the use of graphical expressions, people from low-context cultures prefer simple emoji while people from high-context cultures prefer stickers that are more complex.

1.3 Aim and Research Questions

This article aims to design a new communication aid called SeeCC, which can help users see culture in communication. SeeCC can provide individual-level cultural orientation information and real-time communication tips, to facilitate OCCC. We designed and developed this tool and applied it to text-based online collaborative tasks, to evaluate its effectiveness in improving skills and performance. The evaluation is conducted with two more specific research questions:

RQ1. Can SeeCC improve users' online cross-cultural communication skills?

RQ2. Can SeeCC improve users' online cross-cultural collaborative performance?

First, we introduced the function and interface design of SeeCC in Sect. 2. Then, we introduced the design of an online collaboration experiment with 60 participants from multiple cultures in Sect. 3. In Sect. 4, t-tests evaluated the effects of SeeCC in improving users' OCCC skills and performance. Finally, the results were discussed, and suggestions for further OCCC aid design were given in Sect. 5.

2 Design of SeeCC

2.1 Function Design

We designed the SeeCC to be embedded in an online messaging platform. The SeeCC supports three functions: cultural portrait, tips, and recommendation. The design concept of SeeCC is shown in Fig. 1.

The cultural portrait function is intended to describe the communication partner's cultural orientation. The portrait is described based on the cultural orientation of the specific partner rather than the culture of his/her nationality. The portrait is given according to the partner's orientation in cultural dimensions such as communication style, individualism-collectivism, power distance, uncertainty avoidance, masculinity-femininity, long-term orientation, and indulgence-restriction. The descriptions are given in everyday language, which users, who have never heard of Hofstede's or Hall's cultural theories, have no problem understanding. Please see some examples of cultural portrait descriptions provided by SeeCC in Table 1.

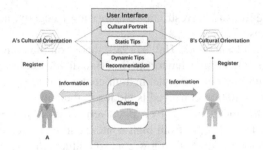

Fig. 1. Concept script of SeeCC

Table 1. Some examples of portrait descriptions (Take user Ben for example)

Cultural dimension	Level	Portrait descriptions
Communication style (Hall 1989)	Low	Ben prefers implicit, straightforward communication
	High	Ben prefers indirect, tactful communication
Individualism (Hofstede et al. 2010)	Low	Ben values the collective
	High	Ben values the individual interest and uniqueness
Power distance (Hofstede et al. 2010)	Low	Ben tends to accept and agree that people are equal
	High	Ben tends to accept and agree with the status differences between people
Uncertainty avoidance (Hofstede et al. 2010)	Low	Ben prefers flexibility and he thinks that rules can always be changed depending on the situation
	High	Ben can't quite stand the uncertainty
Long-term orientation (Hofstede et al. 2010)	Low	Ben values short term benefits over long term benefits
	High	Ben values long term benefits over short term benefits

The tips function provides real-time tips on communication and collaboration behavior. There are two types of tips: static tips and dynamic tips. Static tips are provided based on the two users' cultural portrait, while dynamic tips are provided based on both users' cultural portrait and their dynamic chatting content. The tips are given according to previous research on cultural differences in OCCC behavior. Some examples of the tips given by SeeCC are shown in Table 2.

The recommendation function can influence a user's nonverbal communication behavior in a more natural and undisturbed way. The SeeCC will recommend an emoji or a sticker according to the current chatting content and partner's communication style.

Table 2. Examples of tips provided by SeeCC

Static tips		
Triggering conditions	Tips	Reference
When the chatting partner's age is more than the user's age, and at the same time the partner has a high power-distance	Show respect to the senior, and the senior may want to lead	(Qie et al. 2019)
When the partner has high collectivism	Use more "We" than "I", more "Our" than "My"	(Na & Choi 2009)
When the partner is high-context in communication	Use proper stickers to express emotions Pay attention to read between lines	(Hall 1989; Lim & Urakami 2018)

Dynamic tips			
Triggering conditions	Chatting	Tips	Reference
When the partner's age is more than the user's age, and at the same time the partner has a high power-distance	The other person: Hi/Hello User: Hi/Hello	Try to use a respectful way to greet the senior	(Qie et al. 2019)
When the partner has high collectivism	User: I prefer/I think/my opinion/my idea	Use terms like "it is better for us" to show group sense	(Na & Choi 2009)

When a user expresses emotions, such as gladness or sadness, and some salutation words, such as hello or bye, in text, the corresponding emoji or stickers will pop up. Then, the user can decide whether to adopt it with a click or ignore it by simply continuing to type. If the partner is high-context in communication style, a sticker is recommended, and if the partner is low-context in communication style, an emoji is recommended (Lim & Urakami 2018, examples of emoji and stickers are depicted in Fig. 2).

Emoji   Stickers

Fig. 2. Examples of emoji and stickers used in the system

2.2 Interface Design

The SeeCC consists of three main interfaces: login interface, questionnaire interface and chatting interface. The login interface is for the user to register or log in the system. The questionnaire interface is to collect the users' cultural orientation. The layout of the chatting interface is made up of three parts: the information presentation part on the left, the chatting part in the middle, and the notes part on the right. The information presentation part presents the partner's age, gender, nationality, cultural portrait, and tips. The chatting part is designed according to a common layout of messaging apps, such as Line and WeChat online. The interaction design, such as hotkey and usage of emoji, is the same as in common messaging apps, so that users can quickly adapt to it. Participants can choose and use emoji or stickers in the chatting part, and the system supports the recommendation function of emoji and stickers. The notes part is designed for the user to manage local notes during collaborative tasks. The interface for the participant system is shown in Fig. 3.

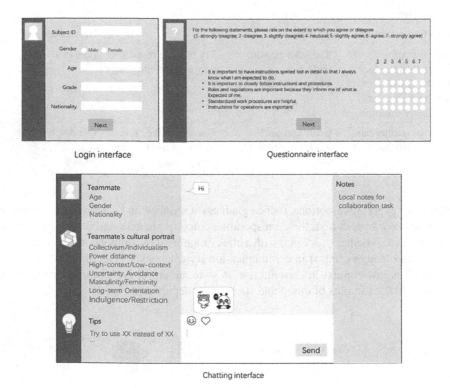

Fig. 3. Interface of the participant system with SeeCC

3 Experiment Methods

We designed an experiment to test the effectiveness of SeeCC in improving users' OCCC skills and performance. Each participant finished two collaborative tasks in sequence, one with SeeCC and one without SeeCC. Then, the data on online cross-cultural communication skills, skill improvement, and OCCC performance were collected.

3.1 Participants

We recruited 60 participants from multiple cultural backgrounds, and divided them into teams of two. The two participants in a team should be from different cultural backgrounds to simulate an OCCC scenario. Because the research team was in China, we recruited a Chinese sample of 30 Chinese participants, and an international sample of 30 participants from 17 different non-Asian countries. We set the Chinese sample as a single country sample and set the other one as a non-Asian sample to avoid arranging two people with close backgrounds in one team. A qualified participant should (1) be born in and living in the respective country for more than 18 years, and (2) be able to type and communicate fluently in English. Furthermore, for the international sample, a qualified participant should (1) have been in China for less than six months, and (2) be from a non-Asian country, to avoid cultural homogeneity with Chinese culture.

All the participants were undergraduate or graduate students recruited through Sojump.com (an online questionnaire platform). Participants were asked to assess their own ability to type and communicate in English, with a 10-point scale (1 for the least ability and 10 for perfect ability). Participants who rated their English ability lower than 6 were excluded. Each participant was offered 90 CNY as a reward for participation. The demographic information of the participants is summarized in Table 3.

Table 3. Participants' demographic information

	Chinese sample	International sample
Age	M = 24.2, SD = 2.37	M = 23.2, SD = 3.37
Gender	14 males, 16 females	16 males, 14 females
Average English level	M = 7.6, SD = 1.46	M = 8.8, SD = 1.07
Nationality	30 Chinese	2 Americans, 1 Belgian, 1 Bolivian, 4 Brazilians, 1 Canadian, 2 Frenchmen, 6 Germens, 1 Ghanaian, 1 Greek, 4 Italians, 1 Dutchmen, 1 Norse, 1 Polish, 1 Romanian, 1 Spanish, 1 Swiss, 1 Ukrainian

3.2 Experiment Procedure

Participants were divided into four groups of 14 or 16 people, with the number of Chinese participants equaling the number of international participants in each group. One group participated in the experiment at a time. The experiment was conducted in a large classroom. Each participant was provided with a desktop computer. The participants were arranged to sit separately to ensure that they did not interfere with each other, and cannot see the screen of each other.

First, the participants were asked to sign on an informed consent document. Second, they were instructed to login to the experiment platform and fill in a questionnaire about their age, gender, nationality, and cultural orientation. Third, to compare between collaboration with or without SeeCC, each participant was supposed to finish two collaborative tasks in sequence. In each task, the system randomly arranged a Chinese participant and an international participant to form a team. The experiment was designed to ensure that each participant would be assigned two different partners for the two tasks.

The two tasks were designed to have the same procedure; however, with different topics, to avoid the influence of task order on performance (please see Sect. 3.4 for task design details). The order of collaboration with or without SeeCC and the order of the two tasks were cross-balanced, to avoid the influence of the learning effect After each collaborative task, the participants filled in a questionnaire to evaluate their team collaboration performance. Before the SeeCC supported collaboration, the participants' online cross-cultural communication skills were measured. After the SeeCC supported collaboration, the participants' online cross-cultural communication skill improvement was measured. The whole experiment took about 90 min for each participant. Every participant can get 90 CNY as a reward.

3.3 Experiment Platform

The experiment platform is developed with html5. The platform consists of the host system and the participant system. In this experiment, we used the Chrome browser to run the platform. The backend is deployed on the Tencent cloud server (https://cloud. tencent.com), which can support up to 30 participants to be online at the same time. The system backend recorded participants' login information and all experimental process data, to facilitate the analysis of participants' communication and cooperation behavior.

The host system is divided into three main functional modules: experiment management, system management, and data management. The experiment management module is used to control and monitor the experiment progress. The system management module is used to manage the cultural orientation questionnaire, which can insert, delete or modify questions, add or delete cultural dimensions, as well as set up the logic for the system to model cultural portraits based on questionnaire data. The data management module is used to manage the experimental data, which records all the participants' personal information, cultural orientation information and chatting records.

The participant system has two versions: one with SeeCC functions and one without SeeCC functions. The design for the participant system with SeeCC is as shown in Fig. 3. Interface of the participant system with SeeCC. The participant system without SeeCC has the same login interface and participant interface, while for the chatting interface, the information presentation part presents only the partner's age, gender and nationality. The chatting part does not support the recommendation function of emoji and stickers.

3.4   Collaborative Task Design

The collaborative tasks should be able to trigger participants' creativity and collaborative behavior. We designed collaborative tasks consisting of three subtasks: brainstorming, justification, and analysis. These three subtasks corresponded to creativity, decision-making, and intellective tasks, respectively, according to McGrath's (1984) classification. The tasks were generally designed to be proposal writing tasks. In the brainstorming subtask, each participant was supposed to generate eight ideas according to the given topic. In the justification subtask, the two people discussed their ideas and chose three out of the 16 ideas to put into the proposal. In the analysis subtask, they further discussed the pros and cons of the three chosen ideas and summarized them into the proposal.

We generated six potential topics from previous literature and classic group interview questions, and designed a survey to collect opinions about these topics from 38 raters from diverse professional backgrounds, to ensure that the topics were appropriate for the research purpose. The raters were asked to rate each topic according to three criteria: (1) The participants' professional backgrounds should not determine their performance. In this case, topics such as "how to design a database for inventory management" are not suitable. (2) The participants' cultural backgrounds should not determine their performance. In this case, topics such as "how to design a three-day trip to Beijing" are not suitable. (3) There should be a specific target for collaboration. In this case, topics such as "imagine what will happen if humans had three eyes" are not suitable. For each topic, raters scored from 1 (not suitable at all) to 7 (very suitable) on the three criteria, respectively, and ranked the six potential topics from the most to the least suitable. We deleted topics with a score below 5 on at least one of the criteria and chose the top two ranked topics to be used in this experiment. The two tasks are:

Amusement Park Task. Suppose that you and your teammate are working for a big international amusement park. You two are going to collaborate on a project in the coming year. During the summer holiday, the amusement park is crowded, and the weather is hot. In this part, you and your teammate are supposed to generate ideas on "how to improve the customer experience in the summer holiday".

"Go Green" Team Task. Suppose that you and your teammate are working for a "Go Green" Team. You two are going to collaborate on a project in the coming year. You two are supposed to generate ideas on "how to spend $5000 to support environmental sustainability". The ideas should be effective and should be reasonable to achieve with limited funding.

The participants were asked to write the proposal with a pre-designed template on a synchronous text editor. They were given 10 min for brainstorming, and another 25 min to discuss and collaborate on proposal writing. Once the time was over, they were asked to move to the next step immediately, regardless of whether the previous step was completed.

3.5 Measurements

Cultural Orientation Questionnaire. In the current experiment, the system collected communicators' cultural orientation in individualism-collectivism, power distance, uncertainty avoidance, long-term orientation (Yoo et al. 2011), and communication style (Richardson & Smith 2007) in 7-point Likert scales. The average rating of all question items on each cultural dimension was used as the communicators' rating on that dimension. If the rating on a dimension is higher than or equal to 5, we considered the communicator to have a high-level orientation on that dimension; if the rating is lower than or equal to 3, we considered the communicator to have a low-level orientation on that dimension. For dimensions with scores between 3 and 5, corresponding tips for that dimension are not provided.

Online Cross-Cultural Communication Skill Measurement. To measure participants' online cross-cultural communication skills, we generated seven items from previous research on computer-mediated communication skills (Derks, Bos, & Von Grumbkow 2008; Rourke et al. 2001; Wang 2016, summarized in Table 4). The Cronbach's alpha coefficients for the scale of these eight items reached 0.88, which met the Nunnally and Bernstein's (1994) threshold.

Online Cross-Cultural Communication Skill Improvement Measurement. The online cross-cultural communication skill improvement scale also adopted these seven items, with a slight adjustment of the item description. For example, "I know how to use proper emoticons" was modified to be "I know more about how to use proper emoticons", Both the skill and the skill improvement were measured with 7-point Likert scales.

Table 4. Items in online cross-cultural communication skill scale

When communicating online with people from different cultures...
I know how to express my emotions (e.g., appreciation, anger) properly
I know how to use proper emoticons
I know how to use proper stickers
I know how to express my values, beliefs or attitudes properly
I know the limits of sharing private information, feelings and opinions
I know how to express and respond to humor properly
I know the proper greetings and salutations

Online Collaboration Performance Measurement. Collaboration performance was assessed from two aspects: self-evaluation and expert-evaluation. The self-evaluation was measured by a virtual team efficiency measurement designed by Fuller and his colleagues (2006). The self-evaluated performance can be further divided into three dimensions: outcome satisfaction, teammate satisfaction, and outcome quality. Three items about outcome satisfaction (e.g., I am satisfied with the project outcome produced by my team), three items about teammate satisfaction (e.g., I was pleased with the way my teammate and I worked together), and three items about perceived outcome quality (e.g., the work produced by my team was of high quality) were asked. The expert-evaluation refers to the evaluation of the co-written proposal quality. As the deliverable of team collaboration, the quality of the proposal can objectively represent collaboration performance. Two raters assessed the proposals independently, according to uniform criteria we developed from the Bouchard Jr & Hare (1970) brainstorming assessment criteria. The proposals were assessed in three aspects: idea quality, analysis quality, and proposal quality (Table 5). The final score of a proposal was the sum of the three scores.

Table 5. Evaluation criteria for the proposal quality

Category	Scoring criteria	
Idea quality (For each idea)	Amusement Park Task	The idea can improve experience (1 point) The idea can solve the hot issue (1 point) The idea can solve the crowded issue (1 point)
	"Go Green" Team Task	The idea will have a public influence (1 point) The idea is practical with $5000 (1 point) The idea can support environmental sustainability (1 point)
Analysis quality (For each idea)	Reasonable pros (1 point for 1 pro) Reasonable cons (1 point for 1 con)	
Proposal quality (For each proposal)	Distinct reasonable ideas (if two or more ideas talk about the same thing then it can only get 1 point)	

4   Results

4.1   Correlation Analysis

We first conducted a correlation analysis to obtain an overall impression of the relationship between online cross-cultural communication skills and performance (Table 6). The results showed that the participant's skills were significantly positively correlated to the self-evaluated outcome satisfaction ($p = 0.002$, $r = 0.27$), self-evaluated outcome quality ($p = 0.016$, $r = 0.27$), and the expert-evaluated outcome quality ($p = 0.037$, $r = 0.26$). The self-evaluated teammate satisfaction was not correlated to the participant's own skills; however, it was correlated to the communication partner's skills ($p = 0.004$, $r = 0.26$). The self-evaluated outcome satisfaction, teammate satisfaction, and outcome quality were highly correlated to each other ($p < 0.01$), while they were not significantly correlated to the expert-evaluated outcome quality ($p > 0.05$).

4.2   The effects of SeeCC in Skill and Performance Improvement

We tested the effectiveness of SeeCC in improving participants' OCCC skills and performance, by comparison analysis using t-tests. The self-reported skill improvement was

Table 6. Means (M), Standard deviations (SD), and correlations of the variables (N = 60)

Variables	M	SD	1	2	3	4	5
1. Skill	5.3	0.85					
2. Communication partner's skill	5.3	0.85	−0.11				
3. Outcome satisfaction (self-rated)	6.0	1.19	0.27**	0.09			
4. Teammate satisfaction (self-rated)	6.2	1.01	0.14	0.26**	0.73**		
5. Outcome quality (self-rated)	5.6	1.40	0.27*	0.12	0.87**	0.73**	
6. Outcome quality (expert-rated)	16.0	5.09	0.26*	0.26*	0.15	0.07	0.11

*Notes. * p < 0.05; ** p < 0.01*

directly measured using a 7-point Likert scale in the experiment. Participants reported whether they perceived their skills improved by giving scores greater than 4 (improved), equal to 4 (neutral), or less than 4 (not improved). We compared participants' ratings with the mid-point 4. The results showed a positive improvement in skills (M = 5.3, SD = 1.99, t = 9.53, p < 0.001).

The self-evaluated outcome satisfaction, teammate satisfaction, and outcome quality were reported twice by each participant, once after collaboration with SeeCC, and once without SeeCC. We compared each participants' two ratings on these three variables by paired t-tests. The outcome satisfaction with SeeCC (M = 6.2, SD = 1.14) was higher than without SeeCC (M = 6.0, SD = 1.00), but the difference was not statistically significant (t = 1.27, p = 0.590). The teammate satisfaction with SeeCC (M = 6.2, SD = 1.00) was higher than without SeeCC (M = 6.1, SD = 1.03), but the difference was not statistically significant (t = 0.84, p = 0.411). The teammate satisfaction with SeeCC (M = 5.6, SD = 1.39) was higher than that without SeeCC (M = 5.3, SD = 1.42), but the difference was not statistically significant (t = 0.19, p = 0.738). Although the self-evaluated evaluation for the outcome and teammate were all better with SeeCC than without SeeCC, no statistically significant difference was found.

The two experts evaluated the proposals in three aspects: idea quality, analysis quality, and proposal quality, and we summed the scores in all these three aspects as the score for expert-evaluated outcome quality. The scores given by the two raters achieved a strong agreement with the weighted Cohen's kappa = 0.90 (LeBreton & Senter 2008). We compared the expert-evaluated outcome quality score between collaboration with or without SeeCC by a paired t-test. The result showed that the expert-evaluated outcome quality was significantly higher when communicating with SeeCC (M = 17.1, SD = 4.85) than without it (M = 15.0, SD = 5.18, t = 2.12, p = 0.039).

4.3 Influences of SeeCC on Chatting Behavior

From the analysis above, we found that the participants perceived an improvement in their skills; however, they did not perceive a significant improvement in the outcome satisfaction, teammate satisfaction, and outcome quality by themselves after using SeeCC. At the same time, the expert evaluation results showed a significant improvement in outcome quality. We need to investigate the participants' behavior further to explain this phenomenon. In an online chatting scenario, chatting records can be a good representation of participant behavior.

We chose two typical behavior indicators: the use of personal pronouns and the use of non-verbal expressions. These two indicators were unambiguous and corresponded to the tips and recommendations of SeeCC. If the participants adjusted their behavior according to SeeCC, we should observe participants behave more consistently with the tips and recommendations when collaborate with SeeCC than without SeeCC. That is to say, (1) when communicating with a high-collectivism person, use more plural personal pronouns (we, us, or our) than singular personal pronouns (I, me, or my), and verse visa; (2) use more stickers when communicating with a high-context participant, and use more emoji when communicating with a lower-context participant.

We summed the number of "I", "me", and "my" as the I-indicator, and the number of "we", "us", and "our" as the We-indicator, for each participant in each chat. We defined an I/We indicator as the we-indicator divided by the I-indicator. When communicating with a low-collectivism partner, the I/We indicator in OCCC when supported by SeeCC (M = 2.73, SD = 1.630) was marginally significantly larger than when not supported by SeeCC (M = 1.90, SD = 1.320, t = 1.62, p = 0.053). When communicating with a high-collectivism partner, the I/We indicator in OCCC when supported by SeeCC (M = 2.85, SD = 1.314) was not different from that when not supported by SeeCC (M = 2.85, SD = 1.653). The results showed that participants' behavior in using personal pronouns were partially influenced by SeeCC.

We calculated the number of emoji and stickers used by each participant in each chat. The result showed that when communicating with a low-context partner, the participant used significantly more emoji in chatting when supported by SeeCC (M = 1.4, SD = 1.80) than when not supported by SeeCC (M = 1.3, SD = 1.62, t = 3.35, p = 0.001). When communicating with a high-context partner, the participant used significantly more stickers in chatting when supported by SeeCC (M = 1.7, SD = 1.66) than when not supported by SeeCC (M = 0.9, SD = 1.26, t = 4.10, p < 0.001). The results showed that participants' behavior in using non-verbal expressions were influenced by SeeCC.

5 Discussion

5.1 Effects of SeeCC in Improving Skills and Performance

People reported improvements in online cross-cultural communication skills, indicating that SeeCC is an efficient tool to improve cross-cultural skills (RQ1). In this research, we asked participants directly about their online cross-cultural communication skill improvement, like MacNab and Worthley's (2012) did, instead of comparing skill ratings at different times, which is in line with our focus on the immediate effect of SeeCC. It is easier for the participants to report whether they feel their skill is improved, than to report differences in two same questionnaires within an hour.

SeeCC significantly improved the co-written proposal quality, confirming the positive effects of this tool in improving the performance of actual collaboration (RQ2). The self-reported perceived outcome quality did not show significant improvement. Some participants gave feedback that because of the time limitation, they perceived themselves as not paying much attention to the cultural portrait and suggestions provided, but the improvement in proposal quality indicated that they behaved differently with or without SeeCC.

We further analyzed the chatting behavior to investigate how they behaved differently during OCCC. We chose the use of personal pronouns and the use of non-verbal expressions as the two indicators. The use of personal pronouns is mainly influenced by the tips function, while the use of non-verbal expressions is influenced by both the tips and recommendation functions. The analysis of these two indicators showed that both tips and recommendation functions had influenced users' behavior. Compared to tips, the recommendation function had a more direct and significant influence. Although not quite clearly perceived by the users, their behavior and deliverable quality were influenced, providing evidence for the significant application potential of SeeCC in facilitating OCCC.

5.2 Design of OCCC Supporting Tools

SeeCC provided users with individual-level cultural orientation of the chatting partner, rather than about the partner's national culture. Previous cross-cultural improvement tools focused on geo-based cultures and equaled cultural differences to differences between national cultures. However, recently, more researchers have criticized the national-based cultural framework (Baskerville 2003; McSweeney 2002, 2009). There can be multiple cultures within a country (McSweeney 2009), and people from countries far away can be similar in culture. Cross-cultural skills should refer to the skills to deal with culturally different individuals (Patel & Salih 2018), especially in an online context, where geographical information is not significant. This research confirmed the value of providing individual-level cultural orientation information in OCCC. We suggest that more cross-cultural tools targeted at online and offline scenarios should pay attention to non-geo-based cultural differences.

Although we intended to provide cultural orientation at an individual level, the theoretical and cultural dimensions we relied on were established from a national cultural framework. These dimensions can be applied to describe individual cultural differences (Yoo et al. 2011); however, if we only rely on these theories, some cultural information specific to the individual level may be lost. Now, technologies such as machine learning provide new possibilities for cross-cultural research (Bail 2014). Analysis of user behavior at the individual level can provide more comprehensive data, which can be applied to the future design of online cross-cultural supportive tools.

5.3 Limitation and Future Research

This research has some limitations. First, we only conducted a short-term experiment. Previous research showed that the length and comprehensiveness of the cross-cultural training impact its effectiveness (Koo Moon et al. 2012). The potential of SeeCC for long-term applications and for integrating with other tools requires further examination.

Second, all the participants were students. In this experiment, we recruited students to carry out proposal writing tasks. Further investigation is needed for potential users from more diverse backgrounds. More task conditions could be investigated, such as international customer services and online classes.

Third, although we have a participant group of individuals with varied international backgrounds, the participants were all in China at the time the experiment was conducted. In online cross-cultural communication, people may communicate with a person from cultures they have never experienced. Further investigation can be conducted on participants who are residing in different locations.

The future will require increasingly extensive online cross-cultural collaboration in international business. Limited by the scope of this study, the SeeCC provides only a general cultural portrait of the communication partner and limited number of communication tips. This design can be further applied in specific contexts, such as manual customer service of multinational companies and class discussion in a global online classroom, by providing more context-specific cultural portrait and communication tips. The idea of SeeCC can be further applied to a broader range of communication media. For example, a virtual agent with a detailed image can be applied in further communication and training scenarios for virtual reality.

6 Conclusion

We designed SeeCC, which can provide individual-level cultural portrait and real-time communication tips during online cross-cultural communication. We evaluated the effects of SeeCC in improving online cross-cultural communication skills and performance by using an experimental approach. Sixty participants from multiple cultural backgrounds conducted online collaborative tasks through online chatting. The experiment results confirmed the system's effects in improving online cross-cultural skills and collaboration performance. Based on the results, we suggested that future online cross-cultural supporting tools should be designed based on a non-geo-based cultural framework. SeeCC has great potential to be implemented in cross-cultural training and global collaboration support, and the design of SeeCC can be applied to more diverse online interaction scenarios.

References

Agar, M.: The biculture in bilingual. Lang. Soc. **20**(2), 167–182 (1991)

André, E.: Preparing emotional agents for intercultural communication. In: The Oxford Handbook of Affective Computing, pp. 532–551. Oxford University Press London (2015)

Aritz, J., Walker, R., Cardon, P.W.: Media use in virtual teams of varying levels of coordination. Bus. Prof. Commun. Q. **81**(2), 222–243 (2018)

Bail, C.A.: The cultural environment: Measuring culture with big data. Theory Soc. **43**(3–4), 465–482 (2014)

Baskerville, R.F.: Hofstede never studied culture. Acc. Organ. Soc. **28**(1), 1–14 (2003)

Bouchard Jr, T.J., Hare, M.: Size, performance, and potential in brainstorming groups. J. Appl Psychol. **54**(1p1), 51 (1970)

Carlson, J.R., Zmud, R.W.: Channel expansion theory and the experiential nature of media richness perceptions. Acad. Manag. J. **42**(2), 153–170 (1999)

Davison, S.C., Ward, K.: Leading International Teams. McGraw-Hill Publishing Company (1999)

Derks, D., Bos, A.E., Von Grumbkow, J.: Emoticons in computer-mediated communication: Social motives and social context. Cyberpsychol. Behav. **11**(1), 99–101 (2008)

Fuller, M.A., Hardin, A.M., Davison, R.M.: Efficacy in technology-mediated distributed teams. J. Manag. Inf. Syst. **23**(3), 209–235 (2006)

Hall, E.T.: Beyond culture. Anchor (1989)

Hofstede, G., Hofstede, G.J., Minkov, M.: Cultures and Organizations: Software of the Mind. Revised and Expanded. McGraw-Hill, New York (2010)

Jarvenpaa, S.L., Shaw, T.R.: Global virtual teams: Integrating models of trust. Organ. Virtual. 35–52 (1998)

Johnson, W.L., Zaker, S.B.: The power of social simulation for Chinese language teaching. In: Proceedings of the 7th International Conference and Workshops on Technology and Chinese Language Teaching in the 21st Century (2012)

Kayan, S., Fussell, S.R., Setlock, L.D.: Cultural differences in the use of instant messaging in Asia and North America. In: Proceedings of the 2006 20th Anniversary Conference on Computer Supported Cooperative Work, pp. 525–528 (2006)

Koo Moon, H., Kwon Choi, B., Shik Jung, J.: Previous international experience, cross-cultural training, and expatriates' cross-cultural adjustment: Effects of cultural intelligence and goal orientation. Hum. Resour. Dev. Q. **23**(3), 285–330 (2012)

LeBreton, J.M., Senter, J.L.: Answers to 20 questions about interrater reliability and interrater agreement. Organ. Res. Methods **11**(4), 815–852 (2008)

Lim, T.S., Urakami, J.: Cross-cultural comparison of german and japanese mobile messenger communication. In: International Conference on Applied Human Factors and Ergonomics, pp. 626–635 (2018)

MacNab, B.R., Worthley, R.: Individual characteristics as predictors of cultural intelligence development: the relevance of self-efficacy. Int. J. Intercult. Relat. **36**(1), 62–71 (2012)

Mak, A., Barker, M., Logan, G., Millman, L.: Benefits of cultural diversity for international and local students: Contributions from an experiential social learning program (The EXCELL Program). International Education: The Professional Edge, pp. 63–76 (1999)

McGrath, J.E.: Groups: Interaction and performance, vol. 14. Prentice-Hall Englewood Cliffs, NJ (1984)

McSweeney, B.: Hofstede's model of national cultural differences and their consequences: a triumph of faith-a failure of analysis. Hum. Relations **55**(1), 89–118 (2002)

McSweeney, B.: Dynamic diversity: variety and variation within countries. Organ. Stud. **30**(9), 933–957 (2009)

Moreno, R., Mayer, R.: Interactive multimodal learning environments. Educ. Psychol. Rev. **19**(3), 309–326 (2007)

Na, J., Choi, I.: Culture and first-person pronouns. Pers. Soc. Psychol. Bull. **35**(11), 1492–1499 (2009)

Nunnally, J.C., Bernstein, I.H.: Psychometric Theory. MaGrawHill, New York (1994)

Nyman Gomez, C., Berg Marklund, B.: Games for cross-cultural training: a game-based tool for cross-cultural discussion: encouraging cultural awareness with board games. Int. J. Serious Games, **5**(4), 81–98 (2018). https://doi.org/10.17083/ijsg.v5i4.259

Patel, T., Salih, A.: Cultural intelligence: a dynamic and interactional framework. Int. Stud. Manag. Organ. **48**(4), 358–385 (2018)

Qie, N., Patrick Rau, P.-L., Wang, L., Ma, L.: Is the Senpai—Kouhai relationship common across China, Korea, and Japan? Soc. Behav. Personal. Int. J. **47**(1), 1–12 (2019)

Richardson, R.M., Smith, S.W.: The influence of high/low-context culture and power distance on choice of communication media: Students' media choice to communicate with professors in Japan and America. Int. J. Intercult. Relat. **31**(4), 479–501 (2007)

Rourke, I., Anderson, T., Garrison To, A.W.: Social Assessing Presence In Asynchronous Text-based Computer Conferencing Journal of Distance Education. Revue of l'enseignement à Distance (2001)

Schuller, B.W., Dunwell, I., Weninger, F., Paletta, L.: Serious gaming for behavior change: the state of play. IEEE Pervasive Comput. **12**(3), 48–55 (2013)

Scollon, R., Scollon, S.W., Jones, R.H.: Intercultural Communication: A Discourse Approach. Wiley (2012)

Shirts, R.G.: Bafa bafa. Del Mar, Calif.: Simulation Training Systems (1977)

Trevino, L.K., Daft, R.L., Lengel, R.H.: Understanding managers' media choices: a symbolic interactionist perspective (1990)

Wang, S.S.: More than words? The effect of line character sticker use on intimacy in the mobile communication environment. Soc. Sci. Comput. Rev. **34**(4), 456–478 (2016)

Yoo, B., Donthu, N., Lenartowicz, T.: Measuring Hofstede's five dimensions of cultural values at the individual level: Development and validation of CVSCALE. J. Int. Consum. Mark. **23**(3–4), 193–210 (2011)

Capabilities Influencing Cross-Cultural Communication in Digital Contexts: Exploration with a Chinese Sample

Nan Qie and Xinyue Kang[✉]

Department of Industrial Engineering, Tsinghua University, Beijing, China
kxy20@mails.tsinghua.edu.cn

Abstract. This study aims to understand the capabilities that an individual needs to better communicate with people from different cultural backgrounds in digital contexts. From a literature review, an initial pool of knowledge, skills, abilities and motivations needed in online cross-cultural communication was gathered. Then, a survey was conducted with 345 Chinese participants to identify the factor structure of the necessary capabilities. The results derived a seven-factor model named BESTCIM, comprising behavior, external motivation, social-oriented knowledge, task-oriented knowledge, cultural-theoretical knowledge, intrinsic motivation and metacognition. Further, the factors' influences on participants' online cross-cultural communication performance were examined. The regression results indicated cultural-theoretical knowledge, social-oriented knowledge, intrinsic motivation, external motivation, and behavior can positively predict the self-rated cross-cultural communication performance. Overall, our findings established a structured foundation to better understand factors influencing cross-cultural communication in digital contexts, providing a theoretical basis for empirical studies on virtual team collaboration and international talent training.

Keywords: Cross-cultural communication · Cultural intelligence · Survey · Factor analysis · Cross-cultural performance

1 Introduction

Today, people interact more frequently and intensively across cultures, largely due to the popularity and accessibility of the Internet. Computer-mediated communication (CMC) is an integral component of interpersonal communication. According to Statista, by February 2020, the world's top three Instant Messengers (WhatsApp, Facebook Messenger, and WeChat) had more than four billion active users alone, among which more than 1 billion are Chinese (Statista 2020). The popularity of these chatting tools helps physically distributed people and teams communicate more conveniently and less expensively. The Internet overcomes space constraints, making it more common to interact with people of diverse cultural backgrounds.

Cross-cultural interaction poses challenges due to cultural diversity, in online and offline settings alike. These challenges have been well documented (Kankanhalli et al.

© The Author(s), under exclusive license to Springer Nature Switzerland AG 2023
P.-L. P. Rau (Ed.): HCII 2023, LNCS 14023, pp. 126–141, 2023.
https://doi.org/10.1007/978-3-031-35939-2_10

2006; Shachaf 2008; Staples and Zhao 2006). People from different cultural backgrounds may use different verbal and nonverbal communication methods, lead different lifestyles, and hold different opinions on what values are important or unimportant, right or wrong. These diversities can lead to incompatibility and misunderstanding in cross-cultural interaction. Previous researchers have identified factors at an individual level that are related to dealing with cross-cultural challenges, such as personality and self-efficacy (Harrison et al. 1996). Further, researchers have even developed a specialized concept to describe necessary capabilities in successful cross-cultural interaction. Earley and Ang introduced the concept of cultural intelligence (CQ), to describe the capabilities that can allow individuals to deal effectively with cross-cultural scenarios (Earley and Ang 2003). Such a structured description of the necessary cross-cultural capabilities can help identify qualified people for cross-cultural business, and help develop cross-cultural training programs.

The online contexts differ from offline contexts, leading to more challenges in cross-cultural communication. Theories indicate that CMC conveys less rich information (Daft and Lengel 1986), and is less natural than face-to-face interaction (Kock 2004). CMC, especially text-based communication such as email, instant messaging, forum or chat, is restricted in richness because of the lack of nonverbal cues. This lack of richness can make it more difficult to cope with cultural diversities. For example, when a Japanese says "yes", it can either mean "yes" or a polite expression of "no". A face-to-face partner may detect the latter from a hesitant tone or a frown, but neither is available to a partner in text-based CMC. Although the recent advanced communication technology can support richer CMC media, such as pictures, audio and video, due to a lack of broader contextual information and facilitation of physical interaction, the naturalness of these media still doesn't quite equate to face-to-face communication. In addition, the cross-cultural interaction scenarios involved in CMC are more limited and special compared to those in offline interaction scenarios. Instead of issues such as long-term cultural adaption, people usually communicate online in more fragmented time to either fulfill social needs, or collaborate/negotiate on specific tasks. These differences raise the need to define the factors that influence cross-cultural communication specifically tailored to digital contexts, where not enough research attention is currently devoted.

Therefore, this research aims to construct a new multi-factor model to describe an individual's capabilities that affect cross-cultural communication in digital contexts. The context to be considered in this study is restricted to text-based CMC, where people communicate by sending and receiving text and some symbolic expressions such as emoticons. First, text-based CMC is still an important part in online interaction. Although new communication technologies such as voice and video chat are now gaining popularity, research indicated that in both interpersonal context and organizational context, even with the availability of richer communication media, people sometimes prefer text-based CMC, considering formality (Trevino et al. 1990), social influence, and individual experience (Carlson and Zmud 1999). According to Sheer, adolescents preferred text-based communication because it is more convenient for self-image presentation control (Sheer 2010). Further research indicated that text-based communication is more helpful in in-depth communication to develop close friendships (Sheer 2011).

In a business context, people sometimes preferred text-based communication for convenience in embedded tools and backtracking changes (Aritz et al. 2018). All these studies indicated that text-based communication is still of great value for research. Second, the gap between text-based CMC and fact-to-face communication is assumed to be larger, which makes it more necessary to establish a target model rather than using the traditional CQ model.

We restrict our scope to an individual's personal traits that can be developed through experience or training, such as knowledge, skills, abilities and motivations. We focus on these factors because an understanding of them is instructive for talent development and skill enhancement. Some personal traits such as personality may also have influence on cross-cultural CMC, but these factors will not be brought into our model, because they are antecedents to the cross-cultural capabilities, but not a part of the capabilities (Ang et al. 2006).

To make our model more adaptable to a wide range of contexts, the factors should be able to describe how an individual generally deals with different cultures, without limiting the scope to one or two particular cultures. Thus, capabilities on a particular language, or a particular custom in a particular culture, is beyond the scope of this research. Finally, the model should be able to guide practice, so the sub-dimensions of the model should have practical meaning and should predict cross-cultural CMC performance. From the above, this research aims to answer the following two research questions:

RQ1. What are the capability factors that influence cross-cultural communication in digital contexts?

RQ2. Can these factors predict self-reported cross-cultural CMC performance?

To answer these two research questions, we conducted an exploratory study with a convenience sample. Three steps were conducted. First, we identified items related to online cross-cultural communication from literature and designed a questionnaire. Second, we conducted a survey and established a multi-factor model by explorative factor analysis. Third, we examined the effect of the factors on self-rated cross-cultural CMC performance by regression. Finally, there was a general discussion of the results. The results indicated the influencing factors of cross-cultural CMC, established a structured foundation to better understand self-rated cross-cultural CMC, and provided a theoretical basis for cross-cultural communication training and development in the digital age.

1.1 Computer-Mediated Communication

In addition to CQ components, knowledge and skills leading to good CMC performance are required in a digital context. Text-based CMC is usually limited in media richness, and lacks nonverbal cues like gesture and facial expression. To overcome these limitations, people use affective expressions and cohesive expressions. Affective expressions contain personal expressions of emotion, feelings, values, beliefs, or attitudes. In CMC, emotions can be expressed through verbal expression or non-verbal displays, such as emoticons (Derks et al. 2008; Wang 2016). Emoticons can help to emphasize a tone, to clearly express a current mood, or to clarify textual messages (Derks et al. 2007). Cohesive expressions are communication behaviors that build and sustain a sense of group commitment, such as greetings and salutations (Kehrwald 2008; Swan 2002).

If a person can do well in CMC, it must be because he/she wants to do well. Motivation can drive people towards achieving goals. The motivations in cross-cultural CMC can be divided into the motivations to communicate cross-culturally, and the motivations to communicate through the Internet. The latter can be explained by technology acceptance. Technology acceptance describes users' attitude and intention towards certain technology. In Davis's technology acceptance model (TAM), perceived usefulness and perceived easiness significantly influence users' acceptance (Davis 1989). Venkatesh claimed that perceived anxiety and perceived enjoyment are determinants of perceived easiness (Venkatesh 2000). Venkatesh and Davis extended the TAM by introducing social influences (Venkatesh and Davis 2000). When a person perceives that most people important to him think he should or should not perform a behavior, he will follow them. These motivations can drive people to try a technology or use a technological way to accomplish their goal.

There are other variables that can influence communication, which may still matter in CMC. In communication, it is necessary to know the limits of sharing private information, feelings, and opinions, defined as the degree of self-disclosure (Schug et al. 2010). People communicate online not only for social purposes but also for tasks. During collaborative decision making, which is a very common scenario in cross-cultural CMC, one needs to learn about the decision-making style and risk preference tendency in another culture to perform appropriately. People hold different decision-making styles such as rational, intuitive, dependent, and avoidant (Scott and Bruce 1995). Risk preference is related to how people frame gains and losses (Kühberger et al. 1999).

1.2 Culture and Communication

Researchers have established frameworks to describe cultural differences in a structured and theoretical way (Hall 1989; Hofstede et al. 2010; Trompenaars and Hampden-Turner 2011). Knowledge of these frameworks can lead to a more systematic understanding of cultural differences. Hofstede's (Hofstede et al. 2010) and Hall's (Hall 1989) frameworks are the most cited and widely used. Hofstede's framework depicts cultural differences in six dimensions. The collectivism-individualism dimension describes how much importance people attach to the group versus the individual; the power distance dimension describes to what extent people accept and agree with the unequal distribution of power; the uncertainty avoidance dimension describes to what extent people can get along with uncertainty; the masculinity-femininity dimension describes how much importance people attach to success/money versus love/care, and how serious is the sexual stereotype; the long-term orientation dimension describes how important people think future gains are compared to current gains; and the last dimension, indulgence-restriction describes how people think of satisfying human natural desires. In Hall's framework, the most mentioned dimension is the communication style dimension. Hall divided communication style into high-context style and low-context style. People in high-context cultures communicate more implicitly and the information conveyed is hidden in the context, while people in low-context cultures communicate by explicit verbal expression.

Both Hofstede's and Hall's frameworks have been found to function well in explaining and predicting at least certain kinds of phenomenon in CMC. Hermeking found that

Hofstede's collectivism and uncertainty avoidance is correlated to Internet usage (Hermeking 2005). Callahan found relationships between Hofstede's cultural values and web design (Callahan 2005). Hall's high/low-context communication style has been proved to be related to web design and usage (Würtz 2005). Besides, masculinity-femininity influences how people treat different gender roles and power distance influences how people treat different status roles; long-term orientation and indulgence/restriction affects what matters in decision making. Knowledge of the differences in these values can lead to better understanding of people in a different cultural background, and lead to better cross-cultural communication.

1.3 Cultural Intelligence

Earley and Ang introduced the concept of cultural intelligence (CQ) to describe "a person's capability for successful adaptation to other cultural settings, that is, for unfamiliar settings attributable to cultural context" (Earley and Ang 2003). Ang and his colleagues considered CQ as a four-factor construct, consisting of metacognitive CQ, cognitive CQ, motivational CQ and behavioral CQ (Ang et al. 2007). Metacognitive CQ refers to mental processes that individuals use to acquire and understand cultural knowledge; cognitive CQ refers to knowledge related to cross-cultural settings; motivational CQ refers to the capability to direct attention and energy to learning about and functioning in cross-cultural situations; and behavioural CQ refers to the capability to employ appropriate verbal and nonverbal actions when interacting with people from different cultures.

Based on the four-dimensional structure, a 20-item cultural intelligence scale (CQS) was developed to measure CQ (Ang et al. 2007). Van Dyne and his colleagues further divided the four dimensions into 11 sub-factors and developed a 37-item extended cultural intelligence scale (E-CQS) (Van Dyne et al. 2012). In the E-CQS, metacognitive CQ is subdivided into planning, awareness, and checking; cognitive CQ is subdivided into cultural-general knowledge and context-specific knowledge; motivational CQ is subdivided into intrinsic interest, extrinsic interest, and self-efficacy to adjust; and behavioural CQ is subdivided into verbal behavior, non-verbal behavior, and speech acts.

Most previous research on CQ has considered non-digital conditions, such as collaborating in a cross-cultural team (Chua et al. 2012; Mor et al. 2013), working in international cooperation (Deng and Gibson 2009; Jyoti and Kour 2015), and studying, working, or living abroad (Chen 2015; Guhmundsdóttir 2015; Lin et al. 2012). Although some researchers have discussed online virtual teams (Erez et al. 2013; Li et al. 2017), they simply collected data on the participants' abilities to deal with the non-digital cross-cultural context. Previous research indicated that the knowledge, skills, abilities and motivations required in face-to-face communication and CMC are distinct (Schulze et al. 2017), so the factors influencing cross-cultural communication may also have difference between digital and non-digital contexts. Therefore, it is of great necessity to specifically explore factors that influence cross-cultural communication in digital contexts.

1.4   The Influence of CQ on Performance

CQ has been found to have influence on cultural adjustment, cultural adaption, cross-cultural leadership, intercultural cooperation, intercultural negotiations, intercultural creative collaborations, and cross-cultural performance (Ott and Michailova 2018). Among these CQ outcomes, we are particularly concerned with cross-cultural performance, because the general performance can be simply measured by self-reported questionnaire, and because it is key to cross-cultural communication.

The conclusions of previous studies indicated that both the overall CQ and the sub-factors of CQ can contribute to cross-cultural performance. Ang and his colleagues found that metacognitive and behavioral CQ predict performance (Ang et al. 2007), while Malek and Budhwar found that motivational and behavioral CQ predict performance (Malek and Budhwar 2013). Further research has shown that CQ does not directly influence performance; instead, it directly influences cultural adjustment, which itself influences performance (Lee et al. 2014). Previous research has paid attention to the effects of CQ on virtual team performance (Erez et al. 2013). For example, research showed that in virtual team collaboration, lower CQ in a dyad predicts collaborative satisfaction, while higher CQ predicts performance. However, these studies simply adopted the traditional CQS without considering the digital context (Li et al. 2017).

2   Materials and Methods

2.1   Research Design

This is an exploratory study of the capability factors influencing cross-cultural communication in digital contexts. The data for the exploratory analysis were collected from a questionnaire survey. The potential items for the questionnaire design were collected from previous literature. In the survey, responses were collected regarding potential cross-cultural CMC capability factors and cross-cultural CMC performance. The valid data were put into an exploratory factor analysis (EFA), and a structured model was established to describe the capability factors influencing cross-cultural communication in digital contexts. The factors derived from EFA were put into a regression analysis to test their effects in predicting cross-cultural CMC performance. Next, we will describe the methodological approach of questionnaire design and the survey.

2.2   Questionnaire Design

Based on the literature review, potential items were identified from CQ, CMC and related literature. We collected CQ related items mainly from the CQS (Ang et al. 2007) and the E-CQS (Van Dyne et al. 2012). Some items such as the metacognitive items were put directly into the questionnaire because they generally describe an individual's personal traits without considering the context. Some items concerning the marriage system, arts, and crafts were deleted because they are more relevant to living in a different culture, which were not applicable in CMC. Some items were slightly modified to suit the text-based CMC context. We designed CMC related items according to affective expressions, cohesive expressions (Kehrwald 2008; Swan 2002), and TAM model (Venkatesh and

Davis 2000). Items asking about Hofstede's and Hall's cultural values, self-disclosure, decision-making style and risk preference were added to the questionnaire. In total thirty-two items were produced.

Two experts with a psychological background, two with a cross-cultural research background, and one with a measurement design background reviewed the drafted questionnaire. Based on the experts' suggestions, three additional items were added. The first item concerns the proper use of memes, which is representative of online culture. The second item concerns understanding of ethics and morality. The third item concerns understanding of humor, which varies across cultures and is complicated by the lack of nonverbal cues in the online context.

The questionnaire was divided into four parts. The first part was an informed consent stating the purpose and the general content of the survey. The participants had to read the consent and decide whether they agreed to participate. The second part sought demographic information, including age, gender, overseas experience, as well as cross-cultural CMC experience and frequency. The third part measured the 35 items with 7-point Likert scales (1-totally disagree, 7-totally agree). The fourth part comprised a single question on self-reported cross-cultural CMC performance: "I am good at online cross-cultural communication".

2.3 Participants

A convenience sample was used in this exploratory study. The participants of the survey were all born and raised mainly in China. Only the responses of the participants who had cross-cultural CMC experience were screened as valid. The valid sample comprised 345 responses, including 156 males and 189 females, with ages ranging from 18 to 60 years ($M = 25.57$, $SD = 6.58$). The participants' demographic information, overseas experience and cross-cultural CMC experience are summarized in Table 1.

Table 1. Survey participants' basic information ($N = 345$)

		Number of people	Percentage
Gender	Male	156	45.2%
	Female	189	54.8%
Age	18–25	172	49.9%
	26–30	117	33.9%
	31–40	36	10.4%
	41+	20	5.8%
Overseas experience	More than one year	127	36.8%
	Less than one year	195	56.5%

(continued)

Table 1. (*continued*)

		Number of people	Percentage
Cross-cultural CMC experience context (one person can choose several)	None	23	6.7%
	Interpersonal social	323	93.6%
	Online courses	76	22.0%
	International teamwork	148	42.9%
	Contacting overseas office	130	37.7%
Frequency of cross-cultural CMC	Everyday	40	11.6%
	Several times a week	114	33.0%
	Several times a month	113	32.8%
	Less than once a month	78	22.6%

2.4 Survey

The questionnaire survey was conducted both online, via SoJump (www.sojump.com) and WeChat, and offline, by disseminating printed questionnaires. It took about 15 min to finish all the questions. Every respondent was given either 10RMB for participating. The survey was approved by the institutional review board at the Institute of Human Factors and Ergonomics at Tsinghua University.

3 Results

3.1 Constructing the Multi-factor Model

We constructed a model through EFA on survey data, using varimax as the rotation method. Three items were dropped from the model because they failed to load on any factor at a 0.50 level (Hair 2011). Eventually, a seven-factor structure containing 32 items was extracted that explained 65% of total variance (see Table 2). The Cronbach's alpha coefficients for the seven factors were 0.88 (social-oriented knowledge), 0.88 (cultural-theoretical knowledge), 0.83 (behavior), 0.80 (intrinsic motivation), 0.58 (metacognition), 0.80 (task-oriented knowledge), and 0.87 (external motivation). All the alphas were larger than 0.50, thus meeting the threshold for acceptable EFA (Vaske et al. 2017).

Factor 1, labeled social-oriented knowledge, comprises seven items explaining 12% of total variance. It contains items on the knowledge of proper expressions (e.g., expression of emotions, values, greetings, and humor), proper use of Internet expressions (e.g., emoticons and memes), and degree of self-disclosure. Factor 2, labeled cultural-theoretical knowledge, comprises seven items explaining 12% of total variance. These seven items of this factor describe understanding of Hofstede's cultural values. Factor 3, labeled behavior, comprises four items explaining 10% of total variance. It describes behavior adjustments of different types (verbal or non-verbal), and behavior adjustment when performing different interactions (social-oriented or task-oriented). Factor 4, labeled intrinsic motivation, comprises four items explaining 10% of total variance.

Table 2. Explorative factor analysis results of cross-cultural communication in digital contexts.

When communicating online with people from other cultures…	Loadings of factors						
	1	2	3	4	5	6	7
Social-oriented knowledge							
I know how to express my emotions (e.g., appreciation, anger) properly	0.77	0.19	0.19	0.15	0.11	0.08	0.08
I know how to use proper emoticons	0.74	0.10	0.04	0.13	0.23	0.13	0.13
I know how to use proper meme	0.72	0.09	0.04	0.03	0.17	0.20	0.21
I know how to express my values, beliefs or attitudes properly	0.67	0.15	0.28	0.12	0.15	0.11	0.02
I know the proper level of self-disclosure (limits of sharing private information, feelings and opinions)	0.63	0.30	0.26	0.15	0.11	0.18	0.07
I know how to express and respond to humor properly	0.56	0.21	0.06	0.18	0.14	0.35	0.13
I know the proper greetings and salutations	0.52	0.18	0.37	0.31	0.12	0.08	0.06
Cultural-theoretical knowledge							
I know how people in the other culture view their relationship with family and group	0.16	**0.80**	0.15	0.07	0.11	0.17	0.11
I know the attitude towards individual independence of people in the other culture	0.13	**0.76**	0.30	0.07	0.11	0.01	0.12
I know the relative importance between masculinity values (e.g., money, success) and femininity values (e.g., caring for others, life quality) in the other culture	0.18	**0.76**	0.13	0.22	0.03	0.16	0.05
I know the superior-subordinate relationship in the other culture	0.11	**0.73**	0.13	0.03	0.14	0.24	0.03
I know the attitude of balance between indulgence (enjoying life and having fun) and restraint (human desires regulated by strict norms) in the other culture	0.21	**0.54**	0.11	0.05	0.17	0.36	0.06
I know how much importance people in the other culture attach to the future	0.27	**0.51**	0.07	0.16	0.18	0.32	0.11
I know the attitude towards uncertainty of people in the other culture	0.17	**0.50**	0.06	0.27	0.11	0.46	0.20
Behavior							
I will adjust my verbal behaviors (e.g., phrasing,) according to the cultural background of the others	0.21	0.23	**0.78**	0.13	0.12	0.18	0.17

(*continued*)

Table 2. (*continued*)

When communicating online with people from other cultures…	Loadings of factors						
	1	2	3	4	5	6	7
I will adjust my social-oriented behaviors according to the cultural background of the others	0.14	0.17	**0.74**	0.25	0.20	0.13	0.10
I will adjust my task-oriented behaviors according to the cultural background of the others	0.17	0.14	**0.70**	0.15	0.22	0.24	0.09
I will adjust my non-verbal behaviors (e.g., emoticons, frequency of sending message) according to the cultural background of the others	0.20	0.19	**0.68**	0.10	0.07	0.11	0.26
Intrinsic motivation							
I feel comfortable when communicating with people from other cultures through the Internet	0.18	0.11	0.20	**0.81**	0.10	0.14	0.17
I enjoy communicating with people from other cultures through the Internet	0.12	0.13	0.18	**0.78**	0.21	0.08	0.13
Communicating with people from other cultures through the Internet attracts me	0.13	0.12	0.24	**0.74**	0.14	0.07	0.32
Communicating with people from other cultures through the Internet is easy	0.31	0.15	0.03	**0.59**	0.04	0.23	0.22
Metacognition							
I check the accuracy of my cultural knowledge	0.16	0.13	0.19	0.15	**0.77**	0.03	0.07
I am conscious of the cultural knowledge I apply	0.26	0.11	0.04	0.27	**0.75**	0.03	0.01
I adjust my cultural knowledge	0.14	0.14	0.14	0.02	**0.71**	0.08	0.17
I am aware of how my culture influences my interactions	0.16	0.11	0.22	0.10	**0.66**	0.09	0.05
Task-oriented knowledge							
I know the legislation in the other culture	0.17	0.19	0.24	0.05	0.01	**0.72**	0.04
I know the risk preference of people in the other culture	0.19	0.27	0.03	0.23	0.05	**0.67**	0.12
I know the decision-making style in the other culture	0.29	0.32	0.20	0.17	0.02	**0.64**	0.01
External motivation							
If my superiors communicate online with people from other cultures, I would follow them	0.17	0.18	0.19	0.29	0.11	0.08	**0.75**
If my family communicate online with people from other cultures, I would follow them	0.19	0.11	0.25	0.29	0.14	0.01	**0.72**

(*continued*)

Table 2. (*continued*)

When communicating online with people from other cultures...	Loadings of factors						
	1	2	3	4	5	6	7
If my friends communicate online with people from other cultures, I would follow them	0.11	0.10	0.26	0.43	0.13	0.05	**0.71**
Variance explained	0.12	0.12	0.10	0.10	0.08	0.08	0.07
Cronbach's alpha	0.88	0.88	0.83	0.80	0.58	0.80	0.87

It includes items on comfort, enjoyment, attractiveness, and perceived easiness. Factor 5, labeled metacognition, comprises four items explaining 8% of total variance. These four items are exactly the same as the CQS metacognitive items. Factor 6, labeled task-oriented knowledge, comprises three items explaining 8% of total variance. It includes items on understanding of legislation, decision style, and risk preference. Finally, factor 7, labeled external motivation, comprises three items explaining 7% of total variance. Its items describe the influence of family, friends, and superiors. The model is named as BESTCIM, an acronym derived from the names of the seven factors (B-"Behavior", E-"External motivation", S-"Social-oriented knowledge", T-"Task-oriented knowledge", C-"Cultural-theoretical knowledge", I-"Internal motivation" and M-"Metacognition").

3.2 Predicting Cross-Cultural CMC Performance with BESTCIM Factors

A multiple linear regression model was formulated to examine the extent to which the seven factors can explain self-reported cross-cultural CMC performance. All item ratings under the same factor were averaged as this factor's rating, and the ratings on the seven factors were entered into the model as seven independent variables. The performance rating was entered as dependent variable. The data passed independence and multicollinearity tests. Table 3 summarizes the regression results.

The seven factors explained 47.3% of variance in self-reported online cross-cultural performance ($F_{7,547} = 72.11$, $p < 0.001$, adjusted $R^2 = 0.47$). Intrinsic motivation ($\beta = 0.29$, $p < 0.001$) and behavior ($\beta = 0.28$, $p < 0.001$) are the strongest positive predictors of cross-cultural CMC performance, followed by cultural-theoretical knowledge ($\beta = 0.21$, $p < 0.001$), social-oriented knowledge ($\beta = 0.20$, $p < 0.001$), and external motivation ($\beta = 0.09$, $p < 0.012$).

Table 3. Multiple regression predicting the self-reported cross-cultural CMC performance.

BESTCIM factors	β	p-value
Social-oriented knowledge	0.20	<0.001***
Cultural-theoretical knowledge	0.21	<0.001***
Behavior	0.28	<0.001***
Intrinsic motivation	0.29	<0.001***
Metacognition	-0.04	0.372
Task-oriented knowledge	0.01	0.763
External motivation	0.09	0.012*

Notes. * Significant at 0.05; *** significant at 0.001

4   Discussion

4.1   The BESTCIM Model

The multi-factor BESTCIM model is established to describe an individual's capabilities that affect cross-cultural communication in digital contexts. The model comprises seven factors: metacognition, cultural-theoretical knowledge, social-oriented knowledge, task-oriented knowledge, intrinsic motivation, external motivation, and behavior (RQ1). Among them, cultural-theoretical knowledge, social-oriented knowledge, and task-oriented knowledge refer to the cognitive aspect, while intrinsic motivation and external motivation refer to the motivational aspect. The model fits Sternberg's theoretical framework of multiple loci of intelligence, that mental capabilities consist of metacognition, cognition and motivation and behavioral capabilities.

Perceived usefulness is an important determinant of technology acceptance (Davis 1989). However, perceived usefulness is dropped from the BESTCIM model. This outcome may be due to the cross-cultural CMC experience of our participants. Among the 345 respondents, 93.6% reported cross-cultural CMC experience in interpersonal social context; thus, their intrinsic motivation for cross-cultural CMC highly overlaps with their intrinsic motivation to socialize through the Internet. This is in line with Wirtz and Göttel's (2016) research on the technology acceptance of social media, which shows that perceived easiness and enjoyment are more important than perceived usefulness in social-oriented Internet usage.

4.2   Predictors of Cross-Cultural CMC Performance

Among the seven factors, cultural-theoretical knowledge, social-oriented knowledge, intrinsic motivation, external motivation, and behavior positively predict self-rated cross-cultural CMC performance, while metacognition and task-oriented knowledge fail to show a significant effect (RQ2). Among the 345 respondents in the survey, 93.6% reported cross-cultural CMC experience in interpersonal social contexts, while only 47.9% reported experience in International teamwork. In the BESTCIM model, task-oriented knowledge is mainly related to decision-making, which is more important in teamwork than in interpersonal social context. This may be one reason for social-oriented knowledge rather than task-oriented knowledge predicting their self-rated performance.

Previous research on the relationship between CQ facets and performance provides inconsistent results. Metacognitive CQ, motivational CQ, and behavioral CQ have all been found to predict performance (Ang et al. 2007; Malek and Budhwar 2013). However, Lee et al. (2014) concluded that CQ has no direct influence on cultural effectiveness; instead, CQ positively influences adjustment, which in turn influences effectiveness. In CMC, people do not need to enter another cultural environment, so the role of cultural adjustment may vary from in the traditional context, and the path through which CQ influences performance may differ.

Research on cultural-diverse virtual teams has demonstrated the effect of CQ on team performance (Li et al. 2017). However, all these studies used the CQS in the CMC context without any modification, and none examined the effect of individual CQ factors. Our research provides a more context-specific model for further empirical research on multicultural virtual teams.

5 Study Limitations

This research has several limitations. First, in the EFA, three items failed to fit into the model. Although deleting these items is mathematically reasonable, it is not sufficient to rule them out as potential components. The dropped items should be further investigated. Second, this study used a convenience sampling approach, although the age range is large (from 18 to 60), the average age for the sample is about 26, indicating that young people made up the bulk of the sample. Young people's cross-cultural communication experience can be limited. According to their responses, only 42.9% of the sample has experience in International teamwork, which is important in International business. Besides, all the participants were born and raised up mainly in China, thus limiting the generalizability of our findings. Further validation of this model with more diverse samples should be conducted. Third, the performance data in this study is collected by self-reported questionnaire survey. Support from experimental study is required to further investigate the influence of these BESTCIM factors in practice.

6 Future Implications

The future will bring increasingly extensive cross-cultural interactions through the Internet. The traditional CQ structure is not sufficient in the digital age. To the best of our knowledge, this is the first study to explore the model of factors influencing cross-cultural CMC. By establishing BESTCIM model and introducing context-specific items, we believe our approach can help to build a clearer and more complete understanding of cross-cultural CMC. Further empirical studies based on our model can provide more detailed insight into how these factors affect virtual team performance, compared to previous studies that treat CQ as a one-dimensional concept in traditional scenarios (Erez et al. 2013; Li et al. 2017).

In practical terms, our model provides a solid foundation for developing an online self-rating cross-cultural communication measurement. Limited by sample size, we cannot claim that our seven-dimensional, 32-item model can be directly used as a mature scale, while we believe in its great potential. Researchers can test the model's reliability and validity with larger and more diverse samples, thereby generating a robust measurement.

The BESTCIM model can be used to guide human resource development. Although the model should not be cultural-specific, our model can aid the design of training programs with respect to a specific culture, by simply introducing more cultural-specific issues and scenarios.

Our results also highlight the importance of an individual's cultural-theoretical knowledge, social-oriented knowledge, intrinsic motivation, external motivation, and behavior for cross-cultural CMC performance. This provides valuable insight for developing talent training programs considering global management and leadership. By facilitating understanding of each person's BESTCIM factors in a structured way, our findings can aid the targeted design of relevant training and development courses, workshops, and applications.

7 Conclusions

This research constructed a seven-factor (metacognition, cultural-theoretical knowledge, social-oriented knowledge, task-oriented knowledge, intrinsic motivation, external motivation, and behavior), 32-item model to identify influencing factors of cross-cultural communication in digital contexts. Among the seven factors, cultural-theoretical knowledge, social-oriented knowledge, intrinsic motivation, external motivation, and behavior can positively predict self-reported online cross-cultural performance. This research focused on the increasingly international Internet environment. The model has valuable theoretical and practical implications with respect to measurement design, virtual team collaboration, and Internet talent training.

Acknowledgements. We thank Professor Pei-Luen Patrick Rau for his guidance and advice on this research. We thank Zhi Guo, Hanjing Huang, Jian Zheng, Xin Lei and Xiaofang Sun for their contribution to the review of the draft questionnaire and discussion of potential items.

References

Ang, S., Van Dyne, L., Koh, C.: Personality correlates of the four-factor model of cultural intelligence. Group Org. Manag. **31**(1), 100–123 (2006)

Ang, S., et al.: Cultural intelligence: Its measurement and effects on cultural judgment and decision making, cultural adaptation and task performance. Manag. Organ. Rev. **3**(3), 335–371 (2007)

Aritz, J., Walker, R., Cardon, P.W.: Media use in virtual teams of varying levels of coordination. Bus. Prof. Commun. Q. **81**(2), 222–243 (2018)

Callahan, E.: Cultural similarities and differences in the design of university web sites. J. Comput.-Mediat. Commun. **11**(1), 239–273 (2005)

Carlson, J.R., Zmud, R.W.: Channel expansion theory and the experiential nature of media richness perceptions. Acad. Manag. J. **42**(2), 153–170 (1999)

Chen, A.S.: CQ at work and the impact of intercultural training: an empirical test among foreign laborers. Int. J. Intercult. Relat. **47**, 101–112 (2015). https://doi.org/10.1016/j.ijintrel.2015.03.029

Chua, R.Y., Morris, M.W., Mor, S.: Collaborating across cultures: cultural metacognition and affect-based trust in creative collaboration. Organ. Behav. Hum. Decis. Process. **118**(2), 116–131 (2012)

Daft, R.L., Lengel, R.H.: Organizational information requirements, media richness and structural design. Manag. Sci. **32**(5), 554–571 (1986)

Davis, F.D.: Perceived usefulness, perceived ease of use, and user acceptance of information technology. MIS Q. **13**, 319–340 (1989)

Deng, L., Gibson, P.: Mapping and modeling the capacities that underlie effective cross-cultural leadership: an interpretive study with practical outcomes. Cross Cult. Manag. Int. J. **16**(4), 347–366 (2009)

Derks, D., Bos, A.E.R., von Grumbkow, J.: Emoticons and social interaction on the internet: the importance of social context. Comput. Hum. Behav. **23**(1), 842–849 (2007). https://doi.org/10.1016/j.chb.2004.11.013

Derks, D., Bos, A.E., Von Grumbkow, J.: Emoticons in computer-mediated communication: social motives and social context. Cyberpsychol. Behav. **11**(1), 99–101 (2008)

Earley, P.C., Ang, S.: Cultural Intelligence: Individual Interactions Across Cultures. Stanford University Press, Stanford (2003)

Erez, M., Lisak, A., Harush, R., Glikson, E., Nouri, R., Shokef, E.: Going global: Developing management students' cultural intelligence and global identity in culturally diverse virtual teams. Acad. Manag. Learn. Educ. **12**(3), 330–355 (2013)

Guhmundsdóttir, S.: Nordic expatriates in the US: the relationship between cultural intelligence and adjustment. Int. J. Intercult. Relat. **47**, 175–186 (2015)

Hair, J.F.: Multivariate data analysis: an overview. In: International Encyclopedia of Statistical Science, pp. 904–907 (2011)

Hall, E.T.: Beyond culture. Anchor (1989)

Harrison, J.K., Chadwick, M., Scales, M.: The relationship between cross-cultural adjustment and the personality variables of self-efficacy and self-monitoring. Int. J. Intercult. Relat. **20**(2), 167–188 (1996)

Hermeking, M.: Culture and internet consumption: contributions from cross-cultural marketing and advertising research. J. Comput.-Mediat. Commun. **11**(1), 192–216 (2005)

Hofstede, G., Hofstede, G. J., Minkov, M.: Cultures and organizations: Software of the mind. Revised and expanded. McGraw-Hill, New York (2010)

Jyoti, J., Kour, S.: Assessing the cultural intelligence and task performance equation: mediating role of cultural adjustment. Cross Cult. Manag. **22**(2), 236–258 (2015)

Kankanhalli, A., Tan, B.C.Y., Wei, K.-K.: Conflict and performance in global virtual teams. J. Manag. Inf. Syst. **23**(3), 237–274 (2006). https://doi.org/10.2753/MIS0742-1222230309

Kehrwald, B.: Understanding social presence in text-based online learning environments. Dist. Educ. **29**(1), 89–106 (2008)

Kock, N.: The psychobiological model: towards a new theory of computer-mediated communication based on Darwinian evolution. Organ. Sci. **15**(3), 327–348 (2004)

Kühberger, A., Schulte-Mecklenbeck, M., Perner, J.: The effects of framing, reflection, probability, and payoff on risk preference in choice tasks. Organ. Behav. Hum. Decis. Process. **78**(3), 204–231 (1999)

Lee, L.-Y., Veasna, S., Sukoco, B.M.: The antecedents of cultural effectiveness of expatriation: moderating effects of psychological contracts. Asia Pac. J. Human Res. **52**(2), 215–233 (2014)

Li, Y., Rau, P.-L.P., Li, H., Maedche, A.: Effects of a dyad's cultural intelligence on global virtual collaboration. IEEE Trans. Prof. Commun. **60**(1), 56–75 (2017)

Lin, Y., Chen, A.S., Song, Y.: Does your intelligence help to survive in a foreign jungle? the effects of cultural intelligence and emotional intelligence on cross-cultural adjustment. Int. J. Intercult. Relat. **36**(4), 541–552 (2012)

Malek, M.A., Budhwar, P.: Cultural intelligence as a predictor of expatriate adjustment and performance in Malaysia. J. World Bus. **48**(2), 222–231 (2013)

Mor, S., Morris, M.W., Joh, J.: Identifying and training adaptive cross-cultural management skills: the crucial role of cultural metacognition. Acad. Manag. Learn. Educ. **12**(3), 453–475 (2013)

Ott, D.L., Michailova, S.: Cultural intelligence: a review and new research avenues. Int. J. Manag. Rev. **20**(1), 99–119 (2018)

Schug, J., Yuki, M., Maddux, W.: Relational mobility explains between-and within-culture differences in self-disclosure to close friends. Psychol. Sci. **21**(10), 1471–1478 (2010)

Schulze, J., Schultze, M., West, S.G., Krumm, S.: The knowledge, skills, abilities, and other characteristics required for face-to-face versus computer-mediated communication: similar or distinct constructs? J. Bus. Psychol. **32**(3), 283–300 (2017)

Scott, S.G., Bruce, R.A.: Decision-making style: the development and assessment of a new measure. Educ. Psychol. Measur. **55**(5), 818–831 (1995)

Shachaf, P.: Cultural diversity and information and communication technology impacts on global virtual teams: an exploratory study. Inf. Manag. **45**(2), 131–142 (2008). https://doi.org/10.1016/j.im.2007.12.003

Sheer, V.C.: Hong Kong adolescents' use of MSN vs. ICQ for developing friendships online: Considering media richness and presentational control. Chin. J. Commun. **3**(2), 223–240 (2010)

Sheer, V.C.: Teenagers' use of MSN features, discussion topics, and online friendship development: the impact of media richness and communication control. Commun. Q. **59**(1), 82–103 (2011)

Staples, D.S., Zhao, L.: The effects of cultural diversity in virtual teams versus face-to-face teams. Group Decis. Negot. **15**(4), 389–406 (2006). https://doi.org/10.1007/s10726-006-9042-x

Statista. Messaging App Usage Statistics Around the World | MessengerPeople (2020). https://www.messengerpeople.com/global-messenger-usage-statistics/

Swan, K.: Building Learning Communities in Online Courses: The Importance of Interaction, vol. 2 (2002). https://doi.org/10.1080/1463631022000005016

Trevino, L.K., Daft, R.L., Lengel, R.H.: Understanding managers' media choices: a symbolic interactionist perspective (1990)

Trompenaars, F., Hampden-Turner, C.: Riding the Waves of Culture: Understanding Diversity in Global Business. Nicholas Brealey Publishing, Hachette (2011)

Van Dyne, L., Ang, S., Ng, K.Y., Rockstuhl, T., Tan, M.L., Koh, C.: Sub-dimensions of the four factor model of cultural intelligence: expanding the conceptualization and measurement of cultural intelligence. Soc. Pers. Psychol. Compass **6**(4), 295–313 (2012)

Vaske, J.J., Beaman, J., Sponarski, C.C.: Rethinking internal consistency in Cronbach's alpha. Leis. Sci. **39**(2), 163–173 (2017)

Venkatesh, V.: Determinants of perceived ease of use: Integrating control, intrinsic motivation, and emotion into the technology acceptance model. Inf. Syst. Res. **11**(4), 342–365 (2000)

Venkatesh, V., Davis, F.D.: A theoretical extension of the technology acceptance model: four longitudinal field studies. Manage. Sci. **46**(2), 186–204 (2000)

Wang, S.S.: More than words? the effect of line character sticker use on intimacy in the mobile communication environment. Soc. Sci. Comput. Rev. **34**(4), 456–478 (2016)

Wirtz, B.W., Göttel, V.: Technology acceptance in social media: review, synthesis and directions for future empirical research. J. Electron. Commer. Res. **17**(2), 97 (2016)

Würtz, E.: Intercultural communication on Web sites: a cross-cultural analysis of Web sites from high-context cultures and low-context cultures. J. Comput.-Mediat. Commun. **11**(1), 274–299 (2005)

An Analysis on Design Strategy of Traditional Process in Global Digitization

JinMeng Zhang[1], Rui Xu[1,2]([✉]), and ZiQiong Yang[1]

[1] School of Art and Design, Fuzhou University of International Studies and Trade,
Fuzhou 350200, China
635524937@qq.com
[2] The Graduate Institute of Design Science, Tatung University, New Taipei, Taiwan

Abstract. Traditional crafts in a materialized form for us to use, but also our spiritual needs, is our emotional expression carrier, in the rapid development of the current society, traditional crafts have cultural characteristics and aesthetic concepts, and ideological values will change with the development of society, should be combined with actual life and fashion needs, through modern expression to activate its fresh vitality. Deeply explore the cultural connotation and contemporary value of traditional crafts and promote the use of practical fields and research methods in public cultural services and meeting people's spiritual and cultural needs. In the full use of the Internet, big data and other rich digital resources, by studying the comparison of traditional crafts and digital informatization to reduce the contradiction between traditional crafts and art design, through the expression of traditional crafts in the digital age and the confusion between the audience and the confusion between the audience, this paper aims to explore how to achieve the transformation of digital traditional crafts in the context of globalization (multi-distance, technical, sensual), reflect modern values and aesthetic taste, build an interactive platform, and enhance audience participation Through the combination of culture, art and science and technology, expand the new experience of people's participation in traditional culture and the characteristics of the times.

Keywords: Traditional Process · Digitization · Integrated Development · Interactive Experience

1 Introduction

As a medium for the continuity of culture, the craft development and presentation as well, traditional crafts facilitate the integration of traditional and modern crafts to drive the innovation of the cultural industry chain and provide spaces for the diversified development of modern technologies. Therefore, the issues on continuity shall not be considered on the inheritance of traditional crafts only, we must stand from a cross-cultural perspective (herein it refers to the development of global transformation and the height of world diversification to understand). Back to the civilized society nowadays, traditional handicrafts were discovered first as a product of history, and they have been affected by

P.-L. P. Rau (Ed.): HCII 2023, LNCS 14023, pp. 142–154, 2023.
https://doi.org/10.1007/978-3-031-35939-2_11

conflicts internally during the transformation of industrial and commercial civilization (namely the transformation of technological industry) [6]. In order to use the combination of digital technology and art to change the concept and behavior on traditional crafts, this article will study and analyze the art of crafts and their object itself, as well as the value of the era, international exchanges and integrated development experience contained in, the importance of the article in the research of innovation and development based on the traditional craft system, and the lack of development of traditional industries under the digital transformation. In the research on modern technology development, we explore how to better enable the audience to properly understand the connotation and core value of traditional crafts in the context of the new era, and to integrate new technological innovations in the digital age for providing feasibility of development of traditional crafts, providing models and theoretical systems to facilitate the transformation and upgrading of traditional crafts [2].

2 Challenges Faced by Traditional Crafts in Digital Era

2.1 Insufficient Traditional Craft Works and Methods

The development of folk handicrafts strictly requires the technical capacity and their own regional characteristics as well as cultural customs. We found that some valuable craft works may not be able to give full play to their value via investigation an research, and now an unbalanced development in the "Trust" and "Famousness" of such works are always existed, especially for some works (products) that do not have quality supervision and geographical labels, leading to their substandard quality and hindering the cultural connotation and value of handicrafts [5]. From above, it is concluded that the only way for traditional crafts to be effectively inherited is to meet the requirements on the packaging for the product itself (herein it refers to the development of traditional macro-structure and craft inheritance relying on modern platforms), and to reinforce the propaganda for the product.

2.2 Conflicts Between Modern Technology and Traditional Laboring

The rapid development of science and technology becomes one of the main reasons hindering the development of traditional handicrafts, in which the most prominent problem is that the current society is facing a series of backwardness such as the lack of traditional handicraft talents, hindering the development of the industry and talent. In this regard, in order to protect the future development of traditional crafts, examine the development environment of traditional crafts in recent years. Although the rapid development of modern crafts has brought great convenience to people's lives, for those who love to chase (fast) collections or (rapid) understanding of the active behavior will also lead to a certain extent that the rapid active behavior cannot make a real understanding, which will also lead to its core values such as innovative consciousness and cultural connotation contained in traditional crafts. Factors have not been well understood, inherited and developed, seriously affecting the future expectations of traditional crafts.

2.3 The Development of Media Has Distracted People's Attention to Traditional Crafts

In the new media era, various forms of artistic expression have reduced people's learning and notability to traditional culture and works. With the improvement of network speed and the popularity of online videos, more and more people are accustomed to learning about the products they are interested in through simple adaptations or quick explanations of short videos. To a certain extent, the media makes people lose the seriousness and attention to traditional crafts, and also the ability to think independently. As compared with reading ancient books or history books, etc., the easy-to-understand adaptation seems to be more in line with the information of people to accept the habit in this era.

3 The Impact and Application on Traditional Craftsmanship in the Trend of Global Digital Transformation

3.1 The Evolution of Traditional Craftsmanship in the Digital Transformation System in the New Era

In the context of the new era of modern social economy, production conditions, environmental conditions, fashion culture, etc., the review and development of traditional crafts also tends to develop from traditional crafts to modern forms of modern traditional crafts. At present, with the development of the "Global Development Economic Belt" and the communication of the "Community of Shared Future for Mankind", the enthusiasm and attention of the whole society and even the world to traditional handicrafts has greatly improved the audience's enthusiasm and attention to traditional handicrafts. The industrialized model is constantly facilitating the advancement of mass consumption. This article highlights the problems between the rich materials that facilitates the protracted development of fashion and the conflicts between industrialized productions that destroy the development of traditional handicrafts, bringing us new challenges and vitality while solving problems. In addition, with the continuous development of industrialization, personalized design is also ushering in new handwriting, and there will also be major changes between consumption and designers.

The concept of "traditional craft system" has formed "handicraft" culture in the narrow sense and "handicraft" culture in the broad sense (namely the folk handicrafts, cultural tourism, stage art, graphic, video, etc.), media network, film and television performances and other cultural activities carried out in the name of traditional handicraft culture) [6]. In various cultural contexts, the incarnation of "traditional crafts", CIS image, audios, commercial brand, image ambassador, landscape concept, regional characteristics, visual language, advertising symbols, OTOP (One Village One Product) and other referents, successively appeared, or even broke through the limitations of attributes, and traditional crafts turned into a kind of "Spirit" [2]. Under the background of the new era, cultural affiliation and spiritual identity are gradually expanding, and the traditional craft system is transformed into a modern form in the correct way, and evolved into a representative traditional craft system, a regional traditional craft system, and a modern transformed traditional craft system.

3.2 Integration of Digital Intelligent Manufacturing and the Multi-dimensional Art Industry

As a unique type of technology in the digital age, 3D digital technology can create virtual 3D image data and print out intuitive product models with the help of advanced design software and scanning equipment, using analog operation functions. These products derived from the digital age have great influence on art design. Important role. With the rapid development of three-dimensional digital technology, there are still contradictions between the health and development of traditional craft technology. This article discusses how to make full use of modern science and technology to give new vitality to traditional craft technology, how to become a new engine of digital application (manufacturing) that will also become an excellent handicraft industry.

Digital Technology Provides Value Guarantee for Traditional Handicrafts. Traditional handicrafts are ornamental objects and memorials with certain meanings, symbols or pictograms. It is an art that reflects social life and expresses the artist's aesthetic feelings, aesthetic emotions, and aesthetic ideals. For example, sculpture works (products) have complex and fine textures, and the carving cycle of the product is comparable to the difficulty. Therefore, a simple and fast 3D modeling method has emerged in the sculpture industry. 3D scanning technology is a digital model acquisition method by obtaining 3D coordinate data on the surface of the measured object. It is featured as high precision, high resolution, and high point cloud density. The 3D data of the sculpture can be directly collected without pasting points, and the automatic processing function of the software can be used. 3D data (1:1) and color information of the model. It is a method of importing the triangulation network model into the model to build and repair the model data, to re-divide the surface texture coordinates, and output a 3D model with real texture [9]. The application of 3D scanning technology has been well inherited and developed for the preservation of core value factors, such as traditional craft innovation consciousness and cultural connotation.

Fig. 1. Image courtesy of Artec's website

3D Digitization Achieves the Inheritance and Development of Handicrafts. The use of 3D digital technology in traditional handicrafts is beneficial for designers to record the procedures of the production process, and to imitate and produce the handicrafts by means of mechanical production. Traditional craft learners (enthusiasts) can also use digital technology to simplify complex craft techniques and present a more direct way, which is conducive to learning and mastering (including experiential consumers who have no handmade experiences). The effectiveness of the entire teaching has been greatly improved.

ZHU Sendi emphasized in "Process Innovation in the Digital Transformation of Manufacturing Industry" at the 2019 Smart Manufacturing Conference: following the old process management model, process drawings and simple process cards have limited guidance for production, and product data are also limited. The association and integration with various systems has not been realized, thus forming a data fault and unable to update in real time, which greatly reduces the accuracy and effectiveness of the data. This shows the necessity of digital technology. Nowadays, the process links can already be empowered by high technologies, such as industrial Internet, AI, cloud computing, and big data, so we have the ability to solve complex process problems.

The introduction of 3D digital intelligent technology in the development of traditional arts and crafts can realize the effective combination of traditional arts, crafts industry, modern science and technology, and improve the contradiction between the design and manufacturing process efficiency and production quality of art products as well.

3.3   The Driving Force of 3D Digital Manufacturing Technology for Traditional Crafts

With the development of computer information technology, IT has rapidly penetrated into many fields of human social and economic development. Some exquisite handicrafts have not only expanded international exchanges, but also cultural influences produced. The emergence of digital technology has enabled digital protection of handicrafts, such as digital storage, digital display and dissemination. In this regard, the article focuses on how to effectively inherit and protect these precious cultural heritages by applying modern science and technology.), AR (augmented reality), interactive experience and other advanced science and technology to protect it digitally. For example, the Italian researcher Pesci used TLS and digital images to complete the damage detection of Palazzo D'Accursio and Piazza Maggiore; Armesto detected the damage of the carved surface of the murals in the Santo Domingo Church and digitized them.

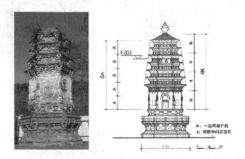

First, for example, ancient pagoda carvings, a precious cultural heritage, have been severely damaged after thousands of years of weathering, erosion and historical changes, and some ancient pagoda carvings can no longer be repaired. It takes a lot of manpower and material resources to train a senior craftsman with proficient carving skills, and the most serious problem is the loss of traditional craftsmanship, which will not be resolved in a short period, causing serious limitations to the development of the sculpture. As well as the increasingly prominent difficulties in the works and exhibition of handicrafts, the use of 3D digital technology can effectively solve the production technical problems in the engraving industry. Through accurate scanning and digital modeling technology, computers are used to design handicrafts to be manufactured, and 3D printing and digital output equipment are used to complete the restoration and digital preservation of handicrafts [8]. During this period, stone carving masters who do not need work experience are reduced. The cost of manual carving and the uncertainty of human error.

Fig. 2. Of Chinese Architecture - "Changing Flowers"

Second, with reference to the current digital technology for the processing of sculpture works, with the support of accurate data, in order to further analyze its aesthetic value and value; to provide a solid basis and support for the inheritance, development and protection of the sculpture industry; The 3D model from the Tianning Temple's sculpture is shown in Fig. 1 and Fig. 2. Where, ① 3D laser technology is used: accurate 3D point cloud data for engraving works is collected and information database storage is set up; VR: a digital management storage system for the electronic files of documents is set up, digital images and 3D data is archived in this work [11].

The application of 3D scanning technology has enabled to realize the healthy and feasible transformation from 2D to 3D in the field of traditional crafts. Above mentioned technologies not only makes proper utilization for the protection and value of traditional crafts, but also greatly improves the coverage of dissemination, which has made great contributions and future support for the management and redevelopment of traditional crafts. People understand such technologies from a new perspective, a new way to be used for storage, and new demands for use, presenting handicrafts a powerful vitality [9] (Figs. 3 and 4).

South   West   North   East   South West   North West   North East   North South

图 2   塔身雕刻三维模型

Fig. 3. 3D Tower Body Sculpture Model

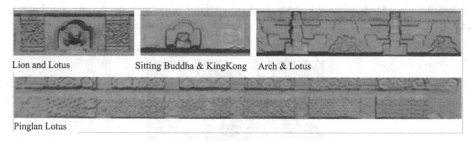

Lion and Lotus   Sitting Buddha & KingKong   Arch & Lotus

Pinglan Lotus

Fig. 4. 3D Tower Base Sculpture Model

4   The Development and Application of Interactive Art in the Digital Ear

With big data as the support of intelligence–upgrading the field of technology empowerment, this makes digitization and intelligence the link between traditional craft design and production. The maturity of the digital revolution means moving closer from technology application to the field of art. Under the interaction of many corresponding factors, the digital art form based on art has formed a new situation in the relationship and thinking of art, technology, and the public.

Interactive art refers to the art itself and an art form that includes audience participation in the appreciation process of art works. It is an artistic form of expression completed by the joint participation of creators and audiences. The artist Duchamp believes that the act of artistic creation cannot be completed by the artist alone. An independent and single work does not have artistic attributes, and the audience shapes the integrity of the work [4]. Through in-depth interpretation, research, and contact with works of art, the audience becomes the key factor for the integrity of the work, while interactive art is trying to challenge the traditional boundary between the creator and the audience, using space as a carrier to explore the relationship between the audience and the work [16], making the audience a partner of the creator and using the physical medium to influence the perception of the participants. This is considered as the most powerful result of interactive art output. Meanwhile, the development of technology has also given interactive art a larger display stage. Under the help of Internet technology and multimedia technology, the creative concept of interaction and digital technology communication media are organically combined to form a comprehensive art [5]. The intervention of information technology has made interactive art no longer a superficial ornamental art. It has more forms of expression, breaking the way of existence on traditional art forms such as design, works, and products based on 2D planes, creating a multi-dimensional subjective ideology [15]. This article uses digital technology to inject new blood into the art ecology under the new art form of traditional crafts.

4.1 The Emergence of Interactive Art in the Digital Era

The complementary relationship between design and art, innovative thinking at the artistic level, aesthetics and expressions is interacting with each other. Therefore, only when continuous interaction (idea) between design and art produces better design works, its core lies in the interaction between people or between people and objects, which is also a behavioral response combining psychology and physiology, or changes among audiences. Such changes in attributes and relationships all exist together. Therefore, in this process, relying on the development of computer technology and other technologies, interactive art and these art forms are combined in the creation process, generating interaction and connecting functions and functions, making audiences more closely related to traditional art than traditional art [13], through special interactive experience forms, and the audience's participation and interactive experience process in interactive art works realize the audience's creation of interactive art works, and also enable the artist to share their creation with the audience.

4.2 The Application of Interactive Art in the Digital Era

The Application of Digital Art in Traditional Handicrafts - Interactive Products for Children The "OPPO" exhibition about Japanese traditional craft toys held by WOW, a visual design studio in Tokyo, Japan. This is a digital art exhibition mainly aimed at children's entertainment, and its contents from local folk traditional handicraft products.

For example, the contents of the exhibition: "OPPO Forest", "POKURO", "Yadodo". WOW Studio hopes that modern technology can better interpret and convey the culture, meaning contained in these traditional handicraft toys. The main reason is that in the Tohoku region of Japan, there are some local toys with a long history, such as woodcuts and eagle claws. Although they are commonly seen everywhere in daily life, as time goes by, they are gradually ignored and become more and more rare. But the significance contained in these traditional craft toys is profound. We take the "OPPO Forest" as an explanation, highlighting the key content of this work as "Eagle", which corresponds to the local traditional woodcarving toys. Sasano District, Yamagata Prefecture is Ittobori. In severe Winter, covered with snow trees Koshiabura and raw materials, farther northeast from the capital, many unique crafts are born. Toy birds live in the Northeast in such winters. When experiencers (children) stick the props with magnetic force similar to tree trunks to the picture, the "Eagle" will stay on the "wooden stake" to stop and rest (Fig. 5).

The Application of Digitization in Art Museums - "Time Brilliance Porcelain Paradise" Light and Shadow Art Exhibition The works exhibited this time are mainly based on China's thousand-year-old porcelain culture, using the most advanced digital

Fig. 5. "OPPO" exhibition held by WOW, a visual design studio in Tokyo, Japan

means to "activate" history, let traditional culture enter the life of the younger generation, and create a visual sense of cultural belonging for them.

Such as one of his works - blue and white porcelain. There are also three dishes hanging on the wall, each of which records a piece of blue and white porcelain history, showing blue and white porcelain styles in different periods and blue and white patterns under different styles in the form of a 3D Mapping show, leading people into a blue and white world, creating a strong visual cultural feast for the audience (Fig. 6).

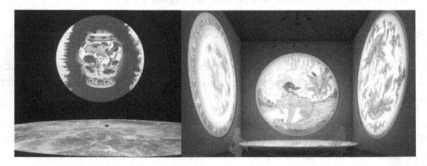

Fig. 6. Brilliance from Time · Porcelain Paradise Light and Shadow Art Exhibition

In addition, another composition of the exhibits - Gaoling Cliff. It also uses 3D Mapping to design an art installation in which stones burst instantly, using multi-angle projections. It interprets the dynamic changes of ceramic materials during the firing process of pottery and porcelain, creating a poetic and fantastic immersion for the audience with traceability space (Fig. 7).

The exhibition exhibits numerous murals spanning various time dimensions across the western regions, throughout the East and West—from the Central Plains to the Western Regions, and spanning thousands of years—from Wei, Jin to Song and Yuan Dynasties. Through a series of pictures and multimedia scenes, as well as carpets, mineral pigments and other real objects, the exhibition shows the exquisite mural art on the Silk Road to the audience in an all-round way (Fig. 8).

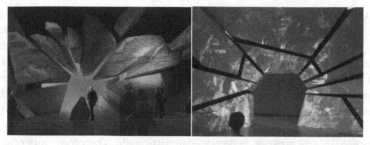

Fig. 7. Brilliance from Time · Porcelain Paradise Light and Shadow Art Exhibition

Fig. 8. Audience from Time · Porcelain Paradise Light and Shadow Art Exhibition

The development of multimedia technology has brought about subversive changes in the design thinking of museums, from the original single item to the interaction between "people" and "things". The interactive design is more able to make the audience participate in the museum, which forms a meta-immersive digital interactive space through the multi-dimensional, 3D and interesting digital interactive space, the 360-degree surround + ground visual technology in the preface hall of the exhibition. This new type of Interactive design can not only stimulate the curiosity of the viewers, but also facilitate cultural transmission. The Augmented Reality (AR) technology and Virtual Reality technology (VR), holographic projection, somatosensory interaction and other high-tech means used in it increase the experience fun and sense of presence [14], so that the cultural relics collected in the museum are displayed and developed in public culture.

4.3 The Impact Produced from Interactive Art in Digital Era

For traditional crafts, the emergence of digitization firstly changes the carrier of artistic creation, which greatly shortens the time consumed by artistic creation, and at the same time enriches the expression forms of artistic creation, namely it has a positive impact. Therefore, the integration of digital technology into artistic creation also means the integration of various modern technologies into the multi-dimensional art [11], combining various technologies to create modern technological and traditional artistic beauty.

A Trend of Healthy Development Integration. Compared with traditional art communication, the development of digitalization is more conducive to enhancing the interaction in the process of art communication and avoiding negative factors such as singleness and inflexibility. Therefore, digitalization has enhanced the link between art and ordinary people. For example, the Rijks museum of the Netherlands launched an online gallery on its new official website in 2013, and successively fully opened up HD collection pictures for users to download for free without any restrictions. The museum publishes its collection information, HD images, encourages users to use them creatively, and holds an international design award every two years. They invite the public to create their own art inspired by the museum's collections, regardless of form. From graphic design to installation art, applied art, to costume design, photography and videography, as long as you are inspired by any artwork, audiences can participate. Therefore, under the inspiration of famous paintings, some people designed blindfolds, made hats, and so on. This way is undoubtedly another way of inheriting traditional culture and handicrafts.

Second, when art uses digital related technologies, it can directly intervene in people's real life and triggers people's enthusiasm for exploring their own mysteries. For example, Turkish artist Anador's "Memory Melting" transforms the elusive memory retrieval process in the human brain into a data set and presents it in an immersive and creative way. The entire project consists of E-painting, augmented data sculpture and light projection. The LED media wall and CNC foam present visitors with a visual interpretation of the inner movement of the human brain. In the past three years, the American artist Kaws and the art organization Acute Art have launched the AR art project "Vacation" (Extended Edition), which uses location-based in Doha, London, Melbourne, New York, Paris and Hong Kong etc., on the basis of principle of geographic information, viewers open the Acute Art App, and they can see a huge doll image (named Companion) mischievously covering its eyes, appearing in the space they are in (Fig. 9).

Fig. 9. KAWS "Expanded Holiday" Art Experience

To sum up, the development of the digital transformation process is not only the further creation of art forms, but also the continuation and expansion of the audience's acceptance. Whether it is popular online art or physical art, the expansion of art is constantly being mediated. In the process of development, with the support of digitalization, the contradiction between tradition and modernity is gradually merging as it recedes, and the rich generative nature between them is further enhanced, while improving a broad cognitive platform for the public, it forms a formal framework of space navigation (operation guide), which contains a variety of public perception conditions, perspectives and even concepts.

5 Conclusions

This article firstly analyzes traditional craftsmanship as a material and spiritual life need of different classes, first of all as a production method with memory, on the other hand, as a carrier of historical creations, it appears in the public eye, accompanied by the diversified development of modern ideology. After analyzing the current difficulties faced by traditional crafts, it is found that although there are contradictory negative influences in the development process of traditional and modern forms, in the process of diversification of information dissemination forms, carriers and the impact of tradition. It also breaks through the rigid thinking of traditional carriers, facilitates the diversification of its expressions, makes up for the shortcomings of traditional crafts in the process of creation. In the development of traditional crafts, 3D digital intelligent technology is introduced to restore, reinforce traditional handicrafts, relying on digital surveying, modeling and other technological means to protect and restore historical relics, using 3D data for non-contact, fast, high-precision, high-resolution imaging effects and many other strengths, systematically and accurately collect various information of cultural relics, such as size, texture, details, etc., and finally realize the electronic data conversion of work information, turning boring data into The vivid model leads the development of the museum into a new era of public participation and interaction. It is not only a supplementary upgrade to traditional protection methods, but also provides more possibilities for the protection, publicity, development and research of traditional crafts analysis. In order to realize the effective combination of traditional craft industry and modern science and technology, the 3D technologies promote the development and progress of traditional craft in China. Finally, digital technology and interactive art are integrated and developed, which better stimulates the digital value contribution of art, solves the conflict between traditional crafts and digital technology, and realizes the interaction and mutual influence of art and technology to a certain extent. It achieves the healthy integration and development of modern technological beauty, traditional arts and crafts, lead the leap of traditional crafts from 2D space to multi-dimensional space, pays more attention to the changes in the relationship between the audience's experience and emotion, and breaks the original art and audience, stimulates the creative inspiration of the participants and cultivates the participants' aesthetic awareness and emotional expression. It is more convenient and acceptable to convey the cultural connotation and value behind the works through such activities, so as to achieve the inheritance, development and upgrading of traditional crafts under the digital transformation.

Fund name. Campus level longitudinal research project topic "Localization strategy analysis of traditional artworks, taking porcelain for example" (FWXXS21123).

References

1. Ma, H.: Research on the development of traditional crafts under the new media technology environment. West. Radio Televisi. **8**(16), 8–9 (2014)
2. Luo, C.: Analysis on the inheritance and development of traditional arts and crafts from the perspective of modern culture. Chin. Handcraft (3), 113–115 (2022). https://doi.org/10.3969/j.issn.1672-6766.2022.03.032

3. Liang, J.: The development strategy of traditional porcelain carving technology in the new era. Ceram. Sci. Art **56**(11), 14–15 (2022)
4. Wu, J., Yu, S., Yu, T.: Digitization and artistic expression of Mogao Grottoes sculpture——taking the three-body sculpture in cave 158 of Mogao Grottoes as an example. Dunhuang Res. **6** (2009)
5. Zhao, Y.: Analysis on inheritance and development strategy of traditional arts and crafts in the new era. J. Putian Univ. **28**(6), 76–81 (2021). https://doi.org/10.3969/j.issn.1672-4143.2021.06.0
6. Li, Y.: The contemporaneity and regionality of traditional arts and crafts——revisiting the protection and development of traditional arts and crafts. J. Nanjing Univ. Arts (Art Des. Ed.) (1), 5–9 (2008). https://doi.org/10.3969/j.issn.1008-9675.2008.01.003
7. Shi, Z.: Digital technology and video art. J. Beijing Film Acad. (2), 54–60 (1993)
8. Ji, Y., Xu, X.: Digital reconstruction technology of 3D cultural relics. J. Beijing Inst. Technol. **34**(6), 565–569 (2014)
9. Song, P.: Integration and practice of 3D digital technology and traditional crafts in architectural modeling course. Ceramics (7), 152–153, 158 (2020)
10. Li, S.: Analysis of traditional arts and crafts design based on 3D digital technology. J. Chifeng Univ. (Nat. Sci. Ed.) **33**(20), 36–37 (2017). https://doi.org/10.3969/j.issn.1673-260X.2017.20.016
11. Yang, X.: Chinese ancient tower chinese photography, vol. 4 (1994)
12. Jiang, H.: Viewing between the virtual and the real - the digital trend of art exhibitions. Natl. Art Res. **30**(2), 63–70 (2017). https://doi.org/10.21004/issn.1003-840x.2017.02.063
13. Su, Z.: The application of virtual reality technology in the teaching of new media animation——comment on "virtual reality technology and application". Chin. J. Educ. (5), Post-insert 41 (2021)
14. Dai, Y.: Digital interactive art experiment under the aesthetic concept of "artistic conception and virtual reality". Art Res. (3), 122–125 (2020)
15. Chu, X.: The impact of technological progress on multiple interactions between art creation and aesthetic appreciation. J. Southeast Univ. (Phil. Soc. Sci.) **23**(1), 111–127 (2021)
16. Wang, X.: Research on social interaction forms of new media art. J. Huaqiao Univ. (Phil. Soc. Sci. Ed.), (2), 156–160 (2013). https://doi.org/10.3969/j.issn.1006-1398.2013.02.020

The Effects of Timbre on Voice Interaction

Ruiqing Zhao[1], E. Erleke[1], Linbao Wang[1], Jun Huang[1], and Zhe Chen[1,2(✉)]

[1] School of Economics and Management, Beihang University, Beijing 100191, People's
Republic of China
zhechen@buaa.edu.cn
[2] Beijing Key Laboratory of Emergency Support Simulation Technologies for City Operations,
Beihang University, Beijing 100191, People's Republic of China

Abstract. With the development of voice interaction and speech synthesis technology, the impact of different audio timbres on user experience is particularly important. This study focuses on the voice transmission of news information, taking users' subjective emotional experience as the starting point, and conducts relevant experimental research to investigate the impact of different timbres on user experience in the process of voice interaction. This study conducted an experiment in which two types of data were collected from 30 participants each, including PAD scale data and behavioural questionnaire data to measure subjective emotional experience, and skin potential data to measure objective physiological indicators. The experimental data showed that different timbre gender and type elicited different emotions from the users. The timbre gender had a significant effect on the standard deviation of the skin conductance, i.e. the level of emotional arousal; the timbre type had a significant effect on the participants' interest; the news type also influenced the level of interest and the users' evaluation. Timbre gender and news category had a significant interaction effect, as did timbre type and news category, which influenced the degree of matching and user evaluation. Finally, based on the results, this paper further discusses the conclusions related to timbre gender, timbre type and news type, and gives practical suggestions for the design of speech interaction systems.

Keywords: Timbre · Voice interaction system · User experience · News broadcasting · PAD emotion scale

1 Introduction

1.1 Voice Interaction System

In the production and life of the information age, people are using smart devices more and more. As smart devices become more intelligent, how people can interact with them in a more natural way and in line with people's communication habits becomes an important research question. From the user's point of view, voice is the most natural user interface and offers hands-free operation [1].

Voice messages can show more emotion by expressing information in different dimensions [2]. Different acoustic and prosodic characteristics show different personality and emotions of the speaker, i.e. speakers with louder voices are perceived as more outgoing and lively [3]; speaking speed affects the personality perception of people with voices of the opposite sex [4]; men with a wider range of pitch variations are perceived as having a softer temperament and aesthetic ability, while women with a wide range of variation are perceived as more lively and outgoing [5].

1.2 Timbre

Timbre is an acoustic concept commonly used in psychoacoustics. In this paper we measure the timbre of the human voice in two dimensions: gender and personality characteristics.

Gender. Some studies have concluded that the timbre of women's voices is inappropriate for broadcasting compared to men's voices, because women's voices are higher in pitch, faster in speech, and have more personal characteristics than men's, so people pay too much attention to their timbre rather than the content of the broadcast. In the field of voice assistants, on the other hand, people prefer female voices [6], and that's why female voices are used in most of the intelligent voice interaction systems designed.

Much of the research on the impact of timbre on interaction design and user experience focuses on gender as a variable. Changes in the vocal characteristics of voice interfaces (i.e., voice gender and manner) are seen as key determinants of user experience, and voice gender (male vs. female) and voice mode (calm vs. passionate) as variables can have a significant impact on the psychological and behavioral outcomes of voice interactions, including message credibility [7].

Personalization Characteristics. The concept of timbre personalization comes from social psychology. People will have a specific impression of people with certain character traits in social life, perhaps influenced by many film and television works, and people's impressions of different character groups have certain commonalities.

Relying on intelligent speech synthesis technology, major manufacturers have given their virtual voice assistants unique voice characteristics, through comparison, you can clearly feel the obvious difference in their voice, these different timbre is set by manufacturers to match their personalized virtual assistant's personality, for example, Apple's voice assistant female voice is biased towards cold and loyal professional women; Xiaomi's voice assistant Xiaoai's voice is biased towards the cute girl next door. That is, the personalization characteristics design of timbre is necessary to consider in voice interaction system design to improve users' experience.

1.3 Intelligent Voice Broadcast

With the rapid development of mobile Internet and the emergence of self-media, people are not satisfied with obtaining information from traditional text reading, and the new media communication form with sound as the carrier has gradually become the mainstream. According to Deloitte's 2020 forecast, the global audiobook market size will grow by 25% in 2020 to reach \$3.5 billion, the global podcast market will grow by 30% in 2020 to reach \$1.1 billion. The United States and China rank first and second respectively in the global audiobook market, accounting for 75% of the global market.

In the United States, Edison Research and Triton Digital found that by 2020, 27% of Americans over the age of 12 (76 million) will own at least one smart speaker, 62% will have used at least one voice-activated smart personal assistant, and 60% will have listened to online audio in the past week, with the percentage of the population listening to online audio increasing each year. The 169 million Americans who listened to online audio in the past week spent an average of more than 15 h per week listening [9]. In addition, podcasts, which have been described as "the new radio", have grown rapidly in recent years [10], with podcast subscribers expected to reach 155 million in the US by 2020, representing 55% of the population, up from 33% five years ago [9, 11]. Podcast listeners tend to be "loyal, affluent and well-educated" (PodcastInsights.com, 2020), with a roughly balanced gender structure (51% male, 49% female) and an average listening time of 6.7 h per week, while the proportion of podcasts listened to, listening time, etc. will continue to grow with the further development and popularity of smart speakers (nielson.com, 2020).

2   Methods

This study was reviewed and approved by the Human Research Ethics Committee of the School of Economics and Management, Beihang University, and informed consent was obtained from each participant.

2.1   Participants

In this study, 30 participants from a university in Beijing were invited to take part in the experiment. The average age of the participants was 21, and all the participants were undergraduates who had passed the Chinese college entrance exam and had normal hearing. 30 participants rated themselves as 'very good' in Chinese hearing and memory, 29 of them were right-handed and 1 was left-handed. The experiment used a full within-group design. Each participant was asked to complete 12 experimental tasks. To counterbalance the effects of order and to avoid learning effects, a Latin square design was used in this study (Table 1).

2.2   Experimental Design

Independent Variables. In this study, we investigate the impact of different timbre effects on user experience in the task scenario of news broadcasting. Therefore, we classify the types of independent variables in the experiment into three types, i.e. the type of news broadcast, the gender of the voice used to broadcast the news, and the type of timbre used to broadcast the news.

We divide the news into three categories, science and technology news, entertainment news and epidemic-related news, according to the different channels through which

Table 1. Latin square

Number	Number of the task											
1	1	2	3	4	5	6	7	8	9	10	11	12
2	2	3	4	5	6	7	8	9	10	11	12	1
3	3	4	5	6	7	8	9	10	11	12	1	2
4	4	5	6	7	8	9	10	11	12	1	2	3
5	5	6	7	8	9	10	11	12	1	2	3	4
6	6	7	8	9	10	11	12	1	2	3	4	5
7	7	8	9	10	11	12	1	2	3	4	5	6
8	8	9	10	11	12	1	2	3	4	5	6	7
9	9	10	11	12	1	2	3	4	5	6	7	8
10	10	11	12	1	2	3	4	5	6	7	8	9
11	11	12	1	2	3	4	5	6	7	8	9	10
12	12	1	2	3	4	5	6	7	8	9	10	11

users access the news; the gender of the voice is two types, male and female; the type of timbre used to broadcast the news is two types, the usual timbre when broadcasting news and the ACGN timbre. Non-serious news has become an important form of media in today's Internet culture environment, and ACGN timbre is the representative of a more entertaining one. ACGN culture lovers are mainly young users, and as reported by Guangming Daily, the number of ACGN lovers in Chi-na reached 340 million. Therefore, the selection of the above two types of timbre is significant and valuable for this study.

Dependent Variables. There are three dependent variables, including the PAD Emotional Scale, behavioral questionnaire, and skin conductance, which are used to measure and evaluate the voice perception experience. There are three questions in the behavioral questionnaire: The degree of interest in the news; How well the voice matches the news; Overall evaluation of the news.

Control Variables. Considering that different participants have different levels of acceptance of different types of news, the selection of news should be controlled to be relatively neutral, objective and avoid negative news.

Considering that the length of the task would have an impact on the cognitive load and performance of the participants, each news item should not be too long or too short, the broadcast time should be limited to 25–30 s.

Tasks. A 2 × 2 × 3 experimental design was conducted according to the variable settings, as shown in the following table (Table 2).

Table 2. Tasks of the experiment

Task	Gender	Timbre Type	News Type
1	Male	ACGN	Epidemic
2	Male	ACGN	Technology
3	Male	ACGN	Entertainment
4	Male	Broadcast	Epidemic
5	Male	Broadcast	Technology
6	Male	Broadcast	Entertainment
7	Female	ACGN	Epidemic
8	Female	ACGN	Technology
9	Female	ACGN	Entertainment
10	Female	Broadcast	Epidemic
11	Female	Broadcast	Technology
12	Female	Broadcast	Entertainment

2.3 Procedure

Once participants have agreed to take part in the experiment, they will be asked to provide written informed consent. Before the experiment begins, participants are asked to complete the first page of the questionnaire with their personal information and relevant background checks. Each participant completed 12 tasks, and each task required the participant to listen to the audio and then complete a PAD scale [12] and a Likert scale [13]. Skin conductance was measured and both video and voice recordings were collected throughout the experiment.

2.4 Apparatus

The experimental messages were collected from the internet. The audio (12 segments) used in the experiment was exported from the human voice narration function in the Tik-tok APP, and the questionnaire used in the experiment was created using Questionnaire Star. A NeXus-10 MKII from MINDMEDIA was used to measure skin conductance and the recording APP is called BIO-Trace. A video recorder (Sony) and an audio recorder (Sony) were used for the experiments.

3 Results and Discussion

The experiment produced a total of two sets of data: one was the skin conductance data recorded by the skin electrical device during the experiment, and the other was the PAD Emotional Scale and Behavioral Questionnaire data completed by the participants during the experiment. The skin potential data record the degree of arousal of the participant's objective emotions when performing different tasks, while the questionnaire is the participant's subjective emotions based on their own feelings. A total of 30 participants were recruited in this experiment, so the sample size of the PAD questionnaire, the behavioral questionnaire and the skin conductance data was all 30, which met the conditions for statistically small sample testing, so the data collected was statistically significant.

In this experiment, there are 3 items in the questionnaire, and the Cronbach's alpha coefficient calculated by the reliability of the questionnaire is 0.745, indicating that the reliability is good (Table 3 and Fig. 1).

Table 3. Descriptive results of PAD emotion scale, behavioral questionnaires

Factor	Level	P		A		D	
		Mean	SD	Mean	SD	Mean	SD
Gender	Male	0.09	2.04	−2.26	3.80	0.30	3.22
	Female	−0.31	2.09	−2.33	3.66	0.15	2.70
Timbre Type	ACGN	−0.11	2.17	−2.27	3.77	0.36	3.02
	Broadcast	0.06	1.80	−2.31	3.69	0.08	2.91
News Type	Entertainment	−0.26	1.91	−2.59	3.74	0.21	2.58
	Epidemic	0.24	2.02	−2.24	3.71	0.22	3.12
	Technology	−0.05	2.02	−2.05	3.73	0.23	3.19
Factor	Level	Interest		Matching		Evaluation	
		Mean	SD	Mean	SD	Mean	SD
Gender	Male	3.34	1.05	3.30	1.20	6.19	2.08
	Female	3.41	1.08	3.15	1.32	6.14	2.30
Timbre Type	ACGN	3.47	1.05	3.22	1.20	6.29	1.99
	Broadcast	3.28	1.07	3.23	1.32	6.04	2.38
News Type	Entertainment	3.32	1.05	2.63	1.16	5.42	2.06
	Epidemic	3.70	1.04	4.03	0.90	7.34	1.80
	Technology	3.09	1.03	3.00	1.27	5.71	2.21

The PAD scale data show that most of the participants were more relaxed when they participated in this experiment, and the experimental task did not impose a greater cognitive load on the participants' subjective feelings.

Behavioral questionnaires show that the average degree of interest in each news item was 3.4, i.e., they were generally interested in the news program; the average degree of match between tone and news was 3.2, i.e., the tone and type of news were almost matched; and the average overall rating of the news was 6.1.

Due to the significant differences between individuals' skin conductance data, we focus on the mean, standard deviation, and maximum value of an individual's skin conductance data rather than discussing the population mean versus standard deviation, Table 4 shows the results.

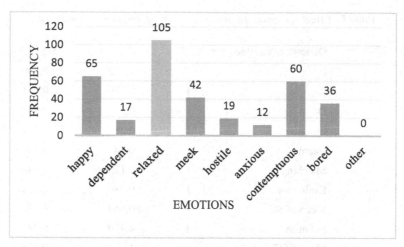

Fig. 1. PAD sentiment category histogram

Table 4. Descriptive results of skin conductance

Factor	Level	Mean of skin conductance		SD of skin conductance		Maximum of skin conductance	
		Mean	SD	Mean	SD	Mean	SD
Gender	Male	9.11	3.67	0.73	0.55	10.47	4.37
	Female	8.80	3.54	0.61	0.47	9.91	4.15
Timbre Type	ACGN	8.91	3.59	0.65	0.47	10.10	4.18
	Broadcast	9.00	3.63	0.70	0.56	10.28	4.35
News Type	Entertainment	8.98	3.65	0.73	0.56	10.35	4.42
	Epidemic	8.71	3.65	0.62	0.48	9.82	4.21
	Technology	9.19	3.61	0.66	0.51	10.41	4.18

Looking at the overall trend of the skin conductance data as each participant performed different tasks, the data showed a downward trend at the start of the task, indicating a trend towards a decrease in the level of emotional arousal. The trend in skin conductance is synchronized with the progress of the task.

Repeated measures analysis of variance (ANOVA) was performed to assess the significance of the effects of the three dependent variables, and the results are presented in Table 5.

The results of the ANOVA show that gender had a significant effect on the standard deviation of skin conductance ($F = 4.479$, P-value $= 0.035$), among which the standard deviation of male skin conductance ($M = 0.7321$, STD $= 0.55474$) was greater than that of female skin conductance ($M = 0.6425$, STD $= 0.50916$), indicating that male timbre had a greater effect on the fluctuation of emotional arousal level.

Table 5. Effects on emotions, interest, matching and skin conductance.

Source	Dependent variable	df	F	Sig
Gender	P	1	1.122	0.290
	A	1	0.019	0.891
	D	1	0.202	0.653
	Emotion	1	0.28	0.597
	Interest	1	0.34	0.560
	Matching	1	2.125	0.146
	Evaluation	1	0.086	0.769
	Mean of SC	1	0.664	0.416
	SD of SC	1	4.479	0.035*
	Max of SC	1	1.473	0.226
Timbre type	P	1	0.681	0.410
	A	1	0.007	0.935
	D	1	0.797	0.373
	Emotion	1	0.199	0.655
	Interest	1	2.967	0.086
	Matching	1	0	0.986
	Evaluation	1	1.372	0.242
	Mean of SC	1	0.039	0.844
	SD of SC	1	0.942	0.332
	Max of SC	1	0.151	0.698
News type	P	2	1.816	0.164
	A	2	0.621	0.538
	D	2	0.002	0.998
	Emotion	2	1.36	0.258
	Interest	2	10.181	<0.001*
	Matching	2	60.384	<0.001*
	Evaluation	2	31.888	<0.001*
	Mean of SC	2	0.509	0.601
	SD of SC	2	1.444	0.237
	Max of SC	2	0.657	0.519
Gender * TT	P	1	0.638	0.425
	A	1	0.725	0.395

(*continued*)

Table 5. (*continued*)

Source	Dependent variable	df	F	Sig
	D	1	0.282	0.596
	Emotion	1	0.16	0.690
	Interest	1	0.069	0.794
	Matching	1	2.774	0.097
	Evaluation	1	0.325	0.569
	Mean of SC	1	0.014	0.905
	SD of SC	1	0.003	0.957
	Max of SC	1	0.004	0.948
Gender * TT	P	2	0.01	0.990
	A	2	0.147	0.863
	D	2	0.126	0.882
	Emotion	2	0.622	0.538
	Interest	2	1.22	0.297
	Matching	2	20.636	<0.001*
	Evaluation	2	4.405	0.013*
	Mean of SC	2	0.226	0.798
	SD of SC	2	0.52	0.595
	Max of SC	2	0.211	0.810
TT * NT	P	2	2.115	0.122
	A	2	2.621	0.074
	D	2	0.209	0.812
	Emotion	2	2.516	0.082
	Interest	2	1.157	0.316
	Matching	2	8.858	<0.001*
	Evaluation	2	2.746	0.066
	Mean of SC	2	0.222	0.801
	SD of SC	2	0.996	0.370
	Max of SC	2	0.364	0.695

* Significance level < 0.05.

The timbre type had a significant effect on the level of interest (F = 2.967, P = 0.086), among which the ACGN timbre (M = 3.3258, STD = 1.05287) was greater than the broadcast timbre (M = 3.2768, STD = 1.06982), indicating that the participants' interest in the ACGN timbre was greater than that of the broadcast timbre.

Besides, the results of the ANOVA show that the type of news has a significant effect on the level of interest ($F = 10.181$, P-value < 0.001). Among them, epidemic news (M = 3.6975, STD = 1.03788) was greater than entertainment news (M = 3.3248, STD = 1.04905) and greater than technology news (mean M = 3.094, standard deviation STD = 1.02539), indicating that participants were most interested in epidemic news.

(a)

(b)

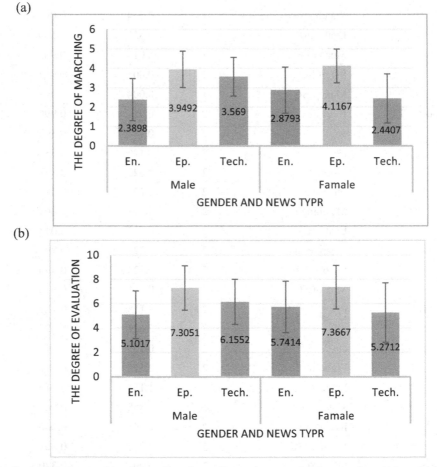

Fig. 2. (a) The interaction effect of gender and news type on the degree of marching. (b) The interaction effect of gender and news type on the degree of evaluation.

Moreover, there was a significant interaction effect between gender and news type on the degree of matching ($F = 20.636$, P-value < 0.001) and evaluation ($F = 4.405$, P-value < 0.013). The highest degree of matching was that the female voice broadcast epidemic news (M = 4.117, STD = 0.865), and the lowest degree of matching was that the male voice broadcast entertainment news (M = 2.389, STD = 1. 083); and the highest matching degree was that the female voice broadcast epidemic news (M = 5.102, STD = 1.962), and the lowest matching degree level was that the male voice broadcast entertainment news (M = 7.3667, STD = 1.794), indicating that the female voice is more suitable for broadcasting epidemic and entertainment news, while the male voice is more suitable for broadcasting technology news (Fig. 2).

Timbre and news type also have a significant interaction effect (F = 8.858, P-value < 0.001). The highest degree of matching was that between entertainment news and broadcast timbre (M = 4.1186, STD = 0.93005), and the lowest degree of matching was that between epidemic news and ACGN timbre (M = 2.4068, STD = 1.10045), indicating that women are more likely to match broadcast epidemic and technology news, which are more serious, while ACGN timbre is more likely to match broadcast entertainment news (Fig. 3).

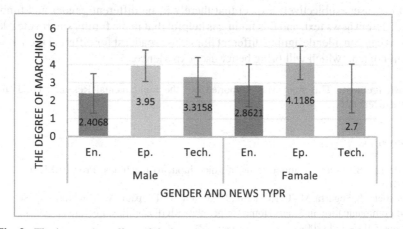

Fig. 3. The interaction effect of timbre type and news type on the degree of marching.

4 Conclusion

The experimental results show that gender has a significant effect on the standard deviation of skin conductance. The reason why the standard deviation of the male voice is larger than the standard deviation of the female voice is that the number of females in this experiment is larger than the number of males, and relevant studies have shown that when the gender of the male voice is used to broadcast news information content, the female group has a higher degree of liking than the male group, indicating that the male timbre has a greater effect on the fluctuation of emotional arousal level in this experiment where the female participants are the majority.

The timbre type has a significant effect on the participants' interest in the whole news, and the participants prefer the ACGN timbre to the broadcast timbre, which may be due to the experimental group consisting of young students who have a higher degree of acceptance of novelty. The ACGN timbre is more interesting than the broadcast type, which corresponds to the perception of traditional media broadcasting, so that young people have a stronger sense of subjective experience and higher interest.

The type of news had a significant impact on the level of interest, and the participants' interest in the type of news was ordered from high to low: epidemic news, entertainment news, and technology news. Since the selection time of epidemic news is close to the start time of the experiment, and the news is selected as local epidemic information in Beijing, this news is very timely, and the experimental participants are all college students, whose social activity status is closely related to the form of epidemic, so they are more interested in epidemic news among the three. Compared with entertainment news and technology news, technology news has too many technical terms and is too abstract and difficult to understand, so it is difficult to arouse interest and ranks last.

The whole experiment proves that timbre has an impact on users' emotions when interacting with smart devices. In the scenario of smart voice broadcasting studied in this article, users subjectively expect that there will be different gender and timbre to match different news text, and this finding is helpful that in the future, smart voice device designers can consider designing different timbre to broadcast for different scenarios and different content, which will bring better user experience.

Acknowledgement. This study was supported by "the Fundamental Research Funds for the Central Universities".

References

1. Martin, T.B.: Practical applications of voice input to machines. Proc. IEEE **64**, 487–501 (1976)
2. Ghorbel, M., Segarra, M.-T., Kerdreux, J., Keryell, R., Thepaut, A., Mokhtari, M.: Networking and communication in Smart Home for people with disabilities. Lecture Notes in Computer Science. 937–944 (2004)
3. Hildebrand, C., Efthymiou, F., Busquet, F., Hampton, W.H., Hoffman, D.L., Novak, T.P.: Voice analytics in business research: conceptual foundations, acoustic feature extraction, and applications. J. Bus. Res. **121**, 364–374 (2020)
4. Gocsál, Á.: Female listeners' personality attributions to male speakers: the role of acoustic parameters of speech. Pollack Periodica. **4**, 155–165 (2009)
5. Norman, D.: Emotion & design. Interactions **9**, 36–42 (2002)
6. Scherer, K.R.: Personality inference from voice quality: the loud voice of extroversion. Eur. J. Soc. Psychol. **8**, 467–487 (1978)
7. Borkowska, B., Pawlowski, B.: Female voice frequency in the context of dominance and attractiveness perception. Anim. Behav. **82**, 55–59 (2011)
8. Jeong, J., Shin, D.-H.: It's not what it speaks, but it's how it speaks: a study into smartphone voice-user interfaces (VUI). In: Human-Computer Interaction: Interaction Technologies, pp. 284–291 (2015)
9. Edison Research. The Infinite Dial 2020. https://www.edisonresearch.com/the-infinite-dial-2020
10. McHugh, S.: How podcasting is changing the audio storytelling genre. Radio J. Int. Stud. Broadcast Audio Media **14**, 65–82 (2016)
11. Pew Research Center. Audio and Podcasting Fact Sheet. https://www.journalism.org/fact-sheet/audio-and-podcasting
12. Mehrabian, A., Russell, J.A.: An Approach to Environmental Psychology. M.I.T. Press, Cambridge (1976)
13. Westie, F.R.: A technique for the measurement of race attitudes. Am. Sociol. Rev. **18**, 73 (1953)

Future-Focused Design

The HCI Technology's Future Signals: The Readiness Evaluation of HCI Technology for Product and Roadmap Design

Tikfan Chan[1] and Zhiyong Fu[2(✉)]

[1] Department of Information Art and Design, Tsinghua University, Beijing 100084, China
[2] Springer Heidelberg, Tiergartenstr. 17, 69121 Heidelberg, Germany
fuzhiyong@tsinghua.edu.cn

Abstract. This research study will collect information from experienced HCI designers and product managers in the electronic consumer product industry to study their way of receiving information, making predictions, and identifying the progress of HCI technology. We will analyse their participation experience, propose the sequence of technology signals' maturity, and develop practical tools to evaluate those signals. The framework could support the HCI designer and product manager in designing the product roadmap on the technology side; Further studies and case studies about these future signals that could benefit product roadmap design would be helpful.

Keywords: Human Computer Interaction (HCI) · Electronic Consumer Product · HCI Technology · Future Signal · Feasibility Study of Technology

1 Background

HCI designers and product managers in the technology industry are frequently required to navigate multiple HCI technologies to convert their design ideas into actual products. In addition, they need to create a competitive roadmap for a series of products. They make decisions about which HCI technology to use and when to deploy it.

Currently, their companies rely on their experience, sneak information from competitors in the market, or direct orders from high-level management with personal preference. Evaluation and speculation on the potential of emerging HCI technologies is left to the insight and intuition of a few people [1]. Once it is a success, their knowledge is not well documented, and their cases may not be repeatable next time. It limits the application of emerging HCI technology to innovative design ideas. Once a failure occurs, they can change their strategy to become more conservative and limit innovation. Applying the latest technology to promote innovation could present risks in project management [2]. It is not an easy decision to make in the business world.

To assist them in selecting the right HCI technology for the design or to monitor emerging HCI technologies, this research study will collect information from experienced HCI designers and product managers to study their way of receiving information,

P.-L. P. Rau (Ed.): HCII 2023, LNCS 14023, pp. 169–179, 2023.
https://doi.org/10.1007/978-3-031-35939-2_13

making predictions, and identifying the progress of HCI technology. It covered the following questions: How do they collect emerging HCI technology signals? How do they use or prioritise these signals? How do they justify the implementation of HCI technology in their design?

We will conduct a literature review and questionnaire to collect information from the frontline HCI participants in the electronic consumer product industry to summarise their experience receiving the new technology signals, identifying the maturity and risk of the latest technology, how they decide to deploy it into the current design, and how they design the future product roadmap.

As expected from this research, we will summarise and conclude the information from the frontline HCI participants. We will analyse their participation experience, prioritise the sequence of maturity of technology signals, and develop practical tools to evaluate these signals. We expect that the framework could support HCI designers and product managers in designing the product roadmap on the technology side. In addition, it should be capable of developing technology for future foresight.

2 Literature Review

2.1 Diffusion of Innovations Theory

In the 1960s, social psychology scholar Everett Rogers wrote "Diffusion of Innovations [3]" to explain how innovations or technological advances spread over time within a society. The adoption process is typically illustrated as a classical normal distribution. Generally speaking, there are five types of adopters in society: innovators, early adopters, early majority, late majority, and laggards. An innovator is eager to take on the latest technology and does not require much persuasion to try the new technology. Those who are early adopters, also known as opinion leaders, do not require much convincing to make them change their minds. To adopt an innovation, an early majority of the population needs to demonstrate that it is effective in the long term. As a result of the late majority, an innovation is adopted after it has already been tried by the majority and is viewed sceptically. As a group, laggards are conservative and sceptical of change and require statistics, fear appeals, or pressure to accept any upcoming technology. Different strategies are used to appeal to other groups of adopters. The article illustrates a broad picture of the diffusion process concerning the adoption and acceptance of innovative technology by societies worldwide. Despite this, no specific signals indicate that a technology is ready, making it difficult for designers to assess its readiness.

2.2 Technology Readiness Level (TRL)

In the 1970s, the National Aeronautics and Space Administration (NASA) in the United States developed the concept of "Technology Readiness Levels" (TRLs), which is an assessment scale to evaluate and communicate the current development signals of new technology development without disciplinary barriers. The TRL scale was further detailed in definitions and examples of each level in 1995. Later, TRLs were adopted by the U.S. Congress' General Accountability Office (GAO), the U.S. Department of Defense (DOD), and numerous other organizations [4] (Table 1).

Table 1: Technology readiness level (NASA) [1]

	TRL	
System Test, Launch & Operations	TRL 9	Actual system "flight proven" through successful mission operations
System/Subsystem Development	TRL 8	Actual system completed and "flight qualified" through test and demonstration (Ground or Flight)
	TRL 7	System prototype demonstration in a space environment
Technology Demonstration	TRL 6	System/subsystem model or prototype demonstration in a relevant environment (Ground or Space)
Technology Development	TRL 5	Component and/or breadboard validation in relevant environment
	TRL 4	Component and/or breadboard validation in laboratory environment
Research to Prove Feasibility	TRL 3	Analytical and experimental critical function and/or characteristic proof-of-concept
Basic Technology Research	TRL 2	Technology concept and/or application formulated
	TRL 1	Basic principles observed and reported

Nevertheless, NASA's TRL technology evolution helps assess the status of space technology. As a result of their complexity, these projects may be broken down into several subsystems, parts, and subsystems. The level of concern and criteria may differ between NASA's space technology projects and general HCI technology in commercial products. A generalization and suitability perspective suggests that the TRL approach may not be suitable for developing and designing HCI technologies. Alison and Steven conducted studies and interviews to identify 15 challenges from practitioners' perspectives related to TRL [5]. Connectivity, interface, visualization, and product road mapping are highly associated with the design of HCI technology applications. The evolution of TRL technology is technology-centric and not user-centric [6].

2.3 Chris Harrison's S-Curve of New HCI Technology

Chris Harrison conducted a comparison of Rogers' technology lifecycle S-curve [3] with Utterback's dynamic model of process and product innovation [7] during the design and implementation of the new HCI technologies to determine changes in market size and rate of innovation [8]. Myers' work [9] also included a collection of timelines of various HCI subjects illustrating how research can be transformed into commercial applications. There has been a significant separation in time, and Bill Buxton said that "any technology that is going to have a significant impact in the next ten years is at least ten years old." This long period of incubation is what Buxton describes as a "Long Nose of Innovation [10]".

Through their work, we were able to gain a better understanding of the life cycle of the upcoming HCI technology, including Glint (ideation), Embryonic (research development), Growth (industrial development and application), Maturity (well-accepted by the market), and Ageing. There are specific future signals that designers and engineers need to identify to determine the current status and future trends of those upcoming HCI technologies.

2.4 Gartner Hype Cycle

Gartner Group started releasing Gartner's Hype Cycle in 2009. It depicts a typical pattern for each upcoming technology or innovation in a specific domain. Each year, Gartner creates around 90 Hype Cycles to illustrate an overview of the maturity, adoption, application, and disuse of technologies in the various domains [11].

Although Gartner's Hype Cycle presented technologies' life cycles and predicted emerging technologies, it only reflected general expectations within a specific domain rather than the feasibility of technologies. Some articles argue about applying Gartner's Hype Cycle to technology planning and prioritisation [12].

HCI designers and product managers need practical tools to classify the readiness of emerging HCI technology signals on their tables. They need the most effective solution to translate their design idea into an actual design or to illustrate a competitive roadmap for product series. A questionnaire survey was conducted in January 2023 to better understand how industry participants predict future HCI technologies.

3 Methods

3.1 Overview

Based on the literature review, there has not been a systematic way to present the current development signals of HCI technology. In January 2023, we conducted an online questionnaire survey. There were 66 industry participants who shared their understanding and experience in predicting the upcoming HCI technology. We also suggested a set of future signals to indicate the progress in the development of the next technology in HCI. Participants were asked to arrange these future signals sequentially to present the development process.

3.2 Research Aims, Questions, and Hypotheses

The research is based on the assumption that professionals with over ten years of industry experience, with their understanding of HCI technology developments, would benefit our work. A wide variety of possible technology solutions are available in the supply chain. Participants and their companies rationally choose HCI technology.

During the survey and interview, we focused primarily on the following areas:

- What is your experience in the industry?
- How have you been involved with product development and companies in the past?
- Is there any information channel that informs them of the status of technology development so that you can predict the future?
- What signals were received from these channels?
- In addition, what is the sequential order in which these signals relate to technology readiness?
- As a result of their experience, how accurate are these predictions about your company and yourself?

3.3 The Participants in the Survey

The survey is designed in the form of a questionnaire that invites industry professionals to complete it online. The questionnaire with the same ten questions in content is available in three different languages, including simplified Chinese, traditional Chinese, and English, for participants from different locations. After they were available online for one week, 74 samples were submitted. We removed eight samples that completed the questionnaire in less than 100 s to ensure quality. The simplified Chinese questionnaire was completed by 56 participants, while another 10 participants completed the traditional Chinese or English version. We grouped all the samples for the following analysis.

Based on the survey results, participants have been participating in those projects for an average of 10.1 years (see Fig. 1).

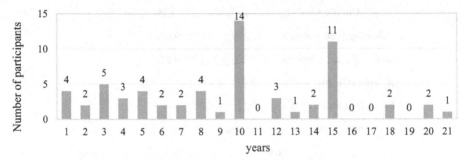

Fig. 1. The number of years that the survey participants have been involved in the industry. (n = 66)

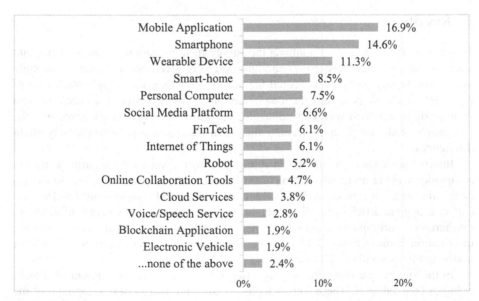

Fig. 2. Experience with technology projects of survey participants in the past. (Multi-select answer options provided, n = 213)

Survey participants have already participated in over 14 types of HCI technology-related projects in the industry, of which 16.9% are mobile applications (see Fig. 2).

In addition, they have performed more than ten different roles in these projects, 19.7% of them playing the role of detailed design (see Fig. 3).

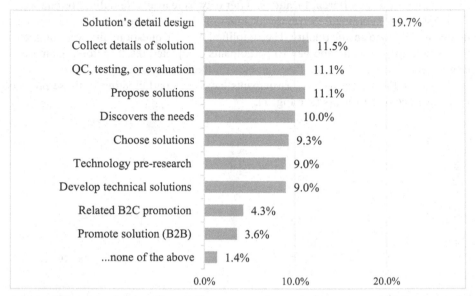

Fig. 3. Survey participants' responsibilities in these past technology projects. (Provided multi select answer options, n = 279)

4 Results

To describe the accuracy level among the survey respondents, we used a seven-point Likert scale. One point represents strongly disagree; seven points represent strongly agree. The survey participants scored the accuracy of their company's prediction of future HCI technology development at 4.74 points. It is somewhat more accurate than their prediction, which was 4.65 points. Survey participants generally agree that the company's prediction is more accurate than their own, although there are only slight differences.

Internet searches are a significant source of information for both participants and companies seeking more information (22.0% and 21.5%, respectively). Due to a company's resources, it is more likely to work with professional consultations (20.1%) and collect academic articles (19.6%) to obtain more reliable and convincing information. Furthermore, participants could rely on their social networks in the industry to receive information from insiders (13.4%). They could also access paid subscriptions (7.8%) or traditional news media (9.1%) (see Fig. 4).

In the survey questionnaire, we suggested future signals from different HCI technologies [see Table 2]. These signals represent different stages of development of the

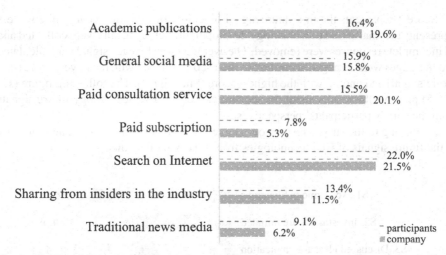

Fig. 4. The list of channels used by survey participants and their companies, for receiving the latest information about HCI technology and supporting their decision making. (Multi-select options provided, participant: n = 232, company: n = 209)

upcoming HCI technology. They are randomly listed in the survey. Survey participants are invited to reorganise these signals to reflect their understanding of HCI technology in the progress from early ideation to commercialisation on the market.

Table 2. Future signals of HCI technology suggested

	Name of future signals	Description of future signals
S1	Academic publications	Published academic articles explain or illustrate how it works;
S2	Investments are initiated	Investments are initiated, businesses invest in R&D resources;
S3	Discussed ideas of application	Ideas for applications are discussed verbally or in brainstorming;
S4	Registration of patents	Patents show different ways to achieve the same goal;
S5	Applicable to other types of product	It indicates the possibility of commercialising;
S6	Workable prototypes demonstrate	A workable prototype shows the technical solution;
S7	Applied to similar products	Even though it has limitations, similar products use it;
S8	The technology is widely used	There is widespread use of technology on commercial markets;

Score 1 represents the first future signal of technology development, while score 8 represents the final signal of technology development. Survey results were collected and all incomplete responses were removed. The average score for each signal was calculated and the stages were arranged according to their score, starting with the lowest score (first future signal) and ending with the highest score (final signal). The following figure (see Fig. 5) presents the results about the sequential order of HCI technology future signals from the survey participants' perspectives.

According to the survey results, our suggestions are similar to the sequential order of the future signals of HCI technologies from survey participants.

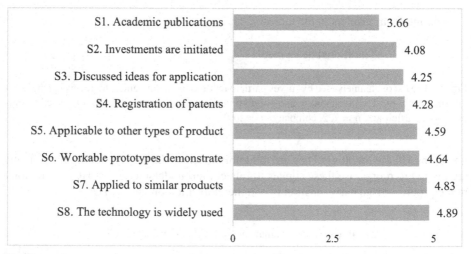

Fig. 5. Suggested ranking order of the future signals of HCI technology by survey participants. (n = 58)

5   Discussion

5.1   The HCI Technology's Future Signals

As we have discussed, HCI designers and product managers will investigate various technologies to determine which is most suitable for their latest design. Designers can use these future signals as a reference point to make decisions regarding the feasibility of the design and the risk associated with the project (see Fig. 6).

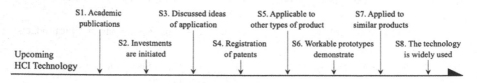

Fig. 6. The future signals of HCI technology.

5.2 The HCI Technology's Future Signals with the Company's Capability

From an internal perspective, companies may have different resources, capabilities, and cultures to take risks in their product design. Externally, a robust competitive market would lead these companies to accept more risks to choose cutting-edge technology. Therefore, they collectively form a range that covers future technology signals so that we can select the appropriate technologies. The following figure (see Fig. 7) illustrates various examples of technology with different signals and demonstrates a specific range of future signals the company can take. Visually presented the status of the HCI technology and the acceptance range of the company. Communication, management, and decision-making in product development could be enhanced.

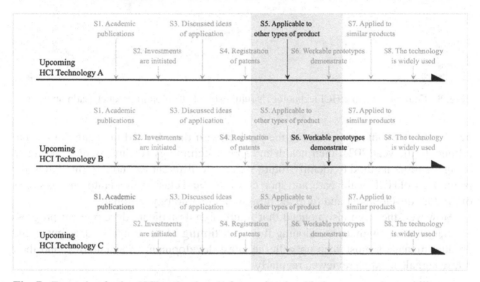

Fig. 7. Example of using HCI technology's future signals with the company's capability range

5.3 The HCI Technology's Future Signals in Product Roadmap

Additionally, designers and product managers are required to design upcoming products and create a product roadmap and portfolio. They could develop and allocate various new HCI technologies to different generations of products based on the future signal of those HCI technologies. It would be a visionary product roadmap to support the development of future designs. In addition to establishing a clear goal for the development team, the upcoming HCI technologies would be developed with a clear objective (Fig. 8).

5.4 Case Study of Product Roadmap Design

Since 2019, one of the technology companies in China, as a newcomer to the related health and sports technology industry. They seek a way to manage their research and

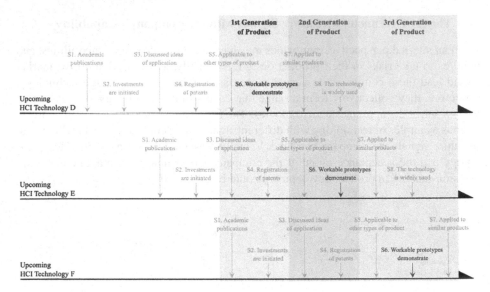

Fig. 8. Example of using HCI technology's future signals to support product roadmap design

development resources and design the product with their limited biotechnology capabilities. In the year 2021, their health and sports technology roadmap will be designed using a similar method to identify future signals of different technology (including the technology of HCI, health care, and sport coaching) and classify them into various stages of product development and form the design of a technology roadmap.

However, the team also noticed that future signals indicate development progress in relative terms without mentioning the exact timing of the progress. Designers and product managers must keep up with the latest development of technology, and their future signals must be reviewed regularly.

6   Future Work

As the samples are chosen from personal networks in the industry, the distribution may not be normal for all industries related to HCI technology. Some results may not show significant variations (i.e., the difference between S3 and S4 is only around 0.03) due to the small number of samples. Large-scale industry surveys could be conducted to increase the credibility of the findings. In addition to expanding the sample size, statistical data on future signal activities could be collected. It could be applied to studying certain phases of the development of HCI technologies.

We suggested using future signals of HCI technology to support product roadmap design; however, how these future signals could benefit product roadmap design remains unclear; more case studies would be helpful.

Acknowledgements. The authors would like to thank all survey participants and Tsinghua University. This study was supported by Graduate Education Innovation Grants, Tsinghua University.

References

1. Kim, H.-C.: Acceptability engineering_the study of user acceptance of innovative technologies. J. Appl. Res. Technol. **13**, 230–237 (2015)
2. Shenhar, A.J., Dvir, D.: Reinventing Project Management: The Diamond Approach to Successful Growth and Innovation. Harvard Business Press, New York City (2007)
3. Rogers, E.M.: Diffusion of Innovations, 3rd edn. Free Press, New York City (1983)
4. Mankins, J.C.: Technology readiness assessments: a retrospective. Acta Astronaut **65**(9–10), 1216–1223 (2009). (in English). https://doi.org/10.1016/j.actaastro.2009.03.058
5. Olechowski, A.L., Eppinger, S.D.: Technology readiness levels: shortcomings and improvement opportunities. Syst. Eng. **23**, 395–408 (2020). https://doi.org/10.1002/sys.21533
6. Salazar, G., Russi-Vigoya, M.N.: Technology readiness level as the foundation of human readiness level. Ergon. Des. **29**(4), 25–29 (2021). (in English). https://doi.org/10.1177/106 48046211020527
7. Utterback, J.M., Abernathy, W.J.: A dynamic model of process and product innovation. Omega-Int. J. Manag. Sci. **3**, 639–656 (1975)
8. Harrison, C.: The HCI innovator's dilemma. Interactions, 27–33 (2018)
9. Myers, B.A.: A brief history of human-computer interaction technology. Interactions, 44–54 (1998)
10. Buxton, B.: The long nose of innovation. Bus. Week (2008)
11. Inc, G.: Hype Cycle | Information Technology Gartner Glossary. https://www.gartner.com/en/information-technology/glossary/hype-cycle
12. Linden, A., Fenn, J.: Understanding Gartner's Hype Cycles (2003). http://www.ask-force.org/web/Discourse/Linden-HypeCycle-2003.pdf

Haptic Cognition Model with Material Experience: Case Study of the Design Innovation

I-Ying Chiang[1]($\boxtimes$) (iD), Po-Hsien Lin[2] (iD), and Rungtai Lin[2] (iD)

[1] Department of Arts and Design, College of Arts, National Tsing Hua University, Hsinchu 300044, Taiwan
iychiang@mx.nthu.edu.tw
[2] Graduate School of Creative Industry Design, College of Design, National Taiwan University of Arts, New Taipei 220307, Taiwan
{t0131,rtlin}@mail.ntua.edu.tw

Abstract. Humans have been pushed to change their communication interfaces and dissemination methods during this post-pandemic era. People are increasingly relying on digital-technology devices and reducing their various perceptions of tangible material experiences synchronously. However, this study aims to explore the receive, comprehension, expressions, and application of tactile perception derived from material experiences. The authors propose three sections of the research procedures for developing the haptic cognition model (HCM) by exploring material experience (MX) and haptic semantics (HS). Moreover, there are five stages during the HCM application procedures: (1) Understanding the material via the material experience, (2) Extracting haptic semantics derive from the material understanding, (3) Manifesting MX-to-HS design, (4) Evaluating by experts, (5) Reflecting by designers. Based on the theoretical foundation, this study invites young designers to participate in the empirical design project with the haptic topic. Eventually, this research clarifies how the material experience and haptic semantics can be applied to a cognition model and which relevant components are needed for a haptic cognition model.

Keywords: Haptic Cognition Model (HCM) · Material Experience (MX) · Haptic Semantics (HS) · Process Innovation · Product Innovation

1 Introduction

At the beginning of the 21st century, people just declared the coming of a global aesthetic economy and the return to a haptic era; the product designers also had been encouraged to focus on exploring the influences of physical perceptions and sense of touch [1, 2]. However, since 2019, people have been pushed to change their interactional methods and increasingly rely on digital devices via virtual interfaces due to the impact of epidemic prevention and the quarantine limitation. Therefore, humans are reducing their various perceptions of tangible material experiences synchronously. Meanwhile, the new concerns about how people will keep receiving or shifting their corporeal feelings and tactile

© The Author(s), under exclusive license to Springer Nature Switzerland AG 2023
P.-L. P. Rau (Ed.): HCII 2023, LNCS 14023, pp. 180–193, 2023.
https://doi.org/10.1007/978-3-031-35939-2_14

awareness expression have roused the authors' research interests. This observation also reveals the related frontier of haptic cognition lacks an innovative exploration during this post-pandemic era.

The aesthetic experience derived from sensory perception joined the precious channels of body feeling and self-consciousness to the cognitive approach [1]. Tangible materials are essential mediums of bodily sensations. People interact with the materials by directly touching them, and the physical action of "touching" could transform and accomplish a satisfying "Qualia" [1]. Furthermore, materials also carry spiritual significance or extended associations. By means of semantics, the denotation and connotation extended from the somatic sensations, and perceptive awareness in material experiences help people understand and express their tactile feelings as well as haptic imageries more clearly [1, 3]. Therefore, designers should thoroughly realize the characteristics of material experience and the capabilities of haptic cognitions to advance the various connections between materials and humans.

This research aims to clarify and realize how the material experience (MX) and haptic semantics (HS) can be applied to a cognition model and which relevant components are needed for a haptic cognition model (HCM). Figure 1 shows the research processes of three sections for developing the HCM by exploring material experience and haptic semantics.

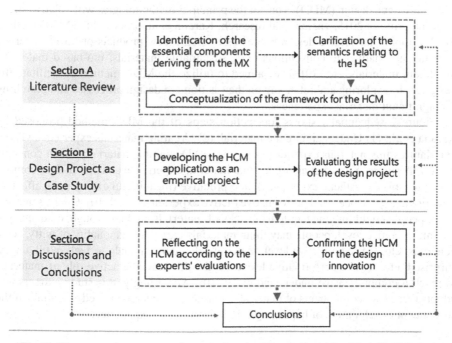

Fig. 1. The research processes of developing the "Haptic Cognition Model" (HCM).

First, in section A, based on the literature retrospections, the authors implement the reviews of three categories as follows: (1) Identification of the essential components deriving from the material experience, (2) Clarification of the semantics relating to the haptic expression with material experience, (3) Conceptualization of the framework for a haptic cognition model. Furthermore, in Section B, this research executes a craft design project to explore the application possibilities of the HCM and examines the case study results. Finally, in Section C, this study discusses and summarizes the conclusions as well as proposes a confirmed and feasible HCM for the designer in process and product innovation.

2 Literature Review

2.1 Material Experience and Innovative Design

Since the 1980s, Ezio Manzini has attempted to clarify the complexities between materials and design. In *"The Material of Invention,"* he creates and links essential communication between researchers, designers, and engineers [4]. To reinforce the innovation of product design and its process, scholars and designers have constantly discussed and developed "Material Experience" strategies for decades [5, 6]. Although the functional need is always the first concern of the product industry in choosing material for commercial success, some researchers believe the material should go beyond its practical assessment and extract meaningful user experiences [5, 7, 8]. Among these explorations, the material-driven design (MDD) is one of the principal methodologies with relative structural integrity. In 2015, via material research, Karana et al. proposed the MDD method for developing innovative design processes to create new products or novel materials as better alternatives to conventions (e.g., sustainable materials, bio-based materials, intelligent materials, etc.) [9]. They aimed to utilize the MDD method to facilitate the designers in exploring and reflecting on their actions in design processes and searching for significant material experiences.

Figure 2 sequentially shows four action steps of the MDD method proposed by Karana et al.: (1) Understanding the material, (2) Creating materials experience vision, (3) Manifesting materials experience patterns, (4) Designing material/product concepts [9]. Furthermore, Karana et al. argued that material experience consists of four components: sensorial (aesthetic experience), interpretative (meaningful experience), affective (emotional experience), and performative (active experience) [7, 9, 10]. On the sensorial level, people could find the tactile feedbacks of materials are hard, rough, cold, etc. On the interpretative level, people may think materials carry the personality of witty, sexy, generous, etc. On the affective level, materials also cause people to feel joyful, angry, surprised, etc. On the performative level, we should know the active role of materials to reach a comprehensive understanding [9, 10]. Accordingly, this study extracts and adopts these four components of material experience as interconnected essentials of the subsequent development of haptic cognition via material experience.

2.2 Haptic Semantics

People percept the external world by relying on the bodily senses and express their feeling or thoughts via verbal language or lexical description. Osgood et al. proposed the semantic analysis study in the early 1950s and published *"The Measurement of Meaning"* in

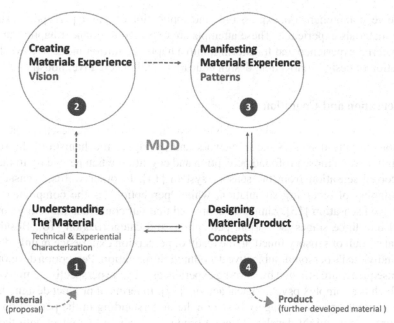

Fig. 2. Four stages of Material Driven Design (MDD) method [9]. (re-illustrated in accordance with the map proposed by Karana et al., 2015)

1957 [11]. The semantic analysis aims to reinforce the comprehensive understanding of the tendencies or purposes derived from certain concepts and ideas. It is usually used to assess qualitative information or documentation via a specific evaluation scale, allowing researchers to obtain significant meaning through analysis, discussion, and inference. Designers also employ the method of product semantics to explore the artificial objects related to the users' cognitive and social contexts. They treat the verbal expression or lexical description of the sensation and awareness derived from the design object as important messages. According to this, they provide further suggestions or active interventions during the design innovation process [12]. Furthermore, this study advocates the semantics approach to facilitate designers' understanding and reinterpreting materials via the material experience.

Language empowers humans to create and disseminate significance. The contextual description shows our realization of the living world and is the cultural evolution approach. As Lakoff & Wehling addressed, meanings carried or stashed in the words and sentences bear much more than the eyes (sight) can catch [13]. Syntax guides the canons of how words can be combined into sentences; nevertheless, semantics indicates what they mean. Denotation and connotation compose the meanings of words. Denotation is a word's precise, literal meaning, the same as the dictionary definition, whereas connotation is the emotional association extending from a word [14]. For example, "hot" might be used to express the feeling of "high temperature" and also could convey the meaning of "sexually attractive."

Diverse materials with various texture characteristics may physically cause unique corporal sensations and spiritually convey their significant meaning. This study explores the receive, comprehension, expressions, and application of haptic perception extracted via the materials experience. These attempts are expected to connect haptic semantics with material experience and transform it into a haptic cognition model (HCM) for the application of design innovation, design education, and the creative industry.

2.3 Sensation and Cognition

People generate sensations when receiving external stimuli. The research on human sensations usually discusses the framework and its trigger mechanism of the sensory system. It drives a more profound perception and cognition when people try to interpret the received sensation from the sensory system [14]. In other words, "sensation" is the beginning of receiving stimulation, while "perception" is the comprehension of the received sensation [15]. Zimbardo addressed that our conscious trajectory could be divided into three stages: sensation, perception, and categorization [16]. Besides the physical stimuli of sensory function, the result of perception experience mainly depends on the individual's personal, subjective decoding/interpretation. Perception development and consequence are affected by learning experiences, diverse perspectives, motivations, etc., which is a complex psychological activity [17]. In terms of product design, the user will generate the product imagery based on the understanding in the perception stage. Therefore, people might develop different product imageries in contact with the same product via diverse receiving channels.

This study aims to explore the sense of touch, which refers to the tactile impression of receiving pressure when the skin surface touches or sustains something, also called the "sense of pressure" [17]. For humans, the haptic feeling is the first and most direct channel to help people receive the external environment [18]. The sense of touch is the advanced herald among all senses, treating the most complicated mechanism but with the least apprehended [19, 20]. There are three ways to perceptions of touch: cutaneous sense (pressure, vibration, temperature), kinesthesis (movement), and proprioception (location) [21]. For most people, touch mainly refers to the feeling derived from pressure, vibration, and temperature of cutaneous sense via external stimuli through receptors on the skin's surface [22]. Regarding the interaction between the individual and the object, the purpose of touch could be divided into two categories: active touch and passive touch [23]. Based on the same stimuli, touch with active intending is more sensitive and capable of recognizing external objects than passive touch [24]. The ability of cognition aids people to identify, classify, remember, sequence, and learn, then become the concepts. People can identify the touched object and explore its attributes via the tactile sensation of hands. Namely, according to the assistance of haptic cognition, people percept the external world and present the appropriate behaviors [3]. Therefore, the researchers believe haptic cognition crucially influences human behaviors and judgments [25, 26].

Since the 1980s, scholars have discussed that user engagement and experiential sensation will synchronously occur when people interact with objects directly [27–30]. Norman roused the concern of user-centered design; based on cognitive psychology, he proposed the advanced concept related to user experience (UX) in 2004. As he suggested in the book *"Emotional Design,"* three levels of emotional processing compose the design procedure: visceral level, behavioral level, and reflective level [31]. Besides the outer perception of aesthetic elements, the concerns about the semantic cognition and inner spiritual of the user's emotional effect influence the process and quality of product design. This advocacy has become mainstream and impacts contemporary product design. Norman has pointed out that each product will generate three types of psychological imagery to construct the cognition and dissemination models: the Designer's Conceptual Model, the User's Mental Model, and the System Image. The designer model emerges as the designer's vision of the product during creation. The user model reveals the user's cognition of how a product or equipment should be used or operated. The system image transits the product impression, which conveys the information and appearance via the product manual [31–33]. Usually, the designer assumes the designer's model will match the user's model, but the user's understanding does not always perfectly meet the designer's expectations [33, 34]. Based on the communication theory and Norman's emotional design, Lin et al. integrated and extended the product cognition and dissemination models, as shown in Fig. 3 [31–34].

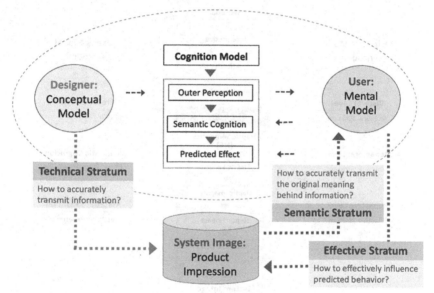

Fig. 3. Cognition and Dissemination Models of Product Design [31–34]. (re-illustrated for this study)

3 Materials and Methods

3.1 Research Framework

Based on the previous studies [7, 9, 10, 31–35], this study proposes a Haptic Cognition Model (HCM) research framework, as shown in Fig. 4. Two different models will recure interactively during the communication process between the designer's concept and the user's cognition. Furthermore, this framework illustrates the essential components from material experience (MX) to product design via haptic semantics (HS). Material experience comprises four parts: sensorial, interpretative, affective, and performative. During the encoding process, the designer's conceptual model goes through three levels: visceral (technical stratum), behavioral (semantic stratum), and reflective (effective stratum). Rather than directly relying on the visual form, the designer describes and translates the material experience via haptic semantics during the process of "MX-to-HS design." According to the haptic descriptions, which correspond to four parts: haptic feeling, imagery, impact, and action, the designer creates the haptic design product. During the decoding process, the user's mental model also goes through three stages: material sensation (aesthetic experience), semantic cognition (meaningful experience), and predicted effect (emotional, active experience). However, applying haptic semantics has changed the design path and cognition model.

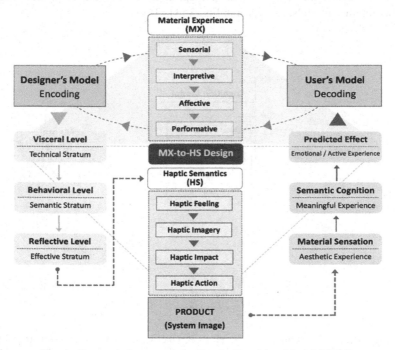

Fig. 4. Research framework for Haptic Cognition Model (HCM).

3.2 Stimuli and Empirical Design

Based on the Haptic Cognition Model (HCM) research framework, this study demonstrates an empirical design project in which exploring and applying haptic semantics derived from material experience is the primary intention. There are 6 kinds of materials (wood, cement, wool, resin, glass, and ceramic) were chosen as the original stimuli by 10 designers. Then, this empirical design project developed 10 haptic topics with 30 haptic objects (Fig. 5), which generate from the original stimuli materials. This study chooses the cup sleeve as the particular design item to focus on the haptic discussion according to the hand's touch. Furthermore, these 30 annular objects imitating cup sleeves are the advanced stimuli for experts' evaluations.

3.3 Participants and Procedures

There are 10 designers, 1 project organizer, and 3 consultants participating in this design project on the particular topic. The designers are third-year students from the Department of Arts and Design in the University with diverse craft creation and product design experiences who designed the cup sleeves via the haptic cognition approach with the material experience. The organizer has been a skilled crafter and design educator for years, organizing and directing the HCM application procedures. The consultants are the senior experts in craft creation, design education, and cognition psychology, who supervise this experimental project and evaluate the design results.

There are five stages during the HCM application procedures: (1) Understanding the material via the material experience (MX), (2) Extracting haptic semantics (HS) derive from the material understanding, (3) Manifesting MX-to-HS design, (4) Evaluating by experts, (5) Reflecting by designers. First, in the material experience (MX) stage, the project organizer indicates the young designers to choose one interested material as their initial stimuli. Through hand touch, the designers contact the raw material and also perceive and establish personal material understanding respectively. Second, in the stage of extracting haptic semantics (HS), the instructor guides the designers to express their tactile feelings by describing and writing down the haptic adjectives in four parts: sensorial, interpretative, affective, and performative. Third, in the empirical design stage, the designers try to interpret, transform, and design a product corresponding to the HS derived from the MX stage. Fourth, three experts inspect and evaluate the haptic products according to the HS targets each designer extracted. Finally, the designer executes the reflection on the MX-to-HS design, referring to the experts' evaluation.

3.4 Research Instrument

This study proposed an inspection form as the research instrument that guides and checks the MX-to-HS design procedures, as shown in Table 1. The designer applies and notes the haptic semantics of four parts: sensorial, interpretive, affective, and performative keywords that connect to the description of MX in outer perception, extensional meaning, inner emotion, and associate scenario. Besides, this form also integrates and records the experts' evaluation results and the designer's reflections.

Table 1. The inspection form exemplifies the MX-to-HS design procedures via the HCM.

Material	RP Resin	Participant	Designer 08
Material Experience (MX) to Haptic Semantics (HS)			
Sensorial	Outer Perception	Haptic Feeling	Brittle, Crispy
Interpretive	Extensional Meaning	Haptic Imagery	Witty, Clever
Affective	Inner Emotion	Haptic Impact	Joyful, Amusing
Performative	Associate Scenario	Haptic Action	Fiddle, Fondle
Haptic Keywords	**Brittle / Witty / Joyful / Fiddle**		
Design Element	Lamina	**Technique / Skill**	3D Printing
Haptic Control (1–5: weak / low – strong / high)			
Control Factor	**I** (reduced)	**II** (medium)	**III** (enhanced)
Layers Density	1	3	5
Wave Curvature	2	3	4
Texture / Shape			
Product Outcome			
Dimension (L x W x H)	90 x 90 x 36 mm	90 x 90 x 36 mm	90 x 90 x 36 mm
Product Code	P08-1	P08-2	P08-3
Product Evaluation (Expert) (1–5: weak / low – strong / high)			
Sensorial (Brittle)	3.33	4.67*	3.67
Interpretive (Witty)	3.00	4.00*	3.33
Affective (Joyful)	3.00	4.67*	3.67
Performative (Fiddle)	3.33	4.67*	3.33
Overall Mean	3.17	**4.50***	3.50
Reflection (Designer / Creator)			

a. The thickness of each sheet could rearrange in changing dimensions in order to create various layers and gaps vividly for generating a crispy or brittle feeling of touch.

b. The thickness limitation of 3D printing technology should be conquered or combined with the handcraft to fulfill the thinning quality for a friable tactile need.

c. The highness of the cup sleeve could be extended to fit the size of the adult's palm.

* The best result recognized by experts' evaluation matches the designing semantics.

4   Results and Discussions

4.1   The Application of HCM

Applying the haptic cognition model (HCM), 10 designers developed 10 haptic topics generated from the 6 stimuli materials (wood, cement, wool, resin, glass, and ceramic), respectively. Each designer completes 3 haptic products (a series of cup sleeves) according to each haptic topic. These topics are mainly related to the sensorial semantics (haptic feeling) derived from outer perception when experiencing a specific material. This empirical design project has developed ten topics: angular, gravelly, coarse, fluffy, puffy, bumpy, smooth, brittle, ample, and gentle, as shown in Fig. 5.

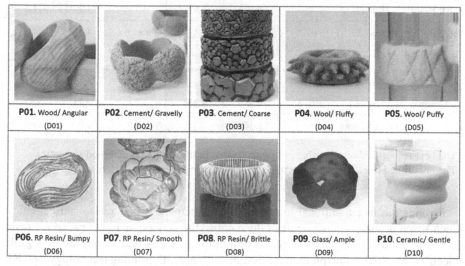

Fig. 5. Project outcome of HCM application on Cup Sleeve Design (P01 ~ P10).

Besides the sensorial semantics of haptic feeling, interpretive semantics of haptic imagery, affective semantics of haptic impact, and performative semantics of haptic action co-compose the four essential parts of haptic keywords that orient the design execution. After the experts' in-person inspection, one product was chosen from each haptic topic as the best-recognized result by the experts' evaluation that best matches its designed semantics, as shown in Table 2. According to the overall mean of the experts' evaluations, the sensorial result of 4.30 shows that the outer perception is the best part of haptic feeling expression by designers. Secondly, the affective result of 4.07 shows that inner emotion is vital to the haptic impact on designers. As well as, the performative result of 3.97 associated with the scenario and haptic action is the challenging part for designers. However, the interpretive presentation of 3.83 related to the extensional meaning and haptic imagery is the most difficult part of defining and transforming by designers. Although some designers chose the same material as the stimulus, they respectively developed different haptic topics derived from personal material experience.

Table 2. Evaluation results of the HCM design project (P01 ~ P10).

Material	Haptic Topic	Best Recognized Product	Sensorial*	Interpretive	Affective	Performative	Overall Mean
Wood	Angular	P01-2	4.00	3.67	4.00	4.67*	4.08
Cement	Gravelly	P02-3	5.00*	4.00	4.00	4.33	4.33
Cement	Coarse	P03-2	4.33*	3.67	4.00	3.33	3.83
Wool	Fluffy	P04-2	4.00	3.67	4.00	4.33*	4.00
Wool	Puffy	P05-3	3.67	3.33	4.33*	4.33*	3.92
RP Resin*	Bumpy	P06-3	4.67*	4.67*	4.33	4.00	**4.42***
RP Resin*	Smooth	P07-2	4.67*	4.00	4.67*	4.33	**4.42***
RP Resin*	Brittle	P08-2	4.67*	4.00	4.67*	4.67*	**4.50***
Glass	Ample	P09-3	3.67*	3.00	3.33	3.33	3.33
Ceramic	Gentle	P10-3	4.33*	4.33*	3.33	2.33	3.58
Overall Mean			4.30*	3.83	4.07	3.97	4.04

* The best-recognized result evaluates by experts that best matches its designed semantics.
_ The underlined marks the worst-recognized result among the experts' evaluations.

Besides the five traditional materials (wood, cement, wool, glass, and ceramic), which seven designers chose, another three chose the new-era material called RP resin as their stimulus. These three designers design the products and manufacture tangible objects by employing computer-aided design software, 3D-printing technology, and RP resin. As Table 2 illustrates, P08–2 is the best-recognized product that best matches its designed semantics with an overall mean of 4.50 score in four inspection parts (sensorial, interpretive, affective, and performative). Simultaneously, P06–3 and P07–2 are the second-recognized product that fits their designed semantics, both with an overall mean of 4.42 score. Coincidentally, these top three products are made with RP resin. Although three designers (D06, D07, D08) chose the same material of RP resin, they developed three different haptic topics (bumpy, smooth, and brittle) derived from the material experience. Nonetheless, these three haptic topics generated from the same material of RP resin all get a well-recognized evaluation corresponding to their various haptic semantics. However, designer D09 chose the glass as the stimulus during the MX stages, the haptic topic of "ample" with its extracting HS that transforms as a series of products (P09) with an overall mean of 3.33 score is the most difficult-recognized result.

4.2 The Innovation via MX-To-HS Design

This study aims to accomplish process innovation and product innovation via manifesting the MX-to-HS design of the haptic cognition model (HCM). Usually, people generate exuberant sensory feelings derived from the touches of tangible material. Without guidance or practice, those tactile feelings are hard to express in words and often get confused and ignored by designers and users. Based on the material experience (MX), this study explores and develops the path toward tactile expression by adopting haptic semantics (HS). At the beginning of MX, the project organizer encourages the young designers to probe and express their haptic feelings by describing and writing freely. Besides the physical sensation from outer perception, these designers also endeavor psychological prospecting of inner emotion, extensional meaning, and associate scenario to extend the material understanding via related haptic keywords. Furthermore, those cognition abilities on haptic interpretations transform into a unique product design capability by controlling the haptic factors, as demonstrated in Table 1. Meanwhile, this study constructs the process innovation with "MX-to-HS design" and executes the product innovation via HCM, as shown in Fig. 4.

5 Conclusions

From theory to practice, the design industry and education have been searching for design innovation methods for decades [30]. This study employs a haptic semantics approach to enhance the sensation of material experience and improve tactile awareness via verbal expression and lexical documentation. Focus on the MX-to-HS design method, designers clarify their haptic feeling and construct haptic cognition via explorations in four aspects: sensorial, interpretive, affective, and performative. Based on the connection and interaction between MX and HS, the HCM is established and comprises the designer's and the user's models. As previous researchers mentioned, the designer who can deliberately understand and integrate the relationships between the material, product, and user will make the MX much more meaningful [8]. The authors address that MX understanding facilitated by the HS will converge the cognition models between the designer's encoding and the user's decoding.

Based on the theoretical foundation, this study invites young designers with more than two years of experience in crafts creation and product design to participate in the empirical project of the cup sleeves design with the haptic topic. They are familiar with traditional craft materials and know how to manipulate them by hand. But, three of them chose the new material of RP resin as their vivid stimulus and created the cup sleeves by employing computer-aided design software and 3D-printing technology. Unexpectedly, those cup sleeves using RP resin became the top three best-recognized products that match their designed HS, as shown in Table 2. The RP resin's three series of haptic objects perform well in experts' evaluations. The extraordinary result of this project assessment caused a new reflection on the trends and influences of novel materials, molding technologies, and haptic needs. During this post-pandemic era, people increasingly rely on new interfaces of digital-technology devices and generate new haptic experiences. Meanwhile, people are gradually reducing their real perceptions of traditional material experiences.

According to the experts' evaluation and discussion of the empirical design project, the HCM (Fig. 4) is unique and dynamic in cooperating with each designer, especially in the sensorial exploration of personal perception and flexible application of process innovation. Moreover, the HCM may be more mentoring for the novice or young designer lacking the plentiful MX, who needs to enhance more meaningful perception and consider manipulation skills for creating Qualia products. Regarding the individual case, the stages of the MX-to-HS design processes can be rearranged to bridge the designer's encoding and the user's decoding via the haptic product with coincided system image. As many researchers declared, many purchases are encouraged by hedonic impulses. Haptic feelings are the most direct response aroused and received when people touch a product; in other words, the tactile sensation often promotes hedonic motivations. This research clarifies how the materials experience (MX) and haptic semantics (HS) can be applied to a cognition model and which relevant components are needed for a haptic cognition model (HCM). The authors suggest that future research could further execute the advanced design project adaptively using the HCM and get more evaluation data. Eventually, this study believes that new generations need to undertake inclusive innovation via the process innovation of HCM with MX-to-HS design for the new era.

Acknowledgments. This research was supported by the National Science and Technology Council, Taiwan [Grant ID: NSTC 111–2221-E-007–049]. The authors would like to thank all the designers who participated and contributed their creations. In addition, the authors also appreciate the valuable suggestions of Prof. Han-Yu Lin from the Department of Industry Design at the National Kaohsiung Normal University.

References

1. Chiang, I.-Y., Sun, Y., Lin, P.-H., Lin, R., Lin, H.-Y.: Haptic semantics in qualia product. In: Rau, P.L.P. (eds) Cross-Cultural Design. Interaction Design Across Cultures. HCII 2022. Lecture Notes in Computer Science, vol 13311. Springer, Cham (2022). https://doi.org/10.1007/978-3-031-06038-0_2
2. Masayuki, K., Wang, X.: Design Focus Product Masayuki Kurokawa. China Youth Press, Beijing (2002). (Chinese version)
3. Chen, Y.-T.: A Study on Tactile Image and Style (Doctoral dissertation). National Chiao Tung University, Institute of Applied Arts, Hsinchu (2016). (in Chinese)
4. Manzini, E.: The Material of Invention. MIT Press, CambridgeA (1989)
5. Ashby, M., Johnson, K.: Materials and Design: The Art and Science of Material Selection in Product Design, 2nd edn. Butterworth-Heinemann Elsevier, Oxford (2009)
6. Yao, R.-K.: An introduction to the material experience design method and its promotion report in Taiwan crafts. J. Craftol. Taiwan **1**, 69–86 (2022). (in Chinese)
7. Karana, E., Hekkert, P., Kandachar, P.: Materials experience: descriptive categories in material appraisals. In Proceedings of the Conference on Tools and Methods in Competitive Engineering, pp. 399–412. Delft University of Technology, Delft (2008)
8. Karana, E., Pedgley, O., Rognoli, V.: On materials experience. Des. Issues **31**(3), 16–27 (2015)
9. Karana, E., Barati, B., Rognoli, V., van der Laan, A.Z.: Material driven design (MDD): a method to design for material experiences. Int. J. Des. **9**(2), 35–54 (2015)
10. Giaccardi, E., Karana, E.: Foundations of materials experience: an approach for HCI. In Proceedings of the 33rd SIGCHI Conference on Human Factors in Computing Systems, pp. 2447–2456. ACM, New York (2015)
11. Osgood, C.E., Suci, G.J., Tannenbaum, P.H.: The Measurement of Meaning, 9th edn. University of Illinois Press, Champaign (1975)

12. Tewari, S.: Product semantics. In: Edwards et al. (Eds.), The Bloomsbury Encyclopedia of Design, vol. 3. Bloomsbury Academic (2016). https://doi.org/10.5040/9781472596154-BED-ONLINE-002

13. Lakoff, G., Wehling, E.: The Little Blue Book: The Essential Guide to Thinking and Talking Democratic. FREE, New York (2012)

14. Sternberg, R.J.: Cognitive Psychology, 5th edn. Wadsworth, Belmont (2009)

15. Solso, R.L., Wu, L.-L.: Cognitive Psychology. Hwa Tai, Taipei (1998). (Chinese version)

16. Gerrig, R. J., You, H.-S.H.: Psychology and Life, 20 edn. Wunan Publishing, Taipei (2019). (Chinese version)

17. Chang, C.-H.: Modern Psychology, 1st edn. Tung Hua, Taipei (1995). (in Chinese)

18. Ackerman, D., Zhuang, A.-G.: A Natural History of the Senses. China Times Publishing, Taipei (1993). (Chinese version)

19. Prytherch, D., McLundie, M.: So what is haptics anyway? research issues in art design and media, no. 2. Spring (2002). ISSN 1474–2365

20. Kreifeldt, J., Lin, R., Chuang, M.-C.: The importance of "Feel" in product design feel, the neglected aesthetic "DO NOT TOUCH." In: Rau, P.L.P. (ed.) IDGD 2011. LNCS, vol. 6775, pp. 312–321. Springer, Heidelberg (2011). https://doi.org/10.1007/978-3-642-21660-2_35

21. Loomis, J.M., Lederman, S.J.: Tactual Perception (K. Boff, L. Kaufman & J. Thomas Eds.). John Wiley & Sons, Inc., New York (1986)

22. Chang, C.-H.: Modern Psychology: The Modern Science of Their Own Problems. Tung Hua, Taipei (2009). (in Chinese)

23. Sonneveld, M.H., Schifferstein, H.N.J.: The tactual experience of objects. In: Schifferstein, H.N.J., Hekkert, P. (eds.) Product Experience. Elsevier, San Diego (2008)

24. Gibson, J.J.: Observations on active touch. Psychol. Rev. **69**, 477–491 (1962)

25. Lederman, S.J., Klatzky, R.L.: Hand movements: a window into haptic object recognition. Cogn. Psychol. **19**(3), 342–368 (1987)

26. Hinckley, K., Sinclair, M.: Touch-sensing input devices. In: Paper Presented at the Proceedings of the SIGCHI conference on Human Factors in Computing Systems: the CHI is the Limit, pp. 223–230 ACM, Pittsburgh (1999)

27. Hutchins, E.L., Hollan, J.D., Norman, D.A.: Direct manipulation interface. Hum.-Comput. Interact. **1**, 311–338 (1985)

28. Norman, D.A., Draper, S. (eds.): User Centered System Design: New Perspectives on Human-Computer Interaction. Erlbaum, London (1986)

29. Norman, D.A.: Cognitive artifact. In: Carroll, J.M. (ed.) Designing Interaction. Cambridge University Press, Cambridge (1991)

30. Chiang, I.-Y., Lin, P.-H., Kreifeldt, J.G., Lin, R.: From theory to practice: an adaptive development of design education. Educ. Sci. **11**(11), 673 (2021). https://doi.org/10.3390/educsci11110673

31. Norman, D.A.: Emotional Design: Why We Love (or hate) Everyday Things. Basic Books, New York (2004)

32. Norman, D.A.: The Design of Everyday Things: Review and Expanded. Basic Books, New York (2013)

33. Lin, C.L., Chen, C.L., Chen, S.J., Lin, R.: The cognition of turning poetry into painting. J. US-China Educ. Rev. B **5**(8), 471–487 (2015)

34. Chiang, I.-Y., Lin, R., Lin, P.-H.: Placemaking with creation: a case study in cultural product design. In: Rau, P.-L. (ed.) HCII 2021. LNCS, vol. 12771, pp. 244–261. Springer, Cham (2021). https://doi.org/10.1007/978-3-030-77074-7_20

35. Lyu, Y., Wang, X., Lin, R., Wu, J.: Communication in human–AI co-creation: perceptual analysis of paintings generated by text-to-image system. Appl. Sci. **12**, 11312 (2022). https://doi.org/10.3390/app122211312

Design Futurescaping: Interweaving Storytelling and AI Generation Art in World-Building

Zhiyong Fu[✉] and Jiawei Li

Tsinghua University, Beijing 100085, China
fuzhiyong@tsinghua.edu.cn

Abstract. In a time of rapid change, innovative ideas are urgently needed to examine the changes of the times in order to meet the new challenges of the Anthropocene. As a result, exploring future trends, mapping Futurescaping and creating future value has become a key focus for future developments and applications in the field of design. Although there are already powerful design concepts such as anthropocentric design, transitional design and systems design, research in the field of Design Futurescaping has mainly focused on social and humanistic fields to generate discussion and reflection, and has not yet developed a mature practical approach to guide design practice. Therefore, this paper will discuss an art project called 'AI City Park' as a design paradigm, and incorporate a storytelling perspective based on Rhizome Thinking to construct the shape of the future world, so as to generate various methods and concepts of Design Futurescaping. The paradigm has been applied and feedback has been positive. The paradigm has been used with some success to help audiences imagine the future at an early stage of their practice, to stimulate creativity and imagination, and to provide new ideas for the future of the design field. At the same time, the paradigm focuses on exploring the deep integration of artificial intelligence and future cities, and through the construction of Futurescaping, it can inspire the audience to pay attention to and reflect on the current environment, society and culture, and help them to make better choices about their actions in the present.

Keywords: Design Futurescaping · World-Building · Rhizome Thinking · Storytelling · AI Generation Art

1 Introduction

1.1 Designing for the Challenges of the Anthropocene

The dominant role that humans now play in shaping the Earth system indicates that our planet has entered a new geological era, the Anthropocene. The Anthropocene challenges facing the world today, including but not limited to climate change, ecological crises, resource depletion and urbanisation, have forced humanity to begin to move from a focus on itself, to a focus on natural ecology, to a focus on the harmonious coexistence of humans and nature. "The 21st century Earth will enter the Anthropocene, and the world will face two major challenges: population explosion and climate warming.

P.-L. P. Rau (Ed.): HCII 2023, LNCS 14023, pp. 194–207, 2023.
https://doi.org/10.1007/978-3-031-35939-2_15

A range of emerging technologies such as genetic technology, artificial intelligence, robotics and space exploration technology will play a greater role in helping people to meet the challenges, but of course innovative technology is also a double-edged sword that brings new uncertainties. We have an obligation to promote the beneficial applications of the results of their work and to warn of their drawbacks" [1]. Martin John Rees made this point in his keynote speech "Perspectives on the future of humanity" at the Global Grand Challenges Forum 2019 in London. The application of artificial intelligence technologies in human-computer interaction and design has led to new discussions on human relationships, prompting researchers and practitioners to rethink the harmonious co-existence of technology, society and culture [2].

At the same time, in this process, how to judge uncertainty in change, how to seek possibilities in uncertainty, how to analyse future trends in possibilities and how to build Futurescaping in trends are the main questions that humanity needs to think about and explore. The field of design should continue to evolve, creating new disciplines, acquiring new knowledge and developing new tools to help answer the questions raised by this new era, which includes the well-being of people, the resilience of organisations, the shortcomings of sustainable living: depletion of natural resources, desertification, ecological extinction, widespread pollution, migration, and social and environmental injustice.

1.2 Designing Future Well-Being in a Symbiosis of Virtual Reality

In 1995, the American scholar Nicholas Negroponte proposed in his book Being Digital: "Humanity is about to live in a virtual, digital living space where people will use digital technology to communicate, exchange, learn, work and do other activities with information. This is the digital world" [3]. In terms of the attributes of digital life, it can be divided into four characteristics: namely decentralisation, globalisation, the pursuit of harmony, and empowerment. Based on this, more and more internet users can have the power to master tools as a way to influence and change their digital lives.

With the intervention of new ICT technologies, the urban environment has become more sensual, interactive and flexible. The integration of the physical space and the invisible network of the city can support human activities at all levels and create a highly complex ecosystem [4]. Humanity is increasingly eager to find a new perspective on the balance of technology in complex systems and to find the subtle but real 'digital well-being'. Take, for example, the emerging field of metaverse. This means that the virtual reality of the online world has become a new social and ecological model. Based on the new changes in life and communication in the metaverse, it is a new challenge in the design field to create more possibilities for future digital life and design future well-being for human beings from the virtual dimension to the real dimension, and to help users rebuild a virtual symbiosis environment that is suitable for the sustainable development of human beings in a world where carbon-based and silicon-based civilisations coexist.

We try to study the "AI City Park" art project from the perspective of design innovation, conceiving a deep integration of artificial intelligence and the city, further considering the relationship between society, humanities and technology, and through the construction of Futurescaping from the perspective of virtual and real symbiosis, we can inspire the public to pay attention to the current environment, social culture and other aspects, and to reflect on this, helping the public to make better choices on the current actions.

2 Related Concept Analysis

2.1 Futurescaping as a Design Goal

In 2009, Bruce Sterling published an article in Maker Magazine called Designer Futurescape in which he excitedly mentioned that 'a networked, interactive and increasingly speculative future world' has arrived [5]. He refers to Arjun Appadurai's statement that 'imagination has become an organised field of social practice' [6] as a 'speculative culture', which represents Design Futurescaping as a hybrid practice at the intersection of design foresight and critical design [7]. Design Futurescaping is a hybrid practice first pioneered by Superflux and presented by Anab Jain, one of the founders of Superflux, at the Lift09 conference. Under this hybrid practice, the tools and insights of critical design are deployed in rich, nuanced, collaborative forms of foresight research and exchange. Design Futurescaping uses collaboration, co-creation and Storytelling to sort out the unevenly distributed fragments of the future. Embracing the organic, messy and localised social conditions of the present. These fragments of the future can fuel a hybrid, human vision and replace the deterministic, policy-driven, and business-as-usual consensus future. In short, we can understand its nature as an attempt to make similar small-scale interventions in the technological imagination. Using 'micro-targeting, low-cost, democratic and empowering strategies' to realise the details of the programme, promote a shift in public discourse and ultimately achieve lasting behavioural change [8]. Futurist Jamais Cascio uses the phrase 'plausibly surreal', while Steven Johnson speaks of 'adjacent possible': a phrase that 'simultaneously captures the limits of change and innovation and the potential for creativity' [9]. Whatever the terminology used, the increasing visibility of these faint signals and early warnings in an information-rich online culture makes Design Futurescaping an effective practice to address the problem.

2.2 World-Building Leads to a Better Future

World-building is a narrative technique commonly used in science fiction that involves the creation of detailed, immersive fictional worlds with their own unique rules, cultures and histories. Although world-building is often associated with Storytelling, it can also be a valuable tool for designing futures, providing a framework for envisioning and designing plausible Future Scenarios.

Peter von Stackelberg and Alex McDowell suggest in 2015 that World-Building is the process of constructing an imaginary world that is complete, makes sense and can serve as a backdrop for a story. It is "the creation of imaginary worlds with coherent geographical, social, cultural and other features" [10]. World-Building provides a detailed set of contextual rules for design, developing a larger reality that goes beyond a single story, while potentially providing a deeper understanding of the underlying systems that drive these worlds. World-building can inform visionary practice and can also help build a stronger relationship between vision and systems design. Leah Zaidi likens world-building to the story of social constructivism and systems design [11]. Similar to how our social-ecological systems emerge, co-evolve and 'interconnect in a never-ending adaptive cycle of growth, accumulation, and 'reorganisation', the world of science fiction instils a sense of wholeness [12]. World-Building need not be narrow or artefact-centric; it can and should aspire to be systemic. Despite World-Building's tendency to be systemic and its association with foresight in the context of science fiction, World-Building is an under-researched act of intentional design that has potential for real-world application. Raven and Elahi note that "there is little literature that applies narrative as understood by writers, filmmakers, and cultural scholars strategies and logics to the methods that future scholars and practitioners will employ in creating their final output" [13]. The field of design combining the three domains of World-Building, storytelling narrative, and Design Futurescaping is therefore highly likely to offer great value for the future.

2.3 Commonalities Between Rhizome Thinking and Social Networks

Gilles Louis Réné Deleuze argues that traditional Western philosophical thinking is a tree-like pattern, with a strong unity that follows the laws of nature to two or more, and that the 'branches' that grow out of it follow a strict hierarchical order, presenting a linearly ordered and closed structure. 'Rhizome' is a critique of the traditional tree-like mode of thinking, where Deleuze sees things as an uncentralised plurality, and uses the new metaphor of the 'Rhizome' to interpret his philosophical ideas [14]. By comparing Rhizomes with tree-like structures, Deleuze reveals the complex interconnectedness of things in constant flux that the Rhizome system reveals, and constructs an open and dynamic way of thinking that is free of centres and priorities. Things become fragmented 'chaos', growing into an extraordinary variety of forms, stretching and connecting on surfaces that bifurcate in all directions, ultimately leading to an infinitely open and smooth space.

Manuel Castor summarises the social structure of the information age as "Network Society", i.e. unlike the disparate patterns of agricultural and industrial societies, the new information technology paradigm brings about a flattened and distributed society, manifesting itself as a decentralised network. The new information technology paradigm brings about a flat, distributed society, manifesting itself as a decentralised network [15]. In short, the emergence of virtual worlds has degraded the basic unit of social interaction from the organisation to the individual, reshaping social interaction in a de-organised way and making social forms particulate and networked. This characteristic coincides with the philosophy of decentralisation and pluralism advocated by Deleuze's 'rhizome' concept.

Non-linear, Interconnected AI-Generated Art. The use of artificial intelligence in the creation of art has become increasingly common in recent years. Art produced by artificial intelligence is created using machine learning algorithms that are trained on large data sets of images, music or other types of media. These algorithms learn to recognise patterns and relationships in the data and use this knowledge to generate new, original works of art. Although Deleuze's Rhizome Thinking and AI-generated art are two different concepts, they share a common connection in challenging traditional hierarchical structures and promoting non-linear, interconnected modes of thinking. Like Rhizome Thinking, AI-generated art challenges traditional hierarchies and categories, creating new connections and associations between different forms of media. AI-generated art often blurs the boundaries between different art forms, such as music and visual art, or between different cultural traditions. One example of the use of AI in the creation of rhizomatic art is the project "AIArtists.org" by Mario Klingemann, which uses machine learning algorithms to generate original artworks that combine different styles and media [16].

3 Creation of the AI City Park Project

3.1 Paradigm Design

AI City Park is a design paradigm that constructs the shape of the future world from the perspective of storytelling narratives to generate a multifaceted, open and non-hierarchical structure of Futurescaping. The paradigm is pre-designed as an illustrative guide that guides the viewer through an autonomous exploration and creation of a series of virtual and real symbiotic spaces, with behavioural data collection and multiple scenarios to present generative alternatives, resulting in a continuous, differentiated, distributed, egalitarian and generative World-Building. Digital spaces, etc. The aim is to reconstruct the relationship between users, objects and scene elements in order to help the audience migrate to the virtual world, adapt and balance the emerging environment, and provoke the audience to pay attention to and reflect on the current environment. The AI City Park design paradigm is composed of four stages. World-Building based on Rhizome Thinking; Designing the core future elements of AI City Park; Distributed Narrative Selection Mechanism; Design Futurescaping Generation (Fig. 1).

The Futurescaping generation process is based on six elements: 1. Worldview construction, 2. Future Scenarios, 3. Future Artifacts, 4. Future Personas, 5. Storytelling 6. AI Art generation. Each essential element is described more specifically below in relation to the guide illustrations and post-creation results.

3.2 World-Building Based on Rhizomatic Thinking

Deleuze's Rhizome Thinking offers a new perspective on how we perceive virtual worlds: the idea that things are intertwined and interpenetrating relationships that should not be confined to a fixed hierarchical structure. Therefore, we need to construct a pluralistic, open and non-hierarchical view of the world in order to facilitate the unfolding of distributed narratives. First, our thinking spatialises the concept of the 'rhizome', a spatialisation based on Table 1, which explains the principles of Connection, Heterogeneity, Multiplicity, Asignifying Rupture, Cartography, Decalcomania.

Similarly, Rhizome Thinking provides the conceptual underpinning for AI City Park's World-Building, which is embodied in the operation of expansion, conquest, capture, and branching for construction. According to Deleuze and Guattari, Rhizome Thinking is a concept of knowledge and community that allows for "multiple, non-hierarchical entry and exit points in the representation and interpretation of data". Networks are used to describe methods of connection and emphasise processes of flow,

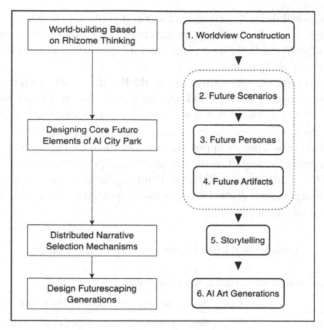

Fig. 1. Components of the AI City Park Design Paradigm

Table 1. Characteristics of Rhizome Thinking

Rhizome Thinking	Explanation
Connection	The ability to aggregate by establishing connections on itself and at any point within itself
Hetrogeneity	The ability to connect anything to anything else, the linking of different elements
Multiplicity	The elements of the rhizome coexist with each other without any structure. No point in the rhizome can change the whole
Asignifying Rupture	The rhizome may be broken off, but will start again on the old or new line
Cartography	The rhizome is similar to a map, has no starting point, can be manipulated at will, and has multiple entrances and exits
Decalcomania	The rhizome does not fit into any structural or generative model; it is a "mapping rather than a tracing"

change and interaction, and it is in this uncertainty of heterogeneity and plurality that networked societies are constantly reorganised and formed, arguing against hierarchical structures and that everything is in a state of constant change. Rhizome Thinking breaks down borders and boundaries and constitutes a state of openness and continuity, which is in line with the essential characteristics of the network society, highlighting its openness and the infinite possibilities it contains, and more crucially, the changes in practices and the internal logic formed by different entities connected through the network society. Table 2 shows the World-Building principle and its application in Futurescaping based on the Rhizome Thinking feature.

Based on this principle, the form of the World-Building shifts from a closed, purely geometric state to one of disorder and openness, establishing a relationship between people, architecture and nature that is mutually decontextualised and heterogeneously connected, offering more possibilities for the next art projects to re-jurisdiction the form of the world and create Futurescaping. We innovate the traditional design cognition of 'Being' into a generative cognition of 'Becoming' and propose a series of design inspirations for AI City Park based on Rhizome Thinking, namely: interconnected modules, heterogeneous aggregation, hybrid configurations, potential evolution, deconstructive layout, and nomadic iconography.

Table 2. World-Building based on Rhizomatic Thinking

Principles of World-Building	Applied to Futurescaping
Modularity	Connections, self-organised derivations, new connections
Differentiation	Heterogeneous reconciliation, evolutionary iteration into new objects
Symbiosis	Decentralised, inclusive aggregates, group intelligence
Proliferative	Jurisdictions, fractured divisions, escaped resurgent boundaries and unbounded domain
Territoriality	Dissolution domains, mapping, smooth, open maps
Generativity	Tracing, dynamically generated collage-pattern mapping

AI City Park's World-Building. After applying the above design inspiration to the creation, we visualised the World-Building based on Rhizome Thinking in the form of a guide (Fig. 2). A futuristic, durable and distributed 'builder's park' is created spontaneously in this world, from the formation of the ground to the architectural structures, to the biogenetic recombination and the birth of a digital human being. But as far as creative activity is concerned, making this world a platform for otherworldly creative expression is the prominence of the unstructured nature of artistic activity, the gathering of tangible and intangible, documented and forgotten information that forms the various ligne de uite and is subsequently used as a trajectory point for the creation of related rituals, Storytelling and fantasy role-playing, exploring Depiction and construction of futurescaping.

Secondly, we have designed four levels of world-building, as the entrance to the hybrid space and the universal carrier, each of which stores data and information about the better future of human life. They are built as the basis for the development of the future city, and are the basis for our infinite imagination of the future world. They are the Civilisation and Harmony City, the Ecological Symbiosis Layer, the Digital Technology Layer and the Free Art Layer (Fig. 3).

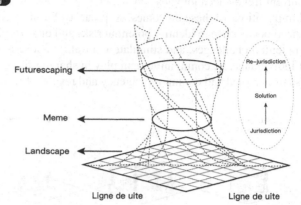

AI City Park's World-Building

It is a futuristic, enduring, distributed 'builder's park' in which the world is created spontaneously, from the formation of the ground to architectural structures, to biological genetic recombination and the birth of the digital human. But in terms of creative activity, allowing this world to serve as a platform for otherwise-attractive creative expression is the prominence of the unstructured nature of artistic activity, where these aggregated tangible and intangible, documented and forgotten messages form various escape lines that are subsequently used as trajectory points for the creation of relevant rituals, storytelling and fantasy role-playing, exploring the depiction and construction of Futurescaping of form.

Fig. 2. AI City Park's World-Building

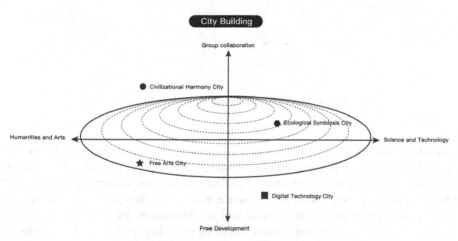

Fig. 3. City Building

Designing the Core Future Elements of AI City Park. Based on the current challenges of the Anthropocene, we have extracted Future Life, Future Mobility, Future Education and Future Health as the four core themes, and based on these four themes we have created Future Scenarios, Future Artifacts and Future Personas, the three core future elements that make up AI City Park, with the aim of demonstrating the different possibilities of the future through the extraction of risk signals from the real world.

Future Scenarios. Future Scenarios are an important tool in world-building, which involves the creation of fictional or imaginary worlds. In literature, film and other forms of media, Future Scenarios act as a central element of world-building, providing a plausible framework for imagining what the future might look like. In Future Scenarios enable people to consider the implications of current choices and make more informed decisions about how to move forward. Allows creators to explore the possible outcomes of current trends, technologies and societal shifts, and to imagine the human and societal implications of these outcomes. Approaches Future Scenarios with a balanced and nuanced perspective to identify potential risks and opportunities, anticipate and prepare for potential challenges, and stimulate innovation and creativity, emphasising the role that individuals and communities can play in shaping the future and helping to foster a sense of personal and community agency and responsibility (Fig. 4).

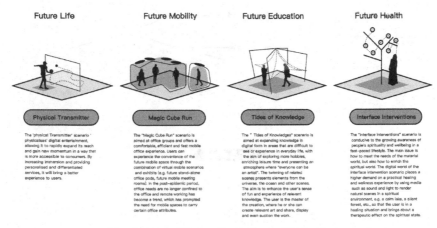

Fig. 4. Part of *Future Scenarios in AI City Park*

Future Personas. Future Personas are the collection of characteristics, traits, behaviours and preferences that individuals in a future society are likely to possess. These personalities are often used as central elements of world-building to create a coherent and believable future society. Whether in science fiction or other genres, world-building often involves imagining a future world and its inhabitants. Future Personas help to create a more fully realised and realistic world by providing a framework for character development and social norms. By identifying what people in a future world would be like, authors and creators can explore how society would function, how people would interact with each other, and the challenges they might face. If a future society values individualism over collective action, it can prompt us to consider the implications of our current emphasis on individual freedom, and the impact it might have on the future. At the same time, it could also reinforce existing social norms and prejudices and perpetuate stereotypes or assumptions about certain groups of people. It is important to recognise that these imagined futures are not inevitable; they are shaped by the views and prejudices of their creators (Fig. 5).

Future Artifacts. In the design process, it is vital that we consider the impact of future tools and their impact on society and people. We need to engage in ethical and responsible design practices that prioritise social and environmental sustainability, diversity, equity and inclusiveness. By doing so, we can ensure that the tools of the future are designed and deployed in ways that promote human well-being and advance the common good. The role of Future Artifacts, which evolved from discursive design, is thus to help us imagine

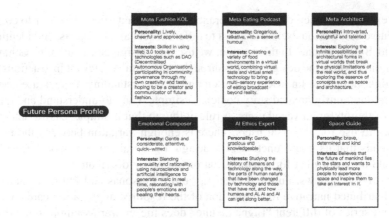

Fig. 5. Part of *Future Personas in AI City Park*

and shape a better future. These props are even new social systems that have the potential to address current and future challenges. They can enable new forms of communication, change the way we work and help us solve problems that cannot be solved in reality, such as global issues like climate change, inequality and social injustice. The aim is to stimulate and inform a broader dialogue about the future and to enable people to imagine and shape it in a more intentional and deliberate way, helping us to explore new possibilities, challenge existing assumptions and create a more just, equitable and sustainable future (Fig. 6).

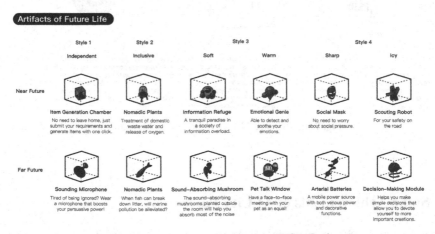

Fig. 6. Part of *Future Artifacts in AI City Park*

Distributed Narrative Selection Mechanism. If the traditional narrative approach is a 'formula' developed by humans through practice, the narrative approach based on Rhizome Thinking requires complex 'programming' to mutate, expand, conquer, capture and branch in a morphological way that allows The narrative needs to be programmed to mutate, expand, conquer, capture, and branch in a way that allows the user to complete the narrative autonomously, and to adapt to different scenarios, objects, and identities of the World-Building state. In this section, we use the 'design heuristic' approach, which provides direction to the design process through contextually relevant instructions based on intuition, default to knowledge, and empirical understanding, to increase access to unique autonomously created story content, a simple, easy to understand and quick to use rule of thumb for universal users. A rule of thumb that is simple, easy to understand and quick to use for universal users. There is enough variation between the multiple story threads that its main function is to design a general context (worldview) for all stories and a master plan for the direction of the many distributed stories. The user's selection of Worldviews, Future Scenarios, Future Personas and Future Artifacts will form a distributed narrative representation of the resource aggregation cards. Only by selecting a series of different "Ligne de uite" does the viewer assemble some of these pieces into a story, with each person's choice leading to a different presentation of the story threads (Fig. 7).

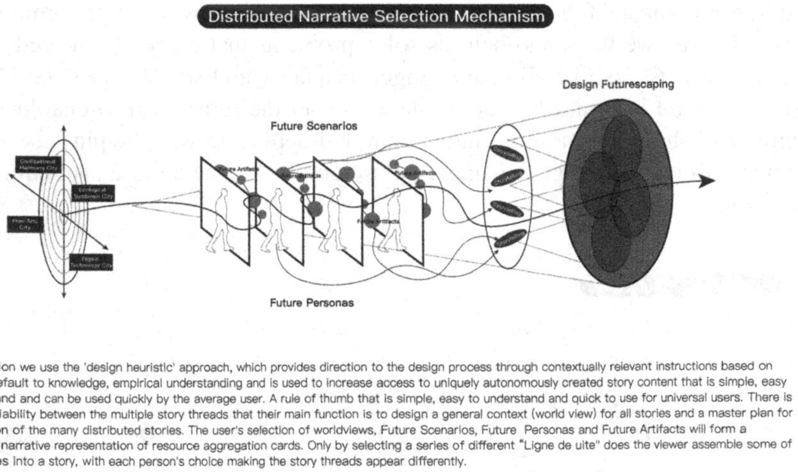

In this section we use the 'design heuristic' approach, which provides direction to the design process through contextually relevant instructions based on intuition, default to knowledge, empirical understanding and is used to increase access to uniquely autonomously created story content that is simple, easy to understand and can be used quickly by the average user. A rule of thumb that is simple, easy to understand and quick to use for universal users. There is enough variability between the multiple story threads that their main function is to design a general context (world view) for all stories and a master plan for the direction of the many distributed stories. The user's selection of worldviews, Future Scenarios, Future Personas and Future Artifacts will form a distributed narrative representation of resource aggregation cards. Only by selecting a series of different "Ligne de uite" does the viewer assemble some of these pieces into a story, with each person's choice making the story threads appear differently.

Fig. 7. Distributed Narrative Selection Mechanism

4   Some Achievements of AI City Park

Based on a study of future urban trends, the projection of the future direction of the city is made through a collection of political, economic, social and future technological trends, as well as from technological, educational, economic, environmental and human aspects. Four different world views of the future are explored, critically thinking about urban access, life, community, mobility and education. The direction of the deep integration of AI is explored, realising the meme of the vision of AI fully participating and sharing the social scene of human life.

Based on the AI City Park design paradigm described above, we have allowed a series of ideas to evolve and iterate into new design projects through discussion and using various forms. We co-create a collaborative and presentational platform for participation in the mapping of future cities, incorporating hints of engineering and meme [17]. This is manifested through guidelines to guide the user in the correct way to use the distributed narrative, thereby enhancing the user experience. In this space, the user will first make an autonomous choice between Future Scenarios, Future Personas and Future Artifacts respectively (Fig. 8). Finally, the system analyses the user's selections and generates a discursive story out of the content (Fig. 9). Having used this design project to derive the paradigm, we also combined storytelling with Ai generation again, using Midjourney to produce a range of new outputs, including serialised comics, three-dimensional mapping and other forms (Fig. 10).

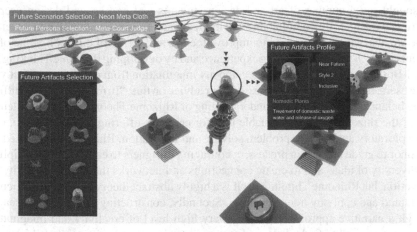

Fig. 8. Users Select Future Artifacts in the Space

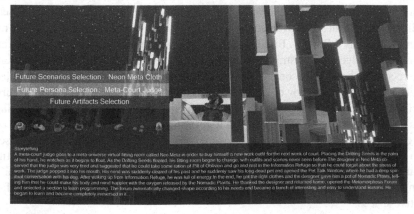

Fig. 9. Storytelling Generation Based on Selection

Fig. 10. Designed after Midjourney

5 Discussions and Future Works

We sought out a number of art and design students and non-art and design users to experience the tool. By combing through the feedback from students and non-specialist users, we also gained inspiration to improve the use and set-up of this tool. Some of the students said." It was an interesting experience and by developing Rhizome Thinking into World-Building, I could choose to develop my imagination from multiple perspectives". Some users, on the other hand, expressed their advice on this: "In my opinion, it is difficult to find balance in it without prior understanding of Rhizome Theory". Overall, Deleuze's idea of the rhizome can be a valuable tool for creators, offering a more flexible, open and exploratory approach to problem solving and innovation. Rhizome can be used as a metaphor to guide the design process, encouraging designers to embrace the multiplicity and diversity of ideas and to create connections and networks that foster creativity and innovation, but Rhizome Thinking itself is a highly abstract theory that can be difficult to understand and apply by non-specialists. Secondly, constructing Design Futurescaping through a narrative approach requires a very high level of creativity and imagination, and designers need to find a balance between complexity and uncertainty, which is not possible for everyone. There is also a risk that this approach is overly theoretical and detached from reality, and designers need to maintain a good balance between theory and practice in order to truly achieve the goal of innovation. We conclude that the design paradigm needs further improvement if it is to be used as a practical method to guide more design practice, as follows.1. Building Design Futurescaping is a process of integrating existing knowledge in an abstract way. It depends on each individual's past experiences and perceptions. For this reason, we are planning to create a library of AI City Speculative Artifacts. Harnessing the power of crowd-sourced creativity, we will collect discursive knowledge from multiple fields and create a repository of source stories. 2. We plan to create an extended version of AI City that will further iterate into creative tools and open source platforms to support more designers and non-professionals to participate in scene development and building Design Futurescaping. It will further promote and investigate virtual creation tools and research platforms for AI-human interaction and symbiosis, leading more people to understand and experience the new experience of distributed narrative spaces.

6 Conclusion

Design, in whatever form, is the conscious organisation of elements to create a product, service or system with certain functional and aesthetic values. Through World-Building, based on Rhizome Thinking, a more flexible, open and exploratory approach to problem solving and innovation is offered. This paradigm exploration can be used as a metaphor to guide the design process, encouraging designers to embrace the multiplicity and diversity of ideas and to create connections and networks that foster creativity and innovation. In the future, the message of fan kui will be communicated to a wider range of participants in the form of workshops, thus enabling participants to embrace and have a sense of autonomy and innovation, providing the opportunity for the next stage of deeper design transformation and further shaping the design paradigm. Through the lens of narrative, experience the World-Building based on Rhizome Thinking and further reflect on the relationship between society, humanity and technology. At the same time, it is hoped that through the design and construction of Futurescaping, the public will be well inspired to pay attention to the current environment, society and culture, and to reflect on this, helping the public to make better choices about their actions in the present.

References

1. Rees, M.: On the future: a keynote address. Engineering **6**(2), 110–114 (2020)
2. Sustar, H., Mladenović, M.N., Givoni, M.: The landscape of envisioning and speculative design methods for sustainable mobility futures. Sustainability **12**(6), 1–24 (2020)
3. Joi, I., Howe, J.: Whiplash: How to Survive Our Faster Future, p. 51. MIT Media Lab, Boston Herald (2012)
4. Negroponte, N.: Being Digital. Alfred A. Knopf, United States (1995)
5. Sterling, B.: Designer futurescape. Make Magazine **18**, 28–29 (2009)
6. Appadurai, A.: Disjuncture and difference in the global cultural economy. Publ. Cult. **2**(2), 1–24 (1990)
7. Dunne, A., Raby, F.: Speculative Everything: Design, Fiction, and Social Dreaming, p. 9. The MIT Press, Cambridge (2013)
8. Guardian Professional Network, http://www.guardian.co.uk/sustainable-business/urban-acu puncture-community-localised-renewal-projects. accessed 2011/01/09
9. Johnson, S.: Where Good Ideas Come From. Penguin Books, New York (2010)
10. Stackelberg, P., Alex, M.: What in the world? Storyworlds, science fiction, and futures studies. J. Futures Stud. **20**(2), 25–46 (2015)
11. Zaidi, L.: Building Brave New Worlds: Science Fiction and Transition Design. https://openre search.ocadu.ca/id/eprint/2123/. accessed 2023/2/20
12. Eriksen, T.H.: An Introduction to Social and Cultural Anthropology. Pluto Press, London (2001)
13. Raven, P.H., Elahi, S.: The new narrative: applying narratology to the shaping of futures outputs. Futures **74**, 49–61 (2015). ScienceDirect
14. Deleuze, G., Guattari, F.L.: A Thousand Plateaus: Capitalism and Schizophrenia (B. Massumi, Trans.). University of Minnesota Press, Minneapolis (1987)
15. Castells, M.: The Rise of the Network Society, 2nd edn. Blackwell Publishers, Malden (2000)
16. AIArtists.org. https://aiartists.org/mario-klingemann. accessed Feb. 2023/2/20
17. Boyd, R., Richerson, P.: Culture and the Evolutionary Process. The University of Chicago Press (1985)

Building Experience Management Body of Knowledge: Responding to the Challenge

Manhai Li[✉], Yixuan Zhou, Lianyu Huang, and Haiwei Wu

Chongqing University of Posts and Telecommunications, Chongqing 400065, China
limh@cqupt.edu.cn

Abstract. Under the background of the booming of experience economy, enterprises attach more and more importance to the customer experience. At present, there are two problems in improving experience management ability. Firstly, the knowledge of the experience management is miscellaneous but unstructured; Secondly, the knowledge of the experience management is abundant but not systematic. In order to solve the above problems, this paper attempts to build a set of experience management body of knowledge. The goal of the body of knowledge is as follows, the content should be not only progressiveness, but also can lead the development of the user experience industry; Moreover, the content of the experience management body of knowledge should be easy to implement and be able to match the organizational structure and decision-making mechanism of the enterprise. In order to achieve the above goals, this paper adopts the nine-grid array of "three levels - three ranges" to make the knowledge more structural; at the same time, this paper adopts the three-level model of "project level - system level – culture level" to make the knowledge more systematized.

Keywords: Experience Management · Knowledge · Experience Design · Experience Economy

1 Introduction

Enterprises from selling commodities, to processed goods, additional value-added services, and experience that can resonate with the hearts of consumers. This development process was first described in detail by B. Joseph Pine II and James H. Golmore in the "Welcome to the Experience Economy" of Harvard Business Review in 1998 [1]. The common practice of enterprises selling experience to consumers is to provide certain services as a stage for consumers to interact and participate in, while providing certain products as props during the consumer interaction. A typical example is Disneyland, where consumers queue up and spend money to buy a wonderful, warm, and joyous individual experience for a whole day. The experience product revenue of Disneyland in the third quarter of fiscal year 2022 reached 7.394 billion US dollars, with 70% year on year growth. In 2021, Super Office interviewed 1920 businesspeople around the world to analyze their business priorities for the next five years. According to the data, the customer experience ranked first with a proportion of 45.9%. Therefore, it can be seen that the experience economy with broad market prospects is developing in full swing.

P.-L. P. Rau (Ed.): HCII 2023, LNCS 14023, pp. 208–220, 2023.
https://doi.org/10.1007/978-3-031-35939-2_16

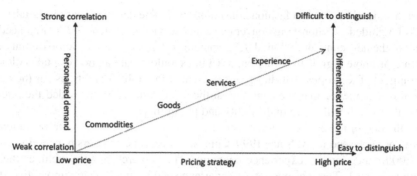

Fig. 1. Characteristics of Experience Economy.

As shown in Fig. 1, under the circumstance that the product functions or service features provided are difficult to show differentiation, if the enterprise wants to meet the personalized needs of consumers as much as possible, and achieve high profit at the same time, it is an inevitable choice to sell experience to consumers. In the context of the experience economy, with the development of the definition of customer experience, the customer experience management (abbreviated as CEM or CXM) has emerged, which means that companies use to track, monitor and organize customers and organizations in each interaction process during the entire customer life cycle [2]. The experience economy involves the transformation of corporate culture and organizational strategy, and digital experience management platform based on data has been applied. In 2018, Qualtrics, a provider of experience management platform, was acquired by software giant SAP for $8 billion in cash, creating the most expensive acquisition record of SaaS platform ever. This event made the concept of "experience management" widely mentioned worldwide. Tangshuo, Bestcem, Isal and other experience consulting companies actively follow up the experience management digital platform investment and propose experience management solutions. Traditional user research companies such as IPSOS and Digital 100 accelerated the recruitment and acquisition of talents in the field of experience management, and expanded their experience management teams.

Under the background of the booming of experience economy, relevant concepts such as 'customer experience' and 'experience management' are constantly enriched and demonstrated by relevant experts and scholars, and the importance of experience management is also reflected in the research.

2 New Challenges Faced by Experience Management

Although experience management started late in China, it has a good development environment and sufficient social conditions.

In 2021, the 14th Five-Year Plan for National Economic and Social Development of the People's Republic of China and the Outline of the Long-range Goals for 2035 issued by China government, put forward the goal arrangement of the development of digitalization. The relevant contents are mainly divided into the following aspects: 1. China should insist on encouraging the development of new models such as customization, experience, intelligence and fashion consumption; 2. The development of digitalization should be guided by improving convenience and service experience; 3. China needs to adhere to the new concept of digital development; 4. China should develop digital economy and promote digital construction; 5. China should create a good digital ecological environment. The proposal of this goal has created favorable conditions for the development of experience management, and at the same time, it has provided the relevant practical research with more malleability and possibility.

At the end of the 20th century, Chinese experts and scholars began to pay attention to the experience economy. Since 1999, Chinese experts and scholars have written more than 3000 papers on the experience economy. The research mainly includes the following aspects: 1. The introduction of experience economy; 2. The comparative study of experience economy and service economy; 3. The exploration of experience economy thoughts from different subject field and the significance of economic growth in the market operation; 4. The application of experience economy thought in tourism, sports, enterprise management, marketing and other production and life fields, and its development prospects and social values were studied to a certain extent.

In China National Knowledge Infrastructure (CNKI), the number of essays containing the subject words of "experience management" and "enterprise economy" in the search scope limited to "general database" has increased significantly since 2009 and maintained a certain amount. In 2019, the number of researches entered the peak, and in 2022, the number has increased by leaps and bounds.

However, the development of experience management is also faced with challenges at the same time. Although the current research on experience management has made some achievements, it is still not mature. At present, there is no unified guiding framework for the relevant theories and practical applications of experience management. The knowledge is miscellaneous but not systematic and unstructured, and most enterprises and practitioners are still in the stage of lack of appropriate methodology systems and practices for the current situation.

2.1 Experience Knowledge is Miscellaneous, but Unstructured

The miscellaneous and unstructured experience knowledge makes it difficult to solve complex problems in reality.

Current research mainly focus on the elements of a certain level or block of an enterprise, but the boundary between levels and departments is not so clear in actual application, and there are elements that penetrate each other and overlap or contain each other in each level and department. Enterprise experience management cannot be solved by dealing with a single element, but needs to go through different levels, adjust multiple departments at the same time, cooperate with each other, test repeatedly to achieve [3]. The vertical functional system in an enterprise is seriously separated from the horizontal business process. Each level or block mostly considers whether a work can be seriously implemented in its own level or department, but seldom considers how to assist the smooth implementation in relevant level and departments. It is less work oriented, and it is not the department that supports the process, but requires the process to be transferred around the department, so that the work cannot be completed smoothly, and needs repeated coordination which increases the management cost. These actual difficulties are complex and difficult to sort out, therefore, it is very necessary to have a structured experience management body of knowledge for reference, so as to deconstruct the problem, dismantle the problem, clarify the elements and dimensions, and solve the problem quickly and accurately.

2.2 Experience Knowledge is Abundant, but Unsystematic

Experience is a hot topic nowadays which has abundant knowledge but there are few interpretations that comprehensively analyze the development context and trend of the development of experience knowledge. Most papers focus on sorting out researches on "experience" in economics, management, engineering, design and other fields, and a unified body of knowledge has not been completely formed. Breakthroughs in the field of single contact are difficult to effectively guide practical problems. It is urgent to build an enterprise management body of knowledge that covers the whole cycle, the whole contact points, and the whole process.

An enterprise is a collective of relevant interests, and every employee is an internal stakeholder. Enterprises through the cooperation of each employee, internal control to achieve the target of economic activities. The internal control system is an important system in the enterprise overall management system, and the division of rights and responsibilities is the key link in the internal control. Confusion of rights and responsibilities often occurs in the internal control of enterprises. The responsibilities and rights of the internal stakeholders of various departments and posts are unclear, which will not only easily cause chaos in the personnel system and management, but also makes the productivity of enterprises unable to be effectively guaranteed. In a serious way, it also leads to a series of disputes and the disintegration of personnel. For example, there are endless situations where many Internet company developers are also engaged in demand analysis, research and development, testing, delivery, communication, and reception, etc. There are frequent cases where no clear responsible person for the work, the enterprise meeting becomes meaningless repetition, the same work task repeatedly proposed for many times with no progress or even failed to finish, management promotion is very difficult, leaving great hidden dangers. Some employees have excessive labor intensity, frequent switching of multiple tasks, resulting in very low efficiency, while some employees have very few tasks. Faced with such internal chaos, a systematic theoretical knowledge is urgent needed to guide.

3 Approaches to the Problems

XMBOK, the eXperience Management Body of Knowledge, is a general description of the knowledge content and ability advancement required by experience management, which integrates ideas, tools, and methods.

Combining with the new environment of experience economy, integrating multidisciplinary, achieving the building of the experience management body of knowledge from the Nine Squares Path and the three levels including project level, system level and culture level of capabilities of experience management, in order to meet the challenges faced by the current experience management.

3.1 The Nine Squares Path Making XMBOK Structured

The Nine Squares Path of experience management is borrowed from the social design path initiated by WinterHouse Organization in 2013. This organization is a practical community of design educators, and the social design path provides a clear and powerful framework for social impact design educators, students, and practitioners to plan the resources and expertise knowledge needed to solve complex social problems at different levels and scales (Fig. 2).

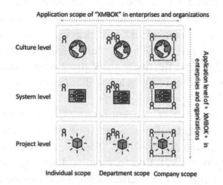

Fig. 2. The Nine Squares Path of Experience Management.

The purpose of establishing the Nine Squares Path of experience management is to solve the complex multi-level and multi department management problems encountered by enterprises by clarifying the unstructured and mixed experience management related experience, expertise knowledge and skills. The X-axis of the model is the scope that the experience management body of knowledge can influence in the enterprises, which is in the order of individual scope, department scope and company scope from small to large. The three scopes represent different behavior participants, and achieve different levels of influence by learning targeted enterprise experience management knowledge respectively. Among them, the individual scope refers to that the experience management body of knowledge only affects the individual ability, and individuals can improve their management level; The department scope means that the experience management body of knowledge can affect a group of people in the department, and the department can collectively improve the experience management ability; The company scope refers to that the experience management body of knowledge can affect everyone in the company, and everyone in the company can improve the experience management awareness. The Y-axis is the level at which the experience management body of knowledge can influence the enterprise organization. The order from low to high is project level, system level, and culture level. Among them, the project level refers to that the experience management body of knowledge affects a single project team, helping the project team to improve product and service quality from the perspective of customer experience; At the system level, it means that the experience management body of knowledge affects multiple project groups and helps the project groups have the ability to make overall experience planning and evaluation system construction; At the culture level, it means that the experience management body of knowledge has affected the corporate culture, helping the company to formulate experience strategies and build experience organizational structure from strategic perspective.

To solve the problem of the experience knowledge is miscellaneous and unstructured, it's needed to construct problems from various perspectives through the Nine Squares Path, design intervention measures, and let employees and various departments participate effectively, so as to jointly build the common goals. The enterprise aims to establish a user centered service experience management platform to achieve changes at different levels. The views of outstanding scholars and practice pioneers are constantly developing, which will be summarized in the Nine Squares Path of experience management. For example, the Swiss International Organization for Standardization defined the concept of "user experience" in "User centered interaction system design", the 210th part of ISO 9241-210:2009. William H. Leffingwell, in his book Scientific Office Management (1917), proposed the classification of service objects and applied scientific management methods to each type of service. This makes user centered service experience management clearer.

The Nine Squares Path can not only establish the direction on the whole, but also integrate different basic skills in each quadrant, so as to achieve the purpose of effective participation and preparation of each stakeholder. By spanning multiple quadrants, the experience, expertise knowledge and skills required by each department can be effectively combined, thus solving the problem of disorder of experience management contact points. For example, the marketing department and the planning department of an enterprise have been set up separately, while the marketing department is subordinate to the marketing headquarters. In terms of product promotion functions, the marketing department is responsible for planning and implementation, but at the same time, the planning department is responsible for planning. The responsibilities of these two departments overlap. However, the enterprise has no clear authority provisions for these overlapping responsibilities and overlapping works, which leads to mutual buck passing among departments and seriously inhibits the improvement of organization and work efficiency [4]. At this time, all departments can cooperate smoothly through the Nine Squares Path.

In real life, the frequent mistake made by enterprises is to form a "department wall", and another mistake is what is commonly called "the bottom commands the head". In fact, these two problems are caused by the disorganization of experience knowledge. The reason why corporate departments cannot cooperate effectively is that they cannot adjust local interests and overall interests. Experience management is closely related to this element and makes enterprise services specific and clear. The failure of experiential knowledge to play a role is also the biggest problem that hindering the development of enterprises. The development of design innovation tools for experience touchpoints will be one of the key directions of service optimization and differentiated design. The Nine Squares Path is a good design innovation tool for touchpoints.

3.2 Three-Level Capability Model Making XMBOK Systematic

The three-level capabilities of experience management refer to the respective positioning of job position and inter-relationship of the three level development channels of

XMBOK. According to the depth and breadth of knowledge, the content of XMBOK can be divided into project level, system level and culture level.

The three-level development channel is intended for all personnel and members in professional fields involved in software, mobile terminal, or Internet application development, including R&D managers, demand analysts, software developers, software testers, UI designers, agile management masters, quality management personnel, etc. (Fig. 3).

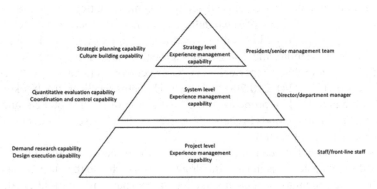

Fig. 3. Three-level Capability Model of Experience Management.

The three-level model can be understood from two different perspectives. From the horizontal perspective of project operation, the three-level development channel corresponds to the demand for experience management ability in the process of project operation. Among them, project level talents focus on the demand research capability and design implementation capability of experience management, system level talents focus on the quantitative evaluation capability and coordination and control capability of experience management, and culture level talents focus on the strategic planning capability and culture building capability of experience management. From the vertical perspective of the enterprise organization, the three-tier development channel corresponds to the experience management talent echelon in the enterprise organizational structure. It is specifically divided into project level experience management capability, system level experience management capability and culture level experience management capability.

In the era of experience economy, improving enterprise management plays an important role in the long-term development of enterprises [5]. Firstly, through the three-level model, a quantitative and qualitative system can be established within the enterprise, refining task decomposition and individual responsibility. To clear rights and responsibilities, sub task objectives, responsible persons, time points and deliverables. To make task information transparent. Let each stakeholder in the enterprise know or have a place to know who is responsible for each task and who is related to the task they are responsible for. Secondly, the three-level model can improve the enterprise experience management, which can fully apply modern knowledge and technology to practical work, so that every stakeholder in the enterprise can have a clear goal and reach consensus, and ensure that every work and everyone in the project is contributing to the realization of this goal. If everyone does not know what direction they are working towards, most of the time they can only work passively, and it is difficult to make more contributions to the whole project.

The division of power and responsibility of many enterprise stakeholders is chaotic. In an enterprise, employees will encounter great difficulties in performing their duties because they only emphasize the formulation of the goals and plans of the enterprise and departments, and the realization of the goals and plans does not have the support and cooperation of the corresponding departments or positions. Due to unclear understanding of the scope of responsibilities between departments or positions, and between superiors and subordinates, employees have unclear assignment of tasks and inaccurate understanding of assessment standards. These overlapping rights and responsibilities and overlapping tasks have no clear authority provisions and specific assessment standards, which lead to the phenomenon of "everyone is responsible, and everyone is not responsible" and "overstaffed institutions and superfluous staff". This phenomenon can be solved by three-level model. First of all, from the horizontal perspective of project operation, the three-level development channel corresponds to the demand for experience management ability in the process of project operation. Project level talents focus on the demand research ability and design implementation ability of experience management, system level talents focus on the quantitative evaluation ability and coordination and control ability of experience management, and culture level talents focus on the strategic planning ability and cultural construction ability of experience management. By dividing layer by layer and focusing on individual rights and obligations, each thing will have a clear person in charge.

4   Building Experience Management Body of Knowledge

The XMBOK was first proposed in November 2021 by China Southwest Branch of UXPA International User Experience Professional Organization, in conjunction with the Experience Management Talent Special Committee of Chongqing Enterprise Talent Development Research Association.

The experience management system is based on the enterprise's foundation (operation and organizational structure), through the design of the entire experience system (brand, marketing, product, service, and other links), delivers the value proposition of the enterprise to the target customer group, and gets the recognition and symbiosis of the customer group.

4.1   Project Level of Experience Management

The knowledge of project level talents mainly covers the experience management ability of front-line personnel, and carry out research and studies on experience strategy formulation, user experience research, experience design execution, experience effect evaluation and other knowledge around "how front-line business operators perform tasks with users as the center", so that the key actions to improve user satisfaction can be effectively implemented [6]. The project level experience management capability is divided into four modules: experience strategy formulation, user experience research, experience design execution and experience effect evaluation. It is not only necessary to start from the overall project management, systematically formulate experience strategies, decompose experience objectives, promote experience implementation, and achieve experience evaluation [7]. In addition, it is necessary to continuously insight into user pain points, comprehensively measure the internal and external conditions of the enterprise, accurately improve the sustainable competitiveness of products, so as to positively affect the brand strength of the enterprise, and provide scientific and systematic practical guidance for the enterprise to partially implement experience management [8]. The four modules form a closed loop, as shown in the following figure (Fig. 4).

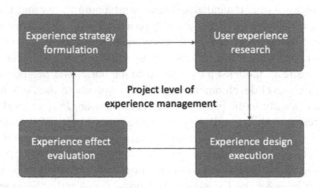

Fig. 4. Project Level of Experience Management.

The development of experience strategy can be carried out through two aspects: user journey map and decision chain map: user task journey map is a visual analysis tool that can show the process of users utilizing products or services to complete a certain task and the behavior of each stage, thus helping the team to find multi-dimensional innovation opportunities from the perspective of the overall user [9]. Decision chain map is a concept when studying user profiles, and is an important content to promote service implementation. Improve customer satisfaction, loyalty, and support by responding to customer interactions to meet or even exceed customer expectations.

User experience research can be carried out through six aspects: user role analysis, task step decomposition, competitive product analysis, demand definition, scenario definition, and user experience map [10].

Experience design execution can be carried out through five aspects: information architecture, pattern analysis, prototype design, design principles, and the construction of design system.

Experience effect evaluation refers to an activity that analyzes and studies products, process or services according to certain procedures and judges their experience effects according to certain goals, standards, technologies or means [11]. On this basis, a written evaluation report is formed to decide whether to adopt the scheme or iteration direction etc.

4.2 System Level of Experience Management

The knowledge of system level talents mainly covers the experience management ability of department heads, focusing on "how the middle managers conduct management with users as the center", so as to complete the research and study of experience management mechanism planning, experience indicator system construction, experience management platform construction and other knowledge, so that managers can improve satisfaction purposefully, systematically, and gradually.

The system level experience management capability is divided into three major modules: experience management mechanism planning, experience indicator system construction and experience management platform construction. The three modules form a closed loop, as shown in the figure (Fig. 5).

Fig. 5. System Level of Experience Management.

The experience indicator system construction refers to sorting out experience indicators, building a monitoring system based on the user perspective, and managing customer experience related data end-to-end.

The experience management platform construction refers to the construction of a digital experience management platform to realize automatic collection, integration, and intelligent analysis of omni channel data and form experience optimization actions.

The experience management mechanism planning can be carried out from six aspects: defining experience goals, formulating experience plans, declaring value propositions, reaching team consensus, building collaborative platforms, and designing agile experience. The plan of experience design project mainly includes design analysis, design implementation, design verification and design optimization. The value proposition will determine the overall tone of the whole project implementation. The value proposition is the delivery value of the product to users, and how the product or service will benefit your users. Team consensus refers to the common cognition reached by the managers and ordinary members of the team when they are working hard to achieve a certain goal, which is the awareness of cognition, discussion, interpretation, and decision-making through the whole design team. The collaborative design platform is a cloud collaboration center that meets the requirements of multiple scenarios of the design team. Agile experience design is based on agile development, which requires designers to modify the design scheme in a timely manner according to changes in user needs [12].

The experience management platform can be built from two aspects: multi-channel data collection and customer experience measurement analysis: multi-channel data collection refers to the use of data from different sources to reflect the experience level [13]. Customer experience measurement and analysis is the process of analyzing and seeing through the collected experience data [14].

4.3   Culture Level of Experience Management

The knowledge of strategic talents mainly covers the experience management ability of the senior management team. Focusing on "how senior managers develop strategies with users as the center", to carry out research and studies on experience strategy planning, experience organization evolution, experience management maturity and other knowledge, so that experience driven organizations can be built from the corporate strategy and culture level. Strategic experience management refers to a dynamic management process in which an enterprise determines its mission, sets its experience strategic objectives according to the external environment and internal conditions of the organization, to ensure the correct implementation of the objectives and achieve progress strategy, and implements such plans and decisions based on the internal capabilities of the enterprise, as well as conducts control during the implementation process (Fig. 6).

Fig. 6. Culture Level of Experience Management.

The planning of experience strategy can be carried out from two perspectives: insight of experience strategy and the design of experience management system. The design of experience management system is to further practice the ideal user or customer experience management, and comprehensively optimize the enterprise experience management by creating a closed-loop experience strategy.

The implementation of the experience strategy must be undertaken by an organization, driven by the strategy of "user or customer centered", but the original organization of the enterprise may not be able to adapt. Organizational evolution is indispensable to ensure that the experience strategy is implemented and moving towards the established goals. The evolution of experience organization can be carried out from three aspects:

the establishment of experience organization, the budget of experience organization, and the construction of experience culture.

The maturity of experience management refers to the enterprise's ability to attract and retain lifelong customers, who can not only reuse the businesses launched by the company, but also encourage others to do the same. This step can be carried out through digital management and experience management maturity. EXperience Management Maturity (hereinafter referred to as XMM) sees experience management as a project, to describe the various development stages of an organization in terms of strategy definition, organizational design, measurement improvement, data management and cultural precipitation. In accordance with this principle, the experience management process is monitored and studied to make it more standardized and scientific, so that the organization can better achieve its business or social goals.

5 Summary

With the rapid development of the national economy, the living standard and consumption level of residents are constantly improving. The needs of users are no longer focused on specific problems, the consumption habits have changed, and the change of thoughts has led to the arrival of the experience economy era. Under the background of experience economy, the business model of experience management is rising. At present, the experience management of enterprises is still in the early stage of development, and building a complete experience management body of knowledge is the only way for the future development of enterprise experience management. In order to solve the dilemma of current user experience change, from the perspective of experience management, structuring experience knowledge through the Nine Squares Path, and systematizing experience knowledge through the three-level model. It is believed that after the construction and improvement of the enterprise experience management body of knowledge, experience management will be more and more valued and acquire better development.

Acknowledgement. This work was supported by Doctoral startup fund and talent introduction fund project of Chongqing University of Posts and Telecommunications -- Research on the cost and benefit distribution of big data productization (K2020-201) and Chongqing educational science planning project -- Research on the talent training system of "social theme" in Colleges and Universities (2020-GX-284) and Research Center for network social development of Chongqing University of Posts and Telecommunications -- Research on the cost of network big data production (2020SKJD06).

References

1. Pine, B.J., Gilmore, J.H.: Welcome to the Experience Economy, vol. 76, no. 4, pp. 97–105 . Harvard Business Review (1998). https://doi.org/10.1080/00076799800000334
2. Margaret Rouse. customer experience management [EB/OL]. https://searchcustomerexperie nce.techtarget.com/definition/customer-experience-management-CEM-or-CXM. 2021–10–01

3. Peterme. Interface Design [EB/OL]. https://peterme.com/index112498.html 1998–09–24, 2019–09–05
4. William, L.: The Pocket Universal Principles of Design: 150 Essential Tools for Architects, Artists, Designers, Developers, Engineers, Inventors, and Managers (2015)
5. Gartner. Customer Experience Management [EB/OL]. https://www.sas.com/en_us/insights/marketing/customer-experience-management.html 2021–10–01
6. Susan, W.: 100 Things Every Designer Needs to Know About People. New Riders Publishing (2011)
7. Olsen, D.: The Lean Product Playbook (2015)
8. Hartson, R., Pyla, P.S.: The UX Book: Process and Guidelines for Ensuring a Quality User Experience. Morgan Kaufmann Publishers Inc. (2012)
9. Patton, J., Economy, P.: User Story Mapping: Discover the Whole Story, Build the Right Product. O'Reilly Media Inc. (2014)
10. Sauro, J.: Quantifying the User Experience: Practical Statistics for User Research. Morgan Kaufmann Publishers Inc. (2012)
11. Richter, M., Flückiger, M.D.: Usability Engineering kompakt Benutzbare Produkte gezielt entwickeln. DBLP (2013). https://doi.org/10.1007/978-3-642-34832-7
12. Dan, O.: The Lean Product Playbook: How to Innovate with Minimum Viable Products and Rapid Customer Feedback (2015)
13. Albert, B., Tullis, T.: Measuring the User Experience (Interactive Technologies): Collecting, Analyzing, and Presenting Usability Metrics. Morgan Kaufmann Publishers Inc. (2013)
14. Barnum, C.: Usability Testing Essentials: Ready, Set. Test!. Morgan Kaufmann Publishers Inc. (2011)

Research on Natural Objects and Creative Design from the Perspective of Phenomenology

Yonghui Lin[⊠] and Hailin Liu

Beijing Institute of Technology, Zhuhai, China
53907024@qq.com

Abstract. With the rapid development of digital technology and artificial intelligence, designers' design methods have also changed, including educational cognition, knowledge category, way of thinking, design logic and design value. The use of point fragment knowledge is shielding the inheritance, learning and innovation of inherent systematic profound knowledge. The inherent mode of conversation between people and the world is being replaced by the mode of conversation between people and AI and other tools. The inherent pattern of design and implementation, in which human beings collide with souls to enhance rationality, is being replaced by the interactive pattern of human beings, tools and machines. The inherent design ethics generated by the interaction of spiritual intentions between people in a specific field is being replaced by the self emotional value system of information presented by people and digital tools. As time goes by, designers lose their basic thinking ability as human beings.

The basic spirit of phenomenology is to "return to the thing itself". To return to the thing itself is to transcend the words and opinions of empiricism, explore the thing in the giving nature of the thing itself, and get rid of all the "foresight" that does not conform to the thing, so as to return to the thing itself. Husserl's phenomenology does not simply return to the phenomenal world, nor empirically recognize the phenomena of visible objects, or simply state some experience about the phenomenal facts, but returns to the matter itself, returns to the life world, and super empirically visualizes the essence of its intentions (spirit, outlook, reason).

This topic takes Husserl's phenomenology as the methodology of design, so as to guide the practice of original art design. With the concept of "great art and design", it extends the unknown and possibility of design development experimentally. In terms of specific modeling, through in-depth observation and experience, some natural forms and form elements are transformed into design elements. Information is transmitted through images, emphasizing the insight into the form representation and life organism from the natural form, so as to transcend the surface description, understand the potential relationship between form and function, and strengthen its form language and form consciousness. Through the research and analysis of natural objects, we can intuitively experience their growth process, laws and many phenomena that affect their lives, and clarify their internal essence. Open up the real natural phenomenon covered by the design itself, and truly reveal the possibility of diversified creation of design art through the personal understanding of designers.

Keywords: Phenomenology · Natural objects · Life world · Experience · Creative design

P.-L. P. Rau (Ed.): HCII 2023, LNCS 14023, pp. 221–236, 2023.
https://doi.org/10.1007/978-3-031-35939-2_17

1 Introduction

The contemporary Chinese design industry has gradually become mature from its initial start. The maturity of design is not based on the specific experience gained from repeated practice, nor can it be achieved by virtue of the expanding market capacity. As large as a country or a region, as small as an enterprise or a team, the energy and level of design must be determined by their understanding and research depth of design.

Today, China's design industry is growing rapidly. At the same time, growth will inevitably bring many problems. In the field of design theory, green, information, experience, sustainable design, integrated design, emotion and other western theoretical trends have been rising one after another, and have become the popular words of designers and educators for a period of time. Everyone is adding attributive to "design" to redefine the "scientific paradigm" of design. The "noumenon" of design has been eroded and disintegrated by external fashion knowledge, and has become blurred. Compared with the theoretical development of academia, Chinese enterprises are more "pragmatic". They regard design as a means of market competition, a tool to stimulate consumption and serve the appreciation of capital. The purpose of design activities is alienated, and the method is understood as a shortcut. In the era of copy and paste, the internal design of enterprises is represented by collage, transplantation and imitation. At the same time, design education has shown the trend of "Great Leap Forward" in recent years. Therefore, there is a need for scientific methodology to guide design practice, improve design value, return to the origin of design, and change the design thinking and plagiarism of original concepts.

2 Background and Significance of the Study

2.1 Imprisonment of Chinese Traditional Thought on Design Creative Thinking

Back in ancient times, Chinese design is a "precocious child". As early as in Shuowen Jiezi, the ancients have defined the "work" that is intrinsically related to design, that is, "people and things that are handmade according to a certain French scale". And in Kaogongji, the Chinese ancients have summarized the materials, dimensions and patterns of design at a very early time. However, there is a lack of necessary scientific classification after synthesis and necessary quantitative analysis after qualitative analysis. Therefore, discrete experience cannot be upgraded to a systematic scientific theory. In addition, in ancient China, although there were "six state-owned posts", there was no further scientific and systematic division of the handicraft industry, and the purpose of the establishment of the "six posts" was to maintain the feudal unified politics, which was the product of agricultural civilization and the tool of the feudal system. Under the control of religious ideology, patriarchal ideology and feudal etiquette, people have no independent personality and thinking. They are deeply bound by feudal ideology and are closed. The theoretical summary can be described as a matter of "sages and sages", and the "sages" entrusted with the important task are just to transform scientific intuition into the macro metaphysics between "heaven, earth and man". Therefore, the thinking of Chinese people has been imprisoned at this time, and their behavior ability has also been limited.

2.2   The Influence of Modern Design Education on Design Creativity in China

In modern times, the Opium War opened the door of the country, and the Qing government sought self-rescue in the defeat. The Westernization Movement was launched by the Westernization Movement. In order to achieve self-improvement, it set up industrial schools and recruited and trained a large number of design and drawing talents. The seemingly prosperous education also hides various problems. First of all, in the industrial education at the end of the Qing Dynasty, only attention was paid to the cultivation of students' skills, but not to the construction of their thinking consciousness and moral ethics; Secondly, the Westernization Movement basically copied foreign models mechanically and failed to quote them on the basis of its own digestion and absorption; In addition, the training of both drawing and painting courses in the industrial school was separated from traditional Chinese crafts at the beginning. Therefore, Chinese design lacks its own language and thinking ability at the very beginning. At the beginning of the 20th century, some new art schools were established in succession. Many domestic design education pioneers went abroad to study and learn from foreign mature experience, such as "taking the law as a teacher", and introducing the Japanese "pattern study" system. The design education has developed slightly, but in terms of teaching methods, each college still takes painting skills as the basis and "sketch changes" as the main technique. The current situation of emphasizing skills and neglecting thinking in China's design education has not changed, and the teaching model that has been used for reference has also become a stereotype of misunderstanding. Since China's reform and opening up, the popularization of higher education has been promoted, and the art and design education has developed rapidly. However, from the perspective of the curriculum of art and design education in most colleges and universities, it is basically to copy the existing design professional courses in some developed countries, and some have made major or minor adjustments and reforms in the traditional art education curriculum, and some colleges and universities simply offer courses according to their own teachers, It completely disregards the actual situation of talent training. Many colleges and universities pursue "marketization" one-sidedly, and they have become good skill training centers for investment and marketing. Social, humanities, science and technology comprehensive courses are lacking, and design planning, business application and other courses are also lacking. Colleges and universities and society are more or less trapped in the "utilitarian trend of thought", and students' comprehensive ability cannot be improved, and their way of thinking cannot be exercised. Chinese design has gradually lost itself, but still continues to "mass production" without paying attention to quality. China's design education has not figured out what should be brought to students, nor has it solved its own problems from the root cause. The phenomenon of design plagiarism is serious.

2.3   Impact of Artificial Intelligence Intervention on Design Creativity

With the continuous involvement of artificial intelligence (AI) and its profound impact on the design field, a significant change is the improvement of designers' efficiency and the liberation of labor force. AI has been able to assist designers to achieve enviable design results. Its powerful function paints a desirable future for designers: designers' work will become unimaginably easy, and design results will become more creative.

However, as the film "Terminator" has triggered for more than 30 years, the debate about whether the future AI robot will replace human beings has not ended. Now, while AI technology benefits the design industry, it also triggered designers' thinking about the development of the future industry. The publication of Herali's "A Brief History of the Future" has played a role in fuelling this topic, and has once again aroused designers' reflection on AI. Will AI be competent for design and replace the role of designer? The result of this role transformation includes not only the change of AI in the form of design expression, but also the optimization of the derivation process of design thinking, that is, whether AI can ultimately think, analyze and solve problems like designers. Design thinking and its value evaluation are the core power of design innovation. Human design activities are accompanied by subjective feelings such as analysis, reasoning, analogy and imagination, that is, their own creativity, as well as their unique emotions, emotions and understanding of things that are formed by both innate and acquired. Therefore, under the impact of artificial intelligence technology, the original creativity of human beings is particularly important.

2.4   The Guiding Significance of Phenomenological Methodology to Design Creativity

To explain the design problem from the perspective of phenomenology is no longer to define "what design is". This is because in the view of phenomenology, the existing design is to objectify "things", that is, people take themselves as the main body and send out a certain "object" to him. The things considered by the design are regarded as "objects", which means that things appear in their non-authentic state and become the appendages of the subject. Therefore, we must abandon the prejudice and foresight in the traditional thought, that is, we should not think about the design problem in the way that "subject" and "object" are separated and opposed to each other. We should no longer regard the design as an external object that is the same as the general existence, but should treat the design activity as a process of mutual generation of human and object. Therefore, design, as a kind of picture presented in the world of human life, is the result of the self-expression of human creativity and vitality. Using the philosophical method of phenomenology, the author thinks about the contemporary design phenomenon and its problems on the philosophical and aesthetic level, distinguishes the boundary for design, understands how the design phenomenon occurs, analyzes various existing design phenomena, and states the historical evolution of design. As a way of human existence, design needs to be restored to the world of life.

3   Research Methods and Steps

3.1   Design Methods and Learning Methods from the Perspective of Phenomenology

Through an overview of the main characteristics and methods of phenomenology, the author finds that the relevant theories and methods of phenomenology have a positive reference and guidance role for the construction of designers' learning view.

First, the choice of design content. In the process of design and learning, we will encounter complex learning content. How designers learn more valuable knowledge in a limited time, which involves the choice of learning content. The practice of phenomenological research shows that the more freedom the researcher gives the research object to choose their own life experience, the richer the information the researcher obtains. When choosing the design content, try to choose the content that is consistent with your own life experience, so that you can find rich knowledge and experience from the limited design content.

Second, the choice of design methods, which play a very important role in the composition of designers' design concepts. The effective design method can make the design get twice the result with half the effort, while the bad design method can only make the design get twice the result with half the effort. Therefore, the selection of design methods should be very careful. The research methods of phenomenological reduction, construction and deconstruction still have reference and guidance for design methods. Restore the acquired knowledge. In the design process, when meeting new knowledge and new content, if you only stay in the new knowledge itself for learning and thinking, that kind of knowledge is inert knowledge without vitality, and the effect of learning and design will not be too obvious. At this time, we should restore the new knowledge to the basic principles and methods we have learned, and lead back to the source of knowledge itself for thinking. To construct the whole knowledge system, the learning content is easy to obtain, but the construction of the knowledge system abstracted from the learning content needs to go through a long and arduous process. From the perspective of phenomenology, learning content is a kind of "being", while knowledge system is a kind of "being". The learning content is easy to be "accessible". The knowledge system as the "existence" cannot "simply meet it". Therefore, in order to better grasp the learning content and improve the effectiveness of learning, it is necessary to build our own knowledge system. According to the overall knowledge construction method of phenomenology from individual to general, we can start with specific learning contents, increase knowledge reserves, conduct in-depth processing on the basis of detailed knowledge accumulation, and gradually build our own personalized overall knowledge system. Deconstruct learning and design purposes, which have the function of guiding design practice and effective design. Different learning and design purposes will lead to different learning and design results. The designer should deconstruct the learning and design purpose until the source of the design purpose. Through constant questioning and dismantling, we can conceptually explain the design purpose, grasp the significance of the quality of the design purpose, better stimulate the designer's design motivation and creativity, and strive to achieve the design purpose with practical actions.

3.2   The Principle and Construction of Design Artistic Conception

Heidegger's phenomenological thought and Taoist Laozi's thought have some similarities. Using his thought to explain the principle of artistic conception has both the charm of traditional Chinese culture and the characteristics of western philosophy. Heidegger believed that we always "face the existence of...". This is a dynamic process with a certain trend. From the big point of view, people must die, so life is born to be "dying"; From a small point of view, people always set their own goals, big or small, and spend a long life in the process of constantly reaching these goals. Therefore, the "existence towards…" is the actual life situation of people, which constitutes our daily life world, from which we can obtain the meaning of life. In this sense, the world of life is the artistic conception of life. Our state of existence in the artistic conception of life is shown in Fig. 1.

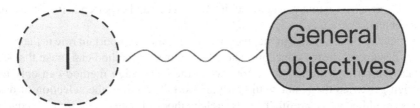

Fig. 1. Existence state in the artistic conception of life

In Fig. 1, there is no clear boundary between "I" and the surrounding daily life scenes, but it is not a whole, so "I" is separated from the surrounding by dotted lines. "I" will always set some goals in life, but this goal is only a general trend, without a mandatory development line. The process from "I" to the goal is uncertain, infinite and convoluted. It can make "I" produce infinite meaning. Therefore, there is no lack of meaning in the life world. "The complete and rich life world itself is the only theme and purpose. Life is not for other purposes, but for 'living'." Living is the meaning of life. In the world of science or design, due to the separation of the subject and the object, the opposition is caused. The "I" as the subject is separated from the scientific knowledge as the object, and the "I" forms a solid line relationship with the surrounding, and the scientific knowledge becomes the objective design goal. In order to achieve the best design effect, these goals are often clear, limited and measurable. At the same time, in order to make designers "take fewer detours", many designs have even designed the track to achieve the goal, and try to be "straight". This state of existence is shown in Fig. 2.

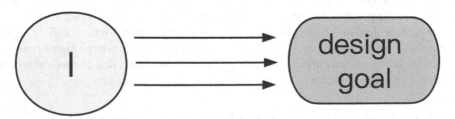

Fig. 2. Existence state in the design world

In this seemingly fast and unrestrained track, the past "towards the existence of" has been broken. Although we have reached the scientific goal, we may have missed the meaning. In fact, many years of design practice has proved that it has led to serious consequences, such as lack of design spirit, rigidity, thinness of thought, lack of vitality, short-sighted, eager for quick success and instant benefit, and other chaotic phenomena are all meaningless manifestations.

Of course, it seems obviously unrealistic to abandon the scientific world or the design world and return to the primitive, self-sufficient, small country and few people era that is integrated with the natural world. Humans can no longer part with the scientific world or the design world. Scientific knowledge has long been integrated into our soul and into our blood. In this case, according to Heidegger's statement of "towards the existence of", on the premise of achieving the established design goal, we can change the process of tending to it, and in this process, try to integrate the designer as the main body into it, forming a situation similar to the existence of "I" in the meaningful life world. This is the artistic conception that design should strive to create - the conception of meaning occurrence and comprehension. This process is shown in Fig. 3.

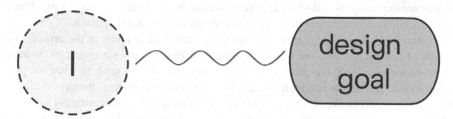

Fig. 3. Existence state in design artistic conception

3.3 Da VINCI'S Design Manuscript is the Embodiment of the Existing State of Design Artistic Conception

Leonardo da Vinci is the most famous artist, sculptor, architect, engineer, scientist, scientific master, literary theorist, great philosopher, poet, musician and inventor in the Italian Renaissance. He is a profound, knowledgeable and versatile artist. Because he is an all-rounder, he is also known as "the most perfect representative of the Renaissance". In the process of scientists and artists engaging in creation, whether they grasp the world in a rational way or in an aesthetic way, they always consciously or unconsciously realize the unity of sensibility and rationality in human beings. The subject of creation has a strong desire for knowledge and aesthetic appreciation. In the process of seeking, there will be a primitive disturbance arising from surprise. Science can break through the inherent thinking framework with the help of artistic imagination, Realize the leap of concept. With the help of scientific fantasy and rationality, art can break through perceptual intuition and realize emotional leaps. The artist's passion and the scientist's idea are integrated to expand the new space of nature, life and spiritual world, just like the realm of "Zhuang Zhou Mengdie". As for the relationship between art and science, Leonardo da Vinci handled it best.

Da Vinci took notes every day throughout his life. After his death, he left a large number of unorganized manuscripts, which were written in reverse with his unique left hand mirror image. It was difficult to interpret, mysterious and mysterious, such as superstition, and the cipher word set was annotated around the deconstructed accurate and beautiful pictures. These "mirror books", which need to be reflected in a mirror to be read smoothly, were lost for more than 200 years in the world, and were not seen until 1817. The manuscript is more than 7000 pages long, with more than 5000 existing pages, covering topics including astronomy, anatomy, optics, painting skills, mathematics and even human-controlled flight. His understanding of human body, natural laws and physiological functions transcended that era for several centuries, and still affects scientific research. He is a prophet of the modern world and an epic of the long history of human development. Today, the aircraft, tanks, and even robots invented by humans have already been involved in the 15th century Da Vinci manuscript. His manuscript page is called a true encyclopedia of science and technology in the 15th century. He studied all the mysteries of nature and life with the never-ending spirit of exploration, fused art and science, intelligence and emotion, body and spirit, inherited and developed the humanistic thoughts and realistic expression methods of predecessors, pushed art to an unprecedented height, and made great contributions to natural science.

Leonardo da Vinci's design manuscript is the state of existence in the artistic conception of design, and also the true embodiment of Heidegger's statement of "towards the existence of...". On the premise of determining the design goal, he attaches great importance to the whole research process and personal experience, integrates himself into the life world in the design process of the manuscript, and constantly improves and improves his design manuscript with the drive of curiosity, This is the artistic conception that design should strive to create - the conception of meaning occurrence and comprehension, and stimulate the generation of design creativity. As shown in Figs. 4 and 5.

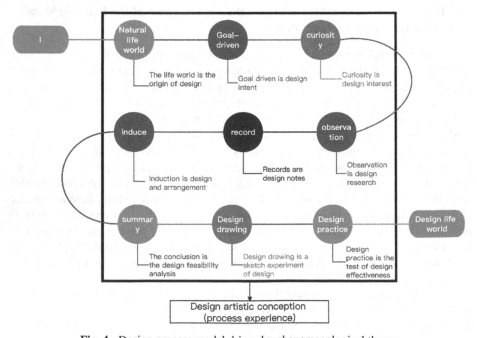

Fig. 4. Design process model driven by phenomenological theory

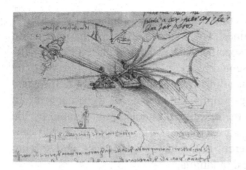 

Fig. 5. Da Vinci's design manuscript

4 Implementation and Case Study

The beauty of lacquer is reflected in its properties and appropriate operating techniques. The higher the technical difficulty, the more challenging and higher aesthetical value it is and has. Chinese lacquer has many limitations. For example, it is expensive, requires complicated techniques, easy to cause skin allergy and has many limitations in colours. But without these limitations, the soul and beauty of lacquer will disappear. The value of lacquer art lies in its irreplaceability. Lacquer creation should first apply the rule of lacquer itself. We should realize and accept its limitations before any creation.

Modern lacquer art integrating into modern space requires us to use traditional techniques and combine new design concepts. Due to change of concepts, there are certain differences in aesthetic standards and production techniques between modern and traditional lacquer art. Traditional lacquerware pays more attention to the neatness, preciseness, and symmetry of shapes, as well as the practicality and decorations. While modern lacquerware design emphasizes the aesthetic value of lacquerware. The shape and decoration of modern lacquerware are integrated, in other words, combined perfectly. The modern lacquer art breaks the boundaries between painting and craftsmanship, absorbs modern design concepts in the design, attach significance to the texture of the material itself and applies the characteristics of the lacquer to combine various techniques to express the unique charm of lacquer. Hegel once said that implication is more profound than visible presence. A work of art should have implication. We should create lacquer works with a sense of the times, and the unique oriental charm. Innovating and expanding on the basis of elegance and quietness and ancient charm will better meet the aesthetic characteristics and development path of lacquer itself.

4.1 Design and Implementation of Deep Experience of Life World as a Person in the Emotional World

With the rapid development of digital technology and artificial intelligence, the way of design has changed. The use of point-like fragment knowledge is masking the inheritance, learning and innovation of inherent systematic and advanced knowledge. The inherent design mode of human-world conversation is being replaced by the conversation mode of human-AI and other tools. The inherent mode of design implementation in which human and soul collide to improve rationality is being replaced by the inter-active mode of human and tools and machines. The inherent ethics of the interaction of spiritual intentions between people in a specific field is being replaced by the self-emotional value system of information presented by people and digital tools. With the passage of time, the progress of the times, the adjustment of the industrial structure, and the demand for talents. The reform of design implementation needs to be carried out. The reform of design behavior is based on the emotional interaction generated by the direct contact between human beings and nature and the world, presenting the process of creating beautiful life and world as different individuals of designers, and solving different design problems with their own design language.

The unknowns and possibilities of the development of experimental extension design. In terms of specific modeling, some natural form and form elements are transformed into design elements through observation. Through images to transmit information, it emphasizes to obtain insight into the form representation and life organism from the natural form, so as to transcend the surface description, so as to understand the potential relationship between form and function, and strengthen its form language and form consciousness. We sometimes confuse the aesthetic and plastic knowledge contained in the form. It can be understood that aesthetics is a sufficient condition, that is, a designer should have aesthetic knowledge and a good sense of beauty. And modeling is a necessary ability. One of the main activities of design is modeling, so designers need to create beauty while recognizing beauty. The scope of the concept is the broadest. In addition to some ways of thinking that can be summarized in language, the concept is largely related to its own background knowledge, such as the social environment, learning and working atmosphere, thinking mode, and so on. Attitude is also a sociological aspect. From a horizontal perspective, we can think that attitude is the source of forming a style, and we can also see the world outlook and values of designers from design works. Klaus Lehman, a famous German design educator, said in his book Design of Design Education Education that inspiration must play an important role in design education. The ideal goal of education is to explore individual talents, consolidate and develop them. He believes that the shape, appearance and emotional value of design are the essential content of basic practice. In addition to functional requirements, we should focus on the development and research of form and structure. Different from Bauhaus' more artistic basic course practice mode, it develops and perfects its own system by finding practical problems in the design process. Basic practice is a test ground for personal learning methods. Through practice, we can find a methodology suitable for ourselves.

4.2 Design Creative Process Based on Nature

People and nature coexist harmoniously. Designers often draw inspiration from nature in the process of creation. Many disordered elements in nature can bring people different visual experience and even affect people's aesthetic taste after orderly processing by designers. Nature is the best inspiration pool for designers. The animals, plants and microorganisms in nature are all worth exploring and learning from. Bionic design is based on the "shape", "color pattern", "sound", "function", "structure" and "material" in the natural world, and selectively applies these characteristic principles in the design process. In terms of refining plant elements, the ingenuity of nature has brought us a lot of enlightenment. In terms of refining animal elements, our ancestors were inspired by bird nesting and invented "nesting" to resist the attack of beasts. In ancient times, Luban invented a sharp saw based on the experience of being cut by a leaf once entering the mountain and the saw teeth of locusts inadvertently observed, thus changing the way of doing things and improving the efficiency of doing things. The process of design is also the process of transforming disorder into order. Through this process, designers can extract some disorder from the nature on the basis of following the laws of nature, and replace it with an orderly design process. The natural forms, even though abstract, in the final analysis, their creative points are from nature, but higher than nature, and should be able to serve humanity.

The re-recognition of natural forms requires us to put aside our visual inertia and understand and interpret natural forms from a completely different perspective. With the help of advanced scientific means, we will experience an exciting new visual experience and also a natural form different from the previous impression. Obtaining design inspiration from natural forms is the basic way of visual design. From the perspective of visual thinking, try to combine and transform concepts, visual images and natural forms creatively. As shown in Fig. 6.

Design creative implementation process model

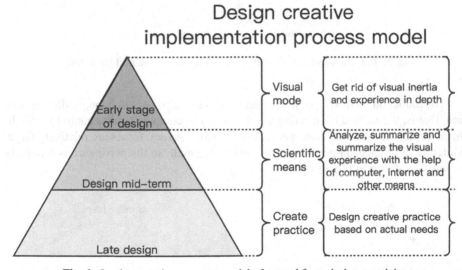

Fig. 6. Implementation process model of natural form design creativity

Starting from the natural form is because the natural form is simple, straightforward and common, which can make people quickly find materials and make associations. It is low in difficulty and easy to use. Select a natural object of interest, and express it in multiple design languages from the object's own analysis, growth process, living environment, existence significance, etc. to train the ability of integrated design (as shown in Fig. 7). Learn to observe natural forms. Through in-depth analysis, comparison and induction of natural forms, we can find the formation rules of natural forms, and then provide basis and reference for the research and creation of design forms. It can also improve the ability of designers to observe and analyze problems. (As shown in Fig. 8).

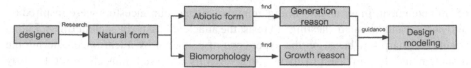

Fig. 7. Design purpose based on nature

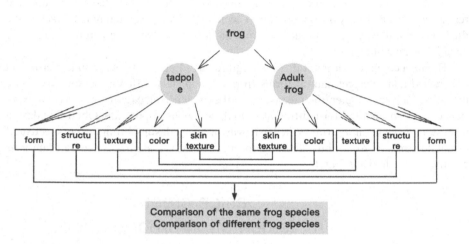

Fig. 8. Induction and comparison of many elements in natural form design

The induction method of similar natural forms can also be called longitudinal induction, that is, the method of selecting a certain level to compare similar natural forms. In this method, the common elements between various natural forms are relatively large, while the differences in personality are relatively small, so the pertinence is relatively strong. (As shown in Fig. 9).

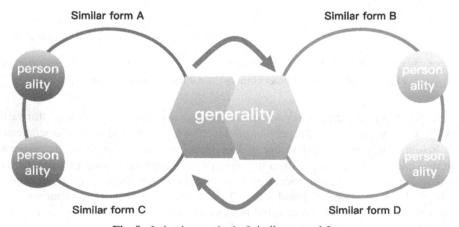

Fig. 9. Induction method of similar natural forms

4.3 Design Case Analysis Based on Nature

The natural form focuses on the designer's curiosity about natural things, and returns the visual subject to the nature itself. Through the research and analysis of natural things, it can intuitively and experience its growth process, laws and many phenomena that affect its life, and clarify its internal essence. Open up the real natural phenomenon covered by the design itself, and reveal the possibility of multiple creation of design art through the personal understanding of designers. Figures 11, 12 and 13 are the classroom assignments of the first-year students majoring in visual communication design in the College of Design and Art. The students bring the natural objects into the classroom. First, the students are required to understand and record the natural phenomena of the natural objects studied through comprehensive literature retrieval, and then analyze the different local forms of the natural objects by dissecting the natural objects and observing them from multiple angles (as shown in Fig. 10), Growth mechanism analysis and internal morphological unit analysis are classified and drawn on the design sketch. All elements of visual form hidden in nature, such as symmetry, proportion, rhythm, rhythm, balance, coordination, variation, unity, etc., are recorded through vision to lay the foundation for subsequent design. Finally, it is required to develop artistic expression or design expression as the professional basis of visual communication design according to the research results and the sudden inspiration in the composition. (As shown in Figs. 11, 12 and 13).

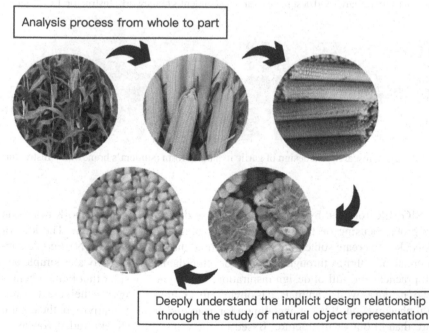

Fig. 10. Different local morphology analysis and multi-angle observation of natural objects

Fig. 11. Analysis, research and design of natural form corn (student's homework) Instructor: Lin Yonghui

Fig. 12. Analysis, research and design of natural fig (student's homework) Instructor: Lin Yonghui

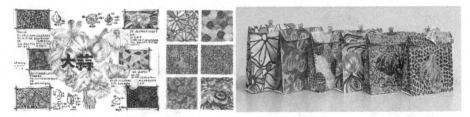

Fig. 13. Analysis, research and design of garlic in natural form (student's homework) Instructor: Lin Yonghui

NOSIGNER, founded by the famous Japanese designer Hideki Tadao Kawa, is an activity group focusing on the symbiosis and evolution of social design. The idea of NOSIGNER is to create something invisible behind the shape (NO-SIGN). People constantly create new things through design to develop themselves. Advocates simple and natural, practical and full of design inspiration. When you consider that human beings are part of nature as well as animals, it is obvious that human beings use their creativity as a natural phenomenon. It is not uncommon for us to find greater creativity in the natural structure than in our own structure. Based on these insights, Hideki Tadao Kawasaki concluded that human creativity is a phenomenon similar to biological evolution, and continues to seek to build creativity through evolution. This makes him systematize evolutionary creativity, which is a creative thinking method that applies biological evolutionary structure to design and innovation. Mr. Tadao Kawasaki Yingfu believes that "learning from nature" can carry out more sophisticated design, and we still need to learn from nature again. Creativity is everyone's innate instinct. We must create and change all existing things. We all live in an era that must be redesigned and changed. Sustainable development is inevitable. We must make changes and think about the needs of society with design philosophy.

The evolutionary thinking of Taidao Chuan Yingfu is also a philosophical thinking. Every evolution process of human beings is a great design creation. Every real creation is the result of life experience and human progress, not the result of design, but the design inspiration generated by human beings in the interaction between nature and survival. It is also the important philosophical essence of phenomenology "back to the thing itself", Only go back to the matter itself to understand the purpose and significance of design, understand the nature of design, understand the needs of people, and return to the premise that there is no design experience and case to learn from, how to communicate with the natural world again, understand, experience life, and create creative design works that belong to different designers' personal characteristics. (As shown in Fig. 14).

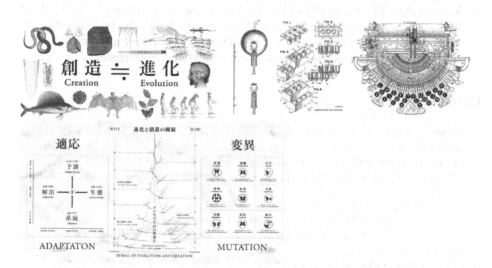

Fig. 14. Some works of the book "Evolution Thinking" by Taidao Chuan Yingfu

5   Conclusion

Design itself is a world, and only by removing the cover can we open our own existence. The contemporary design phenomenon is complicated and has expanded to all aspects of our life world. At present, the research of design theory in China is largely biased towards the description of a phenomenon, lacking the analysis of design problems and a philosophical speculation. Therefore, using phenomenological methods to analyze design problems has very important theoretical and practical significance. In terms of theoretical significance, because most of the current research on design theory in China still stays in the general description of brief history, classification and so on, the introduction of interdisciplinary knowledge often stays in the stage of explanation and application of nouns and principles. The use of phenomenological methods combined with Chinese design practice to reflect the general nature of design will play an important role in promoting the in-depth development of basic design theory. In terms of practical significance, because behind the seemingly prosperous appearance of the contemporary Chinese design community, there are various crises caused by design activities that are divorced from specific human background knowledge, such as the crisis of technology, the crisis that deviates from the sustainable development of human beings, and the crisis of value nihility. Reflecting on the deep relationship between design and human life world and survival experience from the perspective of phenomenology will help to break the unreasonable and outdated design concepts, It plays a positive role in guiding the design practice in contemporary China. Nature is the resource pool of design, and natural elements are also the regular visitors of design. The integration of natural elements into the design reflects that designers introduce the beauty and charm of nature into the design. As a successful designer, the process of observation is also the process of thinking. In daily life, we should be a conscientious person who loves life, care about the flowers and plants around us, maintain a keen sense of design observation and smell, and obtain design inspiration from nature, Inject innovative thinking and natural vitality into the design, and promote the continuous innovation and development of the design.

References

1. Husserl, E.: Methods of Phenomenology (translated by Ni, L.). Shanghai Translation Publishing House (2005)
2. Liu, G.: Thoughts on China's Industrial Design. Jiangsu Phoenix Art Press (2018)
3. Lehman, K.: (Germany) Design Education Design (translated by Zhao, L, and Du, H.). Jiangsu Phoenix Fine Arts Press (2016)
4. Husserl, D: Phenomenology of the Living World (translated by Ni, L. and Zhang, T.). Shanghai Translation Publishing House (2005)
5. Du, Y.: Unity of Knowledge and Action, Wang Yangming. Jiangsu Phoenix Literature and Art Publishing House (2017)
6. Liu, G.: On Juice Culture. Heilongjiang Science and Technology Press, Harbin (1995)
7. Kening, S.: Architectural Phenomenology. China Construction Industry Press, Beijing (2008)
8. Wang, W., Zhong, H.: The principle and construction of teaching artistic conception - from the perspective of Heidegger's phenomenology. Education and Culture Forum (01), 112–118 (2022). https://doi.org/10.15958/j.cnki.jywhlt.2022.01.017

A Discussion on Sound Field Optimization with Utilizing Design Thinking Framework

Wei Lin[1](✉) and Hsuan Lin[2]

[1] School of Architecture, Feng Chia University, Taichung, Taiwan, Republic of China
`wlin@fcu.edu.tw`
[2] Industrial Design, ChaoYang University of Technology, Taichung, Taiwan, Republic of China
`t2020021@mail.cyut.edu.tw`

Abstract. The purpose of this study is mainly to solve indoor acoustics problems, with the goal of optimizing indoor sound field practice as the guidance, for complex topics such as room types and material properties, put forward effective module to optimize sound field strategies, and further understand the practical field topics and modular development process. The research content mainly starts from the spatial narrative framework of design thinking, and analyzes the environment of different sound fields through the object intervention and situational conditions in the narrative process. The research method and framework system of integrated with "Design Thinking" is introduced with practical cases, hoping to stimulate interior designers' interest in acoustic-oriented performance issues, and share the prediction results of the effectiveness results through computer simulation software verification and analysis of design solutions. Based on the sound field scenario and design process, this study aims to introduce another feasible thinking to the room acoustics planning partners engaged in related professional topics in the process of practical operation.

Keywords: Room acoustics · Design thinking · Computer simulation

1 Introduction

1.1 Research Background

With the advent of Industry 4.0 toward the 5.0 era, the demand for talent cultivation has changed from professional knowledge orientation to cross-field innovation and integration ability, and higher education has also changed and adapted accordingly. In order to cultivate talents capable of challenging the future industrial transformation and changing society, the Design thinking model and method advocated by Stanford University D school, The Project based learning (PBL) is designed for cross-field courses that are widely referred to by educational institutions, guiding innovative thinking, problem definition, teamwork and problem solving ability, so that real problems can be solved through professional application, and cultivating employability. The future of jobs report (World Economic Forum), published by the World Economic Forum in 2018, addresses the core

P.-L. P. Rau (Ed.): HCII 2023, LNCS 14023, pp. 237–251, 2023.
https://doi.org/10.1007/978-3-031-35939-2_18

competencies required by different generations. In addition to creativity, critical thinking and collaboration, The most important is the ability to solve Complex problem. Continuously, in the process of problem solving, through solving complex problems of strategy and action plan, seeking cross-field professional support and cooperation, is the primary key, for the interaction of professional verification field must also be adjusted accordingly. In recent years, "design thinking and integration" has been frequently adopted and discussed. It is a mode of thinking that emphasizes experience and implementation, and reconnects users from different walks of life through feedback from user experience and empathy. This study attempts to change the one-way verification model of the "formula derivation form of room acoustic optimization performance". Starting from the spatial narrative structure, based on the materials and scenes of the sound field in the narrative process, the indoor performance of different sound fields is analyzed by situational learning, and the actual cases are used for learning. At the same time, the concept of CDIO integration design is integrated to make the practical development closer to the core sound field verification results. Through Conceive, Design, Implement and Operate of the teaching mode of engineering education in the process of design thinking, it is the whole thinking process, and this teaching mode is not only applicable in the field of engineering, but also widely used in professional courses in other fields. In the teaching process to induce students to participate in the actual design, play an important basis in the teaching process. Especially from the conception stage, objects required for the indoor sound field are introduced, and the acoustic field performance and sound insulation are taken as the guidance for the initial planning. The learning method for the construction of indoor sound field comfort level is shown in Fig. 1.

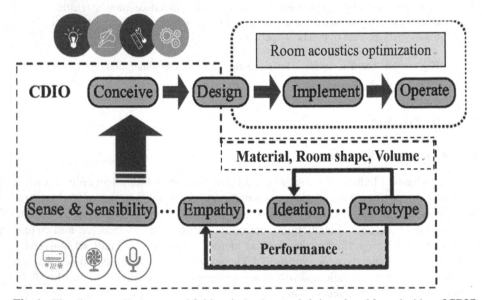

Fig. 1. The diagram of indoor sound field optimization mode is introduced from the idea of CDIO design thinking

"Design thinking" was originally proposed by Tim Brown, CEO of IDEO, a former product design company. It helps original products to have different changes and innovative thinking, and re-proposes innovative ideas based on traditional product design needs and feedback from user experience, so as to transform them into designer experience. Starting a new trend of design service (Brown & Wyatt, 2010) [1], in view of this, it is necessary to integrate the learned knowledge from the overall perspective while considering the essence of the task and solving the condition. Since 2000, MIT and other higher education institutions have jointly developed and promoted the CDIO engineering education model and established the CDIO International Cooperation Organization. Through the teaching mode of CDIO engineering education in the process of Design thinking [2], Conceive, design, Implement and Operate is the whole thinking process. This mode is not only applicable in the field of engineering, but also widely used in professional courses in other fields. Architectural and indoor sound field optimization plays an important role in the development of indoor acoustics by inducing the actual sound field to participate in planning and design. Advocate MAPS (Mind mapping, Asking questions, Presentation, Scaffolding instruction) through innovative thinking methods, is used to guide the acoustic performance and get close to the core goal of acoustics profession. Problem-oriented professional strategies, the first part, based on Problem-based Learning (PBL) deal with problems in the process of understanding and solving problems. The second part, based on Project-based Learning, investigates and explains the actual problems, and produces the final solution to the problems. The third part, based on case-based Learning, is the process of solving practical problems in the case, and learning by means of practical exercises, analysis, solutions and proposing solutions. Finally, through peer support, action learning continuously reflects on the feasibility of its solutions to real problems.

In the traditional case study, projects mainly connect from the past experience and case situations to conduct. Especially in the current professional field of study, projects must integrate other professional knowledge, based on the establishment of more links knowledge and conditional links, need to back support in approach activities. Linkage is not just a case-by-case discussion, but a professional issue that can describe the knowledge of the case-by-case situation to the issues with perspectives of optimization. In addition, according to Siemens [3], "Learning is a process of connecting special notation with knowledge sources." Establish connections between notations in the design process that establish knowledge systems and processes. The depth and breadth of the discussion from the perspective of ideal approaches depends on the degree of connection of the concept, and if the node (Domination, concepts, profession) is recognized by more disciplined experts. The possibility of cross-pollination of learning communities will have more opportunities to present. As opposed to strong ties and weak ties, they are two paths with different information. In traditional case study, conditional knowledge transfer occurs when ideal scenario is induced. Downes [4] mentioned that situational knowledge Emergence and transfer include four elements: (1) Context, (2) Salience, (3) Emergence and (4) Memory, as shown in Fig. 2.

Spatial narrative method is a kind of image situation to describe a presentation of its professional knowledge pedigree, through the narrative process, objects and conditions complete record, knowledge transfer. The disclosure of design-related problems, the

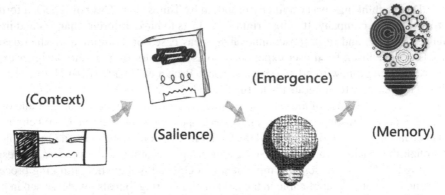

Fig. 2. Contextual knowledge Emergence and transfer includes four elements: Context, Salience, Emergence and Memory (Downes, 2006) [4].

designer's existing knowledge links are strengthened, and the shortcomings of the case are made up by the application of design optimization and performance scenarios. The thinking method of memory and concentration was first developed by Buzan [5], which is a structural and diffuse cognitive memory method mainly based on images. Gerard [6] developed a narrative connotation of spatial text in order to strengthen and connect the information transmission between readers, and summarized five characteristics: (1) Spatial, (2) Temporal, (3) Substantive, (4) Pragmatic and (5) Functional.

The spatial narrative method also emphasizes its connotation, including diachronic and synchronous, selectively reducing the scope of analysis to perform several projects, or integrating each conceptual thoughts to strengthen critical thinking and analysis ability from the implementation exercise, and to conduct in-depth investigation and systematic analysis of selected topics. In the field of innovation and practice, professionals play the role of director and screenwriter. The most challenging is to fully understand the project and the target content, design the specialty as the topic development, and guide the exploration of the practical field. Instructors' contextual guidance, within its role of creativity and complex problem solving, is helping Process engagement to improve contextual outcomes, Whether situational guidance affects designers' complex problem solving self-efficacy, and develop practical solutions based on their complex problem solving ability.

1.2 Research Purposes

In Taiwan, the trend of "flip" is emerging in creative thinking, trying to change the previous one-way linear way, with innovative design thinking methods, so that the design profession and performance orientation, closer to the core value of optimization. Based on the process of "Design thinking", this research enables designers to better understand the sound field design and material planning in interior space. Based on the spatial narrative structure of creative thinking, this research analyzes the performance of different scenarios according to the objects and conditions in the narrative process. Induce the designer to explore the process of one of the results of performance optimization by design planning and sound field performance. The objectives of this research are as follows:

1. Indoor acoustics planning, based on the spatial narrative concept, to explore the effectiveness of the process, according to the analysis of different scenarios, understand the principle of performance design, improve the indoor sound field according to the degree of compliance, to obtain the required professional ability.
2. Based on the "CDIO" design thinking method, designers are induced to discuss the indoor of different performance. The situation and conditions generated by the narrative process are discussed according to the situational analysis, and the implementation cases are analyzed to support the performance optimization effect in practice.
3. In this study, the concept of sound field optimization is based on the spatial narrative structure known in interior design, peer structure and interaction.
4. Get the maximum learning benefit in a diversified way to improve the understanding of interior acoustics design planning, and move forward towards the goal of broad professional technology indoor.

2 Literature Review

2.1 Design Thinking

In order to further master the professional cooperative operation method, Conceive, Design, Implement and Operate with CDIO design thinking mode as the whole thinking process, and this operation process mode is not only applicable in the engineering field. Also widely used in other fields of professional courses. As shown in Fig. 3, introduce the Double Diamond adopted by Stanford D School to develop the feasibility proposal of multiple thinking by Diverge and Converge in different teaching development stages. In the two stages of Conceive and Design, the first Loop (1st Loop) corresponding to the design development should be started and the check point of the first problem setting should be set. The check point task should conceive whether consensus or opinion has been generated. To confirm consensus building before moving into the Implement phase. The equipment planning and performance prototype developed from the first loop was further developed to develop operational solutions. In the process of carrying out the 2nd Loop, Workable project was workable to continuously grasp practical technology and application and gradually turn to workable project. Meanwhile, the second Check point of feasibility correction was carried out. Finally, the spatial narrative structure discusses the sound field performance required by different functional spaces. Through the actual real field to verify the completion, optimization performance discussion derivation, to verify the case, expect in the field practice ability training, to achieve the set performance results.

2.2 Room Acoustics Theory

When sound waves are incident obliquely with contacting the interface of an object, the incident angle will be equal to the reflection angle. The reflection is like a mirror-reflection effect, specular reflections will occur [7]. The reflecting surface of acoustic

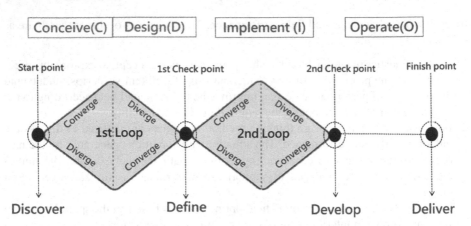

Fig. 3. The framework of research methods and implementation steps of room acoustics optimization.

energy has concave and convex texture and decoration, so the intensity of the reflected sound will be reduced, and the reflected energy will be scattered at various angles, which is called diffuse reflection [8, 9]. The physical characteristics of the natural sound field are limited, and the use of sound amplification can enhance the condition, especially in large hall spaces. Loudspeaker equipment is used to compensate for sufficient volume, adjust the characteristics of the sound and the balance of parts during the performance, while recording and reproducing in other spaces. The sound amplification system must provide a volume of 85 dB or more in a general auditorium and 110 dB in a rock venue. In addition to providing sufficient volume, improve sound clarity, a wide range of output frequencies to meet the requirements of high standards. The acoustic properties of the interior space radiation causes a series of reflections. The volume of sound is mainly distributed by direct sound and reflected sound. Except for distance, the volume of sound will not decrease significantly. The scale of space is also related to the characteristics of sound distribution. Understand the detailed relationship between subsequent reflections (e.g., early reflections) and the direct sound, including the late energy response that records the arrival time and acoustic energy of the direct sound, as well as subsequent reflections [10]. The recommended reverberation time (RT) is planned according to the volume of the chamber. The acoustical parameters that are subject to physical quantities, such as RT30, C80, D50, Ts and EDT, are regulated based on the impulse response of international standard ISO 3382 (Bradley, 2004) [11].

3 Methodology

Starting from the spatial narrative framework, this study integrates the design thinking concept of CDIO integrated design and is close to the core value of sound field optimization practice. Through the implementation steps starting from the spatial narrative structure, including the introduction of sound insulation performance, indoor sound field performance and sound field verification, room acoustics development and practical implementation of different sound fields and uses are carried out. The research and implementation steps are divided into three stages. First, after the situational derivation of sound field optimization performance is introduced, the situational analysis of different indoor sound fields is discussed based on the sound insulation conditions and sound field performance of the narrative process, and the different phases of logic connection and relationship combination for performance optimization are induced. In the first phase, the current situation of the sound field is revealed. The second phase is the discussion of sound insulation and sound field performance. In the third phase, the technical application feasibility scheme of sound field verification is verified and presented. The framework of research methods and implementation steps of this research is shown in Fig. 4. The indoor sound field should be designed for the first Loop (1st Loop) to confirm the performance and set the first problem check point. Check point task be confirmed whether consensus has been reached. 2nd Loop, continuously grasp practical technology and application, gradually turn to indoor sound field-oriented scheme (Workable project), carry out the second check point of feasibility correction, finally, the workable application is workable.

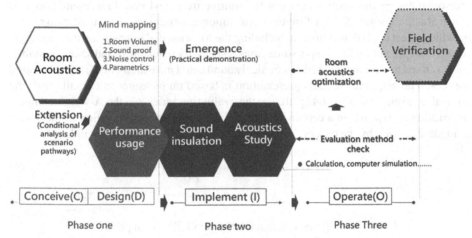

Fig. 4. The framework of research methods and implementation steps of room acoustics optimization.

3.1 Sound Performance Usage

In addition to the adjustment of indoor space, sound energy provides considerable information on the distribution of sound field. In order to further determine the objective of indoor sound field performance planning, the independence and correlation of acoustic parameters were confirmed. Evaluation techniques through computer simulation include several oriented discussions, including the evaluation of indoor sound insulation performance in diffusion sites. After the verification measurement is completed, the physical properties in real time are collected through objective testing, and the corresponding relationship between objective physical measurements is explored. In this stage, the indoor sound field model and sound insulation performance are predicted and evaluated by computer simulation. With the continuous advancement of software and hardware technology, the computer simulation software for hall sound quality has matured and is widely used in hall research on sound quality design and evaluation of sound field characteristics. Computer simulation of indoor sound field according to geometric acoustics, the actual hall model is established to simulate the propagation law of sound wave in the room. In order to reduce the time required for generating noise contour map by computer simulation, a kind of contour map drawing software based on measurement is developed. The CAD file of indoor space can be used as the base map for future evaluation. NoiseAt-Work software is used to analyze the actual measurement and draw the distribution map of sound energy. The research results can be used to establish the optimization scheme of the overall distribution of sound field. The computer model realizes the visual correspondence of the measured results, and further draws the image of sound pressure level. By verifying the sound field model, the future sound field and standard can be predicted, and another stage of subjective evaluation can be carried out. Using the computer to simulate the sound field environment results, using the grid calculation method to draw the sound energy distribution curve, with intuitive trend and visual representation, and can evaluate the sound field in different environmental conditions. The simulation results provide a great deal of information, including the location and intensity of sound energy. It has trend prediction function in some cases, especially when the sound source is stable, such as fixed noise source (fixed mechanical sound), and measurement of multiple sound sources. The mapping contours presentation is based on measurement results with the equivalent average volume $LAeq$ (dB) as the evaluation index and the A-weighted noise intermittently exposed in a certain period of time in the selected position in the sound field are averaged by the energy. The parameter index formula is shown in Eq. 1.

$$LAeq = 10\,log\frac{1}{T}\int_{t}^{t+T}(\frac{Pt}{P0})^2dt \tag{1}$$

$LAeq$: A-weighted average energy level dB (A) in period time;
T : measurement time in seconds;
Pt: measure sound pressure in Pa;
P0: reference sound pressure, based on 20μPa

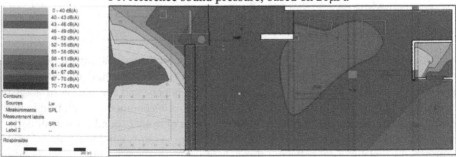

Fig. 5. Results of calculation within the occupational noise sector and present the visualization of mapping contour.

For different sound sources, according to the size of sound energy results to draw, ceaseless measures to reduce sound energy and discuss. NoiseAtWork software is used to simulate and draw the sound energy distribution curve to establish the overall distribution of sound field. Use individual environmental factors to verify and hypothesize, build a model. Through the realization of measurement correspondence, the sound pressure level image and sound field model are verified, and the future scenario is predicted to explore the influence of sound source energy. Results are discussed and evaluated (See in Fig. 5).

3.2 Sound Proof for Interior

The building structure reduces the noise interference between conjunction indoor rooms through the performance of sound insulation. There are many reasons for the treatment of the indoor acoustic environment, including adjacent space and outdoor air noise and noise vibration generated by the equipment. Noise is introduced which is penetrated into the room through building doors, windows, walls, and floors, and the vibration of building internal equipment and indoor activities of residents constitute the increase of environmental noise, which has become one of the reasons for disturbing life and affecting environmental quality. The existing standards and specifications for sound insulation aim to strengthen the whole system of sound insulation, not to regulate individual components or materials, reduce the disturbance and influence of residents' living sound independently, and improve the quality of the quiet environment of the residential area. Air insulation design and floor impact insulation design, according to the code has its scope of application. 150 mm thick reinforced concrete walls were used for the interior space in Taiwan; Surface cement mortar paint, the field sound insulation grade can reach more than 42 dB, has good sound insulation performance, the glass sound insulation performance specification standard is also more than 36 dB, can provide professional manufacturers in the development of materials in the process of benchmark reference. As long as the mass per unit area (m) and the Modulus of Elasticity (E) of the panel are known, the sound transmission through a single-layer plate can be approximated to a good accuracy. At low and mid frequency bands, the acoustic transmission loss (TL) is calculated according to the mass law [12, 13]. The prediction formula is shown in Eq. 2.
The prediction formula is shown in Eq. 2.

$$TL = 20 \ \log{(mf)} - 48 \, dB \tag{2}$$

At high frequencies, the coincidence effect weakens the acoustic transmission, and the transmission loss is given by Eq. 3.

$$TL = 20 \ \log{(mf)} + 10 \ \log{(f/fc)} - 44 \, dB \tag{3}$$

Another computer simulation software evaluates the sound insulation of partitions, floors, ceilings and Windows. This method can estimate the sound transmission loss of 1/3 frequency and A-weighted sound insulation (STC or Rw), which can provide acoustic consultants with suggestions on the structural sound insulation of space in detailed design. The low frequency acoustic transmission effect of small building structures is considered in the calculation of sound insulation, and it is applied to the estimation of small building structures such as windows and common building structures. It takes into account finite size effects, which are important when predicting small samples (such as windows) and low-frequency normal elements. The material database is provided in the software as a practical reference. The main source is laboratory data provided by professional material vendors, which is widely used in various countries and regions. The database is updated regularly through the technical support of software vendors, and users are welcome to provide feedback to expand and improve the material base. As with other estimation tools, simulation is not a substitute for actual measurements. However, based on the results of comparison with the predicted data obtained from the database, the difference in sound insulation performance can be within 3 dB for most building structures and components. For example, in the dual-panel construction system, the calculation results of the predicted transmission loss can refer to four different frequency regions. At medium and high frequencies, the transmission loss is mainly determined by the plate quality law. When the two plates are coupled, the transmission loss TL can reach 18 dB. At the same time, the resonant frequency (fo) is determined by the mass of the panel and the mass of the boundary gap, but in the air layer between the plates,

Table 1. The results of sound insulation calculation for double layer of lightly structure

Freq.	TL	Result of S Chart and illustration
50	12.6	
63	12.4	
80	10.6	
100	9.7	
125	15.0	
160	20.9	
200	26.1	
250	30.4	
315	34.1	
400	37.3	
500	40.1	
630	42.4	
800	44.5	
1000	46.5	
1250	48.3	
1600	49.9	
2000	51.2	
2500	51.9	
3150	51.1	Wall: + 1 x 9 mm Plasterboard + Timber stud (132 mm x40 mm) +
4000	42.0	132 mm Fiberglass (10kg/m^3) + 1 x 9 mm Plasterboard
5000	44.4	
Rw		39
C		-4
Ctr		-11

the low frequency fL has the same wavelength, the cavity and the panel are coupled together, and the low frequency transmission loss can be increased by 12 dB. The results of sound insulation prediction was derived from INSUL v9.0.20. Double layer with 9 mm plasterboard +132 mm Fiberglass (10 kg/m^3) +9 mm plasterboard of lightly structure for sound insulation calculation as shown in Table 1.

4   Results

First of all, the sound field issues are analyzed and left with important themes as the main discussion guideline and as the basis for the design of the next stage. The purpose of indoor sound field use is taken as the context guidance, such as home, office, audio-chamber, etc. After the tasks and themes are established, the sound field influence factors of indoor environment, including room volume, surface area, sound absorption coefficient and room space type, are used to evaluate the sound field environment under different conditions by visualization and disassembly system (Opening parts). The measured values reflect the actual state of the space and explain its related performance. The professional solution of indoor sound fields corresponding to space function, single-use, or multifunctional compound problems is discussed. This study explores and documents the processes and steps of planning and configuring thinking in the process of problem-solving between different interfaces, and analyzes the rational (performance system view) and emotional (spatial aesthetic view) problem-solving approaches adopted by the case as the content of the optimized analysis. An open-office space is initiated as an example in this study as shown in Table 2. In terms of sound field environment, an open office space with good potential for comfortable work field. Air sound transmission has limited effect, and there is no solid sound transmission. Sound field measurement results show that the outdoor balcony can meet the standard volume, indoor sound field verification also meets the indoor sound field comfort sound energy, for the partition wall and office area outward window recommended to meet the sound insulation performance standards.

Table 2. The results of approaching sound filed with phases of design thinking

Phase	Sound filed Issue addressing
Con-ceive	1. The project is located on the 6th floor, adjacent to the quiet lane, with limited impact of air transmission. 2. The sound field of long-distance elevators and equipment in the office space has no impact of solid sound transmission on the preliminary field zoning.
De-sign	1. The household wall should conform to the sound insulation performance (Rw $\geqq$ 45dB) 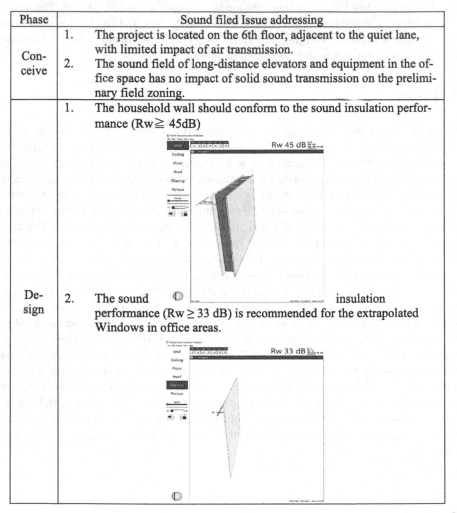 2. The sound ⬤ insulation performance (Rw $\geq$ 33 dB) is recommended for the extrapolated Windows in office areas.

(*continued*)

Table 2. (*continued*)

Imple-ment	1.	Entrance door, airtight glass door (D1).
	2.	As for the design suggestions, the glass door (D2) is in line with the sound insulation performance (Rw≧ 33 dB).
	3.	As the cross door (D3) belongs to the office area environment, it is recommended to maintain the status quo.
	4.	The balcony floor door (D4) is recommended to meet the sound insulation performance (Rw≧ 33dB).
	5.	The walls of the office and other adjacent rooms (P1) should conform to the sound insulation performance (Rw≧ 45dB).
	6.	It is recommended to combine the sound insulation performance of furniture with the partition wall (at P2) to optimize the current situation.
	7.	The external window (W1) in office area is recommended to meet the sound insulation performance (Rw≧ 33 dB).
		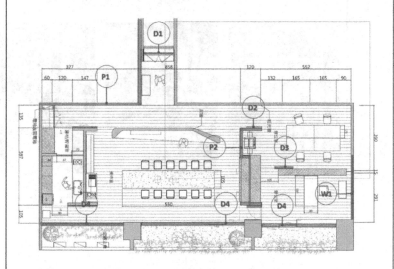
Oper-ate	1.	The LAeq(dB) of the outdoor balcony is 45.6dB;
	2.	The outdoor sound field was more than 99% 42.0dB during the sampling and measurement time.
	3.	Measured results of LAeq(dB) are below 74dB during the day, below 70 dB at night and below 67 dB at night.
	4.	The average sound energy of the average energy is LAeq(dB) 26.2dB(A), which is consistent with the comfort of the indoor sound field.
	5.	On-site verification conforms to the standards of the second type of residential quiet sound control zone.
	6.	In the process of indoor sound field measurement, the window is closed and the sound field is silent.

(*continued*)

Table 2. (*continued*)

Parameter Verification point	LAeq (dB)	LAF max (dB)	LAF min (dB)	L 99% (dB)
P1	45.6	52.1	41.3	42.0
P2	25.5	32.2	22.6	
P3	34.1	36.5	32.0	
P4	24.8	29.9	19.6	
P5	28.1	30.6	25.7	
P6	20.6	23.7	18.0	
P7	24.2	28.4	20.6	
Average	26.2	30.2	23.1	

P1 measurement point is located on the outdoor balcony of the office

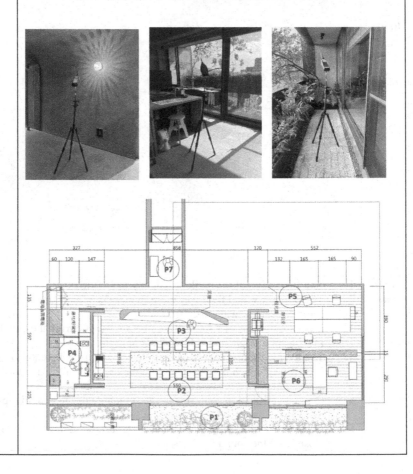

5 Discussion

This study attempts the problem-based PBL mode of "Design thinking". Based on the spatial narrative framework, the indoor sound field situational planning analysis is carried out, and the practical case is used for teaching and learning. The educational concept of CDIO integrated design is more consistent with the core value of indoor sound field optimization. Room acoustics design planning is often discussed in terms of performance and numerical calculation. Under the guidance of space narrative creativity approaches, interior designers can systematically understand the nature of interior sound field and effectively engage to support the design plan systematically. Differ from the indoor sound field discussion, the paper proposes a kind of solution to issues, which will bring out a jade effect for interior designers engaged in the field of specialized indoor sound study.

Acknowledgements. This study was subsidized and supervised by Research Project of Feng Chia University, and Grace Liu who are kindly share the verification of design office venue for achieving the results. At the same time, the author hereby extends sincere gratitude to the reviewers who gave many valuable suggestions for revision of this paper.

References

1. Brown, T., Wyatt, J.: Design thinking for social innovation. Development Outreach **12**(1), 29–43 (2010)
2. Yeh, S.-C., et al.: Diverged preferences towards sustainable development goals? A comparison between academia and the communication industry. Int. J. Environ. Res. Public Health **16**(22), 4577 (2019)
3. Siemens, G.: Connectivism: a learning theory for the digital age. Int. J. Technol. Distance Learn. **2**, 1–8 (2005)
4. Downes, S.: Learning networks and connective knowledge. Collective Intell. E-learning **20**, 1–26 (2006)
5. Buzan, T., Abbott, S.: Mind Maps for Kids: Max Your Memory and Concentration. Thompsons, London (2015)
6. Genette, G.: Paratexts: Thresholds of Interpretation, Trans. Jane E. Lewin. Cambridge UP, New York (1997)
7. Barron, M.: Auditorium Acoustics and Architectural Design. E & FN Spon, London (1993)
8. Beranek, L.L.: Concert Halls and Opera Houses: How They Sound. Springer, New York (1996)
9. Beranek, L.L.: Concert Halls and Opera Houses: Music, Acoustics, and Architecture, 2nd edn. Springer, New York (2004). https://doi.org/10.1007/978-0-387-21636-2
10. Long, M.: Architectural Acoustics. Elservier Academic Press, London (2006)
11. Bradley, J.S.: Using ISO3382 Measures to Evaluate Acoustical Conditions in Concert Halls (2004)
12. Sharp, B.H.: Prediction Methods for the Sound Transmission of Building Elements. Noise Control Engineering **11** (1978)
13. Cremer, L., Heckel, M., Ungar, E.E.: Structureborne Sound. Springer Verlag (1988)

Application of Mathematical Logic in Modern Design

Jie Tang[1,2] and Xing Ji[1,2(✉)]

[1] Beijing Technology Institute, Zhuhai, Zhuhai 519088, People's Republic of China
54619184@qq.com
[2] Bangkok Thonburi University, Bangkok 10170, Thailand

Abstract. Rationality and sensibility have been complementing and restricting each other in the process of design. Mathematicians have used mathematics for thousands of years to uncover the secrets of beauty, and it has long been an invaluable tool for composition and design. Many artists and designers derive infinite possibilities from mathematical thinking. Early geometry used empirical principles of figure, length, Angle, area, and volume to meet the practical needs of mapping, architecture, astronomy, and various crafts. That's why ancient Greek architects used the Golden Section at the Parthenon, and Byzantine architects elegantly combined geometric concepts like square, circle, cube and arched hemisphere in the design of Istanbul's Hagias Sophia (Stichel, 2010) [1]. Nowadays, with the in-depth study of the design discipline, the position of mathematical logical thinking has become more and more prominent in the teaching of design and design foundation. It is not only a knowledge resource of design, but also a means to reduce experiments and eliminate technical errors. Design allows algorithms and laws to be embodied in a more concrete way in space. In the same way, modern design relies on points, lines, surfaces, proportion, symmetry, geometry and structure, which are often used in mathematics.

Keywords: mathematical logic · Natural form · Design thinking

1 Introduction

Throughout history, nature has inspired the principles of science and technology as well as major inventions. Due to the pressure of survival competition, individual differences in nature have their own long evolution and thus have the ability to adapt to changes in nature. By using the ability of observation, thinking and design, human beings began to imitate these creatures, and through creative thinking and labor, made simple and practical tools, which enhanced their ability to fight against nature and the ability to survive. The appearance of early human tools is not imaginary, but a direct simulation of the existing form or a certain way of composition in nature. Although the production process is relatively superficial and simple, on the other hand, it also proves that the origin and embryonic form of the ability of logical thinking has already existed in the primary stage of human creation. With the progress of human civilization and the more extensive

P.-L. P. Rau (Ed.): HCII 2023, LNCS 14023, pp. 252–259, 2023.
https://doi.org/10.1007/978-3-031-35939-2_19

and in-depth study of natural science, human beings have classified these studies in detail, thus giving birth to philosophy, mathematics, physics and other academic fields, which have been influential to this day. In modern times, human beings derive mathematical theorems and formulas from the analysis of the forms of natural objects, and apply them in all directions and fields of modern design through mathematical logical thinking, and constantly explore the inherent causal relationship between the two (Dai, 2007) [2]. At the present stage, the design can be more scientific and rational based on mathematics. In the future design means, we can draw lessons from the mathematical logic thinking to carry on the in-depth study of parametric design and digital modeling. Mathematical logical thinking is an indispensable part of design thinking, and rigorous digital logic is a kind of rationalism. In the basic design teaching of colleges and universities, a large number of mathematical logical thinking subject exercises are needed, because only with rigorous thinking design can make it better serve the public.

2 Literature Review

The ancient Greeks attached great importance to mathematics and logic, and their achievements occupy an extremely important position in the history of mathematics. With human's understanding of objective things rising from experience to theory, Thales, the ancient Greek thinker, scientist and philosopher, advocated that science should not be satisfied with intuitive, perceptual and special understanding, but should advocate abstract, rational and general understanding. This advocacy also laid the foundation for the creation of rational mathematics by Pythagoras. The contributions made by the mathematicians of ancient Greece made great contributions to the development of mathematics, physics and physics and the progress of practical disciplines in the later world, from geometry to engineering, from geography to astronomy.

Starting from the Pythagorean School, ancient Greece, through the combination of deductive reasoning and induction, believed that mathematics was no longer a set of static rules, but a dynamic system capable of complex development, and put forward the idea that "beauty is a kind of harmony of numbers". From the perspective of the development history of western aesthetics, ancient Greek sculpture to the most core aesthetic principles of neoclassicism in the 19th century are basically based on this idea, and even include the thinking and practice of the beauty of design in modern design (Lin, 2021) [3]. In life, everything needs logic, and mathematics represents the most basic logical thinking in life. The design with mathematical logical thinking can not only make it more scientific and rational, but also make the design present the eternal beauty of mathematics.

2.1 Mathematical Logic and Art

Mathematics is a knowledge that abstracts specific problems into the relationship between spatial form and quantity, and mathematical thinking is a thinking method that examines and studies objects according to mathematical laws. Mathematical thinking is abstract thinking and belongs to higher logical thinking form. But there are no strict boundaries between forms of thought and they often permeate each other. Symbols used in thinking activities can be images in perceptual thinking, that is, memory elements, including the estimation of quantitative and spatial relations. Therefore, mathematical logical thinking is often permeated in artistic activities.

The harmony based on quantitative relations can explain the universality of mathematical logical thinking in the field of art. The same is true in art. The application of perspective in painting based on mathematical principles is an important milestone in the development history of western art (Ni, 2018) [4]. The Renaissance master Leonardo Da Vinci, who made a great contribution to perspective, said, "No human endeavor can be a science unless it opens its own path through the expression and proof of mathematics." He believed that the purpose of painting was to reproduce nature, and that the value of painting lay in its accurate representation. Therefore, painting was a science, which, like other sciences, was based on mathematics.

The aesthetic evaluation of form also relies on quantitative description. For example, big eyes, slim figure and so on. And vice versa, negative aesthetic judgments such as short body shape, slanted eyes and crooked mouth are also based on mathematical relationships such as quantity and location. Therefore, the structure and proportion of the form should be considered in the composition of painting. The use of the famous golden ratio in painting and design fully proves this point. In addition to simple physical composition, the design of color and shade also reflects mathematical thinking. For example, there is a proportional relationship between the cool and warm degree of the tone, the color system or the transition of light and shade. Beyond a certain percentage is exaggeration, deviating from the truth of art.

Of course, artistic reality is not the same as objective reality. The quantitative relationship of things in art such as painting need not be exactly the same as that of real things. The symbolic form used in artistic creation itself contains appropriate elasticity in scale. For example, it is true that painting can reflect the original appearance of things in reality, but it does not need to pursue 100% "reality", including various quantitative and proportional relations.

Ancient Chinese architecture is symmetrical and square. Among them, not only the aesthetic pursuit, but also the use of mathematical thinking. "Dougong" structure is a unique form of ancient Chinese architecture (Tao, 2020) [5]. Dou and arch, all are supporting members in the building of wooden structure in our country, at the column and beam junction. The arched elbow protruding from the top of the column is called the arch, and the square cushion between the arches is called the bucket. Dougong bearing structure, can make a large degree of eaves extension, not only beautiful form, and symmetrical structure can achieve the balance of forces, so that the building has stability (see Fig. 1). The application of Dougong immortalized ancient Chinese architectural art, which cannot be separated from the precise mechanical calculation and other mathematical thinking.

Art cannot be separated from mathematical thinking. The form of art has a quantitative attribute, and the harmony of art is essentially the harmony of quantitative relations. Therefore, the creation and appreciation activities of art are permeated with mathematical thinking. The communication between different art departments can rely on mathematical thinking, and the educational activities of art also benefit from mathematical thinking.

Fig. 1. Dougong (picture from the network)

2.2 The Influence of Mathematics on Ancient Greek Architecture

In the field of mathematics, many Western scholars are fascinated by the golden ratio. The ancient Greek mathematician Euclid described the golden section in his "Elements" written in the third century BC, which became the earliest recorded example of the golden Section. Ancient Greeks even believed that mathematics was the most fundamental logic for the operation of the world. They not only learned and applied these logic in the field of architectural design, for example, in the proportion of the Parthenon Temple (see Fig. 2), they strictly followed and applied this logic (Zhao, 2021) [6].

Fig. 2. Parthenon Temple (picture from the network)

2.3 Aesthetics in Mathematics

When we were still thinking about the boundaries between arts and sciences, our pioneers probably anticipated long ago that knowledge was what kept the arts alive. Pythagoras said, "The most beautiful of all three-dimensional shapes is the sphere; the most beautiful of all planar shapes is the circle." Because the two shapes are symmetric in all directions. Symmetrical beauty can be traced back to the patterns of the Mesopotamian civilization (Launay, 2016) [7].

In the process of mathematical exploration, mathematicians strive to establish the research direction of mathematics according to the aesthetic standards of simplicity, harmony, unity and abstractness. They then put the fruits of their labor in the most rational form, namely, mathematical formula. This is a very important beauty in mathematics – the beauty of simplicity. Simplicity is also evident in the design world, such as the appearance of Apple products and the design of MUJI products (Cao, 2017) [8].

Mathematical language shows mathematical content succinctly by means of mathematical symbols, which embodies accuracy, orderliness, generality, simplicity and organization. The unified beauty of mathematics refers to the internal relations or common laws between different mathematical objects or different components of the same object. The common law of unifying beauty is also an important law in the design process.

3   The Practice and Research of Mathematics in Design

3.1   Mathematics in the Hive

The shape of the hive is a perfect hexagon, which is the inspiration for many designs. In a Honey packaging design named HONEY, the designer directly uses hexagons in the honeycomb as the shape of the entire packaging bottle, and uses high transparency of high-quality glass, which can show the honey inside the jar at a glance (see Fig. 3). This design is just a simple imitation of the appearance of the beehive, but the mathematics contained in the beehive has benefited mankind a lot, thus achieving more scientific and technological development (Ruan, 2021) [9].

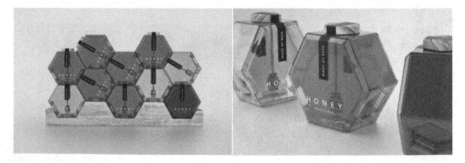

Fig. 3. HONEY packaging design (picture from the network)

Hexagons exist everywhere in nature, from beehives to snow crystals, and they have the laws of physics as well as mathematical geometry. In fact, strictly speaking, the honeycomb is a strict hexagon column shape, one end is flat hexagonal opening, the other end is closed hexagonal diamond chassis, composed of three identical diamond obtuse Angle of 109°28', acute Angle of 70°32'. The wall of the nest is made of beeswax, and the thickness of each side is 0.073mm, which is quite accurate with minimal error (Cao Z., 2005) [10]. All the hives are tilted slightly horizontally because of the direction of the Earth's magnetic field, which prevents honey from leaking out of the hives.

Darwin once noted that the perfect hexagon of a beehive was "the least labor-intensive and least material-intensive choice." In his view, since the hexagonal hive requires the least amount of energy and time, the survival of the fittest is a natural way for bees to evolve this way of building (see Fig. 4).

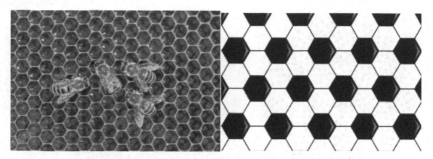

Fig. 4. Hive and Hexagons (picture from the network)

Mathematicians have also worked out that if a plane is covered with figures of the same shape and size, with no gaps between them and no overlap, only equilateral triangles, squares and hexagons can solve this geometric problem. At the same time, the use of honeycomb structure is a way to save materials because the sum of the girth required to use the regular hexagon is the least when the same area is covered.

In daily life, mobile phone signals are transmitted between different areas through base stations in the form of electromagnetic wave, but the electromagnetic wave transmission distance is limited, and gradually fades with the increase of distance. So in order for the signal to reach a wide enough range, you need to set up a lot of base stations. The distribution of the base station is not random (Wei, 2021) [11]. In order to save costs and maximize the use of resources, the distribution of the base station has been carefully calculated, and this calculation process is precisely from the mathematical thinking of the hive.

The structure of the hive is not only high strength and light weight, but also has a good reflection in sound insulation and heat insulation. Now in the field of aviation, the space shuttle, artificial satellites, spacecraft have a large number of internal honeycomb structure, even the shell of the artificial satellite is almost all honeycomb structure, after all, this is the most material saving structure.

3.2 Mathematics in Sunflowers

Sunflowers are very interesting plants in nature. They will always follow the sunlight and turn themselves. The artist Van Gogh also left many paintings about sunflowers. The sunflower is also a very famous plant in the mathematical community, because the arrangement of the seeds in the disk of the sunflower was found to be very consistent with the Fibonacci series (Ye, 2014) [12]. Modern mathematicians use computer equipment to replace sunflower seeds with dots to simulate computer experiments, after continuous verification found that the divergence Angle must be 137.5° golden Angle, because no matter the divergence Angle is greater than or less than 137.5°, there will be gaps between dots. Such verification results have inspired many designers to apply the principle of Fibonacci series to the design field, such as the mini audio system launched by Xiao MI (see Fig. 5).

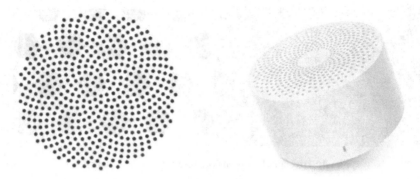

Fig. 5. Xiao MI Bluetooth speaker (picture from the network)

3.3 Imitation Shark Skin Swimsuit

In 2010, FINA banned high-tech swimsuits from competition, referring to the imitation shark-skin suits. Biologists have found that the shark is very fast in the water and one of the dominant ocean, because the rough V-shaped wrinkles on the surface of its skin can greatly reduce the friction of the water, so that the water around its body is not only fast and efficient flow (Liang, 2020) [13]. The ultra-stretch fiber surface of the suit mimics the shark skin structure. In the last generation of high-tech swimsuits in competition, designers and developers reduced the water resistance of the high-tech suits by 3%, and athletes used this advantage to set a number of new records in the event. This turned the Fair play of the Olympics into a high-tech competition, so FINA had to ban imitation shark-skin swimsuits from competition. Although high-tech swimsuits are banned, it is easy to see that both mathematics and fluid dynamics have contributed greatly to the design of this swimsuit.

4   Conclusion

Because mathematics is the primary subject of the development and progress of western society, logical thinking such as observation, comparison, analysis, experiment, abstraction, conjecture, synthesis and generalization in mathematical thinking appear in the daily life of Western people, and they make good use of induction, analogy, and deduction for logical reasoning. When such behavior in turn affects other disciplines, it can also make other disciplines become more reasonable and rational in the process of thinking. In the theory of design, we often mention the professional words such as proportion, symmetry, geometry and so on. In fact, they all come from the discipline of mathematics. Therefore, the essential way of thinking in design thinking should also be mathematical logical thinking. Secondly, philosophy represents the ability to think about the whole aspect of things, while mathematics represents the ability to solve specific points of things, which is exactly the same in the thinking process of designing and solving problems.

In today's rapidly changing technology, every time designers draw inspiration and modeling analysis, there needs to be the corresponding technology as support. Each technological progress requires further in-depth development of the form. We not only need to draw lessons from the logical thinking of mathematics for in-depth exploration and research of design, but also can make use of the advantages of other disciplines to carry forward the design.

References

1. Stichel, R.H.: Volker Hoffmann der geometrische entwurf der Hagia Sophia in Istanbul. Nexus Network J., 531–535 (2010)
2. Dai, J.: Research on bionic method in product design. Nanjing University of Aeronautics and Astronautics (2007)
3. Lin, Z.: The Aesthetic Thought and Historical Role of "Harmony" in Pythagorean School. Peony (08), 30–31 (2021)
4. Ni, M.: Art and Scientific Rationality: A Study on Renaissance Perspective and Its Influence. Shanghai University (2018)
5. Tao, R.: Structural characteristics analysis of ancient wooden buildings in China. Green Build. Mater., 110+114 (2020)
6. Zhao, S.: Aesthetic Algebra. Book City (03), 40–48 (2021)
7. Launay, M.: Le grand roman des maths. FLAMMARION (2016)
8. Cao, X.: How can design move people. Art Educ. Res., 65–67 (2017)
9. Ruan, Z.: Mathematical beauty in nature - honeycomb. Math PHS (03), 42–44 (2021)
10. Cao, Z.: Mathematical secrets in honeycomb. Math. World (03), 43 (2005)
11. Wei, N.: Mathematics in nature. New Century Intell., 2 (2021)
12. Ye, W.: Research practice of mathematical problems in sunflower. J. Fujian Univ. Educ., 61–63 (2014)
13. Liang, Y.: Performance analysis of high-tech swimsuit with new materials and its influence on competitive swimming and prospect. J. Bond., 64–67+84 (2020)

Practice of UX Design's Scale Improvement Under Multi-product Line Enterprises

Emma Wu[✉], Zhiyuan Wu, Yilan Zhang, and Shengbin Zhu

Beijing Yuanian Science and Technology Co., Ltd., Haidian District, Beijing 100086, China
wum@yuanian.com

Abstract. Under the wave of enterprise digitalization, users have higher and higher requirements for enterprise product experience, and product experience has become an important part of competitiveness. UX teams and designers face great challenges, especially in enterprises where small-sized UX teams support complex and multiple lines of business. This article elaborates how we try to solve this problem in order to achieve the goal of rapid and large-scale improvement of the overall product line experience by following 5 aspects: Design system that fit the business domain; Agile and easy-to-use front-end component library; Product development collaboration process; Full staff experience culture creation; UX design quality control.

Keywords: enterprise products · multiple product lines · user experience design · design system · UX culture · design implementation

1 Background

Yuanian is a company with the mission of "driving the progress of Chinese enterprise management". It is a leader in Chinese management accounting, financial management, business operations, data analysis and other digital fields and a promoter of the digital transformation of Chinese enterprises. With the rapid iteration of Yuanian products, Yuanian itself and customers have higher and higher requirements for product user experience, and the requirements for experience designers engaged in enterprise products are also getting higher and higher.

Yuanian has multiple product lines with financial digital products as the core. To improve the overall product experience on a large scale in a short period of time, we need to actively explore UX practice methods suitable for our company (Fig. 1).

It has been nearly 20 years since the first year of self-developed products, but the role of interaction designer has only been introduced in the last two years, and the team has grown from 5 people last year to about 15 now. However, in the face of 4 major product systems and more than 10 product lines, the scale of this UX team still faces

© The Author(s), under exclusive license to Springer Nature Switzerland AG 2023
P.-L. P. Rau (Ed.): HCII 2023, LNCS 14023, pp. 260–284, 2023.
https://doi.org/10.1007/978-3-031-35939-2_20

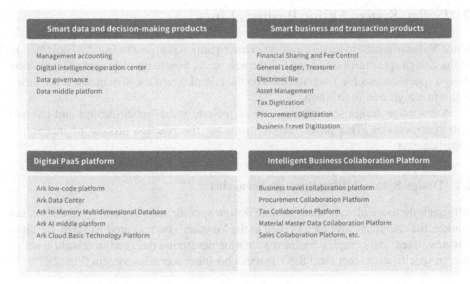

Fig. 1. Four major categories and more than 10 product lines in Yuanian

many challenges, and it is necessary to actively seek and explore best practices suitable for our situation. At the beginning of the team, we faced the following problems:

- In the past, it was mainly functional, basic "usable," lacking platform specifications and consistency, and insufficient experience.
- Mandy product lines, large volume of features
- Customers are increasingly demanding product experience
- Product history burden, difficult to change
- Different perceptions of experience, high cost of collaboration and communication
- Repetitive development costs
- Poor match between third-party components and business

Taking the opportunity to start the ark platform and front-end technology architecture upgrade in the first year of the establishment of the team, we started the work of building specifications and developing component libraries in the first year, so that the specifications and component libraries became part of the solid base of the ark platform of each product line. At the same time, in the running-in with the product team, constantly make up the shortcomings: make up the process, make up the way of collaboration, continuously optimize and improve the internal requirements of the team and the influence in the company, build the experience culture, empower the front-end and product managers, and promote the product experience upgrade together with the QA force.

The following shared practices apply to small and medium-sized UX teams supporting complex, multi-line businesses like Yuanian. This paper tries to summarize and refine the practical experience of the first year in this process from the following aspects, and discuss with the industry peers.

2 Design System Fitting Business Lines

Since Yuanian started to set up a user experience team, it is urgent to face the construction of the design specification system. For the new team, how to develop a set of interaction design specifications for Yuanian based on the complex and massive business scenarios is the first high wall to to climb.

A complete design specification should include visual specifications and interaction specifications. This paper mainly discusses the practice process of interaction specifications.

2.1 Design System Fitting Business Scenarios

Although there are already many mature design specification systems available on the market, the comprehensive factors such as the Yuanian's current product stage, multiple business lines, and complex business scenarios determine the need to rebuild a set of design specifications that meet the Yuanian's business scenarios system (Fig. 2).

Fig. 2. Specification Development Strategy

2.2 Maximize Specification Benefits

"Once we decide to make a specification, we should do it as a product. To sort out a set of efficient and reasonable, reusable production process, to analyze what kind of "standardized products" can produce the greatest value." (Fig. 3).

According to the normative benefit model, the commonality of the specifications should be improved as much as possible to 90%. Then solve the scenario segmentation), create a high-quality common pattern library to improve quality and efficiency, and strive to let more people benefit from this design system, so as to make the specification system play a greater value.

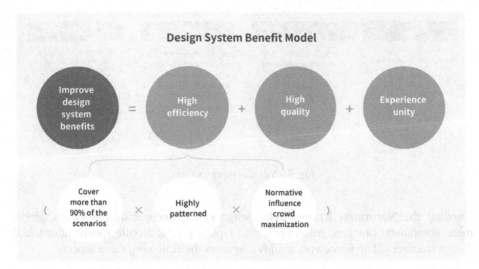

Fig. 3. Design System Benefit Model

2.3 Regulatory Policy

Clarify User Requirements for Design System. To build an interaction specification suitable for Yuanian's products, first of all, it is necessary to clarify the user groups. After several rounds of research by the design team, it is determined that the target users for the design specification are the design team, product managers, front-end developers, Test engineers, implementations / consultants. Based on the demands of core users, it provides a basis to develop the subsequent normative content framework (Fig. 4).

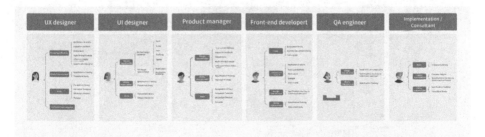

Fig. 4. Interaction design system target users and requirements

Identify Design Values. There's historical burden for the product, the system structure is complex, While improving the user experience, it is the first priority to express the table of contents clearly. For example, we should respect the user habits that have been formed and pay attention to the connection between the versions when we optimize the transformation, make the user clear. That is why we take clarity as the first value. In addition, improving efficiency is the eternal theme of enterprise product user experience, while taking into account the simplicity and consistency of the system (Fig. 5).

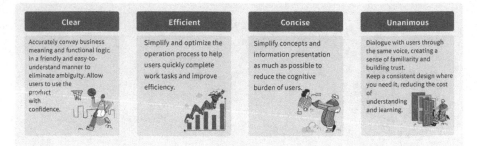

Fig. 5. Yuanian design values

Carding the Normative Framework. Design system include design values, global rules, component libraries, pattern libraries, typical pages, mobile specifications, and design resources. The framework mainly considers the following three aspects:

- Sort out existing components and remove parts that are not used
- Learn from the framework of similar competing products reference, identify gaps and fill the gaps

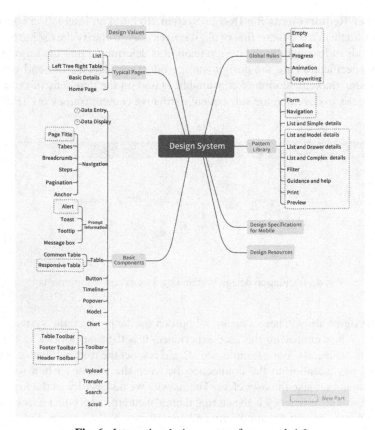

Fig. 6. Interactive design system framework 1.0

- Scenario validation, deeply intergrate with business scenario

After sufficient argument and combing, the normative framework has been redefined and the missing content has been added. As shown above. Examples include frequent toolbar additions, typical page additions, pattern libraries, and global rules. At present, the first version of the specification framework is based on the content with the highest priority of business scenarios, and more specification content increases relying on continuous iterations to gradually improve the specification framework (Fig. 6).

Formulation and Critique of Design System Content
1. Content of components in design system

- Change records
- Component definition
- When to use

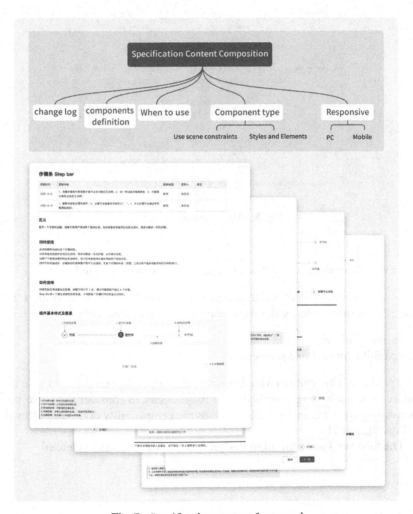

Fig. 7. Specification content framework

- Types of components: Basic style elements, usage constraints
- Component's response: PC response and mobile response (Fig. 7)

2. Principles for the formulation of normative content

- There are clear scenarios to follow
- Eliminate unnecessary branches

For example, while defining the form specification, the alignment of the form labels is unified: the label is aligned to the right, the input box is aligned to the left, and the overall situation remains uniformd (Fig. 8).

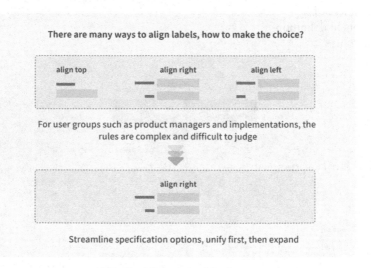

Fig. 8. Alignment of the form

- Logic is self-consistent and rules are clear and easy to understand

For example, the name of a common alert is adjusted to a permanent alert, and the semantics is more suitable for the scene and easy to understand (Fig. 9).

- Extensibility of rules
- Compatibility of multiple scenarios

The product architecture of Yuanian is an automatic adaptation from PC to mobile. Therefore, when designing components, it is necessary to consider the corresponding relationship between PC and mobile as well as the compatibility of the scenarios at both ends (Figs. 10 and 11).

3. The first version of Yuanian design system was officially released

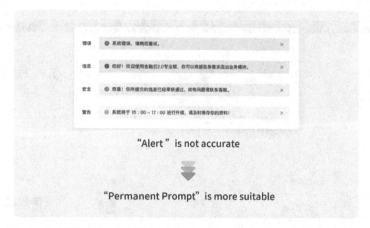

Fig. 9. "Alert" is changed to "Permanent Prompt"

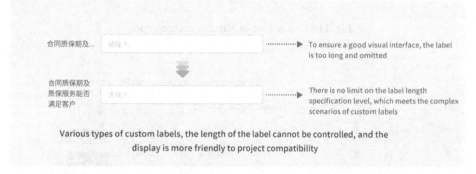

Fig. 10. Compatible with multiple scenarios, take labels as an example

2.4 Collaboration and Agile Iteration

After the release of the first version of the specification, with the inspection of the actual project, the expansion and business scenarios, how to iterate the design specification efficiently, determines whether the design system can continue to go further (Fig. 12).

The content of the specification is reviewed periodically, and must pass business, technical, and design reviews to ensure that the specification is usable, applicable, and easy to use.

In the future, our design system will have different owners based on product modules, at the same time each person has backup, who can help to do peer-review, double guarantee the specification quality.

Fig. 11. First release of Yuanian design system

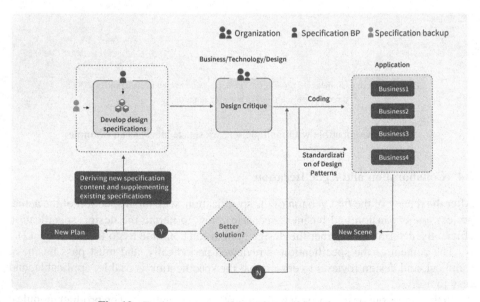

Fig. 12. Design system collaboration and iteration patterns

3 Agile and Easy-to-Use Front-End Component Library

Combined with the complex business scenarios and multi-product line characteristics of the Yuanian, the rapid creation of a set of agile and easy-to-use, high-quality front-end component libraries that meet the actual business scenarios of the Yuanian is the key to improving product development efficiency, improving UI quality, and improving user experience.

3.1 Front End Component Library Creation Goals

• **Improve development efficiency**

Code package for high-frequency use and common components to avoid duplication of development work.

• **Improve the quality of development**

Through the Yuanian of various business scenarios and business lines of temper, precipitation component code best practices.

• **Improve product experience**

The code can be coded to reduce the uncertainty and uncontrollability of results caused by understanding deviation and information transmission problems in multi-role collaboration. Different business lines, no projects, share a set of basic code to ensure the consistency of experience.

3.2 Organization of Components

Combining the actual business scenario and atomic design theory in the Yuanian, the components are divided into different granularity: basic components, business components, typical page components, in order to apply to different R & D scenarios (Fig. 13).

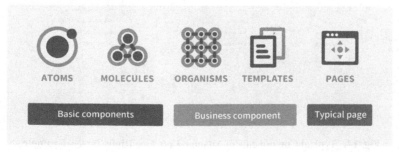

Fig. 13. Abstract Process of Component Library Combining Business, Ref. 1

- **Basic components**

The basic component is the minimum granularity of the Yuanian component library, which constitutes the basic component of the Yuanian system interface.

- **Business components**

On the basis of the basic components, combined with the business scenarios with common business characteristics in the Yuanian, the business components with the business characteristics in the Yuanian are sorted out.

- **Typical page components**

Combing the typical page with the characteristics of the Yuanian of business, compared with the basic components and business components, the typical page is more specific, providing users with representative content and framework, and accurately describing the content that users ultimately see. Such as the Yuanian list and the "left-tree-right-table" typical page components, as the most common page structure in the Yuanian. Each business scenario can reuse the page component with maximum granularity, ensuring the consistency of the basic components within the page component, and achieving the consistency of the page experience in different product lines to the greatest extent (Fig. 14).

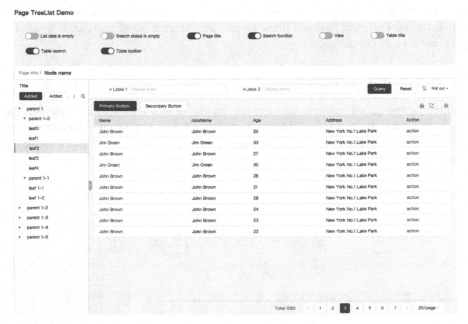

Fig. 14. Typical Components of Yuanian Left Tree Right Table - Example

3.3 Promote the Implementation of Front-End Component Library

In the process of landing the design specification in the early Yuanian to the component library, there are many problems and obstacles, such as low quality of development landing, content omission, inconsistent understanding of all parties, acceptance and repair problems are not in place. Dealing with these issues is a huge drain on UX team resources. By summarizing the experience and lessons of the early component library landing, combing the implementation process, under the new collaborative process, a new batch of component development has been qualitatively improved in terms of collaboration efficiency and development quality.

Layered Propulsion

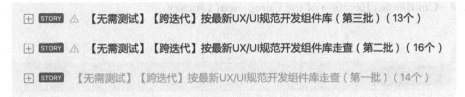

Fig. 15. Batch development landing

Component library development is a continuous iterative process, considering that component library development resources are extremely limited and there is no dedicated staff responsible for it. In the process of cooperating with the component library development team, we solve the problem of updating and optimizing the component library through step-by-step development, and help the component library to be implemented efficiently by continuously optimizing the collaboration process. The principle of step-by-step development of front-end component libraries (Fig. 15):

- **Priority** principle: Prioritize the development of components for line-of-business pervasive scenarios
- **Urgency** principle: Priority development of components required for business lines that urgently need the mobile version
- **Quickly achieved** principle: Develop and implement costly components that defer processing

Self-check acceptance list

The component UX responsible person sorts out the interaction details of subordinate components that need to be developed and collated into a document. After the developer completes the component development, Refer to the self-inspection documents provided by UX, check loopholes and make up for deficiencies, ensure that the front-end components entering the UX acceptance process will not have more defects, reduce the workload of post-inspection and communication modification, and supervise developers to improve the degree of reduction and quality of component landing (Fig. 16).

	验收点（开发自查点）	UX owner	备注贴图	开发owner	自查结果	开发自查贴图
日历选择	日历-区间选择显示共计多少天	熊冬迎		@李壮	符合要求	
日历选择	日历-日期不可选样式	熊冬迎		@李壮	符合要求	
日历选择	日历-日期向上滚动月份跟随变化	熊冬迎		@李壮	符合要求	
输入框-文本框	支持类型：基本文本框、前/后置标签、前/后缀	熊冬迎		@程正法	符合要求	
输入框-文本框	标签字段左对齐，必填样式右对齐	熊冬迎		@程正法	符合要求	

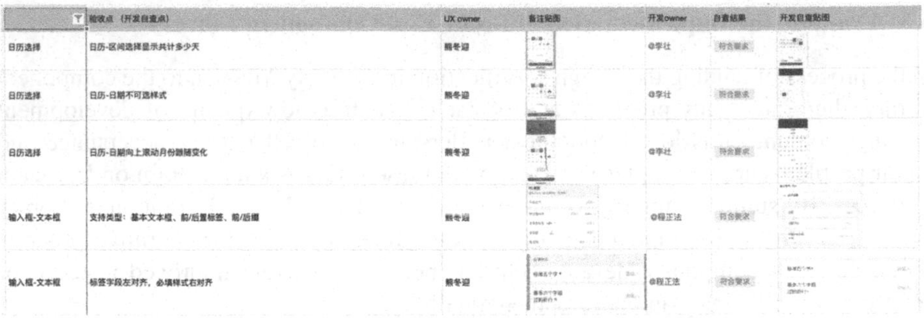

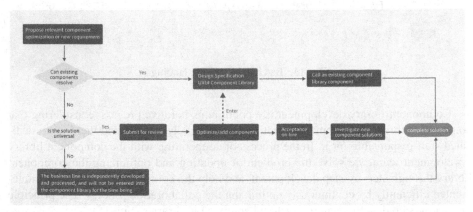

Fig. 16. UX provides a self-cooling table for front-end development

3.4 Continuous Iteration of the Component Library

Fig. 17. New component and optimization of component process of Yuanian front end component library

The UX team controls the quality of component library iterations through a set of standard processes, and in their daily work, they often receive new component requirements from product managers or project partners or improvements to existing components. The UX department, as the core link to promote the construction of component libraries, needs to judge from a global and deeper perspective to ensure the universality and high quality of front-end component libraries, avoid redundancy of component libraries, and reduce R & D and maintenance costs (Fig. 17).

4 Product R & D Collaboration Process as the Assurance

A good process is a strong guarantee for good results, and a product feature needs to go through multi-role coordination and a series of steps from generation to development. A disciplined R & D collaboration process must be relied upon to ensure that each role is clear about its responsibilities and how it will interface with upstream and downstream. At the same time, in Yuanian, we also hoped that the collaborative process would ensure that design resources could be tilted towards key business modules, and that each role could play to enhance the product experience together.

4.1 UX Role Needs to Be Integrated into a Standardized R & D Process

At the beginning of the UX team, the first problem we faced was that the demand was random and entirely dependent on the individual product lines and product managers. Because the UX role has just been introduced, some product managers know that there are UX resources, whether important or not, the requirements are handed over to UX design, and some product lines are not familiar with UX and have not cooperated, regardless of the multiple experience modules. In order to solve this problem, we have developed a first UX integration process to solve the problem of rational and effective use of UX resources (Fig. 18).

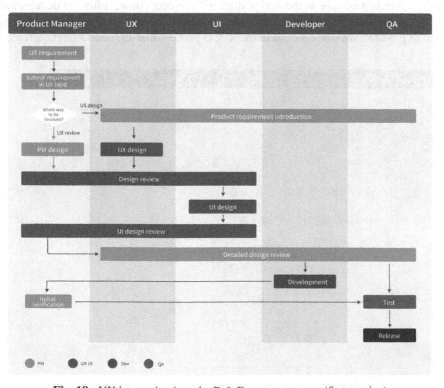

Fig. 18. UX integration into the R & D system process (first version)

The characteristics of enterprise-class products in the first year, multiple business lines, a large number of business modules with similar page structure and interaction mode for administrator users, and the ratio of product managers to interactive teams have determined that not all requirements need to flow to the interactive team for design. In judging "**what needs to flow to the UX team**" when designing, we gave the following guidance:

- **Number of users** angle: Scenarios used by a large number of end users, such as booking, reimbursement, purchase page
- **Importance of users** angle: Core, key user scenarios (eg. Company leaders, decision makers)
- **Generality** angle: Common components or frameworks that require UX to be designed with the needs of each line of business scenario in mind

Other requirements are mainly designed by product managers, with UX slightly involved in review.

4.2 Collaborative Process Iteration - UX Acceptance is a Necessary

Then we are faced with a new problem: design reduction degree is poor, the company boss vividly described as: look at the design draft is "fine decoration," after the development of landing became "blank room." In order to ensure the design restoration quality as much as possible, we made it clear in the R & D process that all functional requirements

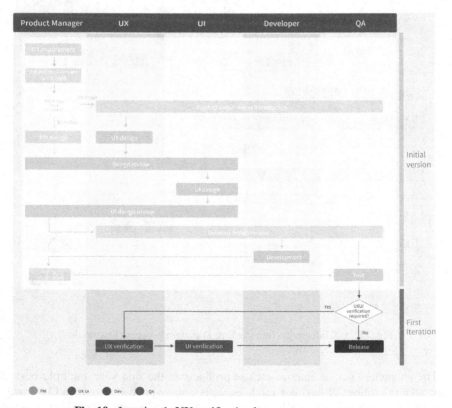

Fig. 19. Iteration 1: UX verification becomes a necessary step

related to the front page need to be transferred to the UXUI responsible person in the development collaboration tool for acceptance. Record the UX defect in the product team TAPD, indicate the severity, for UX defects above the "serious" level, prohibit the release (Fig. 19).

4.3 Collaborative Process Iteration - Joint QA Resource

After UX participates in the acceptance check of the collaboration process, it effectively improves the problem of poor product reduction, but at the same time, it will occupy a lot of team energy, and it will also face the problem of too short a time reserved for UX UI acceptance.

In the first year of R & D system there are more than 100 people in the test team, full use of the power of the test team to test a clear point in the design document is one of the methods we are practicing and exploring (Fig. 20).

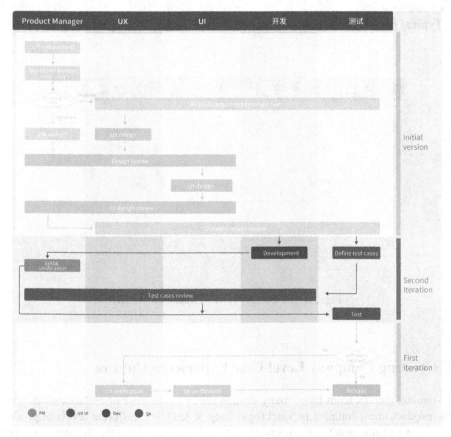

Fig. 20. Iteration 2: Joint QA effort for UX implementation validation

4.4 Rationalization of UX Effort Assessment

In order to coordinate with each product line iteration plan and strive for reasonable UX design time and ensure the quality of output, reasonable evaluation of design cycle is particularly important for UX manpower management. In this regard, we divided the design requirements into three ABC levels.

For A and B level requirements, usually the module is larger, the first UX design and then phased iterative development, for these two types of requirements, in the evaluation model is given the approximate duration concept, such as in months, greater than 1 month or 2 months.

For C-level requirements, it is usually for the product manager to arrange a certain iteration before mentioning the UX design requirements, the design scope is relatively clear, and we combine the **"typical page count factor"** and **"design difficulty factor"** the approximate evaluation formula of UX duration in days is given.

- **Design difficulty factor**: Range (0.8 to 1.5), depending on the complexity of the line of business;
- **Typical page count factor**: Assess Need Scope Scale (N) (Fig. 21)

Rank	Definition	General period
A	Develop new products Overall upgrade of existing products eg. · Expense reimbursement experience upgrade · Brand-new design of business travel PC terminal	⩾ 2 months
B	Key module experience optimization and upgrade eg. · "To-do" Module UX new design · 2.0 Mobile Console	⩾ 1 month
C	Partial single or several task functions, experience optimization	Page No. (N) *Business complexity (0.8~1.5) Day Business complexity can be assessed by product managers based on experience

Fig. 21. UX Design Cycle - Evaluation Model

5 Creating Company Level User Experience Culture

In Yuanian, the UX team faced many challenges in the process of collaboration.: multiple product lines, complex product logic, long R & D link, different levels of product awareness and attention,Good experience design is difficult to landHigh communication costsTo solve these problems, if only the UX team's own strength is not enough, it is necessary to mobilize all aspects and personnel of the company to pay attention to the user experience and jointly promote product experience improvement. Therefore, we have carried out the construction of the full experience culture system, and infiltrated the concept of experience culture. After nearly 6 months of experience culture promotion, the company's full attention to product experience and recognition of the value of experience have been greatly improved, and ultimately reflected in all aspects of product development, product experience grinding has been greatly improved.

5.1 Building an Experiential Culture Irrigation Mechanism

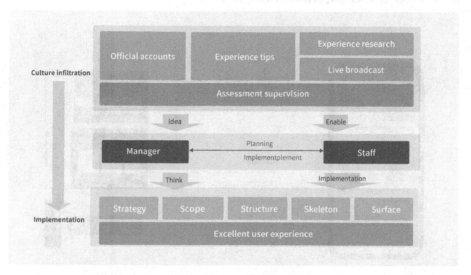

Fig. 22. Model of experiential culture irrigation mechanism

UX department through the multi-dimensional experience knowledge content matrix, multi-channel and multi-scene full coverage, Popularize and deepen the company's understanding of the value of product experience at all levels, improve product experience thinking and insight, help leaders think about the relationship between business, product development and user experience from a new perspective, and empower product managers and R & D personnel to produce high-quality output. The values of "user-centered" and "creating the ultimate product experience" are rooted in the corporate culture, guiding the work in the R & D process and ultimately affecting the five product experience dimensions of the product: the strategic layer, the scope layer, the structural layer, the framework layer and the presentation layer. In order to achieve the "ultimate product experience" goal of the Yuanian product (Fig. 22).

By building an experiential culture irrigation mechanism and enhancing the awareness of all employees, it can bring long-term value to product development:

- Improve design reducibility
- Reduce training costs
- Improve cross-departmental communication efficiency
- Enhance the UX department's image force
- Increase customer satisfaction

5.2 Practice of User Experience Evangelist

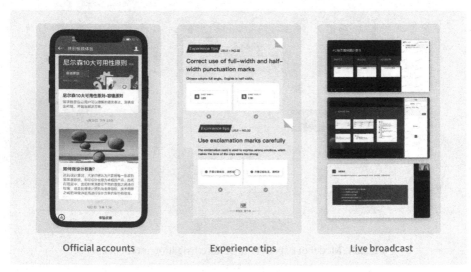

Fig. 23. Content matrix

For different types of experience knowledge, we take different communication channels to penetrate, in order to achieve the best effect, avoid formalization, experience culture penetration, learning to implement, and ultimately affect all aspects of product development. The following are the main channels and methods of UX team in the Yuanian of experience culture promotion (Fig. 23):

- **The best experience official account**

Mainly release the basic principles of product experience, experience value, project review, common experience problems and other in-depth long articles. Let people at all levels of the company know the user experience and value, so that the concept of user experience is deeply rooted in the hearts of the people.

- **Experience knowledge small card**

Organize the product experience small knowledge points, low cost of reading and learning. The use of staff fragments of time, the small experience of learning knowledge points, step by step, to thousands of miles.

- **Live sharing**

For key and complex product experience content, such as interactive specification presentation, key issues replay, product managers and developers should know the knowledge points, using the way of preaching live, better detailed explanation of the content and difficult problem communication.

- **Experience research sharing**

UX department members conduct experience research on core competitive products, and share with product manager and related personnel after finishing analysis, empowering product manager, and providing new ideas for product experience design.

6   UX Design Quality Ensurence

The professional level of the UX team determines the upper limit of the company's product experience to a certain extent, and continuous improvement of UX's own professional output capabilities can improve the company's product experience from the source.

6.1   Design Self-inspection

A large number of experience related issues of enterprise-level products violate the basic design consensus. Therefore, it is necessary for designers to keep in mind the design principles no matter before or during the design critique, check for omissions and make up for gaps, and keep the bottom line. We have developed a set of UX self-inspection tables suitable for Yuanian products in the UX department to review the design. The UX designs ensure the design quality through these self-inspection points to avoid basic experience issues in the product (Fig. 24).

In daily work, the UX self-inspection form always occupies a prominent position in the work area. During the design critique, everyone will also check the items of the design principles one by one in the form of online documents (Fig. 25).

6.2   Do Well of UX Design Critique

Design critique is a common and classic practice of almost design teams all over the world, which can effectively improve the level of design output and ensure the quality of the team's design output. The method is universal, but how to achieve better results

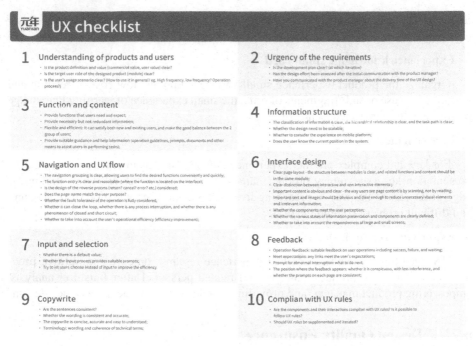

Fig. 24. Yuanian UX checklist

Fig. 25. Yuanian UX checklist in daily work

in diverse implementation is different. We have made the following attempts on how to do a good job in UX design critique.

From "all team member participation" to "design critique committee". Initially, all members were invited to participate in the review within the team, but it was found that only a few colleagues spoke, and some colleagues could not give suggestions due to their junior qualifications, lack of understanding of the product, or lack of enthusiasm. At the same time, as the number of team members increases from a few to more than a dozen, the time costs of the review meeting increase greatly.

Later, we selected relatively senior colleagues in the team who actively raised questions and suggestions to form the design crituque committee, which was carried out in turns on a monthly basis, which could effectively disperse the workload of the committee members on the design critique (Fig. 26).

Time	Design critique committee
May 2022	Zhangyi, Wuzhi, XiongD, Wum
June 2022	Wuzhi, Zhangm, Xiaow, Wum
July 2022	Zhangyi, Wuzhi, XiongD, Wum
Aug. 2022	Zhangm, Zhub, Xiaow, Wum
Sept. 2022	Zhangyi, YangCC, XiongD, Wum

Fig. 26. Yuanian design cirtique committee

And clarify that the related colleagues need to participate in the UX design critique besides the committee members (Fig. 27).

Attendance of design critique   Design critique committee   Backup designer   Related designer

Fig. 27. UX design critique Participation Mechanism

Regarding inviting related colleagues to the design critique, for example, the UX review of "Message Center" module is related to the "Discussion of the news" module which another colleague is in charge of, so you need to invite this colleague to review together to find related issues and consider the design as a whole.

The participation mechanism above is clearly defined in the team's internal collaboration tools to make sure that everyone understands clearly. In addition, there must be records, responses, and follow-ups of the review suggestions, to ensure that the value of design critique is effectively utilized.

6.3   Competency Model for UX Designers

It goes without saying that the cultivation of UX designers' own abilities is an important part of UX quality control. Therefore, we have introduced the following model for the designer's ability cultivation (Fig. 28).

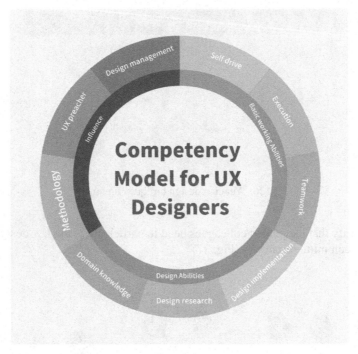

Fig. 28. Competency Model for UX Designers, References 2

We summarized UX designer capabilities into a 3x3 capability matrix. This allows designers to purposely improve their own weakness in the work, and it also makes the company's capability requirements for the designers clearer.

In addition, we required UX designers to learn more about business and front-end knowledge to go one step further, and to better connect with upstream and downstream roles in Yuanian. On one hand, UX designers need to understand the business and have the half business knowledge reserve of a product manager. It would be better if you can have a certain understanding of the business field you serve from a higher industry perspective. On the other hand, UX designers and their downstream, front-end development engineers, also need to be well connected. The UX designers need to know relevant front-end technology concepts, basic layout and interaction implementation logic and methods, and be able to seamlessly translate interface and interaction design into a language understandable by the front-end engineers (Fig. 29).

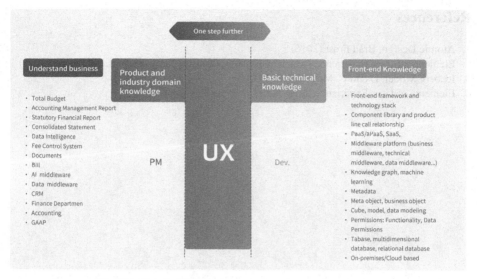

Fig. 29. Yuanian UX designer T-shaped Knowledge model

Epilogue. After more than a year's exploration and hard work, some achievements were made in the following areas:

- At present, the top-down attention to product user experience in Yuanian has been significantly improved, especially the "upper" company executives and product line leaders are paying more and more attention and sensitivity to experience issues.
- "Create the best user experience" has become one of the goals pursued by each product line;
- UX team is growing in influence
- The experience of the new design modules of each product line has been improved significantly, while the consistency and standardization of the experience of the existing products have been improved.

But still face some challenges, such as

- How can UX team change from "passive design execution" to "active experience driven"?
- How to better align product planning and UX priorities from a higher perspective?

The improvement of product experience depends on two important factors: first, the professional ability of the design team; The second is to integrate "continuous improvement of product experience" into the specific work of each relevant role in combination with the actual situation of the enterprise. In the enterprise,Small-scale UX teams have a long way to go to support the rapid scale-up of complex and multi-product line product experience, and we will continue to actively explore practical and effective methods in future practice.

References

1. Atomic Design, Brad Frost (2016)
2. Elements of User Experience:. Machine Fighting Industry Publishing House, Garret (2011)
3. Iceberg Model, David C. McClelland (1973)
4. Elements of User Experience, Jesse James Garrett (2002)

Two Categories of Future-Oriented Design: The Affirmative Design and the Alternative Design

Qing Xia[1] and Zhiyong Fu[2(✉)]

[1] Luxun Academy of Fine Arts, Dalian, China
[2] Academy of Arts and Design, Tsinghua University, Beijing, China
fuzhiyong@tsinghua.edu.cn

Abstract. In the current design exploration of the future, there are two distinct categories, one is the pursuit of what will be possible, and the other is the exploration of what is possible. In order to better distinguish the characteristics and functions of them, this study tries to divide future-oriented design into affirmative design and alternative design from the different future cones explored by them.

Affirmative design takes current solutions as the premise and pursues faster, better, smaller and cheaper solutions. Ostensibly, affirmative design is a pursuit of perfection, but in essence, it is a kind of patching method which may suppress designers' innovation for the future and further restrict people's cognition of the futures. Alternative design is a design method of shelving the reality, trying to seek other possibilities outside the status quo. Its essence is a method of seeking "others". The difficulty lies in that designers need to get rid of the current comfort and complacency, and their works may become castles in the air.

The point of this study is that we need some sort of balance: not to be trapped in a single future, and not to be trapped in an "escape from a single future". On the basis of looking for more possible future, find a path to realize it, so that alternative design will be chosen by people and then transformed into affirmative design.

Keywords: Design futures · Affirmative design · Alternative design

1 Background

In the field of design futures, we can see two types as a whole: First, the new technically enlightened products released by technology companies, or the videos showing the vision of the future; Second, imaginative experiments such as science fiction and speculative design. Typical cases of the former include Microsoft's Future Technology 2020, Corning's A Day Made of Glass, etc. Technology companies use the future vision video as the carrier to demonstrate how we will solve real-life problems through future intelligent products. Representatives of the latter include the Hyper Human machine envisioned by IDEO and the speculative design proposed by Dunne and Raby. Their common feature is to use design as a medium to build a specific worldview and challenge people's current views.

From the comparison between the two, we can find that the former's future is based on the continuation of reality, and in the context of the existing reality, it seeks to achieve a

© The Author(s), under exclusive license to Springer Nature Switzerland AG 2023
P.-L. P. Rau (Ed.): HCII 2023, LNCS 14023, pp. 285–296, 2023.
https://doi.org/10.1007/978-3-031-35939-2_21

better and better life; The latter generally questioned reality as the only solution and tried to find the existence of other possibilities beyond reality by setting futures. For these two driving modes, the former is inward, focuses on the rationality and realizability of the interior of the creation, and bears the realizable pressure from the interior; The latter is outward, looks for possibilities beyond the current existence, focuses on the discussion and review of social and other related factors, and bears the pressure of outward exploration to pursue the future richness.

This study attempts to classify the two from the perspective of the different future zones and make a comparative analysis of them from the view of the possibility of realization.

2 Different Cones of the Future - According to the Possibility

In the concept of linear time, the future is the expected part of the expected timeline [1]. In the special theory of relativity, the future is regarded as the absolute future, that is, the light futures cone [2]. In futures studies, the cone is often used to express the futures, but unlike the light cone of physics, the cone of futures studies expresses the possibilities of the futures. According to how reality and the futures are conceived, futurology researchers question the ontology of time, that is, time is divided into the past, the present and the future. In fact, this tripartite ontology itself can be questioned as a historical and cultural specific hypothesis. As the futures researcher Sohail Inayatullah said, in some cultures, the concept of "future" hardly exists, and "not yet exists" is the future [3]. Similar concepts, such as Grosz's becomings time, explore the concepts of emergence, becoming and virtuality [4]. In the field of futures studies, these ontological issues support the school of "critical postmodern" futures studies [5]. They may question the nature of time, the hegemonic tripartite structure of time, the modern and western clock time paradigm, linear progress and positivist prediction [6]. Therefore, a basic political dimension in futures studies and design is the time ontology and concept that is assumed (and re-generated) [7].

Futures studies believe that "futures" is a dynamic field that includes all things that have not happened [8]. Branches of some possible space are mapped forward from the advance of time. These branches are available paths for a period of time. With the passage of time, the existing possible space withers, but at the same time, new and previously unimaginable branches begin to become dominant [9]. In other words, the "futures" is a space composed of possibilities. The possibility is the whole activity field between reality and fantasy, in which people make choices. In futures studies, it is emphasized to use the plural form of the word "future", and to explore and draw the "possibility space" of alternative futures in more dimensions, rather than to dualize the future in a single dimension of "possible - impossible".

Futures studies often depict the possibility space of the futures as a cone, namely, the futures cone. In 1974, Roy Amara, the head of the Institute for Futures Studies at Stanford University and a computer scientist, proposed a simple three-part framework, namely, "possible", "probable" and "preferable" [10]. He believed that this framework focuses on three driving modes in futures studies, that is, "image-driven" "analysis-driven" and "value-driven". In 1978, Norman Henchey further divided the futures into four types, adding "plausible" space between the original "possible" and probable" futures, and put forward the "cone of plausibility" [11]. On this basis, in 1994, Trevor Hancock and Clement Bezold used the complete "futures cone" model to describe alternative futures [12]. Later, Joseph Voros et.al also defined more alternative future cone segmentation methods [13], but the "futures cone" determined by Hancock and Bezold can meet the analysis needs of this study to the minimum, so the "futures cone" mentioned in this paper refers to this model (Fig. 1).

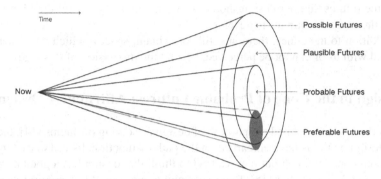

Fig. 1. Futures cone in futures studies

The futures cone is like a flashlight that shines from the present to the future. The luminous point is located in the present, the center is bright, and the edge spreads to the dark. The horizontal axis describes the time, and the vertical axis describes the possibility. Among the multiple cones nested in the futures cone, the space represented by the innermost cone is probable futures, the cone space at the second level describes plausible futures, and the cone space at the third level is about possible futures.

3 Designs in Different Cones of the Futures Cone

The cone of probable futures is the field where most implementation-oriented design practices occur at present. It describes the most likely future except for major changes or extreme situations, including economic crises, biochemical crises, natural disasters, war, etc.

The cone of plausible futures prompts people to think about what can happen. Scenario planning and insight is the field closely related to the plausible futures cone. A typical case is the scenario planning carried out by Royal Dutch Shell in the 1970s. This foresight activity helped the company survive and develop under the circumstances of global economy, political turbulence and other changes. For the design field, the plausible futures role is not an expectation, but to explore the future situation under the influence of a variety of macro factors to ensure that the design can be prepared to deal with a series of new problems that may arise in the future.

Possible futures cone is the field of speculation, such as film, science fiction, social fiction, etc. In design, speculative design, design fiction, etc. also carry out imagination in this space. This cone can be used to establish the connection between the current world and the world where future design is located. The things we design must exist in a future world with specific characteristics; Moreover, no matter how different the future world is from the present world, there must be some way to achieve it, connecting it from the present to the future, so that it can be reached. The satisfaction of these two conditions tempts designers to think about alternatives beyond the conventional ones.

The last conical space is between the plausible futures and the possible futures, which is a kind of preferable futures. "Preferable futures" means the futures that meet people's wishes, the futures that our design should focus on, and the goal and the filter to judge whether the design continues to develop.

In addition to the cones, there are still some blank spaces, which are either rarely connected with us or cannot be perceived, beyond the discussion of this study.

4   Design in the Cone of Probable Futures: Affirmative Design

Since Herbert Simon defined the purpose of design as solving problems [14], the mainstream design methods have embarked on the path of functionalism. James Auger and Julian Hanna once pointed out that we tend to think that design has a good purpose of making people's lives better [15]. Before designing, we should first confirm the current direction and think about how to make the creation more optimized and perfect. Anthony Dunne and Fiona Raby called it Affirmative Design, namely, a design that strengthens the status quo [16].

In the future-oriented design cases, technology companies have adopted the form of vision of the future and preset the future development direction through video scenarios, which is a typical Affirmative Design. In such design, designers often interact with the perfect solution through the ideal humans to present a more convenient, fast and ubiquitous world operation picture.

To carry out this kind of design, firstly, it is necessary to investigate the existing world, including current solutions, user needs, market conditions, technical routes, etc. Then, it should be followed by the coordination of how to arrange the combination of various conditions to meet the needs of users based on the existing solutions, so as to complete the product upgrade (Fig. 2).

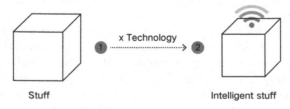

Stuff   Intelligent stuff

Fig. 2. Thinking mode of affirmative design

Therefore, we can understand this kind of perfection-driven design as the design of "multiplication": we have an object, which integrates appropriate intelligent functions to make it become an intelligent or more intelligent object (including reverse operation). The way to create this kind of intelligent product is upgrade, that is, "current" X "new technology" (or new rules). It pursues the advantages of faster, better, smaller, cheaper and so on. In terms of products, it is manifested as: from non-automation to semi-automatic, automation; Or use the technology or rules solving a problem with to solve more problems. A typical representative of this design type is the smartphone. At first, it has the basic call function, and then it has been implanted with more and more additional functions, and the multiplication of this function seems to continue.

The advantage of the affirmative design is that it is relatively easy to predict. In the process of its development and formation, the object itself, human needs, market conditions, technical routes and other conditions are mostly controllable or predictable, and even before being produced, the results can be "predicted" to a certain extent. Therefore, in the futures cone, most of these designs are in the cone of "probable futures", and their driving mode is the optimization and inertia continuation of the present (Fig. 3).

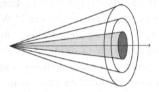

Fig. 3. Distribution space of affirmative design in the futures cone

The design method of establishing the future hypothesis based on the reality extrapolation is very common at present. In such design, the designers mine the requirements from users as a starting point and derive the design scheme. After the processing completed, the designers test and iterate the design based on the user feedbacks. The whole process presents a circular structure, and the user demand is the core content. This also means that the designer's control over the product has been largely transferred to users in the process of product forming and iterating, and user needs play a decisive role. This decision-making mode is very conducive to the landing of products, because all design producing are supported by the user feedback, which is also the reason why it can be widely used in design practice. However, there is a hidden danger in this way of decision-making. When users express their ideas, they mostly take the solution of current problems and the realization of their own short-term interests as the premise. If the development direction of a product has always been the superposition of short-term interests, the consideration and realization of its long-term value must be missing. Similarly, the market and technology are also eager to be realized by catering to users.

This affirmative design driven by existing data, market and technology is seemingly a pursuit of perfection, but it itself is a design method that is directly transformed from reality inspiration into results, and a patching design method. It is depressing for the creativity designers need to create the futures. Charles Eames pointed out in his Design Q & A that design largely depends on the ability of designers to identify as many constraints as possible; his willingness and enthusiasm to work under these constraints, price, size, strength, balance, surface, time and other constraints [17]. Although these factors are often invisible or hidden, they have a significant impact on the potential of design, which leads to the lack of original thinking and long-term neglect of responsibility in design. In addition, there are larger, more systematic and more universal constraints at work, which should be taken into account. Auger and Hanna believe that this pursuit of perfection is a progress dogma [15]. The dogma of progress is a belief in technology. Driven by this belief, it seems unnatural and incompatible to think about the negative impact of (technology) products, which keeps us on the current technological track. Consumers are set to believe that the next generation of products will be better than the current version - therefore, the future is better than the present. However, under the restriction of such positive thinking, it is more difficult for us to realistically understand the complexity of the future.

The consequence is that this driving method will first limit the imagination of design. Usually we predict or imagine the future, sometimes we analyze the latest trends and identify weak signals that may directly affect the near future, but in fact these practices are trying to make a final conclusion for the future [16], that is to say, if the future is designed, what is designed first, and what is not designed, it is determined by "what users need immediately", "what technology can achieve quickly" "What is the recent expectation of the market". As Josefin Wangel, a futures researcher, said, this is a continuation of the research paradigm based on the empirical thinking of causal chain and prediction. These research paradigms advocate evidence-based planning and design, or future prediction based on things that can be known through measurement and aggregation [18]. In this way, design is dominated by technology-center and positivism [3]. According to Jim Dator, a futurist and professor of political science, the idea that the present world will dominate the future is completely understandable, but quite misleading, the result is that other possibilities cannot be seriously considered [19]. The technology can provide the cornerstone and fertile soil of fantasy, and also become the barrier of imagination.

Then, this driving mode will limit people's cognition of futures by limiting imagination. It tends to imagine the future as technology and materials, and depict the future with a determined location, which may be reached through a linear transition path. The development of specific technologies will follow the linear path as the baseline for drawing human maps, and the society and culture [18]. This logic of describing future scenarios and visions will completely penetrate into human cognition. Andrew Feenberg said, the most important question about modern society is what kind of understanding of human life is reflected in the current prevailing technological arrangements [16]. As for the way technology enters our lives and because of its narrow definition of the meaning of human existence, technology imposes cognitive restrictions on human.

In the end, this driving mode will colonize our future by influencing our understanding of development. In 1999, Sardar said that the future had been colonized, and it is already an occupied territory [20]. Western countries have set a standard for the future, such as technological and global. The West coerces countries in other regions to inherit a way they create the future, a technocratic future. Nandy believed that under the guise of "development", the colonial plan was portrayed and sold as the future of developing countries, and any non-western or non-modern cultural ideas and values were suppressed [21]. Similarly, Inayatura uses the phrase "used futures" to metaphor this corrupt transaction. He believed that in this kind of transaction, the dominant culture set the terms of the transaction to encroach on other cultures, thus annihilating the future of other cultures [22].

Although in the social sciences, there have been fierce criticisms of such future exploration and are strongly opposed to exploring the future in a single way, compared with these, the perspective of this design study is to criticize and use, and try other possibilities. If one driving mode is completely denied and another driving mode is purely confirmed, this study will also fall into a single exploration mode of future imagination. Moreover, in reality, in a discipline that looks forward to functional reality solutions, it is difficult for us to pursue a cultural purity, complete decolonization, and total negation of the entered scientific and technological modern civilization, which will be moving from one pole to another.

5 Design in the Cones of Plausible Futures and Possible Futures - Alternative Design

With the market economy becoming the prevailing standard in the mainstream world, and the design also merging into the capitalist trend of the neo-liberal model, the single-dimension criterion of realizability has gradually become the mainstream. However, many designs that cannot match the realizability or bring market benefits are generally assigned to the category of conceptual design. This kind of design shares the principle of shelving reality, that is, the tendency to seek other alternative possibilities beyond the future that is most likely to be deduced from the current situation. Dunne and Raby believe that this is a kind of design that pursues the possibility, encourages inspection, rather than reinforcement of the reality, and seeks the set of expectations and assumptions, which is tentatively named as an alternative design in this study.

Some of the future-oriented design cases come from cutting-edge design fields, such as speculative design, design fiction, vision design, experiential futures, etc. These cases have strong possibility-driven characteristics: when faced with a specific problem, they do not first choose a solution that is more likely to be realized or with higher market value evaluation, but return to the root of the problem and find out the fundamental desire or fear, and conceive an extreme and incredible design to challenge the existing answer. Some design types will further seek appropriate carriers to implement the solution. For design itself, this means the incubation of many new possibilities; For the technical field, it means the breeding of the possibility of new aesthetics; For academic research in the field of science and technology, it is a social, cultural and moral response (Fig. 4).

We can understand this kind of design driven by possibility as a continuous process of seeking the extreme value: When we get an object or a certain demand, we first seek the extreme value of "the most desired", that is, the deep desire and fear of the person behind the object or demand; Next, find the "ultimate solution" which is different from the current way; Finally, if necessary, find a realizable approach of materialization and take the "compromise solution". In this way, we return to the original purpose of using items, and start from the zero point to seek alternative possibilities. In addition, to put aside the technology needed for implementation and build the "most XX" solution with pure ideality, this method suspends the feasible, or pushes down the future of the

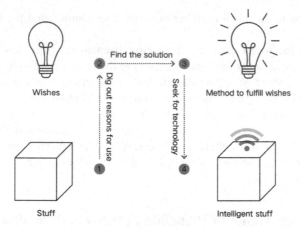

Fig. 4. Thinking mode of alternative design

linear development of the existing solution, to seek "others", from designing for the optimization of the real world to designing for the possibility of the ideal world.

In fact, Affirmative Design is also pursuing possibility, but the possibility dimension is different from alternative design. The former pays attention to the possibility of becoming "real", while the latter searches for "others". In fact, this has replaced the dominant position of "reality" in the space of possibility. Looking back at the futures cone of futures studies, it is to distribute the ordinate by the difference between the "real". On exploring the future, the main difference between design and prediction is that the former is more suitable for exploring other spaces outside the "very likely future", and is a process of using design language to ask, explore or inspire potential, this makes the design have other attributes independent of the single dimension of seeking truth (Fig. 5).

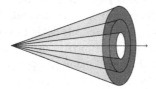

Fig. 5. Distribution space of alternative design in futures cone

"Other" is the core of the alternative design. This kind of design asks whether there is anything else besides "now". When discussing Otherness, Fred Polak once said that the way people envision the future is to deduce and compare it with the present (and the past accumulated by countless present). It enables man to become a citizen of two worlds, this world and an imaginary world. Man has built another field for himself, which is in contrast with the field of his physical existence. In this opposition between imagination and reality, the future kingdom was born [23]. This ability to find the "other" can help the creator get rid of the comfort and complacency of "everything is fine", and maintain the spirit of questioning the current mainstream values and their basic assumptions. Its purpose is to trigger the transformation of ideas and understanding, open a new world for the possibilities that have not yet been thought of, and exercise the creative right of human to formulate and increase the possible futures and pursue another structural world [24].

Because of deliberately keeping the distance from the current existence, an alternative design is easy to fall into the trap of nihilism, and is faced with problems that cannot be proved. First of all, how to imagine unrealistic things and how to persuade others to believe the potential of things not exist. It's a very difficult metaphysical problem, that is, the problem of totality [19]. On what basis can we imagine other things that are not existing? What evidence do we have to prove the possibility of no evidence now? We can recognize the necessity of change, but how can we imagine a surprise change? Grosz believes that if the dominant knowledge model (causality, statistics) cannot foresee absolutely new things, it may be necessary to propose other cognitive models and other forms of thinking [4]. John Rajchman, a historian, art and architectural philosopher, together with Gross, called for another kind of "art of observation and action", rather than those focusing on future causality or determinism, prophecy or prediction. They suggested that art, including design, should be used as other ways to understand, experience and connect with the future [4]. Of course, some exploratory futures studies and design, future literacy, experience futures, etc. are trying to establish theories and methods to cultivate this ability.

On the basis of unimaginable unrealistic things, people are even more unable to choose these other futures. In the social scenario where the market economy is the dominant force, a sustainable development thing must be consumable. People use consumption to make choices about the future. The common feature of possibility-driven designs is to explore an unrealistic existence that breaks through the commercial design, is extremely exploratory, imaginative and encouraging. It is separated from the market and tries to open up a flat space that is free from market pressure and can explore ideas and problems freely. That means they cannot be consumed and selected by the public, so this kind of design is easy to become a castle in the air.

6   Affirmative Design and Alternative Design

In fact, affirmative design and alternative design are not isolated from each other in the long-term evolution of products, but often appear in the form of alternation and combination. If we observe the evolution path of a product (or item) from a relatively macro perspective, for example, from "horse" to "carriage" to "car" to "driverless car", we can find that there are two alternative driving modes: "horse - carriage" and "car - driverless car" are driven by perfection. It confirms that horse and car are the advantageous travel modes at that time, and optimize the travel mode by adding accessories (or intelligent technology); The "carriage - car" is driven by the possibility: The "motor" replaces the "horse" as the driving mode. The two driving modes can meet different product iteration requirements adaptively (Table 1).

The position of this study is to call a balance: We should not be trapped to the pure search for possibility, and should also aim to make the evaluation and transformation of

Table 1. Comparison between affirmative design and alternative design

Affirmative Design	Alternative design
What will happen	What may happen
Perfection-driven	Possibility-driven
Inward	Outward
Practicability	Ideality
Solve the problem	Build the world
Forecast	Extrapolation
Short-term	Long-term
Demand, market and technology	Hope, fear

possibility, otherwise the possibility will always be possibility. Not to be trapped in a single future, and not to be trapped in an "escape from a single future", our research on alternative design is not based on the purpose of negative affirmative design, but to find more possible futures. With the attitude of possibility (or multiple futures), "What kind of possible futures do we expect to develop into?" "What kind of possible futures do we have to guard against?" rather than "How can we get rid of the shackles of a single future?", the purpose of studying or pursuing multiple futures is not to deny or reject the future that is most likely to develop at present but to provide more options, and by providing more choices to stimulate choices which haven't been chosen, to liberate other voices, views and hopes. Of course, if we exhaust (or close to exhaust) the possibility of the futures, and find that the current development is the most preferable, then it is the choice. Just as reality and possibility are not antagonistic, possibility turns into reality as time goes on, alternative design also develops into affirmative design with human choose, and both make contributions in their own path.

7   Conclusion and Discussion

In the process of design exploring the future, there are two categories that we are often exposed to: one is to design products or services that will be realized, represented by future vision videos released by technology companies; One is which builds a parallel future independent of reality represented by speculative design. This study attempts to classify the two from the perspective of the different future cones explored by them and further analysis their characteristics and functions.

In futurology, the "futures" is often partitioned with possibility as the scale, and the futures cone model is used to show the partition pattern. This study borrows Hancock and Bezold's approach to future zoning and help analyze different categories of future-oriented design. The futures are analyzed as a cone of probable futures zone, plausible futures zone and possible futures zone nested. Probable futures cone contains the design that is most likely to be achieved under realistic conditions. Plausible futures cone includes scenario planning and foresight design. Possible futures cone contains experimental designs such as speculative design and science fiction.

From the comparison of the two, it can be found that the affirmative design is located in the probable futures cone. The future ideas are based on the current continuation, and the realization of a complete and better life is sought under the background of the existing reality. Alternative designs located in the plausible futures cone and possible futures cone generally question reality as the only solution and try to find the existence of other possibilities outside the reality through setting the futures. The former aims to solve problems to meet relatively short-term market needs; The purpose of the latter is to create a parallel world to reality in order to explore the possibilities of the long-time futures. The former is driven by user's demand, market and technological development; The latter is driven by human's hopes and fears. The former is conducive to the implementation of the scheme, but it may suppress the designer's innovation for the future and further restrict people's cognition of the future. The latter is good for finding unique and provocative solutions, but the difficulty is that designers need to get out of their comfort and complacency, and their creations may become castles in the air.

What is worth further discussion is how to combine these two seemingly distinct design categories to form a design approach that takes the advantages of both, and strikes a balance in the exploration of future possibilities: not to be trapped in a single future, and not to be trapped in an "escape from a single future". On the basis of looking for more possible futures, find a path to realize the preferable future, so that alternative design will be chosen by human and then transformed into affirmative design.

References

1. Moore, C.L., Yamamoto, K.: Beyond Words: Movement Observation and Analysis. Gordon and Breach, New York (1988)
2. Eddington, A.S.: Space, Time and Gravitation; an Outline of the General Relativity Theory. University Press, Cambridge (1921)
3. Inayatullah, S.: Deconstructing and reconstructing the future: predictive, cultural and critical epistemologies. Futures 22(2), 115–214 (1990)
4. Grosz, E. (ed.): Becomings: Explorations in Time, Memory and Futures. Cornell University Press, Ithaca (1999)
5. Gidley, J., Fien, J., Smith, J.A., Thomsen, D., Smith, T.: Participatory futures methods. Environ. Policy Gov. 19(6), 427–440 (2009)
6. Adam, B. (ed.): Future matters: futures known, created and minded. Twenty-First Century Soc. J. Acad. Soc. Sci. 3(2), 111–116 (2008)
7. Maze, R.: Politics of designing visions of the future. J. Futures Stud. 23(3), 23–38 (2019)
8. Candy, S.: The futures of everyday life: politics and the design of experiential scenarios (2010). https://doi.org/10.13140/RG.2.1.1840.0248
9. de Bono, E.: How to be More Interesting. Penguin, London (1998)
10. Amara, R.: The futures field: functions, forms, and critical issues. Futures 6(4), 289–301 (1974)
11. Henchey, N.: Making sense of futures studies. Alternatives 7(2), 24–28 (1978)
12. Hancock, T., Bezold, C.: Possible futures, preferable futures. Healthcare Forum J. 37(2), 23–29 (1994)
13. Voros, J.: The Futures Cone, use and history. The Voroscope. https://thevoroscope.com/2017/02/24/the-futures-cone-use-and-history/. Accessed 2 June 2022
14. Herbert, A.S., Lincoln, J.: The Ultimate Resource 2, Revised Princeton University Press, Princeton (1996)

15. Auger, J., Hanna, J.: How the future happens. J. Futures Stud. **23**(3), 93–98 (2019)
16. Dunne, A., Raby, F.: Speculative Everything: Design, Fiction, and Social Dreaming. The MIT Press, Cambridge (2013)
17. Eames, C.: Design Q&A. https://www.youtube.com/watch?v=bmgxDCujTUw. Accessed 2 June 2022
18. Wangel, J.: Exploring social structures and agency in backcasting studies for sustainable development. Technol. Forecast. Soc. Chang. **8**(5), 872–882 (2011)
19. Dator, J.: from future workshops to envisioning alternative future. In: Hoffnung, D.T., zu Ehren, R.J. (eds.) Mit einer ausfuhrlichen Bibliographie seiner Veroffentlichungen. Beltz Verlag, Vienna and Basel (1993)
20. Sardar, Z.: Dissenting futures and dissent in the future. Futures **31**(2), 139–146 (1999)
21. Nandy, A.: Cultural frames for social transformation: a credo. In: Nandy, A. (ed.) Bonfire of Creeds: The Essential Ashis Nandy, pp. 17–29. Oxford University Press, New Delhi (2004)
22. Inayatullah, S.: Six pillars: futures thinking for transforming. Foresight **10**(1), 4–21 (2008)
23. Polak, L.: Het hoger onderwijs op de helling, of op een hellend vlak?. Sijthoff, Leiden, Afscheidsrede Rotterdam, Nederlands (1961)
24. Maze, R.: Design and the future: temporal politics of "making a difference." In: Smith, R.C., Vangkilde, K.T., Kjaersgaard, M.G., Otto, T., Halse, J., Binder, T. (eds.) Design Anthropological Futures, pp. 37–54. Bloomsbury, London (2016)

A Review of How Team Creativity is Affected by the Design of Communication Tools

Yan Xia and Yue Chen[✉]

East China University of Science and Technology, Shanghai 200237, China
chenyue@ecust.edu.cn

Abstract. Team creativity can be strongly affected by communication. With the trend of online collaboration, the design of communication tools increasingly affects different creative processes of teams working online. To clarify this effect, this study took the perspective of affordances and reviewed 54 papers to map the needs of teams, the design of communication tools, and the effects of tools on creativity in different creative stages. First, we summarized teams' requirements for communication tools in different stages. Second, we identified key affordances with relevant features. Third, we discussed how these affordances could affect communication and team creativity in different stages and built a mapping of creative teams' needs and communication tools. The mapping can provide insights for both designing communication tools for creative teams and expanding the current team creativity theories to fit the online context and new communication technologies.

Keywords: Communication · Communication Tools · Team Creativity · Creative Process · Online Collaboration

1 Introduction

Team creativity is critical to success in today's rapidly changing business landscape. Though individual creativity is usually defined as a cognitive process, team creativity results from the interplay of many cognitive, social, and motivational factors [1, 2]. Team creativity can be generally promoted by effective collaboration among team members [3]. Through collaboration, communication, and information exchange, team members can bring different knowledge, skills, experiences, and perspectives to create more diverse, novel, and useful ideas [4].

In recent decades, these co-creative processes have been shifting online, and this trend has been accelerated by the COVID-19 pandemic. Increasing teams work online and use various communication tools or applications, including instant messaging, video conferencing, and social media, to facilitate team collaboration and creative performance. Some of them have even been added with functions specifically to support creativity, such as Mural in Microsoft Teams and the Post-it notes on whiteboards in Meta Workrooms. The design of these communication technologies can strongly affect teams' creative processes and performance.

P.-L. P. Rau (Ed.): HCII 2023, LNCS 14023, pp. 297–314, 2023.
https://doi.org/10.1007/978-3-031-35939-2_22

Currently, these communication tools provide various functions and features to support behaviors of team members, such as task-oriented discussion (e.g., idea generation or evaluation), social-oriented or informal talk, and meta-cognitive behaviors (e.g., task management and updates) [5, 6]. The effect of different behaviors on team creativity can vary in different stages of creative processes. A creative process consists of problem identification, ideation, and evaluation [7, 8]. For example, in the early ideation stage, others' ideas may inspire a motivated team member but make an unmotivated member social loafing. Therefore, team members may have different needs for communication and require different functions or features of communication tools in different stages.

However, it is unclear what design features of communication tools team members need in different stages and how these features affect team creativity. Practitioners and researchers have designed various features and explored how these specific features affected social interaction and creativity [10]. However, these results are fragmented and some features may be hard to generalize across communication tools. In addition, these tools increasingly adopt new interactive technologies, such as virtual reality and conversational agents. It is also hard to generalize the findings of previous specific features to the new ones. Designers need a more holistic and general understanding of how the design of tools affects team creativity.

Therefore, this study abstracts specific design features of communication tools and maps them with team creativity from the perspective of affordances. Affordances can be defined as the action possibilities offered by a product [9]. Researchers used the concept of affordance and developed a theoretical framework to map user needs, affordances, and design features of social media [11]. This mapping could help designers to choose or develop innovative interactive features of specific affordances based on the needs of social media users. This study adopted a similar perspective and answers the following research questions:

RQ1. What are the main tasks of team members and the requirements of communication technologies in the different stages of creative processes?

RQ2. What affordances and features are provided by the communication tools used in creative teams?

RQ3. How do the affordances of communication technologies affect communication and team creativity in the different creative processes?

2 Method

This study conducted a literature review. First, we systematically searched two research databases: Scopus and Web of Science. Search phrases include "online collaboration", "collaborative creativity", "team creativity", "creativity support tools" and "collaborative creativity support tools". Second, we preliminary selected relevant papers based on their titles and abstracts. This step resulted in 235 publications. Then, all the publications were screened to find those that focused on the collaborating and communicating processes, tool design, and team creativity. In addition, we manually added some other articles and book chapters in this field that may contribute to answering our research questions from other resources. Finally, we reviewed the full text of 54 publicans. Based on these articles, we mapped the affordances and features of communication tools, as well as the communication module of collaborative creativity support tools, and examined the effect of these features on team communication and creativity.

3 Results

3.1 Main Tasks and Requirements of Every Creative Process Stage

In previous studies, creative process models are predominantly represented in the form of a linear sequence of stages [12].

Zeng et al. summarized the creative process by a four-stage model: analysis, ideation, evaluation, and implementation [7]. Since our study focuses on online communication, and the implementation stage is usually offline, we mainly discuss the first three stages which include more information sharing and communicating process. Similarly, Reiter-Palmon and Leone proposed the three core stages of the team creative process: problem construction, idea generation, idea evaluation and selection [8]. Varieties of creative process models have been proposed, and usually divided the whole creative process into four or three parts.

Analysis/Problem Construction. Generally, the first part of the creative process includes two major sub-processes: problem finding and problem formulating [13, 14]. Instead of routine, presented problems, the creative process involves ill-defined, discovered problems, which makes the analysis (or problem construction) phase indispensable.

During online collaboration, especially cross-border collaboration or interdisciplinary collaboration, individuals are likely to have different backgrounds, which makes them tend to represent the problem in very different ways [15]. On the one hand, different representations of the problem facilitate a more complex and complete understanding of the problem, which can lead to better team creative performance [13]. On the other hand, the representational gaps (rGaps) between team members may disrupt team agreement regarding a solution when not resolved and can lead to the provoke of conflict [63]. Conflicts are inevitable during team collaborative processes, and there are constructive or destructive conflicts [16, 17]. If managed appropriately, constructive conflict can result in the integration of different perspectives, help to identify shortcomings in the discussion of the group and lead to better team creative performance [13]. Team members can also bridge and integrate the different problem representations and potential by discussing the different goals and ways to construct the problem, which can lead to increased creative performance [13].

Open-minded discussions facilitate team members to freely express their views, listen and understand opposing ones, and then integrate them to promote constructive conflict [18]. However, in online circumstances, the lack of support for nonverbal communication, including facial expressions and body language, often leads to misunderstandings, which aggravate destructive conflict, and detriment team creative performance. A survey found that in about two-thirds of the reported misunderstandings, the problem occurred because of the tone of the message and other nonverbal cues, and open communication was used to resolve it [19]. Therefore, it's necessary for teams that work collaboratively online to adapt communication tools that facilitate non-verbal communication which allows team members to express their opinions and share their knowledge adequately and accurately.

In conclusion, during this stage, communication tools are required for:

1. Rich modalities: Enhancing the sharing of non-verbal information to reduce destructive conflicts caused by rGaps and misunderstandings, and support effective communication;
2. Enough responding time: Leaving team members enough time to analyze the problem before responding;
3. Support for rehearsing: Allowing careful crafting of messages (or other types of information), to make it more accurate and understandable for problem integration.

Ideation/Idea Generation. Ideation is defined as idea generation via divergent thinking without evaluation (which involves more reverse thinking) [20]. During this stage, the main purpose is to generate enough novel and appropriate ideas, which is essential for creative performance. In this case, team diversity may contribute to the production of more creative ideas, as team members can provide unique and diverse viewpoints [13].

However, teams are likely to fail to capitalize on their diversity in knowledge and ideas, which may be partly caused by the lack of information sharing [8], which can be caused by certain team dynamics phenomena, such as evaluation apprehension, or concerns about being socially accepted, which inhibit the quality of knowledge sharing [21]. On the contrary, teams with enabling dynamics can support open, respectful, and consistent communication, in which members felt comfortable expressing their viewpoints, and were encouraged to share divergent perspectives [22]. In this case, the action and quality of knowledge sharing can be improved by encouraging certain enabling dynamics, including collaboration, and both open and continuous communication [22].

Besides, exposure to other members' ideas and evaluation apprehension can lead to productivity deficits in the number and categories of ideas, although the novelty of ideas was not affected [23]. Ways of alleviating negative impacts of evaluation apprehension include decreasing team members' stress related to response time management [24], making them feel their ideas are taken seriously and valued by others, especially those in positions of authority [22], and eliminating their feelings of embarrassment and uneasiness by providing different online user-identity revelation modes [25].

While reducing harmful team phenomena like evaluation apprehension can be beneficial to knowledge sharing, thus promoting idea generation during the creative process, it is proposed that knowing how to engage in a knowledge behavior may also facilitate productive knowledge sharing. When team members do not intend to hide their knowledge, the facilitating conditions make it easier for them to perform the knowledge-sharing act [26].

Based on the above findings, during the ideation stage, we concluded several aspects of the main requirements for communication tools for better communication and team creativity:

4. Support for positive interaction and feedback: Alleviating the phenomenon that affects the quality of information sharing, such as evaluation apprehension, can be very helpful. This can be achieved by adding interactive affordance that encourages positive feedback, commonly the like button. Embedding flexible and versatile capabilities of

communication tools by allowing users to use virtual backgrounds and self-image, nicknames, and choose not to be identified [25] can also help to solve the problem.

5. Ease of use: Secondly, provide facilitating conditions that enable team members to record and share their ideas at ease by improving usability, especially features that facilitate users' perceived ease of use, commonly intuitive user interfaces, and rich media channels.

6. Support for continuous communication: Open, respectful, and consistent communication will make team members more likely to share their ideas.

7. Support for simultaneous communication: Allowing team members to share their ideas at the same time.

Evaluation/Idea Evaluation and Selection. Generating ideas alone may not be enough to ensure the implementation of effective and innovative solutions: the team must actively and effectively evaluate the ideas before implementing the solutions. Make unbiased and accurate judgments on the merit of ideas generated. The evaluation stage involves convergent thinking whereby one analyzes, refines, and selects ideas generated [7], and required team members to make unbiased and accurate judgments on the merit of the ideas [13].

An effective evaluation process includes a combination of intuitively analyzing the ideas and then rationally considering the resulting intuition in making the final decision. Both the accuracy of quality and originality are considered during evaluation [27]. When teams assessed solution originality more accurately, they were more likely to be accurate in selecting an optimal solution that was truly creative, while teams that were more accurate in assessing solution quality were more likely to accurately select a solution that was high in quality alone [27]. Teams will consider both the specified evaluation criteria and the explicit solution selection instructions when selecting ideas and solutions [28, 29].

However, studies have found that teams do not always evaluate ideas very accurately and tend to emphasize the quality of an idea over originality [13]. Ways of overcoming this problem include generating a guideline detailing the team's evaluation criteria. This creates a shared framework that supports the team evaluation and selection process, and integrates different ideas and problem representations into the final choice of ideas [13].

To support efficient idea evaluation, communication tools are expected to have the capacity of:

8. Cognitive support: Being able to collect and organize the idea manually or automatically;

9. Easy access: Providing easy access for users to the ideas generated and collected, such as shared documents and group files. Functions that allow quick access to certain ideas, such as tags, likes, or marks may also be helpful;

10. Opinion collection: It's necessary to facilitate team members' interactions and efficiently collect feedback for ideas through certain design functions, such as opinion polls and votes.

3.2 Affordances and Features of Communication Tools

Communication Tools for Creativity. During the team creative process, teams adapted various tools for communication including tools specialized for communication (High synchronicity: IM, video conferencing applications, etc. Low synchronicity: e-mail, etc.), more comprehensive systems (such as enterprise social networking tools, social applications, collaborative creative support tools, etc.), and collaborative creative support system that support highly professional tasks that require specific functions (such as collaborative systems for architecture design, or game development).

The past few years have seen the growing adoption of more complex and comprehensive collaboration support tools, including enterprise social networking (ESN tools, also known as enterprise 2.0), by organizations in an attempt to foster better team communication and collaboration [35, 58]. Compared to Web 1.0 tools such as e-mail, ESN platforms are considered more capable of facilitating effective and efficient team communication and collaboration [36]. A study showed that companies that adapted social media tools for team communication achieved around twice as much innovation as companies that did not [37]. The challenges of using ESN tools in agile virtual teams include language, unbalanced activity, and finding the right ESN workspace structure [38]. Even with a language barrier, tools with face-to-face communication functions were the most recognized media for supporting team communication and enhancing team cooperation [39].

In the field of design, collaborative design technologies are used to support a team of designers to jointly work on a design project either remotely or co-located. During the design process, team members are likely to focus on shared design representations including sketches, drawings, and models, therefore the important features of collaborative design technologies are the types of digital media for design representation, the types of interactions for creating, modifying, and exchanging the shared design works [40].

Relevant Theories

The Creativity Support Index (CSI). CSI is designed for helping researchers and designers evaluate the capacity of creativity support provided by a system, or interface [31]. The CSI measures six dimensions of creativity support: Results Worth Effort, Expressiveness, Enjoyment, Exploration, Immersion, and Collaboration. Users can rate each factor from 1 (highly disagree) to 10 (highly agree) After rating, the factors would be ranked through pairwise comparisons.

Media Richness Theory (MRT). MRT suggests that various types of media differ in their capacity to convey messages and cues. Face-to-face interaction is considered to be the richest medium, while written documents, statements, newsletters, reports, or posters are placed as less rich communication channels. In the middle of the continuum are video conferencing, telephones, IM, and e-mails [31]. A rich medium is especially useful for non-routine, difficult-to-understand messages, and has the immediacy of feedback and dialogue, the use of both verbal and nonverbal cues as well as natural language (gestures, eye contact, and tone of voice), which makes it easier to solve problems and reduce misunderstanding or misinterpretation during communication [34]. Previous research on social media used for teamwork has found that in general, rich communication channels are considered more effective for team communication, and are capable to promote creativity and innovation [35].

Media Synchronicity Theory (MST). MST defines five media capabilities: transmission velocity, parallelism, symbol sets, rehearsability, and reprocessability [43]. Transmission velocity and more natural symbol sets (physical, visual, and verbal) have a positive impact on the tool's synchronicity, whereas parallelism, reprocessability, and rehearsability all have a negative impact [43].

Affordances and Features. Depending on the configuration of affordance, communication technologies will vary in their features and provide functions, which make them fit for different communication scenarios, and ultimately have different effects on communication and team creativity. The fit between the features of the media and the needs of the task influence how users adopt and use them [64]. Practitioners and researchers have designed various features and explored how these specific features affected communication and creativity [9], however, these results are fragmented and some features may be hard to generalize across communication tools.

To help generalize the affordances from various features that may influence communication and team creativity, we referred to MRT, MST, and CSI. Based on these theories, we abstracted affordances from features provided by various communication tools as well as collaborative creativity support tools (see Table 1).

Table 1. Affordance and features of communication tools

Affordance	Definition	Features
Transmission velocity	The speed at which a medium can transfer a message from a sender to an intended receiver	Live preview, instant messaging, etc.
Parallelism	The number of simultaneous communications that can occur through a medium	Group chat, group sending, etc.
Modality richness	The number of ways in which information can be encoded for communication	Emojis, voice messaging, video chat, etc.
Rehearsability	The extent to which the media enables the sender to rehearse a message before sending it	Message editing before sending
Data Persistence	The extent to which the medium enables a message to be reexamined or processed again, during decoding, either within the context of the communication event or after the event has passed	Chat history, group files, etc.
Accessibility	Accessibility refers to the extent to which information can be accessed or extracted easily from the system	A mobile version of the tool, etc.

3.3 The Effects of Affordances of Communication Technologies on Communication and Team Creativity

Transmission Velocity. Transmission velocity refers to the speed at which a medium can transfer a message from a sender to an intended receiver, and can notably support synchronicity not only because it improves behavior coordination, but also because the shared focus exists between individuals working together [44]. Collaborative creativity support tools have offered multiple functions that support the affordance of transmission velocity and synchronicity, such as instant messaging and a live preview of others' work.

On the one hand, faster transmission velocity allows fast information transmission, continuous communication, and quick feedback, and reduce the cognitive effort of team members to interpret information [30, 41, 43], which may be particularly suitable for the idea generation stage for its focus on generating and sharing enough creative ideas. On the other hand, collaboration technologies with low synchronicity allow participants to take more time between the messages, which may help with better analyzing the content of messages [43]. This can be utilized during the stage of problem construction and idea evaluation, which involves more analysis behaviors, and simultaneous interaction is not necessary [30].

During the collaborative creative process, such as game development, live preview is a very popular and helpful feature associated with high transmission velocity. It enables team members to keep up with what other team members are working on, and be instantly aware of progress and updates their partners made during the collaborative creative process [51]. This can foster group awareness [52] and enhance collaboration [64], which ultimately promotes team creative performance.

Other than that, technologies with high transmission velocity, such as IM, enable near real-time communication [30, 54]. The continuous real-time feedback during communication helps to narrow its users' focus on the activity of messaging and makes them easier to concentrate on the content, which brings about flow for team members [54, 59]. Communication technology users' flow comes from both interaction with the technology and social interactions with communication partners and has a significant indirect influence on perceived expected creativity through exploratory behavior and positive affect [54].

To sum up, communication technologies with high transmission velocity facilitate continuous real-time communication and feedback, which not only improve efficiency, but also help users better concentrate on the idea-exchanging content during communication, and bring about flow to make them feel more creative. For collaborative creative support tools, features like live preview serve as a way of communication to let team members know others' progress and update, which promotes creativity by fostering group awareness and collaboration. However, technologies with relatively low transmission velocity are not necessarily ineffective for team creativity, for the ample time it allows for analyzing the information, which may be helpful for the problem construct and idea evaluation stage of the creative process.

Parallelism. Technologies with a high level of parallelism are capable for multiple simultaneous communications [43], which enhance the efficiency of social interactions among users and have an insignificant effect on information capital, and ultimately positively influence team creative performance [9]. Besides, a high parallelism media allows user to seek feedback from different resources simultaneously, which enables a high level of feedback resources for users and facilitate high level of creativity [53].

However, simultaneous communications can lead to multiple unrelated discussion topics from different persons at the same time, and lower shared focus [43]. Studies have found that such a communication process may damage cohesion among team members [43, 60]. Also, parallelism can create an environment where users get exposure to a variety of ideas from other team members. Although being exposed to common or moderately creative ideas was effective in improving creativity [61], during the second half of the group's idea generation, this can reduce the number and type of ideas generated by the groups [23], and have a negative impact on team creative performance.

Modality Richness. Modality richness is evaluated by the number of cues a media can provide in transmitting information [46]. Technologies with rich modality facilitate convey and converge of information [44], which allows effective communication. Rich communication channels are still preferred. According to a survey, business professionals view richer (involving more vocal and nonverbal cues), traditional communication channels as the most effective for team communication [35].

Previous studies have found that technology with rich modalities, such as video conferencing, can help users get to know about the state of other team members and make them feel more connected with each other by offering social cues, both auditory and visual [46]. This promotes certain social processes, such as the establishment of trust, increases collective efficiency [46–48], and further support effective communication [42]. Other than that, the feeling of connection fostered by rich communication cues can also promote the activity of information sharing, including the exchanging of novel information and ideas [49], which is essential for creativity during the idea generation and evaluation stage.

On top of that, non-verbal cues, such as facial expressions, reduce uncertainty and misinterpretation during communication [19, 46], which can be helpful throughout the whole creative process, especially the problem construction stage for its need to integrate different problem representations [13].

In collaborative tasks that are highly visual, modality richness plays an even more important role in improving the tool's capacity to support creativity. An experimental study showed that teams communicating through rich modalities, like video conferencing, generated more useful creative ideas and perceived better collaboration than teams communicating by chatting, and this was especially evident about the share of excellent ideas [50]. Since for creativity, it is usually not the average performance, but the positive outliers that can lead to success [62], this provides another perspective for understanding the positive effect of modality richness on creativity.

Finally, some people suggested that text chat may be more disruptive than a richer modality of communication (e.g., voice chat) during a collaborative working process [51] since it can only convey information when people stop their work to send messages, while voice chat allows communicating and working at the same time. However, for the communication process alone, this may be a minor consideration.

Rehearsablity. Previous studies defined rehearsability as the extent to which the media enables the sender to rehearse a message before sending it [43]. For instance, e-mail, instant messaging, and social media applications allow for the drafting of messages before sending them [44]. And after sending out, it can leave enough time for responding, allowing the receivers to think carefully about how to respond, compared to media like telephone calls and video chat. This may facilitate a better representation and understanding of the message, which is beneficial for the problem construct and idea evaluation stage. Besides, studies have shown that rehearsability has significant and positive effects on information capital, which further supports team creativity [9].

Furthermore, during the communication process, the mentioned affordances of transmission velocity, parallelism, and modality richness can facilitate more efficient communication and sometimes better creativity performance, but may also lead to greater damage when mistakenly releasing important or misleading information, for their capability to support information transmission [43], thus emphasized the importance rehearsability during the creative process, as well as other communication circumstances.

However, the reprocessing ability may delay message transmission and synchronized communication, and hinder cohesion and collaboration [9, 43], which can have a negative effect on team creativity. Therefore, it's necessary to find a balance between the crafting of a message and the time it takes.

Data Persistence. Previous studies used the term reprocessability to describe the extent to which the medium enables a message to be re-examined or processed again [43]. In our study, we refer to the definition of reprocessability, and use the phrase data persistence to describe the extent to which a medium can retain the information generated and shared during communication, including messages, images, files, etc.

In collaborative creative works, reprocessability is an indispensable affordance. Some collaborative support tool provides access to previous working versions, which facilitate team members to easily backtrack to a certain working version, and would be extremely helpful for correcting mistakes during collaborative creative works, for example, fixing bugs in collaborative game development [51].

Like parallelism, reprocessability also has an insignificant effect on information capital, which positively influences user creative performance [9].

During the creative process, it has been proved that ideas and solutions from previous "ideation" sessions can substantially stimulate users' creativity, and facilitate elaborate past knowledge for them to solve new creative problems [55]. Features, such as chat history, meeting records, and shared group files can provide team members easy access to review and reprocess these ideas and solutions, and benefit from the past information, therefore promoting team creative performance.

Last but not least, tools with high data persistence can highlight members' contributions, and thus increase motivation during the collaborative creative process [56], leading to better team creativity.

Accessibility. Apart from the mentioned affordances, accessibility is also a necessary affordance in the team creative process. Accessibility refers to the extent to which information can be accessed or extracted easily from the system, or the medium [57]. Accessibility has a positive effect on the system satisfaction of users, for a collaborative creativity support tool, such as an enterprise mobile application that provides users with simple features and functionalities that help them to work on creative tasks easily, accessibility is positively associated with task-technology fit, which improves user's perceived job performance and job creativity, making it a better creativity-supporting system [57, 58] (Table 2).

Table 2. Effect of different affordances on communication and team creativity

Affordance	Effect on communication	Effect on team creativity	Requirements
Transmission velocity	Allows fast information transmission and continuous communication [43]	1 Foster group awareness [52] and enhance collaboration [51] 2 Allows continuous communication and quick feedback, reducing the cognitive effort of team members to interpret information [43] 3 Bring about flow for team members, which has a significant indirect influence on perceived expected creativity through exploratory behavior and positive effect [54] 4 Media with low synchronicity allows sufficient time to process feedback information [43], which improves the effect of feedback information and improves creativity [53]	2-, 6+,
Parallelism	Allow users to send group messages and provide them with the access of knowing whether a message has been read [44]	1 Parallelism has an insignificant effect on information capital, which positively influences user creative performance [9] 2 Enable users to seek feedback from different persons simultaneously, enabling a high level of feedback source variety and facilitating relatively high level of creativity [53]	7+

(*continued*)

Table 2. (*continued*)

Affordance	Effect on communication	Effect on team creativity	Requirements
Modality richness	Facilitate convey and converge of information [44]	1 Promote social processes, such as the establishment of trust, and increase collective efficiency [46–48], enabling more time for creative work 2 Help team members to feel more connected, hence promoting information sharing and communication of novel information and ideas [49] 3 Reduce the uncertainty and misinterpretation during communication [46], facilitate idea integration 4 Facilitate collaboration, especially the sharing of excellent ideas, and improve team collaborative creativity performance [50] 5 Text chat may be more disruptive than richer modality (e.g. Voice chat) during collaborative work [51]	1+, 4+,10+

(*continued*)

Table 2. (*continued*)

Affordance	Effect on communication	Effect on team creativity	Requirements
Rehearsability	Leaves enough time for responding, allowing the receivers to think carefully about what to respond [43]	1 Contribute to communication performance by allowing senders and receivers enough time to think before communicating [44] 2 Have significant and positive effects on information capital and support team creativity [9] 3 However, the reprocessing ability may delay message transmission and synchronized communication, and hinder cohesion and collaboration [9, 43]	2+ , 3+
Data Persistence	Allows individuals to revisit messages to support information processing [43]	1 A previous working version can facilitate members easily backtrack to that working version and would be extremely helpful for correcting mistakes during collaborative creative works [51] 2 Reprocessability has an insignificant effect on information capital which positively influences user creative performance [9] 3 Facilitate users to elaborate on past knowledge to solve new creative problems [55] 4 Tools with high data persistence highlight members' contributions, and thus increase motivation during the collaborative creative process [56]	2+, 8+, 9+

(*continued*)

Table 2. (*continued*)

Affordance	Effect on communication	Effect on team creativity	Requirements
Accessibility	Allow the information to be accessed and retrieved by users more easily [57]	1 System accessibility is positively associated with task-technology fit, which improves users' perceived job performance and job creativity, making it a better creativity-supporting system [57, 58] 2 Tools with high accessibility facilitate users' accessing and retrieving information from it more easily [57]	4+, 5+, 8+, 9+

4 Conclusion

With the widespread adoption of communication tools in creative teams working online, it is important to clarify how the design of communication tools affects team creativity. This study reviewed 54 papers to map the needs of teams, the design of communication tools, and the effects of tools on creativity in different creativity stages. First, we summarized teams' requirements for communication tools in different stages. Second, we identified key affordances with example features, including transmission velocity, parallelism, modality richness, rehearsability, data persistence, and accessibility. Third, we summarized empirical studies and discussed how these affordances could affect communication and team creativity in different stages.

This study provides a holistic mapping of creative teams' needs and communication tools. Many team creativity theories were developed for face-to-face teams, and thus the role of communication tools is often missing. The mapping in this study connected the psychological theories of team creativity (such as stage models and IPO models) with the design theories of communication tools (such as media richness theory). It provides a potential approach to refining or modifying the theories of team creativity in online contexts with the consideration of new communicational technologies.

This study also provides practical design implications. Designers could develop guidelines based on the mapping for the design of effective communication tools for creative teams working online. Since the mapping abstracted design features as affordances, it could be used to face the ever-changing new technologies. Note that as a limitation of this study, this preliminary mapping was developed by two researchers. Therefore, future research is needed to evaluate or refine the mapping empirically.

For researchers, future studies in HCI can identify the psychological and technical needs motivating the use of specific communication tool functions based on affordances. And for practical design of tools, this study facilitates designers improving communication tools for more creative and commercially competitive use.

References

1. Paletz, S.B., Schunn, C.D.: A social-cognitive framework of multidisciplinary team innovation. Top. Cogn. Sci. **2**(1), 73–95 (2010)
2. Paulus, P.B., Brown, V.R.: Toward more creative and innovative group idea generation: a cognitive-social-motivational perspective of brainstorming. Soc. Pers. Psychol. Compass **1**(1), 248–265 (2007)
3. Hargadon, A.B.: How Breakthroughs Happen: The Surprising Truth About How Companies Innovate. Harvard Business School Press, Boston (2003)
4. Sawyer, R.K., DeZutter, S.: Distributed creativity: how collective creations emerge from collaboration. Psychol. Aesthet. Creat. Arts **3**(2), 81 (2009)
5. Mäntymäki, M., Riemer, K.: Enterprise social networking: a knowledge management perspective. Int. J. Inf. Manage. **36**(6), 1042–1052 (2016)
6. Coursey, L.E., Williams, B.C., Kenworthy, J.B., Paulus, P.B., Doboli, S.: Divergent and convergent group creativity in an asynchronous online environment. J. Creative Behav. **54**(2) (2020)
7. Zeng, L., Proctor, R.W., Salvendy, G.: Creativity in ergonomic design: a supplemental value-adding source for product and service development. Hum. Factors **52**(4), 503–525 (2010)
8. Reiter-Palmon, R., Forthmann, B., Barbot, B.: Scoring divergent thinking tests: a review and systematic framework. Psychol. Aesthet. Creat. Arts **13**(2), 144 (2019)
9. Wu, Y.-L., Li, E.Y., Chang, W.-L.: Nurturing user creative performance in social media networks: an integration of habit of use with social capital and information exchange theories. Internet Res. **26**, 869–900 (2016). https://doi.org/10.1108/IntR-10-2014-0239
10. Norman, D.: The Design of Everyday Things. Basic Books (1988)
11. Karahanna, E., Xu, S.X., Xu, Y., Zhang, N.A.: The needs – affordances – features perspective for the use of social media. MIS Q. **42**(3), 737–756 (2018)
12. Howard, T.J., Culley, S.J., Dekoninck, E.: Describing the creative design process by the integration of engineering design and cognitive psychology literature. Des. Stud. **29**, 160–180 (2008)
13. Isaksen, S.G., Treffinger, D.J.: Celebrating 50 years of reflective practice: versions of creative problem solving. J. Creative Behav. **38**, 75–101 (2004)
14. Lubart, T.I.: Models of the creative process: past, present and future. Creativity Res. J. **13**, 295–308 (2000–2001)
15. Reiter-Palmon, R., Leone, S.: Facilitating creativity in interdisciplinary design teams using cognitive processes: a review. Proc. Inst. Mech. Eng. C J. Mech. Eng. Sci. **233**(2), 385–394 (2019). https://doi.org/10.1177/0954406217753236
16. Dreu, C.D., Gelfand, M.J.: The Psychology of Conflict and Conflict Management in Organizations. Lawrence Erlbaum Associates (2008)
17. Deutsch, M., Coleman, P.T., Marcus, E. (eds.): The Handbook of Conflict Resolution: Theory and Practice. Jossey-Bass, San Francisco (2014)
18. Tjosvold, D., Wong, A.S.H., Feng Chen, N.Y.: Constructively managing conflicts in organizations. Ann. Rev. Organ. Psychol. Organ. Behav. **1**(1), 545–568 (2014). https://doi.org/10.1146/annurev-orgpsych-031413-091306

19. Edwards, R., Bybee, B.T., Frost, J.K., Harvey, A.J., Navarro, M.: That's not what I meant: how misunderstanding is related to channel and perspective-taking. J. Lang. Soc. Psychol. **36**, 188–210 (2017). https://doi.org/10.1177/0261927X16662968

20. Basadur, M.: Managing the creative process in organizations. In: Runco, M.A. (ed.) Problem Finding, Problem Solving, and Creativity, pp. 237–268. Ablex, Norwood (1994)

21. Bordia, P., Irmer, B.E., Abusah, D.: Differences in sharing knowledge interpersonally and via databases: the role of evaluation apprehension and perceived benefits. Eur. J. Work Organ. Psy. **15**, 262–280 (2006)

22. Rosso, B.D.: Creativity and constraints: exploring the role of constraints in the creative processes of research and development teams. Organ. Stud. **35**, 551–585 (2014). https://doi.org/10.1177/0170840613517600

23. Zhou, X., Zhai, H.-K., Delidabieke, B., Zeng, H., Cui, Y.-X., Cao, X.: Exposure to ideas, evaluation apprehension, and incubation intervals in collaborative idea generation. Front. Psychol. **10**, 1459 (2019). https://doi.org/10.3389/fpsyg.2019.01459

24. Mehmood, F., Mahzoon, H., Yoshikawa, Y., Ishiguro, H.: An interactive response strategy involving a robot avatar in a video conference system for reducing the stress of response time management in communication. Presented at the 2021 30th IEEE International Conference on Robot & Human Interactive Communication (RO-MAN), Vancouver, BC, Canada (2021). https://doi.org/10.1109/RO-MAN50785.2021.9515503

25. Yu, F.Y., Liu, Y.H.: Creating a psychologically safe online space for a student-generated questions learning activity via different identity revelation modes. Br. J. Edu. Technol. **40**, 1109–1123 (2009). https://doi.org/10.1111/j.1467-8535.2008.00905.x

26. Serenko, A., Bontis, N.: Understanding counterproductive knowledge behavior: antecedents and consequences of intra-organizational knowledge hiding (2016)

27. Kennel, V., Reiter-Palmon, R., de Vreede, T., de Vreede, G.: Creativity in teams: an examination of team accuracy in the idea evaluation and selection process. In: 2013 46th Hawaii International Conference on System Sciences, pp. 630–639. IEEE, Wailea, HI, USA (2013). https://doi.org/10.1109/HICSS.2013.153

28. Runco, M.A., Illies, J.J., Eisenman, R.: Creativity, originality, and appropriateness: what do explicit instructions tell us about their relationships? J. Creative Behav. **39**, 137–148 (2005)

29. Runco, M.A., Illies, J.J., Reiter-Palmon, R.: Explicit instructions to be creative and original: a comparison of strategies and criteria as targets with three types of divergent thinking tests. Korean J. Thinking Problem Solving **15**, 5–15 (2005)

30. Sundaravej, T., Mirchandani, D., Lederer, A.: Synchronous collaboration technology use in teamwork. In: 2015 48th Hawaii International Conference on System Sciences, pp. 216–225. IEEE, HI, USA (2015). https://doi.org/10.1109/HICSS.2015.35

31. Cherry, E., Latulipe, C.: Quantifying the creativity support of digital tools through the creativity support index. ACM Trans. Comput. Hum. Interact. **21**, 1–25 (2014). https://doi.org/10.1145/2617588

32. Cherry, E., Latulipe, C., Fung, R., Terry, M.: Creativity factor evaluation: towards a standardized survey metric for creativity support (2009). https://doi.org/10.1145/1640233.1640255

33. Lee, Y.: Dynamics of symmetrical communication within organizations: the impacts of channel usage of CEO, managers, and peers. Int. J. Bus. Commun. **59**, 3–21 (2022). https://doi.org/10.1177/2329488418803661

34. Ean, L.C.: Face-to-face versus computer-mediated communication: exploring employees' preference of effective employee communication channel 1 (2010)

35. Cardon, P.W., Marshall, B.: The hype and reality of social media use for work collaboration and team communication. Int. J. Bus. Commun. **52**, 273–293 (2015). https://doi.org/10.1177/2329488414525446

36. Turban, E., Liang, T.-P., Wu, S.P.J.: A framework for adopting collaboration 2.0 tools for virtual group decision making. Group Decis. Negot. **20**, 137–154 (2011). https://doi.org/10. 1007/s10726-010-9215-5

37. Hinchcliffe, D., Kim, P.: Social Business by Design. Jossey-Bass, San Francisco (2012)

38. Stray, V., Moe, N.B., Noroozi, M.: Slack me if you can! using enterprise social networking tools in virtual agile teams. In: 2019 ACM/IEEE 14th International Conference on Global Software Engineering (ICGSE), pp. 111–121. IEEE, Montreal, QC, Canada (2019). https:// doi.org/10.1109/ICGSE.2019.00031

39. Garbajosa, J., Yagüe, A., Gonzalez, E.: Communication in agile global software development: an exploratory study. In: Meersman, R., et al. (eds.) OTM 2014. LNCS, vol. 8842, pp. 408–417. Springer, Heidelberg (2014). https://doi.org/10.1007/978-3-662-45550-0_41

40. Gu, N., Kim, M.J., Maher, M.L.: Technological advancements in synchronous collaboration: the effect of 3D virtual worlds and tangible user interfaces on architectural design. Autom. Constr. **20**, 270–278 (2011). https://doi.org/10.1016/j.autcon.2010.10.004

41. Kratzer, J., Leenders, R., Van Engelen, J.M.L.: The social network among engineering design teams and their creativity: a case study among teams in two product development programs. Int. J. Project Manage. **28**, 428–436 (2010). https://doi.org/10.1016/j.ijproman.2009.09.007

42. Maier, A.M., Kreimeyer, M., Hepperle, C., Eckert, C.M., Lindemann, U., Clarkson, P.J.: Exploration of correlations between factors influencing communication in complex product development. Concurr. Eng. **16**, 37–59 (2008). https://doi.org/10.1177/1063293X07084638

43. Dennis, F.: Valacich: media, tasks, and communication processes: a theory of media synchronicity. MIS Q. **32**, 575 (2008). https://doi.org/10.2307/25148857

44. Wang, W.Y.C., Pauleen, D.J., Zhang, T.: How social media applications affect B2B communication and improve business performance in SMEs. Ind. Mark. Manage. **54**, 4–14 (2016). https://doi.org/10.1016/j.indmarman.2015.12.004

45. Hopkins, M.: Collaborative composing in middle and high school chamber music ensembles. Am. String Teacher. **69**, 47–53 (2019). https://doi.org/10.1177/0003131318816084

46. Reiter-Palmon, R., Kramer, W., Allen, J.A., Murugavel, V.R., Leone, S.A.: Creativity in virtual teams: a review and agenda for future research. creativity. Theor. Res. Appl. **8**, 165–188 (2021). https://doi.org/10.2478/ctra-2021-0011

47. Staples, D.S., Webster, J.: Exploring the effects of trust, task interdependence and virtualness on knowledge sharing in teams. Inf. Syst. J. **18**, 617–640 (2008). https://doi.org/10.1111/j. 1365-2575.2007.00244.x

48. Bos, N., Gergle, D., Olson, J.S., Olson, G.M.: Being there versus seeing there: trust via video. In: Tremaine, M.M. (ed.) Extended Abstracts on Human Factors in Computing Systems, pp. 291–292 (2001). https://doi.org/10.1145/634067.634240

49. Hogg, M.A., Reid, S.A.: Social identity, self-categorization, and the communication of group norms. Commun. Theory **16**(1), 7–30 (2006). https://doi.org/10.1111/j.1468-2885.2006.000 03.x

50. Grözinger, N., Irlenbusch, B., Laske, K., Schröder, M.: Innovation and communication media in virtual teams – an experimental study. J. Econ. Behav. Organ. **180**, 201–218 (2020). https:// doi.org/10.1016/j.jebo.2020.09.009

51. Hossain, Md.Y., Zaman, L.: NCCollab: collaborative behavior tree authoring in game development. Multimed Tools Appl. **82**, 4671–4708 (2023). https://doi.org/10.1007/s11042-022-12307-2

52. Hilliges, O., Terrenghi, L., Boring, S., Kim, D., Richter, H., Butz, A.: Designing for collaborative creative problem solving. In: Proceedings of the 6th ACM SIGCHI Conference on Creativity & Cognition - C&C 2007, p. 137. ACM Press, Washington, DC, USA (2007). https://doi.org/10.1145/1254960.1254980

53. Sijbom, R.B.L., Anseel, F., Crommelinck, M., De Beuckelaer, A., De Stobbeleir, K.E.M.: Why seeking feedback from diverse sources may not be sufficient for stimulating creativity: the role of performance dynamism and creative time pressure. J. Organ. Behav. **39**, 355–368 (2018). https://doi.org/10.1002/job.2235

54. Zaman, M., Anandarajan, M., Dai, Q.: Experiencing flow with instant messaging and its facilitating role on creative behaviors. Comput. Hum. Behav. **26**, 1009–1018 (2010). https://doi.org/10.1016/j.chb.2010.03.001

55. Sielis, G.A., Mettouris, C., Papadopoulos, G.A., Tzanavari, A., Dols, R.M.G., Siebers, Q.: A context aware recommender system for creativity support tools. J. Univ. Comput. Sci. **17**(12), 1743–1763 (2011)

56. Chen, Y., Wu, M., Gao, Q.: Online communication for team creativity in tech companies: barriers and tool design. In: Rau, P.-L.P. (ed.) Cross-Cultural Design. Applications in Business, Communication, Health, Well-being, and Inclusiveness, pp. 13–28. Springer, Cham (2022). https://doi.org/10.1007/978-3-031-06050-2_2

57. Wixom, B.H., Todd, P.A.: A theoretical integration of user satisfaction and technology acceptance. Inf. Syst. Res. **16**(1), 85–102 (2005)

58. Chung, S., Lee, K.Y., Choi, J.: Exploring digital creativity in the workspace: the role of enterprise mobile applications on perceived job performance and creativity. Comput. Hum. Behav. **42**, 93–109 (2015). https://doi.org/10.1016/j.chb.2014.03.055

59. Bakker, A.B.: Flow among music teachers and their students: the crossover of peak experiences. J. Vocat. Behav. **66**, 26–44 (2005)

60. Simpson, J.: Conversational floors in synchronous TextBased CMC discourse. Discourse Stud. **7**, 337–361 (2005)

61. Fink, A., et al.: Stimulating creativity via the exposure to other people's ideas. Hum. Brain Mapp. **33**, 2603–2610 (2012). https://doi.org/10.1002/hbm.21387

62. Girotra, K., Terwiesch, C., Ulrich, K.T.: Idea generation and the quality of the best idea. Manag. Sci. **56**(4), 591–605 (2010)

63. Cronin, M.A., Weingart, L.R.: Representational gaps, information processing, and conflict in functionally diverse teams. AMR **32**, 761–773 (2007). https://doi.org/10.5465/amr.2007.252 75511

64. Dennis, A.R., Wixom, B.H., Vandenberg, R.J.: Understanding fit and appropriation effects in group support systems via meta-analysis. MIS Q. **25**(2), 167–193 (2001)

Online Collaborative Sketching and Communication to Support Product Ideation by Design Teams

Yuting Ye, Hongkun Tian, Tianhang Pei, Yuxin Luo, and Yue Chen(✉)

East China University of Science and Technology, Shanghai 200237, China
chenyue@ecust.edu.cn

Abstract. In recent decades, the team creative process has been shifting online. Many design teams for novel products work together via collaborative software or applications. When generating new ideas, team members sketch to express their ideas and discuss them with each other. However, access has yet to be effectively supported by the current communication tools or creativity support tools online. Therefore, this study aims to clarify the needs of design teams, when they ideate new products online and sketch collaboratively, and the required features of tools to support this process. We conducted individual in-depth interviews with six designers from different design teams in China to identify needs. In addition, after the first two interviews, we demonstrated a preliminary design prototype with potentially useful features for collaborative ideation. The last four interviews also included a heuristic evaluation of the design. The results suggested that design teams working online had several barriers to co-creativity, including collaboration in batches, untransparent processes, and inefficient visual expression. We outlined the features required in an online collaborative tool for product design: integration of creative teamwork and taskwork, version control and visualization, and efficient toolsets.

Keywords: Team Creativity · Product ideation · Communication tools · Creativity Support Tools

1 Introduction

Product design involves a series of creative processes, including problem identification, ideation, and evaluation. These creative processes require the effective collaboration of teams in organizations [1]. Team members need to exchange information and knowledge and also manipulate shared work-in-progress crafts so as to generate more diverse, valuable, and novel ideas [2]. In product design, members often need to collaboratively sketch to visualize and discussion on their ideas [3].

In recent years, increasing product design teams have been working online, and this trend is increasing because of the COVID-19 pandemic. On the one hand, they use communication tools such as Slack, Microsoft Teams, WeChat, and Tencent Meeting. On the other hand, they also use creativity support tools (CSTs) such as XMind, Fabrie,

P.-L. P. Rau (Ed.): HCII 2023, LNCS 14023, pp. 315–330, 2023.
https://doi.org/10.1007/978-3-031-35939-2_23

Sketchboard, and Drawpile. Some communication tools are also integrated with CST features, such as Mural in Microsoft Teams and the Post-it notes on whiteboards in Meta Workrooms. However, most of these current tools need more support specific to product design processes, such as collaborative sketching or quick modeling for effective and efficient discussion.

Some previous studies have proposed collaborative sketching tools, for example, classroom sketching [4, 5], graphic interface design [6] as well as face-to-face product design [7]. Most of these tools are designed for face-to-face collaborative sketching and focused more on taskwork, which is different from the online design team in this study. When working in the online context, on the one hand, team members can interact more in flexible ways, and their discussions can be easier to track and document, providing new opportunities for innovative functions of collaborative tools to support creativity. On the other hand, they lose some extent of media richness, which may reduce social presence, trust, and cohesion in the long term [8]. What is even less clear is the needs of product design team members and their requirements for functions in different processes. Although some researchers [9] identified specific needs of online product design teams based on commercial communication and collaborative tools such as Zoom and MS Team, little attention has been paid to the needs for collaborative sketching and modeling.

Therefore, this study aims to clarify the needs of online design teams when they ideate new products and sketch collaboratively and to identify the required features of tools to support this process. We conducted individual in-depth interviews with six designers from different design teams in China to identify needs. After the first two interviews, we demonstrated a preliminary design prototype with potentially desired features for collaborative ideation. The last four interviews also included a heuristic evaluation of the design. Through the interviews, we identified several current barriers and needs and outlined critical features of an online collaborative tool for product design.

2 Literature Review

2.1 Product Ideation Progress

As a kind of creative design, product design usually includes four stages: problem analysis, conception, evaluation, and implementation [10]. The first step of problem analysis is the most fundamental part of the design. The purpose is to clarify the design objectives and collect and reorganize information [11]. The second step uses various (creative) methods to produce original mental images and ideas for responding to critical challenges [12]. This step has multiple design options, thus requiring a third-step evaluation to screen out the most developmental potential for implementation. A successful product design needs well planned, implemented, and appropriately supported [13].

Product ideation relies on creativity. Rhodes (1961) proposed that creativity was regarded as a dynamic phenomenon composed of four interactive components: person (people), process, product, and press [14, 15]. The four elements listed are also crucial at the team creation level. The flow of information between team members can improve the quality and flexibility of thinking, expand the knowledge and experience resources available between teams, and improve the creativity of teams [13, 16]. Besides, communication may also negatively affect ideation by increasing, for example, social loafing, cognitive load, and social anxiety [17, 18].

The sketch conception stage is the beginning of design activities, which plays a crucial role in the overall development process of design creativity. Designers usually carry out creative activities in the way of sketching to present the thinking process and results [3]. Through the sketches, designers can quickly try out various ideas on paper and use the sketches and their features to build an unexpected virtual world.

Collaborative sketches are significant in product ideation. Collaborative design implies the collaboration of distinct individuals to accomplish common goals simultaneously or chronologically and co-locationally or remotely [19]. Collaborative sketch has the following benefits:

1. Triggering and exploring the iterations of ideas in the dynamics of the product ideation process [20].
2. Encouraging communication between participants about the graphic externalization of ideas challenging to describe in words [21].
3. Highlighting and evaluating graphic proposals developed by the team [20].

In 2016, Wahl and Kitchel concluded that "robust real-time collaboration" tools, so-called "Collaboration 2.0", can be as effective as traditional, in-person activities [22]. Any useful collaborative sketch tool must have four primary attributes: virtual collaborative sketching environment, real-time collaboration, archival record of activity, and widely available [9].

2.2 Creativity Support Tools

Creativity support tools/systems (CSTs/CSSs) are information systems that support creative processes such as ideation and product design [23]. With the guidance of creativity theories, these tools are usually designed for team creativity tasks, decision-making, art design, and knowledge management.

CSTs can be generally categorized into individual or team types [23]. Team-level CSTs can be generally categorized into four classes [11, 24]: idea management systems, group support systems, computer-assisted creativity systems, and virtual team members. Idea management systems are the systems that support collecting, selecting, and evaluating ideas. Group support systems are the systems that support team creativity by facilitating coordination and communication. Computer-assisted creativity systems are the systems that assist the implementation of creative techniques. Virtual team members are artificial intelligence that can help monitor human cognitive processes, simulate human creativity, or generate ideas like human team members.

3 Method

3.1 Participants

We conducted individual semi-structured interviews with six product designers in China. We asked about the typical processes of product ideation and the needs of teams. After interviewing the first two participants, we proposed an initial design of an online collaborative tool for product ideation to demonstrate features fulfilling the potential needs. When interviewing the later 4 participants (P3 to P6 in Table 1), we also conducted a heuristic evaluation as well as the interviews about their needs. Finally, we improved the design as shown in Sect. 5.

Table 1 shows the information of the participants. They aged from 23 to 31 (M = 25.83, SD = 6.99). Five of them were females, and one was male. They worked in different organizations including the design industry, IT industry, and academy. Their team size ranged from 4 to 9, with most between 4 and 6 (N = 4). Three participants worked in a fully co-located team, and other members worked in other cities in China.

Table 1. Summary of the participants.

Participants	Age	Gender	Occupation	Team size	Team was formed	Location
P1	27	F	An HCI designer in a large IT enterprise	9 people	>2 years	CO
P2	31	F	A professor at a university	4 people	>2 years	DT
P3	27	F	An architect in a large design institution	7 people	>2 years	CO
P4	23	F	An industrial designer in a car manufacturing enterprise	4 people	<2 years	DT
P5	23	F	A service designer at a university	4 people	<2 years	DT
P6	24	M	A product design intern in a product design enterprise	6 people	<2 years	CO

Gender: F = female, M = male; Industry: HCI = Human-Computer Interaction, Location: CO = co-located; DT = distributed, but most members were co-located.

3.2 Data Collection

The individual semi-structured interviews included six questions listed below. We asked about participants' needs in the different stages of team creativity, including problem identification, ideation, evaluation, and documentation (Questions 1 and 3). In the interviews with P3, P4, P5, and P6, we also asked questions for heuristic evaluation (Questions 4 to 6). Each interview lasted for around one hour and was audio-recorded and transcribed to texts later. The six questions were:

4. How would you divide your work phases? What is the working process?
5. Which tools were to use in communication? What difficulties were encountered?
6. How to evaluate and organize ideas? Do you use tools? What can these tools do? Will the flash be ignored or forgotten?
7. Does the overall impression of our software meet their needs, does it use smoothly, and how can it be improved?
8. According to Nielsen's usability principles, what issues do you think might be possible?
9. Feelings and suggestions for features like the main interface, custom painting, real-time modeling, social conversations, and more. How do you feel about the main interface, custom painting, real-time modeling, social conversations, and more? Do you have any suggestions?

3.3 Data Analysis

The interview scripts were analyzed by thematic analysis with an affinity diagram. The scripts were coded iteratively for three rounds. In the first round, four researchers read the scripts and initially open-coded for each research question. In the first round of coding, researcher A generated 57 codes, researcher B generated 80 codes, researcher C generated 44 codes, and researcher D generated 39 codes, with 37 (67%) having the same or similar codes. Then, the four researchers discussed and generated an initial codebook. In the second round, researcher A modified and generated 59 codes, researcher B generated 73 codes, researcher C generated 47 codes, and researcher D generated 40 codes, with 51 (93%) having the same or similar codes. They finally discussed and developed a revised codebook with 54 codes. In the final round, Researcher A coded all the scripts.

4 Result

4.1 Product Ideation Progress

The teamwork process and product ideation characteristics were consistent with those suggested in the literature. But after precisely figuring out the workflow, we found some differences and identified the typical processes of ideation and the needs of product design teams. Overall, the current product design teams need more efficiency and visibility of communication, the accuracy and fairness of evaluation, the convenience and efficiency of online design and drawing, and the convenience of traceability after the meeting. These findings revealed a strong need to create online collaborative creative support tools for product ideation.

Problem Analysis. Participants often used the brainstorming approach (N = 4). Most of them could fully express their ideas without the help of tools (N = 5). For parallel innovation teams to explore and find problems together, problems might occur, such as repeated work, because the use of methodology is almost the same. For example, P1 said,

> *"Many times, like in the early days, we need to find a problem. Then we go to research, we may find the same content, and then we will look at some things repeatedly. Although there are differences in the subdivision direction, the background is similar, so the way of thinking is homogenized." [P1, 27, female]*

It also might occur production blocking or extreme divergence. Besides, alternative ideas were mainly evaluated by team members' feelings and experiences (N = 3) or directly decided by the team leaders (N = 5). They lacked systematic approaches to evaluation for better validity and reliability.

Ideation. More than half of the participants (N = 5) said they usually sketched and designed individually, and these alternative ideas were evaluated and chosen by leaders or their feelings later. Two participants said they generated ideas both individually and collaboratively. The possible reason for less collaboration was that participants perceived paper-based sketching as more convenient and faster than computer-based ones. Also, collaborative sketching on a computer is complicated and has few corresponding collaborative CSTs. For example, P6 said,

> *"After the leader releases the task, we each design several sketches and then give them to the leader for evaluation. After selecting the plan, we use the computer for follow-up operations." [P6, 24, male]*

Evaluation and Documentation. More than half of the participants (N = 5) said their ideas were evaluated mainly by their leaders according to experience though they could comment on the alternative ideas before final decisions. One participant noted that parallel teams evaluate ideas based on feelings, and there are no specific criteria. Overall, the evaluation and final decision lack fairness and accuracy and require a specific criterion. For example, P3 said,

> *"Generally, whether our project is feasible or not, the leader will judge it according to his experience. Of course, we will also issue some written feasibility study reports containing some judgments on the project's feasibility." [P3, 27, female]*

Documentation. Half of the participants (N = 4) said that after the meeting, they would organize and document the content of the meeting with the help of mind mapping, semantic map, Nvivo software, or other methods. More than half of the participants (N = 5) said most teams would organize the creative process, relevant documents, project experience, and results after the whole project and then review the summary. Nevertheless, the documentation workload was heavy and tedious, and most people were reluctant to do this job.

4.2 Communication Tools and Creativity-Support Tools

During the product ideation process, the participants communicated with their team members via the following media: communication applications on smart devices, face-to-face communication, emailing, audio or video conferencing, phone calls, and short message service on mobile phones.

When co-located or distributed collaborating, besides the face-to-face method, the most frequently used communication tools were WeChat, Feishu, DingTalk, Tencent Conference, Slack, Microsoft Teams, and so on in China. Their team often used these apps to post notifications, transfer files, and non-face-to-face communication. They used Audio or video for online meetings during remote collaboration. They also used creativity support tools such as XMind, Fabrie, Sketchboard, and Drawpile, which helped them with collaborative sketching and designing. Most participants said the communication applications were practical because:

10. Team members can use these tools to transmit files and communicate accurately and quickly (N = 3).
11. Using shared documents featured with a real-time update function, teams can work together to edit information and increase communication efficiency (N = 4).
12. The information on the tools has data persistence, makes it easy to access these data at any time during the project process, and is also convenient for the evaluation and documentation of the whole project (N = 2).

Although there are many advantages of these communication tools, there are also points worth improving. Besides, most participants said the creativity-support tools for product ideation were efficient but still had problems. The following is something worth improving:

13. Information sharing efficiency is low. Furthermore, in asynchronous interaction, the team members might not be able to reply in time.
14. When communicating, they needed to open various communication and CSTs tools, and information sharing could be more convenient.
15. The sketching and designing tools for product ideation are designed for individual use, so it takes work to sketch and design collaboratively. As mentioned by P3,

"We divide it according to the type of work. Say I draw the plane CAD and then need someone to draw renderings, someone to build a model. Finally, someone to text expression... L the assembly line, this work method is more efficient. Still, its disadvantage is that everyone's work is more limited, unfavorable to the development of their work, everyone to complete the quality of the task has also limited." [P3, 27, female]

16. The CSTs for product ideation were challenging to modify. Because the design on the computer is complex and time-consuming, the cost of the scheme modification is high.

In sum, the CSTs for collaborative sketching and designing have four challenges, interactivity, efficiency of CSTs, team cognition, and device.

Interactivity. As stated in the literature, the interaction between members is significant when creating collaboratively. Interactions between members continue throughout the product ideation process. The need for more interactivity emerged primarily in the ideation and evaluation phases. Some participants said they were independent during the ideation stage, lacking mutual communication. They might put forward several alternative ideas and then evaluate them together. For example, P5 said,

> *"We have leaders in our team. Most of the time, the results of team communication were not the discussion between our team members but what our leaders decided and informed us. And then we will draw some sketches and show them to the leaders." [P5, 23, female]*

The leader sometimes decided on the evaluation stage and was not discussed within the group, which P1 and P6 also mentioned.

Besides, the convenience of using tools can also affect team members' interactions. Most creativity-support tools for collaborative sketching and designing are complicated and need to support online collaboration. More than half of the participants mentioned a possible collaborative use of the CSTs during the problem analysis phase, but they all used the CSTs alone during the ideation phase. For example, P4 said they would use the computer to model after the schemes were decided. Computer modeling took a long time to model and is cumbersome to modify, so they would not model at the beginning.

The Efficiency of CSTs. According to the interview, although the team used communication tools and CSTs for collaborative sketching and designing in the product design process, the level of collaboration was low, even creating individually. Three participants mentioned that this phenomenon is related to the high cost of learning and the use of the software. As P4 said, *"Sketch on paper, you can draw several plans in an hour, but the speed on a computer is halved. Modeling takes even more time, taking at least a few hours to complete a model."*

Besides, the efficiency of CSTs also affects documentation and summary after the whole project is finished. Two participants mentioned that documentation was critical and helpful, which could help them accumulate experience and analyze their shortcomings and weaknesses.

Team Cognition. Two participants said their team members were analogous in majors, so the way to solve problems was similar, which led them to much repetitive work and a lack of innovation. As mentioned by P1,

> *"Although there are differences in the direction of this subdivision, such as psychology, colleagues specializing in industrial design, hardware, and software development. In general, at least in a certain job or study stage, they have*

learned the methodology of human-computer interaction. So, the background is the homogenization of the way of thinking." [P1, 27, female]

Device. Current electronic devices include mobile phones, computers, and tablets. Different devices have different characteristics. Mobile phones are easy to move and communicate with. However, with smaller screens, it is inconvenient to use CSTs and has limitations in performance. Computer performance is the most powerful. A computer is inconvenient to move, so people will only carry it if necessary. Computers support communication, sketching, and modeling. The tablet's size and performance are between computers and phones. Because of the capacitive pen, people can imitate the painting on paper, with the lowest learning cost and more comfortable using feelings. Also, the tablet can model products.

4.3 Evaluation of the Preliminary Design

Participants felt that the tool we designed was generally helpful and improved the efficiency of product conception. Then, they offered further hope. The participants hoped that the painting function could meet the basic requirements of quick sketch design and then have a customized brush to achieve the effect quickly (N = 2). Besides, under the premise of ensuring the running efficiency of the software, the modeling function could realize real-time rendering (N = 3). Moreover, more than half of the participants preferred the model library and component library (N = 4). As mentioned by P6,

"We can make a model material library, which can directly call the related products. For example, the A company is a chair, and he may have designed many chairs by himself, and then he can directly call his previous design in the model library. A new product may have many points related to this design, so we only need to modify his previous design slightly." [P6, 24, male]

Moreover, in the brainstorming stage, participants were reluctant to see other members' online status, which would affect their creation (N = 2). Some participants also emphasized the efficiency of synchronous and asynchronous communication (N = 2). Lastly, half of the participants hoped the whole process could be recorded and documented after the meeting (N = 3). As mentioned by P5,

"After the sketch evaluation process, there can be a section called the display of the evaluation results so that the results can be analyzed. Then we will record the results of this discussion. For example, each person uses a different color to mark it." [P5, 23, female]

5 Collaborative Sketching and Designing to Support Product Ideation

Due to the usage gap between communication tools and CSTs for product ideation, part of the design process's collaboration level was low. We explored the potential design to integrate communication tools with CST features to support team creativity in product design teams. Based on the findings of the interviews, we determined the following design goals:

17. Innovation goal: The tool can enhance the visibility of the team's drawing conception scheme, reduce the omission of ideas and information in the sketching, and promote the collision of the team's creative points.
18. Efficiency goal: The tool can reduce the stagnation of thinking during team communication and promote the progression of the design process. At the same time, it increases the data's durability and organizes the whole process to facilitate traceability after the meeting.

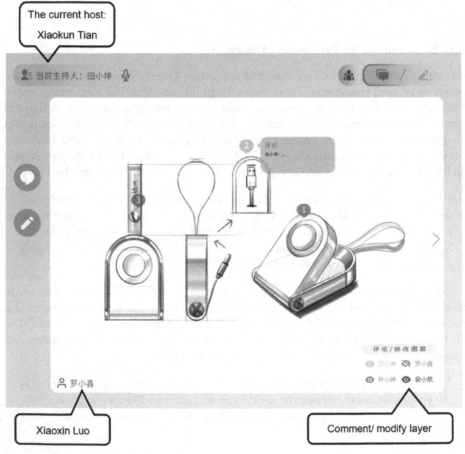

Fig. 1. Interface for sketch evaluation. The group members can hold meetings, comment and modify sketches.

19. Auxiliary goals: The tool can help product designers reduce the difficulty of sketching and modeling.

For these goals, we proposed potential tools which integrate communication, collaboration, and CSTs for product ideation features. According to the product ideation process, we offered three significant components for mobile devices.

First, we integrated communication, whiteboard function, sketch, and modeling functions so that members could design and communicate by voice and video.

Second, on the premise that the tool is functional for synchronous and asynchronous interactions, as shown in Fig. 1. In the upper right corner of the screen, the dual modes of painting and meeting can be switched. A function button is added to the host interface's left side of the dual-mode switch button to cover the whole staff. Click invite members in meeting mode to give members access to comment and modify. According to the specific needs, the members speak and comment in turns. Clicking the annotation function key, members will enter the drawing mode to modify the scheme. The modification results of different members will be presented as a dendrogram below the container, which will be saved in the meeting minutes after the meeting.

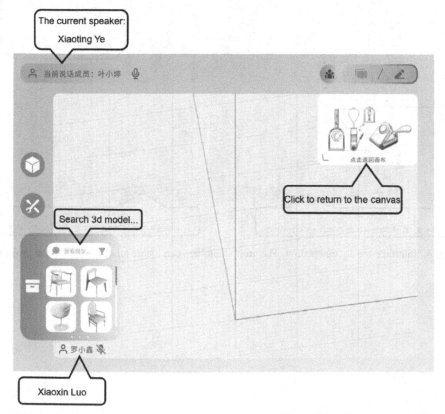

Fig. 2. Interface for modeling. The group members can rapidly model and use the model library.

Third, establish the model library and the product design particular brush material library. Searching for keywords in the model library presents the relevant model, as shown in Fig. 2. Members can modify the selected model's parameters, such as chamfer size, length, and width of different components. The brush material library can quickly show the effect of the product with the selected material when sketching.

Fourth, we have added a post-meeting traceability function. The tool records what the members do during the project and documents the content and process of the meeting. After the project ends, you can view all the operation records for the whole project. Figure 3 shows a clear project record. Figure 4 shows clear meeting minutes.

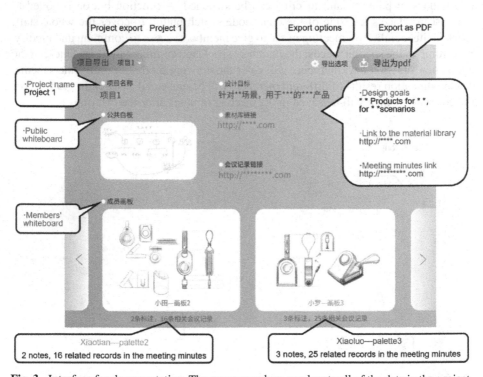

Fig. 3. Interface for documentation. The group members can locate all of the data in the project.

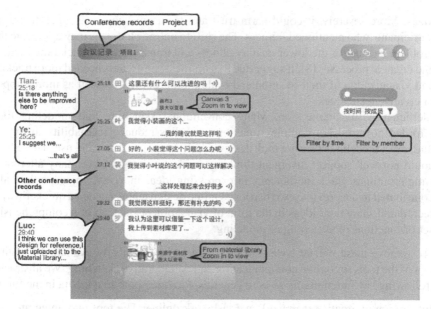

Fig. 4. Interface for documentation. The group members can view meeting minutes.

6 Discussion and Design Conclusion

This study conducted individual interviews with six designers in different product design teams in IT enterprises, design companies, and an academy and proposed a tool for collaborative product ideation for online teams. By qualitative interview analysis, we identified several barriers to creativity during online collaborative product ideation:

1. Collaboration in batches due to the separation of sketching and communication tools. In the ideation and evaluation processes, most of the interviewed teams tended to work in an in-batch fashion, like nominal brainstorming. Typically, team members sketched and formed ideas individually and then submitted alternative ideas in batches to their leader. The leader would summarize ideas and make decisions. This process had some flaws: it could not support members to be inspired by others, merge or expand their ideas and may harm team cognition and mutual understanding. Research suggests that when team members are open to new ideas and effectively communicate, they perceive support for creativity [25], which fosters team and organization [26]. A possible reason for such a process was the lack of convenient online sketching integrated into the communication tools. As a result, most participants still preferred sketching on paper individually. Although researchers have proposed various collaborative sketching tools such as [5, 7], they were not designed to support remote or online teams designing new products. It indicated a need to integrate collaborative sketching and communication functions to support product design teams working online.

2. Untransparent processes and potentially arbitrary selections of the final idea. In most teams, alternatives were selected arbitrarily or based on leaders' experience instead of a more solid evaluation. This arbitrary selection risked burying potentially creative

ideas. More severely, it could harm trust and team cohesion, as suggested by the participants who mentioned fairness. The shift to online platforms may aggravate this problem because of the lower media richness and transparency of social interactions and creative processes [8]. It suggested that online design teams needed more tracking and visualization of their ideation and evaluation processes as well as more support of creative techniques.

3. Inefficient visual expression. Many conventional sketching and modeling tools afforded powerful but complex functions and thus reduced learnability. In particular, most modeling software took designers a long time to learn and use. These tools could not well support divergent thinking or ideation to generate many alternative simple outlines. Such inefficiency in expressing ideas in visual objects online also contributed to the previous two barriers. Online design teams needed a quicker way to record and share their ideas in the form of visual objects instead of a comprehensive set of functions of sketching or modeling.

To remove these barriers, we also proposed and heuristically evaluated an initial design of the tools for online communication and collaborative sketching. We abstracted the following key functionality so as to generalize to other potential media in the future:

1. Integration of creative teamwork and taskwork online: The tool may integrate both synchronous and asynchronous communication functions with creativity supports, including whiteboards, sketching, and quick modeling. Team members need to flexibly choose synchronous (e.g., video conferencing) or asynchronous (e.g., commenting or annotating) interactions in different stages. For example, ideation requires synchronous interaction with both verbal and visual communication [20], whereas in the early stage of evaluation, team members carefully compare and analyze different ideas and thus may need to comment or annotate on others' ideas asynchronously. For example, some recent applications for UI design, such as Figma, supports asynchronous communication by commenting on others' ideas. In addition, some features of electrical brainstorming systems can be integrated to support creative ideation and more effective evaluation, as expected by the participants, and designed in this study.

2. Version control and visualization: The tool may track team members' interactions and manipulations of their alternative ideas, including those interactions in video conferencing. The function of automatic tracking and summarizing meeting minutes can be found in most conferencing platforms. Recently, MS Teams has been integrated with GPT features that can assign tasks to team members based on tracking verbal data [27]. In this study, tracking data involved image data as well as behavioral data and can be further used to support team creativity in many ways. First and most directly, the tracking data can link design alternatives with the discussions during video meetings, and the tool can generate graphical meeting minutes. Second, the tool can afford a higher editability by version control functions, which are available in many current collaborative tools. Third, the tool may further summarize and visualize the team process or alternatives. For example, the alternatives can be clustered manually by team members or automatically by some image processing algorithms or behavior analysis of team members. Some qualitative analysis tools, such as NVivo, provided manual or even automatic coding and clustering functions. Similar functions in co-creative tools can help team members to identify potential patterns and develop a

holistic understanding of their design process. It may also further facilitate better team cognition as well as socio-emotional aspects such as team cohesion.

3. Efficient toolsets: The tool may provide libraries of elements or shortcuts for quick modeling. The libraries may include frequently used brushes, materials, and components. These elements can be customized by team members and automatically recommended by algorithms based on the relevant domains and analyzing the existing alternatives.

This study has two main limitations. First, due to insufficient samples, it only partially covers the target users. The current interviewees are designers, including graduate students and employees from design institutes and design companies. Future research may enroll more product designers to increase the accuracy and reliability of the data. Second, we heuristically evaluated the designed functions of the communication and collaborative sketching tool with a few participants. Future studies may evaluate it more quantitatively, such as through user testing or controlled experimenting.

References

1. Sawyer, R.K., DeZutter, S.: Distributed creativity: How collective creations emerge from collaboration. Psychol. Aesthet. Creat. Arts. **3**, 81–92 (2009). https://doi.org/10.1037/a0013282

2. Carmeli, A., Paulus, P.B.: CEO ideational facilitation leadership and team creativity: The mediating role of knowledge sharing. J. Creat. Behav. **49**, 53–75 (2015). https://doi.org/10.1002/jocb.59

3. He, J.: A comparative study of the effects of tool use on graphic design beginners' sketching behavior. Decorate. **319**, 96–99 (2019). https://doi.org/10.16272/j.cnki.cn11-1392/j.2019.11.020. (in Chinese)

4. Härkki, T., Seitamaa-Hakkarainen, P., Hakkarainen, K.: Line by line, part by part: Collaborative sketching for designing. Int. J. Technol. Des. Educ. **28**(2), 471–494 (2016). https://doi.org/10.1007/s10798-016-9379-7

5. Wallace, S., et al.: Sketchy: Drawing Inspiration from the Crowd. Proc. ACM Hum.-Comput. Interact. 4, 1–27 (2020). https://doi.org/10.1145/3415243

6. Sangiorgi, U.B., Beuvens, F., Vanderdonckt, J.: User interface design by collaborative sketching. In: Proceedings of the Designing Interactive Systems Conference, pp. 378–387. ACM, Newcastle Upon Tyne United Kingdom (2012). https://doi.org/10.1145/2317956.2318013

7. Piya, C.V., Chandrasegaran, S., Elmqvist, N., Ramani, K.: Co-3Deator: A team-first collaborative 3D design ideation tool. In: Proceedings of the 2017 CHI Conference on Human Factors in Computing Systems, pp. 6581–6592. ACM, Denver (2017). https://doi.org/10.1145/3025453.3025825

8. Reiter-Palmon, R., Kramer, W., Allen, J.A., Murugavel, V.R., Leone, S.A.: Creativity in virtual teams: A review and agenda for future research. Creat. Theor. Res. Appl. **8**, 165–188 (2021). https://doi.org/10.2478/ctra-2021-0011

9. Anderson, M., et al.: A Survey of Web-Based Tools For Collaborative Engineering Design. J. Mech. Des. **144**, 014001 (2022). https://doi.org/10.1115/1.4051768

10. Howard, T.J., Culley, S.J., Dekoninck, E.: Describing the creative design process by the integration of engineering design and cognitive psychology literature. Des. Stud. **29**, 160–180 (2008). https://doi.org/10.1016/j.destud.2008.01.001

11. Gabriel, A., Monticolo, D., Camargo, M., Bourgault, M.: Creativity support systems: A systematic mapping study. Think. Ski. Creat. **21**, 109–122 (2016). https://doi.org/10.1016/j.tsc.2016.05.009

12. Puccio, G.J., Cabra, J.F.: Idea generation and idea evaluation. In: Handbook of Organizational Creativity, pp. 189–215. Elsevier (2012). https://doi.org/10.1016/B978-0-12-374714-3.00009-4

13. Brown, S.L., Eisenhardt, K.M.: Product development: Past research, present findings, and future directions. Acad. Manag. Rev. **20**, 343–378(1995)

14. Horn, D., Salvendy, G.: Consumer-based assessment of product creativity: A review and reappraisal. Hum. Factors Ergon. Manuf. **16**, 155–175 (2006). https://doi.org/10.1002/hfm.20047

15. Thompson, G., Lordan, M.: A review of creativity principles applied to engineering design. Proc. Inst. Mech. Eng. Part E J. Process Mech. Eng. **213**, 17–31 (1999). https://doi.org/10.1243/0954408991529960

16. Drach-Zahavy, A., Somech, A.: Understanding team innovation: The role of team processes and structures. Group Dyn. Theory Res. Pract. **5**, 111–123 (2001). https://doi.org/10.1037/1089-2699.5.2.111

17. Kratzer, J., Leenders, oger Th.A.J., Engelen, J.M.L. van: Stimulating the potential: Creative performance and communication in innovation teams. Creat. Innov. Manag. **13**, 63–71 (2004). https://doi.org/10.1111/j.1467-8691.2004.00294.x

18. Maaravi, Y., Heller, B., Shoham, Y., Mohar, S., Deutsch, B.: Ideation in the digital age: Literature review and integrative model for electronic brainstorming. RMS **15**(6), 1431–1464 (2020). https://doi.org/10.1007/s11846-020-00400-5

19. Ozkaya, I., Akin, Ö.: Use of requirement traceability in collaborative design environments. CoDesign **1**, 155–167 (2005). https://doi.org/10.1080/15710880500227958

20. Jimenez-Narvaez, L.-M., Segrera, A.: Creative collaborative strategies of remote sketching on design. In: Taura, T., Nagai, Y. (eds.) Design Creativity 2010. pp. 241–248. Springer London, London (2011). https://doi.org/10.1007/978-0-85729-224-7_31

21. Nagai, Y., Noguchi, H.: An experimental study on the design thinking process started from difficult keywords: modeling the thinking process of creative design. J. Eng. Des. **14**, 429–437 (2003). https://doi.org/10.1080/09544820310001606911

22. Wahl, L., Kitchel, A.: Internet based collaboration tools. Int. J. E-Collab. **12**, 27–43 (2016). https://doi.org/10.4018/IJeC.2016010103

23. Frich, J., MacDonald Vermeulen, L., Remy, C., Biskjaer, M.M., Dalsgaard, P.: Mapping the landscape of creativity support tools in HCI. In: Proceedings of the 2019 CHI Conference on Human Factors in Computing Systems, pp. 1–18. ACM, Glasgow (2019). https://doi.org/10.1145/3290605.3300619

24. Lubart, T.: How can computers be partners in the creative process: Classification and commentary on the Special Issue. Int. J. Hum.-Comput. Stud. **63**, 365–369 (2005). https://doi.org/10.1016/j.ijhcs.2005.04.002

25. Diliello, T.C., Houghton, J.D., Dawley, D.: Narrowing the creativity gap: The moderating effects of perceived support for creativity. J. Psychol. **145**, 151–172 (2011). https://doi.org/10.1080/00223980.2010.548412

26. Santos, C.M., Uitdewilligen, S., Passos, A.M.: Why is your team more creative than mine? The influence of shared mental models on intra-group conflict, team creativity and effectiveness: Shared mental models and team effectiveness. Creat. Innov. Manag. **24**, 645–658 (2015). https://doi.org/10.1111/caim.12129

27. Herskowitz, N.: Microsoft Teams Premium: Cut costs and add AI-powered productivity. https://www.microsoft.com/en-us/microsoft-365/blog/2023/02/01/microsoft-teams-premium-cut-costs-and-add-ai-powered-productivity/. Accessed 09 Feb 2023

New Space Narrative: Responding to Multiple Futures with Design Perspective

Lin Zhu and Zhiyong Fu[✉]

Tsinghua University, Beijing 100084, China
{zhu-120,fuzhiyong}@mails.tsinghua.edu.cn

Abstract. Design fiction is design-based storytelling, a narrative or story that is reflective and speculative on the part of the designer. The framework of rational thinking is further extended to envision the corresponding future under the worldview, thus reflecting on alternative futures and current society, and gradually realizing the concept with the help of technology. It is multi-stakeholder, aims to generate social attention and discussion, and is future-oriented. The new space narrative focuses on how people will live and work in space in the future. Through three iterations of the design space workshop and course, we adapted existing design thinking tools to guide students through the process of conceptualizing future scenarios in space, and reflected on and iterated on the use of the tools in the process. 4 groups of students were selected from "Nature Craving Disorder", "Mars Media Personality", "Earth Odor Missing", and "Irrational Confrontation". The four groups of students worked from the user profiles of four Mars residents, namely "Nature Craving", "Mars Media Person", "Earth Smell Nostalgia" and "Irrational Confrontation", and used Roblox as the main creation platform to shape a new experience of Mars life. The students worked in groups of 4–5, and each group was evenly distributed taking into account their professional background, grade and gender, and completed 4 pieces of work as a group, namely "GreenBot" the green cutie on the Mars base, Mars fitness program: space fitness, "Apollo "Expedition"", and Mars Media Man. The use of the tools and the introduction of the students' works will be expanded in detail in the text.

Keywords: Space design course · Design fiction · Design furues

1 Introduction

Space is a field that is rapidly evolving and holds great potential for innovation and exploration. In the past, space-related design was limited to the constraints of the capsule environment and focused on creating functional and efficient products for use in space. However, with the rise of space tourism, Mars mission programs, and increasing civilian orbital aviation, the field of space design is being re-imagined and expanded. The quality of human existence in a space environment and the comfort of the experience are becoming increasingly important considerations.

Design is a discipline that has the capacity to address the needs of human beings and provide innovative solutions. Inspiration for space design can be drawn from science

© The Author(s), under exclusive license to Springer Nature Switzerland AG 2023
P.-L. P. Rau (Ed.): HCII 2023, LNCS 14023, pp. 331–345, 2023.
https://doi.org/10.1007/978-3-031-35939-2_24

fiction, as well as from space technology itself. This is because design has the ability to balance both the technical and aesthetic aspects of living in space, and to incorporate human-centered design principles.

Recently, a new and emerging field of Space Design has been established, which aims to enhance the research of wellness in Outer Space, increase the comfort of space travelers, and generate innovation through the cross-fertilization of ideas from living in space and on Earth [1]. One such example of this new discipline is the Space4InspirAction (S4I) course, which is the first and only Space Design Course in the world recognized and supported by the European Space Agency (ESA). The course aims to create new professionals who are able to connect technology and beauty languages, increase creativity and visioning, find design solutions by crossing know-how and research, and imagine new cultural and business models for sustainable well-being [2].

Design fiction is a tool that can be used in space design to communicate innovative visions, provide inspiration and motivation for designers, and engage researchers and the general public. Julian Bleecker defines design fiction as "smart, creative, imaginative ways of linking ideas to their materialization" [3]. Design fiction is characterized by its narrative-based approach in which design objects are used as "diegetic prototypes", and its ability to provide a holistic view of the future of life and technology [4]. Tanenbaum notes that design fiction "can be a way to find a more holistic approach to the design of future life and technology [4]. Space design is a rapidly evolving field that holds great potential for innovation and exploration. It is a discipline that incorporates technical and aesthetic aspects of living in space, with a focus on human-centered design principles. Space Design is also a newly emerging discipline that aims to enhance the research of wellness in Outer Space and generate innovation through cross-fertilization of ideas. Design fiction is a useful tool in space design that can communicate innovative visions and provide inspiration for designers, engineers, and the general public.

2 Background

2.1 New Space Economy

The advent of a new Space Era is bringing about a shift in the way we approach and utilize space. As the space economy continues to grow and evolve, partnerships between space agencies and the private sector are becoming increasingly important [6]. According to the Organization for Economic Co-operation and Development (OECD), the Space Economy encompasses the full range of activities and resources that create value and benefits for human beings through the exploration, research, understanding, management, and utilization of space [7]. This growth and evolution of the space industry is leading to new applications and services across sectors such as meteorology, energy, telecommunications, insurance, transportation, maritime, aviation, and urban development, resulting in additional economic and social benefits.

In light of this, reducing our dependence on imports of essential goods from Earth for future space settlements is becoming increasingly important. At the International Space Development Conference (ISDC) 2019, a session was held on Earth Independence off-planet basing to discuss this issue [8]. The core requirements for an Earth Independence base were grouped according to their level of immediacy, including short-term, medium-term, and long-term requirements (Fig. 1). The short-term requirements are necessary for immediate survival, and the medium-term requirements are necessary for weekly survival. The long-term requirements encompass the issues involved in establishing a daily routine in the settlement.

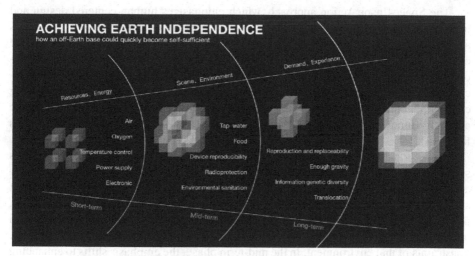

Fig. 1. Achieving earth independence

As we continue to push the boundaries of space exploration and utilization, it is crucial that we consider not just the technical aspects of space settlement but also the design and human factors involved. The comfort and quality of life for those living and working in space must be taken into consideration, and this is where the field of Space Design comes into play. Space Design aims to enhance research on wellness in outer space, improve the comfort of space travelers, and drive innovation through the cross-pollination of space and Earth-based design practices [9]. With the continued growth and expansion of the space industry, the role of Space Design in shaping our future experiences in space will become increasingly important.

2.2 Space Design Course

With the advancement of new technologies such as virtual and augmented reality, space design has become more interactive and immersive in recent years. This has led to the incorporation of these cutting-edge design tools in space design curriculum, preparing students for the use of such tools in the field. The growing interest in human space exploration, such as the establishment of the International Space Station, has brought attention to space design as a specialized field of study, resulting in the creation of dedicated Space Design Programs that focus specifically on designing human habitats in space. Space design courses typically comprise a mix of theory and practice, with curriculum covering design principles, history and theory, building systems, building codes and regulations, computer-aided design, and materials and finishes [10]. Studio-based classes, where students can apply their classroom learning to real-world projects, are also a common feature of space design programs [11]. The student-centered approach, which emphasizes the development of students' design thinking and problem-solving skills through practical projects and case studies, is widely used in space design education [12].

The Space4InspirAction approach, which emphasizes human-centered design and incorporates elements of positive psychology and mindfulness into the design process, is a recent development in space design education [13]. The "Space4InspirAction" course offered by Politecnico di Milano is an innovative program that guides students in developing their concepts related to space design. Studies have shown that space design education enhances students' problem-solving skills and increases their chances of finding employment in the field. Additionally, space design education has been found to promote creativity, innovation, and critical thinking, essential skills for a successful career in this field [14].

Professional astronauts, who are well-trained to adapt and live in space, are today's space travelers. However, with future longer space voyages carrying newcomers, a new and better experience is necessary to balance survival and happiness. The objectives of space habitation design courses can be broadly divided into three phases: short-term, mid-term, and long-term. In the short-term phase, the focus is on designing functional and efficient products for the confined space of a capsule, taking into account the specific constraints of that environment. In the mid-term phase, the emphasis shifts to enhancing the quality of life and comfort of those living and working in space. Students learn to design spaces that promote mental and physical health and provide a sense of home. In the long-term phase, the course focuses on the technical and design challenges of creating self-sufficient habitats on other planets, with the goal of eventually achieving human habitation on other planets."

Today's space travelers are well-trained professional astronauts, able to adapt and live in space. In the future longer space voyages will carry newcomers and require a new and better experience to delicately balance survival and happiness. The objectives of design courses on space habitation can be broadly divided into three categories, oriented to short-, medium- and long-term development phases. In the short-term stage, the focus of the course is on the limitations of the cabin environment and how to design integrated sets of products that are manufactured and placed in the space capsule. Students learn to design products that are functional and efficient in the confined space of a capsule, taking into account the specific constraints of that environment. In the mid-term stage, the focus shifts to people's quality of life and comfortable experience. Students learn to design products and environments that enhance the well-being and comfort of those living and working in space. They explore how to design spaces that are not only functional but also promote mental and physical health, and provide a sense of home. In the long-term stage, the course explores the challenges of designing for human self-sufficiency in off-planet bases. Students learn about the technical and design challenges of creating self-sufficient habitats on other planets such as Mars, with the goal of achieving the long-term goal of human habitation on other planets.

3 The Course

Our course is geared towards a long-term space development plan, considering the lifestyle and community of the Martian settlement. This section first describes the formal course setup, followed by a description of how we apply relevant tools in the space design course.

3.1 The Course Setup

The course on space design is structured in a way that gradually introduces students to the subject matter. The four rounds of one-day course are designed to be interactive and hands-on, allowing students to quickly become familiar with the topic and start exploring the various possibilities of space-related design. During this course, students will experiment with design-thinking and future-thinking tools, learning about their usage and how to effectively apply them in their designs.

The course has been designed to help students develop their design skills, and as such, includes several assignments that challenge students to think creatively and work collaboratively. These assignments include online discussions using the Miro platform, where students can share their ideas and engage in constructive dialogue with their peers. Additionally, students will build scenes in Roblox and participate in community-based scene construction, which will help them move from working individually to working in groups.

The theme of space is unique in that it is not limited by geographical borders or professional boundaries. This offers students a vast imaginative landscape to explore and offers countless possibilities for creative problem-solving. The course takes advantage of this by encouraging students to think outside the box and come up with innovative solutions to space-related problems. Furthermore, the course guides students in generating their Mars life imagination, moving from divergent to convergent thinking over a four-week period. This process helps students to develop their imagination and creativity, as well as their ability to think critically and make informed decisions. The schedule for this process is shown in Fig. 2, which provides a visual representation of the step-by-step progression from divergent to convergent thinking.

3.2 The Teaching Strategies

The course is divided into four phases, namely "Ideate the Future," "Envision the Futures," "Achieve the Future," and "Transform the Future" (Fig. 3). The first phase, "Ideate the Future," involves assigning a mission to the students that prompts them to create a vision for the future of Mars. This phase emphasizes brainstorming and idea generation, encouraging students to think creatively and consider the potential of space design. The second phase, "Envision the Futures," involves refining the ideas generated in the first phase into a scenario that provides a more detailed description of the future of Mars. This phase focuses on developing a narrative that considers the technical, environmental, and social aspects of space design. The third phase, "Achieve the Future," centers around creating a prototype of the future of Mars. Students learn about the technical aspects of space design and apply the scenario developed in the second phase

	Week 1	Week 2	Week 3	Week 4
Knowledge module	Ideate the futures Strategy	Envision the futures Design	Achieve the future Technology	Transform the future Economy
	Vision Planning	Scenario Building	Prototype Construction	Reflection+Transformation
Future signal / Future signal	1. Lecture space design 2. Challenge release (Personas and stories of 5 space travelers, Mission, needs) 3. Introduction to the Technology Platform (Roblox)	1.Design fiction (worldview, object, system) 2. Lecture: Space Art 3. Advanced Technology Platform (Model)	1. Space Traveler Experience Process (UX Cycle) 2. Advanced Technology platform (environment) 3. Space scene construction	1. Space Services (Service Blueprint) 2. Space Verification (Multiple Futures) 3. Preparation of space promotion materials
Research perspective	Meaning construction Story as archetype - attachment	Content translation Object as prototype - common association	Context rendering Scene as prototype - immersion	Value communication Media as prototype - self-actualization
Advanced technology / Science fiction	Product — Story description 1. Guide creative generation (future signals, future signs, vision generation) 2. Lecture: Space Design 3. Determine design direction (from vision to HMW)	Product -- Speculative prototype 1. MVP (least feasible Option) 2. Advanced Technology Platform (Model) 3. Making space objects (3D models)	Services -- Reality simulation 1. Space Operation Manual -- Design expression method (video, tomorrow's headlines, posters) 2. Advanced Technology platform (interaction) 3. Space scene presentation (virtual environment)	Service — scene experience 1. Group report (demonstration, experience and evaluation) 2. Media release (manual release, video shooting, public account push) 3. Designing the Future (Conclusion)
Course assignment	Space mission book	Space database	Space verification module	Space instruction manual

Fig. 2. Time organization that allows for exploration, theory, design practice, and reflection

to create a tangible representation of the future of Mars. The final phase, "Transform the Future," guides students to reflect on their design project and speculate about its impact on the future of Mars. This phase encourages students to think critically about the implications of their design decisions and how they can contribute to shaping the future.

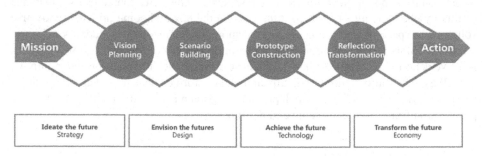

Fig. 3. The process of the space design course

The idea of life on Mars has been active in novels and other books (e.g. [15–17]). In Mary Roach's book "Packing for Mars" [18], she explores the complexities of living on the planet Mars and the unique challenges it poses for artists and designers. Through her presentation of real-life accounts from astronauts and engineers, Roach creates a captivating narrative of the human experience in space, including stories such as an astronaut's newfound love for gardening in the inhospitable environment of Mars. Psychologists use the term "irrational confrontation" to describe what happens when two people are isolated together for more than six weeks [19]. "It's hard to imagine how much you miss nature unless you're deprived of access to it" [20]. These narratives served as inspiration for our project, in which we developed five Personas of potential future residents of Mars, as seen in Fig. 4. Each persona is characterized by distinct traits and labels such as "Martian Media Person," "Nature Craving Disorder," "Earth Temperature Pining Disorder," "Space Environment Friendly," and "Irrational Confrontation." Among these personas, the "Mars Blogger" stands out as particularly fascinating, documenting their experiences on the planet through vlogs and providing a unique view on life on Mars.

Fig. 4. Five Mars Personas

Furthermore, Roach highlights the potential of space exploration to serve as a model for a new environmental paradigm. Engineer Wolfe, for instance, suggests that astronauts may not only be costly heroes but also serve as trailblazers in the development of sustainable technologies such as plastic structures that can be molded to process food. This idea is not limited to containers, but also to the structures that spacecraft usually abandon or leave behind when they return [21]. In our space design course, we aimed to tackle the problems that humans may face when they attempt to migrate to Mars, drawing inspiration from Roach's book and the fascinating stories of those who have ventured into space. The challenges of life on Mars are multifaceted, and understanding the human experience in space is crucial in developing solutions to these problems.

4   Examples of Course Projects:2050 Mars Life

The course is designed to challenge the completion of the first phase of construction of the Mars Migration Program in 2050, when the first passengers are sent to the Mars base to start their new lives. After a month of acclimatization, the first Mars residents have initially adapted to life on the Mars base. In order to effectively and rationally use the materials launched from Earth to Mars, the founder of Trans-Star Creators (FU) proposed to build a co-creation platform connecting the residents of both Earth-Mars. This Space design course focuses on solving the problems of living when humans achieve the Mars migration program. Today's space travelers are trained professional astronauts, able to adapt and live in space. The longer voyages into space in the future will carry newcomers and require a new and better experience to delicately balance survival and well-being. Four groups of students worked on "Nature Craving Disorder", "Mars Media People", "Earth Smells The four groups of students created a new experience of living on Mars with Roblox as the main creation platform, starting from the user profiles of four Mars residents: "Nature Craving Disorder", "Mars Media Person", "Earth Smell", and "Irrational Confrontation". The students worked in groups of 4–5, each group was evenly divided considering their professional background, grade and gender, and completed 4 pieces of work as a group, which were "GreenBot", "Green Cutie on Mars Base", "Mars Fitness Program: Space Fitness", "Apollo "Expedition" and "Mars Media Man". Each group achieved the whole process from idea to prototype scene realization. More detail can be found in an online introduction video [22].

4.1 GreenBot

By the year 2070, the global population has reached 12 billion, and issues such as climate change caused by past carbon emissions have presented significant challenges for humanity. The ocean's circulation has changed, and 30% of the population lives under extreme heat conditions. The United Nations, in an effort to explore the possibility of survival in extraterrestrial environments, has organized a team of experts from various fields to form the first exploratory team to live on Mars. Liu Yang, due to his research and influence in nutrition, agricultural cultivation, and natural environments, was selected for the team and boarded the Mars mission, where he is responsible for crop cultivation and serving as the base's cooking and nutritionist. The first batch of Martian immigrants arrive on the planet. In addition to the need to quickly establish sustainable vegetable cultivation systems, it is also necessary to alleviate the "green longing" of Martian residents (Fig. 5).

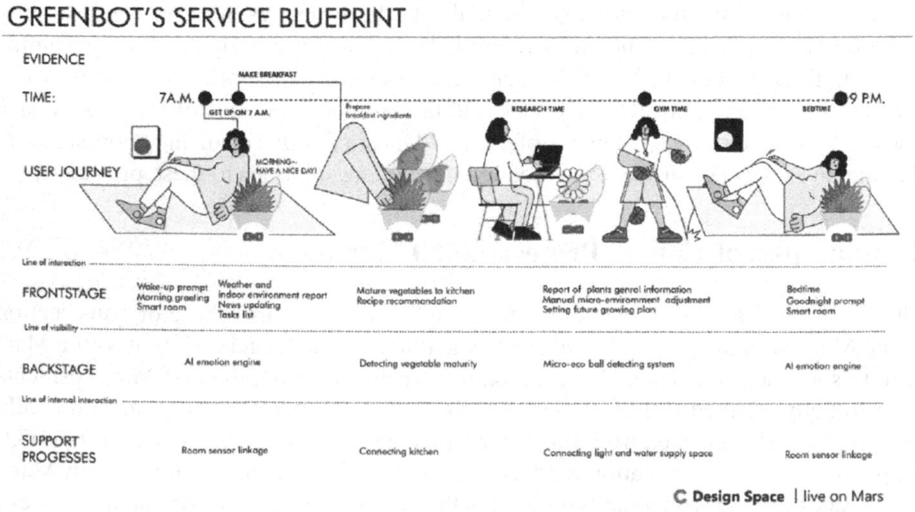

Fig. 5. GreenBot's service blueprint

GreenBot is a mobile, interactive plant cultivation robot that can interact with people. It can, according to the type and characteristics of the plant, go to different Nest (plant cultivation fields) to water the plants, supplement lighting, add nutrients and adjust the soil at specific stages. Based on Mars soil for plant cultivation research, the data, products (plants and materials) and greening effects obtained during the research process are reasonably allocated to achieve maximum sustainable benefits. Nests are located in different locations within the base, and hundreds of GreenBots are busy moving around the corridors and halls, bringing green and vitality to the base (Fig. 6).

Fig. 6. GreenBot future scenarios

4.2 Fitness in Mars

According to past research in the field of space medicine, physical fitness is a crucial aspect of astronaut health and well-being during prolonged periods of weightlessness [23]. The human body undergoes significant physiological changes in response to microgravity, including alterations in cardiovascular function and changes in bone density and muscle mass [24]. Studies have shown that prolonged exposure to microgravity results in a shift of fluids from the lower body to the upper body, leading to facial and head swelling, as well as varicose veins in the neck [25]. Additionally, bone loss and muscle weakening occur as a result of the lack of mechanical loading on the body. Research suggests that astronauts may lose up to 20% of their muscle mass after a short-duration spaceflight and up to 50% during a longer-duration mission if proper countermeasures are not taken.

One effective method for maintaining lower body muscle mass and function in microgravity is the use of resistance exercise equipment, such as a flywheel. However, the limited payload capacity of a Mars mission presents a challenge for traditional flywheel designs, which are often heavy and bulky. To address this issue, our team has proposed a novel solution: using brushless servo motors to create damping for the flywheel, thereby eliminating the need for a heavy flywheel mass [26]. Furthermore, we have designed an exercise teaching system that combines expertise from various disciplines, including human kinematics, artificial intelligence, and meteorology, to assist Mars pioneers in adapting to zero-gravity life and the Mars environment (Fig. 7).

Fig. 7. Fitness in Mars

4.3   For Martian Humans with Earth Odor Misses

In the near future, the human footprint in space is becoming more and more extensive, and several space stations and space bases have been established on Mars. 2060, with the pioneering work of previous generations, Mars has initially become an ideal place to live, welcoming the first immigrants from Earth - however, beyond the space bases, there are still too many uncertainties and potential surprises in the thousands of hectares of Martian landscapes. However, beyond the space base, there are still too many uncertainties and potential surprises in the thousands of hectares of Martian landscape, a vast "oasis" that still needs to be further explored by humans, and Columbus' exploration of the New World will once again be staged. So, while living and working in peace, Mars Base launched an exploration program called "Apollo": a group of experienced and adventurous drivers with a passion for exploration were selected as "Mars Drivers" to undertake the major mission of exploring Mars. They will pilot exploration vehicles like Apollo, the Greek god of the sun, to spread the fire of human civilization to every corner of Mars and to bring light to the continuation of human civilization on Mars (Fig. 8).

Our design content is to help John Young in the cockpit for patrol, terrain collection tasks in the work scenario, through the command, to build immersive scenes in the form of vehicle projection, and according to the user data collected by the sensor to provide a variety of state applicable scenarios, racing car front window for the display, through the manipulation of the driver's seat steering wheel, clutch, throttle, etc. to play, the car will be equipped with audio The car will be equipped with audio, smoke releaser, gasoline smell aromatherapy and other ways to simulate the real driving environment, to solve the problem that the Martian landscape is too monotonous and the pursuit of exciting racing experience, to achieve the goal of adding excitement and companionship to the

Fig. 8. For Martian Humans with Earth Odor Misses

working life on Mars and building a quality immersive working environment according to the mood. Along with the proliferation of human footprints from Earth to space, looking into the future, Mars may become our second home, and the first immigrants will begin their exploration of this vast planet. Based on the Mars Apollo expedition and the first explorer John Young, we designed a new space product system that fully penetrates the needs of the "thought-individual-environment" level, not only breaking through the geographical boundaries of different worlds, but also fully connecting the sensory experiences in the virtual and real worlds. With the new space economy, we are looking forward to a future where "every person is a metaverse".

4.4 Mars Daily

It took nearly 200 years for the Earth to go from near destruction to the ecologically green planet it is now, and mankind, having learned a bitter lesson, decided not to overexploit the Earth and turned its focus to the universe. 2660 years later, human technology continued to develop and began exploring outer space for a habitable second planet. After initial exploration, Mars was selected by the Earth Federation as the first pilot destination. The first four residents of Mars, including Chris, have officially landed last month to start living. The residents' physical needs, such as basic food and clothing, are now well taken care of, while higher-level needs for belonging and self-actualization are beginning to emerge. See future scenarios in Fig. 9.

Mars Daily helps Mars residents to solve the problems of video production, audience feedback and family companionship in a multimedia system to effectively promote Mars while maintaining the physical and mental health of Martians. The Mars Media Station is the connection center and transmission hub between Mars residents and Earth residents, the largest information collection and processing station in the Mars base, and the incubation site of Mars Daily. Surrounded and encircled by giant holographic billboards, the Media Station is the most vibrant place in the Mars colony. The daily newspaper system, linked to the spinach farming program, is able to fully interact with readers from Earth, creating a "Mars-Earth" express line.

4.5 Student Evaluation and Curriculum Reflection

A total of 16 participants were enrolled in the space design course. After completing the course, they were invited to provide feedback through semi-structured interviews.

Fig. 9. Mars Daily

The interview questions focused on their experience in the course, including what they learned, what they found valuable, and areas for improvement. Here lists some insights from the participant.

P1: "I didn't know it was such an interesting topic before this class started, especially in today's era when we're thinking about space, including the metaverse. I think it's very valuable to have the opportunity to do some exploration in this direction."

P2: "This course gave me a deeper understanding of the concept of the future and introduced me to design tools and methodologies that I hadn't encountered before."

P3: "One interesting aspect of this course is studying individuals and then generating a product that can serve the public. It's a unique way to learn."

P7: "Starting with individual personas allows for a lot of space and flexibility in our own design and ideas. It also brings real-world needs into the design process."

P13: "In this class, we learned how to use systematic thinking in product design. We not only considered the functional characteristics of individual products but also took a macroscopic view of the long-term future."

P14: "I also remember a guest speaker who discussed what you need to prepare for a trip to Mars and the attractions you can see there. It was a rare and valuable experience."

The feedback from the students indicated that they found the space design course to be engaging and informative. They appreciated the opportunity to explore the topic of space design, and the use of design tools and methodologies helped deepen their understanding of the future. The approach of starting from individual personas was well received, allowing for creativity and real-life needs to be incorporated into the design process. The course also taught systematic thinking and a macroscopic view of the long-term future. The guest speaker discussing a trip to Mars was a memorable experience for the students.

However, there were also areas for improvement identified by the students. Some suggested that diversifying the content, enhancing hands-on experiences, encouraging critical thinking, and expanding the guest speaker series could further deepen their under-standing and skills. Diversifying the content, enhancing hands-on experiences, encouraging critical thinking, and expanding the guest speaker series could further deepen the students' understanding and skills. These findings highlight the importance of considering both the content and the methodology of design courses.

5 Discussion and Conclusion

Space design is a field of study that has grown in popularity over the years. The field is interdisciplinary and encompasses aspects of architecture, interior design, and environmental psychology. Space design courses vary in their approach to teaching, but most include a combination of theory and practice. The outcomes and benefits of taking a space design course are numerous, but there are also challenges and limitations that need to be considered. This literature review highlights the current state of knowledge and understanding of space design courses and provides recommendations for future research in the field.

Despite the many benefits of space design education, there are also challenges and limitations that need to be considered. One of the main challenges is the lack of stan-dardization in space design curricula, which can make it difficult for students to transfer credits between institutions [27]. Additionally, the field of space design is constantly changing, and it can be difficult for educators to keep up with the latest trends and devel-opments [28]. There is also a lack of diversity in the field of space design and educators are working to address this issue by providing more inclusive and culturally responsive curriculum. Furthermore, the integration of new technologies and sustainability princi-ples into the curriculum is a challenge that needs to be addressed to ensure that students are well-prepared for the future of the field.

According to Clark's 1968 science fiction novel "2001: A Space Odyssey", in the year 2001, which has already passed, humans have built magnificent cities in space, permanent colonies on the moon, and huge nuclear-powered spaceships have sailed to Saturn. And in reality, there is still a long way to go from this great idea. At the same time, information technology is developing at an unimaginable speed, and the network covers the whole world. This does not mean that people are losing interest in space exploration, rather, the VR experience of digital scenarios can be seen as a low-cost and rapid iterative way of testing, which gives designers more room to play, giving them design ideas that can be experienced and better access to the public's will, and to some extent, to allay concerns about the unknown. What we are doing is not predicting the future, but listing out the possibilities in the form of stories, and inviting more people to participate in the process of finding an agreeable future and moving in that direction.

Acknowledgements. This work was, in part, supported by Graduate Education Innovation Grants, Tsinghua University. In addition, we take the opportunity to thank Professor Annalisa Dominoni and Professor Benedetto Quaquaro from Pilitecnico di Milan Design department for sharing their teaching achievements in Space4Inspiraction course. Finally, we thank all students whose project we used as examples: GreenBot team (Figs. 5, 6)- Liu Lairui, Ren Lu, Li liangting, Fu Liqun, and Xu Miao; Fitness in Mars team (Fig. 7) – Fu Zhi, Wang Bingni, Li Zaiyuan, Fu Ruoyu, and Hu Yiran; For Martian Humans with Earth Odor Misses team (Fig. 8) – Wei Ran, Wang Qirui, Xiao

Jieyu, Su Yue, and Cheng Xiran; Mars Daily team (Fig. 8) – Guo Wengjing, Cai Shijie, Chen Changxi, Huang Yangyang, and Cheng Hao.

References

1. Dominoni, A.: Creative design practices. The creative process in product design andenvironment for educational. Esercizi creativi di design / Il processo creativo del design delprodotto ambientale per la didattica. Maggioli Editore, Politecnica Editorial Series, Milan (2008)
2. Donimoni, D., Aversa, S., Maffei, S.: Space4InspirAction: The First Space Design Course in the World. In: Design and the Space Industry, pp. 3–14. Springer, Cham (2018)
3. Bleecker, J.: Design Fiction: A short essay on design, science, fact, and fiction. Near Future Laboratory (2009)
4. Bleecker, J.: Design fiction and the futures of the Internet of Things. In: Proceedings of the 2015 ACM International Joint Conference on Pervasive and Ubiquitous Computing, pp. 797–808. ACM (2015)
5. Jankowski, N.: Design fiction: a manifesto. Sci. Fict. Stud. 37(3), 566–575 (2010)
6. Hufenbach, B.: Space is open for business. Room. Space J 10, Winter 2017:102–107. The Aerospace International Research Center (AIRC). Publishers Press, Vienna (2017)
7. OECD: The Space Economy: Trends, Drivers and Policy Considerations. OECD Science, Technology and Industry Policy Papers, No. 28, OECD Publishing, Paris (2019). https://doi.org/10.1787/9c874d26-en
8. ISDC: ISDC 2019 Proceedings. The International Space Development Conference (ISDC), May 2019, Washington D.C (2019)
9. Hamel, P., Ramspott, U.: The international space economy: an overview and analysis. In: The International Space Economy, pp. 1–20. Springer, Cham. https://doi.org/10.1007/978-3-319-95235-2_1
10. Brown, J.: Integrating sustainability into space design curriculum. J. Interior Design Educ. 12, 45–52 (2019)
11. Chang, S.: The evolution of space design education. Architect. Rev. 12(3), 33–37 (2018)
12. Kuo, L.: Student-centered approach in space design education. J. Interior Design Educ. 15, 35–42 (2022)
13. Liu, L.: The space4inspiraction approach in space design education. J. Inter. Des. 49, 12–19 (2020)
14. Ng, G.: The impact of space design education on creativity and innovation. Design Think. Res. 8(2), 67–74 (2021)
15. The Case for Mars: The Plan to Settle the Red Planet and Why We Must" by Robert Zubrin (1996)
16. Red Planets: Marxism and Science Fiction" edited by Mark Bould and China Miéville (2009)
17. Designing for Habitat: Architecture for the Red Planet" edited by Noah D. Guynn and Sarah J. Fishman (2019)
18. Roach, M.: Packing for Mars: The Curious Science of Life in the Void. W. W. Norton & Company (2010)
19. Burnazyan, A.J., et al.: Year-Long Medico-Engineering Experiment in a Partially Closed Ecological System." Aerospace Medicine, October 1969, pp. 1087–1093.
20. Pesavento, P.: From Aelita to the International Space Station: The Psychological Effects of Isolation on Earth and in Space. Quest: History Spaceflight Quart. 8(2), 4–23 (2000)
21. Worf, D.L.: Multiple Uses for Foods. Paper presented at the Conference on Nutrition in Space and Related Waste Problems, Tampa, Fla., April 27–30, 1964. Sponsored by NASA and the National Academy of Sciences

22. Lin.Zhu (2023, February 7). New Space Narrative/Pruduct and service design course/ Mars futures life [Video]. YouTube. https://youtu.be/x439adIqLGE
23. Sarafin, K., et al.: Exercise countermeasures to mitigate muscle and bone loss during prolonged spaceflight. J. Appl. Physiol. **119**(12), 1439–1447 (2015)
24. Lang, T., et al.: Muscle and bone loss during spaceflight and bed rest: the challenges of countermeasure development. J. Appl. Physiol. **121**(3), 775–782 (2016)
25. Kuznetsov, A., et al.: Cardiovascular adaptation to long-duration spaceflight: current state of knowledge and future directions. J. Appl. Physiol. **126**(4), 937–946 (2019)
26. Smith, J., et al.: Development of a lightweight flywheel exercise system for use in a low-gravity environment. J. Space Explor. **10**(2), 93–102 (2020)
27. Park, J.: Lack of standardization in space design curricula: a challenge for transfer students. J. Interior (2018)
28. Lee, J.: Challenges in keeping up with the latest trends in space design. J. Inter. Des. **45**, 23–28 (2020)

Culturally-Informed Design
of Automated and Intelligent Systems

Synneure: Intelligent Human-Machine Teamwork in Virtual Space

Chiju Chao, Qirui Wang, Hongfei Wu, and Zhiyong Fu[✉]

Department of Information Art and Design, Tsinghua University, Beijing 100084, China
zjr21@mails.tsinghua.edu.cn

Abstract. Researchers have shown that intelligent assistants can improve human productivity in teamwork. With the development of VR technology, such human-computer teamwork will also be able to take place in digital environments. In order to achieve this, this study developed a virtual reality platform called Synneure. The program contains an intelligent assistant that can be configured with a variety of personality traits, skills, and data sets. The platform builds a virtual space with stereoscopic interaction and supports human-machine teamwork between intelligent assistants and humans in virtual reality. Five valid conclusions were derived from prototyping, design fiction, and user testing. For example, reconstructing design tools in a stereoscopic way can help users improve the discussion process in a way that increases the efficiency of spatial manipulation. However, additional instruction is needed. In addition, conclusions are drawn regarding intelligent assistants, such as collaborative functions and emotional functions that follow the discussion phase. Last but not least, people will have a higher expectation of interaction with an intelligent assistant in comparison to the real one, and this will be the next design direction for the follow-up of this study.

Keywords: Intelligent assistant · Human-machine teamwork · Virtual reality · VR · Stereoscopic Interaction

1 Introduction

Known as the era of artificial intelligence, we are currently in the fourth phase of the industrial revolution. Intelligent products surround people in their daily lives, forming a human-machine society where humans and machines live together. These intelligent products are either responsible for mechanized tasks (e.g., floor cleaning robots, transportation robots), bring entertainment and companionship (e.g., smart speakers, virtual pets), or are personal assistants (e.g., automatic car navigation). This mutually beneficial relationship between humans and intelligent products has been described as a symbiotic relationship by researchers in the field of Human-Computer Interaction [1, 2].

Research on artificial intelligence and human-computer interaction has continued to crossover in recent years. While artificial intelligence advances by obtaining data and feedback from HCI systems, it also contributes to the innovation of HCI [3]. As smart products approach the ideal of "intelligence" in the future, designers need to consider

P.-L. P. Rau (Ed.): HCII 2023, LNCS 14023, pp. 349–361, 2023.
https://doi.org/10.1007/978-3-031-35939-2_25

building a social relationship between humans and products. In a human-computer society, if an intelligent product is to be a good collaborator to integrate into human society, it needs to be designed and developed to be a reliable and trustworthy partner in a social team [4]. Therefore, in addition to the rules and behaviors of AI in efficient cooperation, the "emotional intelligence" of AI needs to be considered. This refers to allowing AI to autonomously understand human behavior, thoughts, and emotions, and to provide appropriate feedback. Through this process of emotional interaction, it learns to adapt to human society, which is filled with emotional factors [5]. Many designers have conducted research in this area, for example, combining social psychology and trying to set character attributes for smart products in a role-constructive way [6]. Another example is to set customizable personality trait expressions for products from personality psychology [7].

In 2021, the concept of the metaverse emerged. A metaverse is an online virtual world that is parallel to the real world and maps to the real world. Information from the physical space is used to build the virtual space, forming a two-way communication development between the virtual space and the physical space [8, 9]. Breaking the boundary between the real world and the virtual world through information intermingling, not only makes the virtual world more realistic but also brings new vitality to the physical world [10]. It is anticipated that team collaboration between humans and intelligent products will also have the potential to be transferred to the virtual world as a result of this trend.

In our group's research over the past 2 years, artificial intelligence has been integrated into human co-creation teams. We are studying how to intelligently provide design tools and design cues to help human teams in their design activities. For one study in 2020, we used AI assistants to provide text clues and visual clues during students' design activities [11]. In another study: NEXT! Toaster [12], AI is involved in co-creative activities to provide appropriate design thinking tools. Therefore, based on the research experience, in this study, we will transfer the process of human-computer teamwork to the virtual world and try to give more emotional attributes to it.

2 Literature Review

2.1 Human-Machine Teamwork

For intelligent products, the interaction between humans and machines (or products) is often considered "collaboration". Collaboration between humans is when people carry out activities to achieve a common goal with each other [13]. Today, there is a similar collaborative interaction between humans and intelligent products. The significance of the collaborative interaction between humans and intelligent products is that there is complementarity between humans and machines, which is of significant benefit to team efficiency. In work and life, humans and AI can collaborate on different aspects of team decision-making. Artificial intelligence is well enough to solve complex problems that require mathematical and computational analysis, while humans are more creatively and intuitively focused on uncertainty and ambiguity [14, 15]. A speech recognition system, for instance, could help humans look up needed information materials using voice conversation at work, saving hours of time spent searching the Internet. It is important for HCI researchers to consider how they can work better with humans when designing and developing intelligent products, rather than simply viewing them as tools [1].

For the study of human-machine teamwork, we can apply the theory of teamwork among humans to the study of human-machine interaction [13]. In the same way as human-human teamwork, a similar collaborative framework can be applied to human-machine collaboration. Sub-goals are determined by identifying the current state as well as the goals that the team wishes to achieve. Appropriate actions are then taken to support these sub-goals. Influencing factors of teammates also ought to be taken into account when acting. [5]. To do this, it needs to develop products that can understand and predict human behavior and intentions. And, it needs to communicate this understanding to the human team to create a common perception between humans and the product [16].

2.2 Emotional Human-Machine Interaction

Emotional intelligence is critical to teamwork, in most cases more critical than technical skills. Whether it is motivation, empathy, or social skills, they all play a role in mutual understanding, knowledge sharing, and smooth cooperation among team members. For human-machine teamwork, products today are capable of interacting emotionally with users through affective computing and artificial empathy techniques. Studies have shown that empathic expressions in human-machine interactions have a high social value [17, 18]. Moreover, in the process of human-machine collaboration, empathy can also help to improve the efficiency of collaboration. For example, an intelligent product can make it easier for humans to understand its capabilities through emotional expressions. Humans fully understand what tasks are suitable for intelligent products to do and eventually learn to use them most effectively [19].

Designing intelligent products in such a way that they can communicate empathically with humans becomes a complex problem to be solved. The system of emotions cannot be a copy of the theory of human emotions, but a system of emotions that meets the needs of machines [19]. It is an emotional system tailored to meet both human needs and the needs of intelligent products. At the same time, we need to consider ethical and moral issues. It is particularly pertinent to consider ethical and moral issues when such products enable humans to form strong emotional attachments or even replace emotional interactions between individuals.

2.3 Discussion of Ethical Issues

As HCI designers, we need to pay more attention to the issue of ethics and social responsibility. When these intelligent products are introduced into society [20], our design and manufacturing of these products will also contribute to the changes in society in the future. Therefore, we will be forced to take responsibility for them. When smart products are seen as members of society [21], the moral judgment about AI becomes even more complex. For example, if we have to force them to follow human social norms or impose exclusive social norms on them [22]. Researchers are also concerned about the necessity of anthropomorphizing AI [17, 18].

Although this study was designed out of optimism about AI. However, the concerns about AI are not unreasonable. The more autonomous artificial intelligence becomes, the deeper human cooperation with it will be. A variety of risks may also arise from this [23], including ethical and political issues, data misuse, privacy risks, emotional issues, and so forth.

3 Concept

The purpose of this study is to develop an exploratory design study using some of the previously discussed topics of human-machine team collaboration. We intend to explore the design of human-machine collaboration in virtual environments. In order to elicit unexpected responses from users, this study will combine various types of possible concepts. This exploratory design research is not intended to find definitive conclusions, but rather to point in the direction of being able to find inspiration for subsequent research goals.

3.1 The Character of the Intelligent Assistant

Studies have shown that humans always personify interactable objects [24]. In fact, there is always an emotional connection between the product and the user. The lifetime of a product will depend on the type of emotion between the user and the product [25]. The imagination of product personification is becoming increasingly possible thanks to relevant technologies. For example, Rodrigues [26] proposes an empathic evaluation response model which states that artificial intelligence can empathize with its users. In the model, the generation of empathic responses relies on the moderators set by the user: personality, mood, emotion, and other characteristic attributes.

Researchers in HCI have proposed several different ways to design smart products to express character including voice intonation [27], material appearance, form appearance, and language usage. Or through the design of interactive behaviors such as speech, gaze, and gestures [28]. These design approaches combine personality traits with affective techniques to be able to create intelligent characters with empathic responses [29]. The purpose of this study is to determine if smart products can influence team collaboration by enhancing emotional experiences.

3.2 Virtual Co-creation World

In this study, the physical world and the digital world are combined to explore the concept of human-machine co-creation. Based on the concept of the metaverse, we use VR technology to construct a co-creation platform. We provide users with virtual reality experiences that allow them to communicate and interact with intelligent assistants, environments, and other people. But this design is not only a digital concept. Through the concept of the digital twin, we will first obtain the user's ideas and data from the real world and then construct a VR co-creation platform based on that information.

Through the use of this virtual reality space, this study hopes to investigate the following three issues through this design practice: 1. The design of human-computer teamwork interaction in the virtual reality world. 2. The way data is collected, analyzed, and used in human-computer co-creation. 3. The way in which emotional interaction is expressed in virtual reality.

3.3 Stereoscopic Interaction Tool Design

When conducting design activities in the physical world, we often use paper, pens, sticky notes, and whiteboards. Therefore, the related design thinking tools would also be designed in flat form. But now that we are co-creating in virtual reality, we realize that we need a more advanced perspective on the interaction design of tools. One reason for this is that no research has confirmed that people are equally adept at manipulating flat surfaces in VR. Another reason is that virtual reality enables spatial changes at a much lower cost, so various types of tool design can be experimented with. Therefore, we propose a three-dimensional approach to design thinking tools, where users interact with objects in order to advance the design process.

4 Design

4.1 The User Journey

We used three design tools to guide users during the co-creation phase: Future Signs, STEEP, and Future Triangle.

First, we collected future signs related to the design theme from the users and recorded the data in the form of images and keywords. This data will be transferred to the VR platform and displayed on the wall in VR. After group discussions, users need to pick 8 future signs that match the consistent concept in the second step. Then, keywords for 5 elements of society, technology, environment, economy, and politics will be displayed on 5 pillars in the scenario. These keywords are derived from the future signs chosen by users. Users can select, delete and edit these words and choose the inspired keywords to move to the future triangle in the center of the scene. As part of the future triangle, users must discuss future information in three dimensions: signal, interpretation, and issue (Fig. 1).

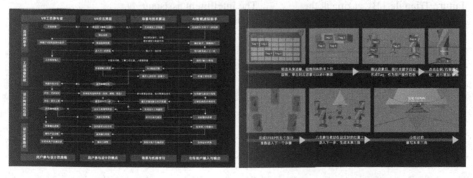

Fig. 1. The User Journey in Synneure.

4.2 Personality and Behavior of an Intelligent Assistant

The smart assistant is the focus of this design and we try to design personality and behavior for it. Users will engage with the intelligent assistant during the discussion process.

In the design of personality, we initially tried two-dimensional attributes: rational and affective, active and passive. The rational assistant displays only the information content required by the user; while the emotional assistant will show different emotional reactions according to the user's state through pre-set tone words. An active assistant responds to user interaction, displays information, and provides voice prompts; a passive assistant does not provide voice prompts and must be elicited by the user Table 1.

In the interaction design, we use gaze interaction, voice interaction, and gesture interaction. There are different interaction behaviors in different scenarios:

Table 1. Interaction Design of Intelligent Assistant in 3 Scenarios.

Scenarios	Gaze Interaction	Voice Interaction	Gesture Interaction
Future Signs	By gazing, some keywords about the target being gazed at can be listed around the target	/	Select a target and place its details in the text box in the head of the intelligent assistant
STEEP	After focusing on a certain keyword, the intelligent assistant will list the images and information related to it around the target	By analyzing what the user is currently saying through NLP technology, the user can get advice from the intelligent assistant at any time	When the gesture points to a keyword, the intelligent assistant conducts an Internet search and displays more detailed information to the user
Future Triangle	By gazing at the keywords, the intelligent assistant displays the relevant information that has been discussed around	The intelligent assistant deduces where the user's input is most likely to be posted and gives the user a hint	/

4.3 Use of Data

The data flow of the platform designed in this study involves collecting, recording, storing, and analyzing. It can be roughly divided into three stages: before, during, and after co-creation.

Before co-creation, the platform collects 2 parts of data from users in advance. The first one is a collection of future signs images and keywords related to the topic selected by the user. The second is the integration and analysis of this platform's past usage data. As a result of the integration of these data into the intelligent assistant's viewpoint database, users will be able to benefit from valuable assistance during the co-creation process.

During co-creation, users' real-time discussion content will be recorded and analyzed. By determining the status of users' discussions, the intelligent assistant can recommend relevant content from the viewpoint library in order to assist users in expanding their ideas.

After co-creation, users will generate ideas. In order to facilitate co-creation by other users in the future, the intelligent assistant records these ideas as a library of ideas Fig. 2.

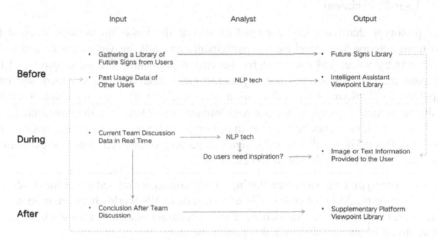

Fig. 2. Data flow in Collaborative Processes.

5   Prototype and Test

5.1   Prototype by Unity3D

We designed three VR spaces for character creation, team discussion, and results presentation.

First, users enter the character creation room. The main function of this room is to generate user characters and select AI assistant characters. After confirmation, the user will be transported to the team discussion room. In this room, the team co-creation process of Future Signs, STEEP, and Future Triangle will occur. Finally, the user enters the display room. All other teams' results are recorded here Fig. 3.

The models were built in C4D and prototypes were developed in Unity3D. We also use DuerOS's open API for speech recognition, intelligent query, and natural language analysis development.

Fig. 3. Prototype model in Unity3D.

5.2 User Experiment

The prototype that has been developed so far has the basic interactions required for the team activity flow developed. 4 participants can talk by voice, use design tools, enter text by voice, and enter text by the virtual keyboard. The development of the AI assistant is, however, influenced by its technical capabilities. The system was only capable of completing basic information searches, and it could not conduct natural dialogue, semantic analysis, or emotional interactions. Therefore, the emotional factor of the AI assistant cannot be tested with prototype experiments. For these reasons, the testing of this design study is divided into two parts. Part one is a prototype experiment test. The second part is design fiction evaluation.

Part I: Prototype Experimental Testing. Participants are invited to use the developed VR prototype platform for co-creation experiences in VR worlds between humans and machines. Participants can experience and evaluate human-machine teamwork and three-dimensional interaction design in this part of the test.

Part 2: Design Fiction's Evaluation. A synthetic movie is used to describe the performance behaviors of AI assistants with different personalities within a team. We used a design fiction approach to create possible stories from the discussion process that would be shown in the film. Those participants who completed the first part of the test were invited to watch the movie. Participants commented on the emotional interactions in the fictional movie in conjunction with the first part of the experience Fig. 4.

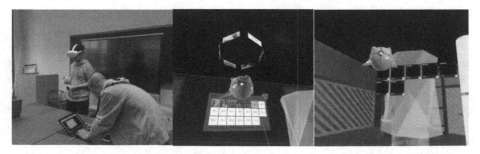

Fig. 4. Prototype Experimental User Test and Design fiction's Evaluation Test.

5.3 Semi-structured Interviews

We used semi-structured interviews to collect participants' perspectives, which are often used to explore 'multiple meanings' and perceptions of 'actions, events, or settings' [30]. Our interview targets were participants who had participated in both parts of the test. The interviews were conducted face-to-face in a quiet indoor environment such as an office and lasted about 30 min. The interview session was divided into two parts. The first part was to understand the participants' perspectives after using the prototype. The second part was to get additional thoughts after watching the design fiction film.

The outline of the interview is as follows:

1. Describe how you interacted with the AI assistant in each session and the various experiences you had.
2. What is the biggest change in the AI assistant's involvement in team co-creation?
3. What are the advantages and disadvantages of using stereoscopic interaction?
4. Which part do you think can be optimized and improved?
5. What is the impact of the emotional performance of the AI assistant shown in the film on team collaboration? Give an example.
6. What kind of personality do you think you prefer in an AI assistant and why?

This interview outline does not need to be followed exactly. To gain a comprehensive understanding of participants' perspectives, questions will need to be adjusted based on their responses.

6 Discussion

After conducting semi-structured interviews with users, we have summarized 5 conclusions. As a result of these conclusions, we have a positive opinion of the design concept as well as some suggestions that can be helpful in further developing it.

6.1 Advantages and Disadvantages of Stereoscopic Interaction

In the Synneure platform, we build stereoscopic design tools in virtual space. The real-world flat tools are represented and interacted with in stereoscopic graphics. This design concept was praised by most of the participants. Virtual spaces are easier to move around, however, they are more difficult to manipulate in detail. Therefore, in terms of interaction experience, this stereoscopic approach is more suitable for virtual space. However, since most people have not had a similar experience of using it, there is some difficulty in understanding and learning, which is something we need to improve. For this kind of stereoscopic interaction design, object design, space size, process arrangement, teaching guidelines, etc. will be the direction of the research.

"Despite the ease of use of the stereoscopic tool, learning is more difficult. In the first place, I did not understand at all what the columns and triangles meant when I entered the space. I had to move to the front to see them. The whole process took me a long time to learn. However, it is true that in the VR world, one cannot quite adapt to the flat interface, such as entering text, pointing to the button, and so forth."

"This type of digital co-creation space is interesting. The three-dimensional tool makes the operation less precise and avoids the problem of not being able to perform fine operations in the VR environment. However, I feel that such an innovative design is not easy to understand. It would be cool to have a process for users to pick a template and create an environment."

6.2 AI Assistants Take on Different Responsibilities Before and After Co-creation

We found that team co-creation in a virtual world has more stages of change compared to reality. These changes come from the gradual familiarization of the user with the virtual world and the gradual acquisition of the required discussion material. Therefore, the role of the AI assistant in the virtual world should also be in line with this change. For example, in the early stages, AI assistants are responsible for session introduction, novice tutorials, and information search. In later stages, the AI assistant is responsible for the organization of information, the elicitation of viewpoints, and the control of processes.

"I would rely more on the AI assistant in the first half of the workshop. Due to the VR world limiting our movement at the time, we had to ask the AI assistant to check some information on the Internet. Later on, during the inspiration phase, it seemed that the AI assistant did not provide much assistance. Because we didn't need any extra info at the time."

6.3 Separate the Two Goals of Information Seeking and Inspiration

The interviews revealed that the AI assistant had the following two main roles in the team discussions: information search and inspiration. Since users are unable to use devices such as computers and cell phones in the VR world, they have to rely on AI assistants to search for Internet information. However, this process actually works better in a controlled way through the search interface. In the later stages of inspiration, the AI assistant plays the role of a different species being invited into the discussion. Therefore, we will separate the information search module from the AI assistant in future work.

"So far, we have only experienced AI assistants that are capable of searching for information. However, in the fictional film, the AI assistant gives some inspirational tips. Perhaps these 2 modules should be separated. It's not necessary to employ an AI assistant since search information can be implemented via a web-like interface. Let the AI assistant handle what he's skilled at."

"Before testing the AI assistant, I was intrigued by it and thought it could provide inspiration. After using it, I realized it could only search for information, so why not just let people call up the web interface?"

6.4 Emotional Interaction Can Be Helpful, but Can also Have a Negative Impact

In the process of prototype testing, we found that once the user has failed to communicate with the AI assistant, the user often feels distrustful of it. Emotional expression makes the AI assistant more human, which helps moderate its use and makes users willing to give it a shot. But it also poses ethical issues. A participant believed that the AI assistant would influence his judgment as a result of this emotional expression. Consequently, he believes that this has a negative impact on the human team.

"I would like an assistant like this based on the emotional assistant shown in the fictional video. Whenever I talk to the AI assistant on the prototype platform, I usually get bored because he often ignores my voice messages in a cold and rational way. However, I may be more tolerant of this AI assistant if it has a personality."

"When the AI assistant has a personality, I worry that it will have an impact on my judgment. For example, I would be very concerned that it would be more positive about some of my ideas. Will AI influence our creative thinking in this case?"

6.5   The Possibility for Interactive Behavior of AI Assistant

In the virtual world, users can interact with AI assistants with more actions. The design and development of these interactions are easier to implement compared to real-world products. For this reason, we found that most users tried to touch the intelligent assistant after entering the virtual world and expected it to give behavioral feedback. However, since this study did not include design in this area, users were not able to obtain feedback on their interaction with the system. As a consequence, we can see a valuable design direction for the future: the design of emotional interaction expressions in virtual worlds for AI assistants.

"The virtual-world AI assistant is definitely more vivid than the real-world voice speaker. It can have different appearances and expressions, for example. However, I have not yet experienced this aspect of the design, which does not seem to highlight the advantages of the virtual world."

7   Conclusion and Future Work

In this paper, we introduce Synneure, a virtual reality co-creation platform. Using this platform, four human users collaborate to complete the process of team co-creation. Each user of the platform is provided with an AI assistant with emotional properties that assists him/her in the search for information and in the prompting of ideas. Through the use of stereoscopic objects in the virtual world, users can complete the discussion process by dragging and editing stereoscopic objects within the scene. By combining multiple innovative design elements, this project explores the topic of AI assistant participation in teamwork in virtual reality.

Three contributions of this study stand out: first, the discovery of a creative interaction design method for executing operations effectively in virtual space - stereoscopic design. The second goal is to explore some future design directions for AI assistants that are involved in discussions in terms of state changes and emotional expression. Last but not least, experimental testing using the prototype platform and a design fiction approach helped participants envision prototypes that could never be realized.

Through prototyping and experimentation, as well as the design fiction approach, we have come to valid conclusions and directions for future work. As a first point, stereoscopic interaction in virtual space is a valuable design element, but further exploration is needed to make it more intuitive for users. Second, AI assistants are limited by technical capabilities and encounter increased challenges in development and testing. Although this study uses a design fiction approach to enable users to evaluate, we will consider experimental testing through the WoZ approach in subsequent work. Last but not least, this study will optimize the AI assistant in three directions: functional modules, emotional expression, and dynamic interaction.

Acknowledgement. This project is supported by Graduate Education Innovation Grants, Tsinghua University.

References

1. Cho, J., Rader, E.: The role of conversational grounding in supporting symbiosis between people and digital assistants. ACM Human-Comput. Interact. **4**(CSCW1), 1–28 (2020). https://doi.org/10.1145/3392838
2. Licklider, J.C.R.: Man-Computer Symbiosis. IRE Trans. Hum. Factors Electron. **HFE-1**, 4–11 (1960). https://doi.org/10.1109/THFE2.1960.4503259
3. Ma, X.: Towards Human-Engaged AI. In: 27th International Joint Conference on Artificial Intelligence, pp. 5682–5686. , Stockholm, Sweden (2018)
4. Paschkewitz, J., Patt, D.: Can AI make your job more interesting? Issues Sci. Technol. **37**, 74–78 (2020)
5. Chakraborti, T., Kambhampati, S., Scheutz, M., Zhang, Y.: AI Challenges in Human-Robot Cognitive Teaming, http://arxiv.org/abs/1707.04775 (2017)
6. ShiJian, L.: Design of Intelligent Product. Publishing House of Electronics Industry (2017)
7. LuxAI: QT Robot, https://luxai.com/
8. Tao, F., et al.: Digital twin-driven product design framework. Int. J. Prod. Res. **57**, 3935–3953 (2019). https://doi.org/10.1080/00207543.2018.1443229
9. Zhuang, C., Liu, J., Xiong, H.: Digital twin-based smart production management and control framework for the complex product assembly shop-floor. Int. J. Adv. Manufact. Technol. **96**(1–4), 1149–1163 (2018). https://doi.org/10.1007/s00170-018-1617-6
10. Gushima, K., Nakajima, T.: A design space for virtuality-introduced internet of things. Future Internet. **9**, 60 (2017). https://doi.org/10.3390/fi9040060
11. Xu, J., Chao, C.-J., Fu, Z.: Research on Intelligent Design Tools to Stimulate Creative Thinking. In: Rau, P.-L. (ed.) HCII 2020. LNCS, vol. 12192, pp. 661–672. Springer, Cham (2020). https://doi.org/10.1007/978-3-030-49788-0_50
12. Xia, Q., Fu, Z.: NEXT! Toaster: Promoting Design Process with a Smart Assistant. In: Rau, P.-L. (ed.) HCII 2021. LNCS, vol. 12773, pp. 396–409. Springer, Cham (2021). https://doi.org/10.1007/978-3-030-77080-8_31
13. Sidner, C.L., Lee, C., Kidd, C.D., Lesh, N., Rich, C.: Explorations in engagement for humans and robots. Artif. Intell. **166**, 140–164 (2005). https://doi.org/10.1016/j.artint.2005.03.005
14. Jarrahi, M.H.: Artificial intelligence and the future of work: Human-AI symbiosis in organizational decision making. Bus. Horiz. **61**, 577–586 (2018). https://doi.org/10.1016/j.bushor.2018.03.007
15. Damm, L.: Moral machines: teaching robots right from wrong. Philos. Psychol. **25**, 149–153 (2012). https://doi.org/10.1080/09515089.2011.583029

16. Grigsby, S.S.: Artificial Intelligence for Advanced Human-Machine Symbiosis. In: Schmorrow, D.D., Fidopiastis, C.M. (eds.) AC 2018. LNCS (LNAI), vol. 10915, pp. 255–266. Springer, Cham (2018). https://doi.org/10.1007/978-3-319-91470-1_22

17. Zong, Y., GuangXin, W.: Anthropomorphism: The Psychological Application in the Interaction between Human and Computer. Psychol. : Tech. Appl. 4(5), 296–305 (2016). https://doi.org/10.16842/j.cnki.issn2095-5588.2016.05.007

18. Liying, X., Feng, Y., Jiahua, W., Tingting, H., Liang, Z.: Anthropomorphism: antecedents and consequences. Adv. Psychol. Issue 11, 1942–1954 (2017). https://doi.org/10.3724/SP.J.1042.2017.01942

19. Norman, D.A.: Emotional Design: Why We Love (or Hate) Everyday Things. Basic Books, New York (2004)

20. Asada, M.: Towards artificial empathy. Int. J. Soc. Robot. 7(1), 19–33 (2014). https://doi.org/10.1007/s12369-014-0253-z

21. Nass, C., Steuer, J., Tauber, E.R.: Computers are social actors. In: Conference Companion on Human Factors in Computing Systems, p. 204. Association for Computing Machinery, New York, NY, USA (1994)

22. Kuipers, B.: How can we trust a robot? Commun. ACM 61, 86–95 (2018). https://doi.org/10.1145/3173087

23. Jianhua, M.: Understanding and theory: the optimistic attitude and pessimistic attitude in the discussion of artificial intelligence. J. Dialectics Nature 40, 1–8 (2018). https://doi.org/10.15994/j.1000-0763.2018.04.001

24. Ishiguro, H.: Studies on Humanlike Robots – Humanoid, Android and Geminoid. In: Carpin, S., Noda, I., Pagello, E., Reggiani, M., von Stryk, O. (eds.) SIMPAR 2008. LNCS (LNAI), vol. 5325, pp. 2–2. Springer, Heidelberg (2008). https://doi.org/10.1007/978-3-540-89076-8_2

25. Jonathan Chapman: Emotionally Durable Design. Routledge (2012)

26. Rodrigues, S.H., Mascarenhas, S., Dias, J., Paiva, A.: A process model of empathy for virtual agents. Interact. Comput. 27, 371–391 (2015). https://doi.org/10.1093/iwc/iwu001

27. Afzal, S., et al.: The personality of AI systems in education: experiences with the watson tutor, a one-on-one virtual tutoring system. Child. Educ. 95, 44–52 (2019). https://doi.org/10.1080/00094056.2019.1565809

28. Zhou, M.X., Mark, G., Li, J., Yang, H.: Trusting virtual agents: the effect of personality. ACM Trans. Interact. Intell. Syst. 9, 1–36 (2019). https://doi.org/10.1145/3232077

29. Cooper, B., Brna, P., Martins, A.: Effective Affective in Intelligent Systems – Building on Evidence of Empathy in Teaching and Learning. In: Paiva, A. (ed.) IWAI 1999. LNCS (LNAI), vol. 1814, pp. 21–34. Springer, Heidelberg (2000). https://doi.org/10.1007/10720296_3

30. Gubrium, J.F., Holstein, J.A.: Handbook of Interview Research: Context and Method. SAGE Publications (2001)

Practical Thinking and Definition of Socially Assistive Robot Design in Smart Care for the Aged

Kuo-Liang Huang[1]([envelope]), Si-Ming Zhang[1], and Hsuan Lin[2]

[1] Department of Industrial Design, Design Academy, Sichuan Fine Arts Institute, Chongqing, China
shashi@scfai.edu.cn
[2] Department of Industrial Design, Chao Yang University of Technology, Taichung, Taiwan, People's Republic of China

Abstract. The aging of population is a common problem worldwide. At present, socially assistive robots (SAR) for the elderly are regarded as the major solution to alleviating care for the elderly, but there are still many problems. This paper tries to put forward suggestions for the SAR design thinking and definition in smart care for the aged, provide more humane service quality and improve the happiness of independent living of the elderly. In this context, this paper emphasizes the human-centered design (HCD) drive, combines the International Classification of Functioning, Disability and Health (ICF) with the nine categories of SAR, and proposes the SAR design procedure, the design ideas of emotion regeneration and enhancement in smart care for the age, as well as the definition of SAR product attributes. The research results can be used as reference and guidance in design practice, so as to provide more human service quality and improve the happiness of independent living of the elderly in the super-aged society.

Keywords: Smart Care for the Aged · Socially Assistive Robot · Human-Centered Design · Smart Product

1 Introduction

Most countries are now entering aging societies and are rapidly transitioning to super-aged societies. It is predicted that by 2050, the global aged population will more than double, which will have a significant impact on the economy and society [1]; as a result, the physical and mental health, living quality and emo-tional needs of the elderly becomes hot research areas [2].

As the elderly grow older, their physical, psychological and cognitive abilities decline year by year [3]. The needs of care for the aged will lead to an imbalance in the traditional elderly care model [4, 5], and form huge so-cial pressure of elderly care; at the same time, the rapid development of artificial intelligence (AI) and other emerging technologies accelerates the reconstruction and reform of the elderly care industry, entering a new stage of "smart care for the aged". Maintaining the independence

P.-L. P. Rau (Ed.): HCII 2023, LNCS 14023, pp. 362–375, 2023.
https://doi.org/10.1007/978-3-031-35939-2_26

of the elderly is a recognized priority for official institutions as well as the elderly themselves [6]; at present, socially assistive robots (SAR) for the elderly have been widely used [4], which are good at completing a series of complex and regular physical tasks [7], and can provide more accurate, efficient and high-quality services for the elderly by reducing labor and time costs, and make up for the challenge from the shortage of nursing labour [8].

However, the development of existing nursing robots is mostly driven by technology, which can alleviate the shortage of nursing staff to a certain extent, but still have many problems in terms of application scenarios, functions, products and service integration of SAR for the elderly in the future development of "smart elderly care"; in particular, there are many deficiencies in providing high-quality service and hu-man emotion [9, 10], which is becom-ing a matter of urgency. In this context, this paper emphasizes human-centered de-sign (HCD) to drive the further discussion and analysis of SAR for the elderly, tries to ask for innovative applications related to science and technology, health and hap-piness, and puts forward suggestions for research on the design thinking and defini-tion of SAR in smart care for the aged, to provide more humane services and im-prove the happiness of independent living of the elderly in the super-aged society.

2   Literature Review

2.1   Smart Care for the Aged and Product Acceptance Barriers

Smart elderly care tries to solve the needs of the elderly in life, medical care and health care in an intelligent, real-time, efficient and convenient way, effectively save the cost of elderly care, and maintain the quality of living and happiness of the elderly for families, communities and elderly care institutions by means of information platforms that combine AI with next-generation information and communication technologies (ICTs) such as sensors, internet of things (IoT) and cloud computing [11, 12]. Smart care for the aged integrates the concept of "health" based on the concept of "smart elderly care", and seeks a state of balance between "body, mind and spirit" [11, 13] to improve the overall well-being of the elderly and achieve the goal of healthy, caring and active elderly care.

Compared with the younger generation, the elderly tend to be less receptive to new smart products, so the challenge of innovative elderly care products lies in how to improve the acceptance of elderly care products [8]. At present, elderly care services are deeply integrated with information and intelligence, and the aging-adaption problem of intel-ligent products is worth paying attention to; although intelligent products can provide operational security, make their life more convenient, and fully care for the elderly users, for the elderly themselves, the cold integrated functions, the complex and impersonal information interfaces and other factors often discourage them from using intelligent products [14].

2.2   Features of the Elderly and Design of Intelligent Products

Due to physiological degradation and loss of agility, the elderly are psychologically and socially different from the past, and their specific features are shown in Table1.

Table 1. Kano model two-way questionnaire

Dimension	Features	Scholar
Physiology	As physical functions gradually decline, the elderly generally move slowly, and their physiological function is not well regulated, with movement disorders and poor reaction abilities. **Sensory system:** visual and auditory ability is degraded, cannot see fine things, cannot hear others speak; **Bones and muscles:** bones and muscles atrophy, decreased flexibility of body movements, cannot withstand too strenuous movements; **Thinking system:** the nerve conduction speed is greatly reduced, so the attention, memory, cognition and comprehension of the elderly decline, and it's difficult for them to learn new knowledge	Charles & Carstensen, 2010; Hui-juan et al., 2020; Hunter, White, & Thompson, 1998; Mao, Wen, & Yang, 2021; Qun & Yu-lan, 2018
Psychology	Due to the decline of physiological sensory function, the elderly also have some psychological changes. Such as (1) **Hearing loss:** cannot hear others speak, easy to misunderstand others, easy to have sensitive, jealous psychology, even many elderly people are reluctant to communicate with others; (2) **Cognitive ability, understanding decline:** need to spend more time to learn and understand in learning new things, therefore, they are easy to have anxiety and inferiority, and are stubborn in some aspects	S. Abdi et al., 2019; Charles & Carstensen, 2010; Mao et al., 2021; Neugarten, 1990
Society	After retirement, the elderly participate less in social affairs, so they feel lonely and empty spiritually, and feel disconnected from the era. In addition, because their children are busy with work, they are easy to feel lonely, lost and anxious. Therefore, they often repose their emotions in a kind of activity, to compensate for the sense of inferiority brought by the body aging	Neugarten, 1990; Charles & Carstensen, 2010; Abdi, Spann, Borilovic, de Witte, & Hawley, 2019

In addition to those described in Table 1, most elderly people have underlying medical conditions that affect their normal lives and therefore require more support in mobility, self-care and family-life related tasks [6], forming more use disorders [15], but many elderly people express a desire for independence despite physical and mental challenges [6]. The intelligent core of intelligent products is based on scenarios and data, and the design of intelligent products is an organic intelligent system that integrates inter-connected perception, data, recognition, expression, learning, calculation, automation, individuation, and self-adaptation, as well as how to collect relevant data and immediately identify, analyze, learn and respond in the contexts of people, things, time, places and things in complex and abstract scenarios [16]. Intelligent products themselves will generate or acquire corresponding data according to user scenarios and self-learn through machine learning model, and they can connect and interact with people or other products, so as to provide better services for users and create greater value.

In summary, people-oriented design should fully consider the features of the elderly, consider user features such as motivation, perception, cognition, action and behavior, and expectation of the elderly in the system composed of "human-product-environment" [17], to stimulate their interest and pleasure in using the product and make the use process simple and pleasant, thus motivating them to remain positive and independent and improving their well-being [10].

2.3 Current Development Situation of SAR for the Elderly

The development of science and technology is aimed at bringing more convenience to people, and to promote the social, mental and physical health of the elderly, improve their quality of living, and achieve the goal of emotional care, health and active aging [1] under the current innovation wave in data technology, especially in computing. SAR is one of the initiatives that provides functions related to supporting independent living, monitoring and maintaining safety, or enhancing health and mental health by providing companionship [10]. Assistive robots that accompany, support or assist the elderly in daily life, caring and social services through ICTs [18, 19], whose typical tasks include cognitive support, such as reminding drug intake, motivating work, engaging the elderly in physical exercise and cognitive exercise [20]. In the future, SARs will play a new role in health and social care to meet the higher needs of intelligent health care [4], and relevant researches have shown that SARs can be used to adapt users' emotions and improve their overall well-being [4].

As for the types of SARs, scholars Shishehgar, Kerr, and Blake [21] divided them into nine categories according to their applications and functions, as shown in Table2.

Reference from: Shishehgar, M., Kerr, D., & Blake, J. (2018). A systematic review of research into how robotic technology can help older people. *Smart Health, 7–8*, 1–18.

2.4 Life Care and Support Needs of the Elderly

After analyzing relevant literature, scholars [21] concluded that there are eight main problems in the life of the elderly: (1) social isolation; (2) dependent life; (3) physical or cognitive disorders; (4) difficulty in moving; (5) poor health monitoring; (6) lack of entertainment; (7) reminding problem; and (8) falls. In terms of elderly care, the "United Nations Principles for Older People" adopted by the United Nations General Assembly in 1991 point out five essential points of care: (1) independence; (2) participation; (3)

Table 2. Types and concepts of SARs for the elderly

Type	Concept
Companion Robots	It aims to provide companionship to help the health and mental well-being of the elderly and has social effects, such as activating communication
Telepresence Robots	It is mainly a means of providing remote connection with video media. Some of them have home navigation features and can provide guidance to remote users
Manipulator Service Robots	Robot with arm-like accessories that handles and carries objects on request, aiming to support the basic tasks of independent living
Rehabilitation Robots	It provides physical assistance without communication, including walking assistive robots and robotic wheelchairs
Health-Monitoring Robots	The main task is to monitor and analyze physical health conditions (weight, sleep patterns, hypertension, etc.) based on clinical and medical knowledge
Reminder Robots	It aims to remind the elderly of relevant tasks, such as taking medicines properly and making appointments
Domestic Robots	Robot that can help the elderly support basic tasks of independent living, such as cleaning, cooking and other housework
Entertainment Robots	Provide or guide leisure and entertainment
Fall Detection /Prevention	Monitor and prevent accidents like falls

care; (4) self-fulfillment and (5) dignity. In terms of the assessment of elderly care and support needs, WHO proposed the International Classification of Functioning, Disability and Health (ICF) in 2001, which aims to provide an integrated view of health and function at the individual and population levels [22], and emphasizes that individual health status must be considered not only from a medical perspective (such as body function and structure), but also from social factors Fig. 1.

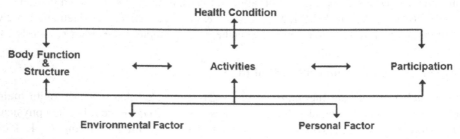

Fig. 1. International Classification of Functioning, Disability and Health (ICF) Framework

To further understand the care and support needs of the elderly, scholar S. Abdi et al. [6] used ICF to conduct scoping review and classification, reviewed a large number of relevant literature in the research, and provided a research framework and a design of practical healthcare actions, which is proved to be an important tool for determining and measuring the efficacy and effectiveness of rehabilitation services through functional analysis and intervention goals [22]. Thus, it can be applied to individual health care, remove or reduce social barriers to increase participation, and provide social supporting and promoting factors.

2.5 Design Concept and Emotional Factors of Products for the Elderly

To understand users, it is necessary to start from human needs, explore their needs and past experience, the changes in their physiological and psychological conditions, as well as economic and social conditions, thus meeting their living needs for food, clothing, housing, transportation, education, entertainment, etc., so as to provide products or services closer to users' needs [23]. However, in the actual development process, it is not easy to design products or services that truly meet the needs of the elderly group; besides age, there are more diverse physiological states and life experience differences. Many designs of elderly products only start from aging's adverse impacts on physiological and cognitive abilities, but it's far from enough. Understanding and respect are more important for elderly products [24]; it's necessary to explore and satisfy elderly people's needs for products and services with empathy [25].

In improving the emotional design of products, scholar Norman [26] proposed the famous three-level theory of emotional design, which divides the emotional dimension into visceral level, behavioral level and reflective level, as shown in Table3:

Table 3. Levels of Emotional Design

Level	Concept	Product design attribute
Visceral Level	Oriented by senses, express the meaning via features	Shape, color, material, texture
Behavioral Level	Situational interactive experience	Echo of scenarios, plots, actions
Reflective Level	Based on the first two levels of personal symbolic thinking association, understanding of the content	Let users transform to form emotional resonance

When people use a product, generally, the design elements based on the instinct level are the first to stimulate their emotions; then users will form experience from the context of the use of the product; finally, they summarize and form emotional associations and understandings with a whole process from perception and cognitive formation (emotion) to behavioral intention. In product design, narrative design means expressing product temperature and emotion through narrative, arousing users' inner feelings, memories and associations, narrowing the distance between users and products, and improving the added value of products [27].

In conclusion, it can be seen that when designing SARs for the elderly, it is necessary to fully understand the pain points and expectations of the elderly, respect their emotional needs, improve their positive emotions as much as possible through perception and interactive experience, enhance self-confidence and other deep emotional needs, improve their sense of self-identity, and support their desire to control life independently.

3   SAR Design and Analysis in Smart Care For the Aged

3.1   Functional Analysis of SAR Products for the Elderly

Based on the nine categories of SARs by the scholar S. Abdi et al. [6] and referring to the ICF framework, this paper further summarizes the key functions of SAR-related products into four categories, as shown in Tables 4 and 5.

Table 4. Key functions and concepts of SAR

Type	Function	Concept
Accompany	**Talk & emotion**	Provide conversational voice interaction, combined with facial expressions, body movements, lighting and other anthropomorphic feedback of emotions, to establish a conversational relationship;
	Entertainment	Lead and promote cognitive and physical leisure and recreation activities;
	Video conference	Act as a hub to assist the elderly to dial the video conference conveniently;
Care	**Daily care**	Assist in daily life, such as feeding, health care, etc
	Physiological test	Detect changes in heart rate, blood pressure, weight, sleep and other relevant data status, and feedback to relevant personnel through analysis information;
	Life management	Remind the elderly of their daily plans, such as medication, eating, activities, etc.;
	Security monitoring	Security monitoring of the home environment through the Internet of Things (IoT), initiate emergency measures to prevent accidents;

(continued)

Table 4. (*continued*)

Type	Function	Concept
	Rehabilitation training	Assist in physical rehabilitation training to help walk around independently;
Daily Housework	**Do housework**	Assist in housework, such as cleaning, etc
Movement	**Accessory**	Mainly used as walking AIDS to improve the adaptability of independent walking;
	Loading	Enhance spatial mobility through an automatic wheelchair

Table 5. SAR design definition

Design goal: Let the elderly live healthily, happily and independently	
VISCERAL LEVEL	
It extracts the common feature elements of the cultural background where the elderly live, and expresses concisely them in modeling, color matching, pattern, etc. by symbolic or metaphorical means, as a partial or overall perceptual image, so as to establish and stimulate the emotional connection between users and the product	
Vision	• Shape: Round shape, simple structure • Color: The overall tone is low-saturation warm colors and grays
Touch	• Material: Comfortable, easy to clean and disinfect • Texture: Texture process or composite material can be added in e range of grip, to improve the touch and comfort
BEHAVIORAL LEVEL	
In the use of SAR related functions, with the behaviors or actions associated with the narrative theme (such as symbolic or metaphorical means, interactive means, etc.), the elderly unconsciously experience the connotation expressed by the narrative theme in the use process and achieve the purpose of narrative. It starts from the inner touching point of the elderly, chooses the appropriate "thing", and creates a good situation atmosphere	
Interaction	• The role can be customized in initial personification, the personality can be shaped, and there will be self-memory and emotional expression of happiness, anger, sorrow and joy; based on the mental model of the elderly, it guides the operation and provides simple and clear positive feedback to reduce the learning cost and improve the operation efficiency; • The conversational voice is the main interface, and there are different local dialects, accents to choose from, as well as facial expression, tone, speech mode, behavior and other changes; • In the corresponding situational elements, by combining plots and memory features, positive emotions are generated by the elderly to actively express themselves;

(*continued*)

Table 5. (*continued*)

Design goal: Let the elderly live healthily, happily and independently
VISCERAL LEVEL
REFLECTIVE LEVEL
Through the interweaving of Visceral Level and Behavioral Level, it combines the growth background and life experience of the elderly, inspires associations and symbols, and activates the positive understanding of the elderly, so as to resonate and sublimate themselves

Activation	• Self-image: real ego, ideal ego…
	• Personal satisfaction: material, social, individual, happiness…
	• Heuristic implication: sensory meaning, semantic memory, event memory…

3.2 Analysis of Service Scenarios

A scenario is a story about people and their behaviors, which consists of the background, role, role goal, purpose, and plot [28]. Intelligent products are intellectual bodies that integrate perception, cognition and behavioral abilities, and the perception of scenario, evolution and context is a key [29]. In addition, in the decomposition of human-object-environment relationship, scholars Kalimuthu, Perumal, Yaakob, Marlisah, and Babangida [30] believed that there are six types of data for analysis: behavior, gesture, event, compound action, person-to-person interaction, and person-to-object interaction; a typical system framework of Human Activity Recognition under data-driven design (as shown in Fig. 2) consists of three components: (1) original data collection for preprocessing; (2) feature extraction and (3) activity classification.

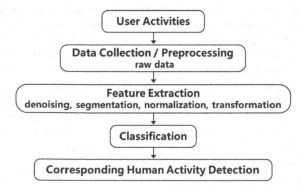

Fig. 2. Program of user scenario data identification

Cutting-edge technologies such as AI have been deeply used in different scenarios of our daily lives, connecting thousands of things and things, people and IoT by devices containing various sensors [31]. Due to the high intelligence of intelligent products and services themselves, a complex relationship of "human-object-situation-data" is formed, in which user-related behavioral data is generated from time to time between people and objects in different scenarios, creating a new design paradigm -"scenario-data" driven design [32].

To enable SAR products to accurately interpret the situation of the elderly, so as to support the provision of appropriate feedback behavior to the user at the appropriate time and in the appropriate way, it is necessary to analyze the user scenario first, mine and extract the demand and expectation, and analyze the scenarios before and after, to predict the user's next demand/behavior. In the analysis of situational empathy, it is necessary to grasp five key points: task, feeling, influence, pain point and goal.

4 Design Thinking and Definition of SARs for the Elderly

4.1 SAR Design Thinking in Smart Care for the Aged

(1) Design program thinking

Combined with the above analysis, the design program proposed in this paper for the SAR product design and development is shown in Fig. 3.

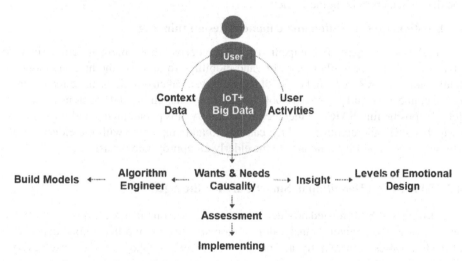

Fig. 3. Design program thinking

First of all, in the initial exploration phase of the design project, according to the design issues and target users, the designer obtains the user big data (including business data and behavioral data) accumulated on the business end related to the application scenario for traceability analysis to understand the user habits and preferences; then, the data in different scenarios (context, role, role goal, goal, plot) and user activities (behavior, gesture, event, compound action, person-to-person interaction and person-to-thing interaction) is interpreted with empathy, which is revealed through visualization skills, a team is organized to interpret the mental model of users and obtain the relationship between pain points, needs and expectations. Then, the design opportunities are explored based on the previous stage, and the algorithm/model engineer transforms the demands, analyzes the original data to form insights, and then connects the demands with the data features; then, in emotional design, the expected sensory and situational interactive experience of the elderly are analyzed based on the three levels of emotional design, and different design attributes and characteristics are found out through qualitative and quantitative analysis according to the corresponding design elements of intelligent products/services, to define the design in an objective way, guide designers to carry out business logic and product logic conception to meet the user experience; at the same time, the algorithm/model engineer uses relevant scenario big data for deep learning to build mathematical models, so that the internal core of intelligent products/services can solve relevant problems in real life.

In the evaluation phase, apart from the designer who verifies the conceptual design of the product/service through the prototype, the algorithm/model engineer also verifies the generalization, accuracy, stability and other capabilities of the model. In the implementation phase, when SARs are commercialized and users begin to use the product/service, the product and service can achieve personalized and adaptive goals through continuous learning of user data through the kernel; at the same time, the algorithm/model engineer can adjust the model parameters based on new insights into the relationships between the data when optimizing the model.

(2) Emotional regeneration and enhanced design thinking

SAR is an inseparable companion for the elderly, whose main functions include companionship, care, daily housework and mobility. To improve the human emotional temperature of SAR, reduce the fear of technology, awaken emotions and enhance emotional connection, and produce a stable human-computer emotional relationship. Therefore, by positioning SAR as a member of the family, it is personalized and possesses its own characters and emotions, which can talk to and empathize with the elderly in life circumstances, and give guidance to the elderly on appropriate occasions.

4.2   SAR Design Definition in Smart Care for the Aged

The attributes of SAR related products are defined based on the three levels of emotional design, so as to effectively transfer information, create and mobilize a good experience of the five senses of the elderly, and promote the elderly to take care of themselves with dignity and live independently in the specific design of subsequent SAR products.

5   Discussion and Conclusions

In this paper, we describe an innovative solution involving a practice-oriented SAR, which aims to let the elderly take care of themselves with dignity and live independently. The practice thinking follows the user-driven method, which is driven by intelligent product design scenario + data, and further defines the design based on the three levels of emotional design, trying to meet the elderly's needs for companionship from perception, behavior to behavior intention, assist in daily care and housework, and improve the elderly users' experience and quality of life. The ultimate purpose of the design is to strengthen the close connection between the elderly and the society, and actively maintain the relationship between the elderly and others. Therefore, nursing robots can have positive personal features, meet the demands of the elderly for companionship from the physical level through emotional design, express social care, guide the elderly to actively accept new things, so that self-identity and social identity complement each other.

In this paper, based on the concept of people-oriented design, the design process and emotional regeneration and enhanced design thinking of SARs for the elderly are described, and the design definition is further made. In terms of research implications, the design thinking and definition of SAR can be used as reference and guidance in the design and development of the SAR in response to the smart care for the aged and the SAR design practice. Finally, we believe that once a product is endowed with some fine emotions, it will shorten the emotional distance between people and the product, which contains not only human physiological and psychological factors, but also social and cultural factors.

Acknowledgments. Supported by the Science and Technology Research Program of Chongqing Mu-nicipal Education Commission (Grant No. KJZD-M202201001), Chongqing University Innovation Research Group "Research on the design of ageing in the scene of smart recreation" and Major Project Cultivation Project for Ph.D. of Sichuan Academy of Fine Arts (Grant No. 22BSQD010).

References

1. Cabreiro, V.: A short note on information and communication technology: aging society. Ann. Aging **1**(1), 1–2 (2022)
2. Wang, J.-S., Liu X.-J., Hou Y.-T., et al.: Mental health status and its influencing factors of the elderly. Chinese J. Disease Contr. Prevent. 308–12 (2019)
3. Menghi, R., Gullà, F., Germani, M.: Assessment of a Smart Kitchen to Help People with Alzheimer's Disease. In: Mokhtari, M., Abdulrazak, B., Aloulou, H. (eds.) ICOST 2018. LNCS, vol. 10898, pp. 304–309. Springer, Cham (2018). https://doi.org/10.1007/978-3-319-94523-1_30
4. Abdi, J., Al-Hindawi, A., Ng, T., et al.: Scoping review on the use of socially assistive robot technology in elderly care. BMJ Open **8**(2), e018815 (2018)
5. Gallagher, A., Nåden, D, Karterud, D.: Robots in elder care:Some ethical questions. Nurs. Ethics **23**(4): 369–71 (2016)
6. Abdi, S., Spann, A., Borilovic, J., et al.: Understanding the care and support needs of older people: a scoping review and categorisation using the WHO international classification of functioning, disability and health framework (ICF). BMC Geriatr. **19**(1), 195 (2019)
7. Hegel, F., Muhl, C., Wrede, B., et al.: Understanding social robots. In: proceedings of the 2009 Second International Conferences on Advances in Computer-Human Interactions, F, (2009). IEEE
8. Hung, J.: Smart elderly care services in china: challenges, progress, and policy development. Sustainability **15**(1), 178 (2023)

9. Huang, K.-L., Jiang, J., Cheng, Y.-Y.: On Improving the Acceptance of Intelligent Companion Robots Among Chinese Empty-Nesters with the Application of Emotional Design. In: Kurosu, M., Yamamoto, S., Mori, H., Schmorrow, D.D., Fidopiastis, C.M., Streitz, N.A., Konomi, S. (eds.) HCI International 2022 - Late Breaking Papers. Multimodality in Advanced Interaction Environments: 24th International Conference on Human-Computer Interaction, HCII 2022, Virtual Event, June 26 – July 1, 2022, Proceedings, pp. 257–270. Springer Nature Switzerland, Cham (2022). https://doi.org/10.1007/978-3-031-17618-0_19

10. Lee, S., Naguib, A.M.: Toward a sociable and dependable elderly care robot: design, implementation and user study. J. Intell. Robot. Syst. **98**, 5–17 (2018)

11. Juhua, Y.: Smart care for the aged: concepts, challenges and countermeasures. Social Sci. J. **2021**(5), 102–111 (2021)

12. Geng, Z., Meng, Z.: Research on evaluation index system of smart elderly care. J. Northeastern Univ. (Social Science Edition) **24**(1), 88 (2022)

13. Fei, W.: Case study of "Integration of young and old" design from the perspective of smart care for the aged. Art Design **349**(05), 52–63 (2022)

14. Hui-Juan, G., Ming-Zhu, D., Hai-Bo, W.: Multi-channel interactive mapping path of intelligent products for elderly users. Packag. Eng. **41**(24), 85–90 (2020)

15. COMMODARI E, GUARNERA M. Attention and aging [J]. Aging clinical and experimental research, 2008, 20(578–84

16. Sun, X., Zhang, Y., Zhou, W., et al.: Review on artificial intelligence products and service system. Packag. Eng. **41**(10), 49–61 (2020)

17. Dianat, I., Adeli, P., Jafarabadi, M.A., et al.: User-centred web design, usability and user satisfaction: the case of online banking websites in Iran. Appl. Ergonom. **81**, 102892 (2019)

18. Reiser, U., Jacobs, T., Arbeiter, G., Parlitz, C., Dautenhahn, K.: Care-O-bot® 3 – Vision of a Robot Butler. In: Trappl, R. (ed.) Your virtual butler, pp. 97–116. Springer Berlin Heidelberg, Berlin, Heidelberg (2013). https://doi.org/10.1007/978-3-642-37346-6_9

19. Tokunaga, S., Horiuchi, H., Tamamizu, K., et al.: Deploying service integration agent for personalized smart elderly care. In: Proceedings of the 2016 IEEE/ACIS 15th International Conference on Computer and Information Science (ICIS), F 26–29 June 2016, 2016

20. Carros, F., Meurer, J., Löffler, D,, et al.: Exploring human-robot interaction with the elderly: results from a ten-week case study in a care home. In: proceedings of the Proceedings of the 2020 CHI Conference on Human Factors in Computing Systems, F, 2020

21. Shishehgar, M., Kerr, D., Blake, J.: A systematic review of research into how robotic technology can help older people. Smart Health **7–8**, 1–18 (2018)

22. Üstün, T.B., Chatterji, S., Bickenbach, J., et al.: The international classification of functioning, disability and health: a new tool for understanding disability and health. Disabil. Rehabil. **25**(11–12), 565–571 (2003)

23. Lo, H.-C.: Introducing Intergenerational Co-creation into Welfare Design Practice Course [J]. J. Design **26**(2), 91–108 (2021).

24. Nunes, F., Silva, P.A., Abrantes, F.: Human-computer interaction and the older adult: an example using user research and personas. In: Proceedings of the 3rd international conference on PErvasive technologies related to assistive environments, F (2010)

25. Wang, D., Chen, S.-Y., Tang, H.-H.: Creating personas through integrating qualitative data: a case study on consumption trend research for the elderly. J. Design **26**(3), 39–60 (2021)

26. Norman, D.: The Design of Everyday Things: Revised and Expanded Edition. Basic Books (2013)

27. Tian-Yu, G., Xue-Ting, R., Mu, J.: Narrative design method in interesting products. Packag. Eng. **40**(12), 168–174 (2019)

28. Go, K., Carroll, J.M.: The blind men and the elephant: views of scenario-based system design. Interactions **11**(6), 44–53 (2004)

29. Liu, A., Teo, I., Chen, D., et al.: Biologically inspired design of context-aware smart products. Engineering **5**(4), 637–645 (2019)
30. Kalimuthu, S., Perumal, T., Yaakob, R., et al.: Human activity recognition based on smart home environment and their applications, challenges. In: Proceedings of the 2021 International Conference on Advance Computing and Innovative Technologies in Engineering (ICACITE), F, IEEE (2021)
31. Ng, I.C., Wakenshaw, S.Y.: The Internet-of-things: review and research directions. Int. J. Res. Mark. **34**(1), 3–21 (2017)
32. Jaramillo, G.S., Mennie, L.J.: Aural textiles. hybrid practices for data-driven design. Design J. **22**(sup1), 1163–75 (2019)

Effects of Robot's Language and Attribute Framing on People's Risky Behavior

Hanjing Huang[1,2] and Pei-Luen Patrick Rau[2(✉)]

[1] School of Economics and Management, Fuzhou University, Fuzhou, People's Republic of China
[2] Department of Industrial Engineering, Tsinghua University, Beijing, People's Republic of China
rpl@mail.tsinghua.edu.cn

Abstract. With the globalization, it is essential to investigate the robot's language on human-robot interaction. The robot's information framing may also affect people's behavior. This study investigated the effects of the robot's language (native vs. foreign) and information frame (positive vs. negative) on people's risky behavior in Balloon Analog Risk Task. The results indicated that participants' behavior was less risky when the robot used the negative frame to represent the information. Furthermore, the effect of the robot's information frame on participants' risky behavior was less obvious when the robot used a foreign language. The use of a foreign language would reduce the framing effects in human-robot interaction. The effects of the robot's language and information frame should not be neglected. The obtained findings can serve as a basis for the design of robots' language and information presentation.

Keywords: Human-robot interaction · Foreign language · Framing effect · Risky behavior

1 Introduction

With the rapid development of robotics, the companies also try to expand their customer base across foreign countries. According to the dataset, more than 7000 languages are spoken in the world in 2022 (Eberhard, Gary, & Charles, 2022). In addition, approximately half of the world's population speak at least two languages. People can use the native language or a foreign language to communicate with others or make decisions. Given the immense number of languages, an interesting question is how robots' languages may affect human-robot interaction. Previous research has proposed the foreign language effect (Keysar, Hayakawa, & An, 2012). People's decisions should be language independent if they understand the option. However, the language would affect people's risky decisions. People tend to be less risk-averse when using a foreign language. The Computers Are Social Actors (CASA) paradigm(Nass, Steuer, & Tauber, 1994) and the Media Equation(Reeves & Nass, 1996) proposed that individuals will interact with computers, social robots in similar manners as with others. For example, Rau et al. found that

P.-L. P. Rau (Ed.): HCII 2023, LNCS 14023, pp. 376–385, 2023.
https://doi.org/10.1007/978-3-031-35939-2_27

the robot's communication style would affect the human-robot interaction(Rau, Li, & Li, 2009). The robot's English accents also affect people's preference (Tamagawa, Watson, Kuo, MacDonald, & Broadbent, 2011). Therefore, it is essential to investigate whether the robot use people' native language or foreign language would affect the interaction.

Moreover, when the robot provides information to people, a critical element is the information frame. Previous research pointed out that people's decisions would be affected by the frame of the information even though the options have equal expected value(Tversky & Kahneman, 1981). There are different types of framing effects (Levin, Schneider, & Gaeth, 1998). The attribute framing refers to the phenomena that people judge an item more positively when the item is described using a positive attribute. For example, people judge the 80% bean beef more positively than the 20% fat beef. It is expected that the frame of the robot's information also affects people's behavior.

In our daily life, many activities involve some degree of risk, from taking medicine to investing in the stock market. The robot can act as a media to provide information to people. The current study, therefore, investigated the robot's language and information frame on people's risky behavior.

2 Background and Research Questions

2.1 Foreign Language Effect

Use of a foreign language affects people's perceptions and choices in risky situations (Costa, Foucart, Arnon, Aparici, & Apesteguia, 2014; Keysar et al., 2012).Previous research found that people perceived lower level of risk when using a foreign language (Hadjichristidis, Geipel, & Savadori, 2015). Researchers found that those using a foreign language were more likely to accept bets with positive expected value than those using the native language (Costa et al., 2014; Keysar et al., 2012). They also found the use of language would affect people's choices in the Asian Disease problem. When people use the native language to make decisions, people tend to be risk seeking when the option framed in terms of losses (e.g., 400 out of 600 people will die), but risk averse when it is framed in terms of gains (e.g., 200 out of 600 people will be saved). However, this asymmetry is reduced when people use a foreign language to make decisions. Overall, the use of a foreign language would affect people's choices. It is also essential to investigate whether the robot using a foreign language would affect people's risky behavior. The research question is as followings:

RQ1. What is the effect of the robot's language on people's risky behavior?

2.2 Attribute Framing

Attribute framing has the requirement that the positive and negative frames are objectively equivalent (Levin et al., 1998). Positive versus negative attribute framing can be achieved through different ways. For example, manipulating the presentation of desirable versus undesirable attributes (hamburger meat is 80% lean vs 20% fat) or manipulating the presence versus absence of a desirable attribute (a treatment is successful 80% of the time vs not successful 20% of the time). Attribute frames consist of three key elements:

the target entity, the attribute label valence (either positive or negative), and the measure of the attribute. The hamburger meat is the target entity, lean or fat is the attribute label valence, and 80% or 20% is the measure of the attribute. The attribute framing effect is defined by the difference between the decisions or judgments obtained from the numerically equivalent positive and negative attributes. Individuals respond more favorably to the positive than to the negative frame. The framing effects have been found in various domains such as medical treatments (Krishnamurthy, Carter, & Blair, 2001; Levin, Schnittjer, & Thee, 1988), purchasing products(Levin et al., 1988), punishment decisions (Dunegan, 1996), environmental conservation(Jacobson et al., 2019).

Researchers have pointed that the attribute framing effects might result from the associations evoked by the attribute label (Krishnamurthy et al., 2001; Levin et al., 1998; Payne, Sagara, Shu, Appelt, & Johnson, 2013). The positive attribute label evokes positive associations in memory, whereas the negative attribute label evokes negative associations in memory. For example, the 80% bean beef invokes associations with the health, whereas the 20% fat beef invokes associations with the unhealth. The information processing is consistent with the priming literature (Putrevu, 2010). When a preceding prime is positive, the attribute would be more favorable. This study aimed to investigate the effects of frame of the information provided by the robot on users' risky behavior. This reasoning leads to the next research question:

RQ2. What is the effect of the robot' information frame on people's risky behavior?

Moreover, previous research has found that the use of the foreign language would diminish the framing effects in Asian disease problem (Costa et al., 2014; Keysar et al., 2012). This study also investigated the interaction effect of the language and the frame on people's risky behavior. The research question is as followings:

RQ3. What is the interaction effect of the robot's language and frame on people's risky behavior?

3 Methods

3.1 Participants

Forty-eight graduate and undergraduate students (men: 24, women: 24) participated in the experiment. The mean age of participants was 23.6 years. All participants were Chinese. All participants passed College English Test Band Six (CET-6). CET-6 is one of the most influential foreign language tests in China. Paired t-tests indicated that the mean age at which participants acquired Chinese (M = 2.6, SD = 2.1) was significantly lower than the mean age at which they acquired English (M = 8.7, SD = 2.4, p < .001). Participants were asked to self-rate their Chinese and English proficiencies in terms of listening, speaking, reading and writing on a 7-point scale from 1 (very poor) to 7 (very good). We used the average score across all four dimensions as a measure of an individual's language skills. Participants rated their Chinese skills at an average score of 6.25 (SD = .75) and English skills at an average of 4.60 (SD = .81). Paired t-tests indicated participants' Chinese skills were significantly higher than their English skills (p < .001). Participants' details are included in Table 1. Participants completed the Negative Attitude Towards Scale towards robots (NARS) (Nomura, Suzuki, Kanda, & Kato, 2006). Participants were randomly assigned to different languages and different frames to complete the tasks. All participants were righthanded. None of them had with any history of psychiatric or neurological disorders. The study was approved by the Ethics Committee of the department. All participants were given a comprehensive explanation of the experimental procedures by an experimenter, and they provided written informed consents for participation.

Table 1. Participants' language proficiency

	Chinese mean (standard deviation)	English mean (standard deviation)
Age of language acquisition	2.6 years (2.1years)	8.7 years (2.4 years)
Self-rating scores for language ability (out of 7)		
Listening	6.44(0.74)	4.56(1.05)
Speaking	6.21(0.90)	3.96(0.94)
Reading	6.38(0.76)	5.31(0.90)
Writing	5.94(1.02)	4.58(0.96)

3.2 Tasks

This study used the Balloon Analog Risk Task (BART) to measure risky behavior (Lejuez et al., 2002). The BART is a computerized, laboratory-based measure that includes actual risky behavior similar to real-word situations where riskiness is rewarded up until a point at which further riskiness results in worse outcomes. The experimental program interface is designed using psychopy3 (Peirce, 2007). The participant was presented with a realistic picture of a balloon on the computer monitor. The NAO robot manufactured by Aldebaran was used in the experiment (Gouaillier et al., 2009). This study used SoftBank Robotics Software and python to program the robot's voice. Nao would use Chinese or English to communicate with the participants. The voice was translated from English to Chinese, and then translated them from Chinese to English for comparison to ensure that the meanings in both Chinese and English are the same (Brislin, 1970). Table 2 represents examples of the information provided by the robot.

Table 2. Example of the robot's information

Language	Frame	Example
English	Positive	The probability of the balloon keeping good is sixty-one percent. What is your choice?
English	Negative	The probability of the balloon explosion is thirty-nine percent. What is your choice?

The specific content of the experimental task is as follows: A balloon was presented on the screen, the robot told the participant the probability that the balloon would explode or remain good, the participant decided whether to inflate it. The participants could press the "space key" to inflate the balloon, each time the participant pressed the "space key", the volume of the balloon would increase a little, and the corresponding amount of the balloon would increase by 10 yuan. Participants could also press the "enter key" to choose not to continue inflating, to save the amount corresponding to the current balloon, and put it into their income account. If the balloon exploded during the inflation process, the reward obtained by the participant on the balloon will be emptied. Each balloon can be inflated up to 10 times, that is, the participant could press the "space key" up to 10 times, and the corresponding maximum amount of each balloon is 100 yuan. The larger the volume of the balloon, the more likely it was to explode. In the formal sessions, there were a total of 30 balloons, and the participant's earnings in the BART task were proportionally converted into the participant's experimental remuneration. In the practice task, there were a total of 10 balloons, the robot would not tell the participant the probability of the balloon exploding or maintaining good, only prompting the participant to make the choice, the participant's income in the practice task would also be converted into the experimental remuneration in the same proportion. Participants completed the practice task first, and then completed the formal task.

3.3 Procedures

The experiment was performed in a demarcated 3 m × 3 m area in a laboratory. Participants completed the BART task on a laptop computer (13.3 inches, with a resolution of 1024 × 768). The NAO robot accompanied the participant and gave information about the balloon explosion and instructions. The experimental environment is shown in see Fig. 1. Participants were individually tested, each experiment lasting for approximately forty minutes per participant.

Fig. 1. Experimental environment.

After the participant came to the laboratory, the participant first read and signed the informed consent form. Then, the participant was asked to fill in the pre-experiment questionnaire, which included personal information, language background information, and a scale of negative attitudes towards robots. Participants were told that their reward for participating in the experiment would be positively related to their task performance in the experiment. The higher task performance of the participant, the higher the reward for the experiment. The average reward was sixty yuan. After the experimenter confirmed that the participant understood the experimental tasks and procedures the participant began to finish the task. Participants were randomly assigned to interact with the robot speaking Chinese or English, using the positive frame or negative frame. When the participant was assigned to interact with the robot speaking English, the introduction and questionnaire in the experiment were also in English. After the participant finished the practice session and formal session, the participant would receive the reward of the experiment according to the task performance.

3.4 Measures

Attitudes Towards Robots. This study used the Negative Attitudes Toward Robots Scale (NARS) to measure participants' attitudes towards robots before the experiment (Nomura et al., 2006). The scale consists of three subscales: attitudes toward interaction with robots, toward the social influence of robots, and toward emotional interactions with robots. The NARS reflects the opinions that people ordinarily have toward robots The scale is a common attitude assessment test that investigates prior attitudes toward robots that may affect participants' evaluations of and interaction with them(Gaudiello, Zibetti, Lefort, Chetouani, & Ivaldi, 2016). This study used the scale to check whether participants in different groups had different attitude towards robots.

Risky Behavior. This study used two primary measures to assess the risk-taking behavior: the adjusted number of pumps and the total number of explosions suggested by previous research (Lejuez et al., 2002). The adjusted number of pumps is calculated as the average number of pumps on the balloons that did not explode. The using the adjusted number of pumps describes a relatively unbiased risk attitude(Seaman, Stillman, Howard, & Howard Jr, 2015). The total number of explosions represents the frequency of making a decision that exceeded the optimal risk level and which was followed by immediate punishment(Hunt, Hopko, Bare, Lejuez, & Robinson, 2005).

4 Results

Manipulation checks. The results from ANOVA showed that there was no significant difference in the negative attitudes towards robots in different language groups of participants (ps > .05).

   Risky behavior. The summary of participants' risky behavior in BART task is listed in Table 3. First, A 2 (language: Chinese or English) × 2 (frame: positive or negative) repeated measures ANOVA revealed that a significant effect of the frame on the adjusted number of pumps (F = 5.87, p = 0.020) (see Table 4). When the robot used the positive frame, the average adjusted number of pumps of participants (M = 5.52, SD = 0.48) was significantly higher than that of participants when the robot used the negative frame

(M = 5.07, SD = 0.81). The results showed that the language and the interaction of the language and the frame did not have significant effects on the adjusted number of pumps (ps > 0.05). Further analysis showed that when the robot used Chinese, the average adjusted number of pumps of participants when robot used the positive frame (M = 5.58, SD = 0.56) was significantly higher than that of participants when the robot used the negative frame (M = 4.82, SD = 0.75, p = 0.011). However, when the robot used English, there was no significant difference between the average adjusted number of pumps of participants when robot used the positive frame (M = 5.46, SD = 0.40) and that of participants when the robot used the negative frame (M = 5.31, SD = 0.82, p = 0.556).

Table 3. Summary of risky behavior in BART task

Language	Frame	Mean of adjusted number of pumps (standard deviation)	Mean of total number of explosions (standard deviation)
Chinese	Positive	5.58 (0.56)	10.67 (5.00)
Chinese	Negative	4.82 (0.75)	5.67 (3.17)
English	Positive	5.46 (0.40)	8.67 (3.09)
English	Negative	5.31 (0.82)	8.58 (3.75)

Table 4. Analysis of effects of the language and the frame on risk behavior in BART task

Dependent variables	Independent variables	F	p
Adjusted number of pumps	Language	0.95	0.334
	Frame	5.87	0.020*
	Language × Frame	2.52	0.120
Total number of explosions	Language	0.17	0.680
	Frame	5.29	0.026*
	Language × Frame	4.95	0.031*

Note. * $p < 0.05$; ** $p < 0.01$; *** $p < 0.001$

Second, a 2 (language: Chinese or English) × 2 (frame: positive or negative) repeated measures ANOVA revealed that a significant effect of the frame on the total number of explosions (F = 5.29, p = 0.026) (see Table 4). When the robot used the positive frame, the total number of explosions (M = 9.67, SD = 4.19) was significantly larger than that of participants when the robot used the negative frame (M = 7.13, SD = 3.71). The results showed that the language did not have a significant effect on the adjusted number of pumps (p = 0.680). The interaction of the language and the frame had a significant effect on the total number of explosions (p = 0.031). Further analysis showed that when the robot used Chinese, the total number of explosions when the robot used the positive frame (M = 10.67, SD = 5.00) was significantly larger than the total number of explosions when the robot used the negative frame (M = 5.67, SD = 3.17, p = 0.009). However, when the robot used English, there was no significant difference between the total number of explosions when the robot used the positive frame (M = 8.67, SD = 3.05) and the total number of explosions when the robot used the negative frame (M = 8.58, SD = 3.75, p = 0.953).

5 Discussions

The results indicated that the robot's language and frame would affect participants' risky behavior in BART task. When the robot used the negative frame to describe the probability of the balloon explosion, participants' average adjusted number of pumps adjusted and total number of balloon explosions were significantly lower, corresponding to less risky behavior. This might result from the negative frame emphasizes the bad outcomes of the inflation. Individuals have the tendency to seek advantages and avoid disadvantages. For example, when the robot told the participant that the probability of explosion was 30%, the participant might avoid the bad outcomes, and choose not to inflate the balloon.

Furthermore, this study found that the influence of the frame mainly existed in the situation where the robot spoke Chinese. When the robot spoke Chinese, participants' risky behavior was more likely to be affected by the frame. This result was consistent with previous research pointing out that the use of foreign language could diminish the framing effect on people's decisions in Asian disease problems and Financial crisis problems (Costa et al., 2014). The farming effect describes the phenomenon that people tend to avoid risk when choices are framed in terms of gain but seek risk when choices are framed in terms of loss (Kahneman, 2011; Tversky & Kahneman, 1981). Such asymmetry would diminish when the problems were presented in a foreign language. Therefore, the foreign language not only diminished the framing effect in Asian disease problem and Financial disease problem, it also diminished the effect of frame describing the outcome on people's risky behavior in human-robot interaction. This study only focused on the attribute framing, even though previous research distinguish frames into three types: risky choice, attribute, and goal framing (Levin et al., 1998). Therefore, further research could choose to investigate the different types of robot's information frames to provide a better understanding of the different framing effects in human-robot interaction.

6 Conclusions

This study investigated the effects of the robot's language and frame on users' risky behavior. The results indicated that the frame of information provided by the robot would affect users' risky behavior. The positive frame emphasizes the positive outcomes, whereas the negative frame emphasizes the negative outcomes. When the robot used negative frame to provide information, participants' choices were less risky. Moreover, the effects of the frame on participants' behavior were less obvious when the robot use English (ie. The foreign language) to provide information. The results suggested that the robot's information frame to provide the information would affect users' risky behavior, and the use of the foreign language would diminish the effect of the robot's information frame. With the large population of bilingualism and globalization, the robot should use appropriate frame and language to provide information to users according to the goal of the tasks. Future research would do well to examine the influence of the robot's information frame and language in different tasks, such as entertainment tasks or examine the influence in users using different languages.

Declaration of Conflicting Interests. The author(s) declared no potential conflicts of interest with respect to the research, authorship, and/or publication of this article.

Funding. This research was supported by the National Natural Science Foundation of China (No. 71942005) and the National Science Foundation of Fujian Province of China (No.2022J05018).

References

Brislin, R.W.: Back-translation for cross-cultural research. J. Cross Cult. Psychol. **1**, 185–216 (1970)

Costa, A., Foucart, A., Arnon, I., Aparici, M., Apesteguia, J.: "Piensa" twice: on the foreign language effect in decision making. Cognition **130**(2), 236–254 (2014)

Dunegan, K.J.: Fines, frames, and images: examining formulation effects on punishment decisions. Organ. Behav. Hum. Decis. Process. **68**(1), 58–67 (1996)

Eberhard, D.M., Gary, F.S., Charles, D. F.: Ethnologue: Languages of the World. Retrieved from http://www.ethnologue.com (2022)

Gaudiello, I., Zibetti, E., Lefort, S., Chetouani, M., Ivaldi, S.: Trust as indicator of robot functional and social acceptance. An experimental study on user conformation to iCub answers. Comput. Human Behav. **61**, 633–655 (2016)

Gouaillier, D., et al.: Mechatronic design of NAO humanoid. In: Paper presented at the 2009 IEEE International Conference on Robotics and Automation (2009, 12–17 May 2009)

Hadjichristidis, C., Geipel, J., Savadori, L.: The effect of foreign language in judgments of risk and benefit: the role of affect. J. Exp. Psychol. Appl. **21**(2), 117–129 (2015)

Hunt, M.K., Hopko, D.R., Bare, R., Lejuez, C.W., Robinson, E.V.: Construct validity of the Balloon Analog Risk Task (BART): associations with psychopathy and impulsivity. Assessment **12**(4), 416–428 (2005)

Jacobson, S.K., Morales, N.A., Chen, B., Soodeen, R., Moulton, M.P., Jain, E.: Love or Loss: Effective message framing to promote environmental conservation. Appl. Environ. Educ. Commun. **18**(3), 252–265 (2019)

Kahneman, D.: Thinking, fast and slow. New York, NY, US: Farrar, Straus and Giroux (2011)

Keysar, B., Hayakawa, S.L., An, S.G.: The foreign-language effect: thinking in a foreign tongue reduces decision biases. Psychol. Sci. **23**(6), 661–668 (2012)

Krishnamurthy, P., Carter, P., Blair, E.: Attribute framing and goal framing effects in health decisions. Organ. Behav. Hum. Decis. Process. **85**(2), 382–399 (2001)

Lejuez, C.W., et al.: Evaluation of a behavioral measure of risk taking: the Balloon Analogue Risk Task (BART). J. Experiment. Psychol.: Appl. **8**(2), 75–84 (2002)

Levin, I.P., Schneider, S.L., Gaeth, G.J.: All frames are not created equal: a typology and critical analysis of framing effects. Organ. Behav. Hum. Decis. Process. **76**(2), 149–188 (1998)

Levin, I.P., Schnittjer, S.K., Thee, S.L.: Information framing effects in social and personal decisions. J. Exp. Soc. Psychol. **24**, 520–529 (1988)

Nass, C., Steuer, J., Tauber, E.R.: Computers are social actors. In: Paper presented at the International Conference on Human Factors in Computing Systems (1994)

Nomura, T., Suzuki, T., Kanda, T., Kato, K.: Measurement of negative attitudes toward robots. Int. Stud.: Social Behav. Commun. Biol. Artif. Syst. **7**, 437–454 (2006)

Payne, J.W., Sagara, N., Shu, S.B., Appelt, K.C., Johnson, E.J.: Life expectancy as a constructed belief: evidence of a live-to or die-by framing effect. J. Risk Uncertain. **46**(1), 27–50 (2013). https://doi.org/10.1007/s11166-012-9158-0

Peirce, J.W.: PsychoPy—Psychophysics software in Python. J. Neurosci. Methods **162**(1), 8–13 (2007)

Putrevu, S.: An examination of consumer responses toward attribute- and goal-framed messages. J. Advert. **39**(3), 5–24 (2010)

Rau, P.L.P., Li, Y., Li, D.: Effects of communication style and culture on ability to accept recommendations from robots. Comput. Hum. Behav. **25**(2), 587–595 (2009)

Reeves, B., Nass, C.: The media equation: how people treat computers, television, and new media like real people and places: Cambridge University Press (1996)

Seaman, K.L., Stillman, C.M., Howard, D.V., Howard Jr, J.H.: Risky decision-making is associated with residential choice in healthy older adults. Front. Psychol. **6** (2015)

Tamagawa, R., Watson, C.I., Kuo, I.H., MacDonald, B.A., Broadbent, E.: The effects of synthesized voice accents on user perceptions of robots. Int. J. Soc. Robot. **3**(3), 253–262 (2011)

Tversky, A., Kahneman, D.: The framing of decisions and the psychology of choice. Science **211**(4481), 453–458 (1981)

Key Factors Influencing the Degree of Acceptance of an Intelligent Customer Service System - A Literature Review

Yunhuan Jia[1] and Zhe Chen[1,2(✉)]

[1] School of Economics and Management, Beihang University, Beijing 100191, People's Republic of China
zhechen@buaa.edu.cn
[2] Beijing Key Laboratory of Emergency Support Simulation Technologies for City Operations, Beihang University, Beijing 100191, People's Republic of China

Abstract. In the context of artificial intelligence offensive markets, intelligent customer service robots have joined the traditional customer service system. Although intelligent customer service is widely used in e-commerce, finance, education and the phenomenon of rejecting intelligent customer service services often turned directly to manual. This article searches and investigates the current intelligent customer service market through a large number of literature. The purpose is to explore the key factors that affect the success of intelligent customer service, and propose the intelligent customer service system that can be more accepted by the public. The work done in the article is to use the existing Systematic Satisfaction Evaluation Model and TAM to explore the key factors affecting the acceptance of the intelligent customer service system. From the analysis of the three elements of tasks, intelligent customer service robots, and users five indicators of Flexibility, Integration, Accessibility, and Timelits' starting points to change the system's perception and usefulness and perception to improve the user experience, and the user is willing to accept and trust intelligent customer service. Finally, make predictions on the customer service industry in the future: intelligent customer service and manual customer service coexist, division of labor cooperation, and complementary advantages, so that intelligent customer service can be used, creating intelligent and empathized customer service systems.

Keywords: intelligent customer service · human-computer interaction · anthropomorphic

1 Introduction

Intelligent customer service refers to a new customer service system based on large-scale knowledge processing technology, natural language understanding technology, knowledge management technology, automatic question and answer system, reasoning technology, etc. And establishes and massive users. The fast and effective technical means can provide personalized suggestions, alternatives and solutions for user problems

P.-L. P. Rau (Ed.): HCII 2023, LNCS 14023, pp. 386–396, 2023.
https://doi.org/10.1007/978-3-031-35939-2_28

through data, and provide relevant enterprises a natural language based on the communication between enterprises and massive users. The fast and effective technical means can provide personalized suggestions, alternatives and solutions for user problems through data, and provide relevant enterprises with statistical analysis information required for fine management (Li and Tao 2020). On January 20, 2022, Wofeng Technology joint Institute of SaaS and Big Data, China Academy of Information and Communications Technology released the "Digital Trends of intelligent customer Service and the Report of the Transformation of the Central State-owned Enterprise" (hereinafter referred to as "Report"), which was digitized into keywords analyze the intelligent customer service industry from the dimensions of market status, technical trends, application scenarios, and industry challenges. The "Report" pointed out that because traditional manual customer service is facing a series of problems such as low labor efficiency, high labor costs, and weak multi-channel service capabilities, intelligent customer service can solve the above pain points, and establish efficient, fast and intelligent communication between customers and enterprises.

The Chinese customer service software market has roughly experienced three development stages: traditional call center software, PC web page online customer service and traditional customer service software, cloud customer service and customer service robot intelligent customer service stage. The traditional call stage appeared at the end of last century, and the customer service system entered China. However, because the Internet has not yet been popularized, customer service communication is mainly telephone, that is traditional manual customer service. After 2000, With the rapid development of China's Internet industry, a variety of customer service channels such as web page customer service have also appeared to enter the PC web page customer service and traditional customer service software stage. In the past 10 years, the development of mobile Internet, SaaS (Software as a Service), Big Data and AI technology has brought traditional call centers and customer service software into the era of SaaS model and intelligent era. Intelligent mode of customer service robots (Zhen Wei 2020). Since 2017, Chinese intelligent customer service robots have been widely used in e-commerce, finance, education and other fields (Zhen et al. 2023).

Intelligent customer service robots have become an important part of establishing a connection with consumers. iiMedia Research predicts that the size of the Chinese intelligent customer service marker will reach 43.6 billion yuan in 2003, and the global artificial intelligence market revenue will exceed $3 trillion in 2024. iiMedia Research shows that in 2021, the proportion of users in China has used intelligent customer service as high as 98.1%, and it is mainly used in common living scenarios: such as handling life payment and other businesses. It can be seen that intelligent customer service almost completely penetrates people's daily life (Sun and Wang, 2019). But the acceptance of intelligent customer service is not high. Some surveys show that in 2021, Chinese users believe that only 45.6% of intelligent customer service can help solve more problems with more problems. Answer a series of bad points such as the same, repeating circulation operations, answering questions, unknown needs, and lag. During the interview, some users said that t "the use of intelligent customer service will not be strengthened after the interview", "hearing the robotic sound, it will directly request manual", "intelligent customer service is the mentally retarded customer service" and so on (Wu 2019). In the comparison of intelligent customer service is almost at a disadvantage, and the number of users of manual customer service is higher (Qianxi Song, Shuang Ma, 2022).

Compared with traditional manual customer service, intelligent customer service has the advantages of immediacy, convenience and low cost, and can provide users with 7×24 h of service in sales, marketing, service support and other fields at a lower cost of customer service (Yi 2021). There are obvious bottlenecks in undertaking capabilities. At the peak period of consultation, users may spend more time waiting, causing customers to lose. However, intelligent customer service can also answer online consultation initiated by tens of thousands of consultation during peak periods, and greatly reducing the waste of customer service resources on repeated issues, which is very efficient. However, in recent years, consumers have had an extremely disgusting effect on intelligent customer service. Consumers are more inclined to people-people talk, and people-machine conversation is more likely to stimulate consumers' irritability, which leads to complaints and reduced complaints. A series of consequences such as purchasing power. In terms of the important factors affecting customer service, such as problem solving degree, service efficiency and user experience, manual customer service is superior to intelligent customer service (see Fig. 1 for specific data). By referring to relevant literature and investigating relevant enterprises, this paper analyzes the causes of people's rejection of intelligent customer service, and explores the main influencing factors that affect the popularity of intelligent customer service, as shown in the following.

Comparison of China's intelligent customer service and manual customer service experience in 2021

	intelligent customer service	manual customer service
Problem resolution degree	9.60%	71.00%
Service efficiency	29.10%	39.10%
Use experience	27.30%	42.30%

Fig. 1. Statistical data

2 Influencing Factors

Since the essence of intelligent customer service is an artificial intelligence technology, in the important factors that intelligent customer service is accepted by users, you can refer to the cause of consumer hate and accepting intelligence technology. At the same time, this article mainly explores intelligent voice customer service system involves important technologies such as human-computer interaction, natural language processing, and Big Data. People and robots, which is interactive objects, convey the information and give feedback on the information. Human participation refers to people in the process of interaction and has the right to accept, judge, decide and operate (Cheng et al. 2020). In the process of human-computer interaction, people's elements are indispensable, and the process of human participation is related to their own characteristics and preferences. It cannot be estimated in advance, and it is also inseparable. The intelligent customer service system organically combines the various voice and behavior of users and intelligent customer service robots by performing tasks. In the discussion of the important factors accepted by the user's service, this article is expanded through the following three elements: task elements, intelligent customer service robot elements, and user elements.

2.1 Task Elements

The task element is the bridge between the robot and the user, and the core design of the intelligent voice intelligent voice customer service system is to complete the task through the voice interaction between users and the robot. Some characteristics of the task itself can affect the user's experience of the user service system and then affect the user's acceptance of intelligent customer service. Among them, the objective and subjective effect of the task (Castelo et al. 2019), the emotionality of the task (Wu et al. 2020), the innovative and programmatic task (Berkeley et al. 2018).

Objectiveness and Subjectivity of Tasks. Studies have found that in more objective tasks, users will have more trust in artificial intelligence, and users will also accept the use of algorithms to complete the task. (Castelo et al. 2019). By investigating the intelligent customer service system of the e-commerce industry and the express delivery industry, the e-commerce industry is represented by JD.com and Taobao. In querying such a more objective task, users choose to transfer manual customer service less times, but for complaints, returns and commodity recommendations. JD.com customer service system directly dispatches these tasks to manual customer service without using it. Intelligent customer service, the stronger the subjectivity of the intelligent customer service execution task, the lower the user's trust, and may have disgust. In the e-commerce industry, the user's purchasing power is reduced and the brand is unpopular.

Emotionality of Tasks. Compared with manual customer service, the advantage of intelligent customer service is that it can save costs and avoid direct contact with consumers with commercial frictions and disputes. Deepen the user's disgust about intelligent customer service. The literature pointed out that while the highly anthropomorphicization of the intelligent customer service system improves user expectations, when the system is no longer "intelligent", it will stimulate user' disgust and exacerbate negative attitudes (Wang et al. 2021). In handing more emotional tasks, although intelligent customer service robots can simulate human sounds, because they do not have high empathy, emotional tasks are often not high, far lower than user expectations. The stronger the emotionality of the task, the lower the solution of the intelligent customer service problem, and the more difficult it is for users to accept intelligent customer service. Studies have found that in those seemingly objective to solve problems; and in those tasks that seem subjective and emotional attributes, users are more inclined to resolve manually (Wu et al. 2020).

Innovation and Programming of Tasks. As mentioned earlier, when users make mistakes in intelligent customer services, the tolerance of intelligent customer service will decrease and disgust will increase. Therefore, when using the intelligent customer service system, merchants are more inclined to entrust programmed tasks to intelligent customer service (Dietvorst et al. 2018; Li 2022). Studies have shown that in the product recommendation task scenario of e-commerce products, users are more willing to accept low-creative product recommendations, and less acceptable high-creative product recommendations (Wu et al. 2020). For innovative tasks, even after the deep learning of intelligent customer service, it may be difficult to give solutions to satisfy users, reduce the sense of problem solving of intelligent customer service in the hearts of users, and greater marginalization of people's needs for intelligent customer service. On the contrary, when the programmatic task is performed by the robot, the error rate is lower than the manual customer service. The problem is more efficient. The programmatic task is handed over to the intelligent customer service. It can liberate the manpower of duplicate work. It provides 24 h of all-day services (Yijing 2018). Reducing the cost of customer service in enterprises is greatly played in customer service services.

2.2   Intelligent Customer Service Robot Element

The essence of the advantages and disadvantages of the intelligent customer service system determines the intelligence of intelligent customer service robots. The stronger the ability and more functions, the more intelligent customer service robots are more popular with users. The quality of the intelligent customer service robot design is manifested in two aspects: internal ability and external image. The internal ability is reflected in the accuracy and intelligence of solving problems. The external image is reflected in its interactive interface settings and anthropomorphic level.

Anthropomorphism of Robots. Studies have shown that for users with high interactive needs, the higher the degree of anthropomorphism of intelligent customer service robots, the user's social desire is satisfied, and the user experience will be better (Ben Sheehan, Hyun Seung Jin, Udo Gottlieb, 2020). However, in the research of intelligent customer service in service failure, the highly anthropomorphism of intelligent customer service will have a negative impact, that is users' psychological expectations for highly anthropomorphic customer service robots are equivalent to real-life dialogue, and intelligent customer service cannot meet user expectations. Instead, it will exacerbate users' disgust (Wang et al. 2021). In summary, the degree of anthropomorphism is an indispensable factor that determines the degree of acceptance of intelligent customer service robots. Quantitative control is needed through data experiments.

In the process of investigating the customer service system of the express delivery industry, ZTO Express customer service has a high degree of anthropomorphicness, mainly manifested in the real estate of robotic sounds, undulating changes in the tone, strong language recognition ability, and strong conversation and communication ability. Under the basic courier query task situation, the user's recognition of ZTO Express intelligent customer Service System is high, and the number of artificial times is small. However, because it is difficult to distinguish whether it is a real person through the tone, it is difficult to solve the difficult problem of the robot and it will exacerbate some customers' rejection of intelligent customer service (Wang et al. 2021). It can be seen that how to control the anthropomorphic and anthropomorphic degree of the robot will significantly affect the user experience. Even if the robot that has been designed, for different task scenarios, it may be necessary to use different degree of anthropomorphic interaction (Fu 2020).

The Accuracy and Intelligent of Solving Problems. The original intention of the intelligent customer service robot design is that intelligent assistance to solve customer service problems, and the accuracy and intelligence of solving problems reflect the inherent core capabilities of the robot. As mentioned earlier, the disgusted dislikes of intelligent customer service robots include "answering thousands of answers", "answering the question", "not solving the problem" and so on. Data shows that the problem of intelligent customer service robots is considered less than 10%, which is far lower than the manual customer service problem solving degree. In the evaluation index model proposed by predecessors or systems, the five indicators of Reliability, Flexibility, Integration, Accessibility, and Timeliness are the key influencing factors of system satisfaction (Wixom and Todd 2005), these five indicators can be reflected in their inherent abilities in intelligent customer service robots, which is the accuracy, reliability and intelligence of the problem solving.

Studies have shown that in the e-commerce industry, the internal ability of robots will significantly improve the willingness to continue to use intelligent customer service: AI flexibility, AI timeliness, and AI reliability meet the customer's expectations to use; AI accuracy and AI flexibility effectively improve user cognitive satisfaction; AI accuracy and AI reliability effectively improve user emotional satisfaction, reduce exclusion effects (Wu et al. 2023). In summary, evaluating the inherent ability of intelligent customer service robots can be used as indicators to solve the accuracy and intelligence of the problem. To improve the satisfaction of users, it is necessary to improve the inherent capabilities of the robot by accurately answering questions and providing intelligent solutions (Fig. 2).

Fig. 2. Systematic Satisfaction Evaluation Model

Interactive Interface Variable Control. The human-machine interaction interface directly contacts the user and intelligent customer service, which directly determines whether the user can and be willing to use the customer service robot. For human-computer interaction interface variable factors, the past research mainly includes whether the expression of robots is emotional (Ma et al. 2021), input and output control (Qu et al. 2021; Fu 2019), whether the interaction process is simple and easy to operate (Fernandes and Oliveira 2021) and so on. For example, in the study of the voice user interface (VUIs), it is found that the subject is found to choose the method of judgment and strategy (rational and emotional) to choose during interaction through experiments, and the emotional answer method is more recognized (Ma et al. 2021). This is also closely related to the degree of anthropomorphicization mentioned earlier, and emotional strategy methods are more likely to be accepted by users. In the inquiry of voice assistant driver factors, it is found that the user's perception and usefulness and perception of ease of use have a positive impact on the user's acceptance of the voice service. The simple and easy operation played a positive role in accepting the system (Qu et al. 2021).

Input and output have many factors. As for as text length is concerned, the current market is more popular with FAQ-based short-text classification technology. This system performs well under the premise of large-scale balanced data. In the research process of the customer service market, the author found that most customer service systems are short texts, but some customer service systems are mostly long texts due to the particularity of the industry. The Chinese railway customer service provided by the 12306-China Railway Customer Service Center answered the output with a very long text, and answered more questions. In addition to answering a specific question, it also extended the answer to the question. The text contains the rich information. However, because the text is too long, it is difficult for users to accept the text, understand the full text, and sort out their own answers to their questions. The user-related feedback evaluation obtained by the platform is not high. Some scholars have also studied the impact of robot dialogue users' claims on the degree of acceptance of users. People are called pronoun preferences. Combined with the specific scenarios of robots and users, people used by robots should change pronouns and promote human-machine voice interaction. Harmony, more close relationships between users and robots (Qu et al. 2021).

There are many interactive interface variables. For different working scenarios and different variables, the role of different variables is different. For specific task scenario and actual technical restrictions, modify and maintain interactive interfaces according to user needs and feedback to create good human-computer interaction conditions, which can effectively improve users' frequency and user satisfaction.

2.3   User Elements

At present, intelligent customer service is almost all over people's lives, but the acceptance of intelligent customer service varies from person to person. User factors have also become an important factor affecting the degree of acceptance of the intelligent customer service system. In a human-machine interaction experiment in predecessors, the research results confirmed that the gender and cultural differences of the user will affect the human-machine interaction process. At the same time, the user's social ability and the relationship between the companion relationship will also have an important impact on users to accept social robots (de Graaf and Ben Allouch 2013). For user elements, this article discusses only the three levels: the gander, age, and psychology of the user. At the gender level, male participants' evaluation of intelligent technology is often higher than female participants (Ma et al. 2021). For intelligent customer service, men can show a more positive attitude to accept. At the age level, compared with young people, the elderly has a greater exclusion of intelligent customer service. Through the technology accepting model TAM (Davis 1989), perception of ease of use determines to use attitude, because the use of AI technology is more difficult for the elderly, the elderly's rejection of intelligent customer service is even worse (Fig. 3).

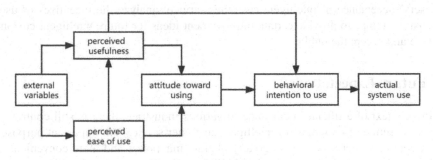

Fig. 3. Technology Acceptance Model, TAM

At the psychological level, psychological factors such as perception of usefulness, perception of ease of use, and perceptual pleasure have a significant effect on users who accept intelligent customer service (Liu Mengxiao, 2018). In addition, some studies have found that users with low individual innovation are not much different from users with low powerful, and the degree of acceptance of intelligent technology (Serenko, 2008). In the inquiry of the influencing factors accepted by new technologies, in 2000, Parasuraman proposed the new concept of technology preparation and found that users with low technology preparation level were even more unwilling to accept intelligent technology (Parasuraman, 2000; Lina Ren, 2022). Through the above literature, the author concludes that users with higher personal innovation and technical preparation level are more willing to accept intelligent customer service. Of course, in addition to the above factors, psychological factors such as personal psychological expectations and optimism will also affect whether users are more willing to accept intelligent customer service, these psychological differences will affect the individual differences are not too obvious so this article does not consider these factors.

3 Summary

In summary, considering whether the intelligent customer service system is more willing to accept, you must start from the three elements of users, robots, and tasks. The task element is the bridge of human-machine interaction. The robotic elements are the essence of the quality of the customer service system. Intelligent customer service system is essentially serving people, and the directly determined by people to improve the "humanity" of intelligent customer service robots, improve the ability to solve problems, efficiently reply to user demands, accurate identification, intelligent allocation, provide personalized services, create intelligent anthropomorphic people. The system makes users more willing to accept trust in intelligent customer service.

At present, although intelligent customer service has caused some users to disgust and exclusion due to some of their own defects, it has a wide range of applications in the market. Compared with manual customer service, it has the advantages of convenient, instantaneous, high efficiency, and low cost. I believe that intelligent customer service will continue to prosper in the customer service market. This article explores the key factors that affect users' acceptance of intelligent customer service, analyze the incentives of users' acceptance of intelligent customer service, analyze the incentives of user's disgust, and hope to provide certain improvement ideas for future intelligent customer service and accept the public.

4 Future Expectations

In the context of artificial intelligence in various industries, there is still controversy about the future development of intelligent customer service. An important purpose of intelligent customer service is to greatly liberate manpower and more convenient and efficiently help users solve problems (Wu et al. 2021). There are not intelligent and bad points such as answering questions and circular circles, and it is not accepted by users, so the development of the customer service industry in the future is still unknown. At present, the intelligent customer service system has a strong form of development in the development of e-commerce and express delivery industries. Repeated work such as querying order business and returns and exchanges business is handed over to the intelligent customer service system, so that human resources are liberated from repetitive and boring work, but for intelligent customer service, for intelligent customer service and for difficulties that cannot be solved, manual customer service will continue to provide customer service services, reduce labor costs, solve user problems efficiently, and future customer service (Cai and Li 2015). In my opinion, the intelligent customer service industry will not decline there, but the customer service industry will not be monopolized by intelligent customer service and manual customer service will not be replaced by robots. Instead, intelligent customer service and manual customer service assist each other. Repeated programmatic tasks were responsible for intelligent customer service, while complex and innovative task were responsible for manual customer service. Reduce the phenomenon of "transferring the intelligent customer service", so that intelligent customer service is used to use, and the market is prosperous.

Acknowledgement. This study was supported by "the Fundamental Research Funds for the Central Universities".

References

Wu, J., Yu, H., Zhu, Y., Zhang, X.: Impact of artificial intelligence recommendation on consumers' willingness to adopt. J. Manage. Sci. **33**(05), 29–43 (2020)

Wu, J., Zhu, Y., Liu, Y., Liang, J.: Research on inducement, psychological mechanism and boundary of the aversion effect of intelligent customer service. Nankai Bus. Rev., 1–23 (2023) http://kns.cnki.net/kcms/detail/12.1288.f.20220629.1011.008.html

Wang, H., Xie, T., Zhan, C.: The negative impact of personification of intelligent customer service avatar in the context of service failure: the mediating mechanism of disgust. Nankai Bus. Rev. **24**(04), 194–206 (2021)

Wu, W., Xiang, D., Li, Y.: Factors influencing intention to use chatbot in E-commerce - a Study mixed SEM and fsQCA methods. J. Chongqing Univ. Technol. (Soci. Sci.), 1–17 (2023) http://kns.cnki.net/kcms/detail/50.1205.T.20230113.1059.002.html

Fu, H.: Research and Implementation of Short Text Classification based on Common and Different Transfer Learning. BUPT (Beijing University of Posts and Telecommunications) (2019)

Li, F., Shao, X., Zhou, L., Jin, Y.: Current situation and development of intelligent customer service robot. Sci. Technol. China Mass Media **277**(04), 67–69 (2016). https://doi.org/10.19483/j.cnki.11-4653/n.2016.04.024

Yi, F.: A preliminary study on the implementation and application of artificial intelligence customer service in express logistics industry. Logistics Mater. Handling **26**(06), 124–128 (2021)

Wu, H.: The future development of operator customer service system. Telecom World **26**(10), 169–170 (2019)

Li, Y.: Research on the Relationship among Artificial Intelligence Technology Stimuli, Social Presence and Customer Stickiness—A Moderated Mediation Mo. North China University of Water Resources and Electric Power (2022). https://doi.org/10.27144/d.cnki.ghbsc.2022.000012

Li, J., Tao, C.: Research on the application of intelligent customer service in securities industry. Financ. Perspect. J. **11**, 64–69 (2020)

Cai, Z., Lin, J.: A intelligent customer service system for mobile e-commerce based on purchase intention. Sci. Technol. Manage. Res. **35**(18), 179–183 (2015)

Sun, S., Wang, Z.: Round in circles, cold... When will Smart customer service really be 'smart'? China Youth Daily, 2019-12-05(008). https://doi.org/10.38302/n.cnki.nzgqn.2019.000269

Song, Q., Ma, S.: A comparative study on the perceived value of intelligent customer service and manual customer service on e-commerce platforms. Trade Fair Econ. **22**, 38–40 (2022). https://doi.org/10.19995/j.cnki.CN10-1617/F7.2022.22.038

Wei, J.: Intelligent customer service innovation ranking. Internet Wkly **18**, 60–61 (2020)

Fu, F.: A Study of Impact of the Anthroporphic Clues of Intelligent Customer Service System on Consumer Purchase Intention. Southwestern University of Finance and Economics (2020). https://doi.org/10.27412/d.cnki.gxncu.2020.001533

Cheng, H., Huang, R., Qiu, J., et al.: A survey of recent advances in human-robot intelligent systems. CAAI Trans. Intell. Syst. **15**(2), 386–398 (2020)

de Graaf, M.M.A., Ben Allouch, S.: Exploring influencing variables for the acceptance of social robots. Robot. Auton. Syst. **61**, 1476–1486 (2013)

Serenko, A.: A model of user adoption of interface agents for email notification. Interact. Comput. **20**(4–5), 461–472 (2008)

Wixom, B.H., Todd, P.A.: A theoretical integration of user satisfaction and technology acceptance. Inf. Syst. Res. **16**(1), 85–102 (2005)

Fernandes, T., Oliveira, E.: Understanding consumers' acceptance of automated technologies in service encounters: drivers of digital voice assistants adoption. J. Bus. Res. **122**, 180–191 (2021)

Dietvorst, B.J., Simmons, J.P., Massey, C.: Overcoming algorithm aversion: people will use imperfect algorithms if they can (even slightly) modify them. Manage. Sci. **3**, 1155–1170 (2018)

Dietvorst, B., Simmons, J.P., Massey, C.: Algorithm aversion: people erroneously avoid algorithms after seeing them err. J. Exp. Psychol. Gen. **144**, 114–126 (2015)

Chen, N.-H., Huang, S.C.-T.: Domestic technology adoption: comparison of innovation adoption models and moderators. J. Commun. Appl. Soc. Psychol. **26**(2), 177–190 (2016)

Parasuraman, A.: Technology readiness index (Tri): a multiple-item scale to measure readiness to embrace new technologies. J. Serv. Res. **2**(4), 307–320 (2000)

Castelo, N., Bos, M.W., Lehmann, D.R.: Task-dependent algorithm aversion. J. Mark. Res. **56**(5), 809–825 (2019)

Ma, Q., Zhou, R., Zhang, C., Chen, Z.: Rationally or emotionally: how should voice user interfaces reply to users of different genders considering user experience? Cogn. Technol. Work **24**, 233–246 (2021). https://doi.org/10.1007/s10111-021-00687-8

Qu, J., Zhou, R., Chen, Z.: The effect of personal pronouns on users and the social role of conversational agents. Behav. Inf. Technol. (2021).https://doi.org/10.1080/0144929X.2021.199 9500

Nie, J., Wang, Q., Xiong, J.: Research on intelligent service of customer service system. Cogn. Comput. Syst. **3**(3), 197–205 (2021). https://doi.org/10.1049/ccs2.12012

Wei, D.: e-commerce online intelligent customer service system based on fuzzy control. J. Sens. **2021** (2021)

Yijing, W.: Intelligent customer service system design based on natural language processing. In: Proceedings of 2018 5th International Conference on Electrical & Electronics Engineering and Computer Science, ICEEECS 2018. Institute of Management Science and Industrial Engineering (2018)

Zhen, R., Song, W., He, Q., Cao, J., Shi, L., Luo, J.: Human-computer interaction system: a survey of talking-head generation. Electronics **12**(1), 218 (2023)

Wu, X., Liu, X., An, Y.: Key technologies of artificial intelligence in electric power customer service. Glob. Energy Interconnection **4**(06), 631–640 (2021)

Road Scene Risk Estimation Using Driving Video

Masafumi Kishimoto and Masaaki Iiyama[✉][iD]

Graduate School of Data Science, Shiga University, Hikone, Japan
s6021111@st.shiga-u.ac.jp, iiyama@iiyama-lab.org

Abstract. In this study, we propose a method for potential risk estimation of road scenes from driving videos and investigate the relationship between the potential risk estimation and the risk perception of humans. We employ a frame prediction method and define scenes where the frame prediction accuracy decreases as risky scenes. We also use the scene depth estimated from the color image and use the prediction error of the scene depth as another risk criteria. The relationship between the proposed risk criteria and the risk perception of humans was evaluated by subject experiments.

Keywords: Frame Prediction · Driving Video · Risk Estimation

1 Introduction

Driving motor vehicles is a scene where many accidents can occur, and understanding by drivers the potential risks of the scene they are driving is essential for safety driving. As a method for evaluating the potential risk of road scenes, systems that display on a map the locations where traffic accidents occurred in the past are widely used. Places where accidents occurred frequently are regarded as risky places, and users can choose to drive more carefully by using this system.

However, such systems can only identify places where accidents occurred as risky places, and cannot identify other risky places. By nature, the risk of the road environment is not static but changes dynamically depending on the environmental factors such as obstacles and parked vehicles and the speed of the vehicle. Therefore, it is necessary to evaluate the risk of the road scene by taking such dynamic changes into account.

The potential risk estimation is also important for evaluating the ability of drivers, that is, how likely drivers are to cause accidents. Methods such as obstacle detection and vehicle position estimation are developed for autonomous driving, and they can detect situations that are obviously dangerous. Although these methods are effective for avoiding accidents, they are insufficient for evaluating the safe driving ability of drivers. This is because accidents rarely occur even if the driver's ability is low, and only detecting situations that are obviously dangerous cannot detect potentially risky driving. In this study, in contrast, we

P.-L. P. Rau (Ed.): HCII 2023, LNCS 14023, pp. 397–406, 2023.
https://doi.org/10.1007/978-3-031-35939-2_29

aim to detect situations that are potentially risky, that is, situations where accidents are likely to occur but do not occur immediately. By detecting potentially risky situations, we can evaluate the safe driving ability of drivers, which can be applied, for example, to determine the risk rate of automobile insurance. The ability to perceive potential hazards in traffic and assess the likelihood of accidents is known as hazard perception. Research [1] has investigated the relationship between hazard perception and factors such as age and driving experience.

A possible method for estimating potential risks is to use the moving speed of the vehicle. However, the moving speed of the vehicle alone cannot evaluate the potential risks. Even if a vehicle is traveling at the same speed, the potential risk is different depending on whether the road is narrow or wide such as a city street and a highway. Instead, our method uses video frame prediction to estimate the potential risk, taking the surrounding road environment into account.

We employ a video frame prediction model, which takes past video frames and predict the next frame, and assume that a high-risk scene is a scene where future frame prediction is difficult. For example, scenes where the speed of the vehicle is high or there are many obstacles are difficult to predict, and even at the same speed, the difficulty of prediction is different depending on whether the road is a narrow road or a highway. Humans recognize scenes where the next scene is difficult to predict as dangerous scenes, and as a result, they drive carefully, e.g., slowing down the speed. Scenes where the accuracy of video frame prediction is low can be considered as scenes where prediction are difficult, and we use the prediction accuracy as the potential risk criteria.

Our method uses two metrics as the accuracy of frame prediction. One is the MAE in the color space, which is calculated by the difference between the predicted RGB frame and the ground truth frame. The other is the MAE of the disparity map estimated from the predicted RGB frame by a monocular depth estimation model. When using the MAE in the color space, the prediction accuracy is affected by lines and road signs drawn on the road, and the prediction accuracy is different between scenes where nothing is drawn on the road and scenes where something is drawn on the road, which may affect the stability of potential risk estimation. In addition, the MAE in the color space does not distinguish between the prediction error in the region close to the vehicle and the prediction error in the region far from the vehicle, so it does not focus on the prediction error in the more dangerous region close to the vehicle. In contrast, using the MAE of the disparity map allows us to focus on the prediction error in the region close to the vehicle.

2   Related Work

Deep learning-based frame prediction [2,3], which takes a sequence of frames as input and predicts the next frame, has been widely studied. It has been used for various applications, such as object location prediction [4], pedestrian trajectory prediction [5], and autonomous driving [6].

Accident anticipation is a task of predicting accidents using driving videos. In [7], Dynamic Spatial-temporal Attention Network is proposed for accident anticipation. In [8], a model for predicting bounding boxes is trained with normal driving video data, and abnormality detection is performed from the viewpoint of the accuracy of the bounding box movement prediction. Bao et al. [9] proposed a method of predicting accident occurrence scores from the relationship features learned by combining graph convolutional networks (GCN) and recurrent neural networks (RNN).

These studies are aimed at predicting accidents in autonomous driving. In contrast, the purpose of our study is to recognize potentially risky driving, not to predict imminent danger.

Scene depth is used for various applications such as autonomous driving and virtual reality, and is generally obtained as a 3D point cloud data from LiDAR and stereo cameras. While there are several methods for depth estimation from such devices, in this study, we use monocular depth estimation, which estimates depth using only images from a single camera using deep learning techniques [10,11]. We use [11] as a monocular depth estimation method.

3   Potential Risk Estimation

We define a degree of potential risk by the prediction error of the frame prediction. PredNet [3] is used as a frame prediction model. PredNet is a recurrent deep neural network and is inspired by predictive coding in neuroscience. It predicts the next frame by updating the state of the hidden layer along the time series.

Let we have a sequence of video frames $I_1, I_2, \ldots, I_T$. PredNet takes $I_1, \ldots, I_t$ as input and predicts the next frame I_{t+1} as $\hat{I}_{t+1}$. Although PredNet is trained so that the prediction error, $E_t = \|\hat{I}_{t+1} - I_{t+1}\|$, is minimized, prediction errors are still observed in the test data.

We consider this error as "uncertainty of the future" and define the potential risk as this error. Figure 1 shows an example of frame prediction by PredNet. Here, we predict the 11th frame I_{11} from the past 10 frames $I_1, \ldots, I_{10}$.

The prediction error is large in a road with many obstacles and small in a wide road. This is consistent with our intuition that a wide road is a safer environment than a narrow road.

There are two problems when using the prediction error as potential risk. One is handling the prediction error obtained in the time series. The prediction error E_t is obtained at each time t, but it needs to be represented as a single indicator. Statistical measures such as mean and variance of E_t can be used as indicators. We will evaluate the performance of these indicators in the experimental section.

Another problem is that the prediction error does not necessarily correspond to potential risk. Figure 2 shows an example. Both scenes in Fig. 2 are similar, but the amount of lines written on the road surface is different. In this case, the prediction error is larger in the upper scene with many lines drawn than in the lower scene. Therefore, if the prediction error E_t is used as potential risk, it may be too high in upper scene.

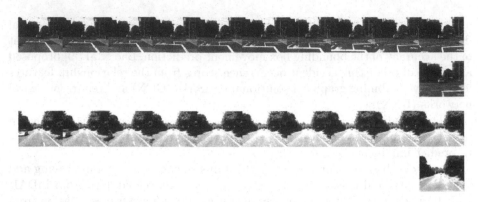

Fig. 1. Result of frame prediction by PredNet. The first and third row: input frames. The second and fourth row: predicted frames.

Fig. 2. Frame prediction of two similar scenes. The first and third row: input frames. The second and fourth row: predicted frames. Both scenes are similar, but the amount of lines written on the road surface is different. In this case, the prediction error is larger in the upper scene than in the lower scene, but it does not correspond to potential risk.

In addition, the prediction error E_t is the sum of the errors of all pixels in the predicted frame. However, not all regions of the image contribute equally to the potential risk. For example, even if an error occurs in the region corresponding to the sky, it has little effect on the potential risk, and the error that occurs in the region close to the vehicle has a greater effect than the error far from the vehicle.

Fig. 3. Estimated disparity maps from ground truth frame and predicted frame.

To solve this problem, we propose to use depth images estimated from RGB frames. For both of grand truth frame I_{t+1} and predicted frame $\hat{I}_{t+1}$, we estimate disparity map d_{t+1} and $\hat{d}_{t+1}$ using learning-based monocular depth estimation [11], and use the error of the disparity $|\hat{d}_{t+1} - d_{t+1}|$ instead of the error in the RGB space. Figure 3 shows estimated disparity maps from ground truth frame and the predicted frame. By using the error of the disparity map, we can reduce the influence of lines and road signs written on the road.

4   Subject Experiment

We conducted a subject experiment to evaluate the effectiveness of our potential risk estimation.

We first trained the PredNet model [3] by using KITTI dataset [12]. The same architecture as the original paper except for the size of the input image (128×416) was used for this training. We also converted the RGB video frames into single channel disparity frames by using the pretrained model [11]. This disparity frames were used to train another PredNet model, which takes disparity frames as input then outputs future disparity frames.

Figure 4 shows the prediction error of the PredNet model trained by using RGB frames. Compared with the left scene (highway scene) in Fig. 4, the right scene (urban scene) has a larger prediction error. In the same scene, the errors are different when oncoming vehicles pass by and when there are few oncoming vehicles, with the largest error at the point where a large truck passes by.

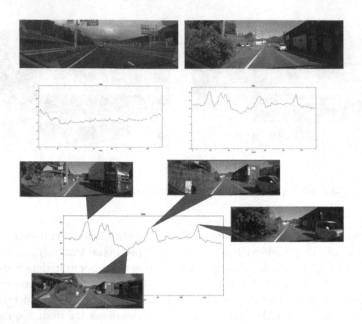

Fig. 4. MAE of the PredNet model trained by using RGB frames. Large errors are shown when oncoming vehicles pass by.

We created the driving video and used it as a dataset. Resolution of the video is 1080 × 1920 and total length is 33 min. This video contains the following five types of driving scenes.

- City street. Thr road is nallower than 5.5 m and is surrounded by houses and buildings.
- Urban area. The road is wider than 5.5 m and is surrounded by houses and buildings.
- Sub-urban area. The road is wider than 5.5 m with sparse buildings around it.
- Rural area. The road is wider than 5.5 m with few buildings around it.
- Highway.

The video is cropped into 5 s frames and the prediction error E_t for each frame is calculated. The following metrics were used to evaluate the effectiveness of our potential risk estimation.

- mean: mean of 5 s prediction error E_t.
- std: standard deviation of 5 s prediction error E_t.
- min: minimum of 5 s prediction error E_t.
- Q1: 25% quantile of 5 s prediction error E_t.
- median: median of 5 s prediction error E_t.
- Q3: 75% quantile of 5 s prediction error E_t.
- max: maximum of 5 s prediction error E_t.

Fig. 5. An example of questionnaries. Subjects are asked to answer which video clip is more risky.

We select 20 pairs of video clips, show them to 26 subjects, and ask them to answer which video clip is more risky. Figure 5 is an example of questionnaires.

Table 1 and Table 2 show the results of the subject experiment and the accuracy of our potential risk estimation by using mean absolute error (MAE) in RGB space, respectively. Using mean, Q3 and max show the best accuracy $(16/20 = 0.80)$.

Table 1. Results of the subject experiment. (MAE in RGB space)

No.	vote	count		mean		min		median		Q3		max	
		A	B	A	B	A	B	A	B	A	B	A	B
1	A(19:7)	5	0	**8.6488**	6.6777	**7.0911**	6.0403	**8.6702**	6.5793	**9.1159**	6.9333	**10.3954**	7.6613
2	A(23:3)	5	0	**6.8417**	4.0422	**5.8869**	3.7511	**6.7868**	4.0011	**7.0439**	4.1497	**8.6332**	4.5162
3	B(0:26)	0	5	4.4041	**5.4978**	3.9924	**5.031**	4.3805	**5.4736**	4.584	**5.6491**	5.3566	**6.1829**
4	B(8:18)	2	3	7.1595	**7.2523**	**6.2015**	6.0007	**7.0822**	6.9476	7.4976	**7.7795**	8.6567	**9.8042**
5	A(23:3)	5	0	**8.0485**	6.6708	**6.8329**	6.1695	**7.6103**	6.5991	**8.0843**	6.7894	**12.898**	8.4254
6	B(1:25)	5	0	**8.8237**	6.4066	**6.9824**	5.6907	**8.7013**	6.2156	**9.7395**	6.4664	**11.0634**	8.0905
7	B(5:21)	0	5	6.849	**11.0565**	5.6629	**8.6966**	6.6915	**10.9499**	7.0578	**11.5889**	9.3884	**14.2315**
8	B(9:17)	1	4	5.6076	**6.0957**	**4.9625**	4.9264	5.5591	**5.8717**	5.8161	**6.4948**	6.9264	**8.9814**
9	B(7:19)	0	5	6.4172	**8.8757**	5.4677	**7.6433**	6.2605	**8.8629**	6.7456	**9.2729**	8.9542	**10.9163**
10	B(10:16)	0	5	4.6455	**7.3243**	4.0246	**6.2263**	4.5228	**7.1496**	4.9228	**7.6717**	5.7335	**8.867**
11	B(7:19)	4	1	**8.0559**	7.3346	5.8381	**6.4191**	**8.1165**	7.1285	**8.7362**	7.7215	**10.2171**	8.9524
12	B(2:24)	0	5	6.8551	**9.1909**	6.1131	**7.8136**	6.8966	**9.2777**	7.0761	**9.8329**	7.7021	**12.3033**
13	A(17:9)	5	0	**7.5629**	6.985	**6.7096**	6.3075	**7.5952**	6.9979	**7.8405**	7.1947	**8.5769**	7.6988
14	A(18:8)	5	0	**6.5715**	6.3223	**5.9539**	5.5808	**6.5337**	6.1472	**6.8099**	6.5597	**8.6533**	8.5088
15	A(24:2)	0	5	5.772	**7.2257**	5.1101	**5.5619**	5.6355	**7.029**	6.0213	**7.8107**	6.8532	**10.9399**
16	A(16:10)	5	0	**8.7833**	4.8616	**6.0859**	4.2084	**8.2793**	4.8773	**10.2717**	5.0448	**14.8078**	5.5782
17	A(20:6)	0	5	5.4842	**7.7857**	5.0197	**6.0085**	5.4184	**7.5246**	5.5824	**8.5222**	6.8826	**10.1422**
18	A(18:8)	5	0	**8.0647**	7.2992	**6.5988**	6.2002	**8.2073**	7.278	**8.5119**	7.5527	**10.5031**	8.3616
19	B(10:16)	0	5	4.4381	**5.0001**	3.6916	**4.3692**	4.4706	**4.9131**	4.749	**5.2562**	5.195	**5.8903**
20	B(3:23)	0	5	6.2057	**6.5695**	5.427	**5.6144**	6.113	**6.3778**	6.4393	**7.3397**	7.7012	**7.9535**

Figure 6 shows a successful case (No. 5). Both cases are in the sub-urban area. Case A has no sidewalk on the left side and the distance to the buildings and trees on the left side is short. In addition, a large truck is running on the opposite lane, which makes people feel more risky. In contrary, case B has no sidewalk on the left side, but the visibility is good and there is no vehicle on the opposite lane, which makes prediction error smaller.

Table 2. Accuracy of the proposed method (MAE in RGB space)

	mean	min	median	Q3	max
accuracy	16/20	15/20	15/20	16/20	16/20

A

B

Fig. 6. A successful case.

Figure 7 shows a failure case (No. 15). Both cases are in the residential area and highway, respectively. Frame prediction error of case B is higher than case A, but the subjects answered that case A is more risky than case B. The reason is that the subjects may think that the highway is safer than the residential area because they know that the highway is safer.

A

B

Fig. 7. A failure case.

Table 3 and Table 4 show the results of the subject experiment and the accuracy of our potential risk estimation by using mean absolute error (MAE) in disparity space, respectively.

Compared with the result of the RGB space, the accuracy of the disparity space is lower. This is due to the accuracy of the disparity estimation. Our method for obtaining the disparity map from RGB image frames utilizes a learning-based approach, and any error in the prediction of the disparity map impacts the accuracy of the feature frame prediction. However, the disparity space is more accurate than the RGB space in some cases such as No. 11.

Figure 8 shows an improved case in disparity space (No. 6). In this case, mean errors in RGB space are $A : 8.8237, B : 6.4066$ but most of subjects answered that case B is more risky than case A (A:1,B:25). On the other hand, mean errors in disparity space are $A : 0.0623, B : 0.0601$, which are smaller gap compared with the RGB space. This improvement can be explained by the representation of differences in road width in the disparity space. Prediction error of disparity,

Table 3. Results of the subject experiment. (MAE in disparity map)

No.	vote	count		mean		min		median		Q3		max	
		A	B	A	B	A	B	A	B	A	B	A	B
1	A(19:7)	1	4	0.0554	**0.0807**	0.0243	**0.0446**	0.0542	**0.0796**	0.0667	**0.0881**	**0.1406**	0.1269
2	A(23:3)	4	1	**0.0412**	0.0253	0.0159	**0.0165**	**0.0322**	0.0246	**0.0521**	0.0281	**0.1107**	0.0368
3	B(0:26)	0	5	0.0355	**0.0426**	0.0225	**0.0282**	0.035	**0.04**	0.0396	**0.0454**	0.0494	**0.084**
4	B(8:18)	5	0	**0.0813**	0.0561	**0.0397**	0.0282	**0.0762**	0.0502	**0.0963**	0.0676	**0.1734**	0.1557
5	A(23:3)	5	0	**0.1071**	0.0801	**0.0449**	0.043	**0.0975**	0.0795	**0.137**	0.0898	**0.2071**	0.1553
6	B(1:25)	3	2	**0.0623**	0.0601	0.0267	**0.0283**	**0.0613**	0.0572	**0.0748**	0.0704	0.1089	**0.1287**
7	B(5:21)	0	5	0.0538	**0.0931**	0.0328	**0.0354**	0.0494	**0.0832**	0.0577	**0.1159**	0.1177	**0.2121**
8	B(9:17)	1	4	0.036	**0.0708**	**0.0202**	0.0191	0.0357	**0.0697**	0.0419	**0.0888**	0.0583	**0.131**
9	B(7:19)	1	4	0.0378	**0.0459**	0.0234	**0.0238**	0.0351	**0.047**	0.0415	**0.0558**	**0.0946**	0.0691
10	B(10:16)	5	0	**0.0779**	0.0504	**0.0408**	0.0193	**0.0698**	0.0448	**0.0928**	0.0688	**0.16**	0.1015
11	B(7:19)	1	4	0.0511	**0.055**	0.0251	**0.0319**	0.0444	**0.0504**	0.0589	**0.0612**	**0.182**	0.1236
12	B(2:24)	1	4	0.0423	**0.0584**	**0.0288**	0.023	0.0413	**0.0556**	0.0468	**0.0671**	0.0748	**0.1106**
13	A(17:9)	0	5	0.0242	**0.0336**	0.0153	**0.0211**	0.0226	**0.0328**	0.0266	**0.0383**	0.0475	**0.0538**
14	A(18:8)	5	0	**0.0456**	0.0368	**0.029**	0.0235	**0.044**	0.036	**0.0499**	0.0416	**0.0767**	0.0627
15	A(24:2)	0	5	0.0489	**0.0525**	0.0204	**0.0225**	0.0491	**0.0517**	0.055	**0.0608**	0.0874	**0.1124**
16	A(16:10)	5	0	**0.0541**	0.034	**0.031**	0.0229	**0.051**	0.0318	**0.0618**	0.037	**0.1111**	0.0633
17	A(20:6)	0	5	0.034	**0.0529**	0.016	**0.0212**	0.0328	**0.0466**	0.0396	**0.0674**	0.07	**0.1159**
18	A(18:8)	5	0	**0.0961**	0.0308	**0.0531**	0.0127	**0.0952**	0.0256	**0.1106**	0.0366	**0.1807**	0.0797
19	B(10:16)	0	5	0.032	**0.0902**	0.0169	**0.0397**	0.029	**0.086**	0.0361	**0.106**	0.0783	**0.1436**
20	B(3:23)	1	4	0.0293	**0.0354**	**0.0197**	0.0174	0.0288	**0.034**	0.0333	**0.0435**	0.0466	**0.0812**

Table 4. Accuracy of the proposed method (MAE in disparity space)

	mean	min	median	Q3	max
accuracy	13/20	13/20	13/20	13/20	13/20

which is the reciprocal of distance, is small even if the prediction error in distance is large in areas far from the vehicle. In other words, prediction errors in areas far from the vehicle, such as roads, do not contribute much to risk estimation. In contrast, the prediction error for objects close to the vehicle, such as oncoming vehicles and pedestrians, has a larger impact on disparity. The use of disparity, therefore, tends to result in a higher risk compared to narrower road width. This aligns with human intuition and may have contributed to the improvement of No. 6.

Fig. 8. An improved case in disparity space. Most of subjects answered that case B is more risky than case A.

5 Conclusion

In this paper, we proposed a method for estimating potential risk of driving scenes using driving video. The key contribution of this paper is to estimate the risk of driving scenes by using the prediction error of the future frame. The proposed method was evaluated by a subjective experiment. The results showed that the proposed method can estimate the risk of driving scenes at accuracy 80%.

As future work, we will use semantic information of driving scenes to estimate the risk of driving scenes. Our method does not take into account the semantic information of driving scenes. For example, the risk of driving scenes is different depending on weather condition, road type (e.g., highway, city street), and type of obstacles. We will use such semantic information for improving the performance of our method.

References

1. Borowsky, A., Shinar, D., Oron-Gilad, T.: Age, skill, and hazard perception in driving. Accid. Anal. Prev. **42**(4), 1240–1249 (2010)
2. Oprea, S., et al.: A review on deep learning techniques for video prediction. IEEE Trans. PAMI **44**(6), 2806–2825 (2022)
3. Lotter, W., Kreiman, G., Cox, D.: Deep predictive coding networks for video prediction and unsupervised learning. In: ICLR (2017)
4. Makansi, O., Ilg, E., Cicek, Ö., Brox, T.: Overcoming limitations of mixture density networks: a sampling and fitting framework for multimodal future prediction. In: CVPR (2019)
5. Bhattacharyya, A., Fritz, M., Schiele, B.: Long-term on-board prediction of people in traffic scenes under uncertainty. In: CVPR (2018)
6. Hu, A., Cotter, F., Mohan, N., Gurau, C., Kendall, A.: Probabilistic future prediction for video scene understanding. In: Vedaldi, A., Bischof, H., Brox, T., Frahm, J.-M. (eds.) ECCV 2020. LNCS, vol. 12361, pp. 767–785. Springer, Cham (2020). https://doi.org/10.1007/978-3-030-58517-4_45
7. Chan, F.-H., Chen, Y.-T., Xiang, Yu., Sun, M.: Anticipating accidents in dashcam videos. In: Lai, S.-H., Lepetit, V., Nishino, K., Sato, Y. (eds.) ACCV 2016. LNCS, vol. 10114, pp. 136–153. Springer, Cham (2017). https://doi.org/10.1007/978-3-319-54190-7_9
8. Yao, Y., Mingze, X., Wang, Y., Crandall, D.J., Atkins, E.M.: Unsupervised traffic accident detection in first-person videos. In: IROS (2019)
9. Bao, W., Yu, Q., Kong, Y.: Uncertainty-based traffic accident anticipation with spatio-temporal relational learning. In: ACM MultiMedia (2020)
10. Yang, X., Gao, Y., Luo, H., Liao, C., Cheng, K.-T.: Bayesian DeNet: monocular depth prediction and frame-wise fusion with synchronized uncertainty. IEEE Trans. Multimedia **21**(11), 2701–2713 (2019)
11. Gordon, A., Li, H., Jonschkowski, R., Angelova, A.: Depth from video in the wild: unsupervised monocular depth learning from unknown cameras. In: CVPR (2019)
12. Geiger, A., Lenz, P., Stiller, C., Urtasun, R.: Vision meets robotics: the KITTI dataset. Int. J. Robot. Res. (IJRR) **32**(11), 1231–1237 (2013)

Study a Driver's Response to Emerging Scenarios Under Different Levels of Perceived Urgency

Hsueh-Yi Lai[✉] [iD]

National Yang Ming Chiao Tung University, No. 1001, Daxue Road, East District,
Hsinchu 300093, Taiwan
hylai@nycu.edu.tw

Abstract. Although intelligent vehicles have filled our daily lives, drivers are still required to take over when automation disengages. To provide effective decision supports in such emerging events with time pressure, how the drivers make reactions deserves more attention. This research aims to investigate the pattern of the drivers' response to emerging events under different levels of perceived urgency. A total of 20 participants were recruited for simulated driving. For the outcomes obtained, three levels of urgency are considered. In cases of low-level urgency, it is found that the average lateral acceleration is the highest, while the values of standard deviation for both lateral acceleration and steering are the lowest. This implies that the drivers can execute active yet cautious operations. For the cases of medium level of urgency, the extent of deceleration is significantly higher. Even though, the driver can maintain the same level of lateral operations as the cases of low-level urgency. Lastly, as for the cases of high-level urgency, not only does the average lateral deceleration decrease but the standard deviation of lateral deceleration and steering increases. This combination implies the deterioration of lateral control, which might affect the overall traffic flow or even result in collisions like the rear end.

Keywords: Emergency driving behavior · Situation awareness · Perceived urgency

1 Introduction

Recent years have seen a rapid advance in automated vehicles. Based on the definition of NHTSA (National Highway Transportation Safety Administration), six levels of automation are defined [1]. Details are shown in Table 1. In general, level 1 or 2 of automation is related to advanced driving assistance technologies, which have gradually filled our daily lives. Automatic emergency braking (AEB) or the lane-centering system are some of the iconic examples. Even though, the research on a higher level of automation never slows down. These few years have seen a surge of research on higher-level automation. For level 3 or even 4 automation, the role of human shifts from a driver to a monitor. Although intelligent vehicles can effectively support driving performance,

© The Author(s), under exclusive license to Springer Nature Switzerland AG 2023
P.-L. P. Rau (Ed.): HCII 2023, LNCS 14023, pp. 407–416, 2023.
https://doi.org/10.1007/978-3-031-35939-2_30

they are likely to go wrong, particularly in situations outside the pre-defined operational domains [2]. Therefore, humans still play a critical role in safe driving. A driver must intervene when automation fails, otherwise, collisions or even accidents are doomed [3, 4].

Table 1. Level of automation

Automation levels	Descriptions
Level 0 (Manual)	Manual driving
Level 1 (Driving assistance)	The driver is fully responsible for the system, while the system provides various assistance to decrease the driver's workload
Level 2 (Additional assistance)	
Level 3 (Conditional automation)	The system is responsible for the vehicle's performance, while the driver must monitor and intervene once the automation fails
Level 4 (High automation)	
Level 5 (Full automation)	The system is fully responsible for the vehicle. The driver does not need to engage the system

To this end, the development of decision support systems attracts the researcher's attention. Although the performance of decision support systems advances rapidly as the relevant technologies and research progress, human-automation interaction still plays a critical role. The sophisticated mechanism of an automated system can be a "black box" for humans. The lack of transparency may degrade one's trust in automated systems or even intensify one's workload in an emergent scenario [5, 6]. Accordingly, a system must be designed in ways that are consistent with the driver's driving behavior or even mental model [7].

With the advances in artificial intelligence, cutting-edge algorithms can consider the distinctive features within driving behavior for providing active support. For example, some researchers have managed to make some strides to predict a driver's intentions, like lane-changing, by considering a driver's real-time eye movements and car maneuvers [8]. Therefore, before developing effective decision support systems for better takeover performance when automation disengages, how the driver reacts to such emerging events under time pressure deserves more attention. Thus, this research aims to provide a preliminary examination of how drivers respond to various emerging events under different levels of perceived urgency.

2 Literature Review

This section provides a comprehensive review of the related work, comprising decision-making during driving and scenario urgency.

2.1 Decision-Making During Driving

To study one's decision-making in a dynamic environment, situation awareness (SA) has been identified as a critical element. SA denotes one's awareness regarding situational changes [3], which consists of three levels. The framework is displayed in Fig. 1. Level 1 of SA considers the cues perceived by the operator. In a driving environment, the environmental cues can be the current speed or the separation among vehicles. Level 2 of SA determines the way a human comprehends the pattern of environmental cues. The process is driven by the mental model developed by one's knowledge and experience. Lastly, one will project the near future in level 3 of SA, which serves as a basis for the upcoming goal determination.

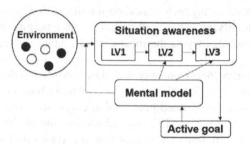

Fig. 1. The framework of situation awareness

Furthermore, the determination and accomplishment of a goal can take several iterations. To execute a goal properly, various strategies are adopted. For example, one may execute competitive driving for more driving benefits, or consider defensive driving for avoiding potential risks [9], which causes shifts in the mental model. The changes in mental model will affect the way one comprehends, projects, or even the way collecting environmental cues. As the environmental cues change, one may also modify the current goal determined. The iterative process ends once the goal is accomplished.

To respond to emerging events properly, a driver must evaluate the current scenario by collecting sufficient evidence from various environmental cues (level 1 of SA). A general tendency of decision-making has been uncovered by relevant research. In general, research suggests that a driver may tend to make brake decisions as the visual angle decreases, while steering decisions are preferred in cases with sufficient distance and time [9, 10]. However, the characteristics of every emerging event can vary owing to the variation of environmental cues. Relevant cues include the changes in the movements, visual angle, brake light of leading vehicles, traffic density, etc. [11, 12]. How a driver responds to various emerging events requires further investigation.

2.2 Scenario Urgency

Based on the discussion above, the combination of environmental cues characterizes the type of event. Despite the variety, the connection among some of the environmental cues helps to examine various scenarios systematically. For example, the brake light and the reduction of separation both imply the occurrence of emerging events. To simplify the design of the experiment, this research emphasizes the urgency of the events.

Among the cues observed in a driving environment, urgency can be a holistic index that considers not only time but also the remaining safety distance. Simultaneously, it also considers the main ideas of various indexes. For example, time-to-collision (TTC), which is computed by dividing the current distance between the obstacles by the current speed [13], is a widely used index to evaluate how close the driver with the obstacles. A lower minimum TTC denotes a higher urgency, showing that the current safety distance is too few to fully decelerate. Aside from the TTC, some research considers a driver's visual angle for examining a driver's reactions upon seeing emerging events [11]. It was observed that drivers may brake for speed adjustment based on the visual angle of the leading vehicle, while the changes in visual angle imply the reduction of safety distance, reflecting a higher level of urgency. Based on the discussion above, urgency can play a suitable role in identifying the overall picture of an emerging event. In fact, recent research has identified urgency as the most critical feature that can predict a driver's response [14].

Aside from the comprehensiveness provided by considering the urgency of an event, urgency is also particularly suitable for decision-making based on the idea of SA. In general, SA is a recognition-primed process that emphasizes the outcomes of pattern recognition rather than analytics [15]. Accordingly, owing to the differences in experience and knowledge, different drivers may treat a certain event in different ways. As a result, compared to the indexes that are quantitatively defined, like TTC or visual angle, perceived urgency might be a better alternative for examining decision-making in a dynamic driving environment.

3 Methodology

This section describes how the experiment is designed and operated. In general, a series of experiments of simulated driving are developed to test a driver's response to emerging events. This section includes equipment, experimental design, experimental procedures, recruitment criteria, and data collection.

3.1 Equipment

To test a driver's response in emergency scenarios, a driving simulator is developed with a triple-monitor setting and a simulated steering wheel (Logitec g923). To develop various driving scenarios, an open-sourced game, Euro truck simulator 2 (ETS2), is adopted to customize the driving environment and the details of the driving scenarios. To record how one corresponds to a scenario, an extra plugin is developed with Python for recording the real-time data of car movements. The layout is illustrated in Fig. 2.

3.2 Experimental Design

In this research, the scene of driving simulations is set to be the highway to avoid potential distractions caused by the environment. Then, the location of obstacles and

Fig. 2. The layout of simulated driving

the distance remaining are two major factors considered. The location of obstacles can be in either current or other lanes, while the obstacles can be constructions, accidents, or even pedestrians that suddenly show up. As for the safety distance remaining, three conditions are designed, including 30, 50, and 70 m. In general, a proper safety distance should be half of the current speed (km/hour). Thus, in the scene of high way, 50 m can be a proper baseline of safety distance. By combing these two dimensions, 6 types of events can be identified. The details are illustrated in Fig. 3. To prevent potential carryover effects or fatigue caused by long-time driving, 6 types of events will be distributed evenly into two driving sessions. To achieve a more realistic driving simulation, virtual vehicles controlled by the software are added. Each participant is required to accomplish two sessions, while 10 min of rest between the two sessions are allowed. All the emerging events, comprising the events pre-defined and those caused by the interactions between virtual vehicles, will be manually recorded by the research team for the following interviews to probe one's level of perceived urgency in each of the emerging events encountered. Furthermore, during driving sessions, the research time will record the driving performance with a sports camera (GoPro HERO10). The recordings can help the participants to recall the conditions of the events (See Fig. 4).

In post-experiment interviews, the research team will replay the videos recorded and ask the participants to label the level of urgency. Three levels of urgency, low, medium, and high, are defined. First, low-level urgency refers to cases with potential risks that can be avoided in advance. In other words, no existing risks are found, while the drivers prefer to be cautious, which shares a similar idea with defensive driving [9]. Second, medium-level urgency refers to cases with existing and obvious risks, however, the relatively sufficient time margins enable the drivers to sort out the proper course of action for risk elimination. Lastly, high-level urgency refers to cases with urgent risks that require

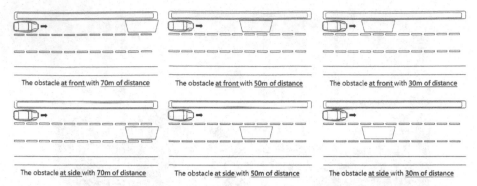

The obstacle **at front** with **70m of distance**   The obstacle **at front** with **50m of distance**   The obstacle **at front** with **30m of distance**

The obstacle **at side** with **70m of distance**   The obstacle **at side** with **50m of distance**   The obstacle **at side** with **30m of distance**

Fig. 3. 6 types of emerging events

Fig. 4. The recordings played for post-experiment interviews

immediate interventions. The drivers must act immediately, otherwise, collisions are doomed. The questions are shown as follows:

1. Do you reckon this event is extremely urgent, while immediate actions should be performed? (Yes: high level/No: ask question 2)
2. Do you have sufficient safety margins to make proper reactions (Yes: medium level)? Or it is just an emerging event that can be avoided in advance (Yes: low level)?

3.3 Experimental Procedures

The experiment can be divided into three parts, including warm-up, simulated driving, and post-experiment interviews. Before the simulated driving commences, a participant must accomplish a warm-up session that helps the participant get used to the control and feedback of the driving simulator. During the warm-up, the research team adjusts the sensitivity of the steering wheel and pedal for a more realistic driving experience. Then, the research team will launch a plugin to record the real-time input delivered by the participants. Simultaneously, the sports camera will be ready to record the experiment. Each participant is required to perform two driving sessions. 10 min of rest is allowed between the sessions. After the two sessions are accomplished, the research team plays the recordings of the sports camera and probes the participants with the interview questions to label the level of urgency.

3.4 Recruitment Criteria

In this research, the participants are required to be licensed drivers for over one year. Simultaneously, the frequency of driving should be at least one time a week, while professional drivers, like taxi or truck drivers, are excluded for better generalization.

3.5 Data Collection

For data collection, three types of driving inputs are collected, including the angle of the steering wheel, and the depth of both the throttle and brake. The sampling rate is set to 10 Hz to record the real-time inputs.

4 Results and Discussion

Table 2. Demographical data

Sex		Age		The month since being licensed		Driving frequency (times/week)				
Male	Female	Ave	St.d	Ave	St.d	1	2	3	4	>5
13	7	27.95	7.17	91.84	77.02	6	3	6	1	4

In this research, a total of 20 participants were recruited, including 13 males and 7 females. The average age is 27.5 with a standard deviation of 7.17, while the average number of months since being licensed is 91.84. Furthermore, most of the participants drive more than one time a week. Relevant details are shown in Table 2. For the emerging events recorded, a total of 144 events are collected. 67 are categorized as a low level of urgency, 29 as a medium, and 48 as a high. The descriptive statistics are shown in Table 3 while Table 4 shows the outcomes of the F-test and post hoc tests. In general, distinct patterns of driving behavior can be observed among the three levels of urgency.

To respond to low-level urgency, it is observed that the drivers tend not to make sudden changes. The significantly lower values of "Speed_ave", "Speed_std", "Acc_ave", "Acc_std", "Brake_ave", and "Brake_std" imply small changes regarding speed control. Noticeably, although lateral acceleration ("L_Acc_ave") is identified to be significantly higher, the standard deviation of both lateral accelerations ("L_Acc_std") and steering ("Steer_std") are both identified to be lower. This pattern implies that the driver does execute active yet cautious operations like detours to avoid obstacles. This pattern does correspond to the driving behavior of defensive driving. As for the medium-level of urgency, some significant changes can be observed. The values regarding speed ("Speed_ave", and "Speed_std") are significantly lower, while the decrement of acceleration ("Acc_ave",

Table 3. Descriptive statistics (Mean/Std)

Urgency	Speed_ave	Speed_std	Acc_ave	Acc_std	L_Acc_ave	L_Acc_std
Low	76.31/26.25	10.04/8.07	−2.20/2.33	1.81/1.40	76.31/0.04	10.04/0.11
Medium	68.49/27.35	13.32/10.17	−3.25/3.28	2.40/1.63	68.49/0.05	13.32/0.18
High	70.33/27.12	15.52/13.37	−4.01/3.69	3.50/4.25	70.33/0.16	15.52/0.89
Urgency	Steer_ave	Steer_std	Throttle_ave	Throttle_std	Brake_ave	Brake_std
Low	−0.0042/0.019	0.0075/0.015	0.17/0.22	0.14/0.14	0.12/0.15	0.13/0.12
Medium	0.0013/0.019	0.0104/0.016	0.13/0.19	0.14/0.16	0.23/0.24	0.19/0.15
High	−0.0048/0.043	0.0262/0.040	0.14/0.21	0.12/0.15	0.27/0.29	0.19/0.17

* **ave: average/std: standard deviation/Acc: acceleration/L_Acc lateral acceleration**

and "Acc_std") and the increment of the depth of braking pedal ("Brake_ave", and "Brake_std") soars. This pattern shows active interventions for speed reduction. However, the variables regarding lateral movement, comprising "L_Acc_ave", "L_Acc_std", "Steer_ave", and "Steer_std" does not show significance compared to the cases of low-level urgency. This pattern can reflect that although one takes acute deceleration due to a higher level of urgency, smooth operations can still be maintained. Lastly, for high-level urgency, compared to the cases of medium-level urgency, no significant difference regarding speed can be found, while the extent of deceleration soars. This pattern can be caused by high time pressure. Furthermore, the features of lateral movements are worth further discussion. First, the average lateral acceleration ("L_Acc_ave") is significantly lower than the cases with low-level urgency. One of the possible reasons can be the limited time available for making sufficient inputs. Interestingly, significantly higher values regarding the standard deviation of lateral movements ("L_Acc_std", and "Steer_std") are observed. The pattern of low average yet high standard deviation of lateral movement shows significant deterioration of lateral control under high-level urgency.

Based on the discussion, some insights can be obtained for providing effective decision support. In general, for longitudinal movements, although deceleration is the most obvious action, the extent of differences among the three levels of urgency is significant. Therefore, ecological interfaces that can visualize maneuver trajectories [16], like deceleration, might be a universal alternative. As for lateral movements, the results show that the drivers can execute smooth maneuvers with higher lateral acceleration yet smaller standard deviation regarding both lateral acceleration and steering. However, as the level of urgency increases, the extremely high time pressure makes the magnitude and control of lateral movements decrease. Improper operations may affect the overall traffic flow, even resulting in collisions like the rear end. Therefore, how to provide timely decision supports to not only avoid obstacles but prevent accidents caused by improper operations can be critical.

Table 4. F-test and posthoc tests

	Speed_ave	Speed_std	Acc_ave	Acc_std	L_Acc_ave	L_Acc_std
F-test	**4.29(0.014)**	**13.89(0.000)**	**17.81(0.000)**	**20.25(0.000)**	**3.31(0.04)**	**26.48(0.000)**
Low vs. Medium	**0.010**	**0.005**	**0.002**	**0.038**	0.764	0.34
Low vs. High	**0.034**	**0.000**	**0.000**	**0.000**	**0.012**	**0.000**
Medium vs. High	0.592	0.092	**0.045**	**0.001**	0.071	**0.000**
	Steer_ave	Steer_std	Throttle_ave	Throttle_std	Brake_ave	Brake_std
F-test	1.89(0.15)	**27.41(0.000)**	1.64(0.20)	0.51 (0.598)	**24.44(0.000)**	**10.97(0.000)**
Low vs. Medium	0.078	0.294	0.133	0.775	**0.000**	**0.000**
Low vs. High	0.828	**0.000**	0.155	0.404	**0.000**	**0.000**
Medium vs. High	0.083	**0.000**	0.878	0.349	0.103	0.955

* **ave: average/std: standard deviation/Acc: acceleration/L_Acc lateral acceleration**

5 Conclusion

Recent years have seen rapid advances in intelligent vehicles, while the roles that a human plays shift from a driver to a monitor. Although the systems of autonomous vehicles can handle most driving scenarios, the driver must take over once the automation disengaged. Under extremely high time pressure and a lack of readiness, how to take over properly has attracted the research's attention. To provide effective decision support that helps drivers to respond to urgencies effectively. This research aims to investigate the pattern of the drivers' response in various emerging scenarios. A total of 20 participants were recruited for simulated driving. For the outcomes obtained, three levels of urgency are considered. In cases of low-level urgency, it is found that the average lateral acceleration is the highest, while the values of standard deviation for both lateral acceleration and steering are the lowest. This implies that the drivers can execute active yet cautious operations. For the cases of medium level of urgency, the extent of deceleration is significantly higher. Even though, the driver can maintain the same level of lateral operations as the cases of low-level urgency. Lastly, as for the cases of high-level urgency, not only does the average lateral deceleration decrease but the standard deviation of lateral deceleration and steering increases. This combination implies the deterioration of the control of lateral movements, which might affect the overall traffic flow or even result in collisions like the rear end.

Acknowledgment. This work is financially supported by NSTC, Taiwan. The grant number is [MOST 111-2222-E-A49-002-MY2]. Sincerely thanks for the assistance provided by the research team.

References

1. NHTSA. Automated Vehicles for Safery. (2021). https://www.nhtsa.gov/technology-innova tion/automated-vehicles-safety
2. Caballero, W.N., Ríos Insua, D., Banks, D.: Decision support issues in automated driving systems. Int. Trans. Oper. Res. (2021)
3. Endsley, M.R.: Situation awareness in future autonomous vehicles: Beware of the unexpected. In: Bagnara, S., Tartaglia, R., Albolino, S., Alexander, T., Fujita, Y. (eds.) Proceedings of the 20th Congress of the International Ergonomics Association (IEA 2018). IEA 2018. AISC, vol. 824. Springer, Cham (2018). https://doi.org/10.1007/978-3-319-96071-5_32
4. Zeeb, K., Buchner, A., Schrauf, M.: What determines the take-over time? An integrated model approach of driver take-over after automated driving. Accid. Anal. Prev. **78**, 212–221 (2015)
5. Karpinsky, N.D., et al.: Automation trust and attention allocation in multitasking workspace. Appl. Ergon. **70**, 194–201 (2018)
6. Xu, Z., et al.: When the automated driving system fails: dynamics of public responses to automated vehicles. Transp. Res. Part C: Emerg. Technol. **129**, 103271 (2021)
7. Degani, A., Heymann, M.: Formal verification of human-automation interaction. Hum. Factors **44**(1), 28–43 (2002)
8. Deng, Q., et al.: Prediction performance of lane changing behaviors: a study of combining environmental and eye-tracking data in a driving simulator. IEEE Trans. Intell. Transp. Syst. **21**(8), 3561–3570 (2019)
9. Zhao, C., et al.: A comparative study of state-of-the-art driving strategies for autonomous vehicles. Accid. Anal. Prev. **150**, 105937 (2021)
10. Gold, C., Happee, R., Bengler, K.: Modeling take-over performance in level 3 conditionally automated vehicles. Accid. Anal. Prev. **116**, 3–13 (2018)
11. McDonald, A.D., et al.: Toward computational simulations of behavior during automated driving takeovers: a review of the empirical and modeling literatures. Hum. Factors **61**(4), 642–688 (2019)
12. Du, N., et al.: Predicting driver takeover performance in conditionally automated driving. Accid. Anal. Prev. **148**, 105748 (2020)
13. Lee, D.N.: A theory of visual control of braking based on information about time-to-collision. Perception **5**(4), 437–459 (1976)
14. Ayoub, J., et al.: Predicting driver takeover time in conditionally automated driving. IEEE Trans. Intell. Transp. Syst. (2022)
15. Lee, J.D., et al.: Designing for people: an introduction to human factors engineering. CreateSpace (2017)
16. Schewe, F., Vollrath, M.: Visualizing the autonomous vehicle's maneuvers–does an ecological interface help to increase the hedonic quality and safety? Transport. Res. F: Traffic Psychol. Behav. **79**, 11–22 (2021)

The Development of China Automotive Human-Computer Interaction

Ruilin Ouyang, Chaomin Ma[✉], and Hao Tan

Hunan University, Changsha 410006, Hunan, China
macm@hnu.edu.cn

Abstract. Since the first automobile appeared in China, the automobile has undergone changes not only in appearance and driving methods, but also in the interaction between the driver and the car. With the advent of new energy and intelligence, the diversity of automotive HCI (human-computer interaction) modes has rapidly expanded. The automobile has moved beyond being just a traditional mode of transportation, becoming a "third space" for people after their homes and offices. To understand the past and present of automotive HCI in China, this paper shares insights into the evolution of automotive HCI in China. This study collects seven representative cases of automotive HCI, adopting a historical research approach, collecting secondary data related to the cases in the form of text and video, and analyzing and comparing them longitudinally to draw conclusions. This study provides a historical review of the development of automotive HCI in China, highlighting the trends and key points in the development of the industry. This research can be seen as a historical review of the development of automotive HCI in China and provides some information and academic references for automotive HCI practitioners.

Keywords: Automotive Industry · Human-Computer Interaction · Historical research · China

1 Introduction

Today, user demand for products is increasingly shifting from availability to ease of use, from functional use to user experience, a trend positively correlated with technological development. The remarkable progress and breakthroughs in new energy and intelligent technologies have also benefited the automobile industry. Around 2014, new energy and intelligent technologies began to play a significant role in the automobile industry. Designers applied different interaction methods to the interior of cars and created the "third space" after one's home and office.

Human-Computer Interaction (HCI) was first proposed by Stuart K. Card, Allen Newel [1], among others, and is an interdisciplinary field of study concerned with the relationship between systems and users, with the goal of making systems both user-friendly and easy to use. Since the invention of computers, humans and computers have been interacting, and the history of HCI is the history of humans adapting to

P.-L. P. Rau (Ed.): HCII 2023, LNCS 14023, pp. 417–429, 2023.
https://doi.org/10.1007/978-3-031-35939-2_31

machines and machines adapting to humans. In the early days, vehicles were merely modes of transportation and their interiors and interaction were relatively simple. With the widespread application of computer technology in the transportation industry and the continuous development of network technology in vehicle information technology, the internal space of vehicles, HCI operation, and interaction are undergoing revolutionary changes 1. Undeniably, the development of the interaction field from the last century to 2022 has brought revolutionary changes to the automotive industry, and the way people interact with cars has changed from traditional physical buttons to touchscreens and now to multi-modal interaction such as voice interaction. More significant changes are to come.

Although some of these changes may already be known to seasoned automotive HCI designers, systematic documentation of these developments is still crucial. This not only bridges the gap between experienced interaction designers and newcomers, but also promotes academic discussions on the evolution of automotive HCI. In addition, as it provides an analysis of the main developments in this field, practitioners in the automotive HCI industry will also find this research interesting. This work will also be of use to academic workers, especially those in the fields of interaction design, automotive HCI, and artificial intelligence.

In this study, we introduce seven representative models in the field of automotive HCI in China, presented chronologically: Hongqi CA71, CHERYFENGYUN, Roewe 350, Volvo XC90, NIO ES8, Traum SEEK5, and WM EX5. A synopsis of automotive information is provided for each model, detailing key interaction modes and innovative patterns, with a final summary of interaction modes. Empirical evidence of their impact is given for the majority of the models. This study is not exhaustive in its scope, as it does not encompass all models that have made significant advancements and innovations within the automotive Human-Computer Interaction industry. However, it provides a valuable foundation and direction for future research.

2 Method

This section describes the key methodology and techniques employed in this study. The methodology of the selected method is first discussed, drawing upon relevant academic resources and previous research examples. Next, the application of the method in this study is described. In this study, a historical research methodology was employed to examine the evolution and transformations of the object of investigation over time. The temporal dimension of social research design, as discussed by Feng 2 in his work on social research methods, is a crucial aspect that can be subdivided into cross-sectional and longitudinal research. The latter, also known as a tracking study, entails the collection of data at multiple points in time to describe the development of a phenomenon and explore the relationships between various phenomena. Based on this definition, longitudinal research was deemed appropriate for the current study. Among various longitudinal research methods, the trend study approach was selected. This method summarizes lateral research at different periods to reveal patterns of change over time. The present study applies the trend study approach to the examination of the interaction design in the Chinese automotive industry, which constitutes the subject of investigation in place of the "social phenomenon".

In the aforementioned article by Xiaotian Feng, it is posited that the methods of data collection in longitudinal studies can be classified into four categories, namely survey studies, experimental studies, literature studies, and field survey studies [4]. In this study, experimental and field investigation methods are difficult to employ. This is due to the objective of the study, which is the automotive HCI, particularly in past vehicles. Many of the vehicles mentioned in the following text have been discontinued or have become symbolic memorabilia that are not displayed to the public. As a result, the method of literature studies was adopted. According to Feng, literature refers to any form of information that pertains to the phenomenon being studied, including but not limited to text materials, and is referred to as secondary data2. The secondary data analysis approach entails the re-analysis and reconstruction of previously collected data [5]. In the context of this study, the secondary data consists of materials and information gathered by journalists and researchers on the seven aforementioned HCI in automobiles, including video, sound, images, and text. In this study, the trend study methodology will be employed to assemble and analyze secondary data.

2.1 AutoHome

Before discussing the development of automotive HCI, it is important to consider the data source AutoHome, as the majority of the quantifiable data utilized in this study is obtained from this source. AutoHome is an online platform that is utilized by automobile enthusiasts for the purpose of evaluating, discussing, and trading various vehicles. The database of AutoHome encompasses over 55,000 automobile models, making it the largest automobile database available at the time of writing this article. As a result, nearly all quantitative data is extracted from the database of AutoHome.

However, due to the characteristics of the AutoHome community, it possesses certain limitations. While AutoHome has administrators to review and monitor all uploaded information, this does not ensure the reliability of the database. A recent study indicated that the accuracy of drug information on a community-run database, Wikipedia, was $99.7\% \pm 0.2\%$ when compared to textbook data, yet its completeness was relatively low at $83.8 \pm 1.5\%$4. As such, AutoHome's database may contain errors in the completeness of its data, primarily in the data of extremely rare vehicle models. The most likely impact on this study would be that the number of published vehicle models within a certain range may be lower than the actual number when citing it. However, if the vehicle model is not present in the AutoHome database, it may have minimal impact on the entire industry.

2.2 Study Case

The second issue addressed in this study is the identification of the vehicle models that have shaped the development of automotive HCI in China. This study aims to select those vehicles that have driven a marked shift in automotive HCI design or have been pioneers in a specific stage of automotive HCI evolution. As mentioned in the introduction, this work does not seek to categorize all vehicles with high impact, but rather considers that without the discussed vehicles, the Chinese automotive industry would be quite different.

As an example, the NIO ES8, which will be discussed later. The NIO ES8 is the first mass-produced vehicle to have an in-car artificial intelligence system, making the car's voice interaction emotional and intelligent. Prior to the NIO ES8, these ideas had never been used in domestic mass-produced vehicle models. With the release of the NIO ES8, emotional intelligent voice assistants became very popular in the automotive market. However, for a vehicle, its impact does not necessarily prove its representativeness. For example, the Wuling Hongguang topped the sales list of AutoHome due to its extremely high cost-effectiveness and solid quality, but it was not particularly influential in terms of interaction, so such vehicle models do not have representativeness.

2.3 Data Collection

In this step, a comprehensive search was performed on the "interaction" and "interior" information of seven representative car on AutoHome. Interaction in early cars was considered a subdiscipline of human factors engineering, and many reports grouped interaction and interior together, thus the "interior" will also be a key piece of information in our search. Reports, news, interviews, journals, videos, user comments, and blogs related to the interaction and interior of the seven cars on AutoHome will be considered as data for this study. However, it is essential to review the data prior to collection to ensure its validity and credibility. The data obtained may be complex and disorganized. It is necessary to extract the content relevant to the research theme, with a focus on key terms such as "interaction design," "interior design," "center console," "HMI (human-machine interface)," and others.

2.4 Data Analysis

Subsequent to the data collection process, a thorough analysis of all valid data will be conducted, drawing upon both longitudinal and trend-based studies. The data will be seg- mented into seven distinct temporal intervals.: Hongqi CA71 1958, CHERYFENGYUN 1999, ROEWE 350 2011, Volvo XC90 2016, NIO ES8 2017, Traum SEEK5 2018, WM EX5 2018, and compared in a sequential manner aimed at uncovering and discovering changes in developmental trends. As emphasized by Feng Xiaotian2, a key factor in trend studies is that comparisons across time points must be directed towards the same research content. To ensure meaningful comparison, it is imperative that the questions posed at each temporal interval are strictly equivalent. Deviations in the questions posed would render comparison unfeasible. This study will undertake a detailed examination of two particular queries within each of the seven vehicle model cases.
1. What is the interaction method for this car?
2. How does this interaction work in this car?
Each automotive case will answer these two questions, as depicted in Fig. 1.

Trend Studies of China Automotive HMI Development

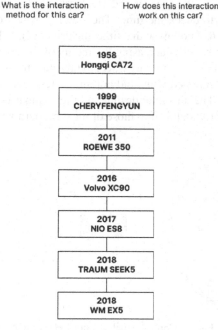

Fig. 1. Research framework

3 Automotive HCI

3.1 HongqiCA72

The Hongqi CA72 is the first car produced in the People's Republic of China since its establishment. The designation "CA" represents "China Automobile," and the number "72" indicates the vehicle category code for passenger cars. The "2" in "72" represents the second generation of the vehicle model. Given the nascent state of China's automotive industry at the time, the Hongqi CA72 was designed and developed based on the Chrysler C69 model, while incorporating elements of Chinese cultural influence in addition to preserving the basic design foundation of the original prototype.

The Hongqi CA72 is also the first numbered sedan in China and was designed as a state limousine, representing the highest level of Chinese automobile design at the time. In 2018, it won the President's Trophy award at the Pebble Beach Concours d'Elegance, becoming the first Chinese model to compete and win at the prestigious event since its inception in 1950. Subsequent design of the Shanghai sedan and other sedans were largely influenced by the Hongqi CA72.

The HCI during this time period was merely based on the arrangement of buttons and screens, as per the driver's posture and operating habits, due to the limited number of operational and feedback projects involved. Figure 2 depicts the central control layout of the Hongqi CA71. Area A comprises the mechanical dashboard and clock, which integrate four instruments for the driver's ease in monitoring the driving status. Area B constitutes the "Global" radio, which can be adjusted through a knob to change the frequency. Area C houses the speaker and clock, primarily intended for the passenger in the co-driver's seat to check the time. The steering wheel of the car is very large. Because of the limited technology at that time, the driver can only save the effort needed to rotate the steering wheel by increasing the radius of the steering wheel. A rearview mirror is also located above the steering wheel to facilitate the driver's gear viewing. The air conditioning unit, equipped with cold/hot air, is designed in the lower right corner of the steering wheel. The air outlet design and the manner of adjusting the direction through a knob are nearly identical to those of most modern vehicles.

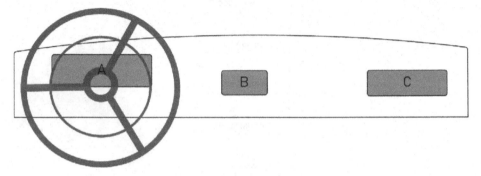

Fig. 2. Control panel layout of HongqiCA72.

3.2   CHERYFENGYUN

On December 18th, 1999, the first Chery automobile, the CHERYFENGYUN, rolled off the production line. CHERYFENGYUN was officially launched at the beginning of 2001, and sales boomed once it was introduced, selling 28,000 units in its first year. CHERYFENGYUN was one of the few vehicles independently developed by China in that era. For a long time prior to the arrival of CHERYFENGYUN, the Chinese automobile market was dominated by the "three old things" (the three most commonly used automobiles) - Jetta, Santana, and Fukang, all of which were developed abroad and produced in China after joint ventures.

With CHERYFENGYUN, the way of HCI inside the automobile cockpit also started to become rich. During this period, the control of the automobile mainly relied on a large number of physical switch buttons, which were arranged around the driver, as shown in Fig. 3. Area A is the dashboard, which displays driving conditions. Area B is the center console screen, which only displays some information from the radio, and the majority of the area accommodates a large number of physical interaction buttons. Area C is three knobs that control the air conditioning system, controlling parameters such as air conditioning temperature. The physical button incorporates ergonomic design principles and employs diverse haptic techniques, including pressing, tapping, and rotating, to demarcate discrete regions and maximize the familiarity of the driver.

Although physical buttons are the most primitive interaction mode, they are the most reliable way inside the vehicle, and even today, physical buttons are still used in parts of the vehicle with higher safety, such as engine start, parking, and door switch. In order to facilitate blind operation of the vehicle, many modern screen-based interactions have incorporated physical button design.

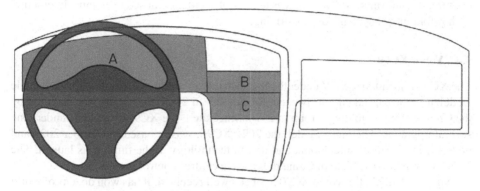

Fig. 3. Control panel layout of CHERYFENGYUN.

3.3   Roewe 350

The Roewe 350, a compact car introduced by the SAIC Group at the end of 2011, was equipped with the iVoka voice interaction system, the first system capable of Chinese voice interaction. Since then, the system has undergone continuous upgrades. The iVoka 3.0, launched in 2013, was awarded the Annual Car Internet Product Innovation Award with a first-place overall score at the first China Car Internet Salon held on October 10, 2013. Through interaction with the voice-controlled iVoka, entertainment interaction between the driver and the car can be achieved, including functions such as navigation, radio listening, and weather inquiry. Like the Siri voice assistant on the iPhone 4S, iVoka can also engage in casual conversation with the driver.

The introduction of the iVoka voice interaction system in the Roewe 350 makes it a milestone in automotive HCI design, as previously mentioned, paving the way for Chinese voice interaction. This is revolutionary in automotive HCI design. Prior to the Roewe 350, the interaction mode between the driver and the car was still dependent on a large number of physical buttons. The Roewe 350 challenged this concept and thoroughly changed the automobile industry in the process. Currently, the in-car voice interaction function has become a standard feature in the cabins of Chinese passenger cars.

The in-car voice interaction system, also known as the voice-controlled infotainment system, plays a key role in improving the driving experience. It allows the driver and passengers to interact with the car's functions using voice commands instead of manual control, such as navigation, music, climate control, and other connected services. The system typically includes a microphone and a speaker, which are integrated into the car's dashboard or built into the steering wheel.

Voice interaction is considered the most natural interaction mode in in-car scenarios, and there are generally three scenarios: quick access, voice-activated control, and voice-controlled entertainment. The prospect of voice interaction in automobiles lies primarily in the ability to minimize driver distraction, thus enhancing safety. By enabling hands-free control, drivers can focus their attention on the road while adjusting the car's settings or obtaining information. This reduces the risk of accidents caused by manual interaction with infotainment systems during driving.

3.4 Volvo XC90

The XC90 is a mid-size SUV under the Swedish luxury automotive brand, Volvo. It made its debut in the capital city of Sweden, Stockholm, in 2014. The brand was acquired by the Chinese Geely Holding Group in 2010. Since then, the XC90 model has undergone several upgrades. The latest model, the 2022 XC90, was released in October 2022 and boasts leading safety, interaction, and design technology at the time of its launch. The XC90 was the first vehicle in China to feature a central control touchscreen.

Since its launch, the Volvo XC90 has been well received. It has won dozens of world awards such as the 2016 NACOTY (North American Car of the Year), The best tech cars of CES (Consumer Electronics Show) 2016, Top Safety Pick+rating from IIHS (the American Insurance Institute for Highway Safety), 2016 Utility Vehicle of the Year Award.

The HMI system of the Volvo XC90, Sensus, has garnered recognition for its innovative design, being awarded the title of "Most Innovative HMI System" at the 2015 Car HMI Concept & Systems conference held in Berlin. The development team behind Sensus sought to revolutionize the driving experience by eschewing traditional physical buttons in favor of a large tablet-style touch screen, a head-up display, and thumb controls integrated into the steering wheel.

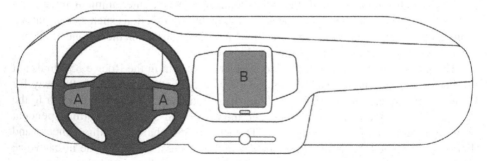

Fig. 4. Control panel layout of Volvo XC90.

As depicted in Fig. 4, the touchscreen in Zone A has replaced the traditional buttons in the center console. All operations can be completed through simple finger swiping by the driver. A "Home" key similar to that of the iPhone 4 is located below the touchscreen, enabling one-touch return functionality. Information, navigation, and media are placed at a highly visible position, making it easy for the driver to view them. The controls for mobile phone, application icons, and climate control are located at a lower position, offering both accessibility and comfort in touch. Furthermore, the information architecture of this interaction system is flattened, reducing unnecessary actions for the driver. When an interaction occurs and one functional module expands on the touchscreen, other functional modules are compressed but still visible and readily accessible. This makes the touchscreen highly user-friendly, eliminating the need to go through the main menu when switching between functions.

The central panel interacts with an adaptive digital instrument cluster positioned in front of the driver, ensuring that critical information is displayed in the driver's line of sight via the head-up display located on the lower portion of the windshield. This design facilitates the driver's access to essential information without the need to divert attention from the road ahead. Furthermore, the user interface incorporates thumb-reach controls on the steering wheel and advanced voice control functionality, reducing driver distractions and promoting driving safety.

The implementation of a touch screen affords a more aesthetically pleasing and intuitive means of automotive HCI, as compared to traditional physical controls. In using this touch screen, drivers are unable to rely solely on their sense of touch for automotive HCI. The variable information displayed on the screen and virtual buttons make it difficult for drivers to rely on touch alone to determine the information being controlled. As a result, automotive HCI has shifted from being primarily touch-based to being visually driven to control the vehicle.

3.5 NIOES8

The NIO ES8 is a sport utility vehicle (SUV) manufactured by NIO, powered solely by electricity. The model designation, "ES8," reflects its place as the eighth model in NIO's performance product range, where "E" stands for "Electric" and "S" for "SUV." With the introduction of the ES8 came the world's first mass-produced in-car artificial intelligence system, NOMI, which offers drivers an intuitive and personalized experience through voice commands for controlling various in-car functions, such as music, navigation, and air conditioning 6. NOMI has received widespread recognition for its intelligent interaction among vehicle owners and NIO enthusiasts.

Currently, Nomi has become one of NIO's unique labels and has a massive fan base. In addition to the Nomi robot itself, NIO has also launched different styles of small hats for Nomi to wear, as well as merch with Nomi printed on it, etc. Currently, Geely, BYD and other manufacturers have launched voice assistant systems that are benchmarked against Nomi.

In the NIO ES8 and all following NIO models, the NIO has left the most central position in front of the cockpit to NOMI6, thus affecting the overall layout and size of the NIO's interior center console. The appearance of Nomi is purely circular in shape, with a high-resolution screen as Nomi's "face" that swings 30° up and down and 50° left and right; In its image, NOMI adopts a minimalist approach, incorporating eyes but no mouth, to mitigate the "Valley of Terror" effect associated with AI. In 2018, NIO introduced NOMI Halo, a second product that uses a halo of light and sound to interact with the user's voice.

The NIO ES8 has been named a "role model" for in-car voice assistants because of its unique Nomi system. More than functionality, Nomi focuses on emotionality. As an artificial intelligence entity, NOMI is able to demonstrate subtle interactions through voice, expressions and movements that virtual assistants cannot accomplish. For example, consider a scenario in which a user engages with the screen through physical contact. In response, NOMI can see what the user is trying to do on top of the screen by slightly adjusting its head orientation. When the user takes his hand back, NOMI's head will be raised again6.

NIO's HCI design with Nomi's emotional voice assistant enables continuous communication between the driver and the vehicle and regulates the atmosphere of the cockpit. Emotional interaction not only enables a more well-rounded development of smart cars and a better user experience for drivers, but also reduces the chance of traffic accidents by improving driver's mood.

3.6   TraumSEEK5

The Traum SEEK5 is a midsize crossover SUV produced by Zotye Auto under the Traum sub-brand and debuted in summer 2018. It is the first produced auto with the intelligent gesture system in China. This system allows drivers and passengers to control various functions and features in their cars through simple hand gestures, without the need for physical buttons or touchscreens.

In-car gesture systems work by using cameras and sensors to detect hand movements and translate them into commands. The Traum SEEK5 gesture control recognition area is located directly below the air vents in the center console of the vehicle, and the vehicle automatically recognizes gestures made by the driver in this area. The gesture recognition distance is set between 15 cm and 35 cm depending on the user's position in the cabin, and the gesture interaction system recognizes eight gestures in the Traum SEEK 5, mainly around multimedia controls. For example, a driver is able to adjust the volume of their music by waving their hand up or down, or switch between navigation screens by making a sweeping gesture.

One of the key benefits of in-car gesture systems is the increased safety they provide. By eliminating the need for drivers to physically touch buttons or screens, these systems reduce the risk of distractions and improve the overall safety of the vehicle. Additionally, gesture control can provide a more ergonomic and intuitive way of interacting with in-car technology, reducing the cognitive load on drivers and making it easier for them to concentrate on the road. Another advantage of in-car gesture systems is that they allow for greater customization and personalization. Drivers can choose from a range of gesture commands, or even create their own, to control various functions in their vehicle. This makes it easier for drivers to find a control scheme that suits their individual needs and preferences.

Interaction gestures in cars are different from those in mobile. The interaction of car not only needs to consider the operation of fingers, but also the high frequency use of wrist. In addition, since the interaction screen is fixed in the car, it is necessary to avoid some inconvenient gestures, such as two-finger upward sliding and upward pushing postures.

3.7 WM EX5

The WM (Weltmeister) EX5 is a compact crossover SUV produced by the Chinese electric vehicle manufacturer, WM Motor, under the Weltmeister brand. WM EX5 integrates window interaction, face recognition, and automatic driving. The car was launched in 2018 and received a great market response, with orders reaching 10,000 two months after launch. In the same year, the WM EX5 won the 2018 iF Design Award, becoming the world's only winning electric mass-production model.

The WM EX5 is the first vehicle to feature window interaction. Prior to this, external automotive HCI have been focused on the utilization of digital car keys and changes in vehicle lights. WM EX5 is the first to incorporate windows into the realm of external automotive HCI. The window interaction functionality of the WM EX5 boasts different modes, encompassing three distinct scenarios, capable of displaying relevant information prior to and after boarding the vehicle. For example, when a user customizes their navigation, the vehicle's windows will recommend a charging plan based on the proximity of the itinerary and display relevant information regarding battery life and mileage. When an account is detected, the windows will display the account name, and in the event of multiple accounts detected, the driver can select the account of their choice.

The WM EX5 is among the first batch of vehicles in China to feature facial recognition technology. This technology is integrated with Weltmeister ID and the driver's facial information, with the facial recognition camera located behind the steering wheel. Upon the driver's entry into the vehicle, the camera automatically activates and scans the driver's face for recognition, triggering the switch of car system and gauge information to the corresponding driver and adjusting the in-car equipment, such as the rearview mirror, seat, and ambient light, to the driver's preferred settings. In the event that the current driver is not the registered owner of the vehicle, the car will automatically initiate privacy mode, masking all associated music, map, and phone information to prevent unauthorized access by others.

The WM EX5 is equipped with an assistance driving function, with its switch button located on the left side of the steering wheel. Upon activation, icons for cruise preparation and distance setting are displayed on the dashboard. The driver can set the cruising speed. Upon activation of the assistance driving system, the vehicle emits a prompt sound of "beep" and the driving display on the dashboard undergoes corresponding changes. Currently, the L2 assisted driving system installed in WM EX5 can only provide driving assistance but not Full automation, with the driving still primarily under the control of the driver. The system does not have strong feedback upon deactivation, requiring the driver to constantly monitor road information and keep a firm grip on the steering wheel.

4 Discussion and Conclusion

This study showcases seven representative vehicle models that demonstrate the evolution of automotive HCI design in China. For each model, their contributions are described and their impacts are exemplified. By showcasing them, we aim for future automotive

HCI designers to learn from these design breakthroughs and improve their own designs. Moreover, there is a scarcity of academic literature on the history of automotive HCI design, despite its significant impact on the entire automotive industry. Finally, by establishing the history of automotive HCI in China, we can help preserve the rich history of automotive HCI.

During the early stages of development of the Chinese automobile industry, due to the absence of industrial capabilities, a majority of vehicle models were modeled after those produced abroad. During the mid-stages, some interactive features, such as the integrated central display interactive mode of the Volvo XC90, were first introduced by foreign automobile manufacturers. Benefiting from the new energy and intelligence policy put forth by the Chinese government in 2014, the Chinese automobile industry rapidly developed, resulting in a concentration of representative interactive vehicle models appearing after 2014.

Although these vehicle models are presented individually, the designs of various vehicle models are interdependent, with many drawings inspiration from advancements made in previous vehicles, including those not explicitly mentioned. Nearly all contemporary vehicles can be traced back to one or more of the models discussed here. A notable example is the BYD-Song PLUS, which currently ranks first on AutoHome, and draws inspiration from various models, such as the Roewe 350 for voice interaction, the NIO ES8 for emotionalized artificial intelligence, the Volvo XC90 for integrated central control display, and the WM EX5 for face recognition.

In conclusion, reviewing the history of the development of Automotive HCI will always be significant, as the development of automotive HCI design is largely a gradual process. By reviewing its past, designers can gain a deeper appreciation for the rich history of Automotive HCI and leverage this understanding to drive future innovations and advancements in the field.

References

1. Olson, G.M., Olson, J.S.: Human-computer interaction: psychological aspects of the human use of computing. Annu. Rev. Psychol. **54**, 491–516 (2003)
2. Becker, S., Hanna, P., Wagner, V.: Human machine interface design in modern vehicles. In: Crolla, D., Foster, D.E., Kobayashi, T., Vaughan, N. (eds.) Encyclopedia of Automotive Engineering, pp. 1–16. Wiley, Chichester, UK (2014). https://doi.org/10.1002/978111835 4179.auto248
3. Feng, X.: Social Research Methods, pp. 81–87. China Renmin University Press (2001)
4. Feng, X.: Social Research Methods, pp. 213–214. China Renmin University Press (2001)
5. Neuman, W.L.: Social Research Methods: Qualitative and Quantitative Approaches. Pearson/Allyn and Bacon, Boston (2006)
6. Reilly, T., Jackson, W., Berger, V., Candelario, D.: Accuracy and completeness of drug information in Wikipedia medication monographs. J. Am. Pharm. Assoc. **57**, 193-196.e1 (2017). https://doi.org/10.1016/j.japh.2016.10.007
7. What is NOMI? Here's everything you need to know – CnEVPost. https://cnevpost.com/2021/03/30/what-is-nomi-heres-everything-you-need-to-know/. Accessed 5 Feb 2023
8. Carsten, O., Martens, M.H.: How can humans understand their automated cars? HMI principles, problems and solutions. Cogn. Technol. Work **21**(1), 3–20 (2018). https://doi.org/10.1007/s10111-018-0484-0

9. Lu, S., et al.: The effect on subjective alertness and fatigue of three colour temperatures in the spacecraft crew cabin. In: Stanton, N. (ed.) AHFE 2021. LNNS, vol. 270, pp. 632–639. Springer, Cham (2021). https://doi.org/10.1007/978-3-030-80012-3_74

10. Stanton, N. (ed.): AHFE 2021. LNNS, vol. 270. Springer, Cham (2021). https://doi.org/10.1007/978-3-030-80012-3

11. 王兴宝, 雷琴辉, 梅林海, 张亚, 邢猛: 汽车语音交互技术发展趋势综述 (2021)

12. 谭浩, 赵江洪, 王巍: 汽车人机交互界面设计研究. 汽车工程学报 (2012)

13. 谭浩, 赵丹华, 赵江洪: 面向复杂交互情境的汽车人机界面设计研究. 包装工程 33, 5 (2012)

14. Stevens, A.: Safety of driver interaction with in-vehicle information systems. Proc. Inst. Mech. Eng. Part D J. Automobile Eng. **214**, 639–644 (2000). https://doi.org/10.1243/0954407001527501

15. de Clercq, K., Dietrich, A., Núñez Velasco, J.P., de Winter, J., Happee, R.: External human-machine interfaces on automated vehicles: effects on pedestrian crossing decisions. Hum Factors **61**, 1353–1370 (2019). https://doi.org/10.1177/0018720819836343

16. Li, H., Lo, C.-H., Smith, A., Yu, Z.: The development of virtual production in film industry in the past decade. In: Rau, P.-L.P. (ed.) Cross-Cultural Design. Applications in Learning, Arts, Cultural Heritage, Creative Industries, and Virtual Reality, pp. 221–239. Springer, Cham (2022). https://doi.org/10.1007/978-3-031-06047-2_16

Investigating Control Method of User Interaction with Multi-device in Smart Home

Yan Shi and Na Liu[✉]

School of Economics and Management, Beijing University of Posts and Telecommunications, Beijing, China
{syan,liuna18}@bupt.edu.cn

Abstract. In order to better understand smart home users' preference for control methods, this study focused on user interaction with multiple smart home devices in daily home use scenarios. This study designed a within-subject experiment with control method as the independent variable and perceived ease of use, perceived usefulness, attitude, intention to use, and satisfaction as dependent variables. The results showed that the centralized control method had a higher positive effect on users' perceived ease of use, perceived usefulness, intention to use, and attitude compared to the decentralized control method, but users were more satisfied with the decentralized control method. These findings provide implications for smart home design in terms of control methods.

Keywords: Smart Home · Multi-device · Control Method

1 Introduction

Smart home refers to a home system with various information and communication technologies such as intelligent automatic systems and household appliances [1]. However, the current smart home systems that people commonly use lack a central control management system or have only subsystem control management systems, and the systems cannot be interconnected as well as unified central management due to the diversity of smart home system protocols. In this context, two types of smart home control methods, namely centralized control and decentralized control have been mainly used when people interact with multiple smart home devices.

The centralized control method refers to that users interact with one intelligent terminal for commands, which then assigns and interacts with each smart home device for tasks; the decentralized control method refers to that users interact with each smart home device directly for commands respectively when they interact with multiple smart home devices.

Previous study has shown that the quality of user-device interaction may vary depending on whether the user interacts directly or indirectly with the device [2]. Direct and indirect interactions with multiple information sources are more likely to be perceived positively than indirect and mediated single information sources for information processing [3]. In addition, when smart devices are distant from the user or used infrequently, users want to interact with a single agent representing such devices [4].

© The Author(s), under exclusive license to Springer Nature Switzerland AG 2023
P.-L. P. Rau (Ed.): HCII 2023, LNCS 14023, pp. 430–439, 2023.
https://doi.org/10.1007/978-3-031-35939-2_32

The different ways in which users control their smart homes can have an impact on their experiences and feelings. For example, previous studies on the interaction styles of smart homes have shown that unmediated interactions are more effective in internal social connections and mediated interactions are more effective in external social connections [4]. It has also been found that the presence of physical attributes during interaction with smart chatbots has a positive effect on the user experience, improving the interactivity of the process and the comfort level of the user [5]. Thus, a centralized interaction method contains an intelligent terminal that can be considered as an interactable entity that can also influence the user experience. We infer that the control method for smart homes could affect on user satisfaction and intention to use.

The technology acceptance model (TAM) [6] is often used to explain user acceptance of new information technology. Based on TAM, this study used perceived ease of use, perceived usefulness, attitude, and intention to use as the dependent variables. In previous studies, researchers have described intention to use as the behavioral response of users to the persuasion of a smart object, i.e., whether users are willing to accept the advice given by the smart object and the degree of acceptance [5]. Extant research focused on interface icons [8], factors affecting intention to use [9], perceived risks [10], smart home technology systems [11], software control [12], smart home Internet of things security [13] and energy conservation [14]. Based on user satisfaction, Yi Liu et al. Proposed a new family load scheduling framework for family energy management based on pricing, which can minimize energy consumption while fully considering the comfort preferences and lifestyle of residents [15]. Studies have also explored the relevant factors that affect the sustainable use of smart homes by users: the service quality and perceived usefulness of smart home services have a positive impact on user satisfaction, and higher satisfaction in turn contributes to the formation of user habits, thus enhancing the possibility of continuous use of smart homes [16]. It showed that social participation is necessary to achieve the satisfaction or enjoyment brought by sharing activities, that is, social participation brought by interaction with devices in the smart home scene will improve satisfaction [17]. Interaction with various objects can establish a certain friendship, which can enable individuals to experience positive feelings and ultimately affect satisfaction [18]. Processes with interactive attributes have been shown to affect outcomes, such as interpersonal attractiveness and satisfaction [19]. However, research on the multi device control mode of smart homes is limited.

In summary, this study aimed to investigate the influence of the control method of user interaction with multiple devices on user satisfaction and intention to use in the smart home usage scenario.

2 Methods

2.1 Participants

A total of 150 valid samples were obtained for this formal experiment (Table 1). The participants came from various provinces in China, with a wide geographical distribution. In terms of age, the mean age of the participants was 30.3 years old; in terms of education, 76.33% of the participants had a bachelor's degree, 12.67% had a college degree, 10.67% had a master's degree, and 1.33% had a high school degree; in terms of occupation,

38.67% of the participants worked in private enterprises, 32.67% worked in state-owned enterprises, 12.67% were students, 8% were institutions, 3.33% were foreign-owned enterprises, 2.67% were self-employed businessmen, and 2% were civil servants.

In terms of smart home use experience, all participants have smart home use experience, among which the frequency of more than one year is 119, accounting for 79.33%; the frequency of six months to one year is 24, accounting for 16.0%; in terms of smart home use frequency, the frequency of at least once a day is 119, accounting for 79.33%; the frequency of at least once a week is 28 The frequency of using smart home was 28, and the percentage was 18.67%, that is, 98% of the participants used smart home more frequently.

Table 1. Demographic information of participants

Item	Category	Frequency	Percentage (%)	Cumulative percentage (%)
Gender	Female	76	50.67	50.67
	Male	74	49.33	100
Age	31–40 years old	69	46	46
	21–30 years old	69	46	92
	0–20 years	5	3.33	95.33
	51–60 years old	3	2	97.33
	41–50 years old	3	2	99.33
	Over 60 years old	1	0.67	100
Academic qualifications	Bachelor Degree	113	75.33	75.33
	College Degree	19	12.67	88
	Master's Degree	16	10.67	98.67
	High School	2	1.33	100
Career	Private enterprises	58	38.67	38.67
	State-owned enterprises	49	32.67	71.33
	Students	19	12.67	84
	Business Unit	12	8	92
	Foreign-owned enterprises	5	3.33	95.33
	Individual Businesses	4	2.67	98
	Civil Service	3	2	100

2.2 Design

This experiment adopted a within-subject experimental design with multi-device control as the independent variable. It had two levels, namely centralized control and decentralized control, where participants will be randomly assigned to complete two trials consisting of centralized and decentralized control. The experiment required participants to watch videos of smart home experiences embedded in the questionnaire, and each video watched by the participants was treated as a task completion. After completion each task, participants filled in the corresponding experimental questionnaire.

Centralized: In the experimental task of the centralized control approach, the simulated participants are asked to interact with the smart terminal, e.g., in task B, the user sends commands to the smart terminal to indirectly control multiple smart home devices. In addition, the simulated participants will passively interact with the smart terminal, e.g., in task C, the smart terminal actively asks the user whether to adjust the room light brightness according to the current scene.

Decentralized: In the experimental task of the decentralized control approach, the simulated participants were required to interact with the smart devices directly, e.g., in Task B, the user issued commands to multiple smart devices separately. In addition, the simulated participants in the decentralized control approach will actively interact with smart devices, e.g., in Task A, the user enters the home and actively issues commands to smart home devices such as lights, air conditioners, and water dispensers separately.

2.3 Procedure

The experiment completed the task scenario building using PowerPoint and the questionnaire platform. Specifically, after determining the interaction scenario, add the voice synthesized by Balabolka voice software as the command issuing and response between the user and the intelligent device, and use the animation in PowerPoint to implement the command execution of the intelligent device, such as turning on the lights, turning on the TV, and other commands. The slides are played according to the established process and a moderate switching speed. The experimental videos are recorded with the screen recording software of Microsoft Windows system. Six separate experimental tasks (Table 2) correspond to six experimental videos.

Each participant is prompted to complete 6 tasks in turn, and the participants will fill in a corresponding matrix scale after each task to measure the satisfaction and intention to use of the participants.

2.4 Data Analysis

ANOVA was used to analyze the effects of control method on perceived ease of use, perceived usefulness, intention to use, attitude, and satisfaction. All data were analyzed using SPSS 26.0 software, and the significance level was set at 0.05.

Table 2. Experimental tasks

Control method	Specific tasks
Centralized	**Task A:** The user enters the room and experiences the entry device activation procedures already set by the smart terminal (smart audio or smartphone), such as turning on the lights, turning on the air conditioner and the water dispenser self-heating
	Task B: The user issues commands to the smart terminal (Turn on the TV, play music, search for movies and play them, etc.)
	Task C: User processing of suggestions given by the smart terminal (Adjustment of room temperature and lighting according to the scene)
Decentralized	**Task A:** The user enters the room and issues commands to the smart home separately (such as turning on the lights, turning on the air conditioner and heating the water fountain, etc.)
	Task B: The user issues commands to multiple smart devices separately (Turn on the TV, play music, search for movies and play them, etc.)
	Task C: The user chooses whether he/she wants to initiate commands appropriate to the scenario (Adjustment of room temperature and lighting according to the scene)

3   Results

3.1   One-Way ANOVA (Control Approach)

According to the results of the analysis (Fig. 1), for user perceived ease of use, there was a significant difference between the centralized and decentralized control approaches (F $(1, 300) = 26.14$, $p < 0.001$, $\eta^2 = 0.081$), with a Cohen's f value of 0.296, indicating a moderate degree of difference in the quantification of the effect of the data.

In addition, for user perceived usefulness, there was a significant difference between the centralized and decentralized control approaches (F $(1, 300) = 17.16$, $p < 0.001$, $\eta^2 = 0.054$) with a Cohen's f value of 0.24, indicating a small degree of difference in the quantification of the effect of the data (Fig. 2).

For user intention to use, there was a significant difference between the centralized and decentralized control approaches (F $(1, 300) = 29.42$, $p < 0.001$, $\eta^2 = 0.090$) with a Cohen's f value of 0.314 (Fig. 3), indicating a moderate degree of difference in the quantification of the effect of the data.

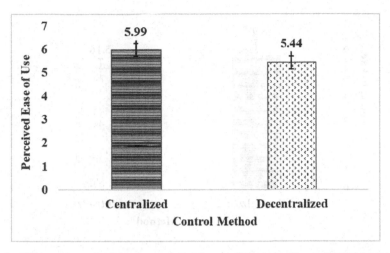

Fig. 1. Effect of control method on perceived ease of use (error line is ±1 standard error)

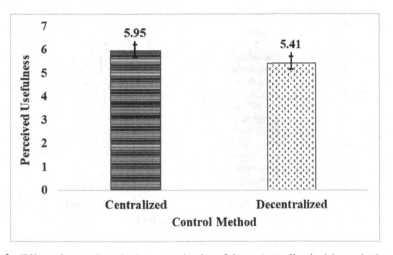

Fig. 2. Effect of control method on perceived usefulness (error line is ±1 standard error)

For user attitudes (Fig. 4), there was a significant difference between the centralized and decentralized control approaches ($F (1, 300) = 17.88, p < 0.001, \eta^2 = 0.057$) with a Cohen's f value of 0.245, indicating a small degree of difference in the quantification of the effect of the data.

For user satisfaction (Fig. 5), there was no significant difference between the centralized and decentralized control methods ($F (1, 300) = 0.93, p = 0.335$).

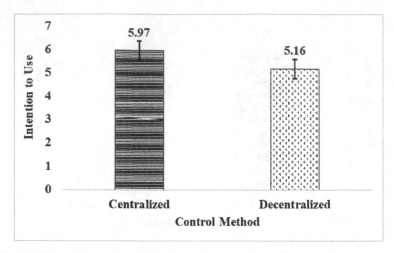

Fig. 3. Effect of control method on intention to use (error line is ±1 standard error)

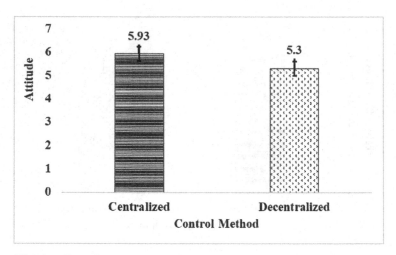

Fig. 4. Effect of control method on attitude (error line is ±1 standard error)

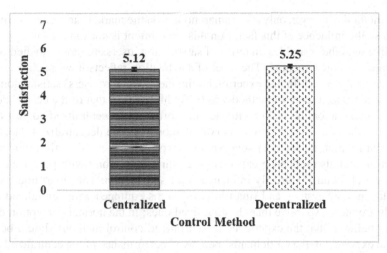

Fig. 5. Effect of control method on user satisfaction (error line is ±1 standard error)

4 Discussion

Overall, in the smart home scenario, users' perceived ease of use, perceived usefulness, intention to use, attitude to use were higher in the process of interacting with multiple devices using the centralized control method, but the decentralized control method scored higher levels than the centralized control method on the variable of satisfaction.

Specifically, perceived ease of use is how easy users perceive it is to use any of the control methods. The centralized control method is easier and simpler for users to use, which is probably due to the fact that the participants have some degree of experience in using smart homes and most of them are more familiar with smart homes due to their higher frequency of use, and therefore their perceived ease of use is lower. On the other hand, according to the technology acceptance model, external variables affect perceived ease of use, i.e., a centralized control approach enhances users' perceived ease of use. For users, a centralized control approach is easier to use than a decentralized one, having a smart terminal that integrates multiple smart home devices, and being able to control multiple devices on one terminal. From the aspect of learning cost, users only need to learn the usage of one smart terminal systematically when using centralized control method, while decentralized control method requires users to learn to master the usage of multiple smart home devices.

In terms of intention to use, from the descriptive statistics, users are much more willing to use centralized control methods than decentralized ones, with a mean difference of 0.81, which is greater than the mean difference of other variables. Combined with attitudes, users believe that centralized control methods are better than decentralized ones in terms of multi-device control. Rational behavior theory [20] suggests that subjective norms and behavioral attitudes combine to influence users' intention to use centralized usage. The subjective norm refers to the influence of the control method usually used by the outside world on individual users, i.e., if the majority of users use the centralized control method, individual users will be more inclined to use the centralized control method. However, only a few smart homes on the market can achieve centralized control, so the influence of this factor on this experiment is not significant.

Unlike the other variables, in terms of satisfaction, users are more satisfied with the decentralized control method. The level of satisfaction reflects how much users like a certain control method. In this experiment, the mean value of users' satisfaction scores for the decentralized control method was 0.134 higher than that of the centralized one, but the concentration interval of satisfaction scores for the centralized control method was higher than the concentration interval of scores for the decentralized one. Expectation confirmation theory [21] suggests that expectations can directly influence user satisfaction and also influence expectation confirmation along with perceived performance, which in turn indirectly influences user satisfaction. The smart home itself is a high technology system, and smart home systems equipped with centralized control methods are more expensive than decentralized ones; in the normal perception of users it is also believed that the experience of centralized control methods should be better. After the experiment, the participants' perceived performance of the centralized control method did not meet their expectations, so the expectation confirmation level was not high and the satisfaction level decreased.

In conclusion, future research can be improved in the following ways. First, optimize the selection of experimental scenes, and let participants choose their preferences for experimental scenes before the experiment, so as to reduce the influence caused by participants' preferences for experimental scenes. Secondly, the offline experimental scenario should be built to include the cutting-edge smart home products available in the market to the greatest extent to enhance the participants' real experience. Finally, we optimize the design of more scientific and reasonable subjective evaluation methods to obtain more accurate and realistic experimental data and obtain more meaningful conclusions and suggestions.

Acknowledgments. This work was supported by a grant from National Natural Science Foundation of China (Project No. 71901033).

References

1. Strese, H., Seidel, U., Knape, T., et al.: Smart home in deutschland: Untersuchung im rahmen der wissenschaftlichen begleitung zum programm next generation media (ngm) des bundesministeriums für wirtschaft und technologie. Institut für Innovation und Technik (iit), Berlin (2010)
2. Kim, K.J.: Interacting socially with the Internet of Things (IoT): effects of source attribution and specialization in human-IoT interaction. J. Comput.-Mediated Commun. 21(6), 420–435 (2016). https://doi.org/10.1111/jcc4.12177
3. Sundar, S.S.: The MAIN Model: A Heuristic Approach to Understanding Technology Effects on Credibility. MacArthur Foundation Digital Media and Learning Initiative, Cambridge (2008)
4. Lee, B., Kwon, O., Lee, I., et al.: Companionship with smart home devices: the impact of social connectedness and interaction types on perceived social support and companionship in smart homes. Comput. Hum. Behav. 75, 922–934 (2017)

5. Ischen, C., Araujo, T., van Noort, G., et al.: "I Am Here to Assist You Today": the role of entity, interactivity and experiential perceptions in Chatbot persuasion. J. Broadcast. Electron. Media **64**(4), 615–639 (2020)

6. Davis, F.D.: Perceived usefulness, perceived ease of use, and user acceptance of information technology. MIS Q. **13**(3), 319–340 (1989)

7. Coskun, A., Kaner, G., Bostan, İ: Is smart home a necessity or a fantasy for the mainstream user? A study on users' expectations of smart household appliances. Int. J. Des. **12**(1), 7–20 (2018)

8. Yu, N., Ouyang, Z., Wang, H., et al.: The effects of smart home interface touch button design features on performance among young and senior users. Int. J. Environ. Res. Public Health **19**(4), 2391 (2022)

9. Pliatsikas, P., Economides, A.A.: Factors influencing intention of Greek consumers to use smart home technology. Appl. Syst. Innov. **5**(1), 26 (2022)

10. Hong, A., Nam, C., Kim, S.: What will be the possible barriers to consumers' adoption of smart home services? Telecommun. Policy **44**(2), 101867 (2020)

11. Robles, R.J., Kim, T.: Applications, systems and methods in smart home technology: A. Int. J. Adv. Sci. Technol. **15**, 37–48 (2010)

12. Piyare, R., Lee, S.R.: Smart home-control and monitoring system using smart phone. ICCA, ASTL **24**, 83–86 (2013)

13. Anthi, E., Williams, L., Słowińska, M., et al.: A supervised intrusion detection system for smart home IoT devices. IEEE Internet Things J. **6**(5), 9042–9053 (2019)

14. Nicholls, L., Strengers, Y., Sadowski, J.: Social impacts and control in the smart home. Nat. Energy **5**(3), 180–182 (2020)

15. Liu, Y., Xiao, L., Yao, G., et al.: Pricing-based demand response for a smart home with various types of household appliances considering customer satisfaction. IEEE Access **7**, 86463–86472 (2019)

16. Gu, W., Bao, P., Hao, W., et al.: Empirical examination of intention to continue to use smart home services. Sustainability **11**(19), 5213 (2019)

17. Rook, K.S.: Social support versus companionship: effects on life stress, loneliness, and evaluations by others. J. Pers. Soc. Psychol. **52**(6), 1132 (1987)

18. Mendelson, M.J., Aboud, F.E.: Measuring friendship quality in late adolescents and young adults: McGill friendship questionnaires. Can. J. Behav. Sci. **31**(2), 130 (1999)

19. Lew, Z., Walther, J.B., Pang, A., et al.: Interactivity in online chat: conversational contingency and response latency in computer-mediated communication. J. Comput.-Mediat. Commun. **23**(4), 201–221 (2018)

20. Fishbein, M., Ajzen, I.: Belief, attitude, intention, and behavior: an introduction to theory and research. Philos. Rhetoric **10**(2) (1977)

21. Oliver, R.L.: A cognitive model of the antecedents and consequences of satisfaction decisions. J. Mark. Res. **17**(4), 460–469 (1980)

Assessing the Cognitive Load Arising from In-Vehicle Infotainment Systems Using Pupil Diameter

Wanni Wei[1], Qing Xue[1], Xiaonan Yang[1(✉)], Hongjiang Du[2], Yahui Wang[3], and Qinglong Tang[2]

[1] Industrial and Systems Engineering Laboratory, School of Mechanical Engineering, Beijing Institute of Technology, Beijing, China
yangxn@bit.edu.cn
[2] Changan Automobile Co., Ltd., Chongqing, China
[3] School of Medical Technology, Beijing Institute of Technology, Beijing, China

Abstract. The purpose of this study is to assess the cognitive load arising from in-vehicle infotainment systems (IVIS) of intelligent connected vehicles (ICVs) by analyzing the changes of pupil diameter of drivers in the simulated driving environment. Cognitive load refers to the amount of mental activity carried out by the working memory of the human brain at any time. The cognitive load here is emphasized by arising from IVIS. Thirty subjects participated in the experiment. The experiment simulated an urban road and asked the subjects to complete three levels of the auditory continuous memory task. Tobii Pro Glasses 3 was used to collect the pupil diameter of drivers, and NASA-TLX was used for subjective evaluation. The results showed that task difficulty level had significant effects on the mental dimension and effort dimension of NASA-TLX, which have been proved by relevant studies to be evaluative dimensions that can reflect cognitive load. In addition, task difficulty level also had a significant effect on the pupil diameter, indicating that the pupil diameter can reflect the cognitive load arising from IVIS. Findings from this study can provide reference and assistance for the design of IVIS.

Keywords: cognitive load · in-vehicle infotainment systems · pupil diameter · NASA-TLX · intelligent connected vehicles

1 Introduction

In-vehicle infotainment systems (IVIS) constitute an important part of automotive human-machine interfaces (HMIs). In most cases, it consists of many screens that can play music, movies and other media, which serve to provide a series of information and entertainment services (e.g., navigation, media, and radio) for the passengers in the vehicle [1, 2]. In recent years, with the rapid development of intelligent connected vehicles (ICVs), a number of IVIS have been added to the smart cockpit to provide a better experience for the drivers. However, the more functions and services provided by IVIS, the drivers need to call more cognitive resources to deal with these large amounts of complex information, thus increasing their cognitive load [3].

P.-L. P. Rau (Ed.): HCII 2023, LNCS 14023, pp. 440–450, 2023.
https://doi.org/10.1007/978-3-031-35939-2_33

When using IVIS, the most important thing is to reduce the cognitive load on the driver while controlling the system [4]. Cognitive load refers to the amount of mental activity carried out by the working memory of the human brain at any time, including intrinsic and extrinsic cognitive load. Intrinsic load describes the use of primary task memory, and it corresponds to the working memory used by people engaged in primary task. Extrinsic load is an unnecessary cognitive load or secondary load, which is accompanied by primary load and has a negative impact on the primary task, making it impossible to complete the task normally. The cognitive load arising from the use of IVIS is actually an extrinsic load. When the extrinsic load exceeds the driver's ability to handle secondary tasks, mental distraction will occur. The consequence of this mental distraction is an increase in the rate of traffic accidents [5]. Therefore, it is particularly important to assess the cognitive load of drivers when using IVIS, which can avoid driving safety hazards caused by excessive cognitive load. Research on driver's cognitive load has shown that real-time information on cognitive load could be used as part of driver assistance systems to warn drivers of possible cognitive overload and thus avoid accidents [6].

Cognitive load can be assessed by monitoring of psychophysiological activities, such as ocular activity [7–9], cardiac activity [10–12], electrodermal activity [13–15] and brain electrical activity [16–18], etc. As an important physiological indicator of cognitive load, pupil diameter has been widely studied [5, 19, 20]. Studies have shown that when people face a challenging cognitive task, their pupils will dilate. This phenomenon is called the Task Evoked Pupillary Response [21]. Pupil dilation is a very precise reflection of cognitive activity, therefore, it is very suitable to assess the current level of cognitive load by measuring pupil diameter size [22–24].

In addition to the objective evaluation of psychophysiological indicators, cognitive load can also be measured by subjective evaluation methods, such as the NASA-TLX questionnaire, which is most commonly used [25]. NASA-TLX includes six subscales: mental demand, physical demand, temporal demand, performance, effort, and frustration. The specific explanation is as follows:

- **Mental demand:** How much mental and perceptual activity was required (e.g., thinking, deciding, calculating, remembering, looking, searching, etc.)? Was the task easy or demanding, simple or complex, exacting or forgiving?
- **Physical demand:** How much physical activity was required (e.g., pushing, pulling, turning, controlling, activating. etc.)? Was the task easy or demanding, slow or brisk, slack or strenuous, restful or laborious?
- **Temporal demand:** How much time pressure did you feel due to the rate or pace at which the tasks or task elements occurred? Was the pace slow and leisurely or rapid and frantic?
- **Performance:** How successful do you think you were in accomplishing the goals of the task set by the experimenter (or yourself)? How satisfied were you with your performance in accomplishing these goals?
- **Effort:** How hard did you have to work (mentally and physically) to accomplish your level of performance?

- **Frustration:** How insecure, discouraged, irritated, stressed and annoyed versus secure, gratified, content, relaxed and complacent did you feel during the task?

Some studies have shown that in these six dimensions, mental demand and effort are closely related to cognitive load, so they can be used as indicators to evaluate cognitive load in NASA-TLX [26]. NASA-TLX generally consists of two main components, rating and weighting. The rating was based on how the subjects felt while completing the driving task, and was rated on a scale of 0 to 20 on six dimensions. In addition to performance, the other five dimensions were rated from "low" to "high"; Performance was rated from "good" to "bad" [27]. Weighting is calculated based on the pairing options considered most relevant to the workload experienced. Weighting is calculated by counting the 15 pairwise combination options of the mental load factor. The value of weighting is between 0 and 5. Overall workload score (OWS) is calculated by weighting the subjective measurement factors of each subject and multiplying by the rating [25].

In this study, we intend to conduct simulated driving experiments in a driving simulator. Complete the lane keeping task on the simulated urban road, and perform the auditory continuous memory task of three difficulty levels at the same time. Use the eye tracker Tobii Pro Glasses 3 to collect physiological data about the size of pupil diameter, and record the NASA-TLX scale. What we expected from the experiment is that the pupil diameter could be considered as an effective indicator to assess the cognitive load arising from IVIS. The findings can provide reference and assistance for the design of IVIS. For example, when designing IVIS, the pupil diameter could be considered as one of the indicators, combined with other psychophysiological indicators and subjective measurement methods to assess the cognitive load arising from IVIS, so as to avoid the potential harm of excessive cognitive load on driving safety.

2 Method

2.1 Participants

The total number of the participants in this study is 30, including 23 males and 7 females. The age of the participants was mainly between 20–50 years old, and the average age is 33. All participants have a driver's license and have been driving more than 2 years. The experiment required all participants to be in good health, normal mental state, good vision (the requirement to wear glasses can reach the normal vision range after correcting the degree), and no eye diseases. In order to ensure that the participants' physical condition is maintained at a good level during the experiment, they were required not to drink alcohol within 24 h before the experiment and not to drink coffee, strong tea and functional drinks within 12 h before the experiment [28]. What's more, they were also asked to sleep more than 7 h the night before the experiment. In addition, the experiment was approved by the Ethics Committee, and the participants of the experiment have been informed in advance of the research conducted in this paper.

2.2 Apparatus

The experiment adopted a driving simulator, as shown in Fig. 1. The driving simulator consists of a Logitech G29 steering wheel with pedals, a HUAWEI 55″ monitor, a Dell

24″ monitor and an HONOR 12″ android pad. The HUAWEI 55″ monitor was used to display simulated road scenes, the Dell 24″ monitor was used to show dashboard, and the HONOR 12″ android pad was used as IVIS. The experimental data of pupil diameter was collected using Tobii Pro Glasses 3 (as shown in Fig. 2).

(a) View 1 of driving simulator   (b) View 2 of driving simulator

Fig. 1. (a) View 1 of driving simulator. (b) View 2 of driving simulator.

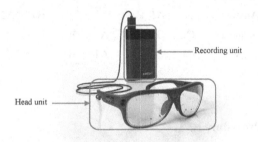

Fig. 2. Tobii Pro Glasses 3

2.3 Driving Scenario

The driving scenario was set as an urban road, which was a two-way three lane urban road. In order to restore the real driving scenario as much as possible, guardrails, grass and lakes were set on both sides of the road, and a small number of two-way vehicles were set on the road that would not affect the normal driving.

2.4 Auditory Continuous Memory Task

The auditory continuous memory task (aCMT) is a cognitive loading task for drivers without any visual stimulus. It can be regarded as an in-vehicle task or a surrogate IVIS (sIVIS). The task required the subjects to maintain a count of their "target" sounds, heard randomly amongst an auditory sequence including non-target presentations. Participants were asked to respond verbally to a count of the target sounds. When the target sound appeared, the cumulative count of the currently heard target sound was loudly reported by participants [29].

The auditory continuous memory task involved presenting 40 letter sounds at a rate of one every 3 s, of which the target sound accounts for about 30% and does not appear consecutively. At difficulty level 1, the target sound that the participants had to remember was A, and when A appeared, the participants had to verbally report the count of A had appeared. At difficulty level 2, the target sound that the participants had to remember was A and B, and when A or B appeared, the participants had to verbally report the count of A or B had appeared. At difficulty level 3, the target sound that the participants had to remember was A, B and C, and when A or B or C appeared, the participants had to verbally report the count of A or B or C had appeared. The example is shown in Table 1.

Table 1. Example of three difficulty levels for auditory continuous memory task

Difficulty level 1	Sequence:	F	D	G	H	A	E	O	A	B	Y
	Answer:					A1			A2		
Difficulty level 2	Sequence:	D	A	G	R	J	B	A	T	W	B
	Answer:		A1				B1	A2			B2
Difficulty level 3	Sequence:	C	G	T	A	B	E	Q	C	R	A
	Answer:	C1			A1	B1					A2

2.5 Experiment Procedure

The experimental procedure is shown in Fig. 3. Each participant was required to sign the consent form first, and then fill in a personal information questionnaire, which includes gender, age, driving age and other information. Participants were instructed to take driving as their primary task and keep the speed at 40–60 km/h. They were also reminded to maintain the vehicle in the center of the lane as much as possible. In addition, they were given a detailed introduction to three difficulty levels of auditory continuous memory tasks to be completed during the experiment, and were told to complete these tasks as best as possible.

Before the experiment, the participants had to undergo a short training process, which consisted of two parts: one was the training of auditory continuous memory tasks, the other was the training of getting familiar with the control and operation of the simulator. For auditory continuous memory tasks, the participants were trained to learn how to distinguish between target and non-target sounds, and the experiment could only be carried out when the success rate reached 95% or higher. For the training of the simulator, as long as the participants felt that they can control and handle the simulator smoothly, they could enter the experiment.

All participants were required to wear Tobii Pro Glass 3 eye tracker for the experiment. The auditory continuous memory task lasted about 2 min for each difficulty level.

After each task, participants were required to fill in a NASA-TLX subjective scale and take a short break before moving on to the next experimental task. At the end of the experiment, each participant was paid 50 yuan as a reward.

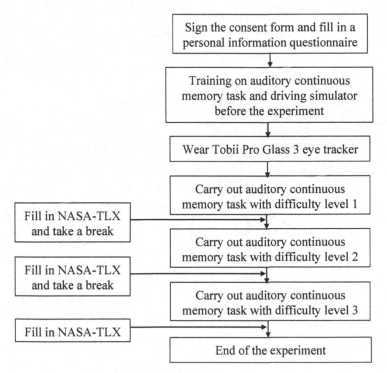

Fig. 3. Experiment procedure

3   Results

One-way ANOVA was carried out on the experimental data of pupil diameter and NASA-TLX. Since the acquisition of pupil diameter is greatly affected by experimental equipment and environment, there may be abnormal data, so abnormal data should be processed first. IBM SPSS Statistics 27 was used here to mark the anomaly cases and then eliminate the outliers.

The results of one-way ANOVA after removing the outliers showed that the difficulty level of auditory continuous memory task had significant differences on pupil diameter, $F(2, 6478) = 44.864$, $p < .001$.What's more, the results showed that the auditory continuous memory task difficulty level had significant differences on the OWS value calculated by NASA-TLX, $F(2, 87) = 5.914$, $p = .004$; And also had significant effects on the mental demand and effort dimensions in the six evaluation dimensions: mental demand dimension, $F(2, 87) = 10.556$, $p < .001$; effort dimension, $F(2, 87) = 11.685$, p

< .001. However, the difficulty level of auditory continuous memory task had no significant effect on the other four dimensions of NASA-TLX: physical demand dimension, F(2, 87) = 1.828, p = .167; temporal demand dimension, F(2, 87) = 1.084, p = .343;

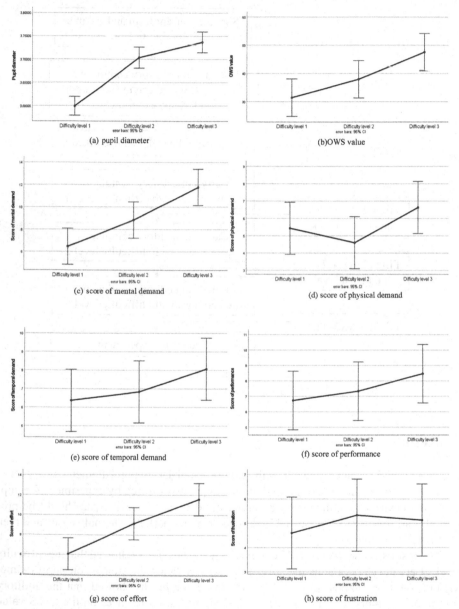

Fig. 4. Change trend of the (a) pupil diameter, (b) OWS value, (c) score of mental demand, (d) score of physical demand, (e) score of temporal demand, (f) score of performance, (g) score of effort, (h) score of frustration with difficulty level.

performance dimension, F(2, 87) = .851, p = .430; frustration dimension, F(2, 87) = .260, p = .772.

Further post-hoc multiple comparisons were performed to obtain more details. The pupil diameter of auditory continuous memory task difficulty level 1 was significantly different from that of difficulty level 2 (p < .001) and 3 (p < .001), difficulty level 2 was significantly different from difficulty level 1 (p < .001) and 3 (p = .039), and difficulty level 3 was significantly different from difficulty level 1 (p < .001) and 2 (p = .039). For NASA-TLX, the OWS value of auditory continuous memory task difficulty level 1 was significantly different from that of difficulty level 2 (p = .001), and difficulty level 2 was also significantly different from difficulty level 3 (p = .045). This also meant that difficulty level 3 was significantly different from difficulty level 1 (p = .001) and 2 (p = .045). However, difficulty level 1 did not differ significantly from difficulty level 2 (p = .171). For the mental demand of different difficulty levels, difficulty level 1 was significantly different from difficulty level 2 (p = .044) and 3 (p < .001), difficulty level 2 was significantly different from difficulty level 1 (p = .044) and 3 (p = .013), and difficulty level 3 was significantly different from difficulty level 1 (p < .001) and 2 (p = .013). The results of effort were similar to that of mental demand. For the effort of different difficulty levels, difficulty level 1 was significantly different from difficulty level 2 (p = .009) and 3 (p < .001), difficulty level 2 was significantly different from difficulty level 1 (p = .009) and 3 (p = .036), and difficulty level 3 was significantly different from difficulty level 1 (p < .001) and 2 (p = .036).

Figure 4 displayed the change trend of the pupil diameter, the OWS value and the score of six dimensions of NASA-TLX with the difficulty levels of auditory continuous memory task. It could be seen that the pupil diameter, score of mental demand and score of effort increase significantly with the increase of difficulty level.

4 Discussion and Conclusion

According to results, task difficulty level had significant effects on the mental demand and effort dimensions of NASA-TLX, but there were no significant differences in the other four dimensions, physical demand, temporal demand, performance and frustration. That might because mental demand and effort dimensions are the evaluation dimensions that can best reflect cognitive load in NASA-TLX. Studies have shown that the rating of mental demand and effort by operators represents the mental effort invested. For different task difficulties, mental demand scale can better reflect participants' perception ability of task requirements compared with other subscales. Regarding the sub-dimension of effort, the perceived effort of the participants is mainly a part of perceived mental demand, and there is a strong correlation between mental demand and effort [26]. These further verified that mental demand and effort were indeed effective indicators to assess cognitive load.

However, although the task difficulty level also had a significant effect on the OWS value, not all task difficulty levels had significant differences. This might be because the OWS value is calculated by weighting the score of the six dimensions, which could not all reflect the cognitive load, so the OWS value could not be used as an indicator to assess the cognitive load.

In addition, task difficulty level also had a significant effect on pupil diameter, and the change trend of pupil diameter with task difficulty level was consistent with mental demand and effort, which were significantly increased. This indicated that pupil diameter can be used as an effective indicator to reflect cognitive load.

In this study, we demonstrated that pupil diameter could be a valid indicator for assessing cognitive load, but we did not take into account the effect of light conditions on pupil diameter[30]. The limitation of this study is that the experimental site was selected in an open space in an office building, and the light intensity would change with time. For future studies, it should be considered to place the experiment in an environment where the lighting conditions will not change. Moreover, the maximum age of participants in this experiment was not more than 50 years old, and with the development of social aging, the age of drivers will also become older and older. Therefore, participants over 50 years old, preferably over 60 years old should be covered in future studies.

5 Conclusion

This study verified that pupil diameter could be used as an effective index to assess the cognitive load arising from in-vehicle infotainment systems (IVIS) by using the effects of auditory continuous memory task difficulty levels on the NASA-TLX subdimensions associated with cognitive load evaluation. The findings of this study can provide reference and assistance for the design of IVIS. For example, when designing IVIS, the pupil diameter could be considered as one of the indicators, combined with other psychophysiological indicators and subjective measurement methods to assess the cognitive load arising from IVIS, so as to avoid the potential harm of excessive cognitive load on driving safety.

Acknowledgement. The authors would like to thank the National Natural Science Foundation (52205513), University-Industry Collaborative Education Program (202101042002, Kingfar), and Changan Automobile Co., Ltd.

References

1. Zhou, S., Lan, R., Sun, X., Bai, J., Zhang, Y., Jiang, X.: Emotional design for in-vehicle infotainment systems: an exploratory co-design study. In: Krömker, H. (eds.) HCI in Mobility, Transport, and Automotive Systems. HCII 2022. Lecture Notes in Computer Science, vol. 13335. Springer, Cham (2022). https://doi.org/10.1007/978-3-031-04987-3_22
2. Marinkov, S., et al.: One solution of a communication manager for connecting advanced driver assistance systems with in-vehicle infotainment systems. In: 45th Jubilee International Convention on Information, Communication and Electronic Technology, MIPRO 2022, May 23, 2022–May 27, 2022. Opatija, Croatia: Institute of Electrical and Electronics Engineers Inc. (2022)
3. Prabhakar, G., et al.: Cognitive load estimation using ocular parameters in automotive. Transp. Eng. **2**, 100008 (2020)
4. Ondas, S., Gurcik, M.: Domain-specific language models training methodology for the in-car infotainment. Intell. Decis. Technol. **11**(4), 417–422 (2017)
5. Kumar, H., et al.: Cognitive load detection on drivers by pupillary analysis. In: 6th IEEE International Conference on Electronics, Computing and Communication Technologies, CONECCT 2020, July 2, 2020–July 4, 2020. Bangalore, India: Institute of Electrical and Electronics Engineers Inc. (2020)

6. Egovnik, T., et al.: An analysis of the suitability of a low-cost eye tracker for assessing the cognitive load of drivers. Appl. Ergon. **68**, 1–11 (2018)
7. Okano, T., Nakayama, M.: Research on time series evaluation of cognitive load factors using features of eye movement. In: 2022 ACM Symposium on Eye Tracking Research and Applications, ETRA 2022, June 8, 2022–June 11, 2022. Virtual, Online, United states: Association for Computing Machinery (2022)
8. Biondi, F.N., Saberi, B., Graf, F., Cort, J., Pillai, P., Balasingam, B.: Distracted worker: using pupil size and blink rate to detect cognitive load during manufacturing tasks. Appl. Ergon. **106**, 103867 (2023)
9. Babu, M.D., et al.: Using Eye gaze tracker to automatically estimate pilots' cognitive load. In: 50th Annual International Symposium of the Society of Flight Test Engineers, SFTE 2019, June 10, 2019–June 14, 2019. Toulouse, France: Society of Flight Test Engineers (2019)
10. Gjoreski, M., et al.: Cognitive load monitoring with wearables-lessons learned from a machine learning challenge. IEEE Access **9**, 103325–103336 (2021)
11. Wang, H., Jiang, N., Pan, T., Si, H., Li, Y., Zou, W.: Cognitive load identification of pilots based on physiological-psychological characteristics in complex environments. J. Adv. Transp. **2020**, 1–16 (2020)
12. Hughes, A.M., et al.: Cardiac measures of cognitive workload: a meta-analysis. Hum. Factors **61**(3), 393–414 (2019)
13. Zihisire Muke, P., Piwowarczyk, M., Telec, Z., Trawiński, B., Maharani, P.A., Bresso, P.: Impact of the stroop effect on cognitive load using subjective and psychophysiological measures. In: Nguyen, N.T., Iliadis, L., Maglogiannis, I., Trawiński, B. (eds.) Computational Collective Intelligence. ICCCI 2021. Lecture Notes in Computer Science, vol. 12876. Springer, Cham (2021). https://doi.org/10.1007/978-3-030-88081-1_14
14. Zihisire Muke, P., Telec, Z., Trawiński, B.: Cognitive load measurement using arithmetic and graphical tasks and galvanic skin response. In: Nguyen, N.T., Manolopoulos, Y., Chbeir, R., Kozierkiewicz, A., Trawiński, B. (eds.) Computational Collective Intelligence. ICCCI 2022. Lecture Notes in Computer Science, vol. 13501. Springer, Cham (2022). https://doi.org/10.1007/978-3-031-16014-1_66
15. Buchwald, M., et al.: Electrodermal activity as a measure of cognitive load: A methodological approach. In: 23rd Signal Processing: Algorithms, Architectures, Arrangements, and Applications, SPA 2019, September 18, 2019–September 20, 2019.Poznan, Poland: IEEE Computer Society (2019)
16. Shakti, D., et al.: EEG as a tool to measure cognitive load while playing Sudoku: a preliminary study. In: 3rd International Conference on Electronics, Materials Engineering and Nano-Technology, IEMENTech 2019, August 29, 2019–August 31, 2019. Kolkata, India: Institute of Electrical and Electronics Engineers Inc. (2019)
17. Meng, X., Zheng, W., Huang, K.: Cognitive load evaluation of human-computer interface based on EEG multi-dimensional feature. In: 25th IEEE International Conference on Intelligent Transportation Systems, ITSC 2022, October 8, 2022–October 12, 2022. Macau, China: Institute of Electrical and Electronics Engineers Inc. (2022)
18. Gomez, L.C., et al.: Studying the generalisability of cognitive load measured with EEG. Biomed. Sig. Process. Control **70**, 103032 (2021)
19. Gable, T.M., Walker, B.N., Henry, A.G.: Cognitive workload, pupillary response, and driving: custom applications to gather pupillary data (2013)
20. Heeman, P.A., et al.: Estimating cognitive load using pupil diameter during a spoken dialogue task. In: 5th International Conference on Automotive User Interfaces and Interactive Vehicular Applications, AutomotiveUI 2013, October 27, 2013–October 30, 2013. Eindhoven, Netherlands: Association for Computing Machinery (2013)
21. Beatty, J.: Task-Evoked Pupillary Responses, Processing Load, and the Structure of Processing Resources. Time-sharing data processing systems (1982)

22. Seeber, K.G.: Cognitive load in simultaneous interpreting: measures and methods. Target Int. J. Transl. Stud. **25**(1), 18–32 (2013)
23. Chen, F., et al., Robust Multimodal Cognitive Load Measurement. Springer, Cham (2016). https://doi.org/10.1007/978-3-319-31700-7
24. Marquart, G., Cabrall, C., Winter, J.D.: Review of eye-related measures of drivers' mental workload. In: 6th International Conference on Applied Human Factors and Ergonomics (AHFE) (2015)
25. Sugiono, S., Widhayanuriyawan, D., Andriani, D.P.: Investigating the impact of road condition complexity on driving workload based on subjective measurement using NASA TLX. In: 2017 2nd International Conference on Design, Mechanical and Material Engineering, D2ME 2017, September 14, 2017–September 16, 2017. Melbourne, VIC, Australia: EDP Sciences (2017)
26. von Janczewski, N., et al.: A subjective one-item measure based on NASA-TLX to assess cognitive workload in driver-vehicle interaction. Transport. Res. Part F Traffic Psychol. Behav. **86**, 210–225 (2022)
27. Braarud, P.O.: Investigating the validity of subjective workload rating (NASA TLX) and subjective situation awareness rating (SART) for cognitively complex human-machine work. Int. J. Ind. Ergon. **86**, 103233 (2021)
28. Wang, J., et al.: Predicting drowsy driving in real-time situations: using an advanced driving simulator, accelerated failure time model, and virtual location-based services. Accid. Anal. Prev. **99**, 321–329 (2017)
29. Jamson, A.H., Merat, N.: Surrogate in-vehicle information systems and driver behaviour: effects of visual and cognitive load in simulated rural driving. Transp. Res. Part F Traffic Psychol. Behav. **8**, 79–96 (2005)
30. Steinhauer, S.R., et al.: Sympathetic and parasympathetic innervation of pupillary dilation during sustained processing. Int. J. Psychophysiol. Official J. Int. Organ. Psychophysiol. **52**(1), 77–86 (2004)

Automotive Head-Up Display Systems: A Bibliometric and Trend Analysis

Chunwang Yang[✉] and Hao Tan

School of Design, Hunan University, Yuelu District, Changsha, China
1545651498@qq.com

Abstract. This study focuses on the analysis and summary of HUD-related studies for the period 2017–2022. Based on the bibliometric approach, the 1009 papers obtained from the WOS (Web of Science) Core library search that were most relevant to the research topic were highlighted for analysis. Based on the traditional bibliometric analysis methods such as keyword frequency analysis and cluster analysis, it was found that the main research hotspots of automotive HUDs in the past five years include human-automation interaction, advanced driver assistance system, crossing behavior and so on. The analysis found that HUDs are closely integrated with assisted driving and autonomous driving scenarios. The analysis is based on a hierarchical analysis of human, automotive and HUD, which reveals that HUDs are applied to a number of scenarios such as early warning, navigation and infotainment in the car, and the driver's attention is allocated to a number of factors. This paper will help future researchers to understand the latest developments in automotive HUDs from a macro perspective, identify key areas for HUD research and application, and provide some insight and useful guidance for future research on the selection of HUD applications in driving scenarios.

Keywords: Design for social change in global markets · Bibliometric Study · Head-up Display · HUD · Literature Review · Automotive

1 Introduction

When driving, the driver needs to look at the interior system and the outside driving environment in order to obtain the necessary driving information. The use of Head-Up Displays (HUDs) brings a new approach to the process of obtaining the necessary driving information. Unlike conventional head-down displays (HDDs), HUDs integrate information about the external environment with system information by projecting visual cues of driving-related information onto a transparent display. As a result, the driver's attention is distributed in a new way.

In recent years, the number of cars equipped with HUD systems has continued to rise [1], and the use of HUDs is expected to increase in the future, with one third of all cars expected to be equipped with HUD systems by 2024 [2]. With the continuous development of various new technologies such as photonics, augmented reality, IoT and autonomous systems, there are more possibilities for diversified applications of HUDs [3].

P.-L. P. Rau (Ed.): HCII 2023, LNCS 14023, pp. 451–469, 2023.
https://doi.org/10.1007/978-3-031-35939-2_34

There has been more extensive research in the past on various automotive HUD applications facilitated by technological advances [4]: some studies have focused on enhancing driving performance and safety through automotive HUDs, such as: driving hazard warning [5–7], navigation scenarios [8–11], etc. at the same time, some studies have also discussed HUDs for non-driving related tasks, such as: infotainment scenarios [12]. Also augmented reality has been progressively advanced as the number of cars equipped with head-up display systems has continued to rise in recent years [13]. The use of HUDs in conjunction with Augmented Reality (AR), a strategy that enhances the use of HUD technology to display driving-related information, is also gaining widespread interest.

Bibliometrics, as applied in this paper, is a quantitative literature review method that uses the bibliometric characteristics of information extracted from literature databases and visualisation techniques in aggregate as a vehicle for research. Bibliometrics is widely used to analyse the published scientific literature, focusing primarily on the research base, hotspots and frontiers of research areas, and to provide a statistical overview of the activities of various scientific communities [14–16].

As there is still a lack of comprehensive understanding of HUD research, it is essential to summarise the current status and perspectives of automotive HUD research, predict and explore future trends, and analyse the direction of future automotive HUD design research. Therefore, we conducted the current study to summarise the current state of research and assess trends in automotive HUDs through bibliometrics. The results of this study can provide researchers and related researchers in the field of driving HMI, especially automotive HUDs, with a new approach to understand the existing research in a relatively systematic and comprehensive manner, helping them to understand the research frontiers and hotspots in this field and explore future directions, thus facilitating the development of HUD research.

2 Methods

2.1 Overview of Bibliometric Methods

In this study, we attempt to quantify the research findings and content of HUDs and to discover the current research frontiers. We conducted a systematic review of research related to the WOS Core library, and used the data processing software BibExcel for data mining and analysis, combined with the analysis software of CiteSpace social network to analyse and quantify the current status and evolution of HUD research [17], and attempted to discuss in depth the research results of high frequencies therein, and the existing HUD-related research results by A relatively systematic analysis and summary was conducted. Figure 1 shows the workflow of this study [18, 19].

2.2 Data Collection and Processing

The bibliometric analysis was preceded by an analysis of the dataset selection for the study. Based on Olawumi et al.'s comparison of the advantages and disadvantages of three databases, Scopus, ISI WOS and Google Scholar [20], this database was finally

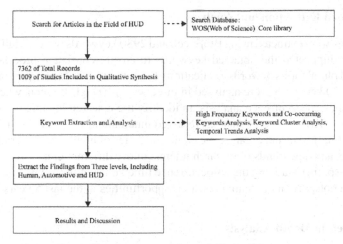

Fig. 1. The workflow of this study.

chosen for this study because the WOS database contains the most comprehensive and influential journals that are scientifically robust. Many scholars have also chosen this database in terms of bibliometrics [21, 22].

All statistics were obtained in November 2021 by identifying search key phrases and using the advanced search function of the WOS database for papers published between 2017–2021 and pre-published relevant papers in 2022. The key phrases used in the search [23] consisted of a combination of two types of topic, "research object" and "research direction", with "research object" includes HUD and its synonyms, related hardware, technology, competing products, driving scenarios, etc., while "research direction" include trends, scenarios, business, applications, technology, user experience, performance, cognitive aspects, etc. To ensure the quality of the literature, the types of research searched are limited to articles, proceeding papers, and reveiew, while other types such as meeting, case report, letter, editorial material, and news are excluded.

The results from the WOS search were imported into Excel for a first round of checking and cleaning to filter out duplicates and ineligible records [24]. For example, an article entitled "Alternative Role of HuD Splicing Variants in Neuronal Differentiation" was not the expected result [25]. Considering that HUD also represents other meanings in other applications, e.g. HuD is a neuronal RNA-binding protein in the field of genetics [26] and HUD is used as an abbreviation for the Department of Urban Development in the field of urban studies [27]. Therefore, the type of search was restricted to exclude as many fields as possible that were not relevant to automobiles, and irrelevant studies retrieved were also removed from the search results.

A total of 7362 records were left after the first round of searching and then, a second round of selection was made by carefully reading the abstracts and information related to the papers. The inclusion and exclusion in this round focused on screening the literature in three dimensions: relevance to the subject content of the current study, frequency of citations of the literature, and journals, and aggregating and de-weighting, resulting in 1009 papers for subsequent in-depth analysis.

2.3 Keyword Extraction and Analysis

The DE fields were extracted using BibExcel, and 2980 keywords were initially obtained. We then de-duplicated the obtained keywords to ensure consistent processing of the singular and plural forms of words, unification of synonyms and cleaning of homophones. The final 2750 keywords were analysed in three ways: (i) high-frequency keyword and high-frequency co-occurrence analysis: to identify the research landing points of HUD in the field of driving research that has received much attention. (ii) keyword clustering analysis: to finely read and organise the eight categories of highly cited literature, so that the hot spots and new trends of research interest under different clusters could be more easily to grasp. (iii) Mapping the co-occurrence time zones of hot keywords: presenting the research hotspots and potential research opportunities in the last 5 years.

2.4 Layered In-Depth Analysis

In step 3, a layered structural analysis is presented by human, automotive and HUD. This is summarised and discussed in more depth through a close reading of the relevant literature, the extraction and reclassification of the specific concerns of the research, e.g. metrics, functional scenarios, features, etc., as well as the research findings. Considering that earlier studies in some scenarios may also be of some help, the conclusions of some papers published in 2015–2016 have been added in a targeted manner to be able to provide a richer and more effective support to the scenario features of the classification analysis. It is hoped that this part of the in-depth analysis will provide a summary and reference to a broader perspective on the existing research findings.

3 Descriptive Analysis

3.1 Influential Research in HUD Studies

Table 1 lists the top 10 highly cited literature screened [16], containing their year of publication, title, TLS, number of citations and subject. The most cited studies were Behnood, et al. for their study on influencing vehicle crash scenarios, noting that there are many influences on the likelihood of serious injury [28]. The second is from Greenwood, BN et al. whose main contribution is from the perspective of carpooling, revealing the importance of combining increased availability with cost savings in car services [29]. This is followed by a paper by Hu, Y et al. which analyses and compares key performance indicators such as measurement principles, system architecture and accuracy, outlines state-of-the-art MFPP works and discusses potential applications of MFPP, making some recommendations for MFPP optical system design [30].

It should be noted that influential articles in HUD-related research have focused on human-machine relationships (e.g., situational awareness, trustworthiness), application scenarios (e.g., intelligent traffic systems, automated intervention for manual driving, etc.), and technical aspects.

Table 1. The top 10 highly cited literature screened.

Ranking	Title	Source
1	Microscopic fringe projection profilometry: A review	Optics and lasers in engineering
2	Planning and Tracking in Image Space for Image-Based Visual Servoing of a Quadrotor	Ieee transactions on industrial electronics
3	AEB effectiveness evaluation based on car-to-cyclist accident reconstructions using video of drive recorder	Traffic injury prevention
4	Dual-focal-plane augmented reality head-up display using a single picture generation unit and a single freeform mirror	Applied optics
5	Micromirror based virtual image automotive head-up display	Microsystem technologies-micro-and nanosystems-information storage and processing systems
6	Conditionally and highly automated vehicle handover: A study exploring vocal communication between two drivers	Transportation research part f-traffic psychology and behaviour
7	The Prediction of Saliency Map for Head and Eye Movements in 360 Degree Images	Ieee transactions on multimedia
8	Omnidirectional Channel Sounder With Phased-ArrayAntennas for 5G Mobile Communications	Ieee transactions on microwave theory and techniques
9	Evaluation of Handheld Scanners for Automotive Applications	Applied sciences-basel
10	Privacy Enabled Noise Free Data Collection In Vehicular Networks	2018 ieee 15th international conference on mobile ad hoc and sensor systems (mass)

3.2 High Frequency Keywords and High Frequency Co-occurring Words

Table 2 shows the details of the top 10 ranked high-frequency keywords resulting from sorting the obtained keywords from highest to lowest frequency. The high-frequency keywords reflect the current hotspots of research in the literature on the topic, and the overall attributes of the keywords or topics can be made clearer based on word frequency and synonym frequency [18].

Clearly, the highest frequency occurrences are in addition to the head-up display and vehicle topic keywords under study and technology applications such as virtual reality, augmented reality, and head-mounted display, the most prominent keywords are advanced driver assistance system (ADAS), automated driving, human-machine interface, human-computer interaction, driver behavior, etc.

In addition, BibExcel was used to analyse the co-occurrence frequency of the keywords obtained, and they were ranked in descending order of co-occurrence frequency. Table 3 shows the top 10 keywords with the highest co-occurrence frequencies. The co-occurring high frequency keywords respond to a major focus of the current research field and these keywords play a key role in shaping the HUD research themes.

The results of the co-word analysis are broadly consistent with the results of the word frequency analysis, with these research themes showing a relatively strong correlation with high frequency co-occurring words. In particular, advanced driver assistance system, automated driving, human-machine interface, augmented reality, head-mounted display, human-computer interaction, etc., which appear in the highest keyword frequency statistics table and the highest keyword co-occurrence frequency table. Human-computer interaction can be considered as representatives of HUD-related user experience research areas. In addition to these, the keywords accidents and artificial intelligence are also directly related to other topics.

According to the data provided in Table 2 and Table 3, it can be seen that scholars have studied a wide range of HUD topics. It is clear that research in the subject area of HUDs is strictly interconnected with each other. HUDs have been extensively studied in the field of advanced driver assistance systems as well as autonomous driving, safety and experience of driving.

Table 2. The top 10 highest-frequency keywords.

Ranking	Keyword	Frequency
1	Advanced driver assistance system (ADAS)	111
2	Head-up display	96
3	Automated Driving	92
4	Virtual Reality	76
5	Human-machine interface	58
6	Augmented Reality	55
7	Head-mounted display	52
8	Human-computer interaction	47
9	Vehicle	38
10	Driver behavior	27

Keyword Cluster Analysis. The results of the cluster analysis using the word frequency co-occurrence and modularity algorithms were visualised using CiteSpace [31], and clusters with mean contour values of 0 and 1 were filtered out, resulting in eight clusters. CiteSpace provides two metrics, module value (Q-value) and mean contour value (silhouette, S-value), based on the network structure and the clarity of the clusters.

Table 3. The top 10 highest-frequency Co-occurrence keywords.

Ranking	Keyword	Frequency
1	Advanced driver assistance system (ADAS)	107
2	Automated driving	95
3	Augmented Reality	80
4	Head-up display	67
5	Head-mounted Display	52
6	Human-computer interaction	46
7	Driving Simulator	29
8	Vehicle	27
9	Accidents	27
10	Artificial Intelligence	16

This is used as a basis for judging the effectiveness of the mapping. In general, Q values generally fall within the interval [0, 1), with Q > 0.3 implying that the clustering structure is significant. Clusters with S values above 0.5 are generally considered reasonable, and if above 0.7, then the clustering is efficient and convincing. The Q-value of this clustering map is 0.5061, and the S-value of all eight clusters after screening is greater than 0.7, with an average S-value of 0.8437, and this clustering map is valid.

The size of the circles in the clustering map represents the number of word frequencies, the number of connecting lines in the circles represents the number of relationships between words co-occurring with other words, and the thickness of the connecting lines represents the number of co-occurrence between word pairs. The different coloured partitions represent different clusters.

Table 4 lists the names of the eight clusters and their corresponding core keywords. The smaller the number, the larger the corresponding cluster. The first three clusters are: human-automation interaction, advanced driver assistance system, and crossing behaviour (Fig. 2).

The literature under the keywords corresponding to the 8 clusters after clustering was read to understand the relevant and important research in the corresponding literature.

Human-Automation Interaction. In this cluster, human-automation interaction is explored in the context of automotive use, with keywords such as human-automation interaction, training, automated driving, young drivers, head-up display (HUD), etc. In the study by Vassilis Charissis et al. a typical touchscreen low head-up display (HDD) interface system is evaluated against a gesture-controlled augmented reality (AR) head-up display (HUD) system. The results of the study showed positive feedback for the gesture-controlled AR-HUDs, with the user keeping his eyes on the road and hands on the steering wheel, improving the effectiveness of collision avoidance [32]. In addition, in a study by Myeongseop Kim et al. the interaction using the In-Vehicle Information Interactive System (IVIS) was discussed using the HUDs as common output feedback

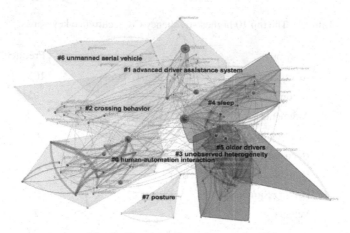

Fig. 2. Keyword clustering network.

Table 4. Keyword cluster information.

	Cluster Label	Keyword
0	human-automation interaction	human-automation interaction, training, automated driving, young drivers, head-up display (HUD)
1	advanced driver assistance system	advanced driver assistance system, driver behavior, autonomous vehicles, stereo vision, adas
2	crossing behavior	crossing behavior, proactive brain, evaluation, oscillation, knowledge
3	unobserved heterogeneity	unobserved heterogeneity, injury severity, frequency, built environment, risk
4	sleep	sleep, sleepiness, fog, age, drowsiness
5	older drivers	older drivers, adhd medication, avoidance, population, ethnicity
6	unmanned aerial vehicle	unmanned aerial vehicle (uav), visual appeal, drone management, trajectory, field test
7	posture	posture, balance, time-to-contact, time-to-arrival, tta

interfaces. The study compared five single modalities (touch, over-the-air gestures, voice, gaze and physical buttons in the steering wheel) typically used for NUI with cascaded multimodal interfaces during a lane change task (LCT). The results showed that the combination of voice + button, voice + touch and gaze + button represented the best cascaded multimodal interface and helped to reduce driver distraction in the HUD-hosted IVIS [33].

Advanced Driver Assistance System. In this cluster, keywords include advanced driver assistance system (ADAS), lane change, driver's intention, artificial neural network (ANN), support vector machine (SVM).

Advanced Driver Assistance Systems (ADAS) are active safety systems that improve vehicle control and thus the safety of drivers and passengers. Clearly, the future of ADAS has a wide range of applications.

The combination between HUDs and ADAS and the resulting impact has been the subject of a number of studies. For example, Luzuriaga et al. found through their study that the HUD had a significant positive impact on the overall driving experience of applying ADAS, especially for in risk averse drivers, older people, students and women, helping to improve the low acceptance of ADAS [34]. Joongjin et al. also suggest that vehicle HUDs will be progressively advanced together with ADAS (Advanced Driver Assistant Systems) for reasons of driving safety and convenience [35].

Crossing Behaviour. Due to technological advances in the field of autonomous and assisted driving and the consequent changes in the urban traffic environment, the study of human behavioural scenarios in traffic has become increasingly important [36]. Crossing behaviour is a category of clusters that contains keywords such as crossing behaviour, proactive brain, evaluation, oscillation, knowledge, etc. To cope with the challenges of modern traffic conditions, explore by paying attention to other road users, such as pedestrians and cyclists, through the behavior scene and perceiving interaction, in order to improve traffic safety.

For example, the study by Karatas et al. addresses the application scenario of displaying potential collisions with pedestrians on the roadside after the application of an autonomous driving system by comparing two kinds of interfaces, AR-HUDs and static head-up displays (S-HUDs), respectively, to explore the impact of their display of pedestrian signals on the speed of pedestrian recognition by the human operator and the perceived acceptability and trustworthiness of this visual cue for automated interventions contribution. The results show that the AR-HUD cue identifies the target pedestrian more quickly and provides a relatively more acceptable perception of automatic intervention [37].

Unobserved Heterogeneity. This cluster contains the following keywords: unobserved heterogeneity, injury severity, frequency, built environment, risk. Heterogeneity is in fact what we often call difference, difference. It can be at the level of the individual or at the level of the group. This clustering study focuses on analysing and examining car crash data to explain the potential heterogeneous effects of explanatory variables in crashes. This unobserved heterogeneity may come from a variety of sources, such as unobserved vehicle characteristics, driver characteristics, road attributes and environmental factors [28].

A comprehensive understanding of the influences associated with the occurrence of different modes of crashes is a prerequisite for the development of safety improvement programmes to effectively reduce traffic crashes [38]. Investigating the risk factors that contribute to crash injury severity in motor vehicles is a thought-provoking and challenging issue. The results could help to better understand and potentially mitigate the risk of serious injuries involved in motor vehicle crashes, thereby improving the well-being of people involved in these crashes [39].

Sleep. This cluster contains the following keywords: sleep, sleepiness, fog, age, drowsiness. Fatigue is a major safety hazard in the transport industry. There are many factors that contribute to driver fatigue, such as long working hours, night and early morning duty hours, and chronic sleep deprivation, among others [39, 40]. Driving fatigue not only has an impact in manual driving, but this problem is even more present with the increased level of driving automation.

It has been noted that there is variability in the effects of fatigue on driving and that different drivers differ in the extent to which drowsiness affects their driving performance [41]. However, regardless of the cause, fatigue can lead to reduced alertness and increased reaction times in driving, compromising safety. It is therefore important to assess the risks and effects fatigue poses to driving and to explore ways to reduce the risk of fatigue.

Older Drivers. This cluster contains the following keywords: older drivers, adhd medication, avoidance, population, ethnicity.

Several studies have discussed factors for older drivers' crashes, for example Pope et al. studied the role of age in distracted driving involvement and found that distracted driving was a widespread phenomenon, evident in all age groups of drivers. No significant differences in distracted driving behaviour were found between younger and middle-aged people [42].

In contrast, one study found that up to 83–95% of age-related differences in driving ability were related to visual and cognitive factors [43]. Older drivers have cognitive factors including slower reaction times, problems with attention allocation and switching, reduced performance in dual or multi-task situations and deficits in the inhibition of irrelevant stimuli and inappropriate responses. Crashes in older drivers are also associated with the cognitive deficits mentioned above, as well as increased visual acuity and substance use.

In addition, several studies have discussed directions and opportunities for improvement in vehicle-related design in relation to the characteristics and human factors of senior drivers [44].

Unmanned Aerial Vehicle. This cluster contains the following keywords: unmanned aerial vehicle (uav), visual appeal, drone management, trajectory, field test. This cluster focuses the research on the scenario of the application of highly automated driving (HAD) functions.

Effective human-vehicle communication plays an important role in the formation of the user's mental model of AV, and the importance of the HMI as an important vehicle for human-vehicle communication is increasing, with Morra et al. showing that exposure to a more information-rich interface, despite a high cognitive load, helps to reduce the user's mental stress, optimise the experience and help to increase the willingness to use the AV experience [45].

Addressing the issue that the unpredictable behavioural patterns of autonomous vehicles (AVs) may also be uncomfortable, von Sawitzky et al. evaluated five augmented reality (AR) user interface (UI) concepts and found that feedback indicating the system state through AR-HUDs significantly increased trust in the AVs [46], which also provides an important reference for subsequent unmanned aerial vehicle information visualisation with an important reference role.

Posture. This cluster contains the following keywords: posture, balance, time-to-contact, time-to-arrival, tta. Driver behaviour is the most important factor in road driving safety and affects traffic safety and efficiency. For intelligent vehicles, it is important to understand driver behaviour and assist in driving tasks based on their state [47].

For example, Hensch et al. explored gaze behaviour during driving: comparing the effects of two display positions, the HUDs and the centre consoles, on the driver's gaze behaviour during partially automated driving after a simulated vehicle task. The results found that although the average fixation duration of HUDs was longer, the distance between HUDs and driving environment might help to identify and respond to emergencies more quickly [48].

Analysis of Temporal Trends. The analysis of the evolution of the research themes provides insight into the context and characteristics of the development of HUDs. Figure 3 shows a timeline view of clustering in CiteSpace, visualising the historical span of clustered themes and the relationships between clustered themes over the course of their evolution [31]. The figure shows the top 21 clustered themes according to cluster size, including 187 nodes and 676 connections, with a network density of 0.0389. With a Q value of 0.5061 (Q > 0.3), the cluster is well structured with clear boundaries and strong domain delineation of the studied themes. The red dots represent keyword emergent nodes, i.e. research frontiers, and the vertical axis indicates the eight clusters, with the number of clusters arranged vertically by size. The more emergent nodes a cluster contains, the more active or emerging trends in research in that area. In addition, the node size represents the frequency of the keyword, while the cluster location year indicates the year in which the keyword was first published since 2017, i.e. the year in which the keyword first appeared from 2017. The connecting line indicates the co-occurrence relationship between this keyword and other articles that contain this keyword.

From a horizontal perspective, it indicates the time span of the study 2017–2022. Cluster 1 (human-automation interaction) continues to receive attention from 2017–2022. Cluster 2 (advanced driver assistance system) and cluster 3 (crossing behavior) remain research active from 2011 to 2019 research, indicating that these 2 topics remain at the forefront of HUD-related research. Research on clusters 5 (sleep) and 6 (older driver) did not persist and entered a silent phase.

Vertically, the links between the different cluster themes represent an intrinsic link between the different clusters. It is worth noting that there are multiple connections between all clusters, indicating that the eight clustered themes are closely related to each other, especially between cluster 1 (human-automation interaction), cluster 2 (advanced driver assistance system) and cluster 5 (sleep).

Figure 4 shows the specific information of the corresponding keyword emergence nodes. As can be seen, collision, motor vehicle, distraction, augmented reality, and adult were the research frontiers at that time in 2017–2018, motor vehicle accident, and road were the research frontiers at that time in 2018–2019, automation, usability, and attention were the research frontiers at that time in 2019–2020, and the research frontiers in 2022 are likely to be grading, technology and algorithms.

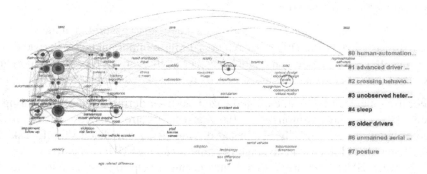

Fig. 3. Literature co-citation network.

Keywords	Year	Strength	Begin	End	2017 - 2022
crashe	2017	0.65	2017	2018	
motor vehicle	2017	0.65	2017	2018	
distraction	2017	0.65	2017	2018	
augmented reality	2017	0.32	2017	2018	
adult	2017	0.32	2017	2018	
motor vehicle accident	2017	0.68	2018	2019	
road	2017	0.62	2018	2019	
automation	2017	1.45	2019	2020	
usability	2017	1.23	2019	2020	
attention	2017	0.92	2019	2020	
classification	2017	2.35	2020	2022	
technology	2017	1.34	2020	2022	
algorithm	2017	0.61	2020	2022	

Fig. 4. Top 13 keywords with the strongest citation bursts.

4   Discussion

4.1   Summary Analysis of Current Research

The above analysis clarifies the research progress, evolutionary trends and hot topics in HUDs in the last five years. However, the generic scientometric results still do not further clearly delineate the multiple directions of multiple studies in the field of lower HUDs. By going back to the specific contents of the relevant papers and conducting an in-depth literature intensive reading analysis based on the results of the bibliometric cluster analysis, it is further proposed to manually extract the main contents and specific findings in individual studies around three levels of human, automotive and HUD, respectively, according to the specific contents of the scenario functions of the studies, and then sort and categorise them according to positive and negative directions. It also explores and discusses the current status and prospects of HUD research (Fig. 5).

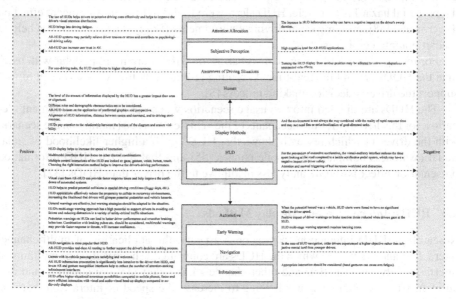

Fig. 5. Important results of HUDs from three perspectives.

4.2 Human: The Impact of HUD Applications on Human-Related Factors

Existing HUD-related research has focused on three main factors: attention allocation, subjective perception, and awareness of driving situations.

HUD applications can help drivers to perceive driving cues effectively and help to improve drivers' visual attention allocation problems [49–51]. HUDs bring about less driving fatigue [52]. However, the increased information overlay from HUDs can negatively affect the driver's sweep duration [53].

Subjectively, AR-HUD systems may partially relieve driver tension or stress and contribute to psychological driving safety [54].

In terms of driving situational awareness, for non-driving tasks, the HUDs contribute to higher situational awareness. However, shifting to the HUD displays from other positions may be affected by unknown adaptation or unexpected side effects [55, 56].

4.3 Automotive: Functional Scenarios for HUDs in Vehicles

Existing HUD-related research has focused on three functional scenarios: early warning, navigation, and infotainment.

Among them, early warning is one of the hot functional scenarios that have received the most attention in HUD applications. Studies have shown that the application of HUDs can effectively reduce the propensity to collide in highway environments [57], increase the likelihood of drivers glimpsing potential pedestrian and vehicle hazards, and when the potential hazard is a vehicle, HUD alerts were found to have no significant effect on driver speed [58], and in special driving environments (foggy days, etc.) HUDs help to predict potential collisions [59].

For the application of navigation scenarios, the HUDs are more popular with users than the HDDs [9] and the real-time AI routing provided by the AR-HUDs can further support the driver's decision making process [8].

The HUDs are divided into two usage scenarios when applied to infotainment scenarios: for the driver or for the occupants of the vehicle. We focus mainly on the scenario with the driver in which research shows that HUDs have a higher likelihood of situational awareness compared to mobile phones [55] and that the AR HUD information presentation effect is significantly less disruptive to the driver than HDDs [32].

4.4 HUDs: Interaction and Display Methods

Research on HUD interaction focuses on 2 aspects: the application of multi-channel interaction and the way in which the HUDs are controlled. The direction of multimodal interfaces between the HUD and other channels has received more attention and discussion, with the HUD displays helping to increase the speed of interaction, but it is important to note that applying the HUDs is not the best choice in all scenarios. For example, the results of one study showed that for preventing over-acceleration, a tactile accelerator pedal system was the most effective, while the visual performance through HUDs, combined with an auditory approach instead reduced the time spent looking at the road, which could have a negative impact on driver safety [60]. HUD control methods, such as gaze, gesture, voice, button, touch, etc. are much also a concern in research. Choosing the right interaction method is beneficial to improve driver performance, but attention needs to be paid to the level of interaction and load [33, 61].

In addition, research on HUD display methods focuses on three aspects: firstly, the type of information displayed by the HUDs: the level of the amount of information displayed has a greater impact than the area or arrangement [62, 63], in addition to considering different roles and demographic characteristics [64]. Secondly, the form of information displayed by the HUDs: the study proposed the need to pay attention to the relationship between the bottom of the figure, to ensure visibility, AR-HUD more attention to the application of conformal graphics and perspective, and the environment combined with the realistic way does not always produce fast response time, and may not be suitable for target-oriented tasks that require fine or strict positioning [65–67]. Thirdly, HUD display information distribution: the alignment of information, the distance between the centre and the surrounding, and the driving environment, all of these factors are the focus of HUD research [48, 62].

5 Conclusion

HUD as an automotive human-machine interaction interface is still a relatively new field, but there is no doubt that the field will continue to update rapidly due to the demand for technological advances and experience upgrades, among other things.

This study provides a bibliometric analysis of publications from 2017 to 2021 (including some pre-publications in 2022) and provides an insight into the current state of HUD research in the driving field over the last 5 years. Based on the keyword analysis, the hotspots and frontiers of HUD research in the past 5 years were identified, and the research results of HUDs were reviewed to provide a reference for subsequent theoretical research in the field. It is worth mentioning that the keyword clustering results also verify the tight integration of HUDs with assisted driving and autonomous driving scenarios. For example, the application of HUDs in autonomous driving scenarios helps to enhance the interpretability of the system, thus improving the driver's trust in autonomous driving [45, 46]. As the research on HUDs deepens, we can continue to consider the combination of HUDs and future autonomous driving scenarios from different perspectives.

After in-depth analysis based on the three levels of "vehicle" function scenario, "human" related factors, and "HUD, we found that the existing research results show that HUD can bring certain positive impact on multiple scenarios like early warning on the vehicle and multiple factors like driver's attention distribution through proper application. The application of AR-HUD has also received some research attention. However, HUDs also have the risk of bringing negative impacts, for example: AR-HUDs can increase the user's trust in AV, but the cognitive load of its application is high. More effective and appropriate human-computer interaction methods need to be targeted according to specific application scenarios and target characteristics. Research on HUDs can focus on three functional scenarios: early warning, navigation and info-tainment, taking into account three major factors: driver's attention allocation, subjective perception and awareness of driving situations to extend the research and mining of HUD interaction and display methods. By analysing the research hotspots and cutting-edge issues in HUDs over the past five years, this paper provides an important reference for future related research and practice.

The innovations in this paper are mainly in the following areas. Firstly, by using bibliometric methods to examine the literature on HUDs, this study systematically summarises the themes and hotspots of relevant research. It reveals the current status of HUD research, as well as the hotspots and research frontiers over the past five years for the target scholars, readers and researchers. Secondly, the research analysis process of the bibliometric methods employed, as well as the research perspective can be used as a reference for subsequent similar studies or extensions to other disciplines. Finally, the quantitative approach of bibliometrics and the qualitative approach of literature research summaries are combined. Our findings are at the same time consistent with subjective experience and highly instructive, while being based on an objective basis, and the relevant information is presented in intuitive and clear tables and visualisations generated by CiteSpace, ensuring the scientific accuracy of the study.

This study has some limitations. Firstly, the analysis in this study is based on the analysis of the selected sample set rather than the results of research in the HUD field as a whole. As the field of automotive HUDs is rapidly evolving, further research in the future could consider combining Scopus, Google Scholar and other databases, or selecting a broader time frame and obtaining a larger dataset for a more comprehensive analysis. In any case, the WOS database is currently the most comprehensive and widely used data available and remains relevant for understanding the current status and development of research in the field of HUDs. Secondly, this paper considers HUD research hotspots and research results mainly from a macro perspective, but does not consider the distribution of authors, micro-analyses between them and their collaborations, institutions, etc. There is no doubt that research on the partnership between researcher characteristics and institutions is also important for understanding the development stages and trends of HUD research. Further research may consider additional studies from the perspective of authorship, country, etc.

References

1. Betancur, J.A., Villa-Espinal, J., Osorio-Gómez, G., Cuéllar, S., Suárez, D.: Research topics and implementation trends on automotive head-up display systems. Int. J. Interact. Design Manufact. (IJIDeM) **12**(1), 199–214 (2016). https://doi.org/10.1007/s12008-016-0350-3
2. Park, J., Park, W.: Functional requirements of automotive head-up displays: A systematic review of literature from 1994 to present. Appl. Ergon. **76**, 130–146 (2019)
3. Gabbard, J.L., Fitch, G.M., Kim, H.: Behind the glass: driver challenges and opportunities for ar automotive applications. Proc. IEEE **102**, 124–136 (2014)
4. Li, R., Chen, Y.V., Zhang, L., Shen, Z., Qian, Z.C.: Effects of perception of head-up display on the driving safety of experienced and inexperienced drivers. Displays 64 (2020)
5. Winkler, S., Kazazi, J., Vollrath, M.: How to warn drivers in various safety-critical situations - Different strategies, different reactions. Accid. Anal. Prev. **117**, 410–426 (2018)
6. Winkler, S., Kazazi, J., Vollrath, M.: IEEE: Distractive or supportive - how warnings in the head-up display affect drivers' gaze and driving behavior. In: 18th IEEE International Conference on Intelligent Transportation Systems, pp. 1035–1040. (Year)
7. Wu, Y., Abdel-, M., Park, J., Zhu, J.: Effects of crash warning systems on rear-end crash avoidance behavior under fog conditions. Trans. Res. Part C-Emerg. Technol. **95**, 481–492 (2018)
8. Bram-Larbi, K.F., Charissis, V., Khan, S., Lagoo, R., Harrison, D.K., Drikakis, D.: IEEE: collision avoidance head-up display: design considerations for emergency services' vehicles. In: IEEE International Conference on Consumer Electronics (ICCE) (Year)
9. Jose, R., Lee, G.A., Billinghurst, M.: A Comparative Study of simulated augmented reality displays for vehicle navigation. In: 28th Australian Computer-Human Interaction Conference (OzCHI) (Year)
10. Pampel, S.M., Lamb, K., Burnett, G., Skrypchuk, L., Hare, C., Mouzakitis, A.: an investigation of the effects of driver age when using novel navigation systems in a head-up display. Pres.-Teleoperat. Virtual Environm. **27**, 32–45 (2018)
11. Topliss, B.H., Pampel, S.M., Burnett, G., Skrypchuk, L., Hare, C., Assoc Comp, M.: Establishing the role of a virtual lead vehicle as a novel augmented reality navigational aid. In: 10th ACM International Conference on Automotive User Interfaces and Interactive Vehicular Applications (AutomotiveUI), pp. 137–145 (Year)
12. Wang, S., Charissis, V., Campbell, J., Chan, W., Moore, D., Harrison, D.: An investigation into the use of virtual reality technology for passenger infotainment in a vehicular environment. In: IEEE International Conference on Advanced Materials for Science and Engineering (IEEE-ICAMSE), pp. 404–407 (Year)

13. Qin, Z., Lin, F.-C., Huang, Y.-P., Shieh, H.-P.D.: Maximal Acceptable Ghost Images for Designing a Legible Windshield-Type Vehicle Head-Up Display. IEEE Photonics J. **9** (2017)
14. Broadus, R.N.: Toward a definition of "bibliometrics." Scientometrics **12**, 373–379 (1987)
15. Diodato, V.P., Gellatly, P.: Dictionary of bibliometrics. Routledge (2013)
16. Mirhashemi, A., Amirifar, S., Kashani, A.T., Zou, X.: Macro-level literature analysis on pedestrian safety: Bibliometric overview, conceptual frames, and trends. Accident Anal. Prevent. **174** (2022)
17. Zhang, S., Wang, S., Liu, R., Dong, H., Zhang, X., Tai, X.: A bibliometric analysis of research trends of artificial intelligence in the treatment of autistic spectrum disorders. Front. Psych. **13** (2022)
18. Bhagat, P.R., Naz, F., Magda, R.: Artificial intelligence solutions enabling sustainable agriculture: A bibliometric analysis. Plos One **17** (2022)
19. Wang, C., Lv, T., Deng, X.: Bibliometric and visualized analysis of china's smart grid research 2008–2018. Front. Res. Metr. Analyt. **5**, 551147 (2020)
20. Olawumi, T.O., Chan, D.W.M., Wong, J.K.W.: Evolution in the intellectual structure of bim research: a bibliometric analysis. J. Civ. Eng. Manag. **23**, 1060–1081 (2017)
21. Yu, D., He, X.: A bibliometric study for DEA applied to energy efficiency: Trends and future challenges. Appli. Energy **268** (2020)
22. Rahman, A.J., Guns, R., Rousseau, R., Engels, T.C.: Cognitive distances between evaluators and evaluees in research evaluation: a comparison between three informetric methods at the journal and subject category aggregation level. Front. Res. Metrics Analyt. **2**, 6 (2017)
23. Wangsa, I.D., Vanany, I., Siswanto, N.: Issues in sustainable supply chain's futuristic technologies: a bibliometric and research trend analysis. Environ. Sci. Pollut. Res. **29**, 22885–22912 (2022)
24. Mulet-Forteza, C., Genovart, J., Merigo, J.M., Mauleon, E.: Bibliometric structure of IJCHM in its 30 years. Int. J. Contemp. Hosp. Manag. **31**, 4574–4604 (2019)
25. Hayashi, S., Yano, M., Igarashi, M., Okano, H.J., Okano, H.: Alternative Role of HuD splicing variants in neuronal differentiation. J. Neurosci. Res. **93**, 399–409 (2015)
26. Dobashi, Y., Shoji, M., Wakata, Y., Kameya, T.: Expression of HuD protein is essential for initial phase of neuronal differentiation in rat pheochromocytoma PC12 cells. Biochem. Biophys. Res. Commun. **244**, 226–229 (1998)
27. Ray, A., Kim, J., Nguyen, D., Choi, J., McElwain, K., Stater, K.J.: Opting in, opting out: a decade later. Cityscape **20**, 63–88 (2018)
28. Behnood, A., Mannering, F.: Determinants of bicyclist injury severities in bicycle-vehicle crashes: A random parameters approach with heterogeneity in means and variances. Analy. Methods Accident Res. **16**, 35–47 (2017)
29. Greenwood, B.N., Wattal, S.: Show me the way to go home: an empirical investigation of ride-sharing and alcohol related motor vehicle fatalities. MIS Q. **41**, 163–187 (2017)
30. Hu, Y., Chen, Q., Feng, S., Zuo, C.: Microscopic fringe projection profilometry: A review. Optics Lasers Eng. **135** (2020)
31. Zhang, X., Liao, X.-P., Tu, J.-C.: A study of bibliometric trends in automotive human-machine interfaces. Sustainability 14 (2022)
32. Charissis, V.: Employing emerging technologies to develop and evaluate in-vehicle intelligent systems for driver support: infotainment ar hud case study. Appli. Sci.-Basel **11** (2021)
33. Kim, M., Seong, E., Jwa, Y., Lee, J., Kim, S.: A Cascaded multimodal natural user interface to reduce driver distraction. IEEE Access **8**, 112969–112984 (2020)
34. Luzuriaga, M., Aydogdu, S., Schick, B.: Boosting advanced driving information: a real-world experiment about the effect of hud on hmi, driving effort, and safety. Int. J. Intell. Transp. Syst. Res. **20**(1), 181–191 (2021). https://doi.org/10.1007/s13177-021-00277-y
35. Joongjin, K.: The Design of an integrated ECU and navigation information based iot head-up display system for vehicles. J. Semicond. Display Technol. **20**, 172–177 (2021)

36. Feldstein, I.T., Dyszak, G.N.: Road crossing decisions in real and virtual environments: A comparative study on simulator validity. Accident Anal. Prevent. 137 (2020)
37. Karatas, N.: IEEE: Evaluation of AR-HUD Interface during an automated intervention in manual driving. In: 31st IEEE Intelligent Vehicles Symposium (IV), pp. 2158–2164 (Year)
38. Wang, J., Huang, H., Zeng, Q.: The effect of zonal factors in estimating crash risks by transportation modes: Motor vehicle, bicycle and pedestrian. Accid. Anal. Prev. **98**, 223–231 (2017)
39. Delen, D., Tomak, L., Topuz, K., Eryarsoy, E.: Investigating injury severity risk factors in automobile crashes with predictive analytics and sensitivity analysis methods. J. Transp. Health **4**, 118–131 (2017)
40. Kosmadopoulos, A., et al.: The efficacy of objective and subjective predictors of driving performance during sleep restriction and circadian misalignment. Accid. Anal. Prev. **99**, 445–451 (2017)
41. Sparrow, A.R., LaJambe, C.M., Van Dongen, H.P.A.: Drowsiness measures for commercial motor vehicle operations. Accid. Anal. Prev. **126**, 146–159 (2019)
42. Pope, C.N., Bell, T.R., Stavrinos, D.: Mechanisms behind distracted driving behavior: The role of age and executive function in the engagement of distracted driving. Accid. Anal. Prev. **98**, 123–129 (2017)
43. Rolison, J.J., Regev, S., Moutari, S., Feeney, A.: What are the factors that contribute to road accidents? An assessment of law enforcement views, ordinary drivers' opinions, and road accident records. Accid. Anal. Prev. **115**, 11–24 (2018)
44. Fernandes, S.C.F., Esteves, J.L., Simoes, R.: Characteristics and human factors of older drivers: improvement opportunities in automotive interior design. Int. J. Veh. Des. **74**, 167–203 (2017)
45. Morra, L., Lamberti, F., Prattico, F.G., La Rosa, S., Montuschi, P.: Building trust in autonomous vehicles: role of virtual reality driving simulators in hmi design. IEEE Trans. Veh. Technol. **68**, 9438–9450 (2019)
46. von Sawitzky, T., Wintersberger, P., Riener, A., Gabbard, J.L.: Increasing trust in fully automated driving: route indication on an augmented reality head-up display. In: 8th ACM International Symposium on Pervasive Displays (Pervasive Displays) (Year)
47. Xing, Y., et al.: identification and analysis of driver postures for in-vehicle driving activities and secondary tasks recognition. IEEE Trans. Comput. Soc. Syst. **5**, 95–108 (2018)
48. Hensch, A.-C., et al.: Effects of secondary tasks and display position on glance behavior during partially automated driving. Trans. Res. Part F-Traffic Psychol. Behav. **68**, 23–32 (2020)
49. Zhang, Y., Yang, T., Zhang, X., Zhang, Y., Sun, Y.: Effects of full windshield head-up display on visual attention allocation. Ergonomics **64**, 1310–1321 (2021)
50. Langner, T., Seifert, D., Fischer, R., Goehring, D., Ganjineh, T., Rojas, R.: Traffic awareness driver assistance based on stereovision, eye-tracking, and head-up display. In: IEEE International Conference on Robotics and Automation (ICRA), pp. 3167–3173 (Year)
51. Park, B.-J., Lee, J.-W., Yoon, C., Kim, K.-H.: IEEE: Augmented reality and representation in vehicle for safe driving at night. In: 2015 International Conference on Information and Communication Technology Convergence (ICTC), pp. 1261–1263 (Year)
52. Grogna, D., Stojmenova, K., Jakus, G., Barreda, M., Verly, J.G., Sodnik, J.: The impact of drowsiness on in-vehicle human-machine interaction with head-up and head-down displays. Multimedia Tools Appli. **77**(21), 27807–27827 (2018). https://doi.org/10.1007/s11042-018-5966-9
53. Oh, H.J., Ko, S.M., Ji, Y.G.: Effects of superimposition of a head-up display on driving performance and glance behavior in the elderly. Int. J. Hum.-Comput. Interact. **32**, 143–154 (2016)

54. Hwang, Y., Park, B.-J., Kim, K.-H.: Effects of augmented-reality head-up display system use on risk perception and psychological changes of drivers. ETRI J. **38**, 757–766 (2016)
55. Gerber, M.A., Schroeter, R., Li, X., Elhenawy, M.: ACM: self-interruptions of non-driving related tasks in automated vehicles: mobile vs head-up display. In: CHI Conference on Human Factors in Computing Systems (CHI) (Year)
56. Wulf, F., Rimini-Doering, M., Arnon, M., Gauterin, F.: Recommendations supporting situation awareness in partially automated driver assistance systems. IEEE Trans. Intell. Transp. Syst. **16**, 2290–2296 (2015)
57. Lagoo, R., Charissis, V., Chan, W., Khan, S., Harrison, D.: Prototype gesture recognition interface for vehicular head-up display system. In: IEEE International Conference on Consumer Electronics (ICCE) (Year)
58. Hajiseyedjavadi, F., Zhang, T., Agrawal, R., Knodler, M., Fisher, D., Samuel, S.: Effectiveness of visual warnings on young drivers hazard anticipation and hazard mitigation abilities. Accid. Anal. Prev. **116**, 41–52 (2018)
59. Halmaoui, H., Joulan, K., Hautiere, N., Cord, A., Bremond, R.: Quantitative model of the driver's reaction time during daytime fog - application to a head up display-based advanced driver assistance system. IET Intel. Transport Syst. **9**, 375–381 (2015)
60. Hibberd, D.L., Jamson, A.H., Jamson, S.L.: The design of an in-vehicle assistance system to support eco-driving. Trans. Res. Part C-Emerg. Technol. **58**, 732–748 (2015)
61. Prabhakar, G., et al.: Interactive gaze and finger controlled HUD for cars. J. Multimodal User Interfaces **14**(1), 101–121 (2019). https://doi.org/10.1007/s12193-019-00316-9
62. Park, K., Im, Y.: Ergonomic Guidelines of Head-Up Display User Interface during Semi-Automated. Electronics **9** (2020)
63. Lin, R., Cheng, Q., Jiang, X., Wang, W.: Novel Design of Head-up display system based on safety control. In: 7th International Conference on Green Intelligent Transportation System and Safety (GITSS), pp. 95–103 (Year)
64. Kim, H.S., Yoon, S.H., Kim, M.J., Ji, Y.G., Acm: deriving future user experiences in autonomous vehicle. In: 7th International Conference on Automotive User Interfaces and Interactive Vehicular Applications (AutomotiveUI), pp. 112–117 (Year)
65. Yoon, H.J., Park, Y., Jung, H.-Y.: Background scene dominant color based visibility enhancement of head-up display. In: 25th International Conference on Systems Engineering (ICSEng), pp. 151–156 (Year)
66. Liu, H., Hiraoka, T., Hirayama, T., Kim, D.: Saliency difference based objective evaluation method for a superimposed screen of the HUD with various background. In: 14th International-Federation-of-Automatic-Control (IFAC) Symposium on Analysis, Design, and Evaluation of Human Machine Systems (HMS), pp. 323–328 (Year)
67. Merenda, C., et al.: augmented reality interface design approaches for goal-directed and stimulus-driven driving tasks. IEEE Trans. Visual Comput. Graphics **24**, 2875–2885 (2018)

Research on Evaluation Index System of Automobile HMI User Experience

Xiaomin Zhang[✉] and Hao Tan

School of Design, Hunan University, Yuelu District, Changsha, China
3241382704@qq.com

Abstract. Under the background of intelligence, networking and experience economy, the user experience of automotive HMI products, as a key point of differentiation of the whole vehicle, affects the purchase decision of consumers. In order to manage and optimize the user experience of automotive HMI products, it is necessary to build a scientific and reasonable evaluation system. This study summarizes the evaluation indexes used in the relevant literature in the past ten years through the content analysis method, and forms a general index library for the evaluation of automotive HMI user experience; and based on this, the evaluation index system of Wuling automotive HMI user experience is constructed by combining user interviews, real-vehicle review and AHP method. The evaluation index system consists of 3 first-level indexes, 6 s-level indexes and 30 three-level indexes; among the first-level indexes, driving compatibility, user satisfaction and HMI efficacy is each given a weight of 0.383, 0.338, and 0.269 respectively. The out-put evaluation index system can provide reference for evaluating the user experience of automotive HMI, which is conducive to the design evaluation and optimization iteration of automotive HMI products; the universal user experience evaluation index library comprehensively summarizes the index types, which can help researchers find the indexes matching their own needs quickly; In addition, the method and process of the evaluation system construction can be a reference and guidance for other manufacturers to build the index system that meets their own needs.

Keywords: Experience evaluation · Index system · Automotive HMI · In-vehicle information system · User experience · AHP

1 Introduction

Automotive human-machine interfaces (HMI), such as central control screens and instrument panels, are important media for information interaction and communication between automobiles and users, enabling the conversion between the internal form of information and the form acceptable to users [1]. With the development of intelligence and network connectivity, the user experience of automotive HMI products is receiving more and more attention. From the user's perspective, the in-vehicle information system (IVIS) with rich functions has become the basic configuration of the car, and the development of assisted driving technology also enables users to have more time and energy

© The Author(s), under exclusive license to Springer Nature Switzerland AG 2023
P.-L. P. Rau (Ed.): HCII 2023, LNCS 14023, pp. 470–485, 2023.
https://doi.org/10.1007/978-3-031-35939-2_35

to interact with it, which makes the user experience of HMI greatly affect the user's evaluation of the whole car; meanwhile, users in the information age have developed the habit and basic cognition of using digital products, and thus put forward higher expectations and requirements for the IVIS. From the manufacturer's perspective, in the face of fierce market competition and technological homogenization, automotive HMI products have emerged as a crucial component of vehicle differentiation; as a result, major manufacturers have recognized the importance of improving HMI user experience to increase brand competitiveness and customer loyalty. At the same time, with the enrichment of functions, the amount of information carried and the structural complexity of IVIS are also growing, which also brings more challenges to the user experience of automotive HMI products.

In the development process of automotive HMI, testing and evaluation is an essential part. By constructing a scientific and reasonable evaluation system to measure the experience of automotive HMI products and then guide their design optimization and iteration, user experience can be effectively guaranteed and improved. However, the industry has not yet formed a mature evaluation system for automotive HMI. On the one hand, it is difficult to apply the traditional technical specifications of the whole vehicle in the field of HMI experience; on the other hand, due to the special interaction environment of automobiles, the evaluation systems of other product areas such as mobile apps and web pages cannot be fully matched. At the same time, there are few specialized studies on automotive HMI product experience evaluation in academic, and the evaluation perspectives, measurement indexes and methods adopted in different studies are quite different, making it difficult for automotive companies to directly refer to them. Therefore, it is important to establish an automotive HMI user experience evaluation system with both generality and individuality by combining the characteristics of the automotive industry.

This study summarizes the evaluation indexes used in the relevant literature in the past ten years and establishes a generic automotive user experience evaluation index library; and invites experts and users to participate in the evaluation practice and iterative optimization, and finally produces a set of automotive HMI user experience evaluation model for a certain brand. We hope to provide reference and help for the experience evaluation and optimization iteration of automotive HMI products, and also provide guidance for the industry to build an index system that meets their needs in terms of methods and processes.

2 Automotive HMI User Experience Evaluation Indexes and Methods

2.1 User Experience of Automotive HMI Products

The concept of user experience was first proposed by Norman [2], and its meaning has expanded constantly as the expansion of user experience in the domain and architecture [3]. Different from the concept of usability, which mainly evaluates whether users can perform a product task smoothly, successfully, and as expected, user experience is a broader concept [4], including but not limited to usability. The most influential definition of user experience currently comes from ISO 9241–210, in which user experience is defined as all the reactions and outcomes of users to the products, systems or services they use or are expected to use [5], including the user's psychological feelings, physical sensation, behavioral performance, and result feedback etc.

It is generally accepted in the literature that user experience involves users, products and interactive environment in these three areas [6]. Different from ordinary products such as cell phones and computers, the interactive environment of automotive HMI products is a special dual-task environment [7], where in quite a few cases, users need to operate HMI products while driving. Driving, including maintaining lanes, controlling speed, and avoiding emergencies, is the primary work, while using the HMI system to navigate on a map, listen to music, or adjust the air conditioning, which are not directly related to driving, is the secondary work [8]. The driver's ability to observe the environment and operate the HMI compete against one another, and the secondary tasks will take up part of the driver's attention and cognitive resources, putting the driver at risk for distraction and causing safety issues. Therefore, in addition to focusing on the usability and operating experience of the system, the evaluator must also pay close attention to the interference caused by the secondary tasks to the concurrent primary tasks when evaluating the user experience of automobile HMI.

2.2 Automotive HMI User Experience Evaluation Index

There is a large amount of academic research in the field of user experience and automotive HMI. In order to comprehensively understand the current situation of user experience evaluation and explore the available indexes and methods in HMI evaluation, this study conducted a large-scale desktop research and literature analysis to collect evaluation indexes as the basis of the whole study. Web of Science (WOS) has very rich literature data, and this study chose the core collection of WOS as the search database, set 2011–2021 as the literature search time, and used "vehicle" or "car" or "automotive" or "automobile" And "user experience" or "UX" or "HCI" or "HMI" as the search keywords. The search results were initially screened based on the type of literature and content relevance, and 1262 papers were ultimately chosen. Our team extracted 236 user experience evaluation indexes from them, but because there were cases that the indexes extracted in different literature were named differently but their meanings were the same or similar, we subsequently analyzed the content of indexes one by one and merged the indexes with similar meanings to finally obtain 91 evaluation indexes.

According to the definition of user experience by ISO [5], user experience can be characterized by several externalized contents such as subjective feelings, physiological reactions, behavioral performance and task achievement of users during interaction with products. The author classifies the indexes according to their data type, dividing them into four major categories: self-reported data, physiological data, behavioral data, and task performance, and briefly analyzes the methods & tools, advantages and disadvantages required for each category, and finally constructs a generic automotive HMI evaluation index library, which is shown in Table 1.

Self-reported Data. The most direct way to understand the user experience of a product is to ask its users. Self-reported data refers to the subjective attitude and feeling evaluation of users during interacting with the product and after using the product to complete tasks, which can be obtained through self-reported methods such as questionnaire, user interviews and vocal thinking. In terms of content, it can be roughly divided into three types of data, such as perceived system usability, enjoyment, and workload. There are already many validated scales that can be used to obtain such subjective data from users. For example, workload, which aims to measure the degree of interference caused by operating HMI products to the main task of driving, can be evaluated with the help of the DALI scale [9], which is designed for driving environments and involves a total of six dimensions, such as attention demand, visual demand, auditory demand, time demand, Interference level, and stress level. In addition, evaluation tools of usability and emotional experience commonly used in other fields are also of great reference value for automotive HMI measurement. For example, SUS [10] is a landmark usability scale proposed by Brooke, which includes ten items such as "I think the system is very complicated to use" and other items that require users' judgment based on their use or

Table 1. Universal automotive HMI user experience evaluation index library

Data Types	Category	Specific indexes	Methods & Tools
Self-reported data	efficacy	Validity, Integrity, Desirability, Understandable, Visibility, Information masking, System performance, Ease of learning, Ease of operation, Error Tolerance, Flexibility, Memorability, Consistency, Feedback, Habit & Intuition, Speed, Fluency, Clearness	Questionnaires, user Interviews, Vocal thinking
	experience	Pleasure, Fondness, Trust, Willingness to use, Willingness to recommend, Satisfaction, Aesthetics, Harmony, Fun, Humanity, Attractiveness, Comfort, Security, Uniqueness, Valuable, Innovation	
	Workload	Attention demand, Visual demand, Auditory demand, Time demand, Interference level, Stress level	

(*continued*)

Table 1. (*continued*)

Data Types	Category	Specific indexes	Methods & Tools
Physiological data	Eye movement data	First entry time, Target gaze time, Resultant hit rate, Pupil diameter, Number of eye jumps, Eye jump distance, Eye movement Trajectory, Blink frequency, Blink interval, Number of retrospective gaze, Number of gaze points	Eye Tracking System, Polysomnography
	Other physiological data	Heart rate (HR), Heart rate variability (HRV), Heart rate high/low frequency ratio (LF/HF), Blood pressure (BP), Skin conductance (GSR), Skin temperature (ST), EEG alpha wave rhythm, EEG beta wave ratio, Respiratory rate, Respiratory speed, Respiratory amplitude	
Behavioral data	Facial expressions	Number of smiles, Number of surprises, Pleasure ratio, Validity value, Arousal degree	Facial expression recognition system, The Finger movement tracking system Video playback & live recording
	Verbal behavior	Positive comments, Negative comments, Number of requests for help	
	Finger movement data	Absolute angular velocity of fingers, Average velocity of fingers, Finger movement distance	
	Visual behavior	Number of sweeps, Frequency of sweeps, Length of single sweeps, Total length of sweeps	

(*continued*)

Table 1. (*continued*)

Data Types	Category	Specific indexes	Methods & Tools
Task performance	Driving performance	Average speed, Standard deviation of speed, Number of brakes during the task; Maximum lane shift, Standard deviation of horizontal shift, Standard deviation of steering wheel angle; Critical incident response time, Critical incident response rate	Driving simulator, Video playback & live recording
	Secondary task performance	Task completion rate, Task completion time, Number of task errors, Number of operation steps, Number of operations without feedback, Effective path rate	

understanding of the system, and the user's evaluation of the usability level of the system through a comprehensive score.

Since user experience itself is highly subjective, inviting users to directly evaluate product experience is the best way to obtain it, and self-reported data is also one of the most common and important types of indicators in experience evaluation; however, due to the differences in a priori knowledge and personal understanding of different users, the evaluation results may have certain individual differences.

Physiological Data. The user's physiological state will alter in response to changes in their emotional state and mental load. These physiological changes are hard to see with the naked eye and must be measured using devices such as oculomotors and multidimensional physiological instruments. Eye movement data, heart rate, blood pressure, and other physiological data are usually applied in evaluating user experience. Due to the maturity of acquisition technology and data interpretation, eye movement indexes have been widely used in many fields. Users receive information through their eyes for cognitive processing, making the eyes a key information channel for users during interaction. Partala et al. [11] showed that changes in pupil diameter can be used to detect emotional responses. In addition, sweat gland secretion and cardiorespiratory function change when the user perceives stimuli [12], which in turn are characterized in skin electrical, cardiac, respiratory, and brain electrical indicators. As Schmidt et al. [13] showed, as workload increases, human heart rate (HR) increases and heart rate variability (HRV) decreases.

Users' judgment of their cognitive state is often inaccurate and often influenced by their subjective will [14]. User physiological data, which has the advantages of objectivity and high data accuracy, can objectively reflect users' physiological and psychological states without being impacted by their subjective will and indirectly evaluate the HMI. However, the cost of collecting physiological data is significant because it requires the use of numerous acquisition devices, and there is still room for improvement in the mapping between some current indexes and user experience.

Behavioral Data. When users interact with HMI products, they are often accompanied by other actions such as frowning, whispering, and looking. Behavioral responses refer to such observable user actions, including facial expressions, verbal behavior, finger movements, and eye shifts. These behavioral data can be gathered by on-site observation logs or by reviewing the experimental videos, which can also provide a lot of valuable information for experience evaluation. The most visible index of psychological states is facial expressions, which are the outward signs of human inner emotions. The complex relationship between facial expressions and emotional responses is described in the emotion analysis dictionary developed by Ekman et al. [15]. When users are using a product, the ratio of positive to negative speech in their speech can be used as a basis for evaluating the overall experience, and the data from their finger movements, including absolute angular velocity of fingers and finger movement distance, can be used as a basis for interaction efficiency evaluation. In addition, visual behavior can measure the interference caused by secondary tasks to the primary task. If the HMI product distracts too much attention, it will cause the driver's eyes to leave the road longer and more frequently, and Riera B [16] verified the mapping relationship between the time of line of sight drift and the difficulty of interaction through driving simulator experiments.

In order to effectively avoid the situation where users' hearts and mouths differ in experience evaluation, user behavior, as objective data that can be directly observed, has good reliability and can complement subjective user data with corroboration. However, because some user behaviors lack clear delineation standards, it is important to make sure that data analysts fully communicate the alignment when processing.

Task Performance. Users use the product ultimately to achieve a certain goal, and task performance focuses on the actual results of users operating the HMI product in the vehicle and is the best way to determine whether users can use the HMI product well [17], which generally needs to be obtained in a scripted task experiment environment. Based on Harvey C et al. [18], task achievements in a dual-task environment can also be divided into driving performance and secondary task performance. An important standard for evaluating the user experience of the automotive HMI is whether the IVIS interferes with the primary driving task. Since interference causes driver distraction, which affects the driver's ability to control the vehicle and perceive their surroundings, driving performance can be used to measure this interference. This interference can be objectively measured by lateral and vertical control of the vehicle and by unexpected event detection. Jin Xin et al. [19] measured the user experience of the automotive HMI in a driving simulator using indexes such as standard deviation of vehicle speed, standard deviation of horizontal offset, and standard deviation of steering wheel turning angle. Secondary task performance focuses on the user's performance when operating secondary tasks, including task duration, completion rate, number of errors, etc. The HMI product's efficiency and efficacy are indicated by how quickly the user completes the work and how few errors are made [20]. These indexes can be collected by on-site observation logs and reviewing the experimental videos.

3   Construction of the Evaluation Index System of Automotive HMI User Experience

The user experience evaluation of products with different brands and development stages has different focuses, and these focuses have a non-negligible effect on the choice of evaluation indexes and methods. The above-mentioned universal index library is a collection of indexes that have recently been used in related fields; it can serve as a basic sources of data for researchers. However, due to the large number and lack of differentiation of priorities, screening and adjustment are necessary to combine with the actual situation of a product if it is to be applied in a certain product. In this study, taking Wuling Automobile as the research object, the author firstly screened the indicators in terms of content fit and method feasibility, then invited users and experts to participate in the evaluation practice to optimize the evaluation indicator structure and content expression, and finally used AHP to build up an automotive HMI user experience index system.

3.1   Initial Screening of Evaluation Indexes

The choice of appropriate evaluation indexes is crucial to the credibility and reliability of the evaluation results, and in addition, previous studies have shown that the evaluation dimensions of user experience are not static, but require flexible adjustment of the components of user experience according to the actual research questions [15]. This research uses the interview analysis method and invites 6 internal enterprise experts to understand the evaluation status, the experience elements of concern, and the preferred evaluation methods of enterprises through the interviews. Based on the interview results, the author then conducts the initial screening of indexes to ensure that they correspond to the actual situation of the enterprises.

In terms of content, enterprises hope to focus on indexes related to "driving safety", "HMI performance" and "satisfaction". In terms of method, self-reported data, behavioral data, and task achievement indexes are preferred because they are less expensive to collect than physiological data that needs specialized equipment. Based on the above conclusions, the author considered the content fit and method feasibility for rough screening, and obtained the preliminary version of evaluation indexes, including 56 indexes and 209 evaluation items. The evaluation item is the specific evaluation medium of a certain index, and an index can correspond to multiple evaluation items. For example, "In the actual operation of the task, have you ever made any mistakes or had any doubts?" is one of the evaluation items of the index "error tolerance".

3.2 Optimization of Evaluation Indexes

The indexes obtained from the initial screening were derived from desktop research, and further validation is needed to determine whether these indexes can fully cover the evaluation needs of enterprises and whether the expression of evaluation items is accurate. Considering that the subsequent users of this index system include both experts and users, internal experts and real users were invited to participate in this tuning process in order to ensure that the expression of the index system can be perfectly matched with the perception of the target users.

Aiming at the problem of adapting the index to the needs of the enterprise, this study invited 12 internal experts from enterprises to collect revision opinions through two sessions: real-vehicle review and card sorting. In the real-vehicle review session, the experts used the preliminary version of the indexes to evaluate the high-frequency functions, such as navigation, music, air conditioning, etc. The team recorded the experts' feedback on the indexes and evaluation items through the method of "voice during evaluation + interview after evaluation". After ensuring that the experts fully understood the indexes, evaluation items and evaluation environment, the team invited the experts to converge and adjust the indexes through the card sorting method. The experts placed the index cards in four quadrants divided by "relevance to user value - relevance to Wuling business" and selected the cards in the first quadrant as the final evaluation index. In addition, the accuracy of the evaluation items, which are the direct reference for the evaluator, has a great impact on the evaluation results. In order to ensure that the evaluation items are accurate and easy to understand, 4 users were invited to conduct user tests and complete the evaluation using the preliminary version of the index in a real-vehicle operating environment, and the team also used the "voice during evaluation + post-evaluation interview" method to record user feedback on the evaluation items.

A total of 132 opinions related to the structure and content expression of the indexes were collected from the expert side, and 30 opinions related to the content expression were collected from the user side. After integrating and analyzing these opinions, the author adjusted the indicators and evaluation items by adding, deleting, changing, splitting and combining, and finally obtained the optimized evaluation indexes. The evaluation indexes involve three dimensions of driving compatibility, HMI performance and user satisfaction, including 30 indexes and 125 evaluation items. See Table 2 for more details.

3.3 Construct User Experience Evaluation Model Using AHP

According to the Law research [21], constructing a user experience model serves as the foundation for evaluating user experience, and user experience evaluation should focus on the distribution of index weights. Different indexes have different influences on the evaluation of automotive HMI experience, and in order to judge the priority of each index for a more reasonable scoring, the weights of each index in the evaluation index system need to be calculated.

Analytic Hierarchy Process (AHP) is a decision analysis method combining qualitative and quantitative analysis [22, 23], which requires top-down dismantling of relevant elements into levels of objectives, principles, and means around the analysis objectives,

Table 2. Automotive HMI User Experience Hierarchy Model

Target level	Criteria level-1	Criteria level-2	Index level	Definition of indexes
Automotive HMI User Experience	User Satisfaction	Emotional experience	Aesthetics	Measuring the aesthetics of the HMI interface
			Fun	Measure how interesting and attractive the HMI product is to the user
			Humanization	Measure the comfort of the HMI product around human needs
			Pleasure	The positive emotional experience the product provides to the user
			Sense of security	The degree to which the user perceives the HMI to be a threat to driving safety
		Attitude expression	Likability	Measuring how much users like the HMI interface
			Trust	Measuring the degree of users' trust in HMI products
			Willingness to use	The user's intention to use the HMI product himself
			Willingness to recommend	The user's intention to recommend the product to others
			Satisfaction	Users' subjective recognition of the quality of HMI products (or the operating experience of a certain task)
	Driving Compatibility	Visual Behavior	Number of sweeps	The number of times the user scanned the dashboard screen during the execution of the task
			Length of single sweep	The duration of the user's eyes on the dashboard screen during the task
			Total sweep time	Total time spent on the dashboard screen during the task

(*continued*)

Table 2. (*continued*)

Target level	Criteria level-1	Criteria level-2	Index level	Definition of indexes
		Driving load	Attention demand	Measure the mental demand (e.g., thinking, deciding, choosing, finding, etc.) and visual-auditory occupancy required to perform the task
			Time demands	Measure the specific constraints due to time demands while running the task
			Emotional level	Measure negative emotions/stress levels while performing the task, such as fatigue, insecurity, anger, frustration, etc
	HMI Performance	Task performance	Task completion rate	Percentage of all users who completed the operation task
			Number of Task Errors	Number of errors made by users while performing the task
			Task completion path	The specific steps performed by the user to complete the task
			Task completion time	Time used by the user from the start of the triggered task to the completion of the task
		Ease of use	Flexible & Efficient	Diversification of information exchange methods between users and the system
			Integrity	The extent to which functions & information cover the specified tasks and user goals
			System Performance	The responsiveness of the system in handling a business request
			Visibility	The extent to which the system output is easy to view and identify

(*continued*)

Table 2. (*continued*)

Target level	Criteria level-1	Criteria level-2	Index level	Definition of indexes
			Error Tolerance	The extent to which the product allows users to make mistakes, prevents them from making mistakes, and helps them recover from errors that occur
			Understandable	The degree to which the system is easy for users to understand and quickly get up and running
			Consistency	The extent to which visual elements, interactions, etc. follow the same standards and specifications at the same level
			Feedback	The feedback and status information given by the system
			Habits & Expectations	The degree to which the design matches the user's mental model/habits/expectations
			Ease of use	The degree to which the product is easy to operate and use for the user

establishing a progressive hierarchy, and weighing the importance of different elements by means of two-by-two comparison. In this study, the AHP was used to construct the model.

Build the Hierarchical Model. Harvey et al. [18] summarized the three main requirements of drivers for IVIS: safety, effectiveness, and enjoyment, and suggested that a good IVIS should avoid distracting the driver's attention to ensure driving safety, provide relevant information and functions to improve efficiency, and and give the driver a pleasant experience when using it.

In the hierarchical model constructed by AHP, the levels can be divided into three categories: the highest level (or target level), the middle level (or guideline level) and the lowest level (or index level), and the elements of the higher level play a dominant role over the elements of the lower level. Focusing on the goal of improving the user experience of automotive HMI products, this study defines three first-level guideline from safety, performance and experience, and builds a top-down hierarchical model of automotive HMI user experience evaluation, which is shown in Table 2. Driving compatibility is concerned with the interference and negative impact of HMI task operation on the main driving task, which can be measured subjectively and objectively from the perspectives of driving load and visual behavior; HMI effectiveness is concerned with the effectiveness and efficiency of performing secondary tasks, which can be measured subjectively and objectively by ease of use and task performance; user satisfaction is concerned with the user's evaluation and recognition of HMI product experience, which is measured by the emotional experience and personal attitude.

The Procedure of Index Weighting

Build Judgment Matrix. Around the 3 levels of the automotive HMI user experience hierarchy model, the judgment matrices under the levels are constructed respectively, and the scale questionnaires from 1 to 9 levels containing the first, second and third level evaluation indexes are output correspondingly.

Invite Experts to Evaluate. Invite experts to evaluate. Ten experts with knowledge of user experience were invited to compare the importance of each index using a judgment matrix questionnaire, while ensuring that all of them had a clear and consistent understanding of the definition of indicators.

Check Matrix Consistency. Collect the expert judgment matrix and calculate the consistency ratio CR so as to check the consistency of the judgment matrix; if it does not pass the consistency test, confirm the adjustment with that expert and reconstruct the judgment matrix.

Construct the Group Judgment Matrix. After ensuring that the judgment matrix of each expert has good consistency, the group comparison matrix is constructed by synthesizing the results of all experts and taking the geometric mean of each expert's judgment value as the final judgment matrix value.

Results. A total of 10 sets of judgment data sets containing 100 matrices were obtained by data aggregation. After calculation, the CR (consistency ratio) values of all judgment matrices are less than 0.1, which satisfies the principle of overall consistency of judgment matrix and indicates that the relative importance relationship between each element in the constructed judgment matrix is established. On this basis, our team used MATLAB AHP software to calculate and output the matrix weight vector calculation report to obtain the weights of each index in Table 3.

The data results show that among the first-level indexes affecting automotive HMI products, the driving compatibility, user satisfaction, and HMI effectiveness are ranked in order of importance, among which the synthetic weight of driving compatibility is the highest (0.393), indicating that driving safety is the most important factor when evaluating the experience in the dual-task environment of a car, and the HMI products should be designed in such a way that they do not interfere with the main driving task as the basic premise. Among the second-level indexes, the synthetic weights of driving load, ease of use, and emotional experience all exceed 0.166, which need to be paid attention to in the evaluation; among the three-level indexes, the synthetic weights of attention demand, emotional level, single scan time, sense of security, satisfaction, and

Table 3. Automotive HMI User Experience Hierarchy Model

Target level	Criteria level-1(Synthetic weights)	Criteria level-2	Relative weights	Synthetic weights	Index level	Relative weights	Synthetic weights
Automotive HMI User Experience	User Satisfaction(0.338)	Emotional experience	0.526	0.178	Aesthetics	0.170	0.030
					Fun	0.075	0.013
					Humanization	0.215	0.038
					Pleasure	0.182	0.032
					Sense of security	0.358	0.065
		Attitude expression	0.474	0.160	Likability	0.176	0.028
					Trust	0.174	0.028
					Willingness to use	0.208	0.033
					Willingness to recommend	0.088	0.014
					Satisfaction	0.354	0.057
	Driving Compatibility (0.393)	Visual Behavior	0.394	0.155	Number of sweeps	0.296	0.046
					Length of single sweep	0.507	0.079
					Total sweep time	0.197	0.030
		Driving load	0.606	0.238	Attention demand	0.381	0.091
					Time demands	0.235	0.056
					Emotional level	0.384	0.091
	HMI Performance (0.269)	Task performance	0.304	0.082	Task completion rate	0.269	0.021
					Number of Task Errors	0.300	0.025
					Task completion path	0.155	0.013
					Task completion time	0.276	0.023
		Ease of use	0.696	0.187	Flexible & Efficient	0.092	0.017
					Integrity	0.105	0.020
					System Performance	0.058	0.011
					Visibility	0.076	0.014
					Error Tolerance	0.086	0.016

(*continued*)

Table 3. (*continued*)

Target level	Criteria level-1(Synthetic weights)	Criteria level-2	Relative weights	Synthetic weights	Index level	Relative weights	Synthetic weights
					Understandable	0.124	0.023
					Consistency	0.079	0.015
					Feedback	0.096	0.018
					Habits & Expectations	0.058	0.011
					Ease of use	0.226	0.042

time demand are high, which should also be paid attention to in the future evaluation of automotive HMI user experience.

4 Conclusion

Automotive HMI devices are playing a significant part in the information flow between users and vehicles in the context of intelligence, networking, and the experience economy. It is crucial to properly manage this user experience by building a reasonable evaluation system. The purpose of this study is to provide a reference for the construction of user experience evaluation system of automotive HMI products including content, method and process, and help practitioners to be able to build an index system that meets their own needs, so as to comprehensively and intuitively discover user experience problems. By collecting and summarizing common indexes in the field of user experience, we sorted them into four categories of indexes, including self-reported data, physiological data, behavioral data and task performance, and built a universal automotive HMI user experience index library; and based on this index library, we gradually established an automotive HMI user experience evaluation system through user interviews, real-vehicle reviews and AHP. The system covers 30 indexes in three dimensions of driving compatibility, HMI performance and user satisfaction, which can evaluate automotive HMI products in a more comprehensive way and hopefully provide some help for relevant design evaluation and iterative optimization. In the future, we will actively conduct empirical research on the index system, carry out experiments in enterprises, collect feedback and continuously adjust and optimize it, and provide feasible suggestions for the experience upgrade of enterprise HMI products.

References

1. Harvey, C., Stanton, N.A., Pickering, C.A., McDonald, M., Zheng, P.: A usability evaluation toolkit for in-vehicle information systems (IVISs). Appl. Ergon. **42**, 563–574 (2011)
2. Norman, D.: The design of everyday things: Revised and expanded edition. Basic books (2013)

3. Scapin, D., Senach, B., Trousse, B., Pallot, M.: User experience: Buzzword or new paradigm? In: ACHI 2012, The Fifth International Conference on Advances in Computer-Human Interactions (2012)
4. Hwang, S., Kim, B., Lee, K.: A data-driven design framework for customer service chatbot. In: Design, User Experience, and Usability. Design Philosophy and Theory: 8th International Conference, DUXU 2019, Held as Part of the 21st HCI International Conference, HCII 2019, Orlando, FL, USA, July 26–31, 2019, Proceedings, Part I 21, pp. 222–236. Springer (2019., 10.1007/978-3-030-23570-3_17
5. Bevan, N.: International standards for HCI and usability. Int. J. Hum Comput Stud. **55**, 533–552 (2001)
6. Quan, W.: Research on development and application of User Experience. Francis Academic Press, UK (2017)
7. Lansdown, T.C., Brook-Carter, N., Kersloot, T.: Primary task disruption from multiple in-vehicle systems. ITS J.-Intell. Trans. Syst. J. **7**, 151–168 (2002)
8. Tan, H., Sun, J., Wenjia, W., Zhu, C.: User experience & usability of driving: A bibliometric analysis of 2000–2019. Int. J. Hum.-Comput. Interact. **37**, 297–307 (2021)
9. Pauzié, A.: Evaluating driver mental workload using the driving activity load index (DALI). In: Proceedings of European Conference on Human Interface Design for Intelligent Transport Systems, pp. 67–77. (2008)
10. Brooke, J.: SUS-A quick and dirty usability scale. Usability Evaluat. Indust. **189**, 4–7 (1996)
11. Partala, T., Surakka, V.: Pupil size variation as an indication of affective processing. Int. J. Hum Comput Stud. **59**, 185–198 (2003)
12. Ward, R.D., Marsden, P.H.: Physiological responses to different WEB page designs. Int. J. Hum Comput Stud. **59**, 199–212 (2003)
13. Schmidt, E., Decke, R., Rasshofer, R.: Correlation between subjective driver state measures and psychophysiological and vehicular data in simulated driving. In: 2016 IEEE intelligent vehicles symposium (IV), pp. 1380–1385. IEEE (2016)
14. Lohani, M., Payne, B.R., Strayer, D.L.: A review of psychophysiological measures to assess cognitive states in real-world driving. Front. Hum. Neurosci. **13**, 57 (2019)
15. Ekman, P., Friesen, W.V.: Facial action coding system. Environm. Psychol. Nonverbal Behav. (1978)
16. Riera, B., Grislin, M., Millot, P.: Methodology to evaluate man-car interfaces. In: IFAC Proceedings Volumes, vol. 27, pp. 425–430 (1994)
17. Albert, B., Tullis, T.: Measuring the user experience: collecting, analyzing, and presenting usability metrics. Newnes (2013)
18. Harvey, C., Stanton, N.A., Pickering, C.A., McDonald, M., Zheng, P.: In-vehicle information systems to meet the needs of drivers. Intl. J. Hum.-Comput. Interact. **27**, 505–522 (2011)
19. Jin, X., Li, P., Yang, Y., Fu, M., Li, Y., You, F.: Touch key of in-vehicle display and control screen based on vehicle HMI evaluation. Packaging Eng. **42**, 151–158 (2021)
20. Swette, R., May, K.R., Gable, T.M., Walker, B.N.: Comparing three novel multimodal touch interfaces for infotainment menus. In: Proceedings of the 5th International Conference on automotive user interfaces and interactive vehicular applications, pp. 100–107 (2013)
21. Law, E.L.-C., Van Schaik, P.: Modelling user experience–An agenda for research and practice. Interact. Comput. **22**, 313–322 (2010)
22. Vaidya, O.S., Kumar, S.: Analytic hierarchy process: An overview of applications. Eur. J. Oper. Res. **169**, 1–29 (2006)
23. de FSM Russo, R., Camanho, R.: Criteria in AHP: a systematic review of literature. Proc. Comput. Sci. 55, 1123–1132 (2015)

Designing Two-Stage Warning Systems: The Effect of Hazard Information

Yaping Zhang[1], Qianli Ma[1], Jianhong Qu[1], and Ronggang Zhou[1,2(✉)]

[1] School of Economics and Management, Beihang University, Beijing, China
zhrg@buaa.edu.cn
[2] Key Laboratory of Complex System Analysis, Management and Decision (Beihang University), Ministry of Education, Beijing, China

Abstract. Warning system design is critical to road safety in the automated driving takeover process. Two-stage warning system had been proposed to be an optimal solution to achieve better takeover performance. However, the two-stage warning system design needs further verification and validation. The primary purpose of this study is to explore the effect of warning content on takeover performance during the automated driving takeover process with a two-stage warning system design. Trust evaluations for the warning systems were also examined to validate the user experience with the alarm design. A within-subject design was used in this study. The within-subject factor was the warning content related to hazard information with two levels: warning with content and warning without content. A driving simulation experiment was conducted, and 32 participants (16 males, 16 females) drove two sessions with the two kinds of warning system design. The results showed that providing warning content to the TOR stage in the two-stage warning system design could result in slower reaction time and shorter TTC_{wpll}. With or without warning content design did not influence drivers' trust evaluation for the two-stage warning system. This finding suggested that warning content should not be provided to the TOR stage when designing the two-stage warning system, which may result in traffic incidents due to an untimely takeover. This study helps design takeover warning systems.

Keywords: Takeover Request Design · Hazard Information · Two-Stage Warning System · Takeover Performance

1 Introduction

In recent years, automated driving systems (ADSs) have increasingly penetrated the consumer market. ADSs are expected to help alleviate modern traffic problems such as traffic accidents, fuel emissions, and road congestion [1–3]. However, conditioned autonomous driving (CAD) also introduces new human factor problems. According to statistics from California's autonomous driving road test data, there were 124 traffic accidents caused by autonomous vehicles from 2014 to 2018 [1, 4]. In these cases, the possibility of the automated driving system failing or exceeding operating limits existed, which requires drivers to be ready to respond to emergencies at any time and complete

© The Author(s), under exclusive license to Springer Nature Switzerland AG 2023
P.-L. P. Rau (Ed.): HCII 2023, LNCS 14023, pp. 486–496, 2023.
https://doi.org/10.1007/978-3-031-35939-2_36

takeover operations to avoid traffic accidents [5–7]. Since the driver (CAD level 3 and above) no longer needs to monitor the surrounding environment all the time and will engage in some non-driving related tasks (NDRT), this reinforces the importance of driver takeover and takeover request design to ensure driving safety. In this case, the warning system design in takeover scenarios becomes even more important.

To verify the influence of different warning designs on takeover performance, many researchers have conducted studies to compare the effect of different types of warnings. There have been some experimental studies [3, 8] and review articles [9–13] investigating the warning system design of the lead time (LT) and warning modality, and the influence factors of NDRTs, takeover scenarios, and some driver factors. The takeover request modality and LT have been most widely discussed [10, 13–15]. Moreover, the warning types, such as the voice type [8], modality of visibility, audition, vibration [3, 16, 17], smell [18], and modality combination [19–23] have been widely studied. The two-stage warning system design has been proposed and proved to be an optimal solution to improve situational awareness, reduce physiological stress, achieve better takeover performance and higher acceptance ratings, and improve takeover safety through simulated driving experiments [24, 25, 28]. However, the two-stage warning system design needs more verification and validation. The broadcast of hazard information is helpful to the establishment of situational awareness of drivers during the takeover process [26]. Then, is it necessary to provide hazard information tips in a two-stage warning system design? Therefore, this study will explore the influence of the design of warning content related to hazard information in a two-stage warning system on takeover performance.

1.1 Two-Stage Warning System

The two-stage design of warning systems means that the warning systems were divided into two stages: the monitor request (MR) and the take-over request (TOR), indicating the ADS will issue an MR warning to prepare the drivers for a possible TOR [27–29]. The MR warning could be "attention please," and the TOR warning is generally "takeover please" [24]. The functions and the urgency of the two warnings are different. The MR stage is designed to bring the driver's attention back to the driving task and is less urgent, while the TOR stage is designed to ensure driving safety and is more urgent. This kind of two-stage warning system design is also called a multistage collision warning system [30] or two-step take-over requests [13, 31].

Recently, some studies have studied the effect of a two-stage warning design on takeover performance and subjective evaluation. Lu et al. [28] compared the effect of the TOR-only (in the LT of 5 s) warning design and the MR + TOR (LT of MR: 12 s, LT of TOR: 5 s) design and found that drivers spent a shorter TOT and a longer minimum TTC in the MR + TOR condition than in the TOR-only condition. In addition, the two-stage or MR (LT: 10 s) + TOR (LT: 7 s) warning design has significant effects on improving the driver's situational awareness, reducing driving pressure, and improving takeover performance and acceptance [24]. The driver's trust and acceptance of the two-stage warning design were significantly higher than those of the one-stage design [24, 25]. However, the two-stage method can also bring some problems. When the MR lead time is 6 s and the TOR lead time is 3 s, a considerable number of drivers take over the vehicle in the TOR stage, resulting in a higher number of accidents [31]. When takeover in the MR stage was allowed, the frequency of vehicle control interventions after the TOR warning was high (22%), which increased the possibility of collision accidents [31]. In addition, the overreliance of the TOR stage may be a new problem [28]. The late TOR warning may cause more collisions [31]. Compared with the time interval (the time between the MR and TOR) of 3 s, 5 s, and 9 s of the two-stage design, the driver had the best takeover preparation (i.e., fast steering wheel operation response and sufficient situational awareness) when the interval between MR and TOR was 5 s [25]. In general, the two-stage warning system design is helpful for effective takeovers, but it needs further verification and validation. Hence, more studies should be conducted to examine the effectiveness of the two-stage warning system design.

1.2 Warning Information

Some research about the hazard information alert in the warning system design has been conducted. A study has proven that semantic output related to the description of the hazard ahead other than warning sounds can shorten the TOT and information processing time [32]. In addition, providing information about the surrounding environment and dangerous subjects in the TOR warning is one way to improve situational awareness [26]. Furthermore, Wright et al. [26] designed four types of warning content. They found that, compared with other types of information, when the ADS provided the driver with an environment cue, the driver was more inclined to decelerate and perform other vehicle behaviors with greater ease (lower speed and greater absolute acceleration) to avoid collisions. Ji et al. [33] divided the types of information into "how message," "why message," and "why + how message," suggesting that the "how message" is more intelligent and attractive than the "why message." Similarly, Du et al. [34] designed three types of TOR warning content in the driving simulator, i.e., "what will, "why," and "why + what will," and found that providing only "why" information is less useful than providing only "what will" information and "why + what will" information.

In summary, it is helpful for drivers to establish situational awareness by providing information about dangerous situations in warning system design. The information conveyed in the warning may be an important influencing factor on the takeover performance. However, in a one-stage warning system, previous studies suggested that providing hazard information or a "what" message does not seem to improve drivers' evaluation. In the two-stage warnings, the presentation of warning content still needs to be further compared and determined.

1.3 The Current Study

The primary purpose of this study is to explore the effect of warning content on takeover performance during the automated driving takeover process with a two-stage warning system design. Trust evaluation for the warning system was also examined to validate the user experience of alarm design. We assume that compared to the without-content two-stage warning design, the with-content two-stage warning design results in better takeover performance and higher trust evaluation. The findings of this study can provide design guidance for the two-stage warning system design. The warning systems can be implemented in autonomous driving systems to increase safety in conditionally automated driving.

2 Method

2.1 Participants

Thirty-two participants (16 males and 16 females) aged 22–45 years ($M = 29.9$, $SD = 6.2$) participated in this study. They all held valid driver's licenses, and had at least one year of driving experience, including highway driving experience, average or corrected-to-normal vision, and normal hearing. All recruited participants had no previous experience with automated vehicle experiments (real-world and simulated). Among these participants, 12 were students with good driving experience, and 20 were employed staff. The average driving experience of the last year was 6,606.50 km ($SD = 7306.78$). This study was reviewed and approved by the Human Research Ethics Committee in the School of Economics and Management at Beihang University.

2.2 Apparatus

The experimental equipment consisted of a simulated driving experiment platform, two loudspeakers, and two iPads. The driving simulator comprised three 27-inch screens subtending a horizontal field of view of approximately 135° and one set of Logitech G27 racing force feedback wheels and pedals (Logitech Inc., US). The driving simulation software UC-win/Road Version 10.2 (FORUM8 Co., Ltd., JP) was used for environment visualization, and the graphics were presented at a resolution of 1920 × 1080 pixels. Two PHILIPS SPA20/93 speakers were placed approximately 100 cm in front of the participants and 45° to the left of the participant's body midline (at an elevation roughly matching their waist level when seated) to play TORs. Participants used two 9.7-inch iPads in this experiment to fill in the questionnaire and perform the NDRT of the Tetris game, respectively. The iPad used for the NDRT was located on the right side of the horizontal desktop. The iPad used to fill out the questionnaire was handed to the participants at the end of each driving road. The experimental scenario is shown in Fig. 1 below.

Fig. 1. Experimental scenario.

2.3 Experimental Design

A within-subject design was used in this study. The within-subject factor was the warning content related to hazard information with two levels: warning with content and warning without content. All participants completed two driving sections with different warning system designs: a two-stage warning system with hazard information and a two-stage warning system without hazard information. The warning design in each driving section was the same. Moreover, the order of the two driving sections was counterbalanced.

In the two-stage warning system (MR + TOR warning system), a monitor request (MR) (i.e., "*Attention please*") was triggered 12 s before the hazard, and a takeover request (TOR) (i.e., "*Takeover please*") was provided 5 s after the MR onset, which was proven to provide the best takeover preparation for the driver [25]. The lead time of the takeover request was set to 7 s [10], which is in the range of 5–8 s to maximize the effectiveness of warning messages [35]. Warning content can only be provided during the TOR warning stage, such as "*takeover please, truck breakdown ahead*" (in Chinese: "请接管, 前方车辆事故").

The warning modality of combining auditory alert (female voice, 300 words/min, and 67 db) and the visual cue was adopted in this study. The visual cue was presented at the top center of the middle screen, which could be seen in Fig. 1. The visual MR warning was white text on a blue background (50-point size font), while the TOR warning was white on a red background (50-point size font).

2.4 Dependent Variables and Measures

Takeover performance measures. The reaction time (RT) and time to collision when passing the lane-dividing line (TTC$_{wpll}$) [13, 24] were calculated. RT was calculated from the time the TOR (or MR, when takeover in the MR stage) was issued to the time the participant pressed the takeover paddle under the steering wheel. The TTC_{wpll} calculation method is shown in Formula (1) [24] below.

$$TTC_{wpll} = \frac{d}{\left(v_{lcp} - v_{dp}\right)} \tag{1}$$

Here, d refers to the distance between the driving vehicle and the danger location when the center of the vehicle coincides with the road edge. The v_{lcp} refers to the speed of the vehicle at that point, and $v_{dp} = 0$.

Trust Evaluation. For the trust measurement, the 12-item human-computer interaction trust scale implemented by Jian et al. [36] was used in the experiment. According to the reliability and validity tests, the factor analysis ($KMO = 0.901$, Bartlett's test of sphericity *Chi-square* $= 705.61$, $df = 66$, $p < 0.001$) suggested that two principal components were extracted, but the first component only contained one item, so the mean score of the remaining 11 items was calculated as the trust evaluation, explaining 61.11% of the variance and the factor loadings ranged from 0.62 to 0.96. The internal consistency was also good (*Cronbach's* $\alpha = 0.942$).

2.5 Experimental Task

The driving scenario was a six-lane highway road (three lanes in one direction), 11 km in length. As shown in Fig. 2, there were four hazard scenarios: (1) a traffic accident (i.e., two collided cars on the main road), (2) a broken-down container truck in the main road, (3) a work zone, and (4) a broken-down truck with seven cargo boxes scattered near the truck. Thus, each driving section consisted of four takeovers at distances of 2.5, 5, 7.5, and 10 km. The obstacles were static (assuming no dodging effect) and were in the center of the right lane. To reduce interference from other vehicles, there was no traffic flow near the hazard. In the driving process, the vehicle was driving in the middle lane except for the situation that needed a takeover. The driving mode switching (automated - manual) was set by the paddle under the steering wheel. In the automated driving mode, the speed of the simulated vehicle was set to 100 km/h, and the participants spent approximately 8 min in each driving section. The ADS issued the MR/TOR when the distance between the car and the obstacle was about 333.33 m/194.45 m (100 km/h $\times$ 12 or 7 s), leaving drivers 12 s/7 s to complete the transition.

NDRT. During the experiment, the participants were required to focus on the NDRT (playing the Tetris game on an iPad) before taking over. Other researchers have also studied this type of NDRT [24]. The difficulty level of the Tetris game was set at level one for all participants. Participants were asked to immerse themselves in Tetris and to ensure the safety of the takeover after hearing the takeover warning.

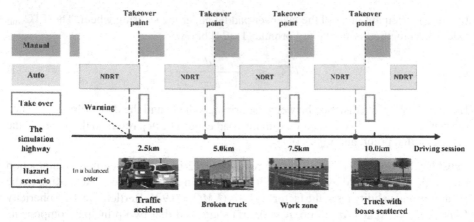

Fig. 2. Driving section and road conditions. In one driving section, each participant had four takeovers, and the warning design in each driving section was the same. The order of hazard scenarios was balanced.

2.6 Procedure

Before the experiment, the participants were asked to fill out a basic information questionnaire. When the participants arrived at the laboratory, they were given general instructions for the experiment and then required to sign an informed consent form.

After that, the participants were invited to sit in the seat of the simulator and were allowed to adjust the angle and position of the seat until they felt comfortable. The participants came to understand the experimental process by reading the experimental instructions and listening to the explanation given by the experimenter. The participants were introduced to using the driving simulator hardware, mainly the steering wheel, brake, accelerator pedal, and driving mode transition paddle. The experimenter reminded them to take over the vehicle after the warning was issued. During the automated driving process, the participants had to do the NDRT task. The Tetris game tasks and operation methods were introduced in detail by the experimenter. Then, participants engaged in a practice section of approximately 6 min to familiarize themselves with the simulator. They could choose to continue the practice until they thought they were already proficient in the operation.

After the practice, each participant participated in two driving sections with different warning designs, which were counterbalanced. Participants were asked to perform the NDRT task before the warnings were prompted. Participants were allowed to take over when they heard the MR or the TOR warnings. There were four hazards in each driving section. After completing each section, the participants were asked to use an iPad to complete a questionnaire measuring their trust in the warning system. The entire experiment took approximately 60 min. The participants received compensation of 150 RMB for their participation.

3 Results

We used IBM SPSS Statistics 22.0 for data analysis. Repeated-measures ANOVA was conducted to investigate the effect of warning content on the dependent variables. A total of 256 takeovers happened in this experiment. Due to an operational error in the experimental process, four takeovers from one participant were unavailable in one driving section. Therefore, the takeover performance data from the participant was removed from the following data analysis. Participants were allowed to take over the vehicle in the MR stage (MR takeovers) or the TOR stage (TOR takeovers). According to statistics, there were 22 MR takeovers in the driving section without content warning design and 20 MR takeovers in the driving section with content warning design. Since the MR phase did not reflect the experimental design of the warning content, the MR takeovers would not be included in the following analysis.

As shown in Fig. 3, for reaction time, the mean RT of the without-content warning system design was 1.44 s ($SD = 0.71$), and the mean RT of the with-content warning system design was 1.64 s ($SD = 0.88$). According to the repeated-measures ANOVA, the RT under the two-stage warning system design without hazard information was significantly faster than that under the two-stage warning system design with hazard information ($F (1, 98) = 5.85, p < 0.05, \eta^2 = 0.056$). For TTC$_{wpll}$, the mean TTC$_{wpll}$ of the without-content warning system design was 2.67 s ($SD = 1.16$), and the mean TTC$_{wpll}$ of the with-content warning system design was 2.48 s ($SD = 1.08$). According to the repeated-measures ANOVA, the difference was not significant ($F (1, 98) = 3.43$, $p = 0.067, \eta^2 = 0.034$). As for the trust evaluation for the two kinds of warning system design, there was no significant difference in the trust scores ($F (1, 31) = 0.56, p = 0.462, \eta^2 = 0.018$), which indicated that warning content design does not affect user trust for the system.

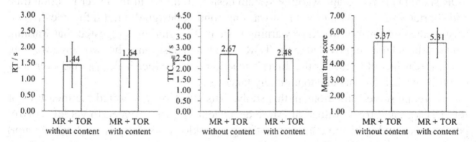

Fig. 3. RT ($n = 99$), TTC$_{wpll}$ ($n = 99$), and trust evaluation ($N = 32$) for the different warning system designs.

4 Discussion

This study conducted a driving simulation experiment to examine the effect of the warning content on takeover performance during the automated driving takeover process. The subjective evaluation of trust for the warning system design was also collected.

According to our results, the reaction time (RT) under the two-stage warning system design without hazard information was significantly faster than that under the two-stage warning system design with hazard information. The mean TTC_{wpll} of the without-content warning system design was longer than the mean TTC_{wpll} of the with-content warning system design. These findings indicated that hazard information should not be provided to the TOR stage in the two-stage warning system design, which could prolong drivers' reaction time and shorten TTC_{wpll}. The reason may be that the participants would wait for the content to be broadcast before taking over, and the content information took up time. As for the trust evaluation for the two kinds of warning system design, there was no significant difference in the trust scores, which indicated that warning content design did not affect user trust in the system. The reason may be that the "why" message provided to the warning had a higher evaluation of perceived usefulness but a lower evaluation of ease of use [34]. According to the information redundancy effect, previous studies believed that the superiority of additional speech output over mere generic auditory output and the additional speech output should be completed before actions of NDRT interruption had begun, which may facilitate drivers' reactions towards the TOR [32]. Since another study proved that providing information about the surrounding environment in the TOR warning can improve situational awareness and increase the detection of latent hazards by almost 40% [26], the warning content design in the MR stage needs further investigation.

5   Conclusions and Limitations

This study examined the influence of the warning content design on the takeover performance and trust evaluation during the automated driving takeover process with the two-stage warning system. The results showed that providing warning content to the TOR stage in the two-stage warning system design could result in slower reaction time and shorter TTC_{wpll}. With or without warning content design did not influence drivers' trust evaluation for the two-stage warning system. This finding suggested that warning content should not be provided to the TOR stage when designing the two-stage warning system, which could prolong the driver's reaction time, reduce TTC_{wpll}, and even may result in traffic incidents due to untimely takeover.

There are some limitations in this study. This study only reported the measures of RT, TTC_{wpll}, and trust evaluation. More dependent variables related to vehicle control performance and subjective assessment (e.g., workload, usefulness, and satisfaction) need to be reported. The LT design of the two-stage warning systems may be optimized. Our study set the LT to 12 s (MR) and 7 s (TOR). When the LT was longer, such as 20 s or more, the driving behavior and the effect of warning content may be different. Future work can concentrate on less urgent takeover scenarios. In addition, warning content design in the MR stage also needs to be further determined.

References

1. Boggs, A.M., Arvin, R., Khattak, A.J.: Exploring the who, what, when, where, and why of automated vehicle disengagements. Accid. Anal. Prev. **136**, 105406 (2020)

2. Eriksson, A., Stanton, N.A.: Driving performance after self-regulated control transitions in highly automated vehicles. Hum. Factors **59**(8), 1233–1248 (2017)
3. Wan, J., Wu, C.: The effects of vibration patterns of take-over request and non-driving tasks on taking-over control of automated vehicles. Int. J. Hum.-Comput. Interact. **34**(11), 987–998 (2018)
4. Arvin, R., Khattak, A.J., Kamrani, M., Rio-Torres, J.: Safety evaluation of connected and automated vehicles in mixed traffic with conventional vehicles at intersections. J. Intell. Trans. Syst. **25**(2), 170–187 (2020)
5. SAE International: Taxonomy and definitions for terms related to driving automation systems for on-road motor vehicles (Technical report No. J3016) (2018)
6. Gold, C., Happee, R., Bengler, K.: Modeling take-over performance in level 3 conditionally automated vehicles. Accid. Anal. Prev. **116**, 3–13 (2018)
7. Gold, C., Berisha, I., Bengler, K.: Utilization of drivetime–performing non-driving related tasks while driving highly automated. In: Proceedings of the Human Factors and Ergonomics Society Annual Meeting, pp. 1666–1670. SAGE Publications, Sage CA: Los Angeles, CA (2015)
8. Bazilinskyy, P., de Winter, J.C.: Analyzing crowdsourced ratings of speech-based take-over requests for automated driving. Appl. Ergon. **64**, 56–64 (2017)
9. Morales-Alvarez, W., Sipele, O., Léberon, R., Tadjine, H.H., Olaverri-Monreal, C.: Automated driving: A literature review of the take over request in conditional automation. Electronics **9**(12), 2087 (2020)
10. McDonald, A.D., et al.: Toward computational simulations of behavior during automated driving takeovers: a review of the empirical and modeling literatures. Hum. Factors **61**(4), 642–688 (2019)
11. Zhang, B., de Winter, J., Varotto, S., Happee, R., Martens, M.: Determinants of take-over time from automated driving: A meta-analysis of 129 studies. Transport. Res. F: Traffic Psychol. Behav. **64**, 285–307 (2019)
12. Weaver, B.W., DeLucia, P.R.: A systematic review and meta-analysis of takeover performance during conditionally automated driving. Human factors 0018720820976476 (2020)
13. Ma, S., Zhang, W., Shi, J., Yang, Z.: The human factors of the take-over process in conditional automated driving based on cognitive mechanism. Adv. Psychol. Sci. **28**(1), 150 (2020)
14. Wu, H., Wu, C., Lyu, N., Li, J.: Does a faster takeover necessarily mean it is better? A study on the influence of urgency and takeover-request lead time on takeover performance and safety. Accid. Anal. Prev. **171**, 106647 (2022)
15. Tan, X., Zhang, Y.: The effects of takeover request lead time on drivers' situation awareness for manually exiting from freeways: A web-based study on level 3 automated vehicles. Accid. Anal. Prev. **168**, 106593 (2022)
16. Cohen-Lazry, G., Katzman, N., Borowsky, A., Oron-Gilad, T.: Directional tactile alerts for take-over requests in highly-automated driving. Transport. Res. F: Traffic Psychol. Behav. **65**, 217–226 (2019)
17. Gruden, T., Tomažič, S., Sodnik, J., Jakus, G.: A user study of directional tactile and auditory user interfaces for take-over requests in conditionally automated vehicles. Accid. Anal. Prev. **174**, 106766 (2022)
18. Tang, Q., Guo, G., Zhang, Z., Zhang, B., Wu, Y.: Olfactory facilitation of takeover performance in highly automated driving. Hum. Factors **63**(4), 553–564 (2021)
19. Bazilinskyy, P., Petermeijer, S.M., Petrovych, V., Dodou, D., de Winter, J.C.: Take-over requests in highly automated driving: A crowdsourcing survey on auditory, vibrotactile, and visual displays. Transport. Res. F: Traffic Psychol. Behav. **56**, 82–98 (2018)
20. Walch, M., Woide, M., Mühl, K., Baumann, M., Weber, M.: Cooperative overtaking: Overcoming automated vehicles' obstructed sensor range via driver help. In: Proceedings of

the 11th International Conference on Automotive User Interfaces and Interactive Vehicular Applications, pp. 144–155. (2019)

21. Kim, W., Kim, J., Kim, H.S., Lee, S.J., Yoon, D.: A study on the driver's response performance according to modality of planned TOR in automated driving. In: 2019 International Conference on Information and Communication Technology Convergence (ICTC), pp. 1471–1473. IEEE (2019)

22. Geitner, C., Biondi, F., Skrypchuk, L., Jennings, P., Birrell, S.: The comparison of auditory, tactile, and multimodal warnings for the effective communication of unexpected events during an automated driving scenario. Transport. Res. F: Traffic Psychol. Behav. **65**, 23–33 (2019)

23. Yoon, S.H., Kim, Y.W., Ji, Y.G.: The effects of takeover request modalities on highly automated car control transitions. Accid. Anal. Prev. **123**, 150–158 (2019)

24. Ma, S., et al.: Take over gradually in conditional automated driving: the effect of two-stage warning systems on situation awareness, driving stress, takeover performance, and acceptance. Int. J. Hum.–Comput. Interact. 37(4), 352–362 (2021)

25. Zhang, W., et al.: Optimal Time Intervals in Two-Stage Takeover Warning Systems With Insight Into the Drivers' Neuroticism Personality. Front. Psychol. 157 (2021)

26. Wright, T.J., Agrawal, R., Samuel, S., Wang, Y., Zilberstein, S., Fisher, D.L.: Effects of alert cue specificity on situation awareness in transfer of control in level 3 automation. Transp. Res. Rec. **2663**(1), 27–33 (2017)

27. Lu, Z., Happee, R., Cabrall, C.D., Kyriakidis, M., de Winter, J.C.: Human factors of transitions in automated driving: A general framework and literature survey. Transport. Res. F: Traffic Psychol. Behav. **43**, 183–198 (2016)

28. Lu, Z., Zhang, B., Feldhütter, A., Happee, R., Martens, M., De Winter, J.C.: Beyond mere take-over requests: The effects of monitoring requests on driver attention, take-over performance, and acceptance. Transport. Res. F: Traffic Psychol. Behav. **63**, 22–37 (2019)

29. Zhang, B., Lu, Z., Happee, R., de Winter, J., Martens, M.: Compliance with monitoring requests, biomechanical readiness, and take-over performance: Video analysis from a simulator study. In: 13th ITS European Congress, pp. ITS-1977 (2019)

30. Winkler, S., Werneke, J., Vollrath, M.: Timing of early warning stages in a multi stage collision warning system: Drivers' evaluation depending on situational influences. Transport. Res. F: Traffic Psychol. Behav. **36**, 57–68 (2016)

31. Epple, S., Roche, F., Brandenburg, S.: The sooner the better: Drivers' reactions to two-step take-over requests in highly automated driving. In: Proceedings of the Human Factors and Ergonomics Society Annual Meeting, pp. 1883–1887. SSAGE Publications, age CA: Los Angeles, CA: (2018)

32. Forster, Y., Naujoks, F., Neukum, A., Huestegge, L.: Driver compliance to take-over requests with different auditory outputs in conditional automation. Accid. Anal. Prev. **109**, 18–28 (2017)

33. Ji, W., Liu, R., Lee, S.: Do drivers prefer female voice for guidance? An interaction design about information type and speaker gender for autonomous driving car. In: International Conference on Human-Computer Interaction, pp. 208–224. Springer, Cham (2019)

34. Du, N., Zhou, F., Tilbury, D., Robert, L.P., Yang, X.J.: Designing Alert Systems in Takeover Transitions: The Effects of Display Information and Modality. In: 13th International Conference on Automotive User Interfaces and Interactive Vehicular Applications, pp. 173–180 (2021)

35. Wan, J., Wu, C., Zhang, Y.: Effects of lead time of verbal collision warning messages on driving behavior in connected vehicle settings. J. Safety Res. **58**, 89–98 (2016)

36. Jian, J.Y., Bisantz, A.M., Drury, C.G.: Foundations for an empirically determined scale of trust in automated systems. Int. J. Cogn. Ergon. **4**(1), 53–71 (2000)

The Roles of Perceived Risk and Expectancy Performance in Passenger's Acceptance of Automated Vehicles

Yiming Zou[✉], Xi Fu, Danlan Ye, and Ruilin Ouyang

Hunan University, Changsha 41006, Hunan, China
874851899@QQ.com

Abstract. The purpose of this study was to investigate the factors that affect passengers riding level 4 autonomous vehicles. By expanding the old TAM model, we propose a theoretical acceptance model: the effects of expected performance and perceived risk on initial trust and use behavior intention. We verified the validity of our model by conducting structural equation modeling analysis on the data collected from 88 survey samples. The final results confirm most of our assumptions that initial trust is the key factor affecting passengers' positive attitude toward using an autonomous vehicle, which together with perceived availability determines a user's intention to use an autonomous vehicle. Initial trust can be enhanced by improving desired performance and reducing perceived risks associated with autonomous vehicles. Theoretically, we add a new perspective of passengers to the traditional car driving acceptance research, and expand the relevant factors that affect passengers' initial trust in the car driving. In terms of practical implications, our results can provide theoretical references for developers of autonomous vehicles and policymakers.

Keywords: automated vehicles · passenger · expectancy performance · perceived risk · culture and psychology

1 Introduction

The era of autonomous vehicles (AVS) is rapidly approaching, offering a new mode of transportation that is believed to be economically and socially beneficial. The widely recognized AV classification standards were established by the SAE (Society of Automotive Engineers International) in 2014, dividing AVS into six levels (L0-L5) as shown in Table 1 [1]. L0 represents traditional human-driven vehicles without AV technology, while levels L1-L5 are graded based on the configuration of AVS technology. Level 3 to 5 are equipped with systems capable of monitoring the driving environment, relying on artificial intelligence, visual computing, radar, monitoring devices, and global positioning systems to work together and allow computers to safely control vehicles without human intervention.

AVS offer numerous advantages over conventional manually-driven vehicles. Firstly, AVS have the potential to significantly reduce accidents caused by human error. Elon

© The Author(s), under exclusive license to Springer Nature Switzerland AG 2023
P.-L. P. Rau (Ed.): HCII 2023, LNCS 14023, pp. 497–511, 2023.
https://doi.org/10.1007/978-3-031-35939-2_37

Table 1. AVS levels and definitions

Level	Name	Definition
Level 0	No automation	The driver performs all driving tasks
Level 1	Driver assistance	The vehicle has one or more systems that assist the driver but do not control the vehicle
Level 2	Partial automation	The vehicle can control certain functions such as acceleration and steering but the driver must still perform the majority of driving tasks
Level 3	Conditional automation	he vehicle can control most driving tasks but the driver must still be prepared to take over in certain circumstances
Level 4	High automation	The vehicle can perform all driving tasks under certain conditions and environments, but the driver must still be available to take over if needed
Level 5	Full automation	The vehicle can perform all driving tasks under all conditions, and the driver does not need to be physically present

Table 2. Fit indices for the tested model.

Fit indices	$\chi 2/df$	RMSEA	CFI	SRMR
Standard	< 2	< 0.06	> 0.95	< 0.8
Value	1.563	0.080	0.952	0.058

Musk has stated that the training of real-world AVS is the quickest, and possibly the only, way to reduce accidents. A study by McKinsey & Company found that AVs could reduce traffic accidents by 90%. Secondly, AVS can effectively reduce road congestion and emissions through more efficient route planning and vehicle operation, resulting in safer roads, less congestion, and less parking. Thirdly, AVS can free people from the task of driving, allowing them to engage in other non-driving activities. Finally, AVS offer new travel options for those who are unable to drive, such as the elderly and disabled, improving their travel experience. Due to these benefits, the global automotive industry has invested heavily in AVS research and development in recent years. Google's AVS prototypes have now driven over 1.5 million miles, and are undergoing testing in several cities in the United States [2] Table 2.

Despite the rapid advancement of AVS technology and the potential benefits it brings, the market is currently reluctant to adopt the technology on a large scale. In an effort to address this issue, a survey of 5000 people was conducted by M. Kyriakidis et al. According to the results of their research, respondents regarded manual driving as the most enjoyable driving method. Currently, the greatest barrier to the widespread adoption of AV technology is not technical but rather public acceptance [3].

To enhance public acceptability of AVS, it is crucial to understand the factors that influence their adoption. According to the research of M. Kyriakidis et al., among all available relevant coefficients, the factors most strongly associated with the intention to purchase an AVS are income, mileage, frequency of driving, and usage of adaptive cruise control systems. For example, it was found that individuals who drive more frequently are more likely to be willing to pay for AVS. This is because those who spend more time driving are more likely to appreciate automobiles and are more likely to purchase a new (automated) vehicle. Furthermore, individuals who currently use adaptive cruise control systems (ACC) are more likely to pay for AV cars. Thus, past experiences (i.e., driving and using ACCs) appear to be the best predictors of future behavior (i.e., purchasing a new car and an AVS car). Designing and testing acceptance models to study the psychological determinants of AVS car acceptance, based on cognitive mechanisms of human behavior, can help explain users' attitudes and acceptability, thereby facilitating a deeper understanding of the factors related to acceptability. They not only benefit businesses in designing intervention measures to alter users' acceptability of certain technologies, but also support policy-making, implementation, and technological development.

The field of AVS acceptability research still has some gaps. Firstly, the factors determining users' psychological acceptability remain unknown [4]. Secondly, although most existing models of acceptability encompass trust construction, the pathways by which it influences acceptability, such as direct, indirect, or mediating effects, have yet to be conclusive. Finally, survey research indicates that perceived risk is one of the most prominent reasons for non-acceptance of AVS [5], but many model-based studies have not explicitly explored perceived risk.

The aim of this study is to fill the gaps in the research field of AVS acceptance by proposing and validating a theoretical model of AVS acceptance. This study focuses on level 4 AVS, which is expected to appear in the future but has limited research available, and the model is based on the Technology Acceptance Model (TAM) and the establishment of initial trust and perceived risk. Trust is a key factor in forming technology acceptance, as it largely regulates the influence of other psychological factors. The results of this study are expected to deepen our understanding of how trust and other factors interact to form acceptance. From a practical perspective, this study will help technology developers, policy makers, and implementers provide better product and service quality, design intervention measures to promote passengers' intention to use AVS, and gain a competitive advantage in the global market. The following section reviews related work and details the process of developing the extended model.

2   Theoretical and Model

2.1   Theories of Acceptance Related to Behavior and Technology

The Theory of Planned Behavior (TPB) was developed by Ajzen. The theory involves five major elements, including Attitude, Subjective Norm, Perceived Behavioral Control, Behavior Intention, and Behavior. The theory suggests that all factors that have an impact on behaviour can indirectly influence behavioural performance through behavioural intentions. [6] The Unified Theory of Acceptance and Use of Technology (UTAUT) is based on a review of the "factors influencing user perceptions" and a summary of previous research on technology acceptance models. [7] Some other factors, such as gender, age, experience and voluntariness have significant effects on the core dimensions (Fig. 1). Acceptance refers to the extent to which people agree or consent to the situation, process or conditions of an event. Based on these models and concepts, it is possible to summarise the theoretical framework: people's trust and perception of new technology have an impact on building acceptance, and the behavioral intention and actual use of innovative technology is a measure of acceptance. The theory of planned behavior states that individual behavior is driven by behavioral intentions, where behavioral intentions consist of a fusion of three main factors, namely attitudes towards a behavior, subjective norms and perceived behavioral control. In addition, perceived behavior also has a direct impact on a person's actual behavior. The Integrated Technology Acceptance Model Theory is developed based on a Unified Acceptance Model, in which Performance Expectations, Effort Expectations, and Social Influence directly influence Behavioural Intentions, together with Facilitating Conditions that predict actual usage behavior.

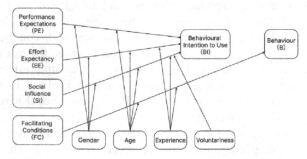

Fig. 1. Integrated Technology Acceptance Model Theory

In order to gain more insight into the results of research on people's attitudes and intentions to use self-driving cars, a certain amount and a certain degree of accumulation of research has been developed. The Technology Acceptance Model (TAM), a seminal and important theoretical model, suggests that perceived ease of use, perceived usefulness and attitudes to using technology have an impact on technology acceptance and that individuals' behavioural intentions are determined by their attitudes to using technology. On the one hand, perceived ease of use and perceived usefulness can influence attitudes, on the other hand, perceived ease of use influencing perceived usefulness, and perceived usefulness directly influencing users' behavioural intentions. (Fig. 2a) [8] Based on the above model, Ghazizadeh et al. took trust and compatibility into consideration and proposed the Automated Acceptance Model (AAM) [9]. In the Automated Acceptance Model, trust and compatibility influence attitudes and behavioural intentions by influencing perceived ease of use and usefulness, while the Technology Acceptance Model (TAM) relationships of perceived ease of use, usefulness and attitudes remain unchanged. (Fig. 2b) However, the validity of the model has not yet been verified. Meanwhile, Choi and Ji and Xu et al. extended the original technology acceptance model and applied it to the study of self-driving car acceptance by incorporating trust and perceived risk factors [10]. (Fig. 2c) It is assumed that trust, perceived risk, perceived usefulness and perceived convenience all directly influence behavioural intentions, while techno-logical trust can also indirectly influence behavioural intentions through each perceptual factor. This theoretical model has received theoretical or experimental support except for the indirect effect of perceived risk on behavioural intention. Kaur and Rampersad proposed the hypothesis that trust and performance expectations are two factors that directly influence the use of self-driving cars; reliability, safety risk and privacy risk influence trust factors indirectly influence intention to use (Fig. 2d) [11]. However, data related to this hypothesis and model are not publicly available. In general, reviewing the available relevant research, the development of acceptance models for autonomous vehicles is still in its early stages. While most studies suggest that consent trust and per-ceived risk are strongly associated with the acceptance of self-driving cars, the specific ways to influence user behaviour still need to be explored.

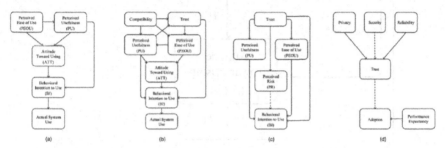

Fig. 2. (a) Original TAM proposed by Davis, Bagozzi, Warshaw (1989) (b) The model presented in Ghazizadeh, Lee, Boyle (2012) (c) The model proposed in Choi and Ji (2015) (d) The model presented in Kaur and Rampersad (2018)

2.2 Model and Hypotheses

To better explore passenger acceptance of self-driving cars, based on relevant literature studies, this study proposes a model of self-driving acceptance involving perceived risk, expected performance, initial trust, attitude towards use, and behavioural intention to use. (Fig. 3) Among them, perceived risk mainly involves perceived safety risk (PSR) and perceived privacy risk (PPR). This paper focuses on the direct and indirect effects of perceived risk and expected performance on attitudes and behavioural intentions to use, and discusses their impact on passenger acceptance of self-driving cars. Moreover, this study proposes hypotheses based on the model.

Initial Trust, Attitude Towards Usage and Behavioural Intention. Behavioural Intentions (BI) refer to an individual's attitude towards a particular behaviour. Behavioural Intentions are influenced by three factors: attitudes towards a particular behaviour, subjective norms that influence an individual's perception of a particular behaviour, and perceived behavioural control. Attitude to use refers to an individual's positive or negative feelings towards the use of a technology. In general, the more pos-itive an individual's attitude towards a technology, the stronger the intention to use it. Therefore, we propose that:

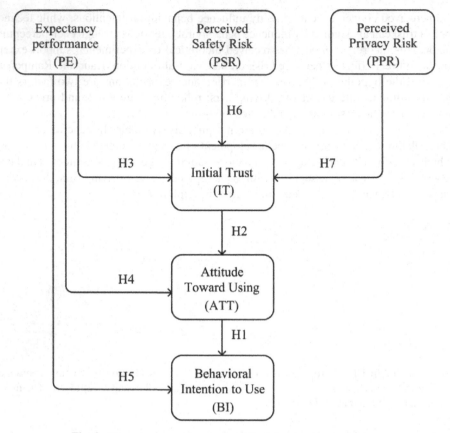

Fig. 3. Passenger acceptance model for L4 autonomous driving

H1: Positive attitudes towards AVS increase behavioural intention to use AVS.

Initial Trust (IT) refers to a state of mind in which an individual trusts a behaviour or technology to a certain extent during the initial interaction. Initial trust is a key factor in human-automation interactions, and distrust of an automated system can lead to refusal to use it, while excessive trust can lead to misuse or abuse. [12] Also, initial trust is influenced by a variety of factors such as personal experience and perception. In general, the higher the initial trust, the more positive the attitude towards use. Therefore, we propose that:

H2: Initial trust has a positive effect on positive attitudes towards using AVS.

Perceived and Expected Performance. Expectancy Performance (EP) refers to the extent to which an individual feels that using the system will help with a task or outcome, a state of mind in which an individual expects a behaviour or technology to be helpful, and has an impact on initial trust and attitudes towards use. The higher the Expectancy Performance, the higher the initial trust, and the higher the Expectancy Performance, the more positive the attitude towards use. Therefore, we propose that:

H3: High expected performance has a positive effect on initial trust in AVS.

H4: High expected performance has a positive effect on positive attitudes towards AVS.

H5: High performance expectations increase behavioural intention to use AVS.

Based on relevant studies and surveys, the public expressed some degree of concern about the risks associated with self-driving cars. Among them, potential Safety Risk and Privacy Risk are the two most important concerns. In terms of safety risk, according to research conducted by Menon and other related scholars, most people are very concerned about the safety risk of the AV users or other road users. [13] Privacy risk mainly involves the user's vehicle driving data or behavioural data etc. being collected and applied illegally by individuals, businesses, companies etc. without informing the user. Therefore, perceived security risk and perceived privacy risk are considered to be the two types of perceived risks that are most likely to affect the use of AVs at this stage [14]. Based on this the following hypothesis is proposed.

H6: Perceived safety risks to passengers have a negative impact on the initial trust in AVS.

H7: Perceived privacy risks have a negative impact on initial trust in AVS.

Related studies have shown that ignoring the direct effect of perceived risk on behavioural intention helps to improve the applicability of the theoretical model, while the direct effect of perceived risk on behavioural intention is not significant. Therefore, this study hypothesises that perceived risk has no direct effect on attitudes or behavioural intentions.

3   Method

3.1   Participants

The experimentation for the study was done via an online questionnaire. The survey of passengers' attitudes toward AVS is the subject of our research at this moment. We did not select the responders in order to acquire sufficiently large amounts of data for analysis because we think that everyone in the future society will surely ride in a vehicle with self-driving technology. Through online social media, we spread the questionnaire, and a total of 88 individuals responded. The respondents had an average age of 29.9 years (SD = 6.2), were overwhelmingly male (55.56%), had bachelor's degrees (65.28%), and most of the passengers had experience driving a car (70.83%). The most frequently used forms of transportation for daily travels were reported to be taxis (20.74%) and subways (22.87%). Only one (1.39%) respondent stated that he had never heard of AVS prior to taking this survey, even though the vast majority of respondents (84.72%) appear to be passengers in their regular trips. The Internet was the most often mentioned medium (95.83%) among those who had heard about AVS, followed by casual talk (58.33%). 37.5%, 12.5%, 27.78%, and 15.28% of respondents said they first learnt about AVS from television, newspapers, books, and other sources, respectively.

3.2   Data Analysis

Confirmatory factor analysis (CFA) was used to investigate the psychometric features of the scales. When the model's fitness indices meet the required thresholds, construct validity is attained.

Kline advised using the ratio of Chi-square value to degree of freedom ($\chi 2/df$), the Comparative Fit Index (CFI), the Standardized Root Mean Square Residual (SRMR), and the Root Mean Square Error of Approximation (RMSEA) as goodness-of-fit indices. In general, the higher the CFI value and the lower the values of the other three indices, the better the model fits. When $\chi 2/df < 2$, CFI > 0.95, SRMR < 0.08, and RMSEA < 0.06 are greater than one, the model is regarded to be a good fit [14]. Convergent validity is the determination of whether or not different indicators of the same notion agree [14]. To ensure convergent validity, an item's factor loading on its theorized underlying construct factor should be substantial and more than 0.6. The Average Variance Extracted (AVE) metric was also used to test convergent validity. An AVE of more than 0.5 is regarded as sufficient. Discriminant validity reflects the extent to which the constructs differ experimentally from one another [15]. The Fornell and Larcker criterion states that discriminant validity is obtained when the square root of AVE (SAVE) for each construct is greater than any of the bivariate correlations involving the construct in the model [15]. Cronbach's alpha and composite reliability were used to assess internal consistency. Cronbach's alpha and composite reliability should be more than 0.7 to be considered strong internal consistency [16]. Finally, the Harman's single-factor test was used to evaluate common method variance (CMV) by entering all items into a principal component factor analysis without rotation [17]. CMV is not an issue if the single factor accounts for less than 50% of total variance. The proposed model's hypotheses were tested using Structural Equation Modeling (SEM). To assess the fit of the proposed model, the same goodness-of-fit criteria (i.e. $\chi 2/df < 2$, CFI > 0.95, SRMR < 0.08, RMSEA < 0.06) were used.

4 Result

4.1 Measurement Model Assessment

Table 3 shows the CFA results after the PE2 item was removed. The fit indeices indicate how well the measurement model matches the data. Table 4 shows that all factor loadings were greater than 0.6, indicating that these items were significantly related to the factors they were supposed to measure. Given that all AVEs were greater than the minimum acceptable value of 0.5 and that each SAVE was greater than any bivariate correlation involving the model's factors (Table 5), it was concluded that the factors retained good aggregate and discriminant validity. Furthermore, all Cronbach's alpha and composite reliability values were greater than the required minimum level of 0.7, indicating that the measures used to measure each factor had good internal consistency. In conclusion, the measurement model has good reliability and validity and is appropriate for structural model analysis.

4.2 Descriptive Analysis of the Constructs in the Model

Respondents expected riding an AVS to improve their expectancy performance (Mean = 3.915, SD = 0.712). Work status had a significance level of 0.05 for initial trust (F = 3.166, p = 0.029), and the specific comparison difference shows that the comparison result of the mean scores of the groups with relatively obvious differences is "currently no job > full-time job; currently no work > student". Expectancy performance (F = 17.326, p < 0.001), initial trust (F = 12.569, p = 0.001), and attitude to use (F = 9.386, p = 0.003) were all significantly related to previous driving/riding of an AVS. Respondents who had previously driven/ridden AVS had significantly higher expectancy performance (Mean = 4.68), initial trust (Mean = 4.09), and attitude to use (Mean = 4.24) than the mean (expectancy performance (Mean = 3.81), initial trust (Mean = 3.19), and attitude to use (Mean = 3.44). With mean ratings of 4.07 (SD = 0.85) and 3.81 (SD = 0.95), respondents rated perceived safety risk and perceived privacy risk as high. These two risk perceptions were consistent across all consumer groups. Riding AVS received a moderately trustworthy rating with a mean trust score of 3.30 (SD = 0.84). The attitudes and behavioural intentions mean values were 3.54 (SD = 0.85) and 3.47 (SD = 0.97), respectively. This indicates that respondents have positive attitudes and plans to ride AVS.

Table 3. CFA results, convergent validity and internal consistency

Construct	Item	Factor Loading	Average Variance Extracted (AVE)	Composite Reliability (CR)	Cronbach's alpha
Expectancy performance (PE)	PE1 PE3	0.696 0.921	0.666	0.796	0.780
Perceived Safety Risk (PSR)	PSR1 PSR2	0.854 0.895	0.765	0.867	0.866
Perceived Privacy Risk (PPR)	PPR1 PPR2 PPR3	0.875 0.887 0.893	0.783	0.916	0.915
Trust	Trust1 Trust2 Trust3	0.874 0.943 0.819	0.775	0.911	0.901
Attitude (ATT)	ATT1 ATT2 ATT3	0.928 0.887 0.823	0.775	0.912	0.909
Behavioural Intentions to use(BI)	BI1 BI2	0.809 0.847 0.681	0.612	0.824	0.813

4.3 Structural Model Assessment

All goodness-of-fit indices of the model met the suggested criteria (Table 3), indicating that the proposed model accurately represented the assumed relationship. Figure 3

Table 4. Results of the discriminant validity test.

	PE	PSR	PPR	Trust	ATT	BI
PE	0.816					
PSR	−0.161	0.875				
PPR	0.050	0.421	0.885			
Trust	0.563	−0.378	−0.118	0.880		
ATT	0.673	−0.290	−0.221	0.792	0.880	
BI	0.569	−0.255	−0.086	0.579	0.707	0.782

PE: Expectancy performance; PSR: Perceived Safety Risk; PPR: Perceived Privacy Risk; BI: Behavioural Intentions to use.

depicts the results of estimating the structural model, where important paths are solid lines and non-important paths are dashed lines. Table 5 summarizes the path coefficients and hypothesis testing results. Attitudes toward using AVS, in particular, were found to have a positive effect on behavioral intention to use ($\beta = 0.707$, $p < 0.001$), supporting H1. H2 is supported by the fact that trust has a significant positive effect on attitude to use ($\beta = 0.792$, $p < 0.001$). Expectancy performance also had a significant positive effect on trust ($\beta = 0.563$, $p < 0.001$), attitude to use ($\beta = 0.673$, $p < 0.001$), and behavioral

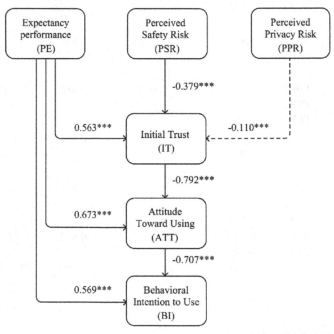

Fig. 4. Results of the structural model. Dotted lines indicate non-significant paths. Note: *** p < 0.001; ** p < 0.01; * p < 0.05

intention to use ($\beta = 0.569$, $p < 0.001$). As a result, H3, H4, and H5 are supported. Among the hypotheses related to trust and perceived privacy risk (H6, H7), perceived safety risk; ($\beta = -0.379$, $p < 0.001$) and perceived privacy risk ($\beta = -0.110$, $p = 0.262$) have a significant positive effect on trust. Not a reliable predictor of trust. As a result, H6 is supported but not H7 (Fig. 4).

Table 5. Results of hypothesis testing

Hypotheses	Standardized Path coefficients	Supported?
H1: ATT → BI	0.707***	Yes
H2: Trust → ATT	0.792***	Yes
H3: PE → Trust	0.563***	Yes
H4: PE → ATT	0.673***	Yes
H5: PE → BI	0.569***	Yes
H6: PSR → Trust	−0.379***	Yes
H7: PPR → Trust	−0.110, 0.262	No

PE: Expectancy performance; PSR: Perceived Safety Risk; PPR: Perceived Privacy Risk; Att: Attitude; BI: Behavioural Intentions to use. ** $p < 0.01$ ***, $p < 0.001$, * $p < 0.05$.

5   Discussion

In this study, we propose a new theoretical AVS acceptance model. This model holds that whether users accept to take AVS depends directly on their initial trust level in AVS to a large extent, and this initial trust is based on a combination of expected performance (PE), perceived security risk (PSR), and perceived privacy risk (PPR). The results support the proposed model, with trust as the strongest predictor of user attitudes, contributing to research and practice in various ways.

5.1   Theoretical Implications

First, most previous studies build models to assess users' attitudes towards AVS from the perspective of drivers, and we innovatively assess passengers' attitudes towards AVS from the perspective of passengers.

In our study, we found that initial trust plays a significantly stronger role than behavioral intention in passenger's attitude towards AVS use. Earle and Cvetkovich [19] explained that trust is "a tool to reduce cognitive complexity", which can well simplify and promote the decision-making process in risky and uncertain scenarios [18]. Trust can be a way to mitigate users' perception of risk when they have to take action in an uncertain and potentially risky environment. This decision process based on TRUST has been proved in the user acceptance experiment in the e-commerce scenario, and the relationship between trust and attitude (ATT) is more stable than risk-attitude (ATT) [19].

But, to our knowledge, for the first time at the driving level, we include passenger trust as a key antecedent of attitudes towards AVS use. It may be due to the influence brought by the limitations of the model proposed by previous researchers or the survey group. Previous studies either suggested that the role of passengers' initial trust in passengers' attitude towards AVS was insignificant [20]. It may be complementary descriptions of the current model [21], or it may be influenced by other factors such as perceived usefulness (PU) [22]. Our research shows that trust not only affects passengers' perception or operational behavior when riding AVS, but also determines whether passengers will ride AVS in the first place. Our proposed model theoretically confirms the importance of initial trust in shaping passengers' attitudes towards AVS.

The second contribution was to demonstrate the impact of perceived risk (PSR) and expectancy performance (PE) on trust. The literature on technology acceptance in the field of information systems tends to model trust as an antecedent of cognitive processes. However, this relationship can only be true if users develop a stable level of trust based on information and interactions they receive from multiple sources. As an emerging technology that has only been perceived by the public in recent years, potential future users of AVS are still building their initial trust in AVS. Previous studies have shown that the initial trust of users is built based on the user's cognitive assessment of the reputation, quality and safety of the technology (Tingru et al. 2019) [23]. Our results extend this theoretical concept further. Specifically, we found that expected performance (PE) and perceived security risk (PSR) are important factors affecting the initial trust built by users. In terms of passengers' initial trust in AVS 'vehicle control, AVS' advantages over traditional cars in improving driving efficiency and driving safety are important and useful. Considering that the basic attribute of the car is as a means of transportation to improve the user's travel efficiency, also it's quite reasonable because the road accident may bring serious personal injury and huge economic loss.

Finally, this study has also explored the effects of perceived security risk and perceived privacy security risk on end-use behavioral intention (BI). In previous studies, perceived risk has often been considered a major issue affecting whether passengers take AVS. Our results refine this conclusion, suggesting that perceived risk indirectly affects passengers' attitudes toward AVS by influencing their level of trust in AVS, and because users' perceived privacy risk does not have a strong effect on initial trust, Therefore, different from the researches in the field of e-commerce, users' perceived privacy risk is not obvious in influencing users' attitudes towards taking AVS.

5.2 Practical Implications

Our results can provide better theoretical support for AVS design for AVS developers and policymakers, because with the improvement of autonomous driving in the future, the passenger attributes of users in travel scenarios will become stronger and stronger in the near future. In our study, trust is an important factor affecting the user's attitude towards AVS, which indicates that the establishment of user initial trust is an essential element for the future promotion of AVS. At the same time, according to our proposed model, a possible design strategy can be provided to improve the user's perceived performance of AVS. Therefore, we suggest that automobile manufacturers should try to reduce the complexity and improve the feedback clarity in the human-computer interaction process, so as to reduce the difficulty of passengers riding the in-car system of automated driving vehicles and reduce the learning cost of users. At the same time, the advantages of AVS compared with traditional cars in driving efficiency and driving comfort should be promoted to users through advertising. Another design strategy is to suggest the car host manufacturer to reduce the perceived safety risks of passengers to improve the initial trust of passengers for AVS cars. AVS should explain the reasons for the failure to passengers in time when the system fails. And policymakers should work closely with academics and manufacturers to develop rules, while ensuring that developers strictly adhere to safety standards.

5.3 Limitations of This Study and Future Work

The current research still has some limitations. First of all, the research results of our research experiment are based on the subjective evaluation indicators of users. Meanwhile, the sample size is small, and the subjective measurement of users' initial trust and behavioral intention to ride an autonomous vehicle may not represent objective behaviors [24]. In the future, we should measure the level of users' trust in autonomous vehicles by measuring behavioral indicators (such as participation in actual tasks) and physiological indicators through offline experiments [25]. In addition, as the current development of autonomous driving technology is still in the stage of incomplete autonomous driving, most respondents have no actual experience in AV. The trust discussed in this study is the initial trust based on the information obtained by respondents from the Internet or daily conversations. As users become more familiar with AVS [26], passengers' trust in AVS and its antecedents will further change due to these factors in the future. Therefore, it is suggested to further elaborate the changes in trust and user acceptance before and after user interaction with AVS by means of longitudinal research. At the same time, future research should also explore the role of other factors such as reliability, perceived cyber-security risk, liability issues, driving pleasure, and the influence of situational awareness on acceptance of AVS.

6 Conclusions

By incorporating the effects of perceived performance, perceived security risk, and perceived privacy risk on initial trust, this study proposes and verifies an extended model based on TAM model to explore the effects of these factors on passenger attitudes and behavioral intentions when using AVS. Trust was identified as a key antecedent to passengers' positive attitude towards AVS use, and expected performance and perceived safety also played an important role. From a theoretical point of view, we further refine the key factors affecting trust in TAM's extended model. It provides a new way to study the initial trust of passengers on AVS. From the perspective of application level, this finding suggests that relevant organizations should enhance public acceptance of AVS by enhancing the credibility of AVS. From the perspective of passengers' perceived performance and perceived safety, designers of AVS can improve passengers' willingness to use autonomous vehicles by optimizing the working efficiency of the interactive system of autonomous vehicles, reducing system defects and adding functions such as driving safety information display, because our research finds that perceived performance is positively correlated with users' initial trust level. The perceived safety risk is negatively correlated with the initial trust level of users. These measures can well promote users' willingness to use self-driving cars from the perspective of passengers.

References

1. National Highway Traffic Safety Administration.: Preliminary Statement of Policy Concerning Automated Vehicles. National Highway Traffic Safety Administration, pp. 1–14 (2013)
2. Waymo, Google Self-Driving Car Project, https://waymo.com 2022/10/20
3. Kyriakidis, M., Happee, R., Winter, J.C.: Public opinion on automated driving: Results of an international questionnaire among 5000 respondents. Transp. Res. part F: Traffic Psychol. Behav. **32**, 127–140 (2015)
4. Talebian, A., Mishra, S.: Predicting the adoption of connected autonomous vehicles: A new approach based on the theory of diffusion of innovations. Transp. Res. Part C: Emerg. Technol. **95**, 363–380 (2018)
5. Sener, I.N., Zmud, J., Williams, T.: Measures of baseline intent to use automated vehicles: A case study of Texas cities. Transp. Res. Part F: Traffic Psychol. Behav. **62**, 66–77 (2019)
6. Ajzen, I.: The theory of planned behaviour. Org. Behav. Human Decision Process. **50**(2), 179–211(1991)
7. Venkatesh, V., Morris, M.G., Davis, G.B., Davis, F.D.: User acceptance of information technology: Toward a unified view. MIS quarterly, pp. 425–478(2003)
8. Davis, F.D., Bagozzi, R.P., Warshaw, P.R.: User acceptance of computer technology: a comparison of two theoretical models. Manage. Sci. **35**(8), 982–1003 (1989)
9. Ghazizadeh, M., Lee, J.D. and Boyle, L.N.: Extending the technology acceptance model to assess automation. Cogn. Technol. Work **14**, 39–49 (2012)
10. Choi, J.K., Ji, Y.G.: Investigating the importance of trust on adopting an autonomous vehicle. Int. J. Human-Comput. Interact. **31**(10), 692–702 (2015)
11. Kaur, K., Rampersad, G.: Trust in driverless cars: Investigating key factors influencing the adoption of driverless cars. J. Eng. Technol. Manage. **48**, 87–96 (2018)
12. Parasuraman, R., Riley, V.: Humans and automation: Use, misuse, disuse, abuse. Human Factors **39**(2), 230–253 (1997)
13. Menon, N., Pinjari, A., Zhang, Y., Zou, L.: Consumer perception and intended adoption of autonomous-vehicle technology: Findings from a university population survey, No. 16–5998 (2016)
14. Zmud, J., Sener, I.N., Wagner, J.: Consumer acceptance and travel behavior: impacts of automated vehicles. Texas A&M Transportation Institute, No. PRC 15–49 F (2016)
15. Kline, R.B.: Principles and practice of structural equation modeling. Guilford publications (2015)
16. Ab Hamid, M.R., Sami, W., Sidek, M.M. Discriminant validity assessment: Use of Fornell & Larcker criterion versus HTMT criterion. In: Journal of Physics: Conference Series, Vol. 890, IOP Publishing (2017)
17. Fornell, C., Larcker, D.F.: Evaluating structural equation models with unobservable variables and measurement error. J. Market. Res. **18**(1), 39–50 (1981)
18. Podsakoff, P.M., Organ, D.W.: Self-reports in organizational research: problems and prospects. J. Manage. **12**(4), 531–544 (1986)
19. Byrne, B.M.: Structural equation modeling with EQS and EQS/Windows. Basic Concepts, Applications, and Programming. Sage, Thousand Oaks, California (1994)

20. Earle, T.C., Cvetkovich, G.: Social trust: Toward a cosmopolitan society. Greenwood Publishing Group, Santa Barbara, California (1995)
21. Kim, D.J., Ferrin, D.L., Rao, H.R.: A trust-based consumer decision-making model in electronic commerce: the role of trust, perceived risk, and their antecedents. Decision Support Syst. **44**(2), 544–564 (2008)
22. Mou, J., Shin, D.-H., Cohen, J.F.: Trust and risk in consumer acceptance of e-services. Electron. Commerce Res. **17**(2), 255–288 (2015)
23. Buckley, L., Kaye, S.A. and Pradhan, A.K.: Psychosocial factors associated with intended use of automated vehicles: a simulated driving study. Acc. Anal. Prevent. **115**, 202–208 (2018)
24. Körber, M., Baseler, E. and Bengler, K.: Introduction matters: Manipulating trust in automation and reliance in automated driving. Applied ergonomics, 66, pp.18–31(2018)
25. Perkins, L., Miller, J. E., Hashemi, A., Burns, G.: Designing for human-centered systems: situational risk as a factor of trust in automation. In: Proceedings of the human factors and ergonomics society annual meeting, Vol. 54, pp. 2130–2134 (2010)
26. Edlund, C., Hume, S., Lewis, M.: Proceedings of the human factors and ergonomics society annual meeting. Human Factors Ergonom. Society Meet. **54**(25), 2130–2134 (2010)
27. Zhang, T., Tao, D., Qu, X., Zhang, X., Lin, R., Zhang, W.: The roles of initial trust and perceived risk in public's acceptance of automated vehicles. Transp. Res. Part C: Emerg. Technol. **98**, 207–220 (2019)
28. Waytz, A., Heafner, J., Epley, N.: The mind in the machine: anthropomorphism increases trust in an autonomous vehicle. J. Exp. Soc. Psychol. **52**(3), 113–117 (2014)
29. Koustanaï, A., Cavallo, V., Delhomme, P., Mas, A.: Simulator training with a forward collision warning system: effects on driver-system interactions and driver trust. Human Factors **54**(5), 709–721 (2012)
30. Balfe, N., Sharples, S., Wilson, J.R.: Understanding is key: an analysis of factors pertaining to trust in a real-world automation system. Human Factors **60**(4), 477–495 (2018)

Research on the Influencing Factors of Autonomous Driving Acceptance

Yao Zu and Na Chen[✉]

Beijing University of Chemical Technology, Beijing 100055, China
chenna@mail.buct.edu.cn

Abstract. Based on the UTAUT and TAM models, this study further enriches the influence of personal traits on the acceptance of autonomous driving, explores the influencing mechanism and the mediating effect of perceived value and perceived risk. A total of 279 questionnaires are collected. The results show that the user's desire for control negatively affect the acceptance of autonomous driving, while hedonic motivation and safety positively affect the acceptance of autonomous driving. Perceived risk and perceived value mediate the influence of personal traits (desire for control and hedonic motivation) and safety on the acceptance of autonomous driving. This study expands the relevant theories related to the acceptance of autonomous driving, enriches the dimensions of factors affecting the acceptance of autonomous driving, and provides reference significance for future autonomous driving design and human-vehicle interaction, as well as reference suggestions for related manufacturing enterprises.

Keywords: Desire for control · Hedonic motivation · Safety · Perceived risk · Perceived value · Acceptance

1 Research Background

In recent years, with the rapid development of Internet deep learning technology and artificial intelligence, autonomous driving, as an important application field of artificial intelligence, has attracted extensive attention from academia and industry. Autonomous driving, as a key driving force for future transportation development and deployment and the basic guarantee of transportation power, is included in the national development strategic goals of more and more countries [1]. At the same time, autonomous vehicles have become one of the most important choices for consumers due to their ability to liberate energy, reduce fuel consumption, reduce traffic congestion and improve the driving environment [2–8]. However, the realization of autonomous driving, in addition to overcoming technical problems, also needs to pay attention to the public acceptance, which is an important factor affecting the realization of autonomous driving in the market to gain wide application [9, 10].

Despite the prospects, the development of autonomous driving also faces new challenges, with safety at the forefront, and research shows that cautious optimism is the general attitude of the public towards autonomous vehicles [11]. On the one hand, the

P.-L. P. Rau (Ed.): HCII 2023, LNCS 14023, pp. 512–530, 2023.
https://doi.org/10.1007/978-3-031-35939-2_38

public has an optimistic attitude towards the development of autonomous driving technology. On the other hand, there are high concerns about the safety and trust of autonomous driving [12–14], and there is still a considerable part of the public that has a negative attitude towards self-driving cars, or even completely reject the technology, believing that cars without human operation will bring great safety risks [15–17]. A study noted that about 38% of participants were skeptical about self-driving cars, and only 25% remained enthusiastic about autonomous driving [18, 19]. Reports related to autonomous driving, including incidents in which autonomous vehicles fail to accurately judge road conditions before an accident and the shutdown of driver assistance systems before an impact, have reduced public acceptance of autonomous driving and raised public doubts about autonomous driving (National Highway Traffic Safety Administration (NHTSA)). As a result, public acceptance of autonomous vehicles still seems to be a barrier, and how to accurately understand and predict the acceptance of autonomous vehicles requires in-depth research.

Many scholars have conducted studies on the acceptance of autonomous driving, mainly from three perspectives, directly using the general technology acceptance model (TAM) or the integrated technology acceptance model (UTAUT), exploring based on TAM [20–23] and UTAUT [24–26] technology acceptance model, and using single dimension measurement. The above three research methods have limitations. Firstly, the research needs to focus on the characteristics of autonomous driving (intelligence, convenience and safety). Existing studies directly using the technology acceptance model to lack the pertinence of autonomous driving technology and its application scenarios, and cannot highlight the impact of its characteristics on public acceptance of the product. Secondly, driving is greatly affected by personality traits, and drivers with different characteristics will have different driving behaviors during driving [27–29]. However, existing studies lack the consideration of factors related to public personal traits. Finally, some psychological determinants of public acceptance are still unclear, and the psychological decision-making process of the public cannot be fully described. Existing studies have not paid more attention to the influence of the public as autonomous driving users themselves on the acceptance of autonomous driving, especially ignoring people's demands for the sense of mechanical control and enjoyment from driving, which are very important personal trait factors in driving. In addition, safety is also very important, and concerns about the safety of autonomous driving have always been a hot issue among the public in relevant surveys.

The above research indicates that our current research on acceptance is still mainly focused on the acceptance of basic general technology. Although there are a few researches on personality traits, the results are not ideal, and there is still a large space for exploration. Therefore, on the basis of TAM and UTAUT, this paper considers the influence of personal trait factors on driving acceptance, and takes the acceptance of autonomous driving as the research object, aiming to explore its influence on the acceptance of autonomous driving and its mechanism from the perspectives of hedonic motivation, desire for control and safety.

2 Literature Review and Theoretical Hypotheses

2.1 Meaning and Measurement Method of Autonomous Driving Acceptance

Autonomous driving acceptance can be defined as the degree to which an individual intends to use the system and, where available, incorporates the system into their driving [30]. Existing studies on the acceptance of autonomous driving generally include three methods: direct adoption, borrowing and single dimensional measurement. Among them, some scholars directly use more relatively mature technology acceptance models for autonomous driving research, such as TAM and UTAUT. The traditional TAM model takes external variables, perceived usefulness and perceived ease of use as the main research objects [26, 30]. On the basis of TAM, UTAUT takes performance expectation, effort expectation, community influence and cooperation as the main research objects [31]. And subjective feelings, such as perceived ease of use, perceived usefulness, perceived risk, perceived benefit, perceived safety and perceived privacy, are important influencing factors for consumers' acceptance of autonomous driving [19, 32–34].

Some scholars have borrowed from TAM and UTAUT to add new variables to the original model and develop a scale to directly measure the acceptance of autonomous driving, such as the UTAUT2 model [35], the Car Acceptance Scale (SCAS) [36], and the Autonomous Driving Acceptance Questionnaire (QAAD). These scales generally also include perception factors, in addition to adding attitudes (positive and negative) to the adoption of autonomous driving technology [37].

There are also scholars who use a single-dimensional acceptance scale to measure, such as the level of autonomous driving [15, 29, 38]. In addition to the factors described above in the traditional acceptance model, a range of activity factors (e.g., work, internal and external socialization, reading, non-driving tasks) were also included in the model and found to have significant effects on perceived usefulness [29, 39].

In addition, some studies have considered the influence of personal traits factors on the acceptance of autonomous driving, but the relevant research is still not in-depth. In a small number of relevant studies, some scholars have considered the Big Five personality traits and found that the correlation between the Big Five personality traits and the acceptance of autonomous driving is weak or even non-existent [27–29]. Other scholars have considered self-efficacy [40]. Therefore, studies on the acceptance of autonomous driving have been studied on typical TAM and UTAUT elements, but there are still few studies on the acceptance from the perspective of personal characteristics, especially ignoring some personal characteristics and psychological feelings of drivers during autonomous driving.

2.2 Desire for Control

Control, as a personality trait, refers to "the motivation to control events in your life" [41], is an important and ubiquitous psychological and cognitive factor, and is one of the hot factors in driving research [42]. Control is very important for the driver, which means being aware of what is happening around them, and losing control means to lose right to control, as well as losing physical sensation and pleasure. Giving up control of the car makes driving less attractive and requires a lot of effort to change behavior and habits [43]. Handing over control creates feelings of pain [44] and leads to safety issues and concerns about taking responsibility for self-driving cars [45]. Surveys have shown that the fear of losing control in drivers appears to be a psychological barrier to support for self-driving cars [46–48].

At present, few studies have explored the influence of control desire on acceptance, and the related studies mainly focus on its influence on driving behavior and driving style [49]. Desire for control was positively associated with an angry cautious driving style [50], control desire was negatively correlated with separation anxiety driving style, while control desire was positively correlated with decompression and caution driving style [51, 52]. High control drivers may reduce their driving speed while driving in order to give themselves more control over their vehicle [53, 54]. In addition, drivers who have not been involved in traffic accidents tend to have a higher desire for control than those who have been involved in accidents [55].

Although the importance of control desire has been mentioned in many driving-related studies, there are few quantitative studies on the relationship between control desire and acceptance, and there is insufficient evidence to show a correlation between control desire and acceptance of autonomous driving [43, 56].

2.3 Hedonic Motivation

Hedonic motivation is an important determinant of users' intention to use new technology, and the degree of pleasure or pleasure they feel when using technology will affect their attitude [57, 58]. Venkatesh et al. [59] proposed the UTAUT2 model based on the UTAUT model, which added three factors, namely hedonic motivation, price value and habit, on the basis of the original UTAUT model, and expanded the application scope and explanatory power of the original model.

There are still few researches related to hedonic motivation in autonomous driving, and the few relevant studies link hedonic motivation with perception. New technologies may bring new pleasures to users, so self-driving cars may also provide new experiences for users [60], however, the existing research suggests that driving pleasure has a negative effect on the enjoyment of users using self-driving cars, the autonomous driving function and degree of cars should be selective, drivers need to undertake certain driving task, and self-driving cars need to balance the management of user security concept and provide them with automated driving pleasure [61]. In addition, some scholars have proposed that hedonic motivation may be an important predictor of the acceptance of automated road transport systems (ARTS) [24].

2.4 Security

Safety is vital to the public and is an indispensable factor in autonomous driving research. Although it is widely believed that safety is closely related to acceptance, there is a lack of studies that incorporate safety into technology acceptance related models. The results of several studies show that safety is the lowest in the score of key factors related to autonomous driving, and the public expresses strong or moderate concerns about the safety of autonomous driving systems and cars [8, 62]. In recent years, public safety concerns about autonomous driving have continued to increase [63].

While self-driving cars can avoid most human error, their driving behavior is unpredictable in many conditions [64, 65], and their effects can be influenced by the surrounding environment and weather conditions. The report by Hardman [66] shows that some respondents felt that autonomous driving was less safe than human driving and were more willing to accept autonomous vehicles with manual driving options than autonomous vehicles without a steering wheel.

2.5 Perceived Value and Perceived Risk

Perceived value and perceived risk are thought to jointly influence technology acceptance in cognitive processes [67] because people always make the choice that human beings pursue low cost and high benefit. Lower perceived risk (cost, effort) and higher perceived value are positive predictors of higher acceptance of various technologies. At the same time, the perceived risk and perceived value influenced by other factors would change the public's acceptance of a certain technology [68].

Perceived value refers to the customer's evaluation of the results of the use of goods/services to achieve their goals and intentions [69]. In a variety of contexts, such as retail, online shopping, mobile services, and innovative technologies, etc. Studies have found that perceived value is one of the most important determinants of consumer acceptance, which has a positive impact on consumers' purchase intention [70–73]. Only when the perceived value of consumers is strong, will there be high acceptance and stimulate purchase intention. Perceived value often plays a mediating role in the related research on the influencing factors of consumer acceptance. For example, a study on the influencing factors of fintech service acceptance shows that performance expectations, effort expectations and perceived risk influence the individual's perceived value, which in turn influences acceptance [74]. A study on the influencing factors of tourism service acceptance points out that perceived value plays a mediating role in the influence of tourism quality (including experience quality, process quality and outcome quality) on tourist loyalty [75, 76].

Perceived value of autonomous driving refers to the user's overall evaluation of autonomous driving, which can only be generated when consumers understand and recognize its advantages and value, and are willing to pay a certain cost to obtain its use. However, the research on perceived value in the field of autonomous driving is still not in-depth. A study of the willingness to use shared autonomous vehicles shows that the perceived value of users is related to technology availability and has an impact on the willingness to use vehicles. When users perceive more value in adopting autonomous vehicles, their willingness to use autonomous vehicles will also increase [77].

Perceived risk is the uncertainty of the outcome of the purchase made by the consumer, and there is no way to confirm whether any purchase behavior is in line with the consumer's expectations, and some results may lead to consumers' unhappiness [78]. Perceived risk consists of two important components, uncertainty (the likelihood of adverse consequences) and loss (the severity of consequences) [79]. Perceived risk is an important barrier to consumption decisions [80], especially in the fields of e-commerce and mobile commerce [81, 82]. There are many studies on the correlation between perceived risk and acceptance. It is generally believed that perceived risk is an important direct predictor of acceptance, and perceived risk has a strong negative impact on acceptance [79].

Autonomous driving perceived risk refers to the possibility of loss perceived by users when using autonomous driving technology. Although perceived risk plays an important role in technology acceptance, there are few relevant studies in the field of autonomous driving. Studies suggest that although autonomous driving can enhance road safety by eliminating human error in driving, users still have serious concerns about the potential risks of autonomous driving, and this perception may be a key obstacle to achieving widespread acceptance of autonomous driving [83]. The study found that passengers' perceived risk of autonomous driving was higher than their perception of driving by human drivers [23]. In addition, in a small number of studies, perceived risk as a mediating variable had an impact on research, and a study on government policy support showed that perceived risk plays an important mediating role in the impact of individual support for government policies [84, 85].

2.6 Brief Summary

There is still a lack of studies on the acceptance of autonomous vehicles. More studies focus on the acceptance and universal technical acceptance of human-driven vehicles, but they still cannot meet the research needs of autonomous vehicles. Among them, there are great differences between autonomous vehicles and human-driven vehicles in terms of technological level, human operability and human-vehicle interaction. The applicability of traditional research conclusions on vehicle acceptance to autonomous vehicles still needs to be tested. However, there are also differences in application scenarios and technologies between autonomous vehicles and other technologies. Traditional studies on technology acceptance are relatively universal, and there is a lack of targeted exploration on the characteristics of autonomous vehicles.

In addition, relevant studies based on TAM and UTAUT model still lack the exploration of the influence of personal characteristics. Based on the UTAUT model, this study focuses on the influence of personal characteristics (desire for control and hedonic motivation) on the acceptance of autonomous driving, and constructs a new technology acceptance model. Future research can expand and explore the influence of more different factors on autonomous driving acceptance.

3 Theoretical Hypotheses

Both the desire for control and hedonic motivation are important personal traits. The former is based on the satisfaction that comes from controlling objects, while the latter is based on the satisfaction and pleasure gained. With the improvement of the level of autonomous driving, the driver's control of the car is limited, and their desire to control the car cannot be satisfied, which leads to the reduction of their desire to use new technology, and has a negative impact on the acceptance of autonomous driving. Therefore, the hypothesis H1 that the desire for control affects the acceptance of autonomous driving is drawn. Autonomous driving, meanwhile, will break the rider to the original state of immersion and enjoyment, which means that for the driver stripped them fun to drive, and the immersion of pleasure is pleasure and motivation, not enough fun to drive may affect the autonomous driving acceptance, so it is concluded hypothesis H2 that hedonic motives influence autonomous driving acceptance. Safety is an important basis for road traffic, and it also has an extremely important impact on the acceptance of autonomous driving. The higher the safety of autonomous driving, the higher the reliability of users, and the more they will accept autonomous driving. Therefore, hypothesis 3 is put forward.

H1: The desire to control is negatively correlated with the acceptance of autonomous driving, that is, the higher the desire to control, the lower the acceptance of autonomous driving.
H2: Hedonic motivation positively affects autonomous driving acceptance.
H3: Safety positively affects autonomous driving acceptance.

When users adopt emerging technologies, they subconsciously assess the potential risks and value. If the perceived risk exceeds the acceptable range, it will lead to a negative willingness to accept. If users think the technology is safe, reliable and has greater value, they will have a positive willingness to accept it. In previous studies, perceived ease of use and perceived usefulness in the traditional TAM model are more used to measure technology acceptance, and only the benefits brought by autonomous driving are considered. We believe that starting from the double-edged sword theory and based on the UTAUT and TAM model, the perceived value and perceived risk are taken as the foothold. Compared with the perceived ease of use and perceived usefulness, the consideration factors for users to accept new technologies can be better illustrated from the perspective of users. In the research on the constitutive attributes of perceived value, it is pointed out that hedonic value is one of the necessary dimensions of perceived value, and hedonic motivation is an important motivation of consumption behavior and brings hedonic value to users [66, 80]. Hedonic motivation may increase due to the shift of attention during the improvement of autonomous driving level, which has an impact on perceived value and perceived risk. Keeping the car within the user's control at all times may affect the user's perceived value and perceived risk, and create a high degree of security within the control range. In the process of driving, safety is closely related to perceived value. The safer the driver feels, the higher his perceived value of driving will be. On the contrary, if the driver feels his safety is threatened, the perceived risk will increase. While perceived risk and perceived value are influenced by many of the above factors, they also have an impact on acceptance. Therefore, based on the UTAUT2 model, the relevant hypotheses H4 and H5 of perceived value and perceived risk are proposed.

H4: Perceived value plays a mediating role among control desire, hedonic motivation, safety and autonomous driving acceptance.
H5: Perceived risk plays a mediating role among control desire, hedonic motivation, safety and autonomous driving acceptance.

Compared with the general technology acceptance, self-driving acceptance is not only affected by automated driving technology itself, but also be affected by the individual drivers' characteristics. This study explores personal traits influence on autonomous driving acceptance, including controlling, hedonic motives and security, and explores the mediation role of perceived value and perceived risk in effect. In this study, a model of acceptance, desire for control, hedonic motivation, safety, perceived risk and perceived value was constructed, and a hypothesis was proposed. The framework of the model is shown in Fig. 1.

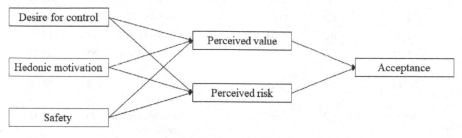

Fig. 1. Research Model

4 Research Methods

4.1 Sample Selection and Procedures

In this study, social software was used to conduct questionnaire survey in the form of snowball. A total of 279 questionnaires were collected, and 260 valid questionnaires were finally obtained after removing invalid questionnaires through careful screening, with an effective recovery rate of 93.18%. Among them, the number of male samples was 134 (48.03%) and the number of female samples was 145 (51.97%). The age group of the sample was mainly concentrated in 21 to 40 years old, among which 124 (44.41%) were 21 to 30 years old, and 102 (36.56%) were 30 to 40 years old. In terms of educational background, junior college accounted for 35.84% and bachelor's degree accounted for 31.18%. Most of the respondents worked in state-owned enterprises, administrative institutions and private enterprises (76.93%). In the total sample, more than half (66.31%) had driving experience. The details are shown in Table 1.

4.2 Measurement Tools

This study included three independent variables (desire for control, hedonic motivation, and safety), one dependent variable (autonomous driving acceptance), and two mediating variables (perceived risk and perceived value). In order to ensure that the quality, reliability and validity of the questionnaire meet the research requirements, the design of the questionnaire in this paper partly bases on and refers to mature scales at home and abroad.

In this study, the control scale developed by Burger and Cooper was used to measure the control desire. The original scale includes five dimensions: control of event situation, prevention of being controlled, self-control, other control, and pressure control. Since this study does not involve other dimensions except self-control, the other dimensions in

Table 1. Sample statistical characteristics

Project	Sample distribution	Numbers	Percentage	Project	Sample distribution	Numbers	Percentage
Age	0–20	14	5.02	Gender	Male	134	48.03
	21–30	124	44.41		Female	145	51.97
	31–40	102	36.54	Job	Students	48	17.20
	41–50	30	10.75		Administrative institutions	85	30.47
	51–60	6	2.15		Private enterprise	102	36.56
	>60	3	1.08		Foreign capital enterprise	26	9.32
Degree	Primary school and below	7	2.51		Freelance	18	6.45
	High school/technical secondary school	52	18.64	Driving experience	Yes	185	66.31
	Junior college diploma	100	35.84		No	94	33.69
	Undergraduate	87	31.18				
	Master's and above	33	11.83				

the original questionnaire were deleted, and only eight items in the self-control dimension were kept, which were translated into Chinese. For example, "At work, I attach great importance to being able to control my office hours and work content". Hedonic motivation was measured using the motivation scale developed by Venkatesh [31], which consisted of five questions. Since this study was based on the autonomous driving scenario. Therefore, the expression of "activity" in the original scale was adjusted to the expression of "autonomous driving activity", for example "I like to seek pleasure in the process of autonomous driving". On the basis of the driving behavior scale constructed by Clapp [86], the safety scale selects the dimension of safe behavior for measurement and contains three items. The questions are appropriately modified according to the actual situation and the specific situation is adjusted to automatic driving, such as "I think self-driving cars are safer than people driving". With reference to the eight-item perceived value scale developed by Sweeney [71], items were modified from four dimensions of emotion, society, performance and value for money, and a total of 8 items were included in the perceived value scale. For example, "the assisted driving function of autonomous vehicles can meet my needs". On the basis of the perceived value scale, according to the types of perceived risks, the items of the perceived risk scale were adjusted from the four dimensions of function, personal, social and psychological, with a total of 8 items [3]. For example, "I am worried that the autonomous driving technology cannot adapt to complex environments and terrain". The automatic driving acceptance scale is derived from the behavioral intention measurement of the technology acceptance model developed by Poortinga and Pidgeon [87]. It contains four items and is adapted according to the use situation of automatic driving, such as "I will introduce autonomous driving to my family and companions". The specific items of the scale are shown in the appendix.

In addition, demographic variables such as gender, age, education, job and driving experience of the respondents were included as control variables in this study. All subjective scales were measured using the Likert 5-point scale, 1 = strongly disagree, 5 = strongly agree.

5 Data Analysis and Results

SPSS and Amos were used to analyze the data. First, the data were tested to verify the validity of the data. Then, the hypotheses were tested successively, the fitness path analysis of the model was tested, and then performed descriptive statistics and correlation analysis between variables. Finally, the mediating effects of perceived risk and perceived trust among control desire, security, hedonic motivation and autonomous driving acceptance were examined.

5.1 Manipulation Check

The reliability test results showed that the Cronbach Alpha values of control desire, hedonic motivation, safety, perceived value, perceived risk and acceptance were 0.909, 0.903, 0.852, 0.937, 0.917, 0.866, respectively, which were all greater than 0.8, indicating that the internal consistency of the above six scales was good. Follow-up data analysis can be carried out.

According to the correlation test results, control desire, hedonic motivation and safety were significantly positively correlated with perceived value (all p < .01), control desire and safety were significantly negatively correlated with perceived risk (all p < .01), and hedonic motivation was significantly positively correlated with perceived risk (p < .01). The perceived value and perceived risk were also significantly correlated (all p < .01), which indicated that further data analysis could be carried out. The reliability test and correlation are shown in Table 2.

5.2 Hypothesis Testing

This study used multiple linear regression with least squares estimation to test the hypotheses. According to the results of regression analysis, control desire, hedonic motivation, and safety all had significant positive effects on acceptance in model 1 without the introduction of mediating variables (Model 1: Control desire, β = -.240; Hedonic motivation, β = .162; Safety, β = .135; all p < .01), which means that hypotheses H1, H2, and H3 are verified.

On the basis of model 1, model 2 added the mediating variable perceived value, and the results showed that the regression effect of perceived value on independent variables was significant (β = .402, p < .001), and H4 was verified. In addition, in Model 2, the significance of control desire and hedonic motivation on acceptance was affected, and

Table 2. Variable mean, standard deviation, correlation coefficient and internal consistency of the scale

	Average	SD	1	2	3	4	5	6	7	8	9	10	11
1. Gender	–	0.501	–										
2. Degree	3.318	0.982	0.053	–									
3. Age	2.646	0.895	−0.057	−0.057	–								
4. Job	2.581	1.079	−0.085	−.404**	.334**	–							
5. Driving experience	1.339	0.474	.338**	−.139*	−0.049	0.066	–						
6. Control desire	3.398	0.896	0.019	.286**	0.055	−.170**	−0.113	(0.909)					
7. Hedonic motivation	3.238	1.002	−0.113	.206**	0.027	−0.115	−.178**	−.675**	(0.903)				
8. Safety	3.188	0.985	0.051	.144*	0.004	−0.023	−0.054	−.628**	.528**	(0.852)			
9. Perceived value	3.298	0.937	0.013	.296**	−0.008	−.177**	−.170**	.744**	.615**	.811**	(0.937)		
10. Perceived risk	3.345	0.945	0.007	.363**	−0.054	−.269**	−.158**	−.223**	.209**	−.196**	.087	(0.917)	
11. Acceptance	3.234	0.903	−0.019	.197**	0.057	−0.092	−0.074	−.556**	.511**	.460**	.634**	.450**	(0.866)

Note: *indicates significant correlation at 0.05 level (two-sided), **indicates significant correlation at 0.01 level (two-sided), values in parentheses on the diagonal are coefficient of internal consistency (Cronbach's α)

the significance of security on acceptance was obvious, namely, partial mediation. At the same time, perceived value had a significant partial mediating effect on the three pathways of control desire, hedonic motivation and safety (Control desire: $\beta = -.412$; Hedonic motivation: $\beta = .333$; Safety: $\beta = .451$, all $p < .001$).

In model 3, another mediating variable, perceived risk, was added, and the results showed that the regression effect of perceived risk on independent variables was significant ($\beta = -.474$, $p < .001$), and H5 was verified. In addition, in Model 3, the original significance of control desire and safety on acceptance was also affected, and hedonic motivation was still significant, that is, partially mediated. Perceived risk had a significant partial mediating effect on the three pathways of control desire, hedonic motivation and safety (Control desire: $\beta = -.156$; Hedonic motivation: $\beta = .148$; Safety: $\beta = -.097$, all $p < .05$). Therefore, perceived value and perceived risk play a partial mediating role in the influence of personal traits (desire for control, hedonic motivation, safety) on autonomous driving acceptance. The specific results are shown in Table 3.

Table 3. Results of linear regression analysis of control desire, hedonic motivation, and safety on acceptance

Variable types	The variable name	Model 1	Model 2	Model 3
Independent variables	Control desire	$-.240^{***}$	$-.073$	$-.097$
	Hedonic motivation	$.162^{**}$	$.085$	$.125^{*}$
	Safety	$.135^{**}$	$.356^{***}$	$-.122$
Mediating variables	Perceived value		$.402^{***}$	
	Perceived risk			$-.474^{***}$
Control variables	Gender	$-.039$	$-.083$	$-.043$
	Degree	$.051$	$.031$	$.017$
	Age	$-.006$	$-.018$	$-.003$
	Job	$-.079$	$-.027$	$-.051$
	Driving experience	$.029$	$.076$	$.044$
	R square	$.377$	$.538$	$.448$
	The adjusted r square	$.358$	$.523$	$.429$
	F	20.161^{***}	34.438^{***}	23.958^{***}

Note: * indicates significant association at the 0.05 level (two-sided), ** indicates significant association at the 0.01 level (two-sided), and *** indicates significant association at the 0.001 level (two-sided)

6 Discussion

Hypothesis 1 of this study is verified, and the public's desire for control is highly negatively correlated with the acceptance of autonomous driving, indicating that drivers prefer low-level autonomous driving systems to high-level autonomous driving systems.

Hypothesis 2 of this study was verified, and hedonic motivation was positively correlated with autonomous driving acceptance. The higher the degree of pleasure-seeking, the more likely the user is to accept autonomous driving. This is consistent with the conclusion of research on the correlation between hedonic motivation and technology acceptance. Hedonic motivation is indeed an important factor of technology acceptance, which is consistent with the study of Venkatesh et al. [59] and the pursuit of new experiences is important for users to accept new technologies. However, this hypothesis is inconsistent with Ernst's [61] view, indicating that although driving pleasure has a negative impact on users' enjoyment of autonomous driving, the degree is lower than that of pursuing new experience. Future studies on hedonic motivation can be further analyzed to explore the positive and negative effects of hedonic motivation in the field of autonomous driving. We can also start from the source of hedonic motivation to study whether hedonic motivation comes from non-driving work or original manual driving, and explore whether different sources of hedonic motivation in driving environment will have different effects on related mechanisms. Hypothesis 3 of this study was confirmed, and it had the most significant impact on acceptance among the independent variables, which further confirmed that safety plays an important role in the acceptance of autonomous driving.

In this study, Hypothesis 4 and Hypothesis 5 are valid, in which the perceived value and perceived risk are correlated with the acceptance of autonomous driving. In the acceptance model, perceived value positively mediates the influence of control desire, hedonic motivation, and safety on autonomous driving acceptance, while perceived risk negatively mediates the influence. The more benefits drivers perceive during autonomous driving, the greater the perceived value will be, which is the same as Kim [88]. Conversely, the greater the perceived risk, the lower the acceptance. In particular, the negative correlation between security and perceived risk is more obvious. Users with higher security have lower perceived risk, which affects the acceptance of technology.

This study focused on the desire for control and hedonic motivation in personal traits, but other personal traits, such as emotional state, cultural background, and type of moral choice, may also have an impact on the acceptance of autonomous driving. Future work can be carried out in this aspect. According to the results of this study, the issue of autonomous driving acceptance should be explored from a multi-dimensional perspective, and more exploratory studies should be conducted based on the application scenarios of different technologies. In addition, in the research on the acceptance of autonomous driving, more exploration can be conducted from the perspectives of consumer behavior and psychology to realize the early landing of autonomous driving.

7 Conclusion

For autonomous driving, it is very important to be accepted by the public, and safety is the primary concern of the public for autonomous driving. On this basis, it is of practical significance to incorporate more user-side factors to discuss the acceptance of autonomous driving. This study is to focus on desire for control, hedonic motivation as the typical representative of personality, based on the UTAUT model, incorporating personality into the autonomous driving acceptance model to explore personal traits influence on autonomous driving, acceptance, and the perceived value and perceived risk in personal attributes and security mediation role of autonomous driving acceptance. A total of 279 questionnaires were collected. The experimental results showed that control desire was significantly negatively correlated with autonomous driving acceptance, hedonic motivation and safety positively affected autonomous driving acceptance, and perceived value and perceived risk played a mediating role in the acceptance model.

This study expands the theories related to the technology acceptance model, especially provides a reference for the related research on the acceptance of autonomous driving. It provides guidance for autonomous driving enterprises in vehicle design and user publicity, and provides development suggestions for related industries.

Acknowledgments. We are grateful for the support of the foundation: the National Natural Science Foundation of China 72201023.

References

1. Balasekaran, G., Jayakumar, S., Pérez de Prado, R.: An intelligent task scheduling mechanism for autonomous vehicles via deep learning. Energies, **14**(6), 1788 (2021). https://doi.org/10.3390/EN14061788
2. Buckley, L., Kaye, S.A., Pradhan, A.K.: Psychosocial factors associated with intended use of automated vehicles: A simulated driving study. Acid. Anal. Prev. **115**, 202–208 (2018). https://doi.org/10.1016/j.aap.2018.03.021
3. Fagnant, D.J., Kockelman, K.M.: Preparing a nation for autonomous vehicles: Opportunities, barriers and policy recommendations. Economics **77**, 167–181 (2014). https://doi.org/10.1016/J.TRA.2015.04.003
4. Perrine, K.A., Kockelman, K.M., Huang, Y.: Anticipating long-distance travel shifts due to self-driving vehicles. J. Transp. Geogr. **82** (2020). https://doi.org/10.1016/j.jtrangeo.2019.102547
5. Sun, Y., Olaru, D., Smith, B., Greaves, S.P., Collins, A.T.: Road to autonomous vehicles in Australia: An exploratory literature review. Road Transp. Res. **26**(1), 34–47 (2017)
6. Körber, M., Gold, C., Lechner, D., Bengler, K.: The influence of age on the take-over of vehicle control in highly automated driving. Transp. Res. Part F Traf. Psychol. Behav. **39**, 19–32 (2016). https://doi.org/10.1016/J.TRF.2016.03.002
7. Janssens, D.: Keynote III empowering citizens with sustainable transportation in the cities of today & tomorrow. Proc. Comput. Sci. **32**, 19 (2014). https://doi.org/10.1016/J.PROCS.2014.05.391
8. Piao, J., McDonald, M., Hounsell, N.B., Graindorge, M., Graindorge, T., Malhéné, N.: Public views towards implementation of automated vehicles in urban areas. Transp. Res. Procedia **14**, 2168–2177 (2016). https://doi.org/10.1016/J.TRPRO.2016.05.232
9. Noy, I.Y., Shinar, D., Horrey, W.J.: Automated driving: Safety blind spots. Saf. Sci. **102**, 68–78 (2018). https://doi.org/10.1016/J.SSCI.2017.07.018
10. Xu, Z., Zhang, K., Min, H., Wang, Z., Zhao, X., Liu, P.: What drives people to accept automated vehicles? Findings from a field experiment. Transp. Res. Part C Emerg. Technol. **95**, 320–334 (2018). https://doi.org/10.1016/J.TRC.2018.07.024
11. Wintersberger, S., Azmat, M., Kummer, S.: Are we ready to ride autonomous vehicles? A pilot study on Austrian consumers' perspective. Logistics **3**, 20 (2019). https://doi.org/10.3390/logistics3040020

12. Hilgarter, K., Granig, P.: Public perception of autonomous vehicles: A qualitative study based on interviews after riding an autonomous shuttle. Transp. Res. Part F Traf. Psychol. Behav. **72**, 226–243 (2020). https://doi.org/10.1016/j.trf.2020.05.012

13. Schoettle, B., Sivak, M.: A preliminary analysis of real-world crashes involving self-driving vehicles. Psychology (2015)

14. Zmud, J., Sener, I.N., Wagner, J.: Consumer acceptance and travel behaviors: Impacts of automated vehicles: final report. Texas A&M Transportation Institute, Bryan (2016)

15. Payre, W., Cestac, J., Delhomme, P.: Intention to use a fully automated car: Attitudes and a priori acceptability. Transp. Res. Part F Traf. Psychol. Behav. **27**, 252–263 (2014). https://doi.org/10.1016/j.trf.2014.04.009

16. Hajjafari, H.: Exploring the Effects of Socio Demographic and Built Environmental Factors on the Public Adoption of Shared and Private Autonomous Vehicles: A Case Study of Dallas-Fort Worth Metropolitan Area. The University of Texas, Arlington (2018)

17. Hudson, J., Orvisk, A.M., Hunady, J.: People's attitudes to autonomous vehicles. Transp. Res. Part A Policy Pract. **121**, 164–176 (2019). https://doi.org/10.1016/j.tra.2018.08.018

18. Nielsen, T.A., Haustein, S.: On sceptics and enthusiasts: What are the expectations towards self-driving cars? Transp. Policy **66**, 49–55 (2018). https://doi.org/10.1016/J.TRANPOL.2018.03.004

19. Liu, P., Guo, Q., Ren, F., Wang, L., Xu, Z:. Willingness to pay for self-driving vehicles: Influences of demographic and psychological factors. Transp. Res. Part C Emerg. Technol. **100**, 306–317 (2019). https://doi.org/10.1016/J.TRC.2019.01.022

20. Osswald, S., Wurhofer, D., Trösterer, S., Beck, E., & Tscheligi, M.: Predicting information technology usage in the car: Towards a car technology acceptance model. Presented at the Proceedings of the 4th International Conference on Automotive User Interfaces and Interactive Vehicular Applications (AutomotiveUI 2012). ACM Press, Portsmouth. (2012). https://doi.org/10.1145/2390256.2390264

21. Ruggeri, K., et al.: In with the new? Generational differences shape population technology adoption patterns in the age of self-driving vehicles. J. Eng. Tech. Manag. **50**, 39–44 (2018). https://doi.org/10.1016/J.JENGTECMAN.2018.09.001

22. Shabanpour, R., Shamshiripour, A., Mohammadian, A.: Modeling adoption timing of autonomous vehicles: Innovation diffusion approach. Transportation **45**(6), 1607–1621 (2018). https://doi.org/10.1007/s11116-018-9947-7

23. Hulse, L.M., Xie, H., Galea, E.R.: Perceptions of autonomous vehicles: Relationships with road users, risk, gender and age. Saf. Sci. **102**, 1–13 (2018). https://doi.org/10.1016/J.SSCI.2017.10.001

24. Madigan, R., et al.: Acceptance of automated road transport systems (ARTS): An adaptation of the UTAUT model. Trans. Res. Procedia **14**, 2217–2226 (2016). https://doi.org/10.1016/J.TRPRO.2016.05.237

25. Kettles, N., van Belle, J.: Investigation into the antecedents of autonomous car acceptance using an enhanced UTAUT Model. In: 2019 International Conference on Advances in Big Data, Computing and Data Communication Systems (icABCD), pp. 1–6 (2019). https://doi.org/10.1109/ICABCD.2019.8851011

26. Nordhoff, S., van Arem, B., Happee, R.: Conceptual model to explain, predict, and improve user acceptance of driverless podlike vehicles. Transp. Res. Rec. **2602**, 60–67 (2016). https://doi.org/10.3141/2602-08

27. Charness, N., Yoon, J., Souders, D.J., Stothart, C., Yehnert, C. Predictors of attitudes toward autonomous vehicles: The roles of age, gender, prior knowledge, and personality. Front. Psychol. **9** (2018). https://doi.org/10.3389/fpsyg.2018.02589

28. Goldberg, L.R.: The structure of phenotypic personality traits. Am. Psychol. **48**, 26–34 (1993)

29. Kyriakidis, M., Happee, R., Winter, J.D.: Public opinion on automated driving: results of an international questionnaire among 5000 respondents. Transp. Res. Part F Traffic Psychol. Behav. **32**, 127–140 (2015). https://doi.org/10.1016/J.TRF.2015.04.014
30. Adell, E., Várhelyi, A., Nilsson, L.N.: The Definition of Acceptance and Acceptability. Driver Acceptance of New Technology, pp.11–21 (2018). https://doi.org/10.1201/9781315578132-2
31. Venkatesh, V., Morris, M.G., Davis, G.B., Davis, F.D.: User acceptance of information technology: toward a unified view. MIS Q. **27**(3), 425–478 (2003). https://doi.org/10.2307/300 36540
32. Lee, J., Lee, D., Park, Y., Lee, S., Ha, T.: Autonomous vehicles can be shared, but a feeling of ownership is important: Examination of the influential factors for intention to use autonomous vehicles. Transp. Res. Part C Emerg. Technol. **107**, 411–422 (2019). https://doi.org/10.1016/j.trc.2019.08.020
33. Garidis, K., Rossmann, A., Ulbricht, L., Schmaeh, M.: Toward a user acceptance model of autonomous driving. In: Proceeding of the Hawaii International Conference on System Sciences, at Maui, Hawaii (2020). https://doi.org/10.24251/HICSS.2020.170
34. Hegner, S.M., Beldad, A.D., Brunswick, G.J.: In automatic we trust: investigating the impact of trust, control, personality characteristics, and extrinsic and intrinsic motivations on the acceptance of autonomous vehicles. Int. J. Hum. Comput. Interact. **35**(19), 1769–1780 (2019). https://doi.org/10.1080/10447318.2019.1572353
35. Korkmaz, H.E., Fidanoglu, A., Ozcelik, S.T., Okumuş, A.: User acceptance of autonomous public transport systems (APTS): Extended UTAUT2 model. J. Public Transp. **24**(1), 1 (2022). https://doi.org/10.5038/2375-0901.23.1.5
36. Nees, M.A.: Acceptance of self-driving cars: an examination of idealized versus realistic portrayals with a self- driving car acceptance scale. Proc. Human Fact. Ergon. Soc. Annu. Meet. **60**(1), 1449–1453 (2016). https://doi.org/10.1177/1541931213601332
37. Weigl, K., Schartmuller, C., Riener, A., Steinhauser, M.: Development of the questionnaire on the acceptance of automated driving (QAAD): Data-driven models for Level 3 and Level 5 automated driving. Transp. Res. Part F Traffic Psychol. Behav. **83**, 42–59 (2021). https://doi.org/10.1016/j.trf.2021.09.011
38. Rodel, C., Stadler, S., Meschtscherjakov, A., Tscheligi, M.: Towards autonomous cars: The effect of autonomy levels on acceptance and user experience. In: Proceedings of the 6th International Conference on Automotive User Interfaces and Interactive Vehicular Applications. ACM Press, pp. 1–8 (2014)
39. Hein, D.W., Rauschnabel, P.A., He, J., Richter, L., Ivens, B.S.: What Drives the Adoption of Autonomous Cars? In: ICIS 2018 Proceedings, p. 4 (2018). https://aisel.aisnet.org/icis2018/practice/Presentations/4
40. Benleulmi, A.Z., Blecker, T.: Investigating the factors influencing the acceptance of fully autonomous cars. In: Proceedings of the Hamburg International Conference of Logistics (HICL), vol. 23, pp. 99–115 (2017). https://doi.org/10.15480/882.1449
41. Burger, J.M., Cooper, H.M.: The desirability of control. Motiv. Emot. **3**(4), 381–393 (1979). https://doi.org/10.1007/BF00994052
42. Baum, A.S., & Singer, J.E. Applications of personal control. (1980)
43. Lee, J., Kolodge, K.: Understanding attitudes towards self-driving vehicles: Quantitative analysis of qualitative data. Proc. Hum. Fact. Ergon. Soc. Annu. Meet. **62**, 1399–1403 (2018). https://doi.org/10.1177/1541931218621319
44. Pettigrew, S., Worrall, C., Talati, Z., Fritschi, L., Norman, R.: Dimensions of attitudes to autonomous vehicles. Urban Plan. Transp. Res. **7**, 19–33 (2019). https://doi.org/10.1080/216 50020.2019.1604155
45. Merfeld, K., Wilhelms, M.P., Henkel, S.: Being driven autonomously a qualitative study to elicit consumers' overarching motivational structures. Transp. Res. Part C Emerg. Technol. **107**, 229–247 (2019). https://doi.org/10.1080/21650020.2019.1604155

46. Konig, M., Neumayr, L.: Users' resistance towards radical innovations: The case of the self-driving car. Transp. Res. Part F Traffic Psychol. Behav. **44**, 42–52 (2017). https://doi.org/10.1016/j.trf.2016.10.013

47. Schoettle, B., Sivak, M.: Motorists' preferences for company's levels of vehicle automation. J. Univ. Michigan Sustain. Worldwide Transp. (2016)

48. Muller, A., Stockinger, C., Walter, J., et al.: Wie wollen wir automatisiert fahren? Technische Universitat Darmstadt, pp. 1–22 (2017)

49. Sun, L., Chang, R.: Research status and prospect of driving style. Ergonomics **19**(04), 92–95 (2013)

50. Taubman - Ben-Ari, O., Mikulincer, M., Gillath, O.: The multidimensional driving style inventory - Scale construct and validation. Accident Anal. Prevent. **36**, 323–32 (2004). https://doi.org/10.1016/S0001-4575(03)00010-1

51. Holman, A.C., Havarneanu, C.E.: The Romanian version of the multidimensional driving style inventory: Psychometric properties and cultural specificities. Transp. Res. Part F Traffic Psychol. Behav. **35**, 45–59 (2015). https://doi.org/10.1016/J.TRF.2015.10.001

52. Juffrizal, K., Nidzamuddin, M., Yusof, J.T., Muhammad, Z.H., Frank, D., Hanneke, H.: The identification of Malaysian driving styles using the multidimensional driving style inventory. Proc. MATEC Web Conf. **90**(1), 01004 (2017)

53. Horswill, M., McKenna, F.: The effect of perceived control on risk taking 1. J. Appl. Soc. Psychol. **29**(2), 377–391 (2006). https://doi.org/10.1111/J.1559-1816.1999.TB01392.X

54. Burger, J.M., Schnerring, D.A.: The effects of desire for control and extrinsic rewards on the illusion of control and gambling. Motiv. Emot. **6**, 329–335 (1982)

55. Kirkcaldy, B.D., Trimpop, R., Cooper, C.L.: Working hours, job stress, work satisfaction, and accident rates among medical practitioners and allied personnel. Int. J. Stress. Manag. **4**, 79–87 (1997). https://doi.org/10.1007/BF02765302

56. Brell, T., Philipsen, R., Ziefle, M.: sCARy! Risk perceptions in autonomous driving: The influence of experience on perceived benefits and barriers. Risk Anal. **39**, 342–357 (2019). https://doi.org/10.1111/risa.13190

57. Alalwan, A.A., Dwivedi, Y.K., Rana, N.P.: Factors influencing adoption of mobile banking by Jordanian bank customers: Extending UTAUT2 with trust. Int. J. Inf. Manag. **37**(3), 99–110 (2017). https://doi.org/10.1016/j.ijinfomgt.2017.01.002

58. Bay, S.: Innovation adoption in robotics: consumer intentions to use autonomous vehicles. Master's Thesis (2016)

59. Venkatesh, V., Thong, J.Y., Xu, X.: Unified theory of acceptance and use of technology: A synthesis and the road ahead. J. Assoc. Inf. Syst. **17**, 1 (2016). https://doi.org/10.17705/1jais.00428

60. Becker, F., Axhausen, K.W.: Literature review on surveys investigating the acceptance of autonomous vehicles. Transportation, **44**, 1293–1306 (2017). https://doi.org/10.1007/s11116-017-9808-9

61. Ernst, C.H., Reinelt, P.: Autonomous car acceptance: Safety vs. personal driving enjoyment. In: AMCIS (2017)

62. Schoettle, B., Sivak, M.: A survey of public opinion about connected vehicles in the U.S., the U.K., and Australia. In: 2014 International Conference on Connected Vehicles and Expo (ICCVE), pp. 687–692 (2014). https://doi.org/10.1109/ICCVE.2014.7297637

63. Nazari, F., Noruzoliaee, M., Mohammadian, A.K.: Shared versus private mobility: Modeling public interest in autonomous vehicles accounting for latent attitudes. Transp. Res. Part C Emerg. Technol. **97**, 456–477 (2018). https://doi.org/10.1016/j.trc.2018.11.005

64. Zhang, X., Wang, X., Ma, Y., Ma, Q.: International research progress on driving behavior and driving risk. China J. Highway Transp. **33**(6), 1–17 (2020). https://doi.org/10.19721/j.cnki.1001-7372.2020.06.001

65. Zheng, D., Jiang, Z., Zhang, Q.: A study on drivers' risky driving behavior and its influencing factors. Ergonomics **20**(1), 20–25 (2014)
66. Hardman, S., Berliner, R.M., Tal, G.: Who will be the early adopters of automated vehicles? Insights from a survey of electric vehicle owners in the United States. Transp. Res. D Transp. Environ. **71**, 248–264 (2019). https://doi.org/10.1016/J.TRD.2018.12.001
67. Midden, C.J.H., Huijts, N.M.A.: The role of trust in the affective evaluation of novel risks: The case of CO2 storage. Risk Anal. **29**(5), 743–751 (2009). https://doi.org/10.1111/j.1539-6924.2009.01201.x
68. Eiser, J.R., Miles, S., Frewer, L.J.: Trust, perceived risk, and attitudes toward food technologies. J. Appl. Soc. Psychol. **32**, 2423–2433 (2022). https://doi.org/10.1111/j.1559-1816.2002.tb01871.x
69. Flint, D.J., Woodruff, R.B., Gardial, S.F.: Customer value change in industrial marketing relationships: A call for new strategies and research. J. Indus. Mar. Manag. **26**, 163–175 (1997). https://doi.org/10.1016/S0019-8501%2896%2900112-5
70. Jin, N.P., Lee, S., Lee, H.: The effect of experience quality on perceived value, satisfaction, image and behavioral intention of water park patrons: New versus repeat visitors. Int. J. Tour. Res. **17**, 82–95 (2015). https://doi.org/10.1002/JTR.1968
71. Sweeney, J., Soutar, G.: Consumer perceived value: The development of a multiple item scale. J. Retail. **77**, 203–220 (2001). https://doi.org/10.1016/S0022-4359%2801%2900041-0
72. Kim, H.W., Chan, H.C., Gupta, S.: Value-based adoption of mobile internet: an empirical investigation. Decis. Supp. Syst. **43**(1), 111–126 (2007). https://doi.org/10.1016/j.dss.2005.05.009
73. Chiu, C.M., Wang, E.T.G., Fang, Y.H., Huang, H.Y.: Understanding customers' repeat purchase intentions in B2C E-commerce: The roles of utilitarian value, hedonic value and perceived risk. Inf. Syst. J. **24**, 85–114 (2014). https://doi.org/10.1111/j.1365-2575.2012.00407.x
74. Xie, J., Ye, L., Huang, W., Ye, M.: Understanding FinTech platform adoption: Impacts of perceived value and perceived risk. J. Theor. Appl. Electron. Commer. Res. **35**(1), 121–127 (2017). https://doi.org/10.3390/jtaer16050106
75. Hussein, A.S., Hapsari, R.D., Yulianti, I.: Experience quality and hotel boutique customer loyalty: Mediating role of hotel image and perceived value. J. Qual. Assur. Hosp. Tour. **19**, 442–459 (2018). https://doi.org/10.1080/1528008X.2018.1429981
76. Keshavarz, Y., Jamshidi, D.: Service quality evaluation and the mediating role of perceived value and customer satisfaction in customer loyalty. Int. J. Tourism Cities **4**(2), 220–244 (2018). https://doi.org/10.1108/IJTC-09-2017-0044
77. Wong, A., Rinderer, P.: Customer perceptions of shared autonomous vehicle usage: An empirical study. Home Int. J. Automot. Technol. Manag. **20**(1): 108–129 (2020). https://doi.org/10.1504/ijatm.2020.10026966
78. Bauer, R.A.: Consumer behavior as risk taking. In: Hancock, R.S. (ed.) Dynamic Marketing for a Changing World. Proceedings of the 43rd Conference of the American Marketing Association, pp. 389–398 (1960)
79. Cox, D.F., Rich, S.U.: Perceived risk and consumer decision-making—The case of telephone shopping. J. Mark. Res. **1**(4), 32–39 (1964). https://doi.org/10.1177/002224376400100405
80. Chang, E.C., Tseng, Y.F.: Research note: E-store image, perceived value and perceived risk. J. Bus. Res. **66**(7), 864–870 (2013). https://doi.org/10.1016/J.JBUSRES.2011.06.012
81. Thakur, R., Srivastava, M.: Adoption readiness, personal innovativeness, perceived risk and usage intention across customer groups for mobile payment services in India. Internet Res. **24**, 369–392 (2014). https://doi.org/10.1108/IntR-12-2012-0244
82. Martins, C., Oliveira, T., Popovič, A.: Understanding the Internet banking adoption: A unified theory of acceptance and use of technology and perceived risk application. Int. J. Inf. Manag. **34**, 1–13 (2014). https://doi.org/10.1016/j.ijinfomgt.2013.06.002

83. Yuen, K.F., Huyen, D.T., Wang, X., Qi, G.: Factors influencing the adoption of shared autonomous vehicles. Int. J. Environ. Res. Publ. Health **17**(13), 48–68 (2020). https://doi. org/10.3390/ijerph17134868
84. Choi, D.: The impact of media use on policy support on fine dust problem in South Korea's atmosphere: The mediating role of attribution of responsibility and perceived risk. J. Risk Res. **24**, 1101–1112 (2020). https://doi.org/10.1080/13669877.2020.1801809
85. Prebensen, N.K., Rosengren, S.: Experience value as a function of hedonic and utilitarian dominant services. Int. J. Contemp. Hospital. Manag. **28**, 113–135 (2016). https://doi.org/10. 1108/IJCHM-02-2014-0073
86. Clapp, J.D., et al.: Factors contributing to anxious driving behavior: the role of stress history and accident severity. J. Anxiety Disord. **25**(4), 592–598 (2011). https://doi.org/10.1016/j.jan xdis.2011.01.008
87. Poortinga, W., Pidgeon, N.F.: Trust in risk regulation: Cause or consequence of the acceptability of GM food? Risk Analysis **25**(1),199–209 (2005). https://doi.org/10.1111/j.0272-4332. 2005.00579.x
88. Kim, Y., Park, Y., Seo, H.H., Choi, J.: An empirical investigation of customer acceptance of self-driving cars. In: Key Challenges and Opportunities for Quality, Sustainability and Innovation in the Fourth Industrial Revolution, January 2021, pp. 73–97 (2021)

Author Index

P.-L. P. Rau (Ed.): HCII 2023, LNCS 14023, pp. 531–534, 2023.
https://doi.org/10.1007/978-3-031-35939-2

Printed in the United States
by Baker & Taylor Publisher Services